The Religion of Israel

The Religion of

From Its Beginnings to the Babylonian Exile

Israel

by
Yehezkel Kaufmann
translated and abridged by
Moshe Greenberg

THE UNIVERSITY OF CHICAGO PRESS

This book is an abridgment and a translation of

יחזקאל קויפמן, תולדות האמונה הישראלית: מימי קדם עד סוף בית שני

Tel-Aviv: Bialik Institute-Dvir, Vol. I (I/1), 1937

Vol. II (I/2), 1937; Vol. III (I/3), 1938

Vol. IV² (II/1), 1947; Vol. V (II/2), 1945; Vol. VI (III/1), 1947

Vol. VII (III/2), 1948; Vol. VIII (IV/1), 1956

The material of Volume VIII is not included in this abridgment

Library of Congress Catalog Card Number: 60-5466

The University of Chicago Press, Chicago 60637
Allen and Unwin Ltd., London
The University of Toronto Press, Toronto 5, Canada

Preface

The need for rendering into a western language Yehezkel Kaufmann's *History of Israelite Religion* has long been felt. Written in Hebrew, this major contribution to biblical scholarship has been largely inaccessible to the many persons here and abroad who have an interest in the subject. The present work, an abridgment and translation of the first seven volumes, has been undertaken to supply this need at least in part.

The planned scope of the *History* takes in the whole of the Second Temple period, and an eighth volume carrying the study to the beginning of the Hellenistic age has already appeared. This abridgment, however, is limited to the volumes treating of the pre-exilic age, which is a self-contained entity and within which Professor Kaufmann places the bulk of ancient Hebrew literature and religious creativity.

This abridgment attempts to convey the essence of the seven volumes. Nearly all the subjects treated in them have received some space here, with the exceptions noted below. Although this has meant a high degree of condensing, I have endeavored as far as possible to preserve the author's original language, preferring omission and combination to paraphrase.

I have selected from the original only such material as is strictly related to the history and character of Israelite religion. Discussions of a purely, or predominantly, literary nature, in which questions of dating and composition take precedence over religious interest, have been drastically curtailed or left out entirely. Two major exceptions to this rule have been made: The literary criticism of the Pentateuch and the literature of classical prophecy is so intimately bound up with the history of religion that it was deemed impossible to omit Professor Kaufmann's position on it. The gist of the original argument has, accordingly, been preserved. For the rest, some

v

remarks were all that could be retained of the extensive critical treatments of the sources that punctuate the original work.

Second, all discussion of disputed points, to which much space is devoted in the *History*, has been greatly abridged or wholly omitted. The author's position, with only a brief, and at times a merely allusive rather than explicit, statement of his grounds for differing with the consensus, has been presented. Reference to the original thus remains necessary for a fair scholarly appraisal of the author's position on any disputed point.

Of other specific items which have been omitted I may here mention the excursus on eschatology at the end of Volume VII, and the treatments of several of the minor prophets. Documentation and references to the scholarly literature have been almost entirely excluded by limitations of space.

In arranging the abridgment I have departed from the original in the first part by placing the morphological, cross-historical treatment of Israelite religion before the source criticism. This material, which in any case lies outside the framework of the historical chapters, has here been placed at the beginning because the distinctive character which the author ascribes to Israel's religion is the central pillar of his thought and underlies much of the later discussion. Professor Kaufmann's own article on the religion of Israel in Volume II of the Hebrew *Encyclopaedia Biblica* follows the same arrangement. For the rest, the order of the abridgment generally follows that of the original, as may be seen in the table below.*

* The abridgment corresponds to the original as in the table. In the body of the text some editorial revisions have been made, and these appear in brackets.

[Footnote continued on following page]

This work could not have been undertaken without the support and encouragement of the Jewish Agency for Palestine, which, through its Book Department (now the Herzl Institute), provided a subvention for the preparation of the manuscript. I wish to record here my deep gratitude for this generous assistance. To my wife I am beholden for constant and unstinting help in every stage of the work.

If "to translate is to traduce," what shall be said of a translation that is at the same time an abridgment! So perilous an undertaking, the more so in view of the relative inaccessibility of the original, would not have been entered upon without the approval of Professor Kaufmann, who passed on the plan of the work and saw the manuscript. But this permission must not be taken to involve him in responsibility for the selection of the material or the manner of its adaptation. That errors of commission and omission have occurred is inevitable in such a work. My hope is that enough has been preserved of the original for its force to overcome these defects, so that this book may not be an unworthy vehicle for bringing something of the contribution of Professor Kaufmann to the attention of a wider audience.

MOSHE GREENBERG

MERION, PENNSYLVANIA

Contents

PART TWO

THE HISTORY OF ISRAELITE RELIGION

PRIOR TO CLASSICAL PROPHECY

Contents

Introduction

Biblical scholarship finds itself today in a peculiar position. There is a view of the history of biblical religion to which the body of biblical scholars subscribe; precisely why this view prevails, however, is not at all clear. At the end of the last century, Julius Wellhausen formulated the now classic theory of the evolution of the literature and of the religion of Israel that to this day goes by his name. Wellhausen's arguments complemented each other nicely, and offered what seemed to be a solid foundation upon which to build the house of biblical criticism. Since then, however, both the evidence and the arguments supporting this structure have been called into question and, to some extent, even rejected. Yet biblical scholarship, while admitting that the grounds have crumbled away, nevertheless continues to adhere to the conclusions. The critique of Wellhausen's theory which began some forty years ago has not been consistently carried through to its end. Equally unable to accept the theory in its classical formulation and to return to the precritical views of tradition, biblical scholarship has entered a period of search for new foundations.

This study is a fundamental critique of classical criticism. It seeks to draw ultimate conclusions, to suggest a new position in place of the prevailing one. It is not undertaken in an apologetic spirit and in the hope of restoring tradition to its lost eminence. Although criticism has, to be sure, often underrated the historical worth of biblical traditions, such of its findings as the analysis of three chief sources in the Torah (JE, P, and D) have stood the test of inquiry and may be considered established. But its basic postulate—that the priestly stratum of the Torah was composed in the Babylonian exile, and that the literature of the Torah was still being written and revised in and after the Exile—is untenable. The Torah—it

*

1

will be shown—is the literary product of the earliest stage of Israelite religion, the stage prior to literary prophecy. Although its compilation and canonization took place later, its sources are demonstrably ancient—not in part, not in their general content, but in their entirety, even to their language and formulation.

Accordingly, we shall have to reassess the conventional view of the origins of Israelite monotheism. Biblical scholars, and historians of antiquity in general, tend to interpret Israelite religion as an organic outgrowth of the religious milieu of the ancient Orient. Some scholars discover the origins of biblical faith in monotheistic tendencies of the religions of the ancient Near East, others point out pagan elements in the religion of Israel. All assume that an organic connection exists, that even the unique elements of Israelite faith must be understood in the light of the surrounding religions. Scholarship has labored prodigiously to lay bare the elements that the religion of Israel had in common with its neighbors, to discover the pagan sources of Israelite creativity. This endeavor is justified by what would seem to be the testimony of the Bible itself, that Israel was a pagan people until the Babylonian exile. Israel's monotheism was, in this view, not a popular creation, but the doctrine of a priestly or prophetic elite. It evolved gradually and reached its culmination only in late times under specific historical circumstances. It was not the religion of the folk, and never the basis of the popular culture. The circles that cultivated this doctrine had always to combat the paganism of the people. Only after the Exile, when the broken nation was reconstituted as a "church" under foreign domination, were the priests and prophets finally able to implant monotheism within it. With this victory, the popular religion was adapted to and overlaid by the ideals of the theocracy. But through the monotheistic veneer, the fundamentally pagan content of the older folk religion can easily be discerned. On the popular level, then, there was no essential difference between the pre-exilic Israelite and the pagan; both were children of the same culture.

This view is here rejected *in toto*. We shall see that Israelite religion was an original creation of the people of Israel. It was absolutely different from anything the pagan world ever knew; its monotheistic world view had no antecedents in paganism. Nor was it a theological doctrine conceived and nurtured in limited circles or schools; nor a concept that finds occasional expression in this or that passage or stratum of the Bible. It was the fundamental idea of a national culture, and informed every aspect of that culture from its very beginning. It received, of course, a legacy from the pagan age which preceded it, but the birth of Israelite religion was the death of paganism in Israel. Despite appearances, Israel was not a polytheistic people. Careful examination of the biblical testimony to Israel's "idolatry" yields an altogether new assessment of this idolatry. It was not genuine, mythological polytheism; foreign elements did not play a substantial, creative role in the formation of the popular culture. Israelite religion developed organically, internally, as does every primary national culture, though it did have to battle a peculiar sort of "idolatry." Israel's world was its own creation, notwithstanding its utilization of ancient pagan materials. To fathom the meaning of this world, we must interpret its symbols from within; the attempts to explain it in the light of pagan models only obscure its real character and bar the way to a true appreciation.

Such an interpretation cannot be founded on the testimony of obscure passages, on ingenious combinations of isolated "hints" and "clues" scattered here and there throughout the Bible, or on learned conjectures, supported by little real evidence. (The habit of developing far-reaching theories from a novel exegesis of an isolated passage—usually an obscure one at that—and of reaching large conclusions literally from jots and tittles, is deeply ingrained in biblical scholarship.) Its proper foundations are the monumental phenomena of the biblical period. Material remains of that age are relatively scanty: no sphinxes, pyramids, temples—not even inscriptions or pictures of biblical Israel have survived in any appreciable quantity. The findings of archeology have therefore limited value for illuminating the thought of that age. But within the Bible itself are to be found data that stem from different periods, various sources and genres of literature (e.g., narrative, laws, prophecy); and these varied materials agree with and complement each other so as to bear certain and compelling witness. Especially significant are the inferences to be drawn from the ideological constants of the literary corpora, from the leading motifs of the various strata, from the several crystallizations of the historical tradition. These are the literary equivalent of geological stratification, and are as conclusive as the material remains of buildings, inscriptions, artifacts, and pottery. Is not the biblical polemic against "idolatry"—consistently misrepresenting the religion of the pagans as fetishism—a monumental piece of evidence? The peculiar biblical conceptions of sin, impurity, sacrifice, magic, dreams, prophecy and inspiration, priest and prophet, and the blanket prohibition of divination, unparalleled in the pagan world, are no less conclusive. That national collapse and exile should have brought on the complete and final extirpation of Israelite idolatry is another datum of tremendous historical import. We have here the record of a unique creation of the spirit.

Yet, as if in stubborn defiance of the very nature of our evidence, biblical scholarship seeks to read it . . . in the light of paganism!

Our inquiry opens with a discussion of the contrast between paganism and Israelite religion, based upon a comparative study of religious forms. Without a proper grasp of this fundamental contrast there can be no understanding of the real problems inherent in the study of biblical religion. Then the history of our documents is examined: specifically, the relationship of the Torah to the historical and prophetic literature, and the formation of the Torah. This lays the groundwork for a historical sketch of Israel's religion—its beginnings, its early popular stage, and its later climax in classical prophecy. Thus we proceed from morphology to literary and source criticism, and, from there, to the unfolding history of the religion of Israel.

PART ONE   The Character

of Israelite Religion

CHAPTER I

The Basic Problem

If one examines the biblical account of the origins of Israelite monotheism and the story of its battle with and eventual triumph over paganism, he will discover a strange fact: the Bible is utterly unaware of the nature and meaning of pagan religion.

The pre-exilic age was, according to the witness of the Bible, the age of Israelite "idolatry." The people repeatedly backslid and worshiped the "other gods" of the nations round about. Biblical literature is dedicated to fight "idolatry," and biblical law, prophecy, and poetry have all left an abundant record of this generations-long battle. Biblical scholars of all shades of opinion have therefore assumed, as a matter of course, that the biblical age was intimately acquainted with paganism. No one, apparently, has ever doubted this assumption or criticized it in the light of the data. It is taken for granted that the biblical age knew the god-beliefs of the pagans and their myths, for were these not part and parcel of the idolatry of Israel? The war upon idolatry is presumed to have struck at the myths as well; monotheism prevailed as Israel's evolving religious consciousness triumphed over pagan mythological beliefs. The time and manner of this victory are the subject of debate among scholars. But it is agreed on every hand that during the biblical period mythological polytheism was prevalent in Israel as elsewhere and that biblical religion proper came into being only gradually as the product of the great struggle against it.

There is, of course, no question that Israelite religion and paganism are historically related; both are stages in the religious evolution of man. Israelite religion arose at a certain period in history, and it goes without saying that its rise did not take place in a vacuum. The Israelite tribes were heirs to a religious tradition which can only have been polytheistic.

7

The religion of YHWH could take hold of the people only after overcoming the ancient faith, and the fossil remains of pagan notions that have been preserved in the Bible testify that it was never wholly eradicated. But what was the nature of this upheaval and what do we know of its history? The study of biblical religion hinges on the answer to this question.

Studies of the origin of biblical religion inquire after the extent to which the popular religion, and even the votaries of YHWH at first, recognized the existence of other gods. It is commonly assumed that the religion of YHWH began as henotheism or monolatry, recognizing him as sole legitimate god in Israel, but acknowledging the existence of other national gods. This stage is said to be attested to in the biblical record. The problem is then posed: when did the idea arise that not only was Israel's worship of other gods illegal, but that those gods had no reality whatsoever; i.e., when did henotheism or monolatry become monotheism?

This view is founded on the tacit assumption that the pagan gods were conceived of identically by both Israelite and pagan. The passage from the earlier to the later stage is taken as the repudiation of the pagan idea of the reality of the gods. But what does the Bible itself tell us concerning the Israelite conception of the.nature of these gods and the nature of their worship?

The pagan conceives of the gods as powers embodied in nature, or as separate beings connected with nature in some fashion. Deification of cosmic forces provides the soil for the growth of mythology. Popular religion conceives of the gods as persons who inhabit the entire universe and are related in specific ways to each other and to men. They are the heroes of popular myths, the subjects of epic poets; to them temples are built, monuments and images erected. In the cult, material objects usually play an important part, the natural or manufactured object being taken as the bearer of divine power, the dwelling place of deity, or its symbol. While worship of material objects is not an essential feature of paganism, it is its natural outgrowth. Homage is done to the god through the care given to his image. The cult of images is thus intimately bound up with the belief in personal gods, who have specific forms, who inhere in natural phenomena or control them.

The polytheism of the ancient Near East during biblical times was highly developed. Its gods and goddesses appear in literature, art, and culture in fairly standardized forms, which were presumably familiar not only to the clergy but to the laity as well. There are gods of sky and earth, of life, love, and fertility, of death and destruction. The gods have specific roles. There are gods of light and darkness, of thunder and lightning, of wind and rain, of fire and water. Mountains, springs, rivers, and forests have their gods also. The gods have sexual qualities, the existence of male and female deities being essential to pagan thought. These characteristics serve as the materials for elaborate myths in which the histories and adventures of the gods are related. Theogonies tell of their birth and lineage. Myths tell of their wars, loves, hatreds, and dealings with men. The cult is closely connected with these myths, which are the vital core of priestly and, in a measure, of popular religion.

What would we know of this had we no other source than the Bible?

The Bible knows that the pagans worship national gods, certain of whom are mentioned by name: Baal, Ashtoreth, Chemosh, Milcom, Bel, Nebo, Amon, etc. But it is remarkable that not a single biblical passage hints at the natural or mythological qualities of any of these named gods. Had we only the Bible, we should know nothing of the real nature of the "gods of the nations." In a few isolated passages the pagans are said to worship spirits and demons, but these are anonymous, whereas what we know to have been mythological gods are, in the Bible, mere names. Not a trace remains of the rich store of popular myths associated with these names.

The Bible has a great deal to say about the image cult that was associated with the named gods. But if the god is not understood to be a living, natural power, or a mythological person who dwells in, or is symbolized by, the image, it is evident that the image worship is conceived to be nothing but fetishism.

A few passages permit the inference that the nations worship living gods. Thus in the ancient poem of Numbers 21:29 (cf. Jer. 48:46), Chemosh may be represented as active. Jephthah too speaks of Chemosh as if he gave the land to the Ammonites (Judg. 11:24). Belief in a living god Baal may be alluded to in the story of Judges 6:25–32, telling of Gideon's destruction of his altar. Elijah's taunts also represent Baal, if only mockingly, as a living god (I Kings 18:27). Similarly I Kings 20:28 has the pagans speak of gods of the valleys and of the mountains, if indeed only with reference to the God of Israel. Apart from this we find the notion that later became widespread among Hellenistic Jews (and passed from them to the Christians) that the gods of the nations are spirits or demons (Deut. 32:16 f.; Ps. 106:37). It must be stressed, however, that this is a vaguely generalized conception; no named god of the Bible is so represented. In the above-cited passages the gods of the nations are alluded to not merely as cult objects, but as active beings, whether so in reality or only in the minds of the heathen. Although it is possible that in some a mere personification of idols is intended, there can be no doubt that in a few there is the suggestion that the pagans worship not only idols but gods and spirits as well.

Biblical writers are also aware of the pagans' belief that their idols have the power to act. The pagans worship and sacrifice to idols hoping to receive benefit and aid from them.

We have now arrived at the limit of the Bible's knowledge of the nature of pagan belief. We find no clear conception of the roles the gods play in nature and in the life of man. No cognizance is taken of their mythological features. The named gods are characterized only by the nations that worship them: "Ashtoreth, god of the Sidonians," "Milcom, the abomination of the Ammonites," "Chemosh, the abomination of Moab," and so forth. No god is ever styled according to his function or place in the pantheon, as so often occurs in the literatures of Egypt, Mesopotamia, and Canaan. Nor is the sexual differentiation of the gods ever alluded to; gods and goddesses are both comprised under the masculine rubric *ᵓelōhīm* (e.g., "Ashtoreth, the god of [*ᵓelōhē*] the Sidonians"), there being, in fact, no word in biblical Hebrew for "goddess."

Observe now what is said regarding the worship of the "host of heaven." Several of the named gods—Ashtoreth (Ishtar), Bel, Marduk, Nebo, etc.— are known from pagan sources to have been astral deities, yet not once does the Bible connect them with the worship of the "host of heaven." The "host" and the idols (i.e., the name-bearing images) are always treated as two distinct classes of pagan deities. Thus Deuteronomy 4:16–18 first forbids worshiping images of any animal, winged or earthbound, following this (vs. 19) with a separate prohibition of the worship of sun, moon, and host of heaven. Again the sun, moon, and host of heaven are repeatedly listed alongside of—not as identical with—"other gods" (17:3; Jer. 19:13). Thus, too, the "queen of heaven" (Jer. 44:17 f.; apparently, the moon) is never identified in the Bible with Ashtoreth or any other deity that the Bible knows by name. And although Ezekiel sees the elders bowing down "eastward to the sun," he fails to link this solar cult with that of the "idols of Israel" which he saw just before (Ezek. 8:16). Nor does he give any hint that this deified sun bears any of the personal mythological traits of the Assyro-Babylonian Shamash. What the Bible calls the "worship of the host of heaven" it apparently understands to be the cult of the heavenly bodies as such. It knows of no connection between the "host of heaven" and the named gods whose idol-worship it condemns.

The mythological motifs that are found in the Bible are considered evidence of pagan influence on Israelite religion during biblical times. The question here is this: Did Israel, after the rise of the religion of YHWH, take over the myths of the pagans along with their idols? The fact is that the Bible recognizes no mythological motifs as foreign, pagan. In all the legends and allusions with such motifs YHWH is the only active divine being. There are no active foreign gods. There are allusions to battles that YHWH fought with primeval creatures such as Rahab and his "helpers," the dragon, Leviathan, and the fleeing serpent (Isa. 51:9; Pss. 74:14; 89:11; Job 9:13; 26:12 f.), but these are not considered by the biblical writers as pagan concepts (whatever be their true historical derivation). They belong to Israel's stock of legends, and may well be a legacy of pre-Israelite times. Such creatures appear in Israelite legends—but never Tiamat, Marduk, Hadad, or the like. The myths of the pagans are not even derided as idle tales, as fabrications, nor are they utilized in poetic figures. No foreign god is counted among the enemies of YHWH. Quite remarkable is the fact that precisely in the creation legends (Gen. 1–11), where the bulk of mythological matter is imbedded, paganism is entirely absent; primeval man knows only the god YHWH. In sum, then, there is no evidence that the writers were conscious of any connection between the mythological motifs imbedded in their narratives and the pagan gods.

These phenomena go too deep and are too pervasive to be explained merely as monotheistic reworking. Moreover, while monotheism could not acknowledge the divinity of the pagan gods, it need not have denied them legendary roles. We have seen that occasionally the Bible does allow them the status of demons; these might have been permitted to play the part of evil spirits or enemies of YHWH. A battle with Bel and Nebo as demons is no more damaging to the unity of God than a battle with Rahab or the dragon. Later Judaism saw no harm in stories of God's battles with rebellious angels.

This is not to say that the Bible knows of no battles of YHWH with the "gods of the nations." Indeed, YHWH does battle with them and "work judgments" upon them. But in every case the objects of his fury are the idols, as we shall see. These complementary phenomena can only be explained on the assumption that the biblical age no longer knew pagan mythology.

THE GODS OF THE NATIONS IN THE NARRATIVES

Just as no foreign god is active in the creation stories, so no god other than YHWH ever appears at work in Israel's early history or in the battles between Israel and its neighbors. YHWH fights Israel's enemies, but no god ever appears as his living antagonist; when the Bible tells us of YHWH's battles with foreign gods, it is always idols that are meant.

Thus YHWH "works judgments" on the "gods of Egypt" (Exod. 12:12; Num. 33:4), and similar expressions are to be found elsewhere (e.g.,

Isa. 46:1, with regard to Bel and Nebo). In several cases it is not clear whether the reference is to gods or idols, but we may interpret these in the light of unequivocal passages. Jeremiah follows, "I shall punish Bel in Babylon" with, "I shall punish the graven images of Babylon" (Jer. 51:44, 47, 52). Nahum warns Assyria, "I shall cut off idol and molten image from your temple" (1:14). And so does Ezekiel prophesy, "I shall destroy idols and put an end to images in Memphis" (30:13). Jeremiah 50:2, "Bel is shamed, Merodach dismayed," is interpreted by the prophet in the very next clause, "her images are shamed, her idols dismayed." From the total absence of any reference to activity (such as, say, flight, which would be appropriate in these cases), we may conclude that such expressions as "trembling" (Isa. 19:1), or "kneeling" (Isa. 46:1) refer to the movement of idols being cut down and removed from their sites. It is characteristic that instead of fleeing, the pagan gods must be borne away on pack animals, or are carried off into exile with their priests (Isa. 46:1 f.; Jer. 48:7; Dan. 11:8).

The account of the humiliation of the Philistine god Dagon (I Sam. 5), the only detailed story of the "judgments" that YHWH wreaked on a "god of the nations" may serve as a model for all such "judgments." The Philistines captured the ark and set it in the temple of Dagon, "beside Dagon." YHWH's revenge strikes at the people of Ashdod through a vile disease, and Dagon is discovered one morning "fallen on his face before the ark of YHWH." On the morrow, not only is he again fallen, but "Dagon's head and his two hands were cut off and lying on the threshold." The Ashdodites decide to get rid of the ark of the God of Israel "because his hand has lain heavily upon us and our god Dagon." We hear nothing of Dagon proper, Dagon the living god; not even the Philistines are said to suggest that the fall of the image portends evil for the god. They, too, see in their idol's fall and mutilation the "judgment" of YHWH on their god. This is how Israel told of the victories of YHWH over the "gods of the nations."

We should not wonder that the Bible speaks of YHWH's "judging" these idol-gods. The idols are "vanities," it is true, but they are more; they are not religiously neutral, but a source of impurity. Even though it is emphasized over and over again that they are "no-gods," as objects of a magical cult the biblical writers hold them in a measure of awe. The Bible does believe in magic and sorcery, and considers the idols as bearers of occult powers. It is as such that YHWH the God wreaks his judgments upon them.

Two stories illustrate vividly the nature of Israel's battle with idolatry:

the story of the golden calf, in which Israelite idolatry is typified (Exod. 32), and the late story of the image set up by Nebuchadnezzar (Dan. 3), in which the worship of the pagans is portrayed.

When Moses delays his descent from the mountain, the people demand that Aaron "make them a god who will go before them"; the priest makes them a "molten calf." The people make a feast in honor of their manufactured god in which they cry before it, "This is your god, O Israel, who brought you up out of the land of Egypt" (Exod. 32:1–6). In this portrayal of Israel's prototypal sin we have a classic representation of the biblical view of idolatry. The sin is not that the people represent YHWH in the figure of an ox. The people, having despaired of Moses and the God who brought them out of Egypt, demand that the priest make them a god in place of YHWH (Exod. 32:1, 4, 8; cf. Ps. 106:20 "They exchanged their glory for the image of a grass-eating ox"; Neh. 9:18; cf. also I Kings 12:28; 14:9). They do not give their allegiance to a living god, one of the gods of the nations or of their own ancient pantheon, but to an anonymous image, just now fashioned out of their own trinkets. In this calf, this idol that was not the image of a god, but a god itself, the Bible embodies its conception of Israelite idolatry as fetishism.

In the later story Nebuchadnezzar sets up a huge image in the plain of Dura and orders all his subjects to worship it under penalty of death in a fiery furnace. Hananiah, Mishael, and Azariah refuse to obey the king's order; they are thrown into the furnace but are miraculously saved by an angel of God. Nebuchadnezzar, beholding this miracle, does homage to the God of the three youths. Here, again, idolatry is the worship of an anonymous idol, an idol that represents no god at all, but is itself to be worshiped. Thus we see that even as late as Persian and Hellenistic times the Jewish attitude toward paganism was determined by the belief that the pagans worshiped idol-fetishes.

THE POLEMIC AGAINST IDOLATRY

A large part of biblical literature is dedicated to the battle against idolatry, striving to expose its absurdity and discredit it in the eyes of its believers. When this material is examined it appears (*a*) that the gods, whom the pagans believe to inhabit heaven and earth, are never said to be non-existent; (*b*) that nowhere is the belief in myths or their telling prohibited; (*c*) that no biblical writer utilizes mythological motifs in his polemic; (*d*) that the sole argument advanced against pagan religion is that it is a fetishistic worship of "wood and stone."

The Bible conceives of idolatry as the belief that divine and magical powers inhere in certain natural or man-made objects and that man can activate these powers through fixed rituals. These objects, upon which magical rituals are performed, are "the gods of the nations." The Bible does not conceive the powers as personal beings who dwell in the idols; the idol is not a habitation of the god, it is the god himself. Hence the oft-repeated biblical stigmatization of the pagan gods as "wood and stone," "silver and gold." Hence also its sole polemical argument that idolatry is the senseless deification of wood and stone images. We may, perhaps, say that the Bible sees in paganism only its lowest level, the level of mana-beliefs.

This view finds clear expression in the prophetic polemics against idolatry.

Literary prophecy brought the religion of YHWH to its climax. Chapter upon chapter records denunciations hurled at apostate Israel for their straying after the gods of the nations. If ever there were a struggle with pagan myths and mythological conceptions of deity, we should expect to find its traces here. But we search in vain: not one word have the prophets for mythological beliefs, not once do they repudiate them. Not only do they fail to brand the pagan gods as demons or satyrs, they fail even clearly to deny their existence. In short, the prophets ignore what we know to be authentic paganism. Their whole condemnation revolves around the taunt of fetishism.

Amos, the first known literary prophet, hardly mentions the belief in gods. In 8:14, he speaks of Ashimah of Samaria; in 5:26, he names gods that the Israelites "made" for themselves. Thus the prophet, who is considered by many to have been the first to arrive at pure monotheism, fails entirely to express himself on the nature of the polytheism which he allegedly leaves behind.

In the first three chapters of Hosea the Baal worship of Jezebel's age is reflected, when court circles in Samaria were influenced by the Sidonian queen's imported cult (see below, pp. 368 ff.). Chapter 2 poetically portrays Baal as an illegitimate lover who has displaced YHWH in the affections of "harlot" Israel. But even here none of the distinctive mythological features of the Canaanite Baal are mentioned. Prosperity is a gift of YHWH which Israel has falsely ascribed to Baal (vss. 7–11). In the later chapters 4–14, Baal worship (9:10; 13:1) is but one among several sins of the past, and the manner in which the prophet conceives of Baal is seen clearly enough in 11:2 where "Baals" are parallel with "graven images." Israel is "joined to idols" (4:17), has made a molten calf of silver, "the work of craftsmen" (13:2), not understanding that "the craftsman made it, it is no god!" (8:6). When will Israel be reconciled with its God? When it says, "Assyria will not save us . . . neither will we say any more 'Our God' to the work of our hands" (14:4). Idolatry is nothing more than the worship of "the work of hands."

It is the same view that we meet with in Isaiah, who speaks of idolatry as the sin of humanity at large. Idolatry entered Israel together with the advent of silver and gold, horses and chariots. As the latter increase, "their land is also full of idols; every one worships the work of his hands, that which his own fingers have made" (2:7 f.). When the Lord humbles man's pride in his final great theophany, "man shall cast away his idols of silver, and his idols of gold, which they made for themselves to worship . . ." (2:20). Isaiah's *Götterdämmerung* is thus the twilight of silver and gold images; he makes no allusion to polytheistic beliefs.

Similarly Micah: On the day of doom all Samaria's "graven images shall be beaten to pieces . . . and all her idols will I lay desolate" (1:7); "And I will cut off your graven images and your pillars out of your midst; and you shall no more worship the work of your hands . . ." (5:12).

Jeremiah speaks of idolatry more than all his predecessors. He mentions anonymous "other gods" (11:10) who are impotent (11:12), whom Israel knew not (19:4); these he represents as the gods of foreign lands (16:13). It has been asserted that Jeremiah acknowledged the existence of other gods, objecting only to their worship in Israel. But Jeremiah amply sets forth his conception of pagan religion: it is the worship of wood and stone (2:27) or the host of heaven (8:2). The "other gods" are not the mythological beings of authentic paganism, nor even demons, but the handiwork of men (1:16), "stone and wood" (3:9), "graven images and strange vanities" (8:19), "no-gods" (2:11; 5:7), and so forth. On the day when the nations repent of the sin of idolatry they will say, "Our fathers inherited naught but lies, vanity and things wherein there is no profit. Shall a man make for himself gods, they being no gods?" (16:19 f.). When men stop worshiping fetishistic "no-gods" idolatry shall come to an end. This conception of pagan religion is expressed most clearly and emphatically in 10:1–16 (cf. 51:15–19). Owing to their resemblance to the viewpoint of the Second Isaiah, these verses have been dated to exilic times. For our purpose, however, the dating is immaterial, inasmuch as all of prophetic literature is unanimous in its conception of idolatry.

In Ezekiel we do find what appears to be an allusion to a foreign pagan myth: the lamenting of Tammuz (8:14; cf. also Zech. 12:11, "the mourning of Hadadrimmon"). Did Ezekiel or his contemporaries know the myth of the death of youthful Tammuz, the beloved of Ishtar? Or did they know only the pagan rites that Ezekiel mentions? The mass of worshipers, even among the pagan nations, had at times only very dim notions of the mythological basis of their rites. Did those "weeping women" know the Tammuz myth? Is it certain that they were Israelites, and not rather pagan priestesses of the royal cult (like the imported pagan priests of Jezebel in an earlier age)? It is certain only that Ezekiel (whom Gunkel believes "filled with mythological material") never once argues against pagan mythology. Despite the fact that he polemizes often and heatedly against idolatry, he has not a word to say about the myths of Tammuz or any other god, nor does he ever employ an argument based on a mythological motif. He, too, characterizes pagan religion as fetishism. His favorite epithet for the gods is *gillūlīm* (dung-pellets); Israel's silver and gold, out of which they "made themselves their abominable images and loathsome things," were their stumbling blocks (7:19 f.). In chapters 16, 20, and 23, the prophet describes Israel's apostasy in detailed visions and allegories; Israel have made "male images" of gold and silver, made offerings to them, even sacrificed to them their sons and daughters. They have adopted the idol-worship of their neighbors throughout their history, from the Egyptian sojourn onward. The imagery is sensual and erotic; the dominant motif is the idol-images, those illegitimate partners of Israel's harlotry, from which the prophet readily passes to the lusty men of the foreign nations—the panoplied soldiery—after whom Israel went a-whoring also. Plastic imagery dominates; in fact, the prophet is so involved with the idols that he ignores the gods entirely. It is most remarkable that Ezekiel, fascinated as he is by erotic symbolism, never once utilizes the sexual themes of mythology. He is silent concerning the strong erotic motif of the Tammuz myths. He uses the awkward image of Israel playing the harlot with stocks and stones, with gold and silver images. But he neglects the mythological store of themes that could have furnished rich material for his imagination. Can it be that Ezekiel knew the myths of the pagans in spite of his failure to employ even one of their motifs in his visions? We are not left to inferences. Ezekiel has himself supplied an epitome of his view of the pagan gods: to the elders of Israel he says, "You say, let us be like the nations, like the families of the countries to serve wood and stone" (20:32). What the pagans worship, then, is nothing but deified wood and stone.

The classic polemics against idolatry found in the Second Isaiah express the biblical conception of pagan worship in its most vivid form. No previous prophet ever arraigned idolatry, ever heaped abuse upon it with such zeal and persistence. And yet, this unremitting attack, this stream of taunts and mockery, plays on one theme only: the monstrous folly of believing that idols can be gods. How much energy and poetic artistry are devoted to prove this single point!

The makers of idols are all of them a mockery, their beloved images are good for nothing. . . .

The workman in wood draws a measuring-line over it, shapes it with a pencil, works it with planes, shapes it with compasses, and makes it into the likeness of a man, with a beauty like that of the human form—to sit in a house!

A man cuts him down a cedar, or takes a plane or an oak, or lays hold of some other tree of the forest. . . . He takes part of it and warms himself, he kindles a fire and bakes bread; then he makes a god and worships it, he molds an image and prostrates himself before it. Half of it he burns in the fire, and on its embers he roasts flesh. . . . And the rest of it he makes into a god—his idol!—prostrates himself before it, worships it, and prays to it, saying, "Save me, for thou art my god!"

They have no knowledge and no intelligence; for their eyes are besmeared so that they cannot see, and their minds are dulled so that they cannot understand. . . . [44:9–18]

Over and over again the prophet ridicules the belief that inanimate objects are gods. Only when the nations perceive that a "block of wood" (vs. 19) is not god will idolatry vanish. This from a man who, so it is alleged, was thoroughly acquainted with the polytheistic religion of his environment and even employed mythological motifs in his writing (51:9). And yet he has not a word about the gods or their myths. It never occurred to him to contrast the sublime God of Israel with the contentious, lustful deities of the pagans and to argue from this contrast that the gods are vanity. If our author had but dipped into the treasury of Babylonian myths, what a mine of material he would have found for his satires: gods who are born and die, who procreate, who eat, drink, and sleep, who make war on their mother, and crowd like flies around the sacrifice. Here was an arsenal which might have armed him to strike at the very heart of paganism: the faith in mythological gods and goddesses and in their dominion over the universe. And yet, in asserting his God's claim, he can say only, "I am YHWH, that is my name, and my glory I shall not give to another, nor my praise to idols" (42:8)—"to idols," not to "a born god," "a dying god," "a lustful god." YHWH evidently has no other rivals beside the idols and the graven images.

IDOLATRY IN THE LAWS

The Pentateuch also represents pagan religion as mere fetishism, and again there is no difference between sources; all agree in their view of idolatry.

There is no law in the Pentateuch interdicting the belief in pagan gods.

or the telling of their myths; in Exodus 23:13, the use of their names in oaths is forbidden (cf. Josh. 23:7). The standing Pentateuchal prohibition concerns the "making" (i.e., the manufacture) of "other gods" and their worship (e.g., Exod. 20:4 f.).

Twice we meet with prohibitions against the worship of beings other than YHWH: the satyrs (Lev. 17:7) and "divine beings" (ʾelōhīm, Exod. 22:19). In both cases, however, foreign gods are not involved, but Israelite demons and divine beings. Whenever foreign gods are mentioned explicitly, it is clear that nothing but idols are meant.

In the Pentateuch, as throughout the Bible, "other gods" include all kinds of images, whether belonging to the cult of YHWH or to pagan cults. Images of the YHWH cult are assumed to be the product of foreign influence, and a cult involving them is regarded as no worship of YHWH at all, but of "other gods" (Exod. 20:3 ff.; Deut. 5:7 ff.). The fetishistic conception is predominant; after banning the worship of Canaanite gods, Exodus 23:24 commands to "demolish them utterly"; Leviticus 19:4 complements "Turn not to the idols" with "nor make for yourselves any molten god." Deuteronomy is particularly illuminating. The two categories of pagan cult objects are the idols and the host of heaven, which God himself has apportioned to the heathen for their worship (4:19; 29:25). The gods of the nations, the "other gods" (6:14 and elsewhere), are unknown to Israel before they learned to worship them from the pagans (11:28; 13:3, 7, 14; 28:64; 29:25). They are "the handiwork of man," "wood and stone" (4:28; 28:36, 64), "silver and gold" (29:16), and the like. The sum total of idolatry is the worship of these fetishes plus the worship of the host of heaven (17:3). Nowhere in all its diatribes does Deuteronomy allude to a belief in living gods and goddesses. What is the folly of idolatry? That its gods "see not, and hear not, and eat not, and smell not" (4:28). It is the same pattern of mockery that we find elsewhere in the Bible (e.g., Pss. 115:4 ff.; 135:15 ff.; Dan. 5:23; Jer. 10:5). Not that they are gluttonous and drunkards—but that they "eat not"! Can we suppose that the biblical authors knew the stories of the banquets of the gods and yet were content with this harmless jeering at the idols alone?

This verdict of the Bible upon pagan religion is too pervasive to be explained as the product of artifice or later editing. Nothing can make plausible the suppression of a polemic against polytheistic beliefs, had such a polemic been in existence.

Does the Bible portray pagan religion as mere fetishism because the writers themselves disbelieved in the gods? If this were so, the writers must have failed in their primary objective, which was to undermine the faith of those who did believe in them. To this end, there was no point in belaboring the fetish-argument to the entire exclusion of the main claim, that the gods were nonexistent. As a matter of fact, it is abundantly clear that the writers naïvely attribute their own viewpoint to the idolaters. The prophets look for the end of idolatry at the time when the idolaters will come to understand that man cannot "make" him gods, and that wood and stone cannot save. When Sennacherib boasts of how he defeated the gods of the nations (II Kings 18:33 ff.; 19:11 f. [Isa. 36:18 ff.; 37:12]), the writer explains, "he cast them into the fire" (II Kings 19:18 [Isa. 37:19]). And Isaiah, too, ascribes this thinking to the Assyrian: "As I did to Samaria and its idols, so shall I do to Jerusalem and its images." The pagan fails to realize that while the gods of the nations are "the handiwork of man, wood and stone," Israel's God is a "living God" (II Kings 19:16, 18 [Isa. 37:17, 19]). There is, of course, no hint that Sennacherib ascribes his triumphs to the god Ashur who triumphed over the gods of these nations.

It may be suggested that the biblical polemic takes this form because, in fact, the mass of people did have this fetishistic concept of the idols, and it was urgently necessary to combat it. Now there was, to be sure, a fetishistic side to paganism: the cult was bound up with an image; the image was, in a sense, the god. This consideration can explain why the fetishistic argument plays an important part in the biblical polemic; it cannot explain, however, the total absence of polemic against the belief in living gods, which was, after all, the root and heart of pagan religion. Greek thinkers in their attacks upon the popular religion gave due attention to its fetishistic aspect, but they did not permit this to distract them from combating the popular myths. Nor did the later Jewish and Christian polemics rest content with the fetishistic argument only. And yet we find that the Bible fails entirely to come to grips with the essence of polytheism— the belief in gods.

Those who have recognized this remarkable peculiarity are too enthralled by the assumption that the biblical writers knew the pagan myths to recognize its significance. The fetishistic argument is said to imply that the biblical writers repudiate the existence of the pagan gods. But where do they? If they meant to say that idols are vain because the gods they represent are nonexistent, why do they persist in arguing that idols are things of naught because wood and stone are of no avail? Why do they conceal the denial of the gods behind the façade of mockery and abuse of images? But the attitude toward the idols is only one aspect of the puzzle. How is the silence of the entire Bible—prophets, narratives, and laws alike—concerning the pagan mythology to be explained? Not only does the Bible fail to deny the existence of the gods, it nowhere repudiates the pagan myths.

In point of fact, as we shall see later, everything in the biblical view of paganism is strangely distorted. It is entirely ignorant of the close relationship between magic and the gods; it knows nothing of the cosmic-mythological basis of the pagan cult; it has no appreciation of the symbolic value of images.

THE BASIC PROBLEM

It seems incredible that Israel should have been totally unaware of the nature of pagan beliefs. For Israel was always in contact with its pagan neighbors and, moreover, had believing pagans in its midst. Certainly there were circles who knew about paganism more than is reflected in the Bible. What is shown by the fact that the Bible bases its whole polemic on the argument of fetishism is that the chief influence of foreign beliefs on Israelite religion did not involve mythological materials and that the age-long battle of the Bible with idolatry did not involve mythological polytheism. This compels us to examine anew the conventional views regarding foreign influences on Israelite religion during biblical times. Moreover, we shall have to re-examine fundamentally the nature of Israelite "idolatry" during this period.

It is clear now that the question as to the origin of Israelite monotheism has been erroneously formulated. We cannot ask whether it was during the preprophetic or prophetic age that the religion of YHWH came to deny the reality of the foreign gods. The Bible nowhere denies the existence of the gods; it ignores them. In contrast to the philosophic attack on Greek popular religion, and in contrast to the later Jewish and Christian polemics, biblical religion shows no trace of having undertaken deliberately to suppress and repudiate mythology. There is no evidence that the gods and their myths were ever a central issue in the religion of YHWH. And yet this religion is non-mythological. Fossil-remains of ancient myths cannot obscure the basic difference between Israelite religion and paganism. It is precisely this non-mythological aspect that makes it unique in world history; this was the source of its universal appeal.

The Bible's ignorance of the meaning of paganism is at once the basic problem and the most important clue to the understanding of biblical religion. It underscores as nothing else can the gulf that separates biblical religion from paganism. A recognition of this gulf is crucial to the understanding of the faith of the Bible. Not only does it underlie the peculiar biblical misrepresentation of paganism, it is the essential fact of the history of Israelite religion.

CHAPTER II

Pagan Religion

THE FUNDAMENTAL IDEA

We designate as pagan all the religions of mankind from the beginnings of recorded history to the present, excepting Israelite religion and its derivatives, Christianity and Islam. This distinction assumes that, on the one hand, there is something unique about Israelite religion that sets it off from all the rest, and on the other, that there is an essential common aspect to all other religions which gives them their pagan character. What is that common essence?

Paganism has embodied itself in an enormous variety of forms: in deification of the animate and the inanimate, in belief in spirits and demons, in magic and incantations. It knows lofty cosmic gods and has produced the longing for knowledge of and communion with the "world soul." It evolved profound religious systems which sought to comprehend the secrets of existence, of life and death, of the destiny of man and the universe. It envisioned the triumph of good over evil at the end of days. Paganism bore such exotic fruit as the religion of the Australian aborigines, and that of the tribes of Africa and America; such delicate flowers as Greek thought; and the speculations of Babylon and Egypt, India, China, and Persia, with all their complex ramifications.

Yet all these embodiments involve one idea which is the distinguishing mark of pagan thought: the idea that there exists a realm of being prior to the gods and above them, upon which the gods depend, and whose decrees they must obey. Deity belongs to, and is derived from, a primordial realm. This realm is conceived of variously—as darkness, water, spirit, earth, sky, and so forth—but always as the womb in which the seeds of all being are contained. Alternatively, this idea appears as a belief in a primordial realm beside the gods, as independent and primary as the gods themselves. Not being subject to the gods, it necessarily limits them. The first conception, however, is the fundamental one. This is to say that in the pagan view, the gods are not the source of all that is, nor do they transcend the universe. They are, rather, part of a realm precedent to and independent of them. They are rooted in this realm, are bound by its nature, are subservient to its laws. To be sure, paganism has personal gods who create and govern the world of men. But a divine will, sovereign and absolute, which governs all and is the cause of all being—such a conception is unknown. There are heads of pantheons, there are creators and maintainers of the cosmos; but transcending them is the primordial realm, with its pre-existent, autonomous forces. This is the radical dichotomy of paganism; from it spring both mythology and magic.

Myth is the tale of the life of the gods. In myth the gods appear not only as actors, but as acted upon. At the heart of myth is the tension between the gods and other forces that shape their destinies. Myth describes the unfolding destiny of the gods, giving expression to the idea that besides the will of the gods there are other, independent forces that wholly or in part determine their destinies. Fate, says myth, apportions lots to the gods as well as to men. This is a great symbol of paganism's fundamental idea: the existence of a realm of power to which the gods themselves are subject.

The limitation of divine powers finds its source in the theogonies that are part of every mythology. The gods emerge out of the primordial substance, having been generated by its boundless fertility. It is not the gods and their will that exist at first, but the primordial realm with its inherent forces. Whether this realm is conceived of as original chaos, or as a kind of primal god, is immaterial. What is decisive is that the gods are born out of it by the natural, involuntary process of procreation. Even the "primal god" is thought of as no more than "father" of the gods and the world, engendering these out of his seed or his substance with no more control over their nature and destiny than a human father has over the nature and destiny of his offspring. His "paternity" does not involve universal rule and power. Indeed, it is typical of the ruling gods that they are usually of the second or third generation. The son who dethrones or murders his father, or rescues him from distress, and thus rises above him, is a standing feature of pagan mythologies.

The god is thus a personal embodiment of one of the seminal forces of the primordial realm. His nature and destiny are determined by the nature of this force. The multiplicity of pagan gods stems from the manifold powers and "seeds" of the primordial realm, each of which is conceived as a self-contained divine entity. Water, sky, light, darkness, life, death, and the like—all derive from the primordial realm; this sets the natural and eternal bounds to the dominion of each pagan deity. It is not the plurality of gods per se, then, that expresses the essence of polytheism, but rather the notion of many independent power-entities, all on a par with one another, and all rooted in the primordial realm. This radical variety finds particular expression in the dichotomies of good and evil, holiness and impurity. Throughout paganism we find good gods and evil gods, equal in their divine rank and power, because both derive independently from the primordial realm. The battle between good and evil, between holy and impure is conceived of as an everlasting struggle between hostile divine twins.

Corresponding to the birth of the gods through natural processes is their subjection to sexual conditions. All pagan religions have male and female deities who desire and mate with each other. The cycles of nature are commonly conceived of as the perennial mating and procreating of the gods. Thus, the gods are subject by their nature to sexual needs. At the same time they are involved in the processes of time. They gestate and give birth, they die and are resurrected; some are young, others old. Moreover, they are subject to physical conditions. They eat and drink, fall sick and require healing, need and invent tools, and so forth. A typical notion is the subjection of deity to powers inherent in matter or to abstract necessity (expressed in terms of numbers, periods, etc.).

Just as the fundamental idea of paganism found poetic expression in myth, so it found practical expression in magic. Since the primordial realm contains infinite forces other than and transcending the gods, their influence and dominion is perforce limited. There are two realms: that of divine powers, another of the metadivine.[1] Even the gods are depicted as calling upon metadivine forces to surmount their own predestined limitations. Pagan man feels himself subject to and in need of both realms. He prays to the gods to enlist their aid, but, conscious that the gods themselves

---

[1] TRANSLATOR'S NOTE: "Divine" and "metadivine" here and in the sequence render (inadequately and misleadingly) Hebrew *ᵓelōhī* and *ᶜal ᵓelōhī*. The former means "of the gods," the latter, "transcending the gods"; the former refers to the individual, personalized pagan divinities, the latter to the transcendent, primordial forces which, while conceived of as numinous, are impersonal and universally pervasive. "Divine" must be understood, then, to mean "of or pertaining to *divinities*" (not *divinity*), "metadivine," "transcending the divinities, the gods" (though divine in the normal sense).

Hebrew *hawāyā*, in *hawāyā qadmōnā* (here rendered "primordial realm"), *hawāyā ᶜal ᵓelōhīth* (here rendered "metadivine realm") has proved to be equally difficult to translate. Our "realm" conveys a notion of a discrete spatial (or temporal) domain which *hawāyā* lacks altogether ("category of being" comes closest to its meaning). No more is intended than a conceptual "realm," a category of being. Thus the forces of the "metadivine realm" (e.g., magic) are universally pervasive and effective.

are specific embodiments of a more generalized power, and learning from his myths that they call upon forces outside themselves, the pagan employs magic also, hoping thereby to activate the forces of the metadivine.

It is owing to this radical dichotomy that paganism could never content itself with being merely "religious"; it could not be satisfied with service to the will of the gods only. Because of the mythological nature of its gods, because of their subjection to a primordial realm, paganism was necessarily and essentially magical as well. The sphere of the gods, the "religious" sphere, was always qualified by the sphere of powers beyond the gods. It is the mythological character of paganism's gods that provides the framework for its synthesis of magical and religious elements.

What we have described as "the fundamental idea" was, of course, never articulated or abstractly formulated as the basis of a systematic world view. And yet we find it in all pagan religions, and in every stage of their development. It is the prime category of pagan thought, the original intuition that shaped religious creativity everywhere. We find it incorporated in many forms—in legends, in speculation, in law and custom. All of paganism serves, in fact, as an expression of this basic idea. Only by appreciating this can we understand the peculiar position of Israelite religion in the history of culture. Hence, we shall devote the following pages to survey in some detail the historic crystallizations of the pagan view in various cultures. The material is ordered formally, in the main, according to motifs and content, disregarding the literary genre or provenance (priestly, popular, etc.). Such a cross-section will serve to strengthen further our contention that the fundamental idea was truly all-pervasive, and found expression in every pagan creation.

THE GODS AND THEIR MYTHS

CosmoGONY—The following features are characteristic of pagan cosmogonies: a primordial realm which harbors the seeds of all being; a theogony telling of the birth of gods who are sexually differentiated and who procreate; the creation of the cosmos out of the primordial stuff—the same out of which the gods emerged, or from some "divine" substance. Also prevalent is the idea of several divine acts of creation; i.e., creation is not a single act, it has several divine "roots."

[Sumerian cosmogony conceived that in the beginning there was the primeval sea, Nammu, "the mother who gave birth to all the gods." Out of it the cosmic mountain, consisting of the male heaven (An) and female earth (Ki), proceeded. From their union the air-god Enlil was born, who begot the moon-god Nanna, who, in turn, begot the sun-god Utu. Man is created later by Nammu, Ninmah, and Enki, god of wisdom. It is Enki who fills the rivers with water and fish, the plain with plants and animals, and creates the tools and techniques of civilization.—M.G.]

Babylonian creation stories—there are several, and not all are wholly preserved—all display these features. According to the main account, *Enuma elish*, only the waters of chaos—Apsu and Tiamat, male and female —were present at first. These "mingled their waters" and begot the successive generations of the gods. Tiamat then tries to destroy her offspring, but Marduk, the head of the pantheon, overcomes her, kills her, and creates the world out of her corpse. Thus, both gods and the world ultimately derive from Tiamat. Another account tells how Anu created the sky and Ea, the sea, for his habitation. There are several versions of the creation of man. In *Enuma elish*, Marduk fashions the first man out of the blood of the slain Kingu, who was Tiamat's consort. Another account ascribes man's creation to the mother goddess Mami with the help of Enki (Ea). According to Berosus, one of the gods, after cutting off Bel's head, fashioned man out of earth kneaded with his blood. Common to all these stories is the idea of a primeval realm out of which the gods have emerged and within which they operate. Their actions actualize the infinite, mysterious powers that inhere in this realm.

Egyptian cosmogonies speak of the primeval waters, Nun, within which the first god, Atum, was formed. Atum engendered upon himself twins, Shu and Tefnet, from whom were born Geb (earth) and his wife, Nut (sky). Shu lifted Nut off her husband, thus creating the world. From these pairs the gods were born. But there are several accounts of creation. Re, Ptah, Neith, Amon, and others are each, at one time or another, represented as creators. Thus, Re, the sun-god, is also said to be the primal god who fathered Nut; yet Nut is his mother, who gives birth to him daily. In Memphis, Ptah was regarded as the first god, as Nun, out of whom the gods emerged. But Ptah himself was divided into the male Ptah-Nun and the female Ptah-Naunet. Another version speaks of a lotus plant that grew out of the primeval waters in which the sun-god was sitting as a child. Yet another has the sun-god emerge from an egg that lay on a hill that rose out of the water. All these stories speak in terms of birth and procreation and derive the gods from a primordial realm.

Canaanite creation stories, preserved in late writings, tell of a primeval spirit and chaos that preceded all. Then desire arose and moved the spirit to mate with "its origin," chaos, They engendered Mot, the father of all creatures. Or, again, we hear that in the beginning there were time, desire, and mist; desire and mist gave birth to air and wind, and these produced the cosmic egg from which all creatures sprang. Or it was the union of ether and air that produced the "youthful god," from whom proceed Chousoros and the cosmic egg. The Canaanite gods were, thus, not considered to have been primary; they were born out of a pre-existent substance by "desire" and the sexual process. They, in turn, had sexual properties and generated accordingly. Of their generations and interrelationships, we now have firsthand evidence in the myths that have been uncovered at Ras Shamra-Ugarit. The deities of Ras Shamra are a community of husbands and wives, fathers and sons, brothers and sisters, who contend with each other, build each other houses, sacrifice, make banquets, and so forth. Their pagan mark is that they are born. Asherah, wife of the arch deity El, is their mother, whose breasts all have sucked; a special ritual celebrates the birth of Dawn and Dusk, offspring of two of El's wives.

Perhaps the most typical expression of pagan thought is to be found in India. There are various Indian cosmogonies, corresponding to their several literary cycles and periods. One of the Vedic creation hymns (Rig-Veda, X, 129) speaks of an indefinable primordial One Thing; there was darkness concealed by darkness, animated by the great power of warmth. Desire was first to arise within it, the primal seed and germ of spirit which links being to non-being. According to another version, at first there were primeval waters within which originated "the golden germ," the cosmic egg containing the gods and the world. Yet another account makes Dyaus (heaven) and Prithiyi (earth) the parents of the gods, although elsewhere the heaven and earth are said to have been themselves generated by gods. In the hymn to Purusha (Rig-Veda, X, 90), the creation of the world proceeds from the substance of a primeval being that the gods sacrificed. His mouth became the Brahman; his arms, the warrior; his legs, the common folk; from his mind the moon was produced; from his eye, the sun; from his head, the sky; from his feet, the earth; and so forth. The Brahmanas contain various legends concerning creation; it is a common notion that the beginning of things was water. Desiring to reproduce, and becoming heated in the process, the waters generate a golden egg, out of which Prajapati, the creator, is born. He utters three holy words; and the earth, air, and sky come into being. Then he creates the good gods and their evil rivals, the Asuras. According to the epic mythology, Brahman is the origin of all: Brahman, the impersonal, absolute reality in which are the seeds of all things, from which all proceeded, and to which all will return at the end of the world. Brahman is, thus, none other than the primordial realm, as yet undifferentiated into gods. As creator, Brahman is personalized in the form of Brahma or Prajapati, who, though styled the creator of all, is depicted as emerging in one fashion or another out of the primordial realm. One version tells of his birth from a golden egg floating on the primeval waters. Another speaks of him springing from a lotus that grew out of the navel of Vishnu, or in the waters. Brahma is spoken of at times as though he were alone and all-sufficient. Yet he has a wife and a daughter with whom he fell in love; he has four faces, in order to be able to gaze upon her always. He is not all-sufficient; he needs the help of other gods, and together with them, he stirs up the ocean to discover its secrets. The Upanishads have another version of the Purusha legend. Here it is Atman who was existent primally, "in the shape of man" (*purusha*). He divided himself in two and became husband and wife; the two engendered humankind. Then this primary couple take on successively the forms of various paired creatures and, mating, give birth to them all. From his mouth, the *purusha* produced fire, from his seed all fluids, including soma (the drink of the gods). From him came the gods also, "for he is all gods."

Zoroastrianism also knows of a primordial realm apart from the gods. The very notion of two primal godheads, Ormazd (light, good) and Ahriman (darkness, evil), implies that there is no one supreme and absolute ruler. Besides these two there are other eternal beings—open space, boundless time (Zervan), endless light, and infinite darkness. Ormazd dwells in the endless light, Ahriman, in the infinite darkness—both realms being conceived of as a kind of primary substance. The Minokhired, a later work, states that Ormazd created the world out of light with the assent and blessing of Zervan, who is thus regarded as independent of and superior to him. But Ormazd and Ahriman not only limit each other, both are born deities. Plutarch reports a Persian belief that the two were born out of light and darkness respectively. Another view—certainly ancient—makes Zervan the father of the twins Ormazd and Ahriman. Later sources preserve various accounts of their birth. Zervan, it is said, made libations one thousand years, but because of his doubt, Ahriman was born along with Ormazd. Zervan, then, is not ultimately sovereign; he makes libations, he doubts, he does not know what will be born to him. Damascius, too, knows of a Persian belief that space or time are the primeval beings out of which the good and evil gods, or their parents, light and darkness, were born. But even in his own realm, Ormazd is not ultimately sovereign. When Ahriman comes to battle with him and his good creation, Ormazd agrees to a combat after nine thousand years, because he has foreknowledge that then he will be able to defeat him. This time-plan is not determined by Ormazd;

he merely has knowledge of what has been foreordained, and bests Ahriman by his superior knowledge. Nor can he fight the plagues that Ahriman has created without the help of other gods and creatures which he brings into being for this purpose.

Greek cosmogony displays the same essential features. While Homer does not offer a systematized theory, we find that Oceanus is represented as the father of all the gods, with Tethys as mother. The pantheon is a lively community of gods and goddesses who love and hate, fight and make peace, eat, drink, and procreate. The ruling gods are a younger generation that seized power from its elders. Hesiod presents a finished cosmogony and theogony. First Chaos came into being, next Gaea (earth) and Tartarus (underworld), and afterward Eros, the delight and master of the gods. With the mating of Gaea and Uranus (heaven), the theogony begins, ending with Zeus, who dethrones Cronus, his father, becomes chief of the pantheon and begets a host of Olympian gods. The various other theogonies, much as they differ in details, are the same in essence. They assume a primeval realm full of various powers, male and female elements, and desire; the world and the gods who rule it come into being by a process of natural (sexual) reproduction.

Gnosticism, while laying aside the pagan deification of nature (in which it saw the domain of evil), is no less pagan in its conception of a primordial realm and sexual differentiation and procreation in deity. The Mandaeans, for example, assume two primeval realms, light and darkness, which are ignorant of each other. The King of Light is born out of the upper realm; other divinities emanate from him. There are male and female gods, who unite and produce offspring. The gods are not all-powerful; they eat and drink, and are dependent on forces outside them. Thus, when the devil Ur tried to storm heaven, it was Hibil, son of the reigning god Hayye Qadmaye, who defeated him and his mother, Ruha. Similar views are to be found in the other gnostic systems.

The obscure Chinese cosmogonies also indicate a belief in a primordial, metadivine realm. A popular view, known however only from late sources, tells of P'an Ku, the creator, emerging from the great chaos. Chinese philosophy speaks of an infinite creative power, Shang-ti, an impersonal, eternal element of the world order, symbolized by the heaven. For the Taoist, the mother of all things which preceded heaven and earth is the Tao—the undifferentiated, ultimate reality which knows no law but its own intrinsic nature. For several philosophic schools, the material principle of the universe is composed of two forces, an active, or male, and a passive, or female; from their interplay all things are engendered. Gods and spirits are not primary; they too were born out of the ultimate realm and are subject to its order.

Japanese accounts preserved in the Nihongi make the origin of the world a chaotic mass in the form of an egg that contained the germs of all being. This substance separated into heaven and earth, and between them the gods were produced. Seven generations of gods passed until the last heaven-born couple, Izanagi and Izanami, appeared. Their union produced the islands of Japan, the nature gods, and finally the gods who rule the universe.

Germanic myths tell of a primeval "yawning gap"—apparently a chaos-image—in which northern rivers of cold and frost met the heat and fire of the south. The union of heat and cold produced the giant Ymir, from whose sweat, in turn, the giants were born. A product of the same union was the monstrous cow Audumla, who suckled Ymir. From the salty stones in the "yawning gap" which she licked, Buri was born. His son, Bur, uniting with a daughter of the giants, begot Odin, "the father of the gods," and his brothers. These killed Ymir, filled the abyss with his corpse, out of which they then proceeded to create the world. But the gods are not omnipotent; their life is somehow dependent upon Yggdrasill, the world tree. At a predestined time, the world and the gods will end; the world tree will go up in fire, and chaos will return.

Fundamentally the same viewpoint prevails among those various Australian, African, and American tribes for whom a kind of "primitive monotheism" has been claimed since the days of Andrew Lang. The discovery that primitive cultures have conceptions of high gods has, to be sure, great significance. It undermines the unilinear theories of Tylor and Spencer, according to which the gods evolved gradually from earlier notions regarding the human soul. The conception of high gods may be quite independent of the ghost-soul concept; the idea of a benign creator is also, apparently, primary. We cannot set up a neat ladder of religious progress through which all cultures passed. As we now see it, religion had many beginnings. Mana-beliefs and faith in gods and spirits can be coeval and coexistent. Yet, this does not support the claim that there existed an ancient monotheism, of which mythological polytheism is a degenerate offspring.

The mark of monotheism is not the concept of a god who is creator, eternal, benign, or even all-powerful; these notions are found everywhere in the pagan world. It is, rather, the idea of a god who is the source of all being, not subject to a cosmic order, and not emergent from a pre-existent realm; a god free of the limitations of magic and mythology. The high gods of primitive tribes do not embody this idea.

To begin with, not all such gods are creators, which is to say that exaltedness does not involve temporal priority. Alongside of the high god there exists the universe of being, with all its forces. Moreover, those who are creators do not always create all things, nor do they always act alone. Baiame (of the Kamilaroi and their neighbors) is the creator of "all," yet there exist among these same tribes other creation stories, with other actors. The crane threw an emu egg skyward which eventually became the sun. Another account tells how Baiame came from far off, turned animals into humans, and went his way. Nurrundere is a creator, but along with him we find the brothers, Nepelle and Waiungare. The latter's birth is recounted thus: his goddess-mother fashioned him out of her dung, played before him and he became a man—a typical account of creation from pre-existent matter. The brothers are creators independent of Nurrundere—one of fish, the other of kangaroo. These notions are far from monotheistic; any one story that speaks of a creation of all must be qualified by the picture that emerges when all the legends are seen together.

The "eternity" which is attributed to these high gods does not imply causal primacy, or freedom from necessity and life processes. The subjection of these gods to a metadivine sphere is expressed here not by theogonies (which are quite scarce), but by their need of external means of subsistence and strengthening. Thus, while Altyira (of the Aranda) is "eternal," he shares this attribute with the sky, earth, water, primeval men, and primeval creators; he also is said to hunt game in the heights of heaven. Nurrundere is a fisherman; he is wounded in battle with a magician, and his old age is marred by deafness and debility. Baiame feeds on the emu bird; his lower extremities are said to have turned into stone in his old age, so that his son now reigns for him. All these gods have families. Puluga, the "eternal" god of the Andaman islanders, makes himself a wife and eats, drinks, and sleeps long in the summers. He descends from heaven to provision himself with various foods. He is omniscient—but only during the daytime. Kaga, the high god of the Bushmen, was at first benign, but his many troubles made him malevolent; he has a wife and two children.

Schmidt believes that the mythological traits of these gods are the product of a later, decadent stage in the history of these religions. From the fact that the gods are also creators who inhabit heaven, control rain, and show concern for morality, he infers an earlier stage in which a pristine concept was free of mythological accretions. The sole support of this argument is the god-idea of the Kurnai, a tribe of southeastern Australia. Concerning their high god, Mungan ngaua, we happen to have no myths— probably owing to the paucity of our data. The Kurnai are culturally very backward; that they should have so refined a god-concept is taken as evidence for the theory of degeneration. And yet, Mungan ngaua has a son, Tundun. Schmidt interprets this sonship "in a moral sense," and rests his case on that basis. But Mungan ngaua is neither a creator, nor originally a sky-god; he only ascends to heaven. The other legends of the Kurnai indicate that their conceptions were far from monotheistic. Their flood story tells of a frog in whom all the waters were stored at first; when a snake succeeded in making it laugh, it disgorged the waters that brought on the flood; Mungan ngaua plays no part. Besides him, the Kurnai know of an evil sky-god, Brewin, who has a wife and son. He is in the storm wind, gives magicians baleful magic, and causes sickness and other misfortunes. Mungan ngaua is but one of several powers of the universe.

Hence, the high gods play a minor role in the cult. It is the totem around which daily religious life of the Australian tribes revolves. The Kurnai make Tundun, Mungan ngaua's son, the center of the cult. The rites are essentially magical; they were established by the high gods, but their potency is intrinsic. The gods themselves play no active part in them. Significantly enough, the gods are also thought to be magicians. Baiame is "a great magician"; Bundyil dances a magic dance around the clods he fashioned into men; Waiungare and his mother are both magicians; and the gods are said to give magic to magicians.

To what extremes the attempt to find primitive monotheism can lead is seen in Schmidt's enthusiasm over the cosmogonic accounts of Californian tribes. At first there were only sea and sky, from which the creator descended, or on which he and Coyote (the evil god) were floating in a canoe. Another account has it that a silver-gray fox, the creator, congealed in a cloud in the primeval sky, while Coyote emerged out of a fog. In these stories Schmidt sees creation *ex nihilo*.

There is then no reason to regard the mythological element in these religions as a result of degeneration. Its ultimate ground is the idea that each god represents only one embodiment of the forces of a universe filled with divine powers. This limitation and plurality produces a tension between powers, hence the events in the life of the gods, their needs and desires. The high god was never conceived as a sole prime cause of all; and so there was room for myth-making. The mythology is a development giving expression to an idea that was fundamental and original; it is not a decay.

THE GODS AND MATTER—Although the will of the gods plays a significant part in the cosmogonies, there is something that transcends it: the power of matter, the innate nature of the primordial order. The gods are conceived in the world-stuff, emerge out of it, and are subject to its nature.

The god has a potent mana, inherited from the primordial stuff through which he acts. But this power is regarded as inhering in the substance of the god, not in his will or spirit. This becomes evident from myths in which the god remains potent even after his death—i.e., after he has ceased being a willing being and has become mere lifeless substance. The various stories of creation out of the corpses of gods and the widespread cult of the graves of the gods are rooted in this concept. Moreover, the god's mana belongs to everything given off by his body; his tears, his spittle, his blood, his mutilated members, his dung—all are represented as sources of life and creation.

The dependence of the gods upon what lies outside them is embodied in the common notion that they are in need of food and drink. Corresponding to the theogony which tells how they were born out of the primeval substance, this makes their continued existence dependent upon the external matter they take in. It is a kind of permanent "theogony." Child-gods imbibe vigor from the breasts of goddesses. Certain substances are often specified as the sources of divine vitality: the Indian soma, the Germanic mead, the Greek nectar and ambrosia. At times the gods have recourse to magical foods and drinks that endow them with special powers, that heal them of sickness, that protect them against evil magic, that rejuvenate them, that act as aphrodisiacs, and so forth.

There are also magical objects that the gods employ for their needs, and that are considered the source of their power. Such are the Babylonian "Tablets of Destiny," possession of which confers supreme authority in heaven. The transfer of these tablets, and with them supremacy, involves a shift in power, as when Marduk takes them from Kingu, or when the Zu bird steals them from Enlil. Again, Marduk arms himself with all sorts of potent weapons before going out to battle Tiamat and her entourage. Ishtar has a girdle with powers of fertility; in fact, all her clothes seem to be magically charged; hence she must be stripped of them before entering the domain of the underworld. Similarly, Aphrodite has an aphrodisiacal girdle which Hera borrows to get the better of Zeus. Hermes has a magic wand which gives happiness and riches. Magic seals, crystals, in which the future can be divined, magic weapons to ward off evil, all these are standard features of mythology the world over. They are a fundamental symbol of paganism, bespeaking the idea that there is no supreme divine will that governs all. The rule of the gods is ultimately grounded on the mysterious forces that inhere in matter, in a realm which lies outside of them.

THE GODS AND NECESSITY—Necessity dominates the universe and the gods who are part of it. Birth, procreation, growth, youth, age, death, and the like—are innate properties of the world-stuff. The fabulous wonderland of myth and magic is bound to necessity; even the gods must bow to the inexorable decrees of fate.

It is this idea, as we shall see further on, that lies at the bottom of the Babylonian astrology which eventually permeated the whole of the pagan world. In Hindu thought, it appears as *rita*—the world order, the principle of pattern and regularity in all phenomena. By *rita*, the rivers flow; the wheel of time runs by it; the righteous man meditates on it; it is embodied in the correct cult. The gods are sometimes called the lords of *rita*, but they are also its servants, guardians, members of its household. The Persians know this concept under the name *asha*. With the Greeks, the ultimate arbiter is *anankē* (necessity) or *moira* (fate). While the gods are spoken of as deciding destinies, they in fact do no more than fulfil the decrees of *anankē*. Thetis foretells to Achilles that he is destined to die after Hector, but it is not Zeus who decides this. Zeus merely weighs the fates of the two in the balance to learn what is destined for them. Nor are the gods above *anankē*; the transfer of authority from Uranus to Cronus and again to Zeus is an irrevocable decree. Cronus must resort to swallowing up his sons so that one of them might not depose him. Thetis is fated to give birth to a son who will surpass his father; to avert this, the gods marry her to the mortal Peleus. Again, Uranus and Gaea tell Zeus that his wife, Metis, is destined to bear wise children; the son she will have after Athena will rule over gods and men. Zeus swallows Metis to forestall this evil. Aeschylus utilizes this idea when he has Prometheus threaten Zeus that his son, stronger than he, will dethrone him through the decree of *anankē*; for even Zeus may not avoid what is destined. The Romans called this sovereign decree *fatum;* similar notions are found throughout the pagan world.

Another reflection of the same concept is the belief that the gods and the world are subject to fixed times and cycles. The course of birth, growth, death, day and night, and the seasons are all conceived as regulated by necessity. It is a widespread notion that the world is destined to pass through various predetermined stages before its destruction or renewal. The gods have no control over this "natural" process; indeed, their fate, too, is usually involved. Seneca, speaking in the name of Berosus, says that the destruction of the world will eventuate from a certain zodiacal configuration which will bring on devastation by fire or water. Paganism here approaches a scientific and mathematical conception of the universe.

THE WISDOM OF THE GODS—The conception of the wisdom of the gods is in full accord with this view of their place in the universe. The wisdom of a deity does not consist in self-awareness, in knowledge of his will and its effect on a world dependent upon it, but rather in a knowledge of the world and its mysterious properties. Its object lies outside the gods; it is knowledge of an order of which they are but a part. The god acquires his wisdom along with his other divine powers from the seed out of which he was born, or by some magical means. Precisely because it is not an essential attribute of the god as god, it may belong as a specific property to certain gods. And so paganism knows of gods who are especially wise in magic, in the therapeutic arts, or in other crafts. Significantly, it is not always the creator or head of the pantheon who is characterized by special knowledge.

In Egypt Thoth was viewed as lord of wisdom and magic; he invented writing and was the great authority in astronomy, medicine, and other sciences. Re himself has recourse to his magical skills to ward off harm and sickness. Isis, who beguiles Re into disclosing his secret name to her, is also a great magician. Similarly, wise Ormazd beguiles Ahriman into postponing their battle because he knows a secret that his rival is ignorant of. A typical expression of the gods' dependence upon matter is the connection of wisdom with primeval waters. The Babylonian Ea, god of the waters, is the lord of wisdom and magic, and the constant counselor of Marduk. He is the inventor and teacher of writing and the crafts. Marduk, Ea's son, is considered wisest of the gods, and Nintu, his daughter, knows how to interpret dreams. In Greek mythology, Thetis, Nereus and his daughters, Proteus, and other water deities are wise, oracular, and law-giving.

The gods can acquire wisdom. Marduk learns medicine and spells from Ea; Cronus learns from Gaea all sorts of tricks; Apollo learns divination from Pan; Hermes learns how to divine with lots from Apollo. Odin learns the runes after he falls from the world tree. Izanami and Izanagi, the Japanese creator-gods, after discovering that they are male and female, do not know how to copulate until a bird instructs them. In the same way ordinary gods, or even men, may surpass the chief gods in wisdom. When the Zu bird stole the Tablets of Destiny from Enlil, one account credits the king of Uruk, Lugalbanda, with finding a way to restore them to the gods. Kothar-wa-hasis, the craftsman of the Ugaritic pantheon, is engaged to build a palace for Aliyan-Baal. Zeus is astounded at the skill shown by Hephaestus in making Hercules' shield. And without Prometheus' cunning, Zeus and his helpers could not have subdued the Titans. Zeus does not even manufacture his own thunderbolts; the Cyclopes (who are mortals) make them for him, or as others have it, the sons of Uranus gave them to him as a gift. It is not Zeus, but Metis who is "wiser than all the gods and men"; to possess her wisdom, Zeus swallows her. This last story is a striking expression of the pagan concept that wisdom is something external to the gods and has to be acquired by them.

THE GODS AND THE WORLD—The outcome of the pagan view that the gods originate in the world stuff is to remove any fixed bounds between them and the world of men and other creatures. For there is a common womb out of which both the gods and all the phenomena of nature have sprung. This confusion of realms manifests itself both in mythology and the cult.

Thus, we find no clear-cut distinction between worship of nature and worship of the gods of nature. What began as worship of natural phenomena, developed into the cult of nature-gods. Even in the theistic stage, however, the worship of nature itself, as the embodiment of the life processes of the gods, lingers on. In one way or another the sun, moon, stars, waters, fire, etc., were always worshiped, even after the myth-makers had created a universe full of gods of whom these were but symbols.

But it is not only the larger phenomena of nature that are deified and sanctified. Various substances—fetishes thought to be charged with mana or viewed as housing gods or spirits—are treated as divinities. The cult of sacred stones, sacred trees, or sacred animals is an important element of paganism. A typical expression of this idea is found in totemism, in which animals or inanimate objects are considered bearers of divine power or lodgings of spirits and gods who are the kin of the tribe. Here we find an actual kinship relation between the god and the world. Similar phenomena appear in higher stages of religious evolution. The cult of various animals was widespread in Egypt,where the gods were incarnate in beasts (the bulls Apis and Mnevis, the ram of Mendes). The belief that gods are incorporated in animals has its counterpart in the idea that animals have been born of gods.

A characteristic expression of this intermingling of realms is the idea of a physical bond between gods and men. We have already noted the Babylonian legends telling how man was created out of the blood of a slain god and the Indian story of the creation of men out of the body of the *purusha*. The Greeks also regarded the gods as genetically related to men, there being no clearly defined boundary between them; the gods were distinguished only by immortality. Paganism knows of unions not only between gods, but between gods and mortals. The Gilgamesh epic tells how its hero spurned Ishtar's advances, throwing up to her the harm she did to all her previous human and animal lovers. In early times, the kings of Sumer and Akkad were considered husbands of Ishtar; Antiochus Epiphanes still maintained this conception, as evidenced by his intention to marry Nanaia (Ishtar) in her temple (taking her treasury as dowry). Rites celebrating the nuptials of gods and women are found in many cultures. Herodotus speaks of a priestess dedicated to Bel who used to sleep in his temple in Babylon; he tells of a similar custom in the temple of Zeus-Amon in Thebes, and in Patara (in Lycia). How popular such notions were can be judged from the story in Josephus (*Antiquities* xviii. 3, 4) about the Roman woman who was violated by her lover in the temple of Isis with the connivance of priests who deluded her into believing that the god Anubis desired her. In Athens there was an annual festival commemorating the marriage of Dionysus with the local "queen." Stories about heroes (i.e., demigods) who mated with women and begot children were also common and were frequently utilized by royal pretenders.

There is widespread belief among pagans that peoples and families have descended from gods. The Germans thought themselves the children of a god who was born of the earth; the Gauls traced their ancestry to Dis Pater; Arabian tribes claimed divine ancestors. Divine ancestry was claimed by aristocratic families of Greece, Rome, and Carthage. Kings of many lands represent themselves as offspring of gods; this is the ground of the common belief that the reigning monarch was begotten by a god who visited his mother.

The continuity of the divine and human realm is the basis of the pagan belief in apotheosis, in the possibility of man's attaining godhood. The idea manifests itself in various forms: in the cult as the worship of deified men; in eschatology as the promise of ultimate immortality, of joining the gods, or even rising above them.

The Babylonians knew of men, such as Utnapishtim, upon whom immortality was conferred, and an early phase of Sumero-Akkadian kingship knew of the deification of kings and their worship. But it was in Egypt that divine kingship found its classic expression in the ancient Near East. The Pharaoh is "the beneficent god," "the great god," the "son of Re," and is worshiped as a god. This notion prevailed during the reign of the reformer Akhenaton as well. The dead king becomes Osiris, reigns with Atum, rises and sets with Re. Deification of dead kings is also found among the Hittites and the Aramaeans. Worship of kings and heroes was current throughout the Roman and Hellenistic world. In Samos, Lysander was worshiped as a god, with altars, sacrifices, and songs; Dion was received with divine homage at Syracuse. Alexander was deified in life and death as the son of Amon or Zeus; in Alexandria, he was worshiped as the local deity until the triumph of Christianity. His Seleucid and Ptolemaic successors maintained the cult of royalty. Roman deification of kings becomes customary after the time of Julius Caesar. Apollonius of Tyana was paid divine honors, and Caracalla even built him a temple.

The mystery religions in particular promised their adherents an apotheosis after death. In the Egyptian Osiris cult the dead person becomes Osiris through various magical rites and dwells among the gods. The aspiration to immortality may also have played a part in the cult of Tammuz and Ishtar. It was the fundamental element in the mystery religions that spread through the Hellenistic world. Their rites of purification, asceticism, and sacraments aimed at union with the godhead, or at enthusiasm—the indwelling of the god in man. Orphic rites promised liberation of the soul from the prison of matter and its elevation to the divine realm. The oriental mysteries, including the gnostic, claimed to make men part of deity. The participant in the cult of Attis became her lover and attained divinity; the devotees of Isis and Serapis became gods; and the complete gnosis made man and god one in essence. These tendencies have their echoes in pagan philosophy as well. The ultimate goal that Plato sets for the philosopher is, after all, to rise above the world of matter to the realm of the divine ideas.

SOCIETY AND MORALITY—The gods normally play a significant role in the social order of all cultures. They are the patrons of families, tribes, and nations; they are ancestors, kings, heroes, founders of culture and civilization. The social order is under their surveillance, and they are both legislators and guardians of justice.

Modern theories give the social element especial prominence in the evolution of religion. For the history of Israelite religion, the interpretation of Robertson Smith and his followers is a case in point. The social role of the deity is regarded as tending to break through the limitations of his natural function. The tribal or national god is involved in all the aspects of the community's life; he gives grain, wine, cattle and sheep, children, sun and rain, victory or defeat. All of nature thus comes to be his domain. With the enlargement of society, with the breakdown of narrow ethnic boundaries, and the realization that all mankind is one, the ethnic god tends to become the god of all men, the one god. The prophetic elaboration of Israelite religion is interpreted along these lines.

But, as a matter of fact, social or moral features in no way alter the basic character of the pagan gods. If the social role of a god elevates him above his natural function, it in no way affects his radical subjection to a transcendent order. For society and its gods are both conceived as belonging to the cosmic order and subject to its laws. There is nothing in a social role that in itself confers total sovereignty. History shows that the social element in paganism was a source of division and multiplicity among the gods no less than their natural functions. Families, tribes, peoples, states, and classes all developed their own tutelary gods. And even after the domain of an ethnic god became enlarged, the nature-gods continued to be worshiped alongside them, the two realms often being quite confused. And, while the great empires (Egypt, Assyria, Rome) did tend to symbolize themselves by a supreme god, they never were led thereby to monotheism.

The ethical moment was equally incapable of giving the gods ultimate sovereignty. For morality is viewed by the pagan not as an expression of the sovereign will of the gods, but as part of the supernal order that governs the gods themselves. Morality, too, is, so to speak, part of nature, and its laws "laws of nature." It is characteristic that a god's moral role be viewed as an adjunct to his natural function. The Sumerian Babbar and the Babylonian Shamash, both sun-gods, are gods of justice and righteousness. The sons of Shamash are Kittu (right) and Mesharu (justice). We find also that moral functions are served, not necessarily by the chief gods, but by lesser divinities, such as the Erinyes—the Greek spirits of punishment.

Being part of the cosmic order, sin and punishment are by nature interrelated as cause and effect. Evil fertilizes the womb of Druj, the Persian goddess of impurity and evil; repentance and purification uproot the seed. Fornication disturbs Ormazd, brings on drought, debilitates man, and so forth. In the Laws of Manu, good and evil works bring on prosperity or misfortune by their intrinsic nature. Evil causes misfortune to a man or his descendants, goodness purifies his soul, raises him to divine rank, and redeems him from the cycle of reincarnations. The Babylonian view also connects sin and punishment innately. Sin involves impurity, disease, and misery; and these are all regarded as the workings of evil demons. Evil is also conceived as brought on by gods, but the role of the gods is, in fact, rather passive; if provoked, they abandon man to the evil demons. Sickness is a curse brought on by evil spirits or magicians. A Babylonian incantation against sickness has Marduk confessing to Ea, "I know not how this man has sinned, or how he can be healed." Sin thus acts automatically without the action or knowledge of the high gods; they have to search for a way to remove its curse from man. At times, sin and its consequences are viewed as decrees of blind fate—as in the tragedy of Oedipus. The acme is reached in the Buddhist concept of *karma*—the self-operating law of moral causality and retribution which binds both gods and men.

The gods themselves are subject to evil forces and impulses, and, having sinned, they too must suffer for their guilt. Thus, the guilty Kingu is slain for his part in Tiamat's attack upon the Babylonian gods. Gilgamesh rebukes Ishtar for her wantonness and cruelty. The Hindu creator Prajapati lies with his daughter, and is punished by the terrible Rudra. Indra, having committed murder, is depressed, and so purifies himself. Cronus castrates his father, and Zeus brings him, in turn, down to Hades. Zeus, Aphrodite, and most of the gods of the Greek pantheon are steeped in promiscuity. The Teutonic Odin is a drunkard, a deceiver, an adulterer, a murderer; it is the same in one mythology after another.

These myths cannot be explained away as the product of a primitive age in which men saw no harm in such acts. Surely murder, theft, and licentiousness were recognized as sins even in earliest times. The fact is that the myths do regard them as sins for which expiation and purification must be made. There is no avoiding the conclusion that paganism ascribed to the gods what it knew to be evil acts. And it is no wonder. For the desires and impulses that rule the gods are a heritage of the substance out of which they have been born. They, no less than all beings, are fated to live under subjection to sin, as they are fated to need food and drink. Although they are the guardians of justice and morality, other forces which are equally rooted in their nature may at times gain the upper hand. The position of the gods is like that of a human king; he, too, is charged with preserving justice and the social order, but on occasion he succumbs to temptation and violates both. The sinning god is thus another characteristic manifestation of the pagan idea.

THE ACME OF PAGANISM—The religions of India—Brahmanism and, especially, Buddhism—express with unparalleled clarity the idea that the gods are subject to a transcendent order and bound to a system of eternal forces and laws. We find, too, the idea that the divine and the mundane are expressions of the same primordial reality. The idea of apotheosis also reached extreme expression there, with gods and men alike seeking to attain a realm of bliss which transcends them both.

These ideas, expressed with varying degrees of approximation in the popular religion, pervade the speculative pantheism found in the philosophic or theosophic chapters of the Upanishads. We find here the conception of an eternal, supreme, impersonal being, the source of all—Brahman-Atman. This is not the creator of the world, but the world itself. It is the life in everything; it encompasses the sun, the elements, nature, man; it has always existed; it is the lasting substratum of all that is transient. Being the cosmic order, it cannot, of course, violate it. There is a tendency, on the other hand, to identify this with the *purusha*, to conceive it as "cosmic man." We likewise find it represented by a personal god, Brahma, who is a typical born and begetting god.

The impersonal conception underlies Buddhist thinking, which, while not denying the existence of the gods, made them subject to a realm beyond them. Buddhism speaks of an impersonal, abstract concept of the cosmic mechanism, the natural law that governs all. Redemption from pain and the cycle of reincarnations is achieved by all-embracing knowledge which even the gods cannot do without. For the gods are bound to cosmic laws, and they also must be released from the bonds of life. The god is but one of the incarnations of eternal being; his soul can be incorporated in man as well, so completely fused are all the manifestations of being. Buddha himself had been a god, and in the course of his transformations he was often an animal. Hence it is not the gods who redeem, but knowledge of the secrets of existence. Brahmanism speaks of the quest of the gods for the key to the cosmic secret; they search, meditate, practice yoga. According to Buddhism, it is not the gods, but the human Buddhas who attain the highest, saving knowledge. Before the Buddha even the gods prostrate themselves. He is their teacher as well as man's. Brahma, the highest of the gods, descends from heaven, bows to Buddha, and pleads that he not conceal his doctrine, but preach it to rescue beings ("human, divine, animal, and hell-dwelling") from the painful cycle of rebirth. It is not, then, the gods who redeem man, but man who redeems himself through knowledge. Knowledge is the means of attaining Nirvana, the goal of gods and men. In this, the ideal of apotheosis reaches its ultimate expression. Yet even the advents of the Buddhas are in accord with the necessities of the impersonal cosmic law. Necessity and eternal law govern even this loftiest manifestation of paganism.

MAGIC

Magic, divination, and cult are the three forms that practical religion takes in antiquity. The magician usually acts in the name of gods and spirits; his techniques have often been revealed to him by the gods, and he is effective through their power. From this viewpoint, magic may be counted among the phenomena of religion, and the magician regarded as a priest who acts with the sanction and help of a potent god.

But magic may also appear in a "pure" form in rites that have no connection with the will of the gods, but are viewed as automatically effective, or even capable of coercing the gods to do the will of the practitioner. There can be a magical basis even to rites involving an appeal to the gods— when they themselves are conceived as skilled magicians who know the secrets of the universe and how to put them to use. It is this ever present assumption of a realm of forces apart from the gods that makes pagan religion, even in its highest manifestations, amenable to belief in magic.

The distinctive mark of all pagan rituals is that they are not directed toward the will of the gods alone. They call upon self-operating forces that are independent of the gods, and that the gods themselves need and utilize for their own benefit. The ultimate symbol of divine subjection to transcendent powers is the god as magician or as diviner.

The organic relation of religion to magic can be illustrated in the religions of Egypt and Babylonia.

Egypt was permeated with magical beliefs. It developed an enormous literature on the subject and a ramified manufacture of magical objects. Magic was called upon at every turn in life: to ward off spirits of the dead, demons, scorpions, serpents, wild beasts, fire, rain, injury, sickness, and enemies; to protect women in childbirth and new-born infants, and to insure the dying man happiness beyond the grave. The gods have an important role as teachers of magical arts to men. Their names, uttered in spells or written on charms, are a chief means of conjuring. They themselves are regarded as charged with the same powers as are found in magical objects and devices. The dead king who "devours the gods," fills his belly with their power and knowledge. Moreover, the gods practice magic in their own right; man merely imitates them. This means that the mana that inheres in the gods and their names is but part of a universally pervasive power which the gods themselves require and know how to use for their own benefit. Thoth recites "the book of the cow of heaven" over Re to protect him. Re is bitten by a snake that Isis created out of his spittle; she cures him by sorcery after she discovers his hidden name. Horus was bitten by a scorpion; Thoth brings "great magic" and cures him. In the magical literature, there is a mythological element—stories of how magic affected the lives and destinies of the gods. The stories telling how the gods were aided by magic are recited in order to ward off demons. The myth of the snake Apophis, the enemy of Re who was defeated by the gods, serves as an incantation. Re, Sekhmet, Thoth, and the god "magic" guarded the body of Osiris in the Nile from wild beasts; this serves as incantation against water animals. A spell on a house-amulet declares that through it the gods kill their enemies. Magic is thus an autonomous force that is operative even in the life of the gods. It is no wonder, then, that the Egyptian magician can threaten the gods, and, if necessary, compel them to do his will.

Babylonian magic displays the same harmonious synthesis with religion. "Black magic," the abomination of the gods, is often, but not always, connected with demons. Witches are allied with the evil demons, but they do not invariably call upon them. There are conjurations in which the sorcerer appears alongside the baleful spirits as the enemy. His evil eye is in itself harmful; so, too, are his evil word and certain baleful plants and liquors whose injurious powers he heightens by a spell. He can work through knots or by actions he performs upon the image of the person to be bewitched. At the same time, the gods play a prime role in Babylonian magic; they assist in warding off evil spirits and magicians. The priest-magician who heals the sick prays to all the gods, exalts their might, and conjures them to help. He is the man of Ea, and of Damkina (Ea's wife), the messenger of Marduk, or Marduk's firstborn, the great *āshipu* of Ea.

Yet here too the gods are portrayed as powerful magicians who use magic for their own needs. Marduk, the great magician of the gods, comes to the sick man, armed with a staff inscribed with the name of Ea, uttering the potent spell of Eridu. Ea comes to the sick man with the life-giving spell of Marduk. The gods in their wisdom know how to combat evil; but they do so as sorcerers, because evil, far from being in their control, threatens them too, unless they fend it off by magic. The seven devils capture the moon god, Sin; Enlil, distressed, sends Nusku with the news to the master charmer, Ea. The latter, after an initial lament, dispatches his son, Marduk, to the rescue with his invincible incantations. Witches have such power as can harm gods as well as men; they can weary heaven, bind up the mouths of the gods, tie the knees of goddesses. The sorcerer conjures against heaven and rises up against earth.

Egypt and Babylonia illustrate what is true for all pagan religions. Everywhere we meet with stories about the sorcery of the gods and the magical implements they utilize for themselves and for men. Here in another form, we see the fundamental idea of paganism—the subjection of deity to a realm beside and beyond them.

DIVINATION

Divination is often defined as the discovery by various means of the will and decree of the gods. But this definition inadvertently imposes upon paganism a unified view of the universe that is foreign to its essence. It presupposes that both the disclosure (by means of a sign, or prophecy, etc.) and the decree (the impending event) stem always from the will of the gods. But paganism was conscious of no such unity, for it did not attribute everything to the will of the gods. Some events and conditions had nothing to do with the gods; others befell the gods themselves as decrees of overriding fate. Even where they reigned supreme, there was no necessary identity between the god who made decrees and the god who revealed them. Pagan divination does not assume, as a matter of course, that the disclosure to man comes from the same god who determines his destiny. Perhaps the most prevalent concept is that certain gods or spirits, who have a particular faculty for discovering what has been decreed, specialize as contacts with man. Shamash, Adad, and Nabu are the Mesopotamian gods of divination and prophecy, although it is not they who determine destinies. The Greeks sought out the will of Zeus, but it is Apollo who is the god par excellence of diviner and prophet. There were, moreover, a host of other oracles—demigods, heroes, spirits of the dead—who revealed what was hidden to man. Plainly, these had no part in shaping destinies; they merely told what they had by way of occult knowledge.

In this separation between the source of the decree and the source of the disclosure, the essential nature of pagan divination reveals itself. It is not his will that the god makes known to the diviner, but his knowledge. Divining is a scientific realm, not only insofar as man is concerned, but for the gods as well; in it the gods manifest their knowledge of matters not necessarily dependent upon them. The limitations of the divine will and the radical division of divine powers are manifest in this conception.

But the diviner need not work always through gods or spirits; he also works through omens alone, or through some native supernatural faculty that frees him from dependence upon the good will of the gods. As such, he is a "scientist" who can dispense with "divine revelation." Here his work enters the category of magic, an occult, self-contained realm of knowledge. The magical side of divination is probably fundamental. Insofar as it is combined with the belief in supreme gods, it is, of course, involved in the ascertaining of their will. But what is divined is not always a matter of the gods' will; on the contrary, it may involve, as we shall see, the fate of the gods themselves. The basic idea appears to be that the system of signs and portents functions autonomously, as a part of nature through which one learns about both the will of gods and the cosmic order which transcends them. Because the system is self-operating, the gods also divine and prophesy to gain knowledge of the unknown. Divination can, therefore, not have been originated by the gods for the purpose of disclosing their will; it is prior to them; it is science of cosmic secrets by which even the gods can serve themselves.

TYPES OF DIVINATION—We may distinguish two main types of divination, inductive and intuitive—as they are termed by Bouché-Leclercq—corresponding to the two types which Cicero called artificial and natural divination (*De divinatione* i. 6). Inductive divination works by observation of external signs, various phenomena of the external world. Intuitive divination is the working of an inner power, a special faculty of the soul to foreknow or to see hidden things.

INDUCTIVE DIVINATION—What is the basis of the pagan belief (vestiges of which survive to this day) that certain external events are signs of things to come?

Insofar as it is the decree of the gods that is being disclosed through these signs and omens, the assumption appears to be that the gods employ specific phenomena as a code for their message to men. There is no natural, inherent connection between the omen and the portended event; the god has in some way intervened in the natural order for a certain purpose. Such a manifestation of divine intentions we may call a revealed sign. If the aim of all divination were to ascertain the will of the gods as revealed by them in signs and omens, there would be only this sort of sign; but this is not the case.

There was ever a strong tendency to assume a natural and causal nexus between the sign and the portended event. One typical view is that coming events cast their shadows before—a sort of inverted causality in which the posterior cause creates a prior effect. Just as the popular mind believes in personal premonitions, so it is with the cosmos: There are in nature anticipations of things to come which can be read by the initiated. Such portents are not special signs revealed by the gods, but rather a product of the natural, mysterious connection between the present and future. We may call them premonitory signs.

There is yet a third view which regards certain signs as in themselves the cause of the coming event; such may be termed causal signs.

These three types of signs are not always distinguished in pagan thought. To the extent that divination involves revealed signs it seeks to disclose the will, or at least the knowledge, of the gods. But insofar as it involves the two other types, it partakes of the nature of a magical or even natural science. Here the essentially pagan presuppositions of divination are manifest.

There is an intimate connection between divination and the gods: it is often the gods who teach men to divine, and it is to the gods that the diviner frequently looks for aid. Enmeduranki, the first priest-king of Sippar, learned divination from Shamash and Adad; they walked with him and taught him the secret of Anu, Bel, and Ea, the mystery of heaven and earth; they gave him the "tablet of the gods." Shamash places the reliable omen in the entrails of the sacrifice; Marduk fixes the heavenly signs and the course of the stars. In Babylonia and Assyria, the gods were inquired of at every turn, and so it is with many pagan peoples. But did the pagan conceive the signs he read as revealed signs, given by the gods to make their will known?

Aeschylus, in *Prometheus Bound*, represents Prometheus as man's instructor in all the sciences and arts, among which are "the many modes of divination." Now inasmuch as Prometheus' actions run counter to the will of Zeus, the modes of divination he has taught men can hardly assume the participation of the gods. They are clearly taken to be a fixed element of the cosmos, quite apart from the will of the gods. The secrets they disclose touch not only the will of the gods, but also matters belonging to the realm above and beyond them. The same view is put forth in Germanic legends. Siegfried asks Odin what signs portend success in battle. He does not ask for revealed signs; on the contrary, he wants to know those signs which herald success for gods as well as men. Odin knows them as part of his omniscience. Mantic knowledge is, thus, the wisdom of the gods. Lecanomancy is the secret of Anu, Bel, and Ea, but it is taught to man by Shamash and Adad. This occult science is one of the mysteries of heaven and earth; it does not exist for man's benefit, for disclosing to him the will of the gods. The gods know how to divine through their great wisdom; they teach it to man just as they teach him magic and incantations.

Akkadian divinatory formulas are phrased as if the intention and decree of the god addressed were being sought. And it is true that often enough this is the case. But there are also cases where inquiry is made concerning something that is obviously beyond control of the god; here the clichéd formula must not mislead us. Such is the case, for example, when Shamash is asked whether king Ashurbanipal will seize the hand of Marduk this year, whether he will go up before Bel to Babylon, "is this pleasing to your godhead and to Marduk, the great lord?" Or, again, when Agumkakrime asks Shamash whether he should restore the image of Marduk from Hani to Babylon, it is not the will or decree of Shamash, but his knowledge which is consulted.

Hemerology plays a very important role in divination. In Assyro-Babylonian civilization, the determination of auspicious days was sought before every sort of activity: building operations, marriages, journeys, sacrificing, warfare, revolution, and so forth. The gods have certain months and days in which they are at peace and benevolent, and others in which they are disturbed and angry. Eventually, lists of good and bad, lucky and unlucky days were drawn up for all kinds of sacred and profane undertakings. The gods also were frequently asked whether a given day was auspicious or not. In Egypt, likewise, hemerology was fully developed. From the Middle and New Kingdoms, we have lists of auspicious and inauspicious days, with attempts at mythological interpretations. Similar beliefs are found among the Persians, the Greeks, the Romans, and many others.

It is plain that the gods have nothing to say about this distinction between lucky and unlucky days. On the contrary, the mood of the gods themselves is determined by days and months. The nature of the day often depends on the position of the stars or the moon. The gods, in their wisdom, know the nature of the days and reveal it to those who ask them.

Hemerology also plays a part in the interpretation of omens, their meaning being contingent on the day. At times it is the day and the portent that are decisive in themselves, quite apart from the gods. If, for example, on the first of Nisan in the morning a snake sees a man before the man sees him, he will die within that year. If the man would live, he must kill the snake, bury its head, and split its sides. Note that this is a causal sign—the snake has an "evil eye" at that moment which can cause death. The means of warding off the dangers are wholly magical; the gods are neither petitioned nor invoked in a spell. More typical, however, is the following: If on a given day a snake sees a man first, he will die; if he would live, he must do as prescribed before. If he calls on Marduk in the morning, he will be delivered from harm. What is interesting here is the equal value assigned to the magical and the religious act. The Assyrian priest Nabua tells the king that a fox was seen in the garden of the god Ashur—an evil omen; but the fox was caught and killed, and the danger averted. Such signs are, of course, not provided by the gods; they are either causal or premonitory signs.

The same holds true for divination by the movements of animals. While it is true that omen-bearing animals may be considered as messengers of the gods, there is also the belief that certain creatures have the natural faculty of foreknowledge. The snake, the dog, and the raven are particularly singled out as possessing this gift. Porphyry speaks explicitly of "mantic animals" whose special quality inheres in their flesh. Men can learn the future from them directly, without the agency of the gods. Indians regarded the cuckoo as an omniscient bird; the Germans divined by the neighing of the sacred horses of the god Freyr; Pliny says that the ravens know the meaning of the signs they give; the lamb that prophesied in the time of Bocchoris spoke out of its own mantic power, and was given divine burial; the horse, Xanthus, of his own accord tells Achilles of his death; the raven brings to Apollo news of the infidelity of Coronis; the raven of the Germanic gods foretells to them the coming end of the world.

Nor were the heavenly signs necessarily regarded as given by the gods for the purpose of making their wills known. The pagan also interpreted them as reflecting events in the life of the gods quite beyond their control. The Babylonians saw in the various lunar phenomena manifestations of the life of the moon-god and his battles with other deities and demons. An eclipse meant that Sin had been captured by the seven evil spirits. Far from being decreed by the gods, the eclipse troubles and puzzles them; they anxiously seek a means to avert its portended evil. Rituals to aid Sin include an element of prayer to the gods, but fundamentally they consist of magical rites designed to ward off the baleful demonic effects of the eclipse. The days of the moon's phases were considered unlucky. The waxing and waning of the moon was viewed by some as portentous. Plutarch tells that the Egyptian priests banned the eating of onions, because they grow when the moon wanes; and the pig was declared unclean, owing to the fact that it mates at that time. The Mandaeans believed that moonlit nights were auspicious, but the child conceived at the dark of the moon was a son of darkness. Such signs also belong to the category of premonitory or causal signs.

From the language of the Babylonian omens, it appears that astral signs, far from being considered as divinely controlled, are portentous for the gods themselves. This comes out most clearly in omens which foretell the moods and actions of the gods. "If there is a double sun with a dim light, divine signs will appear and the gods will rage." "If the sun will darken on one of the days from the first to the thirtieth of Adar II . . . Shamash will accept prayer." "If Venus is dimmed in Kislimu . . . the gods will gather against the land." "If Jupiter rises as *Nibiru* . . . the gods will accept prayers; hear petitions, and will confirm the signs of the *bārū* priests."

Another type of prediction in which the gods play no part are horoscopes. "If a child is born when the moon rises, his life will be bright, happy, firmly established, and long. If a child is born when Venus rises, his life will be tranquil, abundant, and wherever he goes he will be loved. . . ." These too seem to be self-operating causes.

A dichotomy of powers between the gods and a realm beside or beyond them is implicit in all astrology. On the one hand, the heavenly bodies are living gods; therefore, astral phenomena are understood to reflect mythological events. But, besides the gods, immutable laws are operative as well. The influence of the stars follows natural and eternal laws. Within this framework the gods live out their lives. Hence the astral signs can be taken as both divine decisions and fixed laws of the metadivine realm. Because of the growing tendency toward stressing the latter scientific aspect, astrology was able eventually to separate itself entirely from the belief in gods. In Hellenistic times, it was grounded on a doctrine of cosmic sympathy, the mysterious interconnection of all phenomena whose signs are written in the heavens. For many centuries, it was deeply rooted even in the Christian and Jewish worlds. In paganism, however, it served as one of the expressions of the primary, fundamental subjection of the gods to the laws of a higher realm.

The dichotomy is most vividly seen in the Greek concept of divination. Zeus and the other gods are assumed to reveal their intentions to men both through signs and through the agency of Apollo. Yet, in the Prometheus legend, Zeus is not omniscient; he compels Prometheus to disclose to him the secret of his future. Prometheus is represented as teaching men the arts of divining without the consent of the gods. This means that the realm of divination is not bound by the will of gods. In fact, Apollo's utterances are by no means only revelations of the will of Zeus; he also discloses the decrees of fate (although it is true that the Greeks liked to confuse the two). Typical is Proteus' disclosure to Odysseus that fate has decreed he must return to Egypt and make sacrifice there to appease Zeus.

It is particularly significant that the gods are said to practice divination and guide themselves by its disclosures. Zeus divines by the golden balances of fate; Apollo learns divination from Pan; Hermes' theft of Apollo's oxen is discovered by the latter's divining; Apollo teaches Hermes divination by lot; Cronus and Zeus receive oracles regarding their rule. Germanic deities use the runes to discover the future; even the Norans, the goddesses of fate, discover the future by casting lots. The Japanese also tell of gods divining. Izanami and Izanagi, the progenitors of the world, failing at first to produce satisfactory issue, seek aid from the celestial gods; the latter discover the cause by divining. Similar conceptions are found everywhere.

INTUITIVE DIVINATION—Examination of the methods of intuitive divination leads also to the conclusion that divination is not at bottom the disclosure of the will or decision of the gods, but a way of discovering hidden things by means that have no necessary connection with the will of the gods.

ONEIROMANCY—While it is a widespread view that dreams come from the gods, this is by no means the only source of dreams that the pagan recognizes. Oneiromancy is characteristically practiced by means of the dream-riddle. For the Babylonians, it was usually Shamash who inspired such dreams, but so did the "mountain" of the underworld. Again, while the dream is often a sign sent by the gods, it may also be a causal sign, or a spontaneous premonition of things to come. That is why a bad dream is in itself to be dreaded and a good dream is in itself desirable. By magic, one induces good dreams, or the patron god may be petitioned to turn a dream to good. Bad dreams and signs are also sent by sorcerers who wish to harm men; their ill effect can be canceled by an appropriate counterspell.

The Greeks believed that "the dream comes from Zeus," but they also attributed dreams to anonymous demons. Prometheus taught men oneiromancy against the desire of the gods, which implies, again, that dreams are not simply divinely sent signs. Here, too, the bad dream is considered automatically harmful (i.e., a causal sign), but its harm may be averted by specific rites. Moreover, the Greeks believe that a dream vision is conditioned also by the psychic and physical circumstances of man: wine is bad for dreams, whereas water is good for them; onions, garlic, and beans have bad effects. The dream experience is thus made to depend on material properties quite apart from the will of the gods Consequently, we hear not only of gods who send and interpret dreams, but of gods who have portentous dreams themselves.

PROPHECY—The pagan generally regards prophecy as grounded in a special psychic property which enables its possessor to know hidden things immediately, intuitively. Prophecy is a divine attribute in which man can share either by the favor of the gods or by his own magical efforts. But it may also be conceived as a natural gift of the prophet. The ideal of this type is Apollonius of Tyana. As described by Philostratus, his mantic knowledge was acquired, not out of books, or by art, or from the gods, but from natural insight. He has an inherent gift which he perfected by philosophic study and his way of life. He understands all languages without having learned them; he is clairvoyant; he is able to recognize spirits who take on the form of men; without any divine prompting he knows the future. The holy life of the Pythagoreans has filled his eyes with light and empowered him to see hidden things. In his speech before Domitian, Apollonius says that he sees coming events as in a mirror, by means of the ether of his soul.

Pagan prophecy is thus not necessarily dependent upon divine revelation; it may equally well represent a human faculty of sensing hidden things irrespective of the gods. Nor are the gods the sole source of prophetic revelations. To begin with, they too "prophesy," i.e., see hidden things through the special faculty which they inherit from the mana-charged primal stuff out of which they have emerged. The Hindu Agni is a priest and a seer. Furthermore, prophetic revelations are often ascribed to spirits who are not of the ruling pantheon. Thus, the Arab *kāhins* have "friends" who reveal secrets to them. The Greeks, too, knew of other sources of prophetic revelation than Zeus. The oracle of Apollo has a pedigree which extends back generations before the birth of Zeus. Proteus, Nereus and his daughters, and Dionysus are represented as prophets in their own right. Dionysus and Apollo prophesy under the influence of Bacchic frenzy. The human Orpheus competes with Apollo in divining. It is the same power that activates both gods and men.

This power is not a gift of the gods which can be bestowed and withdrawn at their will; it is a natural talent like the gift of wisdom. The idea is expressed by the Arab concept of the "friend" of the prophet, his familiar spirit—a personification of his natural talent, similar to the *jinn* who is thought to inspire the creations of the poet. The Greeks, likewise, believed that once Apollo bestowed his prophetic gift, the recipient was no longer really dependent upon him. Calchas, Tiresias, Melampus, Helenus, Cassandra, and others do not have recourse to Apollo or any other god; they prophesy in their own right. They can even use their gift against the will of the gods: Phineus betrayed the secrets of the gods, for which he was cruelly punished by Zeus, but his prophetic power was not taken from him. Apollo, angered by Cassandra's rejection, decrees that no man shall believe her prophecies; he does not, however, revoke her prophetic power. Once given, it becomes a sixth sense, part of human, as it is part of divine, nature. The clairvoyant, who sees hidden things by his native virtue, without recourse to ecstasy, is a particularly clear expression of this idea. Athena opens Tiresias' ears and endows them with the ability to hear secret things; Melampus becomes a prophet by having his ears licked by serpents; Siegfried, from tasting of the blood of Fafner.

Prophesying in Bacchic frenzy is equally independent of the gods' will; it is the frenzy itself that arouses the latent prophetic faculty. Man initiates the action: he calls down divine influence upon himself, he unites with the gods, he liberates his soul to roam among the gods and listen in on their conversations. It is he who activates his prophetic power by such external stimuli as the dance, the song, and intoxicants. The Pythian priestess of Delphi induced Apollo to take possession of her by artificially stimulated frenzy. The extreme form of this idea is the belief in theurgy, in the power of man to compel the god to dwell in him and make him prophesy.

Because prophecy is not necessarily a divine favor, it may be conceived as passing by inheritance from generation to generation as a power latent in the germ. Just as a god bequeaths his special powers to his offspring (as Apollo does his powers as prophet-physician to Asclepius, his son), so the Greeks knew of families in which the gift of prophecy passed hereditarily from father to son: the Melampodidae (descendants of Melampus), the Iamidae (claiming descent from Iamus, a son of Apollo), and others.

Similarly, prophecy is conceived as having a material basis. Water, the element of wisdom, is also the source of prophecy; hence, water gods are often prophets (the water nymphs, Proteus, etc.). Specific substances induce prophecy: water, various seeds, intoxicating vapors. The Pythia would drink holy water and chew bay leaves. She also is said to have inhaled vapors that arose out of the chasm beneath her. Argive women prophesied after drinking the blood of the sacrifice—a very widespread practice. Mythology contributes further examples. Mimir drinks of the cosmic fountain and learns hidden things; Siegfried is endowed with supernatural hearing powers after tasting the blood of Fafner's heart. The Thriae, the three sister nymphs who dwell in a cave beneath Parnassus, drink honey, which intoxicates them and makes them prophesy. The flesh of certain creatures is endowed with mantic properties, and eating it bestows prophetic powers. Porphyry mentions a custom of eating parts of birds used in augury in the belief that this would make the eaters prophets like the gods. Philostratus tells of an oriental custom of eating the heart or liver of snakes, whereby one became capable of understanding the language and presages of birds.

Paganism also knows prophet-gods. Dionysus is a *mantis:* when he enters into the body of his ecstatic devotees, he fills them with prophetic powers. Apollo too is depicted as crowned in laurel, in a state of Bacchic excitation. Proteus prophesies, apparently in ecstasy. This idea, in characteristically pagan fashion, makes prophecy not a peculiarly human condition, but attributes it to the gods as well. Bacchic intoxication affects them, too, and its prophecy-inspiring frenzy can be transferred from them to men. Thus, prophecy is not only a revelation of the will of the gods; it may also be a revelation of knowledge acquired by them in visions and ecstasy. The human prophet becomes filled with the god, or unites with him; there is no separation of the human and divine realms.

All the various forms of pagan divination are, thus, not limited to discovering the gods' will, but involve the art or gift of reading the signs by which secret things are revealed. This reading may be purely magical, or it may be religious-magical—insofar as it invokes the aid of gods, or seeks to learn their will. Here too we find a realm beside or beyond the gods, whose secrets man seeks to penetrate either directly through magic, or with the help of the gods who know them.

Greek and Roman speculation about divination shows a definite tendency to ground it on natural conditions; to make it, in other words, a matter not of the divine will, but of human science.

Plato distinguishes augury by omens from prophecy, giving preference to the latter. For augury is based on human reason and understanding, while prophecy is a divine madness, the same sort of madness, he believes

which gives rise to poetry. Ominous signs are a part of nature whose meaning
can be arrived at by a study of natural phenomena—a far cry from the idea
that they are ways by which the gods make their will known to man. But
neither is prophecy, according to Plato, anything else than a special manner
of perception, an irrational manner residing in a special sense, which has
been given to men by the gods. Plato locates this sense in the liver, the seat
of the irrational soul, the imaginative faculty. Through this lower soul,
man prophesies in his sleep, when the liver is calm and undisturbed by other
imaginings. It is not by his intelligence that man prophesies, but precisely
when his mind is dormant, when he is asleep, or sick, or in ecstasy. Prophecy
is, then, a divine gift, an added sense, implanted by the gods in a particular
organ, like all the other senses. Plato believes it a universal human faculty,
which becomes actualized, however, only in certain men. Prophecy is thus
not a revelation of the will of the gods, but a perception of hidden things
by means of a special sense.

Cicero also distinguishes two types of divination: artificial (by omens)
and natural (by dreams and prophecy). While he follows the Stoics in regarding the gift of divining as a divine favor, he too regards it as a skill
or a natural talent. Man is able to know the future either through a study
of omens over a long period of time, or by a kind of supernatural instinct
or sense. Omens are based on long experience of an invariable sequence
of certain signs and events. Like the other sciences, divination is grounded
on experiment and conjecture. He says explicitly that nature can indicate
the future without special divine interference, and that it, therefore, can
be discovered without recourse to the gods. Dreams and prophecy are explained as the product of natural faculties of the soul. To be sure, this faculty
is not activated except when the soul parts from the body and comes into
contact with divine powers. These powers are found everywhere; sometimes
within man, sometimes without. Thus, it is a terrestrial power that rouses
the Delphic priestess to prophecy, while it is an internal, natural faculty
that inspires the Sybils. The Delphic oracle failed, he believes, due to the
decline in the mantic powers of the chasm, a natural decay like the drying
up of springs.

Plutarch explains prophecy by the demonic-divine nature of the soul:
just as spirits know hidden things, so does the human soul. The latent
power of the soul is actualized in dreams, or by the mystery purifications
that exalt a man above the material; it is especially aroused in ecstasy.
Various climatic factors also play a part. Plotinus grounds the mantic arts
on "cosmic sympathy." The stars anticipate the future without influencing
it; they are letters written in heaven, a mirror of all cosmic events. For the
universe is like a living organism, whose unity makes that which befalls

one member perceptible in the others. The wise man learns to recognize in one event the symptoms that reveal its fellow. Divination involves an organic, natural law; it has nothing to do with the will of the gods.

Philostratus views prophecy in a similar light. The Pythagorean regimen enables him who is naturally endowed to purify his senses and soul to the point of prophecy. The prophet is the man whose soul is perfect and inspired with ether, whose eyes are filled with penetrating light. This rank is a little less than the gods (for ether, the fifth element, is also "the source of the gods"); in fact, he who attains it is on a par with Apollo. Apollonius of Tyana incarnates the highest philosophic ideal of those times.

THE CULT

The characteristic mark of the pagan cult is not its plurality of worshiped beings, but its view of ritual as automatically efficient and intrinsically significant. The cult is not ordained by the supreme, free will of the deity; its end is not merely to express and embody man's adoration. It is rather a system of rites capable in themselves of working good and evil, whose potency derives from the realm above the gods. It sets into motion magical forces inherent in certain substances (the flesh of sacrifices, blood, incense, oil, water, fire, etc.), certain activities (gestures, dances, processions, songs, dramas, prayers, etc.), and certain forms (numbers, figures, series of actions, pictures, and symbols).

There is always a magical element in the pagan cult, even when it aims at propitiating the gods. For the cult is regarded as playing a vital role in the life of the gods. Its purpose is to benefit man, but it achieves this by serving the needs of the upper realm. The pagan cult not only invokes the blessings of the gods, it also supports them and strengthens them through its rites.

Since the gods are bound to an eternal order of life, procreation, suffering, death, need of food and shelter, and the like, the cult is viewed as man's service to the gods in their crises and needs. Moreover, the cosmic dualism of light and darkness, good and evil, life and death involves the gods no less than men. Men call upon the gods in their struggle with the forces of darkness; but inasmuch as good and evil are alike rooted in the cosmic order, the gods too must constantly fight with evil powers, with demonic impurities. Gods and men are allied in this battle; the cult has been ordained to aid the powers of good in their eternal struggle with evil and impurity. Its ordinances are a product of divine wisdom, its efficacy is rooted in the forces of the metadivine realm.

SACRIFICE AND FESTIVAL—We may distinguish two types of sacrificial rites: those intended to propitiate and do homage to the gods, and those that aim at acting upon or influencing the life of the gods or the cosmos. (Both intentions may be mingled in a given rite.) While submission and homage certainly have a place in the pagan cult, the more fundamental element consists in activities that directly affect the gods, or activate transcendent forces for the good of the gods and the world. A case in point is the pagan festival. Some festivals were held in honor of the gods, but the most solemn celebrate occasions in their lives. The festival is rooted in divine events reflected in nature or in the life of the tribe and recurring in a fixed cycle. All forms of paganism know the cultic drama, in which the gods are both actors and acted upon. The human celebrant participates in the divine mysteries, suffers with the gods, mourns their death, triumphs in their resurrection. His rites crucially affect the destiny and vitality of the gods.

It is a widespread belief that the gods require food and drink; the sacrifice supplies these needs. This notion is not limited to the lower stages of religion; it is found in highly developed cultures as well. Babylonia, Egypt, Canaan, Greece, and Rome all shared the belief that the gods do and must eat. Not only do Akkadian myths tell of the banquets of the gods, but the very creation of man is said to have been undertaken to provide the gods with servants who will wait upon them and sustain them. After seven days of the Flood, the famished gods cluster around the sacrifice of Utnapishtim "like flies." Daily temple rites included the arraying of banquet tables before the images of the gods. The Greeks, too, believed that the gods show favor to men because of the fat offerings they receive from them. The gods partake of the sacrificial meal, sometimes together with the celebrants. Tables laden with food were set before the Roman gods, doubtless under the same assumption.

There is, however, a higher conception of the cult, which views it as a system of rites bringing mysterious powers to bear on the cosmos. The pagan feels himself a partner of mighty gods, with whom his destiny is linked. He performs his duties with piety and awe; his acts have a crucial significance in the life of gods and the world. This conception, too, is found in all levels of religious development. The Aztecs believed that the gods grow old and feeble because they constantly produce rains and food. To revitalize them, the people celebrated a great festival once in eight years in which they performed savage rites aimed at restoring the rain god's strength. To this category belong the rites of death and resurrection of various gods. Several religions know the custom of slaying the god (in the form of a man or animal) from time to time in order to keep him from aging and to enable him to come to life again, young and refreshed. The totemistic common meal is a related notion: the god and his human kin partake together of the flesh of the totem animal; by so doing, the bond between deity and men is renewed. Hinduism provides what is perhaps the most striking case of the mysterious-magical concept of the cult. Nourishing the gods plays no part; here, it is a matter of mystic activity with cosmic significance. The sacrifice is the "navel of the world." The cult is above the gods; through it the gods live, create, and govern; it is *rita*, the secret and inner strength of the world. The Brahmanas represent the sacrifice as identified with the *purusha*, the primal god-man, who was sacrificed and became the stuff out of which all was created. The priest re-enacts the moment of creation at each sacrifice. Such a concept of the sacrifice as creating and maintaining the world is found in Egypt and Persia as well; it is a profound symbol of the pagan idea.

The Battle of Good and Evil—Paganism regards impurity, or demonic evil, as an autonomous, baleful realm as primary as the holy and the good. Death, disease, darkness, and the host of evil spirits who seek to destroy gods and men are the domain of the unclean. The eternal struggle between these two realms is vividly reflected in the cult.

It is a universal belief that a corpse is a prime source of defilement and demonic danger. Harm arising from contact with a corpse can be averted only by certain rituals. The concept of sin is closely bound up with this notion of dangerous impurity. For the Babylonians, sin, impurity, and disease are inextricably combined. Sin is a ritual or moral offense which results in sickness, but this is brought on by evil demons, spirits of the underworld. The Greeks consider that murder defiles and endangers the murderer. He is relentlessly pursued either by the spirit of the victim or by terrible spirits of vengeance. He is unclean and defiles all who come into contact with him. Only lustration can remove his impurity. Similar notions surround the pollution of menstruation, the sexual act, forbidden foods, and the like—all are dangerous and harmful. The Syrians believed that eating forbidden kinds of fish brought on plagues; the Egyptians associated leprosy with the eating of swine (swine are unclean because they mate during the moon's waning, when demonic powers are at their height). Creeping things are defiling because they house evil spirits.

Inasmuch as impurity is a cosmic power, the gods themselves fear it. Death, disease, and misfortune befall the gods as well. The queen of the underworld looses sixty plagues that attack every part of Ishtar's body; only the sprinkling of "waters of life" can heal her. Ahriman sets 99, 900, 9,000, and 19,000 diseases upon Ormazd; Egypt's gods wage an unceasing battle against the evil forces that beset them and sap their strength. Specific impurities are traced to events in the struggle between the gods and the demons. The Persians attribute the origin of them all to Ahriman's desire for allies in his battle with Ormazd.

In Babylonia, the opposition between the realms of purity and impurity is evident chiefly in purification rites. The priest adjures the gods to succor man from evil spirits, using divine names and symbols. Temple lustrations were aimed at driving away the dangerous spirits of defilement that could do harm to the gods too. At the close of the elaborate new year's rite in the temple of Nabu, the high priest adjures the demon in the name of the gods, "Go forth, evil that is in the temple! O evil demon, may Bel destroy you, may you be utterly cut off wherever you are." It was to prevent impure spirits from entering that Babylonian and Assyrian temples posted statues of guardian genii at temple gates.

The two pivots of Egyptian religion are the death and resurrection of the gods and the eternal battle with the baleful demons who menace gods and men. The struggle with Seth, Osiris' murderer; Apophis, the serpent-enemy of Re; and with all the magical forces hostile to the gods and their worshipers is reflected in the cult. Egyptian temples had guardian images, and the gods had personal guards as well: Anubis, who guards the gods in the form of a dog; baboons under the charge of Thoth, who travel in the sun-boat and protect "the eye of Horus," and the like. Spells and rites guard the gods' boat; charms and magic protect the idols in temples and ward off all evil from their bodies. The priest, beginning his daily round of duties in the temple, announces that he is full of magic power and has come to protect the god. His assistant cries: "Guardians of the gate of this temple . . . permit no enemy to enter after him." The opening ceremony is the lighting of the fire, which immediately drives away the power of Seth and cleanses and sanctifies the temple.

Vedic religion also regards the sacrifice as combating demons; the flame and incantations banish them, while the offering gives new strength to the gods. The whole cosmos is founded on the order and the rite of the cult; through it alone can men and gods be cleansed from sin and redeemed from evil.

For the Persian cult, the battle of good and evil, impurity and purity, life and death, light and darkness, is fundamental. Its chief purpose is to heighten the power of Ormazd in his struggle with Ahriman, and to assist him to victory. The man who guards himself against pollution, who keeps the earth and rivers pure, who fulfils the ordinances of religion, strengthens Ormazd. He who prays to the good gods, and offers them proper sacrifices, invigorates them. Prayer and holy incantations are weapons which work against Ahriman and his host of evil demons. To be sure, Zoroastrianism does not limit itself merely to cultic matters. There is a large domain of moral and civilizing duties: zeal for truth and goodness, promotion of agriculture, and fertility in earth, man, and beast. Yet all are ultimately cultic in the sense that they contribute to the power of Ormazd in his fight with Ahriman. This is no mere figure. Because the god of light cannot succeed without the aid of man, he prays that Anahita help him convert Zoroaster to the religion of the truth.

Gods as Priests—The fundamental idea of paganism is most strikingly set forth in the notion that the gods use the cult for their own benefit. Nothing illustrates so clearly the intrinsic value of the cult and the gods' dependence upon it.

Marduk is not only the arch magician, but also the "priest of the gods," as are Shamash, Kusig, Ea, and others. Berosus reports that Oannes (Ea) invented, among other arts and sciences, the building of temples. Ishtar performs the lament for the slain bull of heaven; the sister of Lil, the dead god, performs his cult at his command. The goddess Ninisinna is made priestess by Enki in his temple; she institutes sacred prostitution and establishes the Isin cult. The Anunnaki are said to purify themselves in the lustral waters of the priest.

Much of Egyptian ritual is based on the idea that man merely imitates what has proved efficacious in the case of the gods. The Osirian cult and the funerary cults that are related to it are an imitation of what Horus, Isis, Nephthys, and Anubis did to the dead Osiris. The priest in attendance calls himself Thoth, and says that he will restore life as was done to Osiris. The priest who uses "the book of the sky-cow" as an incantation must anoint his face as does Thoth when he reads it over Re. Horus initiated the sacrifice made on the fourth day of each month. Similarly, all sorcery is but an imitation of the magical practices of the gods.

The Canaanite epic of Ras-Shamra tells how, when Baal died, the gods bewailed and buried him, and made him funerary offerings. Another Canaanite story tells how the hunter-god Usuos erected two pillars to the fire and the wind and poured the blood of his game as a libation upon them.

The gods of India sacrifice, use incantations, practice ascetic rites, and follow *rita* in all their undertakings. They sought vainly to attain immortality by sacrifice; finally Prajapati helped them discover the correct ritual. Another version has them gain immortality by drinking soma or by self-castigation. By sacrifice, the gods heal Vishnu, whose head they have cut off. After Indra killed Brahmani, he was depressed and frightened until he made an offering to Vishnu and purified himself; then his terror left him. Similar stories are found throughout Hindu literature.

Zervan, the primeval Persian god, made libations one thousand years until Ormazd and Ahriman were born. Ormazd sacrificed to the wind and prayed for his help. He offers up milk and *haoma* to Anahita, praying that Zoroaster might accept his religion. In the final glory, Ormazd will appear as the sacrificing priest with Srosh as his assistant-priest; by the formula of the sacred girdle he holds, Ahriman and his demons will be defeated.

The Greeks also regarded the gods as instituting and performing cultic rites. The Homeric hymn to Hermes makes him the inventor of sacrifice; Hermes rid the city Tanagra of a plague with a ram that he led around the wall; henceforth, that rite was maintained there. Rhea taught Dionysus the rites and mysteries of the Great Mother. After Apollo killed the serpent, Python, he went to Crete to purify himself; when Hermes killed Argus, the gods stoned him to remove the pollution of murder from them. The Antiochenes believed that Apollo immersed and purified himself in the streams near Daphne. Goddesses—Demeter, Aphrodite, the Syrian Hera— all are said to have purified themselves after sexual relations, as do human females. Bathing the images of goddesses after the sacred marriage is based on the same idea.

Thus, paganism knows not only the god who is bound to a predestined cycle of births and deaths; not only wise gods and craftsmen, magicians, diviners and prophets; it knew also the priest-god. In no other realm is the subservience of the pagan gods so evident as here. Wisdom, magic, divination, prophecy are all expressions of divine potency and art. But the cult is necessarily an expression of dependence. Gods that purify themselves, offer sacrifices, undergo ascetic penances embody in its ultimate form the idea of divine subjection to a transcendent order.

THE PAGAN WAY TO SALVATION

Subjection of both men and gods to a transcendent realm is symbolized by myth and concretized in the cult. This common lot is what gives meaning to the magical, irrational cult: men share in the life and destiny of the gods, imitate their actions and rites, and commemorate events in their lives. These are the mythological foundations upon which the cult is grounded. And yet, it is a prevalent idea that the rites have autonomous value and innate efficacy. The groundwork is thus laid for bypassing the gods to address the ultimate realm upon which they themselves are dependent. This tendency does not represent a "magical stage" of religion; the notion of the intrinsic efficacy of the ritual is sufficient to turn attention to the meta-divine realm, and to arouse efforts to attain salvation directly through it.

The most advanced manifestations of paganism show a tendency to regard man as able to save himself by his own devices. The cult rises above the commonplace concerns of rain, produce, fertility, and victory to the vision of salvation. At this level, man may be viewed as the ally of the gods in their struggle with evil—that is, at bottom, as co-savior with the gods (Zoroastrianism). Or the tendency may be toward the magical, with the cult regarded as a system of rites capable of exalting man to divine rank and thus saving him from evil. Salvation, however, is his own concern, not the gods'; at most, they but help him find the hidden way (Brahmanism). But paganism may attain the philosophic and meta-physical level. Here, salvation is no longer a matter of ritual, but of knowl-edge of the secrets of being and non-being, life and death. Man liberates himself through his mind and spirit from the prison of the body and the dreary cycle of death and rebirth (Gnosticism and Buddhism). The sub-limest height is reached in the Platonic doctrine, which teaches man how to redeem himself through attachment to the realm of ideas.

Paganism in all its manifestations thus recognizes a transcendent, metadivine realm. There it seeks the key to the destiny of the world and the salvation of man.

CHAPTER III

Israelite Religion

THE BASIC IDEA

The basic idea of Israelite religion is that God is supreme over all. There is no realm above or beside him to limit his absolute sovereignty. He is utterly distinct from, and other than, the world; he is subject to no laws, no compulsions, or powers that transcend him. He is, in short, non-mythological. This is the essence of Israelite religion, and that which sets it apart from all forms of paganism.

This idea was not a product of intellectual speculation, or of mystical meditation, in the Greek or Indian manner. It first appeared as an insight, an original intuition. The Bible, while stressing the oneness of God and his supremacy, nowhere articulates the contrast between its new concept and the mythological essence of paganism. The new religious idea never received an abstract, systematic formulation in Israel. It expressed itself rather in symbols, the chief of which was the image of an omnipotent, supreme deity, holy, awful, and jealous, whose will was the highest law. Taking on popular forms, the new idea pervaded every aspect of Israelite creativity. Working intuitively, it radically transformed the ancient mythological conceptions of Israel. But precisely because it never received a dogmatic formulation which could serve as a standard for the systematic reformation of the old religion, it was unable entirely to eradicate all traces of the pagan heritage. The edifice of biblical religion does, therefore, contain an occasional mythological fragment preserved from the debris of the ancient faith.

THE ABSENCE OF MYTH

The store of biblical legends lacks the fundamental myth of paganism: the theogony. All theogonic motifs are similarly absent. Israel's God has no pedigree, fathers no generations; he neither inherits nor bequeaths his authority. He does not die and is not resurrected. He has no sexual qualities or desires and shows no need of or dependence upon powers outside himself.

Renan attributed this remarkable absence of mythological traits to the poverty of the Semite's imagination and his monotheistic tendency, induced by the monotonous expanses of his desert home. But the ancient population of the desert was by no means monotheistic, nor was Israel exposed only to this environment. For centuries, Israel's ancestors lived among peoples (of Semitic and mixed stock) whose religion was an advanced polytheism; the cultures of Canaan, Babylonia, and Egypt colored Israelite thought profoundly. The Semites of Palestine and Babylonia possess rich mythologies; why did Israel not learn from them? In point of fact, of course, the biblical narrative, far from being colorless, is full of legends about God— even though they differ in kind from pagan myths. One cannot allege, then, either poverty of imagination or a monotheistic tendency among the Semites.

Nor can the phenomenon be explained as belonging to a primitive stage of religion when myths had not yet been developed. Such a stage is not in evidence anywhere in the pagan world. But even if it were, the fact that, whatever its initial level, the religion of YHWH even in later times failed to acquire a mythology through syncretism still would require explanation. We do find vestiges of Israel's ancient mythology imbedded in the Bible, and there was an "idolatry" in Israel; yet the biblical God has no mythological features. It would seem that this reflects a level beyond, not before, mythology.

The absence of mythology in Israel has been explained by the western Semitic conception of deity as king—as divine ruler who marches into battle before his tribe. YHWH, it is said, was originally a lone warrior, without consort or family, like Moab's Chemosh, or Assyria's Ashur. The case of Ashur, however, points in quite another direction. Whatever his original character, Ashur eventually took his place in the dominant Babylonian pantheon. He became identified with Marduk, was provided with a consort, and thus became assimilated into the divine family of ruling gods in the normal syncretistic fashion. Yet there is no evidence that YHWH was provided with a mate, nor is any theogonic or mythological tale related of him. Even if the king-concept were decisive, neither pedigree nor consort are excluded by it.

The peculiar and unique character of Israel's non-mythologism stands out with particular clarity when the biblical stories of YHWH's battles are considered. Here we find that not only YHWH, but his entourage, and even his "enemies" are non-mythologically conceived. YHWH has no companions and his antagonists are lifeless idols.

It is conceded on all hands that by the age of literary prophecy Israelite religion was militantly exclusive; its god was a jealous deity who demanded allegiance to himself alone and unremitting battle with all other gods within Israel. A comparable phenomenon is the war of the Zoroastrians upon other faiths. Other gods, and especially the ancient Indian deities, became its evil demons, the allies of Ahriman, and the enemies of Ormazd. In contrast, the battles of YHWH with the gods of the nations left no mythological residue; YHWH is never represented as winning dominion from any other god. The "judgments" that YHWH wreaks upon the pagans' idols are not regarded as falling upon active, divine antagonists, but on vain images.

Nor is YHWH ever portrayed as world conqueror in the cosmogonic legends of the Bible. There is no biblical parallel to pagan myths relating the defeat of older gods (or demonic powers) by younger; no other gods are present in primordial times. YHWH's battles with primeval monsters, to which poetical allusion is occasionally made, are not struggles between gods for world dominion. YHWH's battles with Rahab, the dragon, Leviathan, the sea, the fleeing serpent, etc. are hardly illuminated by reference to the myth of Marduk's defeat of Tiamat and his subsequent seizure of supreme power. To be sure, the Bible here preserves pagan motifs, but Ugaritic allusions to the defeat of Lotan, the fleeing serpent, Yam, etc. show that it is Canaanite, rather than Babylonian influence that is involved. These motifs belong to Israel's Canaanite heritage, acquired, in all likelihood, before the rise of Israelite religion. In Israel these materials were entirely recast. The Ugaritic allusions do not indicate that these battles had cosmogonic significance (as did the battle of Marduk with Tiamat). Nor does the biblical material speak of battles preceding the creation of the world (like the Babylonian account). They are said to have occurred "in days of old" (Isa. 51:9); Job 26 suggests a time after the creation of the world. The Ugaritic materials indicate that the struggle involved Baal's rule and authority among the gods. There is no hint, however, that YHWH's defeat of Rahab, the dragon, etc. was the beginning of his rule, nor are his antagonists portrayed as primordial or divine beings coeval with him. They are all mentioned explicitly at one time or another as creatures of and subject to YHWH (Gen. 1:21; Amos 9:3; Pss. 104:26; 148:7). The battle is not, then, between primordial divine powers contending over world dominion, but between God and certain of his creatures. An echo of the same idea is the rebellion of the serpent in Genesis 3 or the sinful scheme of men related in Genesis 11. Closer still is the theme of later legends regarding the fall of rebellious angels and Satan.

Thus, the ancient pagan myths were fundamentally transmuted by the Israelite idea. Originally conceived of as mythological beings, born of the primordial realm, divine in their essence, these monsters became in Israel creatures of YHWH, who rebelled against him. This transformation reflects the peculiar Israelite conception of the demonic realm as a whole.

DEMONOLOGY

One of the remarkable aspects of the religion of pre-exilic Israel is that it failed to transmute either its ancient pantheon or the gods of the nations into demons. It is sometimes asserted that the pagan gods became angels, appointed over natural phenomena or patrons of nations. Such a metamorphosis would be quite unique in the history of religion. Ancient gods when displaced may become the elders and progenitors of the reigning pantheon, with little or no place in the cult. At times, they decline into petty tribal or family gods. Or, again, they may be transformed into evil spirits who battle with the new gods and play a part in black magic. But we never hear of displaced gods becoming "angels"—messengers and agents of the new gods—and this precisely in the functions of high gods (gods of the sun and moon, of nations and empires). To be sure, paganism knows agents and servants of the great gods (guardians, craftsmen, bakers, scribes, etc.); however, these are not deposed gods, but deities specialized for these functions. No rejected pantheon ever became transmuted into "angels" appointed over the major phenomena of nature. To say that the biblical angels are pagan gods metamorphosed is to concede the radical monotheism of the biblical viewpoint: the gods have ceased to be gods and have become mere agents of the One.

It must further be noted that if biblical angelology has pagan antecedents, it has lost every trace of mythological features. No angel has a sufficient identity to enable us to see in him his pagan original. The angels of pre-exilic Israel are not yet individualized (as opposed to postexilic conceptions); they are the featureless "host of God" or his manifestation. They lack even the elementary mythological distinction of sexes.

The non-derivative character of Israelite angelology is indicated by the fact that the names of the angels have no antecedents in the old Israelite pantheon or among the gods of the nations. While several mythological names have been preserved in the Bible (such as Terah, Nimrod, and the divine epithets ʾēl, ʾēl ʿelyōn), none appear as angelic titles. The angels of the early sources are nameless; the names they bear later (Gabriel, Michael) fail to connect them with the pagan pantheon.

The nature of Israelite demonology is equally peculiar. Once again, there is no link of nomenclature between Israelite demons and pagan divinities. Evil proceeds either from YHWH himself or from his angels. Destructive agents are sometimes styled by terms that may be taken as proper nouns: *negef* (plague), *mashhīth* (destroyer), *qeṭeb merīrī* (bitter destruction [?]), *reshef* (fiery bolt), and the like. But these are all "messengers of evil" (Ps. 78:49), members of YHWH's suite and his agents. Even Satan is but a member of the divine court (Job 2:1).

Apart from the evil angels are the spirits of impurity called *shēdīm* (demons) or *seʿīrīm* (satyrs, "goats"). These haunt the open country (Lev. 17:5, 7), ruins (Isa. 13:21; 34:14), or the desert (Lev. 16:22). Lilith (Isa. 34:14) and Azazel (Lev. 16:8 ff.) are mentioned by name. Such spirits are not represented in the Bible as working harm. The folk sacrificed to them "in the fields," perhaps believing them to be minor spirits who could be of some benefit. But there is no allusion to positive activity on their part, let alone to their ever playing the role of destructive powers. The *seʿīrīm* are types of Arab *jinn*, a class of beings without individuality who are below the level of deities. They "dance" among ruins and in the desert, together with wild birds and beasts; their shape is goatlike (*seʿīrīm* = goats). They are assigned no function in nature or in the life of men.

What is the relation of the evil angels and the *seʿīrīm* to the pagan gods?

In *reshef*, found as the name of a Canaanite and Syrian god, we have a reminiscence of the ancient pantheon. But it is a verbal reminiscence only, without mythological overtones; for *reshef* is used in poetry as a bare common noun (Job 5:7, Cant. 8:6). The Bible shows no knowledge of Reshef, the mythological god. It is of crucial significance that all destructive agents, *reshef* included, do not constitute a domain opposing YHWH; like the rest of the angels, they are his messengers only.

The *shēdīm* and *seʿīrīm*, however, are in a sense removed from the realm of God; as spirits of impurity they dwell beyond the pale. The nouns *shēd* and *līlīth* hark back to Babylonian origins. Before the rise of the religion of YHWH in Israel, the *shēdīm* doubtless played a special role alongside the gods, as in Babylonia, where they constitute a demonic realm distinct from the gods. It seems probable also that the *shēdīm* have assimilated the ancient Hebrew pantheon. If this be so, the nature of the metamorphosis is altogether remarkable. The old gods did not become evil spirits who rival, or even rebel against, YHWH. Such defiant creatures as Rahab, the dragon, and Leviathan are not numbered among them. The world of old gods has become transformed into the desolate haunts of dancing *seʿīrīm* who keep company with wild animals. All decisive power, divine and even demonic, has been taken from them and given to the messengers of YHWH.[1]

This then was the unique evolution of Israel's pagan beliefs: hostile divine forces (Rahab, the dragon, etc.) who challenged the gods descended to the level of monstrous creatures, while the ancient pantheon was transmuted into shades with no defined functions. No room remains for any divine antagonist of the one God. Even the demonic has become de-mythologized.

Nor can the figures of later Jewish demonology be derived from the pagan gods. Again, it must be noted that not one of the gods after whom Israel strayed left his name to the demons of Second Temple times. Even Rahab, the dragon, Leviathan, and the fleeing serpent have disappeared. Jewish demonology is grounded in an idea that sheds light on the peculiar character of Israelite religion as a whole. Its chief figures are developments not of ancient gods, but of the biblical Satan, the serpent of Eden, and the Nephilim of Genesis 6:4.

What is fundamental and peculiar to Jewish demonology is that its spirits and devils derive, not from a primordial evil root, but from sin. Its Satanic symbol is the land serpent, the tempter of Eden, not the sea serpent (the dragon, or Rahab), the primeval rebel against God. Biblical religion was unable to reconcile itself with the idea that there was a power in the universe that defied the authority of God and that could serve as an antigod, the symbol and source of evil. Hence, it strove to transfer evil from the metaphysical to the moral realm, to the realm of sin. The serpent of Eden is no rival of God, but a "beast of the field" who entices to rebellion against the divine command. That is why he could become a central figure of later demonology. Satan became the chief of the devils, not as the symbol of a cosmic evil principle, but by virtue of his biblical role of seducer and tempter. Later legend connects him with the fallen angels who took human wives; he was "the first of the sinners." His host are his angelic fellows in sin and their illicit progeny. It is they who seduced men to sin, who incited them to idolatry, and taught them divination, magic, and all the other wicked ways. These are no Tiamat or Kingu, no Seth or Apophis, no pri-

---

[1] Hence when the gods of the nations are called *shēḏīm* it is not meant that they are evil spirits, but that they are insubstantial shades, "no-gods," with neither divine nor demonic functions.

meval beings radically hostile to God or capable of challenging his dominion. Judaism's demons are the offspring of sinful *creatures;* their power is only to entice man into sin and thereby bring divine judgment upon him.

The same is true of the "princes of the nations" (cf. Dan. 10:13, 20). Some would see in them the ancient pagan gods, transformed into enemies of YHWH and his people. But, again, not one of their names reveals any connection with the gods mentioned in the Bible. They have no mythological features, nor are they sexually differentiated. Their rule does not rival God's. They are members of the divine court whose part it is solely to advocate the cause of the nations and aid them. Their origin lies in the tendency that gave rise to the later angelology as a whole, to multiply mediators between God and man. If the "princes of the nations" are viewed as hostile toward God, it is only because they personify the enemies of Israel. Their opposition is not that of hostile cosmic principles, but rather of hostile religious and social groupings.

This absence in the Bible of the pagan conception of the demonic is intrinsically linked with the absence of theogony. It is of the essence of theogony that a given god is but one embodiment of the powers residing in the primordial womb of all being. As such, he meets with other independent offspring of the same realm; he fights with them or makes peace with them. Good and evil, Kingu and Marduk, Ormazd and Ahriman, Seth and Osiris, are "brothers"; demonic evil is as eternal and primeval as divine good. Biblical religion, having concentrated divinity in one transcendent being, at once did away with theogony and theomachy. Since there was no "womb" out of which YHWH sprang, he could have no "brothers," divine or demonic. No antagonist could, therefore, be on a par with him.

The insubstantial role of the demonic in the Bible indicates that the absence of theogony is neither an accident nor the reflection of a primitive premythological religious level. Israelite religion conceived a radically new idea: It did not proclaim a new chief god, a god who ruled among or over his fellows. It conceived, for the first time, of a god independent of a primordial realm, who was the source of all, the demonic included.

The history of Israelite demonology complements what was said above concerning the Bible's ignorance of mythological polytheism. While vestiges of ancient pagan beliefs linger on in the shape of Rahab, the dragon, Azazel, and others, the idolatrous cults of biblical Israel left no legacy to Second Temple Judaism. The gods of those cults failed to bequeath even their names to later Jewish demons, let alone their mythological features. This phenomenon can be explained only on the assumption that the folk religion of the biblical period was non-mythological. The ancient myths disappeared from popular consciousness. Pagan influence was superficial and did not work deeply on folk creativity; therefore, it failed to make a mark on demonology. This conclusion will receive further support as we go on.

LEGENDS ABOUT GOD

COSMOGONY—Later Judaism regarded the belief in creation *ex nihilo* as one of the doctrines that differentiated it from paganism. In the Bible, this principle is not yet made explicit. The story of Genesis 1 seems to represent the *tōhū wābōhū* (comprising the watery deep, darkness, and earth) as a kind of primordial stuff out of which God fashioned the world. Herbage and animals spring from the earth, and sea creatures out of the waters, as if these substances harbored the vital seeds of life. In Genesis 2–3, the deity acts particularly like a demiurge. He works upon primary matter, planting a garden, forming man out of the earth, and woman out of his rib. The forbidden trees of the Garden of Eden have strong mythological overtones; life and knowledge may be acquired by eating of their fruit—apparently regardless of God's will. God jealously hoards these treasures of nature, and forbids man to share in them, lest he become "like God." The effect of eating the forbidden fruit is pictured as automatic: the eyes of the guilty pair are opened. God does not then strip them of their newly acquired faculty, but expels them from his garden to deny them the rewards of the tree of life. The primordial world stuff, with its innate powers, seems to be present throughout these stories.

Yet the role of the *tōhū wābōhū* is quite unlike the part played by the primeval matter of pagan cosmogonies. God creates the cosmic phenomena of light, firmament, sun, moon, and host of heaven by fiat alone, with no recourse to primeval stuff. By deriving plant and animal life from the earth, and sea life from the sea, the narrator evidently intends no more than to carry back the natural link between these phenomena to the creative act of God. The perennial processes and interrelationships of nature are themselves established by divine decree. That certain creatures have arisen out of primary substances is not the point; it is the natural connection between them and cosmic elements that is uppermost in the author's mind. In Genesis 2–3, too, creation out of prior matter is intended only to explain the origin of the fixed interrelationships of nature. Subterranean waters (ʾēd), rivers, and trees arise out of the earth; men and beasts are "dust of the earth"; male and female are "one flesh"; the manufacture of clothes is taught to man by God. Not the axiomatic necessity of primary matter, but considerations of etiology motivated the writer to employ the theme of creation out of matter when he did.

Nowhere do we find that the cosmic elements—e.g., earth, heavens, sun— were fashioned out of pre-existent stuff. Hence, it is reasonable to suppose that the obscure passage, Genesis 1:1–2, means: God first created the *tōhū wāḇōhū*, i.e., upper space, darkness, water, and earth which was covered by water. Elsewhere, it is said plainly that YHWH created darkness (Isa. 45:7), the watery abyss (Prov. 3:20; 8:24), sea and dry land (Ps. 95:5; Jonah 1:9; Neh. 9:6). And the conception of Genesis 2–3 seems to be that earth was God's first creation, out of which waters then came forth (2:6). There is also water in heaven (2:5); the four rivers which flow out of the earth apparently empty into what became the sea (cf. Eccles. 1:7). All are created by God (2:4). Job 26:7 depicts God as stretching out the North(ern mountain) "upon the void" and suspending the earth "on nothingness"; he does not raise up the earth out of primeval waters. The idea of creation out of nothing is here given clear poetic expression.

The notion of a pre-existent stuff thus lurks in the background of biblical cosmologies as a vestigial idea which has no meaningful role in the accounts themselves. In pagan myth, however, the primordial realm is the necessary presupposition for theogony. Divine beings and powers must have a derivation—in the spirit of the later philosophic formula, *ex nihilo nihil fit*. Lacking a theogony, the Bible has no need of a pre-existent realm. To be sure, the biblical God fashions some of his creatures out of matter already at hand. But this matter is not alive, charged with divine forces; it neither opposes nor participates in creation.

Biblical cosmology lacks also the basic pagan idea of a natural bond between the deity and the universe. Creation is not depicted as a sexual process, nor does it proceed from the seed of the god, his blood, spittle, tears, or the like. The idea of a material emanation from the creator is foreign to the Bible. Hence, those passages which speak of the world's "being born," or God's "giving birth" to it (e.g., Ps. 90:2), must be understood either as poetic figures or as expressions rooted in forgotten myths; there are no grounds for taking such expressions literally. There is a genuine mythical fragment in the story of Genesis 6:1–4 about the illicit union of "sons of God" (i.e., divine beings) with women, and their giant offspring. It was not felt to be foreign, however, because its protagonists on both sides are creatures of God, not God himself. That any conscious censorship has been at work here to purge these stories of pagan features is improbable in view of the folk naïveté that permeates the legends of Genesis 2–11. It was rather that the religion of YHWH instinctively excluded such motifs and was unable to assimilate them. The idea of a supreme deity who is above any natural connection with his creation found expression in the image of Genesis 1: a deity who creates by fiat.

There is crucial significance in the absence of a demonic realm alongside of God in the creation stories. Formally, there is nothing "unmonotheistic" about having a benign creator opposed by demonic evil. Yet there is no such tension in the biblical cosmogony. The serpent is one of the "beasts of the field"; he is not styled evil but "cunning." The enmity between him and man is referred to a divine curse. Similarly, all physical harm and pain proceeds, not from the decree of fate or the work of demons, but from YHWH. It is he who ordained the pain of childbirth, who cursed the earth so that man must toil, who decreed death, who shortened man's days, who confounded his language, and who dispersed him over the face of the earth. The absence of demons stems from the fundamental idea that prevails throughout these stories. It is not that there were no other celestial beings at hand; there were cherubs and "sons of God." Yet neither they nor the *śeʿirim* play a part even in inciting men to sin—a role which would in no wise have cast a shadow on formal monotheism. Whatever celestial beings there are belong to the suite of the one God; only YHWH is active as creator. The monotheism of these stories is, thus, not the outcome of an artificial adaptation of pagan materials. It permeates their every aspect and finds expression even in passages of artless naïveté.

GOD AND THE WORLD—Like myth, biblical legend utilizes all the vivid coloring of the imagination. Its God reveals himself to man in various forms and by various means. Men see him in day and night visions; prophets see him in his celestial palace surrounded by angelic hosts. But in contrast to pagan myth, biblical legend tells nothing about the personal life of the deity; its subject is always the relationship of God to his creation.

None of the common mythological motifs of divine births, deaths, wars, loves and hates, banquets and amusements is found in biblical legend. Isolated traces of pagan mythology (God walking about in his garden "at the cool of the day"; God's bow; celestial assemblies at "the mount of meeting" alluded to in Isa. 14:13; Ezek. 28:13–16) do not alter this fundamental fact. For even these survivals are imbedded in passages speaking of God's dealings with men, not of his private life.

In several passages YHWH appears among "the sons of God" or host of heaven in congress (e.g., I Kings 22:19 ff.; Isa. 6; Zech. 3:1). These gatherings never involve feasting and entertainment,[2] like those of the

---

[2] "Bread of the mighty" (Ps. 78:25) is rendered by the LXX "bread of angels," probably correctly. The *ʾelōhīm* of "my wine which cheers gods (*ʾelōhīm*) and men"

pagan gods; they are solemn assemblies, concerned with the judgment of men, government of the world, or missions with some moral purpose. When the deity's moods are spoken of ("YHWH repented . . . and was grieved in his heart" [Gen. 6:6], "I shall be angry" [Exod. 22:23, and frequently]), it is always in the realm of his dealings with men. All the portrayals of God as man of war, archer, swordsman, chariot rider, and the like are connected with his judgment and government of the world.

The natural spectacles that serve in biblical imagery to accompany theophanies are not considered aspects of God's life, but external adjuncts of his self-revelation in the world. YHWH does not live the processes of nature; he controls them, and through them displays his might to man. No more than in the creation story is it anywhere assumed that there is a natural bond between God and nature. But nature is the stage and its phenomena the vehicles of his manifestations. Earthquakes and volcanic eruptions are "the finger of YHWH"; he appears in the cloud and in the storm; lightning is his arrow, thunder his voice, wind his breath. In these images, the Bible arrives at, but never crosses, the threshold of paganism. For these are no more than poetic figures. The wind is God's creature, his angel and messenger (Pss. 48:8; 104:4). Thunder is regarded also as produced by heaven (Ps. 77:18), or the storm clouds (Job 28:26; 38:25). In the Sinaitic theophany, the "sounds" precede and herald the coming of God, together with the sound of the horn. The thunders of Exodus 9:23 ff. and I Samuel 12:17 ff. are likewise taken, not as manifestations of God, but his work. That the Bible does not conceive the relation of YHWH to these natural phenomena in a pagan way is clear from its failure to ascribe sanctity to them. Fire, light, storms, clouds, and so forth, are attendant upon theophanies, but are in themselves profane aspects of nature. They proclaim the might of the God who rules them, but there is no bond of life and destiny between them and God. The theophany to Elijah (I Kings 19) gives this idea classic expression: wind, earthquake, and fire precede YHWH, but YHWH was not in the wind, not in the earthquake, and not in the fire.

The connection of the pagan gods with natural phenomena involves

---

(Judg. 9:13), whatever it meant originally, was probably understood in the same way, since ᵓelōhīm applies to celestial creatures as well. The Bible does not hesitate to ascribe eating to angels any more than sexual desire (Gen. 6:1–4; but contrast Judg. 6:18 ff.; 13:16 ff.). Only when YHWH appears in the guise of a wayfarer does he partake of food (Gen. 18:8; 19:3). He is regularly said to smell the pleasing odor of sacrifice—meaning that he accepts it (Gen. 8:21; I Sam. 26:19); but this linguistic fossil is employed only in connection with sacrifice, to signify an aspect of God's relation to men (see below in the text).

a restriction of their domain and the imposition of a fixed pattern upon their actions. The attendance upon YHWH of various natural elements, however, obviously aims at stressing the absence of limitations upon his dominion. This idea is at the root of the biblical tendency to attribute to YHWH both the commonplace as well as the extraordinary and awful. Hence, nothing is to be learned about YHWH's primary "natural" domain from the biblical descriptions of theophanies.

The accounts of the Sinaitic theophany (and its later echoes in biblical poetry) tell of fire, earthquake, and thunder (Exod. 19:16–20; 20:15–18). But this is hardly sufficient to make of YHWH a volcanic deity. Volcanic gods are conceived of as dwelling within the mountain; their element is the subterranean fire that sets the mountain quaking. The fire and thunder of the Sinai legend, however, are adjuncts to the descent of a celestial deity. Thunder and lightning are "over the mountain"; it smokes "because YHWH descended upon it in fire." When YHWH speaks, it is "from heaven." In Judges 5:4 and Psalm 68:8 f., it is heaven and earth, not only mountains, that YHWH shakes. When he appears from Mount Paran, his majesty covers heaven, and his glory fills the earth (Hab. 3:3). Habakkuk portrays him as coming from the desert, from Teman and Paran, but also makes him out to be a sea-god; riding in his chariot over the sea, he stirs up the watery abyss (3:8; cf. Pss. 29:3; 74:13 ff.; 77:17 ff.). Again, the epithet "YHWH of hosts" points to an ancient connection of YHWH with the hosts of heaven. He is god of the desert, the sea, and the host of heaven too, because he is not bound by nature to any of these phenomena. YHWH's especial connection with Sinai and Teman in biblical consciousness is adequately accounted for by the historic circumstances of the rise of the religion of YHWH in Israel.

There is as little merit to the view that the presence of storm features in YHWH's theophanies points to his being originally a storm god. Nothing suggests that YHWH was ever restricted to the atmospheric realm. The early legends of YHWH's battles "in days of old" do not mention lightning and thunder; he subdued his monstrous enemies with his mighty arm and his wisdom (Isa. 51:9; Job 26:12 ff.). In eschatological images connected with these legends, YHWH is said to punish the fleeing and coiled serpents by his great, cruel sword (Isa. 27:1). On the other hand, it is understandable that mighty atmospheric phenomena should arouse the awe of biblical man, and that he should see in them manifestations of the power of his God. But these were no more than tokens of his power; there is no evidence that they were regarded as connected naturally and essentially with YHWH.

The epithet ʾ*ēl shadday* is believed by some to identify YHWH with Hadad, the storm god of Mount Casius. However, precisely in those early narratives of Genesis in which ʾ*ēl shadday* appears, the deity entirely lacks the accouterments of a storm god. He appears as a placid creator and ruler, whose theophanies are unaccompanied by terrifying natural spectacles. Even the Flood story omits mention of divine raging in storm; God brings on the Flood by opening the gates of the deep and the windows of heaven; clouds are not even mentioned.[3] To be sure, the later Pentateuchal stories do portray such features in connection with YHWH's theophanies. The reason for the difference is this: fire, clouds, and thunder are features of God's revelation to a whole people or the entire world; hence they play so large a part in the desert wandering of Israel. In the stories of Genesis, however, public theophanies do not take place.

The original character of the biblical God cannot be deduced, then, from analysis of his names or the description of his theophanies. Images which were originally expressive of natural links between nature and deity became in biblical legend entirely transformed to serve the new idea.

The futility of this method becomes clear when it is observed how in the very earliest period contrary features which in paganism constitute opposing divine realms are united in YHWH. He is lord of plague and death as well as of blessing and life; he rescues and redeems, but has something of the demonic in him too (Exod. 4:24 ff.). These notions demonstrate how early YHWH was made sovereign of all domains. Such an amalgam of natures and roles is possible only in a god who is not regarded as naturally bound to any one of them.

GOD AND MATTER—The pagan idea that the deity derives power and benefit from certain objects and substances is entirely absent in the Bible. The notion of power-charged trees lurks in the Eden legend; it is significant, therefore, that God himself is nowhere said to eat of the forbidden fruit. Along with the theogonic idea, the Bible rejected the thought that YHWH draws upon any external source of power. He has no tablets of destiny, no seal of life, or any other magical object upon which his authority depends. His actions in the world are mediated either through forces of nature (his creatures) or tools such as his bow, arrows, sword, or chariot. He has steeds, cherubs, or "living creatures" upon which he rides. But these are depicted as servants, as means by which he manifests his will, or tokens of his power and activity. They are not mana-filled objects and beings upon

---

[3] In the Babylonian Flood story Adad gathers clouds and thunders loudly; the gods produce lightning, etc. The terror of the storm drives the gods into the highest heaven.

whom he calls for aid and from which he gets power. A "staff of God" is utilized by the man of God, but not by God himself. To be sure Judges 6:21 speaks of YHWH setting Gideon's offering on fire with the tip of his walking stick—but here YHWH has taken the form of a human traveler.

GOD AND FATE—The Bible has no concept of overriding fate and unalterable destiny. Its God is not subject to sexual needs, cycles of growth, life and death, or any cosmic order. The Bible knows only one supreme law: the will of God. Destiny is determined only by God; from him emanate the decrees that bind all. God alone has fixed the laws of heaven and earth, the world and all that is therein (Jer. 31:35; Ps. 148:6; Job 38:33, and elsewhere). Typical is the notion that the order of the cosmos is a covenant which God has imposed upon it (Jer. 33:20, 25). The blessings of fertility, the regularity of nature, the order of the times and seasons have all been ordained by God. He is first and last (Isa. 41:4; 44:6; 48:12); before him there was no god nor will there be after him (43:10). No decree or fate binds him.

From this idea a fundamental difference between the biblical and pagan conceptions of the temporal process arises. Theogony makes the birth of the gods part of the eternal, self-operating process of becoming that governs the universe. Hence the gods—like the rest of the universe—are subject to a succession of ages (ending frequently in annihilation) which are beyond their control. The biblical God, however, is outside of the flux of becoming and change; he controls times and sets seasons.

The prevailing idea in biblical and apocryphal literature conditions the fixing of times not on necessity, but on morality. Merit determines the time of reward, sin the time of punishment, repentance the time of grace. Thus the date of the Amorites' destruction is fixed by the measure of their sin (Gen. 15:16); the forty-year period of the Wandering is determined by the number of days spent in spying out the land (Num. 14:33 f.); the desolation of Palestine must last until its sabbaths have been paid back (Lev. 26:34 f.). Jehu's dynasty is allotted four generations as reward for his destroying the wicked line of Ahab (II Kings 10:30). Jerusalem's redemption is near because "her service has been accomplished, her sin paid back" (Isa. 40:2).

The clearest expression of the moral basis of biblical age-reckoning is found in the book of Daniel, the classical source of all "reckoners of the end-time." To Daniel's inquiry regarding the meaning of Jeremiah's seventy years of exile, Gabriel answers, "Seventy weeks are decreed upon your people and your holy city, to finish transgression, and to make an end of sin, and to forgive iniquity . . ." (Dan. 9:24). It is the same in later Jewish literature where the time of redemption is tied to sin and repentance.

The biblical notion of times and ages thus differs fundamentally from the pagan, in spite of certain similarities. The succession of epochs belongs to the domain of the supreme God; its one determinant is man's moral condition, which to that extent may be viewed as a kind of limitation of divine freedom.

GOD AND MORALITY—The Bible ascribes to God actions that, to our way of thinking, lack moral grounds, or even run counter to our moral sense. Indeed, at times they seem to reflect a ruthless, capricious, demonic being.

The basis of reward and punishment is the assumption that man acts with freedom. Yet several passages represent God as causing man to sin in order to destroy him. YHWH hardens the heart of Pharaoh and the sons of Eli in order to punish them; stiffens Israel's heart to keep them from repenting; entices David to sin in the matter of the census, and then smites the people with a plague.

Nor can we reconcile the dangers of contact with God and his holy appurtenances with a belief in a supreme moral will. Whoever beholds God must die; death threatens all who approach the sanctuary, be they priests or laity; the ark brings on plague and death—as in the case of Uzzah, who was struck down immediately upon touching it (II Sam. 6:6 f.).

Our moral sense is repelled by certain religious obligations and the penalties for their violation. Jephthah sacrifices his daughter to fulfil a vow, and Abraham obeys YHWH's command to sacrifice his son. Moses hangs the chiefs of the people "for YHWH," and David surrenders Saul's seven sons to a similar cruel fate to avert YHWH's wrath. Achan's trespass against the ban at Jericho involves the death of his entire family. The judgment upon Israel's enemies is especially harsh: the Canaanites are to be utterly cut off, and the stories in Joshua have it that this law was carried out. Samuel charges Saul with the extirpation of Amalek "even to infants and sucklings." Jonathan incurs the death penalty for a trivial violation of his father's oath.

Ancient exegetes were troubled by many of these matters, and modern apologetes attempt in various ways to lessen their sting. Our present concern is their significance for religious history. To what extent does a premonotheistic, demonistic conception of deity underlie such notions? If monotheism sprang from a moral conception of deity—as is often asserted —these passages must belong to a prior stage.

It is true that historical monotheism aspired to raise morality to the level of supreme law. Abandoning the amoral universe of magical forces it conceived the idea of a moral cosmos, whose highest law is the will of

God. But this idea arose out of monotheism, and not the reverse. One can discern, therefore, a primary non-moral or supramoral element in monotheistic faiths: the will and command of God is absolutely good. The doctrine of predestination held by some Christian denominations is the most striking form of this idea. God has foreordained who will be saved and who will be damned. At this point the absolute will of God becomes in essence immoral; monotheism approaches paganism. What is important in the present context, however, is the fact that exaltation of the One made it possible for cruelty to develop on a religious basis. God's glory, name, and sacra become the highest values; an offense against them is the supreme crime which justifies any punishment. Israel devoted the enemies of YHWH to destruction; Christianity destroyed idolaters and heretics for the glory of God; Islam fought holy wars. Precisely because of its exclusiveness monotheism can be ruthless. Hence there is no ground for viewing the laws of the ban and the dangers of contact with the holy as notions of an earlier age. They are not demonistic conceptions but express in their own way boundless adoration and reverence of the One.

Some of the legends that lay demonic activity to God (such as the attack upon Moses in Exod. 4:24) are to be viewed as the outcome of the monotheistic tendency to refer every event to YHWH—even such as would formerly have been ascribed to demons. The folk religion evidently took no offense at this notion, and something of this view is retained in biblical literature. That this is what is involved appears from certain passages in which God is said to cause men to sin. Here Israelite religion comes close to the pagan idea that sin is determined by gods or fate, thus removing it from the realm of morality. Yet this notion occurs in plainly monotheistic contexts. The prophet of ethical monotheism, Isaiah, ascribes such activity to God in his inaugural vision (6:9 f.); the thought is expressed by Elijah (I Kings 18:37) and the Second Isaiah as well (63:17). In these passages it is expressed as a general principle, not as a reflex of primitive folk religion. It is the outcome of a desire to comprehend all phenomena as actions of the one God. While it is axiomatic that sin is man's doing, the religious consciousness of the Bible was unable to reconcile itself entirely with this restriction of God's dominion. There is a tension here between the moral demand that sets limits to the working of God and the religious demand that subjects all to divine control. This tension is resolved in the eschatological vision of the new heart that man is to get at the end of days which will render him incapable of sinning (Jer. 31:31 ff.; 32:39 f.; Ezek. 11:19 ff.; 36:26 f.).

Yet there is a basic difference between the Israelite and pagan notions of divine incitement to sin. In the pagan view, the scene of the cosmic drama is the mythological realm with its clashing divine powers. In Israel, however, it is a moral drama arising out of the tension between the will of God and the will of man, who is free to rebel. Sin becomes essentially non-divine; it is grounded entirely in the human heart. The Bible never represents God as causing man to sin in the first instance; he hardens the heart of the voluntary sinner to prevent him from repenting. Pharaoh, the sons of Eli, the Israelites in the time of Isaiah, all began to sin of their own volition. By way of punishment God stiffens their hearts so they cannot repent. Thus the demand for justice is served and the sinner must suffer the full measure of his guilt. This necessity of punishment is at issue in the book of Jonah, where the prophet, not God, refuses to allow the repentance of the sinful Ninevites.

There is a further distinction to be made. The pagan view which links sin with a metaphysical evil principle views its harmful consequences as a natural, inevitable outcome. Sin is itself baleful, polluting; the sinner is automatically its victim. Hence when a god incites man to sin, he utilizes sin as a self-operating harmful force.

The biblical concept is essentially different. Sin never acts automatically; God always intervenes between sin and punishment. It is not the sin that brings on affliction but the will of God. Even demonic harm is ascribed to the hand of God (see, e.g., I Sam. 5:3, 6, 9; II Sam. 6:7). Jonathan wittingly defied the oath of YHWH taken by his father; this excited God's wrath, which was appeased by a ransom (I Sam. 14:24–45). Note that no harm automatically befell either Jonathan or the people for violating the sacred oath. Sin is not a self-operating force, let alone the decree of blind fate. If God causes to sin it is in order to fill the measure of the sinner and justify, as it were, his punishment. Harm does not proceed from sin, but from God. The differences are crucial.

Because sin is not rooted in a metaphysical principle, the notion of a sinning God is foreign to the Bible. While actions are ascribed to God that appear offensive to us, nothing indicates that the Bible regarded them so. Sin in the biblical sense is possible only in creatures; it is rebellion against the will of the Creator.

God and Wisdom—In contrast to the pagan idea that wisdom and knowledge are external to the gods, and can be inherited, acquired, or learned by them, the wisdom of YHWH is innate in him. Wisdom at large is his "first work"; it does not lodge in watery deeps, or in the ocean, in the underworld, or in the earth: it is the possession of God alone (Job 28:12 ff.).

Men have no access to this wisdom unless God bestows it upon them (expert craftsmen and sages, for example, are considered to have been especially endowed by YHWH [Exod. 28:3; 31:2-6; I Kings 3:9]). The Bible knows no figure comparable to the Greek Prometheus or the Canaanite Kothar wa-ḥasis; there is no source of wisdom outside of God. The pagan pride of wisdom is, for Ezekiel (28:3 ff.) and Isaiah (10:12 ff.), rebellion deserving of death.

GOD AND MAN—Inasmuch as the deity is not born out of a primordial womb, and mankind not fashioned either out of divine or primordial stuff, it is impossible, in the biblical view, to become God. There is no bridge between the created universe and God.

At first blush it would seem that the Bible preserves some vestiges of apotheosis: Enoch was "taken" by God; Elijah was transported to heaven in a storm. Reminiscenses of deification of the dead are the term ᵓelōhīm applied to spirits of the dead (I Sam. 28:13) and the popular practice of necromancy. But it is to be observed that strict bounds are set between the realm of YHWH and the host of other superhuman beings (ᵓelōhīm). YHWH is one; the ᵓelōhīm are many. The basic difference is reflected in the cult: only YHWH may be worshiped. "He who sacrifices to the ᵓelōhīm is to be destroyed" (Exod. 22:19). Again, there is no physical link between the world and God, but there is between it and the ᵓelōhīm (Gen. 6:1-4). While there is no desire and procreation in the realm of the deity, there is in the realm of the "sons of God" (*ibid.*). That a mortal should become God is inconceivable; but that he should join the company of celestial creatures is possible, as in the cases of Enoch and Elijah. This is the limit of biblical apotheosis.

The Bible knows of no worship of kings or heroes, nor is ancestor worship evidenced for biblical Israel. To be sure the king has sanctity; to curse him is on a par with cursing God (Exod. 22:27; I Kings 21:10, 13). Poetry styles him a "son" of God (Ps. 2:7). Metaphorically God is his father (II Sam. 7:14) and he is God's "firstborn" (Ps. 89:28), meaning that God is his especial guardian and help. But deification of kings is mentioned only as a heathen custom. Had it existed in Israel the prophets would certainly not have failed to denounce it.

Accordingly the Bible has no concept of salvation through apotheosis in the manner of the pagan mysteries. The idea of mystic union with God is alien to biblical thought. There is fear and love of God, yearning for his grace and revelation; but actual absorption into him is unheard of. On the other hand, later Jewish eschatology does know of aspiration to the status of angels (cf. Matt. 22:30). Even this limited apotheosis is fundamentally non-pagan; it is not achieved by a mystical regimen but by the grace of God toward his faithful servants. It is thus altogether distinct from the Hindu-Buddhist concept of a natural, graded path from the human to the divine, which is typical of pagan thought.

MAGIC AND WONDERS

The Ban on Magic—The Bible bans magic under penalty of death (Exod. 22:17; cf. Deut. 18:10). This ban is quite different, however, from pagan interdictions of black magic. While paganism forbade only that sorcery which was antisocial, which brought injury to men and activated baleful forces, the Bible makes no distinction between "white" and "black" magic. The official functionaries of foreign cults are regarded as magicians (Gen. 41:8; Exod. 7:11; Isa. 19:3; Dan. 2:2), even though they work for the good of society. Balaam is an internationally famous wizard who blesses as well as curses. What is banned in the Bible is therefore not simply the black magic interdicted by paganism.

The Bible recognizes no connection between magic and gods or demons; the magician is not represented ever as invoking their help. The contest between Moses and Aaron and the Egyptian sorcerers is not a contest between representatives of rival gods, for the Egyptians do not work their magic in the name of any god. Unable to produce lice they say to Pharaoh: "This is the finger of God" (Exod. 8:15)—they do not confess, "Their god is greater than ours." In the elaborate preparations made by Balaam for cursing Israel there is no mention of a god or spirit inimical to YHWH; indeed YHWH is Balaam's god too (Num. 22:18). Not even the pagans, in the biblical story, view Balaam as representing hostile powers. Similarly, the Second Isaiah makes no reference to Babylon's gods in his ridicule of her magic and incantations (Isa. 47:9, 12). Because of this the Bible can ascribe a reality to magic that it denies to the pagan gods and demons. For the Bible does believe in magic. The Egyptian magicians can work wonders; Balaam's power to curse is so real that YHWH must intervene to turn his curse into a blessing. This means that the biblical opposition to magic is not based on skepticism, on the recognition that magic is superstitious folly. Unconnected with divine or demonic powers (*shēdīm* and *śeʿīrīm* are never linked with magicians) the biblical conception of magic is fundamentally different from that of paganism. And since it fails to discriminate between "white" and "black" magic, the grounds of its interdiction must be radically different from those of paganism.

The Biblical Conception of Magic—The Bible frequently links

magic with wisdom, and counts magicians among the "wise men" (Isa. 47:10 ff.; Ps. 58:6; Dan. 1:20; 2:2, 13). The contrast between YHWH and the magician is, then, between divine and human wisdom. Magic is one of the aspects of heathen wisdom, reliance upon which seduces man into arrogant self-sufficiency. The Egyptian wizards rely on their magic; only when they fail do they acknowledge the finger of God. Babylon's trust in her wisdom and magic blinded her to knowledge of God. Trust in magic and wisdom is as sinful as trust in might. In a contest with YHWH it is bound to fail, for YHWH "frustrates the omens of the imposters, and makes diviners mad; turns wise men backward, and makes their knowledge foolish" (Isa. 44:25).

While there is a measure of truth to this conception—since magic was essentially a kind of mysterious science—it overlooks entirely the vast role that mythological beliefs played in pagan magic. This can be neither accidental nor the result of a systematic reworking of the early traditions. Such a reworking must presumably have been based on a repudiation of the reality of pagan gods. But then the reality of practices which were linked with belief in those gods would likewise have been denied. Yet the Bible believes in magic. It relates with folkloristic naïveté how YHWH triumphed over the magic arts of the Egyptians, Balaam, and the Babylonians. What prevented it from telling of his triumph over a magician-god of the nations? Such a story, had it existed, would in no way have impugned the idea of YHWH's uniqueness.

The biblical view of magic is explicable only as the outcome of the profound change brought about by the monotheistic idea. Belief in the gods ended; all divinity became concentrated in the domain of YHWH. Since the gods did not become virulent demons hostile to YHWH, their mana was not transformed into demonic magic. This change took place on the popular level; it was guided by instinct and intuition, not by speculation and systematic formulation. Hence we find the belief in the reality of magic persisting. This belief is a vestige of the pagan realm of transcendent powers. But in the non-mythological atmosphere of Israel this realm lost its connection with divinity. Since all power belongs to YHWH its reflex in the biblical idea of magic has no roots in a supernal principle. In the popular consciousness magic was comprehended as a form of human wisdom. It was idolatrous precisely because it was godless, because it represented human rebellion against God. The Bible does not condemn wisdom and science at large (for they are divine gifts to man); it bans only the occult science of magic that enables man to work wonders without recourse to God, thus feeding his ambition "to become like God."

This is, of course, a distorted conception of pagan magic. Yet it does contain a profound insight into its essence. Magic did unlock the secrets of the universe, and did put man on a par with the gods, insofar as he and the gods both had recourse to it. Indeed it even empowered man to coerce the gods to his will. The Bible grasped this essential feature: magic limits the domain of the deity. With the disappearance of the primordial realm, the gods, and the demons the magician-god disappeared too. For the Bible, there remained only man, who exalts himself through his "wisdom" and "designs." Magic is a heathen abomination; its source is not a primordial principle, but the sin of pride.

BIBLICAL WONDERS AND MAGICAL WONDERS—It is a widespread view among students of Israelite religion that in spite of the formal ban on magic the Bible contains a substantial magical element essentially similar to pagan beliefs. There is, in this view, no real difference between the magical conceptions of the Bible and those of paganism, between the magical practices of the biblical man of God and those of the pagan magician. It is only that the gods, demons, and spirits are replaced in the Bible by YHWH.

In examining this view it must be borne in mind that the essence of pagan magic shows itself not in the belief that man can manipulate supernatural forces, but in the idea that the gods stand in need of, use, and benefit from these same forces. Here is revealed the basic pagan idea of a metadivine realm upon which the gods depend. This belief determines the ultimate source of the pagan magician's power. He does not carry out the will of the gods, he imitates them, utilizing the very means employed by them. The magician may therefore act without recourse to the gods. Even when the gods participate, they are viewed as but one among several magical agents. Does the Bible too reflect the belief in an autonomous realm of magical forces beyond or beside YHWH?

Speaking broadly we may distinguish two categories of magic: cultic and technical. Cultic magic is embodied in a system of fixed activities whose purpose is to secure weal and avert woe. Its effect is conceived as quasi-natural—continuous, gradual, slow. Cultic magic insinuates itself, so to speak, into the workings of nature. It aims to reconstitute the natural order in which some fault has appeared or is apprehended. Technical magic, on the other hand, interrupts the natural order, causing marvelous transformations suddenly to take place in some mysterious fashion. This category is especially developed in Egypt and India. The Bible contains reflexes of both categories.

The cultic element of biblical religion is evidently influenced by magical conceptions. The idea that sanctity or impurity adheres to certain substances or emanates from them is grounded ultimately in the notion that given substances possess fixed magical properties. The belief in the purifying effect of specific substances and actions belongs to the same category. All ceremonial regulations have a magical cast; the animal for sacrifice must be of proper age, sex, color, etc.; construction of altars and temples must conform to certain specifications, and so forth.

The wonders performed by biblical men of God recall Egyptian technical magic. There are many allusions to the power of specific objects, gestures, numbers, words, and the like. The sudden marvelous transformation is an important feature of such stories. The staffs of Moses and Aaron, when thrown down, become serpents; the Nile turns to blood, the dust of the earth to lice. Elijah's word miraculously perpetuates flour and oil; Elisha heals the waters of Jericho with salt and raises the sunken iron with a piece of wood. Moses' wonderful staff brings plagues on Egypt, divides the sea, draws water out of the rock; Elijah's staff revives the Shunammite's son. The touch of Elijah's cloak divides the Jordan, and contact with Elisha's bones revives the dead. Of magical gestures we may mention Moses' influence on the battle with Amalek by the position of his arms, or Elijah's crouching earthward to bring on the rain. Numbers play a significant part in the fall of Jericho, accomplished through a seven days' encirclement by the army and seven priests with seven horns. The three arrows that Joash drove into the ground gave him three victories over Aram. The symbolic acts of the prophets also belong here, for they are evidently conceived of as having a part in the realization of events. The magical power of the word is everywhere evident. With a spell Joshua stops the sun; the belief in the efficacy of blessings and curses is a pervasive element of Israelite religion.

A sizable strand of magical conceptions thus runs through the whole Bible. It is present in prophetic as well as pentateuchal literature; priestly concepts seem to be especially saturated. But precisely the fact that prophetic legends likewise contain the conceptions makes it difficult to categorize them summarily as pagan. The prophets were, after all, the zealous champions of YHWH against all manner of Israelite idolatry.

The magical strand of biblical thought is a legacy of paganism. But the ancient materials became in Israel a vehicle to express a new non-pagan idea. This transmutation of magical materials is one of the striking features of the history of Israelite religion.

The characteristic mark of biblical magic is that it lacks a mythological basis. It is the man of God, but never God himself, who uses magical devices. This is a crucial distinction. It means that biblical wonder-working must have a value fundamentally different from that of pagan analogues. As indicated above, magic is regarded by the Bible as a human science of mysterious, quasi-natural forces whose secret is known to the wizard. It is idolatrous precisely because it is godless. Not so the workings of the man of God. The wonder does not originate in his actions and utterances; there is no innate, natural, necessary—in a word, magical—connection between the two. To the Israelite the wonder is "the hand of God." Biblical legend adopted the coloring of Egyptian technical wonders, but the pagan materials have been converted into a fundamentally non-pagan symbol.

THE WONDROUS SIGN—The technical wonder first appears in the story of the burning bush (Exod. 3—4:17). Here it has the special role of being the sign confirming the divine mission of the prophet. This idea has no pagan parallel. Since the pagan magician works by his skill (which may have been bestowed upon him by a god), the wonder he performs betokens only his own power, the power of his magic. The wondrous sign of the prophet, attesting that YHWH has sent him, is a motif peculiar to Israelite religion. It became one of the fundamental motifs of Israelite prophecy.

All the wonders performed by Moses and Aaron attest both the might of God and their mission. When Moses and Aaron appear before Pharaoh claiming to be agents of the Hebrew God and working wonders in his name, the Egyptian wizards duplicate their feats as if to disprove the claim, as if to show that nothing more than ordinary magic was involved. The opening of the sea is a sign of YHWH's saving power and of Moses' "servanthood" as well (Exod. 14:31), It is the same with the miracles of the manna, Miriam's leprosy, the punishment of Korah, the flowering of Aaron's rod, etc. The concept was incorporated in the law: a prophet must adduce signs and wonders to validate his calling (Deut. 13:2). Joshua's dividing of the Jordan confirmed his mission; Gideon tests the truth of his by asking two signs (Judg. 6:17 ff., 36 ff.). Elijah's trial on Mount Carmel constituted a decisive sign that YHWH was God and Elijah his servant and messenger (I Kings 18:36). Isaiah, too, employs signs to confirm his mission (Isa. 7:10 ff.; 38:5 ff.).

When the technical wonder was thus linked with the idea of the apostle-prophet, the nature of its elements was radically transformed. The "magical" actions that precede or accompany the wonder become mere externals. They provide the framework for the working of the divine will without which the wonder would be no sign. These actions relate the divinely wrought prodigy to the apostle-prophet—the wonder taking place when the prophet raises his staff, makes a gesture, or utters his word; or occurring at the time and place that he specifies in advance. Its manifestation in this setting is what makes it a confirmatory sign. The need for a setting found in the magical actions and gestures of the technical wonder an element particularly adaptable for the biblical wondrous sign. But in the Bible this element is no longer the supernatural cause of the wonder. It now serves merely as the setting for the revelation of God's power and the authentication of his messengers.

Let us examine more closely some of the "magical" embellishments of biblical wonder-legends.

One common motif is the wonder-working staff. Such staffs always work at the command of YHWH. At YHWH's bidding Moses' staff undergoes various transformations, and Aaron's staff becomes a serpent (Exod. 4:2 ff.; 7:8 ff.). Whatever Moses or Aaron perform with their staffs is at the bidding of YHWH, and it is YHWH who effects the wonder. Turning to other motifs, Moses casts a piece of wood into the waters at Marah—and YHWH heals the waters (15:25). The brazen serpent that marvelously heals those bitten by snakes is made at YHWH's command (Num. 21:8 f.). Joshua's spell causes the sun to stand still, but the story goes on to say that YHWH listened to his voice because "YHWH fought for Israel." The expression is typical: it is YHWH who causes the miracle; he hearkens to the voice of the man of God and works on his behalf, or on behalf of his people. As Elisha smites the Jordan with Elijah's cloak he cries, "Where is YHWH, God of Elijah?" (II Kings 2:14). Elijah lies upon the child to revive him, praying to YHWH in the meantime—and YHWH hears his voice (I Kings 17:21 f.). Elisha does not utter an incantation to increase the bread; he proclaims the miracle as "the word of YHWH" (II Kings 4:43 f.). In healing the waters of Jericho he utilizes "magical" devices (a new jar and salt); he does not cast a spell in the pagan fashion, however, but announces, "Thus said YHWH: I have healed these waters" (2:21)—as if to say, "I am neither a sorcerer nor a magician, but a prophet, who executes the will of God."

The tale of Elisha's cure of Naaman's leprosy (II Kings 5) is especially illuminating. Elisha recommends a method which appears almost magical: immersion seven times in the river Jordan. But for Naaman this method is all too commonplace and unceremonious. The pagan grows angry; he had expected elaborate magical rites: "Lo, I thought he would surely come out to me, and stand and call on the name of YHWH his god, and wave his hand toward the spot and cure the leper." But Elisha wished to demonstrate that "there is a prophet"—not a potent wizard—"in Israel" (vs. 8). The purpose of the wonder is to show that "there is no God in all the world except in Israel." And Israel's God can cure by any means; he is not bound by any ritual procedure.

A similar fusion of elements is to be found in the account of Hezekiah's cure (Isa. 38). Isaiah seems to effect the cure by a quasi-magical medicine. But it is YHWH who really cured the king because of his prayers and tears; Isaiah merely announced the fact to him. As a prophet he foretells that the shadow will recede ten steps, but as a man of God he performs the wonder; he calls on YHWH and YHWH does his will. Again the wonder is not produced by a magical act, but is a manifestation of the divine will.

It is the same with the magical features of the Samson legend. Samson's locks, the apparent source of his power, are, like the "magical" adjuncts of the prophetic sign, really no more than a setting for the manifestation of God's will. When divine power manifests itself through the consecrated hair of the Nazirite, it is a sign that he is holy to YHWH. There is no independent causal nexus between Samson's hair and strength. Its real source is the blessing and spirit of YHWH (Judg. 13:24 f.; 14:6, 19). When his locks were shorn, YHWH left him (16:20). His strength returned when his hair grew back, yet it is YHWH's answer to his prayer that enabled him to destroy the Dagon temple.

The magical features of biblical religion have thus preserved ancient elements whose original meaning has been radically altered. The Israelite idea stripped magical actions of their autonomous, metadivine potency and made them serve as vehicles for the manifestation of the will of God.

SPELLS AND THE WORD OF GOD—In pagan thought blessings and curses are a variety of incantation; they are regarded as automatically effective, and—since the gods also use and are affected by them—transcendently potent. YHWH neither uses nor is affected by incantations. He acts by the word; but that this is no more than an expression of his will is indicated by the fact that he never uses fixed words or formulas, as do Ormazd or Brahma. His utterances simply say what he wills at a given moment: "Let there be light. . . . Let there be a firmament. . . ."

In the Balaam story (Num. 22–24) the pagan magician and Israelite prophet are combined. Balaam the magician is a potent dispenser of blessings and curses; this is the belief of Balak and his officers, and is accepted by the Bible as part of its belief in the reality of non-divine magical forces. Despite his uncanny power as magician, however, Balaam cannot curse "one whom God has not cursed." But he is also a prophet, in Israelite style, and as such he speaks only the word of God.

The tendency of the Bible is to transform the blessings of inspired men (corresponding to the magicians' spells) into prophecies, and cultic blessings (corresponding to priestly incantations) into commands of God. Thus Balaam's blessing is formally a prophetic vision. Jacob's blessing takes the shape of a prophecy to his children concerning their destiny. The curse that Joshua laid on the rebuilder of Jericho is interpreted as a prophecy (I Kings 16:34). The Israelite priest is charged by God to bless Israel (Num. 6:22 ff.). This blessing is a fixed formula and seems therefore to be close to an incantation. Yet the biblical idea comes through clearly in the charge: "They shall set my name upon the Israelites and I shall bless them." The priest carries out the divine command, but the deity does the actual blessing. God does not reveal to the Israelite priest a magically charged combination of words that act on their own, or that compel the deity to bless. The priest having fulfilled God's command, God on his part will bless the people.

THE MAN OF GOD—The Israelite analogue to the pagan priest-magician is the man of God. Both reveal hidden things, heal the sick, perform wonders, curse and bless. The work of the man of God, however, is never accomplished by any technique, craft or art. Magician, king, judge, counselor, craftsman, and dream-interpreter are all called "skilled" (*ḥākām*); the man of God, or prophet, is never counted among the skilled, nor praised for his wisdom. A sharp line separates him from the priest. The priest's office is hereditary—the prophet's is personal; the priest's work is regulated by established rites and forms—the prophet's is free of all fixed forms. The faculty of the man of God is always dependent on divine grace. By God's will he reveals hidden things, works wonders, heals, blesses and curses. His utterances are free expressions of the spirit. The separation of roles is exemplified clearly in the relation to torah: the prophet reveals torah; the priest "handles" (Jer. 2:8) and transmits it. Whatever can be held and transmitted is the priest's domain; whatever is the product of inspiration and momentary seizure is the prophet's.

Hence there is no learned tradition of wonder-working or healing in Israel, no literature of esoteric science, no magical wisdom. No spells or magical lore are disclosed to Moses at the bush. He asks God's name—in order to tell it to the people; there is no connection between the newly revealed name and his wonder-working. This story is the archetype of all wonder-legends of the Bible. Here and ever after, the procedures of the wonder-worker are altogether commonplace and entirely untraditional. Wood, flour, salt, the waters of the Jordan, fig cakes, are at one time or another employed, without any indication of a fixed tradition. The miraculous staff of Moses, a typical magical motif, is a case in point: the J source makes it an ordinary shepherd's staff that Moses happened to have in hand when God appeared to him in the bush. But even the version that makes it "a staff of God" does not treat it as a fixed magical implement. It never appears after Moses; Joshua does not inherit it. Elijah bequeaths to Elisha not his wonder-working staff, but his cloak. But even the cloak is of moment only because it signified that Elijah's spirit lighted upon Elisha. The only tradition among prophets is spiritual; there is no formulated science, no books, no magical objects.

THE ABSENCE OF MAGIC IN ISRAEL—The biblical laws banning magic, and all other references to magic in Israel, view it as a product of heathen, of foreign, influence. Is this a creditable testimony, or were there also magicians belonging to the native religion of YHWH, using YHWH's name, and transmitting an esoteric lore of Israelite creation?

All the stories concerning Israelite men of God and prophets support the view that magic was alien to native Israelite creativity. Thus while the Bible forbids magic, there is no account of a struggle between prophets and magicians. "True" prophets are ranged against "false"—i.e., against prophets who falsely claim to speak in the name of YHWH—but never against magicians. Even the fact that the sign of the false prophet comes true is construed not as a product of magic, but as an act of God to test Israel (Deut. 13:2 ff.). Magicians are never counted among the courtiers of Israelite kings. When they do appear, in the days of Jezebel and Manasseh, it is under patently foreign auspices. Israel's battles with magicians are always fought with pagans: Moses triumphs over Egypt's magicians; Daniel, over Babylon's magicians, Balaam the prophet, over Balaam the pagan magician.

There is no law prohibiting the use of YHWH's name in magic, nor is there an instance of a prophet rebuking anyone who profaned the name of God in such a way. Indeed, as we have seen, the Bible fails to recognize even that pagan magic is connected with gods or spirits.

A further indication of the insignificant part played by magic in Israel is the absence of apotropaics. No rite is designed to ward off magical or demonic agents of sickness. There is no protective rite at the eclipse of sun or moon (fear of the "signs of heaven" is considered heathenish [Jer. 10:2]). If there were such rites in the popular religion how is it that they are neither opposed nor even mentioned by biblical authors? This can have but one explanation: the religion of YHWH left no room for the pagan fear of magical-demonic powers who attack god and man. Once the mythological roots of magic were cut, it descended to the level of vestigial, underground beliefs. That the magician can work harm is allowed by biblical thought; but his power is no matter for religious concern. The

Balaam story reflects this peculiar attitude; Balaam the arch-magician could have harmed Israel were it not that God intervened and turned his curse to blessing. But even in this isolated incident no recourse is had to any countermagic. Neither Moses nor Aaron battles with Balaam; no apotropaic rite is performed; Israel trusts in its God. The menace of the magician is a theme for legend; in religious ritual he has no place.

To summarize: The Bible is unaware of the mythological basis of magic; we know of no magician caste in Israel; the Bible fails to prohibit magic in the name of YHWH, and contains no apotropaic rites against black magic. This can only mean that in Israel magic was not present in the form we know it elsewhere. What magic was practiced was under foreign influence, a matter of ignorant superstition, not an expression of the national religion. The view that the primitive terror of magic prevailed in Israel, and was a concern of Israelite religion is supported by nothing more than ungrounded analogizing.

DIVINATION AND ORACLES

Israel, like other peoples of antiquity, felt itself close to its God, and believed that he responded to inquiries concerning all aspects of life. In public or private crises, in matters large or small it was the custom to seek an oracle. Kings were appointed and war declared by divine decision. God was inquired of regarding loss of property (I Sam. 9:3 ff.), a painful pregnancy (Gen. 25:22), sickness, or accident (I Kings 14:1 ff.; II Kings 4:22 ff.). Justice was rendered by a word of God (Exod. 22:8), and capital punishment was meted out by it as well (Josh. 7:13 ff.). Failure to obtain an oracle was a token of God's wrath (I Sam. 14:36 ff.; 28:6 ff.). The cessation of the word of God is one of the calamities with which Israel is threatened for its sins (Amos 8:11 f.; Hos. 3:4; Mic. 3:6 f.; Ezek. 7:26; cf. Isa. 29:10; Lam. 2:9).

One of the peculiar features of biblical religion is its ban on virtually all of the techniques employed by paganism for obtaining oracles. This ban applies not only to inquiries addressed to "other gods"; it is an unconditional ban: "There must not be found among you . . . a diviner, a soothsayer, an augur . . . a medium . . . or a necromancer" (Deut. 18:10 f.; cf. Lev. 20:6, 27; I Sam. 28:3, 9; II Kings 23:24; Isa. 8:19; Ezek. 13:17 ff.). Other heathen techniques of divination that are mentioned or alluded to are hydromancy or oleomancy (Gen. 44:5, 15), hepatoscopy (Ezek. 21:26), astrology (Jer. 10:2; Isa. 47:13), divination through idols and teraphim (Gen. 31:19, 34 f.; cf. 30:27; Ezek. 21:26; Isa. 19:3), or by shaking arrows (Ezek. 21:26). These banned techniques, considered heathen customs, are termed divination (*naḥash, qesem*) and are distinguished from legitimate means of obtaining oracles from YHWH (*dārash be-*YHWH, *be-ʾelōhīm* "to inquire of YHWH, of God"). The legitimate means are through the Urim and Thummim (Num. 27:21), the ephod (I Sam. 23:9 f.), lots (Num. 26:55), dreams, and prophecy (I Sam. 28:6).

The ban on necromancy and divination through idols and teraphim is understandable as falling under the prohibition of worshiping the dead and idols. But on what grounds is the distinction made between, say, hepatoscopy, astrology, and cleomancy, which are all banned, and Urim, ephod, and lots, which are permitted, though also involving a technique? It is not that the Bible disbelieves in the efficacy of the banned methods. The witch of En-dor committed a capital crime in raising the ghost of Samuel, but she was able to do it (I Sam. 28:8 ff.). Isaiah believes that the ghost speaks from the earth (29:4); he condemns necromancy not on the ground that it is futile, but that it is rebellion against God (8:19). Laban's divining revealed the truth to him (Gen. 30:27). The laws ban divination on the ground that it is an abomination; they nowhere intimate that it is vain. God can bring to nought "the omens of the imposters" as he can make wise men foolish (Isa. 44:25; cf. 19:3 f.)—but there is substance in omens as much as there is in wisdom.

The current view is that the popular religion at first considered the banned techniques legitimate means of obtaining oracles of YHWH. If this were so the opponents of *naḥash* must have argued that YHWH does not reveal his will by *naḥash* omens and, consequently, that *naḥash* is vain. Yet neither argument is ever found. No champion of the religion of YHWH ever reproaches the people for seeking oracles of YHWH through *naḥash* or argues that YHWH will not respond through its omens. At the same time the efficacy of *naḥash* is never denied. How, now, could the view that *naḥash* is an abomination have arisen alongside the view that it is a legitimate means of disclosing the will of YHWH while belief in its efficacy continued unchallenged?

This distinction between *naḥash* and the legitimate Urim and ephod is explicable only on the assumption that it is primary. Of all mantic techniques Israelite religion adopted from the first only the Urim oracle; the other techniques, called *naḥash*, were never accepted and never regarded as a means of obtaining an oracle of YHWH. *Naḥash* was never employed in Israel to ascertain the will of YHWH. It was always felt to be pagan and foreign, despite the belief in its efficacy. The entire biblical record testifies to the primacy of this differentiation.

Deuteronomy 18:9–22 bans *naḥash* as a custom of the nations, not as a form of seeking oracles from YHWH (whom the nations do not know). More telling are the incidental witnesses to its foreignness. Thus, while diviners and astrologers are time and again named among the courtiers of foreign kings, Israelite kings (even wicked ones, like Ahab) inquire of YHWH only through Urim and prophets. Just as they have no court magicians, so they have no professional diviners. Saul extirpates the mediums and necromancers; only in desperation—after YHWH does not answer him—does he turn to the witch. Ahaziah sends messengers to inquire of Baal-zebub of Ekron, an act regarded as an unheard of sin, and one which brings on his death (II Kings 1). Of the paganizer Manasseh alone is it said that he practiced various forms of divination (21:6). Jeremiah speaks of magicians and augurs when addressing the foreign kings (Jer. 27:9); with Zedekiah however, he knows only of false prophets.

Corresponding to this fact is the absence of any struggle between Israelite soothsayers and prophets, let alone between prophets and soothsayers of YHWH. We hear of no class of professional diviners in Israel. Biblical legend bears the same testimony. The Balaam legend tells of the victory of the word of YHWH over pagan magical augury; no story tells of a corresponding victory within Israel. Augury is always foreign in the legends (Balaam, Laban, and so forth). A striking example is the dual personality of Joseph. As the Hebrew slave he has in him the spirit of God, and with it outdoes the Egyptian magicians; Joseph the Egyptian officer, however, has a silver cup in which he divines. Biblical legend here inadvertently expresses its inner feeling that divination is a pagan custom.

On the other hand, no pagan is ever spoken of as divining by means of the ephod or Urim. Dreams, prophets, teraphim, and lots are common to Israel and the nations; the ephod and Urim are peculiarly Israelite.

The prohibition of all *naḥash* and the legitimacy of ephod and Urim cannot be an accident or the outcome of a tendency that happened to win out in the end. They are grounded in a viewpoint that governed the history of Israelite religion from its beginnings. *Naḥash* is non-Israelite; indeed upon examination it appears that the Bible understands pagan augury no better than it does pagan magic.[4]

[4] The evidence that is adduced to support the view that divination was practiced in the popular religion is either fanciful or based on the assumption that the religion of YHWH contained at first pagan elements. Place names such as En Mishpat (spring of decision), Elon Moreh (instructor's oak), or Elon Meonenim (augurs' oak) point to sacred sites; but that oracles of YHWH were obtained at these sites is unevidenced. Place names may well have been taken over from the Canaanites (cf. names compounded with Anath and Baal). Nor is there evidence of the practice of hepatoscopy. Had such a technique been practiced why should the Bible—which never deals gently with Israel's sinning—have passed over it in silence?

THE BIBLICAL VIEW OF DIVINATION—Just as the Bible is unaware of a connection between magic and gods or spirits, so it knows of no connection between augury and divine beings (aside from ghosts). The Bible mentions divining by idols (II Kings 1; Isa. 19:3), but this is merely fetishistic, as can be seen not only from the entire attitude of the Bible toward the idols, but from the explicit polemic directed against such practices. Idols, we hear, are "molten images" which instruct falsely; they are "dumb idols." To those who divine by them the prophet says, "Woe to him who says to wood, 'Awake,' 'Arise,' to inanimate stone. Will that instruct? It is overlaid with gold and silver, and has no breath in it" (Hab. 2:18 f.). Hosea probably refers to the same practice when he says, "My people asks of its wood, its staff instructs it" (4:12). Divination by idols is thus conceived of as a mantic ritual carried out before or by means of a "dumb" idol. For other ways of pagan divination in the Bible see Isaiah 19:3, Ezekiel 21:26, and Jonah 1:7 f. In no case is any god involved. The only living god with whom Laban comes into contact is YHWH (his "gods" are the teraphim images); he discovers that Jacob has been the cause of his prosperity by "divining"—but no god is mentioned. Balaam has no contact with gods other than YHWH; he uses magic, builds altars, and goes "to meet with enchantments," all without reference to any god. The Philistine priests and augurs do not seek the will and counsel of Dagon; their advice is spoken in the name of no god (I Sam. 6:2 ff.).

The biblical polemic against divination accords with this conception. The prohibitions of *qesem* and *nahash* are unrelated to the ban on worshiping pagan gods. The story of II Kings 1, and perhaps the taunt of Habakkuk 2:18 f. are the only intimations of an awareness that the pagan fetish-idols have to do with oracle-giving. In the many passages speaking of divinatory techniques gods are never mentioned. The Second Isaiah repeatedly mocks the idols for not knowing the future; but in the course of his railing he never mentions *qesem, nahash,* or augury through omens and signs. And when he speaks of the latter he never mentions the former. From the fact that YHWH frustrates the omens of the "imposters" (44:25) and the failure of Babylon's sorceries (47:12 ff.), he does not argue for the nullity of the pagan gods. It is as if the prophet were unaware that the pagans attributed a mantic function to their gods.

How then does the Bible conceive of divination? It is, like magic, a kind of "wisdom" or art; it is an occult science of signs by which man is able to see hidden things and the future. (The fetishistic conception of paganism's gods necessitates this view.) Divination and magic are both aspects of pagan "wisdom": the mediums of Egypt give counsel (Isa. 19:3), the wise men are asked about the future (vs. 12), Balaam is a counselor (Num. 24:14; 31:16). The stories about Joseph and Daniel show that pagan dream-interpretation is also taken to be the domain of sages.

Divination is pagan, an abomination of YHWH, because it aims to reveal the secrets of God in an ungodly way. By his wisdom alone the pagan believes he can discover and interpret signs, and make the dead speak. *Nahash* is another form of rebellion against God, another aspect of man's aspiration "to be like God." The Israelite must be "wholehearted" (*tāmīm*) with YHWH and inquire only of him (Deut. 18:13). To be sure, it is possible to discover the future and reveal hidden things by means of mantic art, but this recourse is abominable and defiling. Moreover the heathen trust in these methods is, in the last analysis, vain. For God can at will frustrate the omens of augurs; in the day of reckoning their counsel will not be able to rescue man from divine punishment.

This view of divination, like the biblical view of magic (and idolatry in general) is distorted. For the gods, as we have seen, did play an important part in divination. Nonetheless, there is a genuine insight here into the magical basis of pagan mantic arts. These were after all utilized by both gods and men; as such they do imply the subjection of deity to a transcendent realm. The religion of YHWH could not assimilate this idea. Hence the biblical opposition to divination involves, not this or that technique, but its very claim to reveal hidden things in a "scientific" way. What offends the Bible is the heathen confidence in human wisdom, the heathen aspiration to metadivine knowledge. The biblical ban on divination did not arise from the gradual disqualification of certain methods of inquiring of YHWH. The banned methods were never recognized in biblical Israel as means of inquiring of YHWH; they were always regarded as foreign to the religion of Israel. The question is, why of all techniques did the Urim and ephod alone remain legitimate, while the rest were rejected as ungodly, pagan practices?

THE METHODS OF INQUIRING OF YHWH—The peculiar feature of Israelite inquiry of God is that it lacks a fixed system of signs and omens. It has no science of signs or library of omens. Its ideal is the direct question put to God, with a clear and simple response in return.

Israelites like to discover the future or the will of God through *ad hoc* signs; they appear to be ignorant of fixed or conventional natural portents. All signs regarded by the Bible as God-sent—such as the signs given to Eliezer (Gen. 24:12 ff.), to Gideon (Judg. 6:36 ff.; 7:4 ff.), and to David (II Sam. 5:23 ff.)—are *ad hoc*. In the latter two cases there is a resemblance to pagan methods (by water and the movement of trees), and yet the difference is manifest; both Gideon's test by water and David's reliance on the rustling of the trees were in obedience to an explicit divine instruction given for the occasion.

The biblical interpretation of natural portents is equally artless. Earthquakes and natural catastrophes signify God's wrath (Amos 4:6 ff.); rain in harvest time means that the people have sinned (I Sam. 12:17 ff.). These are self-evident signs, given for the occasion; they do not require a mantic science for their interpretation.

The Urim oracle is of the same character. Its use as described in the LXX version of I Samuel 14:41,[5] and the verb "cast" (vs. 42) suggest that it was a kind of lot. The Urim and Thummim were placed in the priest's breastplate; according to Exodus 28:25 ff. and Leviticus 8:7 f., this was connected to the ephod and lay on the priest's chest (cf. Prov. 16:33). In Ezra 2:63 the Urim are said to have decided questions of priestly pedigree. The ancient Arab custom of deciding matters of pedigree by casting arrow-lots before the idol Hubal is comparable. The inquiry is framed in simple alternatives which God can select through the lot (I Sam. 14:37, 41 [see n. 5]; 23:10 ff.).

It is no accident that the religion of YHWH preferred lot oracles to all other manner of augury. They are the simplest, most unsophisticated method of decision-making. They address God rather than nature, and express complete reliance upon his decision rather than upon a science of omens. It is true that the Israelite believed the priest to be the only qualified manipulator of the Urim. But this does not alter the nature of the oracle: the priest needed no esoteric knowledge to use the Urim; even as employed by him they remained the ideal vehicle for expressing dependence exclusively on the decree of God.

Israelite religion did not reject divination on the basis of a clear conceptual grasp of its inner essence; here, as throughout all early Israelite creativity, a sound instinct was at work. In this case, however, there may also have been a special historical factor. When the new religion arose in Israel the old Semitic practice—retained long afterward by the Arabs—of divining in temples through lots was still in vogue. This was the origin of the Urim and ephod. The other divinatory techniques were employed by the *kāhin*-type of seer, who was not connected with a temple. But the Israelite prophet-seer, who took the place of the Semitic *kāhin* regarded himself as a spokesman of YHWH, and waited for YHWH's word in dreams

[5] The Hebrew text which may be restored on the basis of the LXX reads: "Saul said, 'O YHWH, God of Israel, why have you not now answered your servant? If the guilt be in me or in Jonathan my son, O YHWH, God of Israel, give Urim; but if it is in your people Israel, give Thummim.' "

or visions; he no longer took omens. The rise of Israelite prophecy, then, marked the end of the mantic techniques of the *kāhin*. A vestigial survival of them appear to be the mediums and necromancers; in the ghosts and familiar spirits which they consulted we are perhaps to see, in transmuted form, the *jinn* of the old *kāhins*. But these practitioners remained outside the religion of YHWH; that religion never developed its own mantic science.

To what extent this is true can be seen from the silence of the Bible regarding the use of any technique except the Urim-lots for ascertaining the will of YHWH. Pagan "scientific" divination (astrology, oleomancy, necromancy, etc.) was practiced among the ignorant masses—as it still is today; this extraneous, superficial foreign influence is condemned by the Bible. But the application of divinatory techniques to learn the decisions of YHWH is neither banned nor condemned, nor is it recorded that there was a native style of mantic arts, or a native class of professional diviners who revealed the will of YHWH. Enthralled by pagan stereotypes, biblical scholarship has failed to appreciate the significance of this monumental testimony to the radically non-pagan character of Israelite folk culture.

DREAMS AND PROPHECY

The general belief of antiquity in the prophetic value of dreams is shared by the Bible. That God reveals himself and his will to man through dreams is one of the foundations of Israelite prophecy.

Two broad categories of dream-revelation are known to the ancient world: the symbolic and the prophetic. The first consists of a symbolic or enigmatic vision whose meaning is veiled; in the second the deity reveals himself and speaks directly to man. The symbol requires interpretation, the prophecy does not. The prophetic dream accords better with the spirit of Israelite inquiry of God, as we have come to know it, inasmuch as its message is explicit and direct. The enigmatic symbolic dream, on the other hand, involves, like the rest of pagan divination, a science of interpretation; dream-interpretation is part of pagan wisdom. And since not all dreams originate with the gods, the mantic value of the dream is not necessarily dependent upon them; basically it is magical.

In spite of the belief in the value of the symbolic dream, a science of dream interpretation failed to develop in Israel. The biblical period feels this science to be fundamentally un-Israelite. This is nowhere explicitly stated, but the Bible obliquely attests to this feeling in an unmistakable manner. We find no reference to oneirocritics, or to a literature of dream-interpretation such as we find, say, in Babylonia. No Israelite seer or man of God interprets dreams. Even the superlatively wise Solomon, expert in judgment and accomplished in parables and riddles, is not said to have been an oneirocritic. Solomon's dream (I Kings 9) is characteristically Israelite; YHWH reveals himself and speaks with him. The dream related in the story of Gideon (Judg. 7:13 ff.) is an interesting testimony to Israelite feeling. Gideon learns of his coming victory over Midian from a symbolic dream. But it is a Midianite who dreams the dream and another Midianite who interprets it. The Midianites and other eastern peoples (cf. vs. 12)—whose wisdom was proverbial—of course have a science of oneirocriticism, but not Israel.

We hear of two Hebrew oneirocritics, Joseph and Daniel. Both belong to the court of heathen kings; the former among Egyptian magicians, the latter among Chaldean astrologers. But, true to its nature, the Bible assimilates their oneirocriticism to prophecy or, at the very least, to the word of God. In the case of Joseph it is emphasized that not through his wisdom was he able to solve the puzzle of Pharaoh's dream, but God revealed its meaning to him (Gen. 40:8; 41:16, 38 f.). Daniel is reckoned among the sages and astrologers of Babylon, but as a Hebrew he works through divine inspiration. God reveals to him in a vision the enigmatic dream of Nebuchadnezzar with its solution (Dan. 2:17 ff.). Instructed by the spirit of God he reads and interprets the puzzling handwriting on the wall (5:11–14). This tendency to assimilate the symbolic dream to prophecy gave rise to a peculiar type of prophetic vision in which God (or an angel) reveals to the prophet a riddle together with its interpretation. Zechariah sees enigmatic visions and dreams, and his angel explains them (Zech. 1:8 ff.; 2:1 ff.; etc.). An angel interprets the vision of the four beasts to Daniel (Dan. 7:16); Gabriel explains to him the vision of the ram (8:16). The visions of Amos (7:1–9; 8:1–3) and Jeremiah (1:11–15; 24) belong to the same category. Here the symbol is the background for the prophecy. The prophet does not apply his wisdom to puzzle out the meaning of the symbol, following an established set of rules; God himself reveals its meaning. The symbolic vision is not regarded as the essence of the revelation; the heart of the matter is the divine interpretation that immediately follows it. YHWH does speak "in riddles" (Num. 12:8), but the highest form of prophecy is "mouth to mouth . . . plainly, and not in riddles" (vss. 6 ff.). Biblical religion preferred that form of dream and vision which suited best its aspiration to set God above all. It is YHWH who causes dreams, and it is he who provides an explanation of their meaning.

ECSTASY AND PROPHECY—The highest form of Israelite prophecy—the apostle-prophet—is, as we shall see later, a peculiarly Israelite conception.

But Israelite prophecy also contains ancient pagan elements that have been refashioned by the Israelite idea. All forms of Israelite prophecy contained, for example, mantic features. Israelite, no less than pagan, prophecy is rooted in abnormal states of the psyche: in ecstasy, Platonic "madness," in certain psychic disturbances and their physical manifestations.

Dionysiac frenzy was known in early Israel. The seventy elders who stand about the tent when God speaks with Moses are seized by the spirit and "prophesy" together (Num. 11:16 ff.). In Samuel's time there is a popular movement of ecstatics; Gibeah has its "band of prophets" who "prophesy" to the accompaniment of psaltery, timbrels, and pipes. The elation is contagious; when Saul meets them, he also is seized, and "prophesies" with them. Ramah has a band of "prophets" over whom Samuel presides. Saul's messengers, upon coming to Ramah, and even Saul himself are infected by their frenzy (I Sam. 10:5 f., 10; 19:20 ff.).

In every age Israelite prophecy displays characteristic signs of ecstasy as we know it from paganism. An extraordinary inner tension seizes the prophet; all his experiences become heightened and his spirit and body are abnormally moved. He senses himself impelled by an external power—"the hand of YHWH." In this state he may perform extraordinary feats of physical prowess (I Kings 18:46), or live alone "filled with indignation" (Jer. 15:17), or fall prostrate (Num. 24:4, 16; Ezek. 1:28). At times the ecstasy takes the form of paralysis and dumbness (Ezek. 3:26 f.). Fear and deep sleep overwhelm him (Dan. 8:17 f.), his aspect changes, pains seize him, his strength and breath leave him (Dan. 10:8, 16 f.). He hears the tumult and rumble of earthquakes (Ezek. 1:24 f.; Dan. 10:6); he feels himself borne on the wind from place to place (Ezek. 3:12, 14; 8–11; 37:1). After the seizure he is shocked and ill (Dan. 8:27).

To "act the prophet" is to behave in a mad and unreasonable manner (I Sam. 18:10). Prophets were popularly called "madmen" (II Kings 9:11; Hos. 9:7; Jer. 29:26) or "fools" (Hos. 9:7). Even the great prophets act peculiarly: Elijah performs a prodigious feat of running before the chariot of Ahab; Isaiah walks about naked and barefoot for three years (Isa. 20:2 ff.); Jeremiah places bands and bars around his neck (Jer. 27:2; 28:10 ff.). Prophets go about unshorn, clothed in a leather girdle, sackcloth, or a hairy mantle (II Kings 1:8; Isa. 20:2; Zech. 13:4).

And yet there is an essential distinction between the Israelite and pagan conceptions of prophecy.

Pagan prophecy is typically regarded as deriving from a specific source of mantic power—from a psychic gift of the prophet, natural or acquired or from particular substances or spirits that inspire him. The Israelite conception knows no such specific power sources, nor are there specific spiritual beings whose function it is to inspire. Not even the prophetic "spirit" is considered the primary source of prophecy, as we shall see presently.

The title "seer" anciently given to Israelite inspired men (I Sam. 9:9) is probably a linguistic survival of the idea that the prophet possesses a natural gift of clairvoyance. However that may be, the Bible nowhere ascribes to its prophets such a faculty. No prophet of Israel has a special sense for discerning the unknown. In fact, the Bible almost goes out of its way to emphasize that prophecy is not a native faculty. The arch-prophet, Moses, is an inarticulate stammerer by nature (Exod. 4:10; 6:12, 30) and Jeremiah is an untried "boy" (Jer. 1:6). Balaam's ass sees more than Balaam until YHWH opens his eyes; Samuel the seer fails to divine which of Jesse's sons has been elected to kingship, for he, like all men, can see only outward appearances (I Sam. 16:6 ff.). Even Elisha, who resembles the pagan magician-diviner most closely, is helpless and ignorant unless YHWH informs him (II Kings 4:27).[6]

Prophecy is therefore not regarded as a native talent; the prophetic spirit is not in the prophet but "comes upon" him. It is a divine effluence that takes hold of him, and that may leave him at any moment. Even less does the religion of the Bible have to do with any material or actional stimuli to prophecy. It knows no regular recourse to wine, water, vapors, or similar inducements to ecstasy. The prophetic bands of Samuel's time use musical instruments; but—as we shall see—this ecstatic movement was, in the first place, entirely a cultic phenomenon, with no mantic function whatever. And even here, neither intoxicants nor dancing is mentioned. Dancing to induce prophetic frenzy is singled out as pagan practice (I Kings 18:26). The prophesying elders who surround Moses employ no external stimulus; it is contact with Moses' spirit that animates them. In all but one of the stories concerning the major prophets, there is no reference to the use of external inducements to prophecy; not even music is mentioned, though music was known to affect the psyche (I Sam. 15:14 ff.; 18:10), and was related to the poetic element in prophecy. Elisha's request for music is the sole exception (I Kings 3:15).[7] This story is important,

---

[6] However the Bible does preserve traces of the belief in the soul's power to see hidden things: persons near death and ghosts know the future independently of divine revelation (Gen. 48:14–20; 49:1–28 [though the prophecy is incorporated in a blessing]; I Sam. 28:19). The biblical belief in necromancy is based on this idea. That Balaam sees divine visions "fallen down, but with opened eyes" (Num. 24:4, 16) may also refer to such a conception of prophecy. But we have here no more than vestigial survivals.

[7] Ezekiel has a pleasant voice and plays an instrument well (Ezek. 33:32); however these are the outcome of, not the stimulus to, his prophecy.

first, as a testimony to the artless candor of the Bible. In view of it, the suspicion that there has been a purposeful and systematic expurgation of deviant materials seems ungrounded. The faithful representation of the popular view of prophecy as madness, the name prophet (*nābīʾ*) conferred impartially on both pagan and Israelite prophets likewise attest the Bible's innocent openness in these matters. It is likely that in reality there was some connection between music and prophecy, since song is the characteristic form that prophecy takes. Yet Israelite prophecy was never bound to fixed stimuli. Arising out of a unique idea, it did not feel itself dependent upon artificial inducements. The Bible, at any rate, preserves no trace of the idea that particular substances, or cultic or magical rites induce prophecy.[8]

THE WORD OF GOD: THE PRIMARY SOURCE OF PROPHECY—The biblical conception of the prophetic spirit is especially illuminating. The Bible never regards the "spirit of YHWH" as the primary source of prophecy. Paganism, as we have seen, views the speech of the rapt prophet as the very utterance of a god who has taken possession of him. Even inarticulate words and sounds have value as the communication of the indwelling god. The words of the ecstatic, being in fact the divine utterance, are the primary source of prophecy. In Israel, however, prophesying frenzy never had primary mantic value. It was considered a sign of having been touched by the divine spirit, but words uttered in that state seem never to have been regarded as divine. We never hear of recording the words of ecstatics to discover their hidden divine meaning, as was done, for example, at the Delphic oracle.

Nor were the lucid words of the prophet speaking in the name of God considered the primary revelation. The prophet repeats the word of God that came to him beforehand. He recounts his experience of the divine revelation—the primary mantic experience—almost invariably in the past tense: "Thus said YHWH," "The word of YHWH came to me," "Thus YHWH showed me," "I saw YHWH." God puts a word in the mouth of the prophet and charges him, "Thus shall you speak" (Num. 23:5). The "parable" spoken later under the influence of the spirit is the prophet's development of the word that was placed in his mouth (22:35, 38; 23:5, 7, 12, 16 f.), or the vision that God showed him (23:3). The figure of eating the words of prophecy, then speaking them forth (Jer. 15:16; Ezek. 3:1 ff.) illustrates the two stages nicely—first the primary revelation, and then the prophet's embodiment of it in his utterance.

[8] The fasting that is recorded of late visionaries (Dan. 9:3; IV Ezra 5:20; etc.) is not conceived of as a mortification designed to induce prophecy, but as part of prayer and entreaty for the favor of a divine response.

In the primary revelation, again, there is mantic value only in the speech of God. This is seen in the symbolic vision where the essence of the prophecy is not the vision but the revealed interpretation, not what the prophet sees but what he hears. Day or night visions provide merely the setting for God's speech (Gen. 15:1; 46:2; Num. 12:6 ff.); so much was prophecy attached to words that *ḥāzōn*, "vision," often means no more than the words of a prophetic message (Isa. 1:1; Obad. 1:1; Nah. 1:1; cf. I Sam. 3:1).

Now this primary revelation of the divine word is never considered to be an effect of the divine spirit.

The effects of the spirit are adjuncts of prophecy; they are not the divine revelation itself. Frenzy, abnormal physical and psychical manifestations— all those features that mark the prophet as a "man of the spirit" (Hos. 9:7)—are produced by the spirit. Being touched by this afflatus, however, does not in itself make a man privy to God's secrets. Neither the seventy "prophesying" elders (Num. 11:16 ff.) nor the "prophesiers" of Samuel's time nor even Joshua (Num. 27:18) and Elisha (II Kings 2:13–15) speak the word of God as a result of contact with the spirit. The spirit prepares a man for prophecy, enables him to frame parables and songs (Num. 24:2), and fortifies him to rebuke the people (Mic. 3:8). But these are not properly mantic activities, nor are they peculiar to prophets.

The spirit works far beyond the domain of prophets and prophesiers. It rests on elders, judges, Nazirites, and kings, endowing them with wisdom and strength without making prophets of them. The spirit of YHWH gives the ideal king of the future the gift of wisdom, power, and righteousness so that he will be able to judge wondrously (Isa. 11:2 ff.). Poetry is likewise considered a gift of the spirit (II Sam. 23:2; cf. Ps. 40:4). It must be recalled in this connection that prophets are pure poets as well, composing not only prophecies but also songs and blessings (Exod. 15; Judg. 5; Deut. 33); liturgical song in general might be called "prophecy" (I Chron. 25:1). The holy spirit in this broad sense is what the psalmist prayed for (Ps. 51:13), and it is in this sense that it is said to abide in Israel (Isa. 44:3; Ezek. 39:29; Hag. 2:5).

The primary revelation of the word of God, however, is not ideally bound up with either the action of the spirit or ecstasy. The stories of God's revelations to Abraham, Jacob, Moses, Joshua, Gideon, Samuel, Elijah, Amos, Isaiah, Jeremiah, Zechariah, Daniel, and many more make no mention of the spirit. When the spirit of God "clothes itself" with Gideon (Judg. 6:34) as when it animates Samson (Judg. 13:25), the effect is to fill them with strength for their trials; but no word of God is involved. The prophetic ideal of the Bible is Moses (Deut. 34:10), of whom no ecstatic phenomena are ever related. To the contrary, the archetypal prophet speaks with God "face to face, as a man speaks with his fellow" (Exod. 33:11); not in vision, dream, or riddle, but "mouth to mouth" (Num. 12:6 ff.). God descends to speak with Moses at the entrance to the tent in the view of all the people, or calls to Moses and speaks with him from inside the holy of holies. Nowhere does the holy spirit play any role. The father of Israelite prophecy was not an ecstatic.

A second embodiment of the prophetic ideal is the Sinai legend (Exod. 19–20). In full daylight, without any ecstatic preliminaries or spiritual manifestations God appears to the entire people out of the fire and clouds and speaks to them. The view of Deuteronomy is that the office of prophecy was then instituted as a substitute for a public theophany, because the terrified people begged that God's word be mediated to them (Deut. 18:15 ff.). YHWH's direct address to the people at Sinai, then, is the ideal form of prophecy. The account of the most sublime theophany of Israelite history says nothing about ecstasy or action of the spirit.

We must thus distinguish the action of the spirit of YHWH from prophecy proper. The spirit is the source of activity and creativity; it animates the ecstatic, the judge, the mighty man; it rests on the poet. It rouses the prophet to act, to speak, and endows him with the ability to harangue and poetize. The spirit of prophecy also prepares him to receive the divine word—to see visions, to hear the divine voice in dreams or ecstatic slumber. But the source of prophecy proper is other than these activities. It is in the revelation of God. In this revelation the prophet ideally is entirely passive; he but listens to what is said to him. The frenzy, the physical aberrations, even the visions are not the essence. Of visions and riddles, too, the important part is the explanation that the prophet receives passively. What makes the prophet is not any faculty of clairvoyance, or the spirit that rests on or in him; it is the word that he has heard from God or his agents.

Accordingly, the essential act of prophecy involves two persons: God who acts and is always outside of man, and man who passively receives his word. The idea that just the laws and prophecies were communicated in this way is the outcome of the biblical view that the laws are the command of God, and that prophecy alone can divulge the secret of God's government. These cannot be ascertained by man on his own, neither by interpreting signs nor by a heightening of his faculties under the influence of the spirit of God. These he can only "hear" directly at the mouth of God.

This conception of prophecy implies the integrity of the prophet's ego. What is said and done in Dionysiac-Delphic ecstasy has no mantic value. Only he is qualified to be a prophet who can hear the divine word and afterward convey it in the language of men. The only "madness" that the Israelite idea allowed was of the Platonic sort—the madness of great men of the spirit whose experiences take religious forms.

THE EFFECT OF THE DIVINE WORD—Dionysiac frenzy, while basically a cultic (rather than a mantic) phenomenon, can, in the pagan view, ascend to the mantic level. The same stimulus that arouses cultic frenzy—wine, dancing, self-castigation—can also bring on mantic prophesying; frenzy can beget prophecy.

In the Israelite conception, however, ecstasy does not induce prophecy; to the contrary, the divine word may cause ecstasy. The word of God is not brought on by the spirit, the spirit is the by-product of the word.

Frenzy never is represented as a preliminary to prophecy. Samuel's ecstatics do not produce a prophet who speaks the word of God. On the other hand, no story concerning the prophets tells of Dionysiac frenzy. The prophetic bands of the times of Elijah and Elisha are never characterized as ecstatic. They comprise a kind of order. They live with the prophet who is their leader, accompany him, serve him, relate his wonders, and perform his missions. Never is a communal frenzy related of them. Even the sight of the transfer of the spirit from Elijah to Elisha does not rouse them to frenzy.

It is typical of the Israelite view that the workings of the spirit are regarded, on the contrary, as by-products of the divine word. The physical and psychical manifestations effected by the divine afflatus are described as results of the prophetic experience, rather than as preconditions to it. Fear, trembling, prostration, languor, dumbness, paralysis, are all effects of the divine revelation. Most important—the onset of ecstasy is often described as *consequent* on the word of God, a striking reversal of the pagan idea.

The classic expression of this reversal is the account of Numbers 11:16 ff. God descends to speak with Moses; an effluence of Moses' spirit falls upon the seventy elders who are with him and they "prophesy." The same idea seems to underlie the picture of the ecstatics with Samuel (I Sam. 19:20 ff.) as well. The transfer of the spirit from the prophet to his disciples and followers is analogous to the spiritual bequest that is made by the laying on of hands (Moses to Joshua) or through contact with the cloak (Elijah to Elisha). This notion also underlies the formation of the prophetic bands; the "sons of the prophets" cleave to the man of the spirit who is privy to the word of God, in the hope that something of his virtue will be caught by them. The prophetic spirit is not an outcome of any activity of the group; but, on the contrary, the divine word that came to the prophet is the source of the spirit that animates the group.

The pagan prophet is endowed with what is conceived of in the first instance as a divine faculty of knowing hidden things. The god knows hidden things by virtue of his mantic power; the human clairvoyant possesses or can attain to the same mantic power; the ecstatic incorporates a prophet-god. Man and god discover hidden things by the same power.

The God of Israelite religion is not endowed with mantic powers. Since there is no metadivine realm, there are no secrets beyond him which he must discover. He knows all because all flows from his will. Neither his knowledge nor, in the last analysis, that of the Israelite prophet is, properly speaking, mantic. The prophet does not share in a special divine mantic faculty. He does no more than announce the "secret" that the sovereign and omniscient God has revealed to him. Hence the actions, the visions, even the speech of the prophet could have no primary mantic value. Hence there could be no mantic value to the action of the spirit on the psyche or body of the prophet. Prophecy was conceived purely as a gift of grace; therefore it was never cultivated or induced. The use of stimuli is grounded in the belief that they harbor a supernatural power of inducing prophecy, of uniting the soul of the prophet with the divine. But Israelite prophecy never sought apotheosis (or enthusiasm) and so never attached itself to ecstasy, though not dogmatically hostile toward it. The spirit prepares to receive and act, and its manifestations may be the by-product of God's word; but it is never more than the background for the divine utterance. Thus was the pagan Dionysiac element transmuted by Israelite religion.

That this transmutation is not a late stage in the religion of YHWH is attested by all of the biblical material on prophecy and related phenomena. It is not the outcome of a studied reworking of written documents. It is never explicitly articulated. There is no biblical doctrine of the relationship between the word and the spirit; there is no explicit repudiation of the pagan conception. And yet Israelite prophecy is in every aspect a new phenomenon. The monotheistic idea has impressed itself instinctively on its entire being.

THE CULT

The biblical cult, like the other aspects of biblical religion, is a composite creation whose roots lie in the pagan prehistory of Israel. Scholars have endeavored to analyze the ancient materials and have found rites embodying

magical, animistic, and demonistic notions. But here especially pagan analogues are apt to mislead. For the pagan religions of the ancient Near East
combined very disparate elements in the course of a gradual and organic
evolution. Beliefs and practices grew old and fell out of fashion without
ever becoming rejected. Polytheism was capable of sustaining its most ancient roots and branches without ever lopping them off as withered members. Biblical religion, however, repudiates worship of gods other than
YHWH, forbids the worship of the dead, spirits, and animals. It broke
with the old religion; hence its relationship to ancient elements preserved
in it was different. All was reformed and brought into harmony with the
new idea. The cult laws of the Bible have no mythological or magic background—that is the heart of the transformation. This was not the product
of an artificial reworking, consciously and rationally undertaken by the
priesthood of a certain age. It is the result of an organic development of
Israelite religion through the course of generations.[9] The Priestly Code of
the Pentateuch allows us to view this development in process.

The attitude of the new idea toward the older elements was not uniform.
All mythological and magical rationales were replaced by historical and
monotheistic ones. Several rites became commemorative of occasions in
which YHWH revealed himself in Israel. Sacrifices and lustrations received
the general sanction of sanctification and exaltation of God. The magical
elements, however, were most difficult to refashion. Paganism valued
these elements as intrinsically potent. Israelite religion while rejecting this
view failed to do away with its product. Precisely because Israel's cult
was not the outcome of a rational, systematic reform it retained magical
features, so deeply rooted as to defy extirpation.

The problem of this material was later solved by the idea of the absolute
command of God. The ultimate sanction of the rite became the divine will.
Judaism thus created a noble symbol for its basic idea that everything is
a divine command; fulfilling the command is an acknowledgment of the
supremacy of God's will. A cult of "commands" evolved; the system of
commands sanctified all of life to the service of the One. To laws for which
no rational explanation could be found the Rabbis applied the general principle: "The commandments were given only for the purpose of purifying
men" (Gen. Rabba 44.1).

[9] The notion that the cult laws are the product of a deliberate and rational adaptation
by religious reformers of basically pagan materials to the ideas of the prophets leaves
unexplained the retention of elements highly susceptible of a pagan misinterpretation:
e.g., the rites of the scapegoat, the release of the purificatory bird of the leper "into the
open field" (Lev. 14:7), the paschal blood daubs; or such expressions as "bread of
God" (e.g., Lev. 21:17 ff.), "a pleasing odor to YHWH," and the like. The whole of
the cult system bespeaks a simple faith in the value of the rites and their divine origin.

But this idea is not yet present in the Torah. The commands are not conceived there as intrinsically indifferent "decrees" whose sole purpose is to discipline man to obey God. On the contrary, there appears a strong and naïve faith in the inner significance of all the rites—though, to be sure, not in a magical sense. This is especially evident in the pentateuchal view of the holy and the impure. These are not conceived of as having only pedagogic or symbolic significance. Impurity is no mere divine "decree" that has fallen on essentially neutral objects. There are things essentially impure. It is no empty thing that the Torah fails to distinguish between moral and ritual impurity; both are regarded as intrinsic. The naïve, popular-priestly feeling that a corpse, a leper, a menstruant woman, etc. are defiling is certainly present in the priestly laws. These venerable beliefs that prevail in all cultures can be found in the Torah nearly in all their pristine force, despite the new religious idea. It is the same with the faith in the purifying and atoning power of given rites. Blood atones because it is "life"; the scapegoat carries off sins to the desert; immersion, the setting of the sun, the water of the red heifer, actually purify. Nowhere is there a hint that all these rites are only "decrees" in the rabbinic sense.

There is thus a recognizable development between the viewpoint of the Torah and that of later Judaism. In between have come the prophets, with their insistence on the conditional value of the cult. Later Judaism incorporated the prophetic view in its evaluation of the cult, but the Torah shows no influence of the prophetic idea. In the priestly laws of the Pentateuch, the first stage of the transformation of pagan materials is evidenced: the mythological-magic basis of the cult has disappeared; impurity ceases to be an autonomous realm—yet something of its ancient substantiality remains. This ambiguous attitude reflects the great resistance of the pagan materials to a full and consistent adaptation in the earliest stage of Israelite religion.

SANCTITY AND IMPURITY—In spite of its belief in the substantiality of impurity, the Bible does not accord to it the status of a primary, demonic force. There is no tension of powers between the holy and the impure. Impurity is no more than a condition—one might almost say a religious-aesthetic state. All power and activity is concentrated in the realm of the holy; the domain of impurity is a shadow. In contrast to the pagan conception impurity is in itself not a source of danger; its divine-demonic roots have been totally destroyed.

The lustrations of paganism are designed to protect men and gods from the demonic or magical action of impurity. The Bible preserves no trace of this idea. There are rites to cleanse the altar, the ark-cover, or the tabernacle from "the defilement of the Israelites." But there is no indication that their purpose is to ward off danger or any sort of demonic force that made its way into the holy. YHWH has no guardians in the pagan sense; no symbol of the Israelite cult expresses the protection of the deity. The "charge" of the holy involves only its separation from the profane. It is an expression of reverence, of supreme awe, entirely different from the pagan idea.

Biblical categories of impurity are quite similar in general to those of pagan religions. Impurity is a condition of negative taboo which is contagious. It inheres in the cadavers of animals and eight types of creeping things, various types of human and non-human "leprosy," men and women who have a flux, or who have had contact with semen, the menstruant, the woman who has given birth and, the corpse; various rites also defile. These pollutions are nowhere represented as intrinsically dangerous. Even the arch defilement of the corpse, so universally dreaded in paganism, is not harmful in the biblical conception. Except for the ban on union with a menstruant woman, no defilement is prohibited to the lay Israelite. It is bringing impurity into contact with the holy that is banned and terribly dangerous. The purpose of the laws is to avert such confusion of the impure and the sacred, to keep the unclean away from contact with the holy, and to guard the holy from defilement by the unclean. To defile the tabernacle of the Lord is to incur death (Lev. 15:31; 22:9).

To be sure, paganism too knows of bans on the commingling of spiritual realms. But these realms are always conceived of as independent and hostile powers. Impurity is no less potent than sanctity; it is essentially and inherently baleful, even more dangerous than the holy. Not so in the Bible. No activity or power is ascribed to impurity in itself. The danger of mingling realms comes only from the holy, the realm of YHWH. Contact with the dead is altogether harmless. But contact, unlawful approach, or even sight of the holy is deadly. The priests must be on their guard at every step lest they transgress and die. Nadab and Abihu die because of an improper offering. Korah and his company die because of their presumption; their fate is a warning for all unqualified persons to keep away from the sacred service. If the Levites so much as behold the dismantlement of the tabernacle, they die. The priest who enters the inner sanctum without the screen of the cloud of incense will die from what he sees. But there is no allusion in the entire Bible to danger or activity of any sort emanating from the realm of impurity.

This becomes especially clear when the images and symbols of the Priestly Code are considered.

One of the leading motifs of this work is the contrast of holiness and impurity. Lepers, gonorrheics, and persons defiled by contact with a corpse are sent outside the camp; "leprous" stones and the dead are removed thither (in Lev. 14:40 ff. "outside the city" corresponds to "outside the camp" [cf. 13:46]). Cultic rites that take place both inside and outside the camp have a double nature. The bullock and goat of sin offering of the Day of Atonement are burned outside and defile the man who burns them (Lev. 16:27 f.). The man who dispatches the scapegoat into the wilderness becomes impure (vs. 26). The red heifer, prepared entirely outside the camp, is a source of several impurities (Num. 19). The Priestly Code preserves traces of the notion that impurity is grounded in the realm of demons and satyrs. Illicit sacrificing "in the open field" is done to satyrs (Lev. 17:5–7); lustral birds of the leper and the "leprous house" are released there (Lev. 14:7, 53). The open field (equivalent to "outside the city/camp" [cf. vs. 53]) is the abode of such satyrs as Azazel, who lives in "the wilderness" (Lev. 16:22) into which the scapegoat (the image of the satyr) is sent. Contact with this domain is apparently the source of the defilements enumerated above.

But it is the source of nothing more than defilement. Removed from the holy the satyrs dwell in their impurity, but they are not destructive or harmful like the demons of postexilic Judaism. The Israelites go astray after them, but they do not actively seduce men to sin or bring trouble on them. Passively they defile and receive defilement. Later Judaism identified Azazel with Satan, but the biblical Satan is a member of the divine court. He is not impure and therefore may be portrayed as an active agent. The biblical Azazel, on the other hand, defiles; he inhabits the desert as a shade whose sole apparent function is to receive the burden of sin and pollution which is annually sent off to him.

The two realms separated by the apotropaic blood of the paschal lamb (Exod. 12:13, 23) are quite a different matter. The blood is conceived of as a protection against the terror that rages without. The distinction here is between the holy, protected realm within and the destroyer outside. But mark who the destroyer is: not a band of demons or satyrs, but YHWH himself or his death-dealing angel. From the realm of YHWH comes all activity—even destruction; no satyrs and no impurity are involved.

The prohibited foods are equally free of dangerous properties. These prohibitions probably had a magical or demonistic origin, but it is crucial that the Bible nowhere suggests it. Blood and fat are forbidden because they are consecrated to the altar of YHWH; the forbidden animal is an abomination and a loathsome thing, no more. The ban on the sinew of the thigh vein has what appears to be a demonistic origin: the "man" who wrestled with Jacob touched it (Gen. 32:33). But this "man" is, in the Bible, not a demon—a *šāʿīr* or a *shēd*—but an *ʾelōhīm* (vss. 29, 31) or an angel (Hos. 12:4 f.), that is to say, a member of the divine suite. Correspondingly, the sinew of the thigh vein does not defile. Again, when activity is involved, it is conceived of exclusively as belonging to the realm of the divine, the holy and pure.

PURIFICATIONS—Biblical and pagan purifications have many features in common. Both employ water, fire, blood, incense, and sacrifice; both involve immersion, laundering, burning, and sprinkling. In both, sin and pollution can be transferred to a particular object which is then destroyed. The offerer lays his hands upon the victim or confesses upon it, charging it with his sin; its immolation destroys the sin. Or the victim, thus charged, may be sent off to an impure place beyond the pale of habitation (as, e.g. in the case of the scapegoat or the birds of the leper). The overall aim of biblical sacrifice is *kappārā* "atonement," much the same as the *kuppuru* or *takpirtu* of the Babylonian *āshipu*-priest. Yet there is a sharp distinction between them.

There are two categories of purificatory rites in the Bible: those designed to ward off real harm or danger, and those intended to remove impurity only. Rites belonging to the first category do not involve the demonic realm, as appears from their lack of purgative or exorcising elements. Rites of the second category do touch upon the demonic realm; they aim to remove impurity, but they are not directed against real harm or danger.

Plagues are removed by incense (Num. 17:11 ff.) or sacrifice (II Sam. 24:18 ff.). To be rid of their pestilence the Philistines send images of boils as a "guilt offering" to YHWH (I Sam. 6:4, 11). If calamity is caused by the sin of an individual, the sinner or his offspring is destroyed in a specific rite the aim of which is to propitiate and purify (Num. 25:3 f.; Josh. 7; I Sam. 14:24 ff.; II Sam. 21:1 ff.). Harassed by enemies, the people fast and make libations (I Sam. 7:6). Immolation of the firstborn was popularly viewed as an extreme propitiatory sacrifice (Mic. 6:7; II Kings 3:27) Elijah's sacrifice on Mount Carmel seems to have as its final purpose to ward off the drought and famine. After offering a bull and making a libation he slaughters the Baal prophets "into the wadi Kishon" (cf. the purifications of Lev. 14:5; Deut. 21:1-9); then rain comes. According to one account Moses purges the people, plagued for having made the golden calf, by burning the idol, grinding it fine, and casting its dust into "the wadi that descended from the mountain" (Deut. 9:21). In the Exodus version Moses slays all the sinners. Placing blood on the doorposts protected the Israelites in Egypt (Exod. 12:13, 23; subsequently the rite was repeated merely as a memorial). The curious story in Exodus 4:24 ff. suggests that circumcision also involved an application of blood (to the foot of the father?) and was considered an apotropaic. The "atonement-money" of the census (Exod. 30:11–16) is apotropaic, as are the bells on the ephod-coat (Exod. 28:33 ff.) and the incense brought into the holy of holies (Lev. 16:2, 13). The common aspect of all these rites is that they have nothing to do with banishing ceremonial impurity.

Such impurity is removed, first, by time. The woman who bears a male child, the leper, the gonorrheic, the menstruant and whoever has connection with her, and whoever touches a corpse, are all impure for a week after separating from the cause of their impurity (a woman bearing a female child is impure for two weeks). Other impurities have no fixed term, but one is not cleansed of them without immersion or laundering, and before the subsequent sunset. Vessels are passed through fire; the leper and profaned Nazirite must shave. Beside these rites various sacrifices are prescribed for purification.

Now the distinctive feature of biblical purifications when compared with those of paganism is that they are not performed for the purpose of banishing harm or sickness. The pagan seeks to avert harm; his purgations are in effect a battle with baleful forces that menace men and gods. Biblical purifications lack this aspect entirely. Lustrations play no part in healing the sick. The woman who bears a child, the leper, the gonorrheic, the "leprous" house, are all purified after the crisis or disease has passed. The laws of the leper are especially instructive. The priest visits the leper during his sickness; he examines the diseased area, quarantines the man, and later pronounces him pure or infected, but he performs no therapeutic or exorcistic activity. Only after the leprosy has healed is a purification rite carried out (Lev. 14).

This absence of a combat with baleful powers accords with the fact that Israelite priests were neither wonder-workers nor healers. Doubtless sacrifices were offered during sickness as they were in every crisis. But there is no evidence of any purificatory act by the priest for or upon the sick person during his illness. That the offering of the gonorrheic and the leper is to be brought only after their recovery, indicates that such acts were in fact nonexistent. Vows of whole and peace offerings were customarily made in sickness and distress; purificatory offerings are unheard of.

Throughout the Bible healing pertains to the man of God, not the priest. Miriam's leprosy is cured not by Aaron, but by Moses, and not by a lustration, but by prayer (Num. 12:10 ff.). Israelites bitten by the serpents are cured by Moses (21:7 ff.) and Naaman is healed by Elisha (II Kings 5), not by a lustration, but by a specially prescribed remedy. The prophet

Isaiah cures Hezekiah with a fig cake (Isa. 38:21). Sickness, like all physical harm, comes, not from the realm of impurity, but from the realm of YHWH and his angels. The evil spirit that troubles Saul is "from YHWH." Even leprosy, which does involve impurity, is not a demonic but a YHWH-sent disease. It is YHWH who makes Moses' hand, and later Miriam, leprous; it is he who infects houses with defiling "leprosy" (Lev. 14:34). Gehazi is made leprous by Elisha, the prophet of YHWH; Uzziah is smitten by YHWH (II Kings 15:5).

Thus we see that no harm—not even diseases that defile—originates in the realm of impurity. The purificatory rites of Israel's priesthood are not directed therefore against that realm.

THE ABSENCE OF SPELLS—The Israelite priest, in contrast to his Babylonian or Egyptian counterpart, never combats evil spirits and powers. Among the detailed cultic regulations of the Priestly Code there is not a single spell or conjuration. It is the same when we examine the biblical counterpart to the Babylonian literature of spells and conjurations, the psalms.

Babylonian and biblical psalmody are historically related. The literary genre, the style, and the general rhythm of biblical psalms clearly show Babylonian influence. Is there a common religious viewpoint as well? Babylonian liturgical poetry is rooted in incantation and conjuration. Have these too become imbedded among the biblical psalms? Mowinckel believes that they have. Interpreting the Bible in the light of pagan analogues he finds in Israel the same "primitive atmosphere" according to which every disease and calamity are ascribed to evil spirits and sorcerers. The Biblical *pōʿalē ʾāwen* are, for Mowinckel, sorcerers. Certain psalms are at bottom purificatory and apotropaic; their aim is to exorcise spirits and release men from spells through the powerful name of YHWH.[10] Following Mowinckel other scholars have discovered further vestiges of spells, conjurations, and allusions to rituals in which they were employed.

Such interpretations rest on nothing more than scholarly romancing. If there were in fact a primitive dread of magic and sorcery in Israel, why has it left so few traces, and these so obscure? The Bible openly acknowledges its belief in the existence of demons and satyrs and in the reality of magic. Later Judaism had room for faith in exorcism and healing through the use of the divine name and amulets. Why then has the biblical period left so meager a residue of such beliefs that not a single outspoken incantation in the style of Babylonia, Egypt, or even later Judaism, survives?

---

[10] S. Mowinckel, *Psalmenstudien, I* (Kristiania, 1922), esp. pp. 29, 78, 157. *Pōʿalē ʾāwen* are taken to be sorcerers in Psalms 5:6; 6:9; 14:4; 28:3; 36:13; 53:5; etc. Psalms 6, 41, 35, 38, 42, 43, 63, 109 are conjurations.

Against Mowinckel's view it must be noted that in all the "magical" psalms no explicit mention is made either of sorcerers, or of specifically magical procedures, or even of demons. The *pōᶜalē ᵓāwen* are accused of the same abominations as the "wicked" and the "enemies" in psalms dealing with social wrongs. They are murderers, liars, and deceivers; flatterers and oppressors of the poor; they plant snares, plot evil, etc.[11] No activity distinctively associated with sorcery such as conjuring, "sowing cushions," binding knots, or the like is ever attributed to them. Never are they represented as causing sickness—a remarkable omission for alleged sorcerers. When sickness is spoken of, it is YHWH who brings it on. The wicked—at times *pōᶜalē ᵓāwen* are among them—merely rejoice at the misfortune of the psalmist-complainant. Incantations are founded on the idea that evil is an autonomous power, personified by spirits and demons who work harm to men and gods. But in the psalms YHWH alone brings on evil; evil spirits are but his agents.

On the soil of Israelite religion incantation became prayer, a plea for mercy to the one God who deals out weal and woe. Accordingly, the psalm became detached from the priestly lustration. Biblical psalms have nothing to do with the priesthood and its functions. This is attested to both by the content of the psalms as well as by their traditional ascriptions.

While baleful angels and spirits are spoken of, impurity is never alluded to as a source of sickness, nor do petitions of the sick contain pleas for purification. Psalms of the sick (6; 22; 30; 31; 32; 35; 38; 39; 41; 102; 107:17–22) are unrelated to lustrations or any other priestly rituals or sacrifices. Prayer and supplication alone are effective against disease; thanksgiving and votive offerings are brought afterward by those whom God has healed. It is likely that sacrifice was offered during the illness too,[12] but this was a general sacrifice (probably a burnt offering) unaccompanied, to the best of our knowledge, by any specific therapeutic rites. The book of Psalms, at any rate, preserves no spell or prayer connected with priestly therapeusis. The style tells as much: such spells are couched in the third person, referring to and making mention of the name of the sick man; but all the psalms of the sick are in the first person. Not the priest or magician, but the sick person himself recited these psalms of prayer and confession.

[11] Compare Psalms 12, 15, 17, 25, 27, 34, 37, 52 with those mentioned in note 8.

[12] Ben-Sira 38:11 speaks of sacrifice made by a sick man in connection with his repentance; he urges the sick man to pray to God, repent of all his sins, and offer a sacrifice —apparently a whole and meal offering. He also makes room for the physician who likewise prays to God for success. Again, there is not a word about the priest and his rituals or purifications. Compare the story of Hezekiah's sickness and his cure by Isaiah, II Kings 20:1–11.

In harmony with this, biblical tradition ascribes the authorship of the psalms neither to priests nor even to prophets as such. The poet-king David and the heads of Levitical families (Heman, Asaph, Jeduthun)—singers and poets—are the chief psalmists of tradition. The Aaronide priests have no part in this creation. Psalmody is a creation of popular poets, and particularly of that body of professional singers who became part of the Levite class. It was not connected with priestly rites. There is no indication that psalms were a part of the sacrificial cult or any other priestly rite. Recitation of the psalms in the temple was a kind of extraneous, lay adjunct to the cult. The Priestly Code makes no mention of it.

The silence of the psalms regarding priestly rites, and the complementary silence of the Priestly Code regarding psalms shows that Israelite psalmody was not a sacerdotal creation. Psalms of the sick can therefore have nothing to do with priests. But even the prophets, who were healers, are not the proper authors of this literature. Psalmody had thus nothing to do with therapeutic arts. Levites, singers, and royal poets had no special relationship to healing; on the other hand, as we have seen, the prophet-healer never employed fixed rites or spells. The Israelite counterpart to the pagan incantation thus became separated equally from the prophetic miracle and the priestly rite. Israel's psalmody was the song of Levites and religious rhapsodists.

The Priestly Code and the psalms of the sick, two utterly different genres, thus agree in attesting to the fact that during the biblical period impurity was not regarded as a demonic force. The Bible knows no tension between hostile supernatural realms; the biblical cult nowhere reflects such a tension.

The absence of a literature of therapeutic incantations complements the absence in Israel of a native magic. This implies that the Israelite world view was essentially non-magical.

SACRIFICE—The question of the primitive forms and significance of sacrifice has no immediate relevance to the study of Israelite religion, since in the environment of Israel's origin highly developed sacrificial systems had long since been in existence. Offerings of produce, whole and peace offerings, lustrations of several sorts, shewbread, libations of wine, oil, and water were known in Babylonia, Egypt, and Canaan. It is to be assumed that all of these forms were part of Israel's legacy from paganism. After the parting of ways it developed its own specific variations on this common material, the peculiarities in detail attesting to the separate and independent development of Israelite ritual. Evidences of Israel's new religious idea are visible here and there in these details, especially so in the sin offering.

But it was in the general conception of sacrifice that the new religious idea of Israel found clearest expression.

The mythological and magical framework that lent cosmic significance to sacrifice in paganism is wanting in the Bible. YHWH is not conceived of as dependent upon food, drink, or any external source of power. This precludes the idea that sacrifice is nutriment for the God. To be sure, popular practice and priestly laws alike treat the preparation of the sacrifice in terms of a meal: choice pieces are selected, the meat is salted and cooked (Judg. 6:19 ff.), and it is accompanied by bread and wine; the altar is a "table." But religion customarily conserves forms that have become emptied of meaning. Such terms and rites mean only that at one time sacrifice was considered food for the god. For biblical religion, however, it is decisive that the mythological setting of this conception is entirely wanting. The ideal basis of these rites has disappeared. Expressions such as "bread of God" (Lev. 21:6 and elsewhere), " a pleasing odor," and the like must therefore be regarded as petrified linguistic survivals which by biblical times had lost their original significance. As late a writer as Ezekiel still calls sacrifice "my bread" (44:7), and the altar "the table that is before YHWH" (41:22; see also Mal. 1:12). Hosea does not shrink from saying, "Their sacrifices will no longer delight him" (9:4); nor does the Second Isaiah shy from the expression, "You did not sate me with the fat of your sacrifices" (43:24). That the classical prophets felt free to use these phrases is the best testimony to their innocence. Had the people at large believed that sacrifice was food for the deity, the prophets and legislators—who surely did not hold this view—would hardly have used such expressions which could only have lent support to what they must consider a gross error. Indeed they would have combated this notion. And yet we find no polemic at all against a mythological conception of the YHWH cult.

The biblical peace offering has been interpreted as a form of communion; part is consumed by the deity (the fat and blood), the rest by the offerer in what is assumed to be a common meal with the deity. But this interpretation has no warrant beyond the pagan models upon which it is based. The Bible itself says nothing about communion. The peace offering is eaten "before"—never "with"—YHWH (cf. e.g., Deut. 12:7, 18; 14:23, 26; 15:20). The Priestly Code makes the flesh of the peace offering the property of YHWH. The human partaker of it is, as it were, a guest of YHWH; this is the nearness to God that is symbolized by eating the peace offering (Lev. 7:20 f.). Nothing supports the notion that man becomes an associate of the deity, is elevated for the moment to divine rank, or shares in the life of the God. Joy, not mystic union, is the basic emotional content of the Israelite cult; this joy too is "before"—not "with"—YHWH (Deut. 12:12, 18; etc.). The difference is fundamental, and its linguistic expression, though subtle, is crucial.

The archetypal legend concerning the meal of the peace offering occurs in Exodus 24:9 ff. As part of the celebration of the covenant at Sinai the chief men of the Israelites partake of a solemn feast on the mountain. This feast is not a common meal with God; the nobles eat and drink by themselves. The sacred moment of the feast is the sight of God. God is seen in varying degrees by all those present on this solemn occasion: by the people at the foot of the mountain, by the nobles who behold and bow down to him "from afar" (vs. 1), and by Moses who alone "draws near" to him (vs. 2). The candid, almost crude, anthropomorphism speaks for the antiquity and popular character of the story. All the more significant, then, is its testimony to the way in which the ancient Israelite idealized closeness to God during the sacred meals. Not mystic union with, but "sight" of, the exalted One whom man cannot see and live; sight "from afar." How deeply rooted this concept was among the people is evidenced by the biblical phrase that expresses the purpose of visiting the sanctuary on festivals and sacrificial occasions: "to behold (read *lirʾōth*) the presence of YHWH" (Exod. 34:23 f.; Deut. 31:11; cf. Isa. 1:12).

Another embodiment of this idea is in the law of Exodus 20:21: Wherever an altar is built to YHWH, and sacrifice and invocation of his name are made, he will come and bless the worshiper. What is looked for is the appearance of God and his blessing, not mystic union with him.

This is the cultic parallel to the prophetic ideal: not inspiration, enthusiasm, or mystic union, but the sight and hearing of God from afar, from across the chasm that separates man from him. Accordingly, the effect of the offering on the divine realm is depicted not in terms of union, but in terms of God's pleasure at man's submission and obedience. The sacrifice is "acceptable," "delightful," and "pleasant" to God. These expressions are found alike in the laws, the narratives, the prophets, and the psalms. Offerings are also a token of honor and reverence (Isa. 18:7; 43:23; Mic. 6:7; Zeph. 3:10; Mal. 1:6, 8, 11). Surely no more than this was conveyed to biblical man by the anthropomorphic phrase "a pleasing odor to YHWH."

THE PURIFICATORY SACRIFICE—The sublimated conception of pagan sacrifice in which the victim is conceived of as the god or his enemy, or the rite is believed to heighten the power of the god in some mysterious way has left no trace in the Bible. That this is no accidental omission is seen from the biblical version of the purificatory sacrifice. Pagan purification rites aim to influence the divine powers, to heighten the powers of good over the demonic powers of evil. When we examine their biblical analogues we find no echo of a struggle between evil and good, no trace of either the mythological or the magical element which underlies the pagan idea.

The sin offering (*ḥaṭṭāth*), like the guilt offering (*ʾāshām*), is prescribed for unintentional sins (Lev. 4–5). But the gonorrheic, the woman who has given birth, the leper, and the Nazirite also must offer a *ḥaṭṭāth*. For essentially the *ḥaṭṭāth* is purificatory; it purifies and sanctifies objects (Exod. 29:36 f.; Lev. 8:15; 16:15 f.; Ezek. 43:18 ff.; 45:18 ff.) and persons (Exod. 29:10 ff.; Num. 8:5 ff.). At bottom the *ḥaṭṭāth* is no offering at all. One type (whose blood is not brought into the sanctuary) may be eaten only by males among the priests, and in conditions which smack of the removal of some dangerous substance (Lev. 6:19–22). Another type (whose blood is brought into the sanctuary) is burnt—not, like the whole or priestly meal offerings, on the altar, but outside the camp, and in its entirety, even its hide and excrement (Lev. 4:11–12, 21; 16:27). Such a disposal seems less a "pleasing odor" than the elimination of some danger. The red heifer—which has nothing to do with sin, but merely cleanses of the defilement of a corpse—is also a *ḥaṭṭāth;* save for the sprinkling of its blood its preparation takes place entirely outside the camp and defiles those involved (Num. 19). The scapegoat is termed a *ḥaṭṭāth*, although it is not a sacrifice in the biblical sense; it, like the *ḥaṭṭāth* goat for YHWH that expiates and is burnt outside the camp, expiates and is sent away outside the camp. Both goats defile the persons who dispose of them (Lev. 16:5, 10, 25–27).

These illustrations suggest that originally the *ḥaṭṭāth* was not a propitiatory offering to the deity, but an exorcising sacrifice directed toward the domain of evil and impurity. The connection of the *ḥaṭṭāth* with various sorts of maladies suggests also that in prebiblical times it had a role in priestly therapeusis, like Babylonian therapeutic sacrifices.

The biblical sin offering, however, is never therapeutic. As pointed out above, it is offered to purge the impurities of disease only after the sick person has recovered. It is not a means of combating harmful spirits, let alone propitiating them. None of its rites are directed toward or against a realm of active virulent demons, but solely toward the domain of YHWH. What is done outside the camp and involves impurity does not recognize another divine or demonic power; the impurity is not an active force. While the *ḥaṭṭāth* has two faces—one turned toward the holy, the other, toward the obscure realm outside the camp—whatever influence it calls down comes from the holy alone. That is why the biblical *ḥaṭṭāth* does have something of the nature of a sacrifice to YHWH. The domain of the unclean has become emptied of power and substantial evil. The *ḥaṭṭāth* is thus a monument to a vanished world; it is a fossil of the ancient paganism that died when the religion of Israel was born.

Of all purifications the most baldly pagan-like seems to be the rite of the scapegoat, directed, apparently, at the demon Azazel. There are many parallels to this practice and there can be no doubt that the biblical rite goes back to the pre-Israelite religion of the Hebrews.

It is a common pagan practice to remove communal impurity by transferring it to an object or animal which is then sent away or destroyed. Plagues, famine, or disease having demonic origin, or the demonic agent himself are usually involved; at times it is sin that is expelled—the intrinsically baleful defilement. The purificatory aspect of these rites is aimed against the evil that comes from destructive demons or spirits. Gods are invoked to aid men in this battle against a common enemy.

The case of the biblical scapegoat, however, is entirely different.

To begin with, despite the correspondence in Leviticus 16:8 between the goat "for YHWH" and the goat "for Azazel," the latter—the scapegoat —is not conceived of as an offering to Azazel. The scapegoat too is placed "before YHWH" (vs. 7), and atonement is made by it "before YHWH" (vs. 10). Together with the goat for YHWH it evidently constitutes a single *ḥaṭṭāth*. Sacrificial rites are performed only upon the goat for YHWH; beyond being charged with sin the scapegoat is free of rites. It is not conceived, then, as an offering but as a vehicle for carrying off sin. What the community sends to Azazel is not so much the goat as the sin it bears. Nor is the rite represented as the expulsion of demonic evil. The sins are viewed merely as religious and moral (i.e., sins before God) not as demonic pollution, as is plain from the role of Azazel. Of all known exorcisms having to do with demons this is unique in being conceived of not as the expulsion of a demon, but as the expulsion of something to a demon. The scapegoat does not bear off Azazel, for Azazel dwells in the wilderness, and does not have to be gotten rid of by a magical rite. The original pagan significance of this rite was surely the expulsion of the satyr Azazel into the wilderness, together with all his evil and harm. But the Azazel of Leviticus 16 is not conceived of either as among the people or as the source of danger or harm; he plays no active role at all. Unless the sin is expelled the deadly wrath of YHWH may be aroused, but no harm will come from Azazel. He is merely a passive symbol of impurity—sin returns to its like. The value of the rite does not lie in exorcising a dangerous demonic power, but in fulfilling a commandment of God. This is not said explicitly, but it is implied by the entire nature of the rite.

Here again we see how the new religious idea radically transformed the ancient religion. The legislator surely did not set about purposely to create this peculiar rite of expulsion. The transmutation came about as a part of the general organic change. Thus an ancient rite, pagan in its roots, was retained after its inner meaning disappeared. On the very verge of paganism the idea of the dominion of one God is symbolized.

The paschal sacrifice involves several rites that are avowedly apotropaic in nature. A pagan substratum is clearly present even if it cannot be reconstructed with certainty. The paschal offering is made on the night of the full moon of the first month. Originally it seems to have been connected with the sacrifice of human and animal firstborn, perhaps to the moon-god. The ancient conception presumably contained the image of a bloodthirsty demon who ravaged until morning. For protection some of the sacrificial blood was daubed with a hyssop on the lintel and doorposts. Blood was also, it seems, placed on the hand and between the eyes (the "signs" and "frontlets").

This sacrifice assumed in Israel an entirely altered form. The night was still connected with a plague danger, but the destroyer was YHWH or his deadly angel. The occasion of the danger also changed. Of old it presumably was the influence of the first full moon of the year that heightened demonic powers; it was a natural event that recurred annually. Biblical legend, however, historicized the danger and made it a unique event that happened by the will of God for a specific purpose. Danger was present only on the night of the Passover of Egypt. The elaborate performance of the rite by later generations was commemorative only; no danger was involved. Yet another change is evident: in paganism the apotropaic sign is a warning set up by one divine power against the inroads of another. Signs, amulets, spells, and the like protect either by virtue of their innate magical power, or as tokens of the gods' protection against evil spirits. The demonic is always an independent realm. The paschal signs, however, are for the angel of YHWH; they serve only to guide him in the correct fulfilment of his mission.

FESTIVALS—Israel's festivals, like the rest of its cult, have a history that long antedates the rise of the religion of YHWH. Their rituals are ancient and grounded in pagan concepts. But in Israel they were cut off from their ancient roots; they lost entirely their magical and mythological rationale.

The nature festivals of Passover, Pentecost, and Tabernacles may be treated as a distinct group. Passover combined two festivals: that of the

firstborn—a herdsman's festival, with that of unleavened bread and the
new grain—a farmer's festival. Pentecost, celebrating the reaping of first
fruits, is in effect the conclusion of the festival of the new grain: the former
marks the start, the latter the finish, of the reaping. Tabernacles celebrates
the ingathering of all produce. It is generally assumed that these festivals
were adopted by Israel from the Canaanites after the settlement, although
there is no evidence for this. The Dionysiac elements of some of Israel's
festivals may just as well go back to the Hebrew tribes' early contact with
Canaan. There are no grounds for supposing that Israel adopted the
Canaanite festivals en bloc. Neither the names nor the rites of the biblical
festivals are found among the Canaanites. Nature festivals are a phenomenon of all cultures; there is no reason to ascribe the origins of Israel's
to the Canaanites rather than take them as indigenous creations. Be that
as it may, what is decisively non-pagan in Israel's festivals is their lack of
mythological features.

The pagan did not consider the produce of field and womb to be simply
the blessing and gift of the gods. Fertility was linked essentially to the life
of the gods; the seasons reflected events in their lives. As we have seen, the
pagan festival is not so much a thanksgiving, as a celebration of the life
processes of the deities.

The predominant idea of Israel's agricultural festivals, however, is joyous
thanksgiving for the gifts and blessings of YHWH. Not the earth, or the
sun, or springtime is celebrated, but the sovereign God who rules all and
bestows all. Israelite festivals lack the dramatic element of mythology.
Pagan ritual dramatized the recurring cycle of the life of the god, not
merely as a memorial, but as a magical rite whose end was to affect the
divine powers and aid them. Such drama is unattested to in Israelite religion.
There is, to be sure, a certain dramatic element in some Israelite festivals,
but it is unique in its kind and therefore most instructive.

Of all festivals, precisely the two great seasonal ones have been most
thoroughly historicized. The Passover commemorates the Exodus (Exod.
12–13; 23:15; 34:18; Deut. 16:1–6); Tabernacles recalls the Wandering
(Lev. 23:43). Since historicization is found in every stratum of the Pentateuch, it cannot be discounted as a later tendency. Paganism seeks to ground
its festivals in the mythological history of the gods; in Israel the same
tendency expressed itself in the peculiar form of commemorating moments
in the history of the nation in which the wonders of YHWH manifested
themselves. This accords with the nature of biblical legends to deal not
with the life of YHWH, but with his relations to men. The historicization

of the festivals is thus a primary tendency arising out of the very essence of Israelite religion.

It is in these historicized festivals (but not in the non-historicized, cosmic Sabbath, new moon, new year, and Day of Atonement) that we find certain dramatic elements. The ancient paschal rite depicted in P and JE (Exod. 12) contains a series of actional prescriptions whose purpose is to re-enact the events of the night of the Passover of Egypt. Blood is to be smeared even though there is no danger of plague; the sacrifice is to be eaten hastily and with preparation for departure; no man is to leave his house even though there is nothing to fear. There is a dramatic element, too, in the injunction to build booths and live in them for seven days. These features are few and peripheral, but they are there, while in the non-historicized cosmic festivals they are not. This is no accident. Dramatization of a cosmic event could easily have become transformed into a representation of an event in the life of God—a motif that had no place in Israel. There was no such danger in re-enacting what had happened to the people. That a sound instinct was at work in the confinement of dramatic elements to the historicized festivals will become plainer when the character of those festivals that could not be given a historical rationale is examined.

The Sabbath—The Sabbath is the only Israelite holyday that possesses a kind of myth. The primary nature and origin of the Sabbath, which has so exercised scholars, is a problem in its own right. In all likelihood there is a connection between the Sabbath and certain days in the Babylonian and Assyrian cultic calendar which were invested with taboos. Here we are concerned, however, with the biblical conception of the day. For the Bible, the Sabbath commemorates the creation. In the etiological legend of the Sabbath (Gen. 2:1–3), there is even a trace of myth: on this day God rested from creating. The idea of the sanctity of the Sabbath thus resembles the pagan belief in the intrinsic value of certain days. Nevertheless the Sabbath legend is not a myth after the pagan manner. We hear only of what befell God in his relation to the world. God is creator; no mention is made of theomachies or procreation. Nor is the sanctity of the day innate; it is God who blesses and sanctifies it. Moreover, corresponding to the historical rationalization of the agricultural festivals, we find here a moral rationale: "That your manservant and maidservant may rest as well as you" (Deut. 5:14; cf. Exod. 23:12).

The New Year—The priestly laws of Leviticus 23:24 and Numbers 29:1 mention the first day of the seventh month as a day of "memorial with trumpet blasts"; it is not called the new year's day. These passages are inadequate to convey an idea of the nature of this holyday. Since only the Priestly Code mentions it, the school of Wellhausen assumed it was a late innovation. More recently the antiquity of the festival has been argued on the basis of its supposed correspondence to the Babylonian new year, in which the myth of the creation and Marduk's battle with Tiamat play a central part.

Originally, it is said, Israel's new year festival celebrated the story of YHWH's battle with Rahab (= Tiamat) and his subsequent enthronement as universal king. All the gods feared Rahab, the primeval dragon, until YHWH went out to fight and conquer him. He put the gods to shame (Isa. 42:17; Ps. 97:7) and thereafter was acknowledged their king. This myth was dramatized on the new year; psalms that sing of YHWH's enthronement (47; 95; 96; 97; 98; 149; etc.) accompanied its presentation. The drama included a great procession in which the ark—YHWH's throne—was led into the temple. These are the essential features of the reconstructed ritual of Israel's new year festival, one of the most remarkable products of the creative imagination of modern biblical scholarship.

That the biblical legend concerning Rahab knows nothing of YHWH's battling divine rivals for supreme authority, that, indeed, there is no reference anywhere in the Bible to YHWH's battling a living god or demon has been shown above. Furthermore, the passages alluding to Rahab are as silent regarding YHWH's subsequent enthronement, as the enthronement psalms are about the battle with Rahab. The combination of the two motifs has no warrant in the sources. Again, the kingship of YHWH, celebrated in the enthronement psalms is over the earth and its inhabitants; that is to say, its setting is historical, not primeval and mythological. YHWH's kingship in the biblical sense means the revelation of his power and authority over his creation; it has nothing to do with a victory over a divine enemy. "God has gone up . . . with the sound of the trumpet . . . God sits upon his holy throne . . . is king over all the earth . . . reigns over all the nations" (Ps. 47); "YHWH is king . . . let many coastlands rejoice . . . and all the peoples saw his glory" (Ps. 97); "YHWH has become king, let the peoples quake" (Ps. 99), and so forth. The ascendancy of YHWH "over all gods" mentioned in these psalms means only the revelation of his supreme godhood before the eyes of the pagan nations (cf. 77:14 f.; 86:8 ff.; 135:5 f.). Neither in Psalms 74:13 f.; 89:11; nor in Isaiah 51:9, are the ancient battles of YHWH said to mark the beginning of his rule. These triumphs are rehearsed along with other past wonders of YHWH with the sole purpose of inspiring faith in his ultimate revelation to all men. Trumpet blasts or acclamations are never mentioned in connection with these battles. When Job 38:7 speaks of the "sons of God" acclaiming the deity, it is the sight of his wondrous creation that stirs them, not his triumph over any enemy.

Nor is there any biblical record of a festal new year's procession with the ark. The Priestly Code, in which the ark plays such a central part, knows nothing of it. Was there any reason for P to conceal it if it had existed? We hear of the ark symbolizing YHWH's presence in the war camp, and of its going out to battle with the armies of Israel (I Sam. 4:3 f.; 14:18; II Sam. 11:11; cf. especially the song of Num. 10:35 f.), but nothing of its being carried during any festival.

Nor do the descriptions of popular celebrations given in the non-legal portions of the Bible support the view that ritual dramas were an element of Israelite festivals. Dance, song, sacrifice, feasting, and rejoicing are all present, but never drama. There were processions—one moved "with the throng" to the temple "with the sound of shouts and thanksgiving" (Neh. 12:27 ff.; Ps. 42:5). There were kneeling, prostrating, shouting, singing, dancing, and circuiting the altar (Ps. 26:6), but there is no hint of drama.

Indeed it is difficult to understand why, if the new year did once commemorate the creation and YHWH's enthronement, these matters were so suppressed as to be discernible today only to the keen eye of the scholar. The memorial day for the creation—as we hear several times—was the Sabbath. Of the new year we know only that it was "the day of trumpet blasts" par excellence (Num. 29:1; cf. 10:10). Now the custom of trumpeting and noisemaking is practiced widely in paganism as a device for frightening away demons. The dark night of the new moon is fraught with demonic terror; the trumpeting on the first night of the month (Num. 10:10; Ps. 81:4) probably originated as such an apotropaic measure. The rites of the new year must have been marked by an unusual amount of trumpeting; hence the style "a day of trumpet blasts" which has survived in the Bible. But in Israelite religion this custom was sundered from its roots.

Since the Bible knows of no activity or influence emanating from the demonic realm, its reason for blasting on trumpets is quite different. Numbers 10:9 f. calls the blasts "a memorial" before YHWH. This is a religious application of the use of the trumpet as an alarm. The blasts call God's attention to man's waiting upon his salvation. There is a popular naïveté even crudeness here (but note the use of this motif in Isa. 62:6 f.), yet there is no mistaking in this transformation the fundamental drive of Israelite religion to do away with all plurality in the divine realm. What was originally a custom of expelling demons became a ceremony of "reminding" YHWH.

The psalms provide another interpretation of the trumpet blast. Here it is conceived as a token of homage to God, like the trumpeting for human kings (II Sam. 15:10; I Kings 1:39; etc.). It celebrates God's kingship, that is to say, Israel's acceptance of his kingship. While there is no evidence that the trumpeting mentioned in the psalms has to do with the new year (though it is not unlikely; see below, p. 308), these passages do make clear how the psalmists understood the trumpet blasts of the new year day; they were "blasts for the king" (Num. 23:21), the acknowledgment of YHWH's sovereignty as king over all the earth, not memorials of his triumphs over primeval monsters and his subsequent enthronement. The Israelite trumpet blast celebrated a kingdom which was "from everlasting to everlasting" but which became known to men only through divine self-revelation. Such was the trumpet blast at the Sinaitic theophany (Exod. 19:13, 16, 19; 20:15) which heralded the God who there revealed himself in all his glory.

THE JOY OF THE FESTIVAL—The pagan festival enables man to experience a participation in the life and destiny of the god. The deity receives as well as gives; he enjoys the festal banquet, decks himself in finery and is borne in a solemn procession. He celebrates his nuptials, he dies, or is resurrected, is sacrificed or eaten. The experience of the Israelite celebrant, however, is quite different; he rejoices in the presence of God.

The solemn meal of the Sinaitic covenant is the archetype of the Israelite festal banquet. The Israelite comes near to YHWH, appears before him, prepares a meal in his presence, and hopes to receive his gracious blessing. The essence of the holyday is to behold the face of YHWH, to appear before him, and rejoice in his presence (Exod. 23:15, 17; 34:23 f.; Deut. 16:16; I Sam. 1:22; Isa. 1:12; Pss. 42:3; 17:15; 21:7). The Israelite is seated before God, dances, sings, and plays before him (II Sam. 6:5, 14, 16, 21), walks in the light of his presence (Ps. 89:16), has fulness of joy in his presence (Ps. 16:11).

This joy is fundamentally different from the emotion of pagan orgiastic rites. The Dionysiac element in Israel's festivals, a legacy of Canaan, is evident in the role played in them by wine-drinking and libation. There was also singing and dancing. Yet the underlying idea is quite distinct from the pagan Dionysiac frenzy. In Israel God does not participate in, and is not affected by the festival, the intoxication, and the enthusiasm. God is not among the throng of his devotees and does not join their frenzy. In Israel, man alone celebrates; the rejoicing is not with God but before him.

GOD AND THE CULT—Thus the Israelite conception of the cult gave clear expression to the idea of the one God's supremacy over all. The pagan notion of the innate value of the cult for the life and destiny of the gods gave way to its evaluation as an expression of God's will, the way man submitted to and related himself to God. YHWH is not a priest, does not purify himself, or celebrate banquets and revels.

To be sure, Israelite religion, too, knows of a celestial cult. But this cult merely expresses the submission of all creatures, including the angels, to the One. The angels praise his holiness in his temple (Isa. 6:3), bow to him and praise him in his heavens (Pss. 29:1; 103:20; and elsewhere). The heavens, earth, sea, and all that is therein tremble before him, pray, and bow down to him. Later Judaism even tends to view the temple cult as an imitation of the heavenly worship. Nowhere, however, is there a trace of the thought that God performs cultic rites for his own need, or that he benefits from a power they embody.

We do find occasional expressions reflecting earlier pagan notions. YHWH is pictured as a priest in the figure of his sprinkling lustral water upon Israel (Ezek. 36:25), or when he is petitioned to cleanse with a hyssop (Ps. 51:9). The non-pagan character of these passages, however, is obvious. In all cases man is the object; the lustral acts are but symbols of forgiveness. Similarly, when God swears by raising his hand, it is by himself that he swears—by his life, his holiness, his eternity. There is nothing like the Greek image of the gods swearing by the Styx. The closest approach to pagan ideas is in the account of the covenant with Abraham (Gen. 15), where God himself is said to pass between the parts. Yet there, too, it is a covenant between God and man; the rite has no cosmic significance, no effect on the vitality of the deity. God acts for man's sake, to implant in his heart supreme faith.

In sum then, the biblical religious idea, visible in the earliest strata, permeating even the "magical" legends, is of a supernal God, above every cosmic law, fate, and compulsion; unborn, unbegetting, knowing no desire, independent of matter and its forces; a God who does not fight other divinities or powers of impurity; who does not sacrifice, divine, prophesy, or practice sorcery; who does not sin and needs no expiation; a God who does not celebrate festivals of his life. An unfettered divine will transcending all being—this is the mark of biblical religion and that which sets it apart from all the religions of the earth.

CHAPTER IV

The Religion of the People

THE NON-PAGAN CHARACTER OF THE POPULAR RELIGION

The characteristic features of Israelite religion as it appears in the Bible have been treated in the preceding chapter. To what extent is this a portrayal of the religion—not of individual thinkers—but of the people at large? The consensus of scholarship is that the popular religion of Israel passed through polytheistic and monolatrous stages before reaching the level of biblical thought. The present chapter will examine this view and the evidence adduced in its support. We shall seek the answers to two questions: Was the popular religion national, limiting the domain of YHWH to the people or land of Israel only? Was it mythological, conceiving of YHWH in pagan terms? The last is the crucial question, inasmuch as the extinction of mythical beliefs is the point of departure for biblical religion. What do we know, then, of the extent to which myth and magic prevailed in the popular religion of Israel?

THE IMAGE OF YHWH IN THE LEGENDS—The biblical battle with Israel's idolatry restricts itself entirely to matters of practice, to rites and cults. There is no battle over the fundamental question: the mythological conception of deity. The significance of this fact can hardly be exaggerated. The Bible has arrived at a non-mythological conception, without a trace of a struggle against popular notions to the contrary. This is the case not only with regard to foreign gods; the Bible does not fight a mythical conception of YHWH either. Not that the Bible keeps silent about what it considers misconceptions. The Bible does oppose human sacrifice (Mic. 6:7; Jer. 7:31; 19:5), idolatrous forms of worship (II Kings 17:8; etc.), the idea that God goes back on his word (Num. 23:19), and so forth. Yet it has not a word against mythological conceptions of YHWH. What mythical vestiges are found in the Bible (e.g., the defeat of Rahab and the dragon) are part of the belief of the biblical authors. There is no myth that is regarded with hostility, as an error that must be uprooted.

Scholars assume that in Israel's idolatrous period Israelite and pagan beliefs were syncretized in the popular religion. Thus, for example, YHWH and Baal became merged into one. Evidences of this are the names of the sons of Saul (Eshbaal), Jonathan (Meribbaal), and David (Beeliada), and the fact that the people called YHWH Baal (Hos. 2:18). But the only syncretism here is titular. *Ba'al* means "lord"; from the mere fact that the people used it as an epithet (which, to be sure, was offensive to later zealots), what can be learned about their religious beliefs? Crucial is the utter lack of evidence that YHWH was given any of the mythological attributes of Baal. We do not hear, for example, that he was mated with Ashtoreth. There is no trace of a battle against mythological accretions to the popular image of YHWH.

The folk character of the creation legends signifies that the people among which they were formed was monotheistic. Gunkel has already shown the error of assuming that the present form of these legends is the result of a literary adaptation of pagan materials.[1] In antiquity adaptation implies an acceptance of and a belief in the material adapted. To suggest that the biblical author worked, as modern man does, with materials that were alien to his beliefs is to misconceive fundamentally the spirit of antiquity. Furthermore, a later adapter would hardly have left so many anthropomorphisms and dangerous ambiguities in his story. The primitive, idyllic—one might almost say provincial—character of these stories, so different from the grand pagan myths of universal forces clashing in primeval times, makes it difficult to discern in them a literary substratum of pagan epics. The homely image of the serpent who is far removed from the later symbol of cosmic evil, of a God who strolls in the garden and sews shirts for Adam and Eve point to a literary genre nearer the folk tale. And yet with all their primitiveness there is no real myth here: no theogony, no sexual differentiation or desire in the deity, no theomachy, no magic, no demonic realm. Too naïve and crude for the prophets, these can only have been creations of the people. Lacking all traces of ideas peculiar to later times, they must be early creations—and they are essentially non-pagan. The ancient materials that Israel inherited from paganism were melted down and recast in the mold of its new idea. These stories are a popular product of this process. They could not have arisen among a polytheistic people, who conceived of YHWH as one of the gods, who knew and believed in pagan myths.

[1] *Genesis*, "Handkommentar zum AT" (1917), pp. 72 f.; cf. pp. lvi f., 39, 127.

MAGIC, DIVINATION, DREAMS, AND PROPHECY—Assuming that the popular religion of Israel practiced magic and divination in the names of gods or spirits, how is it that neither the mythological background, nor the practices themselves are ever mentioned in the Bible? If the people were pagan, can it be that they did not practice magic in the name of YHWH? And if they did, how can we explain the fact that among the long list of sins ascribed to them it is never referred to?

Assuming that the popular religion knew of a science of dream interpretation, why does the Bible—which does not deny the value of oneirocriticism—speak of it always as foreign or as associated with foreigners?

If the popular religion conceived of prophets as men inspired by indwelling spirits, or who spoke the words of an indwelling god in enthusiastic frenzy, could the biblical conception, so different, have arisen without a battle with the old view? Yet the new form appears without ever explicitly repudiating the idea of pagan ecstasy, without formulating its own view articulately, without leaving even a hint of a struggle with the conception it is supposed to have supplanted. How could such a transformation have taken place peacefully if alongside the higher form of biblical prophecy there existed ecstatic prophets who also functioned in the name of YHWH? It is scarcely credible that a clash had not sprung up, and that this clash had not been reflected somewhere in some manner.

THE CULT—It is alleged that the popular religion had priest-healers, who worked with magical incantations or conjurations. Yet they have successfully eluded mention in the narratives or the prophecies. The Bible never hints at an ideological clash with such a conception of priestly function. Is it credible that the biblical image of the priest established itself, in all its contrast to such alleged popular notions, silently and without a struggle of ideas?

The Bible nowhere opposes or denies the view that impurity is dangerous. It simply ignores this idea, so characteristic of all paganism, and proceeds on the assumption that danger and harm come only from the realm of YHWH. Such a procedure could not have been followed had the popular religion embodied rites and beliefs directed against the realm of demonic evil. Worship of satyrs and necromancy are mentioned; but these are the withered remains of Israel's uprooted paganism. It seems that even the folk religion knew of no demons in the pagan sense—independent, autonomous evil beings hostile toward the divine good. At any rate, the Bible, whose interdictions and polemics are our only source of knowledge of the folk religion, never found it necessary to oppose such notions.

The story of Dagon's defeat by YHWH contains a detail that illustrates nicely to what extent the biblical non-recognition of a demonic realm in the pagan sense reflects popular concepts. With a plainness that bespeaks its folk origin, the story tells how the Philistines placed alongside the plague-dealing ark, upon returning it to the Israelites, "boils of gold and mice of gold" as a "guilt offering" to Israel's god (I Sam. 6:3 ff.). Mice are a well-known symbol of the plague-god. The Philistines doubtless intended to expel their plague by making images to which the demon was transferred, and which were then sent away into the land of their enemy. Such expulsion of a demon-bearing object to another city or land is a common mode of sympathetic magic. The Israelites, evidently unaware of this custom, misinterpreted the plague images as a "guilt offering" of propitiation to YHWH—the only way they knew of getting rid of plagues.

The people believed in the efficacy of magic, sacrificed to satyrs, and thought that YHWH accepted human sacrifice. There was idol-worship among them, and an orgiastic element in their cult. All this is reflected in the interdictions and polemics of biblical writers. Was there also a magical-mythological basis to the cult of YHWH? Did the popular image of YHWH conceive him to be subject to magic and theurgy? Was he thought to have needs that were served by the cult? No struggle with magical rites and spells of the popular cult of YHWH can be discerned in the Bible. Nor is there opposition to a cultic drama or indeed any sort of rite with a mythological basis. Most important, there is no polemic against the conception of sacrifice as food of the god—the central concept of the popular cult in most forms of paganism, and especially in the pagan cultures surrounding Israel.

Indeed, the prophetic attack upon the popular evaluation of sacrifice presupposes an awareness that God needs no food. Isaiah's "What need have I of the great number of your sacrifices" (1:11), Jeremiah's "What need have I of frankincense" (6:20) would have had little point to an audience of pagans. Isaiah's "I am sated with the burnt offerings of rams" clearly assumes that its irony is self-evident to the audience. Amos mentions the absence of sacrifice during the Wandering in a rhetorical question that takes the people's knowledge of the matter for granted (Amos 5:25; cf. Jer. 7:22). There is no serious attack on the idea that God stands in need of sacrifice. The reproof of Psalm 50:8 ff. presupposes a general recognition of the fact that YHWH does not eat the flesh of bulls and the blood of goats, else the poet could hardly have dismissed the matter so lightly. It is almost unnecessary to add that there is no struggle with, indeed no awareness of, an idea that the cult is a mysterious means of restoring vitality to, or communing with, the deity. If such ideas had been prevalent among the people what material they would have furnished the diatribes of the prophets! Yet the rhetorical questions of prophecy merely seek to draw the ultimate inference from this commonplace idea: since it is not his food or drink, what value can sacrifice have to YHWH? There is no argument against the mythological concept.

FESTIVALS—The absence of polemic against the mythological conception of sacrifice holds true for the cult in general. The prophetic denial of its intrinsic value nowhere involves an argument against magical or mythological conceptions. Prophets and people appear to share a non-mythological idea of the meaning of the festivals. The prophets merely infer the ultimate consequences of this idea.

The baselessness of the theory that the Israelite new year festival involved a mythological drama motif has been pointed out above. It may here be added that this theory can hardly content itself with the ritual of the new year. If Israel's cult contained one mythological ritual there must have been others. The cultic calendar of the pagan consisted of many mythological rituals: the death of gods, ritual mourning for them, celebration of their nuptials, and so forth. The fact that the biblical authors nowhere condemn the people for such rituals can only mean that they did not exist in Israel.

IMPURE LAND—Amos' warning to Amaziah (Amos 7:17) that he would die in an "impure land," Hosea's threat that the exiled "would eat impure food" in foreign lands (Hos. 9:3 f.) reflect a popular view that the lands of the pagans were "impure." The prophets, with their tendency to universalism, can not be credited with authoring such an idea. The folk religion, then, distinguished two realms: the land of YHWH, holy land, and "impure" foreign lands. This territorial circumscription of YHWH's land has been taken to imply that other lands were believed subject to the rule of other gods.

But if YHWH were really conceived of as one among many gods how could the domains of his fellows—whom the people allegedly worshiped and believed to be essentially as divine as he—have been thought of as impure? On the contrary, the pagan finds holy sites everywhere. Syria is "the land of gods" to the Egyptians; Pharaohs set up temples in Punt, Nubia, and Palestine. The Assyrians hold Babylonian temples sacred, and their kings perform sacred rituals in conquered lands. The Israelite view is a departure from pagan models. It reflects the peculiar notion that YHWH is essentially different from all other gods, that all holiness is limited to him and his terrestrial abode.

The character of the impurity of foreign lands is likewise remarkable.

The idea that powers of impurity may harm a traveler in foreign lands is found among various primitive tribes. It is based on the recognition that the foreigner lacks the special knowledge of how to deal with alien gods and demons. Fear of foreign impurity thus arises from the belief in the plurality of divine realms and the necessity of knowing the peculiar rites of each. The fear that pollution will bring harm is based in turn on an acknowledgment of the divine or demonic reality behind the pollution.

The biblical concept is quite different. Impurity in general is never considered harmful; the impurity of foreign lands is no exception. That impurity is not an independent power but an absence of holiness, an estrangement from YHWH, the source of all holiness. Hence the biblical warning that the Israelites will worship strange gods in foreign lands does not mention any danger or physical harm that this will entail. It is YHWH who will pitilessly force this defiling worship on the people (Deut. 4:28; Jer. 16:13). All activity, even the compulsion to worship foreign gods, comes only from the realm of YHWH. No danger inheres in the impurity of foreign lands because YHWH alone is God. The area of sanctity is circumscribed because only in him is there holiness. This circumscription, so peculiar to Israel, is another expression of folk monotheism.

UNIVERSALISM AND MONOTHEISM

The view that the early popular religion was polytheistic or monolatristic —i.e., that it acknowledged the existence of gods beside YHWH and their rule outside Israel—finds its chief support in certain passages (e.g., Gen. 35:2 ff.; Judg. 11:24; I Sam. 26:19; II Kings 5:17) that appear to restrict YHWH's domain to his land or the affairs of his people. It is assumed that only later under the influence of literary prophecy were the narrow bounds of the popular religion broken so that YHWH could become the universal god of all men. The error of this view arises out of the failure to distinguish adequately between the various meanings of religious universalism.

Universalism in religion may mean either that the dominion and power of the deity are world wide, or that his favor and self-revelation are world wide. The first meaning involves the essence and nature of the deity; the second involves his manifestation among men. Since monotheism asserts that there is but one creator and ruler of the universe, it is perforce universalistic in the first sense. But there is no inner necessity that compels it to distribute the favor of the one God equally among all men. That one God creates and governs all does not of itself imply that all are equal in

Gen. 35:2 - Put away the foreign Gods that are among you.
Judges 11:28 - Chemosh
Sam. 26:19 - go serve other gods
Kings 5:17 - Sacrifice to any god but Y.

his sight. Nothing prohibits his choosing a particular group among men as his elect. Indeed the monotheistic religions have always assumed that he does just that. This idea circumscribes the realm in which God's favor is manifested without, however, affecting the universality of his dominion. Polytheism made an analogous distinction between the realm of a god's natural function and his social role. Marduk is the sun-god, and as such is cosmic; yet he is particularly the god of Babylon. Jupiter is the sky-god, but he is particularly connected with Rome. The question that we must therefore put to our sources is this: Did the limitation set upon the favor and self-revelation of YHWH also circumscribe his dominion?

It must be said at once that those passages adduced above, which are believed to be survivals of Israel's monolatry, are in fact representative of a view that prevails in a great part of biblical literature. The Pentateuch and historical books (Former Prophets) for example, consistently represent the world as divided into two realms, Israel and the nations, with Israel alone "the portion of YHWH." Deuteronomy goes so far as to assert that YHWH himself has ·"allotted" the worship of the host of heaven to the heathen (Deut. 4:19). The distinction discussed above between holy and impure land is the territorial counterpart of this division. Thus while YHWH governs and manifests his activity everywhere—in Sodom, Shinar, Egypt, Nineveh and Tarshish—the area of his sanctity is restricted to the boundaries of the land of Israel. The rest of the lands are the domain of the idols, the host of heaven, or the *shēdīm*—"no-gods" (Deut. 32:17). The early cult is entirely restricted to the sanctified territory of Israel (except for the desert cult, performed in a kind of portable sacred area). Outside it there is no sacrifice and no festival, but only impure ground where idols are worshiped. The Israelite who enters a foreign land is removed from the holiness of YHWH; his very food is impure; he has, as it were, no alternative but to worship other gods.

The book of Jonah contains what is perhaps the most characteristic expression of the inner relationship between monotheism and the territorial limitation of divine grace and sanctity.

The monotheistic idea prevails throughout this work. YHWH is the "God of heaven, who made sea and dry land" (1:9); he rules the sea and commands the wind (1:4); the fish obeys him and he rules Sheol and the abyss (chap. 2); plants and creeping things are under his control (4:6 f.). That YHWH is the sole, universal God is most clearly attested by his solicitude for the pagan city Nineveh and by the judgment that he is about to work upon it. And yet Jonah, a prophet of YHWH, arose to flee to Tarshish "from the presence of YHWH" (1:3, 10). In the light of the author's belief in the cosmic dominion of YHWH this can only mean that Jonah flees, not to the land where other gods rule, but away from the area of divine revelation. He hopes that in the land of the nations the hand of YHWH will not come upon him, and thus he will be freed of his task. Again there are two realms: that of "the presence of YHWH" and that of the idol worshipers. Moreover, Jonah does not admonish the Ninevites for their idolatry, but for "the violence that is in their hands" (3:8). Nor is there a hint of disapproval of the sailors' praying each to his god (1:5). The worship of YHWH, God of the world, is for this monotheistic writer the heritage of Israel only, and can be performed only in its proper place—the land of Israel.

David's complaint that his banishment from the land of YHWH entails the worship of foreign gods is echoed in sources whose monotheistic outlook is unimpeachable. In fact it is there associated (paradoxically it would seem) with the view that such worship is purely fetishistic. Thus the Deuteronomist, who emphasizes the oneness of God, who regards the idolatry of the pagans as divinely ordained, although conceiving of this worship as purely fetishistic, yet threatens Israel with an exile in which "they will serve gods, the handiwork of men—wood and stone" (4:28; 28:64). The notion of a compulsory service of wood and stone in exile is also found in Jeremiah (16:13). Here there can be no question of recognizing the dominion of other gods over foreign lands; wood and stone do not rule. This service is a religious punishment, a ruthless expulsion from the realm of God's sanctity, "For I will show you no favor" (Jer., *ibid.*). David's cursing the men who have driven him from the worship of YHWH to a land where other gods must be worshiped is to be viewed in this light.

The idea is found in even more extreme form in the priestly writings, a context which is uniformly conceded to be monotheistic. The universal creator of the priestly writings has "separated Israel from all the peoples" to be his (Lev. 20:24, 26), has set his abode in its midst and has become its God (Exod. 25:8; 29:44–46). The exclusive sanctity of the land of Israel is as fundamental a part of the priestly laws as the election of the people. The resident alien must accept the laws of YHWH by virtue of his living in the land, even though he is not an Israelite (Exod. 12:48 f.; Lev. 16:29; 18:26). In a story informed with the priestly viewpoint—the episode of the altar built by the two and one-half Transjordanian tribes (Josh. 22)—a most extreme form of this idea is set forth. Those who live outside the holy land fear that their descendants' "portion" in the God of Israel may be denied, and so they build an altar as witness to their belonging to the seed of Israel. The rest of the people are alarmed; to build an altar on impure soil is rebellion against YHWH (vss. 16 ff., 22 f., 29). Verse 25 indicates that one who dwells outside the land of Israel, and is not an Israelite, not only has no portion in YHWH, but *is to be stopped* from worshiping him. This is the most extreme expression of the cultic-territorial limitation of monotheism. Dwelling on impure soil leaves no alternative to idolatry.

We find the same viewpoint in Psalm 137. The psalmist, an exiled Levite who is surely no polytheist, remains faithful to YHWH by the rivers of Babylon. Precisely because of his belief in YHWH's unique holiness he refuses to sing the songs sacred to him on alien soil (vs. 4). In alien lands one cannot worship YHWH.

Again, Naaman recognizes that "there is no God in all the earth except in Israel" (II Kings 5:15 ff.), and promises to worship him in the land of Aram. For this purpose he takes two mules' burden of earth back to build an altar to YHWH. Naaman no longer recognizes his native gods; he wishes to worship YHWH even in Aram. His monotheism is absolute; in fact it goes beyond the priestly laws and Psalms in its universality, for it allows the possibility of worshiping YHWH outside his land. Yet here too a territorial limitation remains in the cultic sphere.

The story of the Samaritan "proselytes" to YHWH (II Kings 17:24 ff.) provides another illustration of this point. The author, the compiler of Kings, is a monotheist. His conception of pagan worship is fetishistic; each of the nations settled by the Assyrians in Samaria "made" (i.e., manufactured) its own gods (vss. 29 f.), which are idols (vs. 41). He tells how YHWH plagued the foreign settlers with lions for their not worshiping him, whereupon they requested and received a YHWH priest who taught them "the rites of the God of the land." That is to say, although foreigners are not obliged to worship YHWH in their own lands, when they come to his land they must worship him. The territorial limitation is, of course, only cultic; it is not the writer's thought that outside of Palestine other gods rule. Even the Samaritans are described as above this level; though exiled they continue to worship their gods in alien lands.

The book of Ruth, surely not the product of a polytheistic environment, displays the same viewpoint. Religion is represented as conditioned by nationality. Orpah returns "to her people and her gods" (1:15), while Ruth says to Naomi, "Your people are my people and your God my God" (vs. 16). The idea here, as elsewhere in the Bible, is that it is natural for the foreigner to worship his idols in his native land. This does not mean that the writer ascribes real divinity to these images. It is YHWH who smites the family of Elimelech in Moab, the land of Chemosh (1:13, 20 f.), and when Naomi begs her daughters-in-law to return home she gives them her blessing in the name of YHWH (vss. 8 f.).

When Jephthah says to the Ammonite king, "That which Chemosh your god has given you as possession. . . ." (Judg. 11:24), he is speaking from the same viewpoint. Jephthah's territorial claim against the king of Ammon is couched in religious terms after the manner of antiquity. It is natural that the narrator put into his mouth a fictitious acknowledgment of the activity of the god of the heathen king. Jephthah merely uses language that the king will understand. But we note that Chemosh's activity is mentioned only in connection with what his believers attribute to him; when Jephthah speaks in his own terms he says, "May YHWH judge, who judges today between the Israelites and the Ammonites." For Jephthah, YHWH alone judges both peoples.[2]

The prevailing conception of idolatry as fetishism and the consequent failure to attribute any activity—divine or demonic—to the gods of nations, show that foreign lands were never considered under the sway of other gods. Impure land was land in which the idol cults flourished. The national-territorial limitation of the religion of YHWH involved only his favor, his self-revelation, and his cult; it did not affect the extent of his rule. This territorial-national phase of monotheism is represented in the literature prior to literary prophecy. This was the monotheism of the popular religion. Passages expressing this viewpoint are not survivals, but faithful reflections of the earliest phase of Israelite monotheism.

[2] Jephthah's statement does not necessarily imply a fictitious acknowledgment of Chemosh as a living god. The biblical idea is that the idolater believes in the power of his fetish to act. The golden calves of Aaron and Jeroboam, which are conceived of as fetishes—nameless "other gods," not symbols of YHWH—are acclaimed as the gods "who took you out of the land of Egypt" (Exod. 32:4; I Kings 12:28). The fatuous idolater does not hesitate to ascribe to his fetish events that took place even before the fetish was made! The Second Isaiah asserts that YHWH revealed the future to Israel lest the pagan say, "My idol made them, my graven image and molten image commanded them" (Isa. 48:5). Jeremiah says (2:27) that the idolater even regards stocks and stones as his progenitors. Accordingly there is no reason to take Numbers 21:29 as proof of a belief in Chemosh as a living god, even if Chemosh is understood as the subject of the verb "has given" (but cf. the version of Jer. 48:46, where the antecedent of "your [sons, daughters]" is Moab, not Chemosh).

In Genesis 31:53 Laban invokes "the god of Abraham and the god of Nahor" as witnesses. If different gods are intended, we have here an allusion to the activity of a foreign deity. But the words are spoken by the Aramaean idolater Laban, and tell nothing about Israelite religion. It is not really clear even here that "the god of Nahor" is not to be understood as a fetish. In all the stories YHWH appears as Laban's god; the other "gods" that he has besides are the teraphim (Gen. 24:31, 50; 30:27, 30; 31:19, 24, 29 f., 49). However the language is unclear, and the reference may actually be to one and the same deity. Jacob, at any rate, swears only by "the Fear of his father Isaac."

The "foreign gods" which Genesis 35:2–4 supposedly acknowledge are fetishes which Jacob buries, along with the earrings, "under the terebinth."

THE ARGUMENT FROM HISTORY

The religion of the Bible is not set forth philosophically. It is urged on Israel on the basis of history; the basic attributes of Israel's God are historical. The first of the Ten Commandments grounds YHWH's claim to be recognized as sole God on the fact that he brought Israel out of the land of Egypt. Israel believed in YHWH and Moses after the miracle of the Red Sea (Exod. 14:31). Israel will have lasting faith in YHWH and Moses because of the Sinaitic theophany (19:9). "Knowledge of God" derives from historical experience: "To you it was shown that you might know that YHWH is God, there is none else beside him" (Deut. 4:35). The Exodus, the theophany at Sinai, the miraculous conquest of Canaan are repeatedly put forth as proofs that "YHWH is God, there is none else" (e.g., Josh. 23; 24; Judg. 2:1–2, 7; 10:11 ff.; I Sam. 12:6 ff.; I Kings 8:16, 53). It is the basis of prophetic arguments as well (Amos 2:9 ff.; Hos. 13:4; Mic. 6:1 ff.; Ezek. 16; 20; and elsewhere). The eschatological events that will proclaim the glory of YHWH to all men are also portrayed in images drawn from the legends of the Exodus.

Biblical faith is thus based on the popular legends. It draws on them even when it battles the people's backslidings into idolatry. The popular legends and the beliefs they imply are the common property of the folk and the authors of the Bible. They constitute the source and substance of early monotheism. In marked contrast to the repudiation of Greek popular religion by the higher religion of Greece's philosophers, or Buddhism's independence of and aloofness toward the religion of the masses, biblical religion neither disdains nor detaches itself from the popular legends. Biblical writers have no quarrel with the people over the image of the deity. The God of the prophets is essentially the same as the God of the popular legends. The fact that both employ the name YHWH is significant. Had the YHWH of the people been a national god after the pagan fashion, a mythological deity, radically unlike the biblical concept of him, would the prophetic cry, "YHWH, he is God, there is none else," have conveyed to the people what the prophets intended it to convey? Would there not have been a grave danger of real syncretism? What the biblical prophets meant by monotheism was not, after all, the exclusive worship of a mythological deity. Had the popular image of YHWH been pagan the first task of prophecy would surely have been to alter this image radically. Who can say that the symbol YHWH could then have served their new concept. Of course the prophets do nothing of the kind. They are zealots for YHWH —the same whom the people know as their savior in Egypt and who has done wondrous things for them throughout their history. Their God is the God of the popular religion; their faith rears itself upon the popular religion and is organically linked with it. Biblical religion is therefore not an esoteric religion of a spiritual elite like the higher pagan religions, but is a growth that is rooted in and nourished by the popular religion of Israel.

THE NATURE OF ISRAELITE IDOLATRY

THE PROBLEM OF THE TRIUMPH OF MONOTHEISM—With the destruction of the temple and the Babylonian exile, the period of Israel's idolatry comes to an end. A spirit of repentance seizes the people and brings about a profound change of heart. Doubtless there were individuals among the exiles who adopted paganism, but the overwhelming bulk of the people "returned" to their God. Even the priests, the nobility, and the royal household, who were the constant object of prophetic reproaches for their backsliding, forsake their idols and cleave to YHWH forever. Later Judaism expressed its astonishment at this transformation in a legend telling how the "Men of the Great Synagogue" captured the "Evil *Yeṣer* of idolatry" and put it to death (Bab. Yoma 69b; Sanhedrin 64a).

The conventional interpretations of this remarkable phenomenon fall far short of accounting for it. If the pagan god of the popular religion went up "in smoke of his temple," how did this lead to the extinction of idolatry? If the people were fundamentally pagan, and regarded YHWH as no different essentially from Baal, Ashur, or Marduk, the catastrophe would only have strengthened their paganism. To be sure, the prophets interpreted it as the chastisement of YHWH, but was no other explanation possible? A pagan interpretation of these events has been preserved for us in the response the women who worshiped the "queen of heaven" made to Jeremiah's censure (Jer. 44:17 f.). Judah's calamity, they assert, is the result of abandoning the cult of the queen of heaven. National collapse, the burning of the temple, and the exile of the people were thus subject to quite another interpretation than that given them by the prophets. To pagans, a more congenial and simple view would have been to take it as the victory of the Assyro-Babylonian gods over the God of Israel. If YHWH were popularly conceived of as the god of Canaan, if his people had worshiped alien deities while still on their own land, now that they were in exile, they should have embraced these foreign gods with doubled intensity. At best one might have looked for a small band of zealots who continued to cling to YHWH even on foreign soil. That a pagan people should have forsaken the "strange gods" precisely at the moment of their greatest triumph, and precisely on their own soil is incomprehensible.

The history of religions knows no parallel to such a phenomenon. The imposition of a new religion upon an entire people always involves the assistance of and promotion by the temporal power. This is the lesson of the spread of Mazdaism, Christianity, and Islam. In Israel, however, the efforts of such royal reformers as Asa, Jehu, Jehoash, Hezekiah, and even Josiah, are said to have failed. Nor did the classical prophets of pre-exilic times meet with success. Only in exile, amidst pagan surroundings, without external compulsion, with scarcely a struggle, out of an inner transformation alone, the Jewish people abandon idolatry forever!

This phenomenon has only one adequate explanation: pre-exilic Israel must have already had a monotheistic faith that was not the property of a narrow elite, but of the entire nation. Israelite idolatry must have been sufficiently shallow for the shock of the catastrophe to uproot it without a struggle. The change that took place spontaneously in the exile and that manifests itself in the community of the Restoration could have occurred only in an environment of popular monotheism.

We must therefore examine afresh the testimony to Israel's idolatry in pre-exilic times.

Nothing seems more established, on the basis of the biblical evidence, than the sin of idolatry that marks the entire pre-exilic age. One of the foundations of biblical historiography is that the evil that befell Israel was caused by this sin. During the period of the judges Israel forgot YHWH and turned to worship the gods of the nations; for this it was repeatedly punished by foreign conquest and oppression. Jeroboam made calves and caused Israel to sin; Judah, too, worshiped idols and the host of heaven. The result of this continuous sin was that YHWH exiled first Israel and later Judah.

Critical examination of the evidence, however, raises doubts as to the historicity of this sweeping biblical indictment. While the period of the judges is represented as wholly infected with the worship of Baals and Ashtoreths, the reign of Saul is strangely free of taint—and this without the trace of a struggle. Saul is a zealot for YHWH; he extirpates the mediums and necromancers from the land (I Sam. 28:3, 9, 21). Yet we hear nothing of an extermination of Baal worship. The Bible seeks to account for his tragic end by ascribing various sins to him (I Sam. 13:8 ff.; 15; 28:18), but the sin of idolatry is not among them. Baal worship has simply disappeared. Is it credible that a popular paganism, adopted, as it is supposed, from the Canaanites, could have vanished so completely merely at the command of Samuel (I Sam. 7:3 f.)? David, a model of devotion to YHWH never attacks idolatry; in his reign, too, it is nonexistent. Idolatrous Ephraim harbors Baal worship only during the reigns of Ahab and Jezebel, and of their sons Ahaziah and Jehoram. The true extent of this worship is suggested by the fact that when Jehu assembles "all the worshipers of Baal" they can be accommodated in one temple (II Kings 10:19, 21), the sole temple of Baal, built by Ahab in Samaria (vss. 25 ff.; cf. I Kings 16:32). Henceforth, until the exile of Israel, no foreign gods are known by the book of Kings to have been worshiped in the north. The sin laid to all the northern kings is the sin of Jeroboam; but this is not the worship of a foreign god. In Judah there is, during the time of Athaliah (Jezebel's daughter), one temple and one priest to Baal (II Kings 11:18). Until the days of Manasseh the presence of foreign gods and attempts to extirpate them are recorded only for the royal city. Manasseh's reign is the first in which we hear of a more general contamination: "Judah, too, did he cause to sin with his idols" (II Kings 21:3, 11). Jeremiah's arraignment of the entire nation for the sin of idolatry is challenged by the people (Jer. 2:23): "I have not become defiled, I did not go after the Baals." His broad indictment in chapter 44 is again qualified by the notice we take that its subjects are men "who knew that their wives were burning offerings to other gods" (vs. 15)—the men lent a hand, but they did not take part in the worship of their wives (cf. 7:18).

It would seem then, that the biblical arraignment is exaggerated; sins of particular groups are ascribed to the entire people. This is an almost necessary consequence of the biblical postulate that Israel's calamities are caused by its sins. The historiographer could not account for what had taken place—the collapse of Israel's monarchy—without sin. Had there been no sin he would have had to invent it. Israel's sinfulness is essential to biblical theodicy; hence the sweeping and generalized nature of the biblical indictment. An analogous case, over which we have a measure of control is the prophetic denunciation of Israelite society. From the prophets one would gather that Israel's society as a whole was unspeakably degenerate. But the historical books make no mention of such widespread moral decay; so far as they know the catastrophe has a religious cause only. Sin was more of a historiographic necessity than a reality; hence the biblical denunciations require careful evaluation before they can be utilized as historical records.

This is not the only allowance, however, that has to be made in treating the Bible as a source for the history of Israelite idolatry.

Idolatry: Dogma and Reality—For the evaluation of Israel's idolatry it is crucial to have a clear idea of what is signified by that term. One may ask, for example: Did Israel's worship accord with the requirements of the Law and Prophets or not? This is the approach of dogmatic tradition, and, to some extent of modern criticism as well. The assumption is that whatever is out of line with Law and Prophets is "idolatry." Hence the popular religion was idolatrous either because it deviated from the Mosaic Law (dogmatic tradition), or because it was as yet unaware of that Law (modern criticism, which affirms that in pre-exilic times the Law had not yet come into existence). But from the viewpoint of the historian the only legitimate question can be, whether the essential idea of Israelite religion as described above was reflected and embodied in the forms of the popular religion. In whatever dress, in however imperfect an expression, does the religion of pre-exilic Israel exhibit the imprint of that idea?

The idolatry that the Bible ascribes to Israel is a congeries of all that savors of "the abominations of the nations." It includes such fundamentally pagan matters as magic, divination, necromancy, and idol cults, but it also embraces such mere heterodoxies as worship at high places and pillars. The biblical criterion is basically external and formal, confusing shadow and substance, essence and historical accident. The prescribed forms of biblical religion are but one set of embodiments of the monotheistic idea that does not by any means exhaust the possible forms by which that idea might have clothed itself. And it must be acknowledged that these forms, selected intuitively and gropingly rather than systematically and consciously have not always been the most felicitous expressions of the monotheistic idea. It is only dogma that makes the biblical selection of forms non-idolatrous. The historian can readily find even in the Bible itself several "idolatrous" elements—shells that have lost their content. That certain of these shells were sanctified and others not seems at times to have been due to mere historical accident.

Thus biblical religion accepted the sacrificial cult, which is fundamentally pagan, in spite of prophetic strictures. Only by accident was it not repudiated as heathen. Or again, out of the various epithets of deity used by the pagans, *ʾēl-ʿelyōn, ʾāḏōn, meleḵ*, and others were adopted by the Bible; *baʿal* was rejected—after a period of acceptance—although it is not intrinsically more pagan than the others. The Bible vacillates with regard to several practices. Pillars and asherahs of the YHWH cult were later banned (Deut. 16:21 f.) and denounced as manifestations of Israelite idolatry (I Kings 14:15, 23; II Kings 17:10; 18:4; 23:14 f.). But in the earlier literature Abraham plants a tamarisk (Gen. 21:33), a kind of asherah, and the pillar appears as a legitimate cultic symbol (Gen. 28:18, 22; 35:14; Exod. 24:4;

Isa. 19:19). At a late period the high-place cult was regarded as pagan (Deut. 12:2 ff.; I Kings 14:23; II Kings 17:9, 11), although the early literature recognizes it. Even the ban on images is not altogether consistent; calves are pagan, but cherubs are not. Before the time of Hezekiah the brazen serpent is sacred; afterward it is an abomination which must be destroyed (II Kings 18:4). Human sacrifice is viewed by the Bible as pagan, but to devote persons to destruction (Lev. 27:29), and to hang ceremonially "before YHWH" (Num. 25:4; II Sam. 21:6, 9; cf. Samuel's slaughter of Agag "before YHWH" [I Sam. 15:33]) is not. Even the account of the near sacrifice of Isaac fails to manifest an outspoken objection in principle to the idea of human sacrifice. That one *can* show absolute submission to God by offering his child to him is, after all, a legitimate inference from the story. Nor does the narrator of Judges 11:30 ff. show repugnance against Jephthah's performance of his vow. Thus, while biblical religion rejected human sacrifice on the basis of its new appreciation of the cult in general and its new moral sense, until this attitude crystallized there was room for regarding even human sacrifice as an expression of highest devotion to the one God.

Even the worship of other supernatural beings, which is for the Bible the essence of idolatry, cannot be considered in necessary contradiction to monotheism. The doctrinal aspect of biblical monotheism is that YHWH is God, there is none else. But the Bible proceeds to infer a drastic cultic consequence of this doctrine: the prohibition of worshiping any other beings or objects (ʾelōhīm-angels [Exod. 22:19], satyrs, demons, the dead, and idols). Monotheism need not inevitably come to this extreme conclusion. The One is not necessarily "jealous" in a cultic sense. There is room in monotheism for the worship of lower divine beings—with the understanding that they belong to the suite of the One. Thus Christianity knows the worship of saints and intercessors, as does Islam. Nor did later Judaism shrink, for example, from conceiving the scapegoat as a propitiatory offering to Sammael (Yalkut Bereshith 44; Aḥare-moth 578; cf. Sifra to Lev. 9:2). Israelite monotheism tended toward cultic exclusivism and was crystallized in this form in the Bible. But during the pre-exilic period Israel was still moving from the basic monotheistic idea to its extreme cultic consequence. Certain of the "idolatries" of Israel are no more than stages left behind on the way. Not even the worship of "other gods" can thus in every case be counted automatically as a departure from the fundamental idea.

The question of the nature of Israelite idolatry can therefore not be answered simply by reference to the formal criterion of biblical dogma. Formulated in accord with the demands of the critical historian the question must be whether YHWH was ever worshiped in Israel as one of many gods, whether he was associated with a mythological pantheon, whether Israelite idolatry was genuinely syncretistic. Only these questions are decisive.

THE WORSHIP OF FOREIGN GODS—That the Israelites worshiped Baals, Ashtoreths, and other foreign gods is the testimony of the schematic editorial framework of Judges and the beginning of Samuel (Judg. 2; 3:1 ff.; 4:1; 6:1; etc.). This generalized indictment—the foundation stone of the editor's historiosophy—always lacks specific details as to when, where, and by whom. The periodic putting away of foreign gods (Judg. 10:16; I Sam. 7:3 f.) after the admonition of a man of God is similarly vague. The site of the purge is never specified; no temples and altars are demolished, and no blood is shed, as in the purges of Elijah, Jehu, Jehoiada, and Josiah. The actual narratives of Judges and Samuel, on the other hand, furnish no certain information concerning the worship of foreign gods. There is, to be sure, "idolatry." Gideon makes a golden ephod (with some sort of an image) in Ophrah (Judg. 8:27); Micah makes an image for YHWH (17–18). But in neither case are foreign gods worshiped. There was an "altar of Baal" in Ophrah, the city of Jerubbaal. But *baᶜal* was an epithet of YHWH in early times (else such loyal devotees of YHWH as David, Saul, and Jonathan would not have given their sons such names as Eshbaal, Meribbaal [I Chron. 8:33 f.], and Beeliada [14:7]). Later (we do not know when) this epithet fell out of favor with zealots (Hos. 2:18). For such zealots altars to "Baal" were idolatrous; the account of Jerubbaal's demolishment of the altar in Ophrah reflects this battle with "Baal." The names of God have always been a crucial matter to religious zealots.[3]

Throughout all the stories of Judges the popular faith in YHWH runs as a powerful current. This faith raises the judges, and inspires poets, prophets, and Nazirites. To be sure, it is different from the religion crystallized in the Law and Prophets. Gideon makes an image in honor of YHWH; Jephthah sacrifices his daughter to fulfil his vow; Samson is an odd sort of Nazirite—yet all these men are moved by a faith in YHWH. It is the same in the stories concerning Eli, Hannah, the adventure of the captured ark, and the Saul pericope. Worship of Baals and Ashtoreths has been schematically interspersed between these chapters, but no trace of a vital,

[3] Baal-berith and El-berith of Judges 9:4, 46 is presumably YHWH. The custom of calling altars and sanctuaries by theophoric names is attested to in early times; cf. YHWH-nissi (Exod. 17:15), YHWH-shalom (Judg. 6:24), and El-beth-el (Gen. 35:7). The Shechem sanctuary was called by the name of Baal or El-berith. That this Baal was a foreign god (Judg. 8:33) is the opinion of the editor based on the "idolatrous" name.

popular belief in any foreign gods can be detected in the stories themselves. Baal prophets appeared in Israel centuries later; but during the age of the judges when Israel is supposed to have been most deeply affected by the religion of Canaan, there are no Baal priests or prophets, nor any other intimation of a vital effect of polytheism in Israel's life.

Neither in the days of Saul and David nor during the first part of Solomon's reign is there worship of foreign gods in Israel. Since the advent of the monarchy was not accompanied by a violent suppression of pagan cults, we have here another indication that the period of the judges was also non-pagan. During these three reigns there is no religious strife. At the end of Solomon's reign a specific and localized foreign cult appears for the first time: the altars to Chemosh, Molech, Ashtoreth, and the other gods that Solomon erects at the instance of his foreign wives (I Kings 11:1 ff.). There is no reason to doubt the historicity of this passage, inasmuch as various other passages attest to precisely the same sort of thing. The queens Maacah (mother of Asa), Jezebel, and Athaliah are responsible for introducing foreign cults into Israel and Judah.[4] The foreign cults of Solomon's time are entirely a matter of the royal household. The altars are erected outside of Jerusalem; there is no attempt to give these private cults official, public recognition, as was done later in the time of Jezebel. It seems that the altars fell into disuse after Solomon's time; none of the reformers, Asa, Jehoshaphat, Jehoiada, or Hezekiah, moves against them. Only Josiah, who seeks to eradicate every vestige of idolatry, finally removes them (II Kings 23:13 f.).

In the time of Rehoboam and Abiam we find high places, pillars, asherahs, and cultic prostitution in the land (I Kings 14:22 ff.; 15:3). But these seem to be corruptions of the worship of YHWH; no foreign gods are mentioned explicitly.[5] Worship of a foreign goddess, Asherah, is specified as a private sin of Maacah, Asa's half-pagan mother (15:13). Thus before the time of Jezebel and Athaliah neither the northern nor southern kingdom had an officially recognized, public cult of foreign gods. The calves of Jeroboam, which the writer of Kings styles "other gods" in place of YHWH (I Kings 14:9; cf. II Chron. 13:8) were evidently regarded by the north as a legitimate symbol of the YHWH cult. Neither Elijah nor Jehu, who,

---

[4] Elsewhere too women are depicted as particularly addicted to idolatry. Rachel and Michal have teraphim (Gen. 31:19 ff.; I Sam. 19:13 ff.), and women bewail Tammuz (Ezek. 8:14). Compare also the phrasing of the ban on intermarriage in Exodus 34:16 (with which cf. Num. 25:1 ff. and 31:15 f.).

[5] The *gillūlīm* that Asa removed (15:12) are apparently the pillars and asherahs of 14:23 f., called there "abominations of the nations."

inspired by Elisha and the Rechabites, rooted out Baal worship, has anything against Jeroboam's calves.

A public cult of a foreign deity was established in Israel for the first time during the reign of Ahab and Jezebel, and in Judah during the reign of Athaliah. For the first time a temple to a foreign deity was built inside an Israelite city (I Kings 16:32). Hundreds of prophets of Baal and Asherah are pensioners of the queen (18:19). The reaction of the people indicates how alien all this was to them; their fury brought on the downfall of the house of Omri. Inasmuch as paganism is by nature tolerant, and in view of the fact that the prophets—the leaders of the zealous opposition—were the main victims of Jezebel's persecution, we must suppose that Israelites initiated the civil strife. In all likelihood it was the prophets who roused the people to rebellion, and it was the people who eventually slaughtered the Baal prophets (18:40). Jezebel reacted by killing the zealots. Elijah's complaint that he is the sole surviving prophet of YHWH is, however, a hyperbole (18:22; 19:10, 14). The persecution was not thoroughgoing, for when Ahab made his expedition against Aram there were some four hundred YHWH prophets in Samaria by whom he inquired of YHWH (22:6 ff.). Jezebel continued her "harlotries and sorceries" until she was put to death by Jehu (II Kings 9:22, 34 ff.). After the dogs picked her bones clean, Jehu set about to destroy all the Baal worshipers (II Kings 10:18 ff.). He gathers them all into the single Baal temple in Samaria and puts them to death. The people demolish the temple and its altars, and turn the site into an outhouse (vss. 26 f.). Because this was the cult of a small circle sponsored by Jezebel, and had no popular roots, it was possible for Jehu to extirpate it once for all (vs. 28). Never again do we hear of an Israelite king who worshiped Baal. The book of Kings thus depicts Baal worship as a brief episode in the history of the northern kingdom. As we shall see, the prophetic literature confirms this testimony.

Baal appears for the first time in Judah in the time of Joram son of Jehoshaphat, who married Ahab's daughter Athaliah. It lasts through the short reign of Ahaziah, their son, until the death of Athaliah. Here too the cult was an alien growth with even shallower roots than in the north. The palace coup, lead by Jehoiada the priest (II Kings 11:4 ff.), puts an end to Athaliah and the single Baal temple and Baal priest in Jerusalem. There is no mention of Baal worship outside of Jerusalem. For a century, between the accession of Joash (836) and the end of Jotham's reign (734), we hear nothing of foreign cults in Judah. Ahaz, however, is said to have gone "in the way of the kings of Israel"(16:3). To judge from II Kings 23:12 Ahaz had private altars built to the host of heaven (cf.

Zeph. 1:5), under the influence of the Assyrian domination. How limited the scope of this deviation was is indicated by the fact that the notice of Hezekiah's purge of idolatry (II Kings 18:4) does not mention the removal of foreign gods. The heyday of Judean idolatry was the reign of Manasseh—the Jezebel of the south. It is not clear what the occasion of Manasseh's conversion to paganism was. Phoenician and Assyrian influence can be detected in his practices, and doubtless a primary motive was his political subjection to Assyria. Again it is a matter of foreign influence, with no roots in the popular religion. Manasseh's idolatry is different from that of Jezebel. He does not build special temples to his gods but converts the very temple of YHWH into a pantheon (II Kings 21:4 ff.). He builds altars to the host of heaven in its courts and sets up an image of Asherah at the north gate, by which women (pagan priestesses?) ritually lament Tammuz (Ezek. 8:14). He is the only king who divined, and promoted necromancy (II Kings 21:6). This pagan reformer spread his cult into the rural area as well, where he seems to have placed pagan priests at the high places (21:11; 23:5). Manasseh's acts appear to have aroused opposition which he suppressed with much bloodshed (21:16; 24:4). Josiah's reaction and reform was also accompanied by considerable bloodshed. Josiah puts to death the pagan priests of the Judean countryside and all the priests of the high places in the cities of Samaria (23:5, 20). We do not hear, however, that any broad circles of the folk were affected. This paganizing interlude, too, was the work of kings (23:5) and had no popular roots. The kings who followed Josiah "did what was evil in the sight of YHWH" but there are no grounds for asserting that they restored the idolatries of Manasseh. Scripture ascribes the fall of Judah not to the sins of its last kings, but to the sins of Manasseh (23:26 f.; 24:3 f.; see below, pp. 405 ff.).

During the 210 years of the northern kingdom (931–722) a public cult of a foreign god was practiced under royal sponsorship for about twenty years. During the 426 years of the southern kingdom (1011–586) a public cult of a foreign god was practiced only during the days of Athaliah and Manasseh, and to a lesser extent at the end of Solomon's reign and in the time of Ahaz. These paganizing interludes appear solely as products of royal initiative. Revolts against them are popular undertakings that are led by the zealots of YHWH. The people are never found on the side of the defenders of paganism.

The conventional opinion that the popular religion was Canaanized and worshiped a syncretistic YHWH-Baal is groundless. Syncretism (the combining of two gods) could have arisen only out of the mutual influence of two cults. But there is no record of an independent, thriving cult of Baal in the period of the judges, nor during the monarchy before the time of Omri. That YHWH had the epithet *ba*ᶜ*al* is no evidence for syncretism. The Baal worship of Ahab's time was altogether new. Its votaries were Jezebel's Sidonian entourage. It was a special phenomenon, entirely apart from the worship of YHWH. The worshipers of Baal and YHWH are two separate groups (II Kings 10:23). Jezebel kills the prophets of YHWH, and the YHWH altar on Carmel is demolished. But Jezebel does not sacrifice to Baal on YHWH's altars nor erect symbols of the Baal cult in the temples of YHWH. Such an amalgam was made by Manasseh, and Josiah's reform consequently involved the purging of YHWH's temple. Nothing of the sort, however, is related of the Baal worship of the north, nor does it appear in the stories of Baal's eradication.

Nor does Elijah confront a syncretizing people. Elijah argues, "If YHWH is God, follow him; but if Baal, follow him" (I Kings 18:21). The underlying assumption is that only one is God, and that a decision must be made as to which one it is. The audience is assumed to have a mono‍theistic, not a syncretistic, outlook. Elijah rebukes them for indecision, as if they could entertain the idea of replacing their God with the god of Jezebel. He rebukes them for permitting Jezebel to plant Baal worship on the holy land. Syncretism has been insinuated into this episode by modern critics. The only attested instance of syncretism is to be found in Manasseh's association of pagan deities with YHWH in his own temple. But his was a royal idiosyncrasy which had no popular roots. The foreign worship clearly did not penetrate below the surface.

THE NATURE OF THE POPULAR IDOLATRY—This does not mean that the biblical denunciations of Israel's idolatry have no ground in reality. It does mean that the popular idolatry was not authentic polytheism, with mythology, temples, and priesthoods. It was vestigial idolatry, a vulgar superstition of the sort that the ignorant level of monotheistic peoples practices to this day. YHWH was God, but the vulgar believed also in the virtue of idols, amulets, spells, and pagan rites; saw no harm in traffic with satyrs and demons; believed in the influence of the host of heaven. They did not practice a genuine, mythological cult of pagan gods, but they did not reject the host of anonymous ᵓ*elīlīm* and teraphim,—figurines of foreign manufacture that archeological excavations have discovered in abundance in Israelite Palestine. Beside this there was at times another form of "idolatry": the worship of YHWH in pagan ways.

The popular idolatry that is described in the literary prophets is, with a few specific exceptions, this sort of vestigial idolatry.

In the book of Amos, only one passage (5:26) deals with idolatry, in this case a type of astral worship. Since this reference to idolatry is isolated, it is suspect, all the more so in view of the fact that astral worship is otherwise attested to only in the reign of Manasseh. The passage may well be from a later hand.

The book of Hosea treats of Baal worship extensively, but the distribution and nature of the allusions to Baal, combined with other features, show that chapters 1–3 which alone speak of Baal worship as a contemporary sin cannot be from the same hand or age as the rest of the book. As will be shown later, chapters 1–3 date from before the reform of Jehu. The Baal worship which is denounced in them is that of the stories of Elijah and Elisha. And like those prophets the First Hosea counts Baal worship as a national sin, although, as we have seen, only court circles actively promoted it.[6] In the last chapters, on the other hand, Baal worship (only in 9:10; 13:1) appears as a sin of the past; the present sin is the calves of Samaria (8:5 f.; 10:5 f.; 13:2), and the other images to which Ephraim cleaves (4:17). Ephraim is not accused of serving any specified foreign god; he inquires of his wood and staff (4:12), bows down to his handiwork (14:4), and cleaves to pillars (10:1 f.). There is no clearly defined pagan cult, no specific mythology, priests, or temples.

Nor do Isaiah and Micah name any foreign deity as an object of popular worship. Idolatry is always portrayed as the service of images of silver and gold, the handiwork of men (Isa. 2:7f., 18, 20; 17:7f.; 30:22), or the worship of asherahs and *hammānīm* (17:8; 27:9). Samaria and Jerusalem worship idols and images (10:10 f.), as they have learned to do from foreigners (2:6 ff.). But this cult has no clearly defined features. The same sort of featureless idolatry is denounced by Micah (1:7; 5:9 ff.).

From the period of Manasseh we find references to a specific form of idolatry. Zephaniah speaks of Baal and his priests, of astral cults on roofs, and the worship of Milcom (1:4 f.). Jeremiah mentions the loathsome things that Manasseh put in the temple of YHWH (7:30; 32:34), the astral and Baal cults (8:1 f.; 19:13; 32:29), and human sacrifice in Topheth (7:31; 19:5; 32:35).

Here we must distinguish the public, royally promoted cults, from the private practices of individuals. To the former belong the "loathsome things" that Jeremiah reproaches Judah for setting up in the temple of

---

[6] The syncretism that is supposedly reflected here is imaginary. There is no commingling of YHWH and Baal; on the contrary, the people are blamed for having forgotten YHWH and gone after other gods (Hos. 2:15; 3:1). The prophet always speaks of two separate realms. Having deserted her "first husband," her true benefactor, Israel foolishly ran after Baal, as if he had given her all her wealth (2:7 ff.).

YHWH or the cult of human sacrifice in Topheth. Such public cults could only have been established under royal authority, and, as is abundantly clear from the prophecies of Jeremiah, were not practiced after Josiah's reform. These are the sins of Manasseh, which Jeremiah still believes to be haunting the people (15:4). To the second category belong the astral cults practiced on rooftops, and the women's worship of the queen of heaven (Jer. 7:17 f.; 44:15 ff.). These were individual practices; the people as a whole in Jeremiah's time worshiped YHWH and trusted wholeheartedly in him—a trust that led them into rash policies that Jeremiah had constantly to combat. Apart from the women's astral worship, the "idolatry" of the time consisted of anonymous images, wood and stone, "lies and vanities," "other gods" which Israel "knew not" (7:9; 19:4; 44:3). The last is a telling phrase; the idolatrous cults are obscure, featureless, not really known to Israel.

Ezekiel, too, refers to these two forms of idolatry. In chapter 8 he speaks of Asherah ("the image of jealousy"), Tammuz, and sun-worship. But these well-defined cults are located in the Jerusalem temple and there only. What he sees in this vision is the work of Manasseh. When Ezekiel speaks of the contemporary idolatry of the people it is the worship of "loathsome things," anonymous "male images" (16:17; cf. 23:5 ff.), or images of creeping things and animals (8:10), "wood and stone" (20:32).

The popular idolatry that the prophetic books depict is thus a magical, fetishistic, non-mythological worship of images, "gods they knew not," imported from abroad. There were also private cults such as that of the women who made cakes for the queen of heaven, but these were performed by individuals without benefit of temple or clergy. The information regarding the idolatry of the earlier periods accords well with this picture. In the original stories of Judges there is scarcely a hint of real foreign gods. The editorial framework however, speaks (doubtless on the basis of valid information) of anonymous idol-worship, "other gods," gods of Aram, Sidon, Moab, Ammon, Philistines, etc., who are comprised under the common rubric "Baals" (Judg. 2:11; 10:10), or, when it is desired to differentiate male from female images, "Baals and Ashtoreths" (2:13; 10:6; etc.). These images have neither priests, prophets, nor temples. Evidently they are the figurines that have been found in such numbers in Israelite Palestine. They were either imported or found on the spot after the conquest, and were the object of superstitious veneration. Such "foreign gods" are what were periodically "put away" from the midst of the people (Josh. 24:14, 23; Judg. 10:16; I Sam. 7:3 f.) without involving the demolishment of altars and temples, and the slaying of priests and prophets, as occurred in the time of Elijah, Jehu, Jehoiada, and Josiah when genuine foreign cults were extirpated. Jacob's household, at his command, surrendered to him "all the foreign gods and the rings that were in their ears," to be buried under the terebinth (Gen. 35:2 ff.). What these "foreign gods" were we know from the story of Rachel's theft of Laban's teraphim-gods.

The zest with which the people took part in the eradication of Baal worship in Israel shows that in the popular consciousness there always was the recognition that "YHWH was God." What the people did not do was to draw the ultimate cultic conclusion from this belief. The magical power of idols, the influence of satyrs or the host of heaven was accepted by the masses without raising these to the divine rank of YHWH. The Bible preserves traces of this stage of belief. The author of Genesis 31 does not shrink from relating how the matriarch Rachel stole her father's teraphim— surely for their religious value—and how Jacob, who is portrayed as a monotheist, did not mind them or any of the other "foreign gods" that his household worshiped. Only before his pilgrimage to Bethel does he become concerned to demand their removal (Gen. 35:1 ff.). Nor does David, who is a paragon of loyalty to YHWH, mind the teraphim of his wife (I Sam. 19:13). At the same time it is clear that neither for the writers nor for their heroes are these teraphim and "foreign gods" real deities. One can hardly miss the indulgent humor in the tale of how Rachel stole the teraphim and then put them in her camel saddle to hide them from her outraged father, or in the story of Michal's placing the teraphim in David's bed to conceal his escape. But this is the limit of the biblical author's tolerance. When it is a matter of a living god even Laban and Balaam, as far as the biblical narrator is concerned, know only YHWH, although this does not stop them from fetishistic idol-worship.

This tendency of the folk religion was fostered by a belief in the reality of magical forces that even biblical religion was unable completely to overcome. The survival of another power realm, if indeed not a divine one, was enough to give room for idolatry. Despite the popular belief in one God, the feeling persisted that there was some magical efficacy to images and rites. How deeply rooted this sentiment was can be seen from the fact that even among the soldiers of Judas Maccabeus were some who bore apotropaic figurines under their tunics (II Macc. 12:40 f.)—and these were zealots who were prepared to die for the honor of their God! The bulk of the people indulged, when they did not deride, this ignorant superstition. This is the attitude of the men of Jeremiah's time whose wives made offerings to the queen of heaven. There was no serious challenge here to the primacy and uniqueness of YHWH.

That is why the biblical battle with idolatry is restricted to the area of the cult. The struggle against idols, calves, pillars, divination, and magic may be said to involve not monotheism but monolatry; at issue is not belief in one God, but the exclusive worship of him. The biblical writers take for granted that faith in one God is common to them and the people; they merely call on the people to consider the implications of this belief, and stop worshiping no-gods. They invoke the popular legends which tell of the mighty acts of the one God, and demand that the people draw the cultic consequence of their belief in him. YHWH is never opposed to other living gods, but to other objects of worship. The biblical battle with idolatry does not involve a battle with myth. YHWH is the only god who has "myths"—the popular legends; the idols and "foreign gods" are myth-less cult objects. Worship of "dumb idols" is, in the biblical view, arrant, sinful foolishness. Such a polemic obviously presupposes a monotheistic viewpoint. In this the biblical writers and the folk are at one. It is only in the cultic implication of this viewpoint that they differ.

Consequently, Israelite idolatry could never take on the character of a genuine syncretism. For genuine syncretism presupposes an essential parity between the deities to be amalgamated. Only so can they be integrated into a single divine order or an enlarged divine family. But when, as in Israel, there is a belief that only one being is supreme, that he is alone of his kind, and that all other cult objects are magical or lesser beings, no genuine syncretism is possible.

Paganism was never a creative force in Israelite culture. National poetry, narrative, prophecy, ethics, and politics were all permeated with the belief in YHWH. Sufficient proof of this is the fact that no prophets of foreign gods ever arose in Israel. Jezebel's prophets are Baal priests who prophesy in ecstatic frenzy (I Kings 18:19, 26, 28 f.); they disappear with the end of their cult.[7] This is sufficient to indicate how far idolatry was from the sources of popular creativity.

Moreover, although there was a cult of images in Israel, archeological remains fail to show a distinctive native Israelite iconography. Those who suppose that Israel was a pagan nation cannot fall back on the Second Commandment to explain this singular lack. That no sculpture developed

[7] Jeremiah refers to prophets who prophesied by Baal (2:8; 23:13), but throughout this book Baal serves to denote idolatry in general (the worship at Topheth is "Baal" worship [19:5; 32:35], the astral cults performed on rooftops are to "Baal" [32:29]), and then, by extension, comes to mean falsity and vanity; with 2:8 compare 5:31, "the prophets prophesy falsely." The prophets with whom Jeremiah has actually to contend all speak in the name of YHWH, and Jeremiah's claim is that they invent their prophecy out of their own heart; Baal does not figure at all (cf. 14:13 ff.; 23:14, 16, 21 ff.; 27:14 ff.; 28:1 ff.; 29:8 ff.; 37:19).

in Israel is a result of the absence of myth which served in paganism as the living fount of religious artistry. If Israelite idolatry failed to produce religious art it can only be that this idolatry was bereft of its life source, mythology. Israelite idolatry was a vulgar phenomenon; it was magical, fetishistic, ritualistic and never attained the level of a cultural force. The fact that the Bible never shows awareness of the symbolic, representative character of images, but takes them to be gods in themselves, reveals how shallow was the impression made by idolatry, and how far Israel was from a true understanding of pagan beliefs.

THE BASIC IDEA AND ITS CULTIC
EXPRESSION

Examination of the thousand-year struggle of the biblical writers against idolatry indicates that already in the time of the judges and the early kings there was no battle with the fundamental idea of paganism, with myth. The pagan idea, the mythological-magical world view of paganism, no longer existed in Israel. The biblical struggle with idolatry restricts itself entirely to the area of cult and ritual. This is decisive proof that from earliest times Israel was no longer a genuinely pagan people.

The passion with which the Bible wages its war against idolatry can easily mislead one into thinking that here the basis of Israelite religion was at stake. The real source of this passion, however, is the desire to concretize and realize in practice what was still an idea. The biblical age is in search of a popular expression and symbol of its new idea of the One. It was felt that without a tangible, popular concretization the idea would remain the property of but a few. The bearers of biblical religion sensed that for the folk the cult is decisive: whatever is worshiped is divine. A plurality of worshiped objects is calculated to foster the erroneous notion of a plurality of divine realms; hence the monotheistic idea needed to be complemented by a monolatrous cult. Even if the cult of idols, satyrs, the dead, etc., did not intend to encroach on the domain of the One, such an outcome was virtually inevitable. The monotheistic idea could never be firmly established with the folk at large unless it were complemented by cultic exclusiveness.

Some stages in the growth of the objection to images are still visible in the biblical record. Gideon's ephod and Micah's image show that at first there was no absolute ban on images in the cult of YHWH. But where these images led to can be seen in the case of the brazen serpent. Tradition ascribed its origin to Moses (Num. 21:8 f.), and for centuries it was a legitimate sacred object, yet Hezekiah was compelled to remove it because the Israelites were making burnt offerings to it (II Kings 18:4). Pillars and asherahs, once licit, eventually were banned, because in their case too, an apotheosis of "wood and stone" developed. The aspiration of Israelite religion to become the common property of all the people is what moved it in this direction. It wished to make YHWH king over all Israel, and the most readily grasped concretization of this absolute sovereignty was an exclusive cult. This is the source of its jealousy for YHWH.

Not the creation of the basic idea of Israelite religion, then, but its symbolic realization in an exclusive cult was the aim and outcome of the biblical battle with idolatry. The basic idea was present and working on every aspect of the national culture from earliest times. It eventually created its necessary cultic symbol as well. Not from monolatry to monotheism, as is the conventional theory, but from monotheism to monolatry runs the path of Israel's religious evolution. Only because monotheism existed long since could it emerge triumphant and even more purified after the political collapse. Only this prevented the people from accepting a pagan interpretation of the catastrophe; only this made them "return" to YHWH. The bulk of the nation believed that the destruction was the work of YHWH, hence there was no escape from the conclusion that they had sinned grievously, and must mend their ways. Foremost among their sins was the provocation of YHWH with "no-gods." Only a thorough extirpation of those idols could assuage his anger. In this way the great shock of the catastrophe aroused the people to accept the final cultic consequence of monotheism and to leave idolatry forever.

That a battle directed solely against idolatrous cults could succeed in Israel is the strongest evidence for the antiquity and primacy of Israelite monotheism. Christianity's battle with paganism involved an attack on myth; with a pagan audience this was inevitable. If the Exile brought about the death of Israelite idolatry without such a battle this can only mean that myth had died out long before. The new idea of Israelite religion took possession of the people in early times and so radically extirpated the pagan mythological outlook that never again could Israel as a whole be influenced by it. The new idea did not arise out of the biblical struggle with idolatry; it is the setting and precondition of this purely cultic issue.

NOTE ON THE RELIGION OF THE JEWS OF ELEPHANTINE

The religion of the Jewish garrison of Elephantine as reflected in the Elephantine papyri is an interesting phenomenon in its own right; it must not, however, be viewed as representative of the ancient popular religion of Israel. The garrison was founded before the Persian conquest of Egypt in 525; the Jews of Elephantine had spent over a century isolated in an alien environment by the time of the papyri. No Israelite writing was found among them, although the pagan Ahikar romance was. They had become assimilated linguistically and intermarried with their neighbors. Whatever "idolatry" they brought with them from their native land cannot but have been heightened in these circumstances. In contrast to the Babylonian colony of exiles they had no prophets among them, though they did have priests. Their religion can therefore be used only in a most qualified way to reconstruct the popular religion of Israel in Palestine.

Despite the various pagan god names in the Jewish onomasticon none of the "gods of the nations" after whom biblical Israel strayed (Baal, Ashtoreth, Chemosh, etc.) are worshiped by the Elephantine Jews. The peculiar divine names found in the papyri (Herembethel, Anathbethel, Anathiahu, Ashambethel) are never found in these forms in the Bible. If they were originally Israelite divinities—and this is by no means certain—they can at most have been akin to the satyrs of the popular religion that had no recognized, public cult in Palestine. How they were conceived of in Elephantine we do not know. Only YHWH is described: he is the "Lord" or "God" of heaven. Only he has a temple and festivals. Ashambethel and Anathbethel have a treasury in the temple of YHWH, but only YHWH is represented as a universal God. The minor deities (if so they be) are given a place in his temple apparently as members of his entourage. It is noteworthy that these Jews feel a distinction between their priests, whom they term *kāhanayyā* and the pagan priests, whom they term, in biblical fashion, *kumrayyā*. But it is not only the subordination of the other divine beings in the YHWH temple that testifies to the unique character of YHWH; what is decisive is the complete absence of a mythological conception of him even at Elephantine.

PART TWO

The History of Israelite Religion

Prior to Classical Prophecy

CHAPTER V

The Sources

THE POSITION OF CLASSICAL CRITICISM

Biblical tradition represents the fathers of the race and the patriarchs of Israel as monotheists. Adam, Noah, Abraham and his descendants all knew God and received his commandments. Idolatry arose as a later degeneration. This view prevails in Judaism, Christianity, and Islam, and was dominant in western thought until modern times. The evolutionary doctrine that changed the face of all sciences during the nineteenth century left its mark on the history of religion as well. If monotheism is the highest stage of religion, it must have been the latest; biblical religion cannot represent the primary stage of Israelite beliefs, but must have emerged only gradually out of lower, pagan forms.

According to the prevailing view, it was under the influence of the literary prophets that Israelite religion slowly evolved its monotheistic character. The Law, which bears the monotheistic idea, must therefore be regarded as a product of prophecy. It is a basic tenet of the critical view of the history of Israelite religion that no monotheistic literature dates to the preprophetic period.

The classic view of the school of Wellhausen distinguishes four chief sources (themselves composites) in the Torah: the J(ahwist), the E(lohist), early combined into JE, the D(euteronomist), and the P(riestly Code). Each source comprises a narrative framework within which a legal element is imbedded. JE was combined and edited in the ninth and eighth centuries B.C.; D was composed in the age of Josiah (last quarter of seventh century); P, during the Exile and the Restoration (sixth to fifth centuries). JE served, both in its narrative and its legal portions, as the basis of D, which elaborated and reworked the earlier document. D is untouched by the spirit and ideas of P. The latter, however, betrays through its conception of the desert tabernacle the influence of D's law of centralized worship, which it dates back to Mosaic times. During the time of Ezra and Nehemiah JE, D, and P were combined; the Torah book was promulgated and became the foundation of the Jewish church of Second Temple times. Occasional novellae were introduced still later—e.g., the law of the Day of Atonement which was as yet unknown in Nehemiah's time.

This hypothesis rests on several mutually complementary lines of evidence. Its methods are comparison of the laws of the Torah with the religious practice that is reflected in the historical books and the later prophets; examination of the interrelation of the legal corpora; and the study of the development of tradition as embodied in the Former Prophets and the later book of Chronicles.

Criticism of the pentateuchal laws is the most significant part of the evidence. To begin with the law of centralized worship—the historical books (Former Prophets) and the literary prophets show clearly that before the reform of Josiah, the idea of centralization of worship was unknown in Israel. The laws of JE do not know it; D inculcates it; P, according to Wellhausen, takes it for granted. This establishes the sequence: JE before Josiah, D contemporary with Josiah, P post-Josiah—more precisely, in Restoration times, when the law of centralization was taken for granted.

Israelite sacrifices show a marked evolution. At first, they consisted primarily of the peace offering, of rejoicing before YHWH; they remain so even as late as D. The sin offering is as yet unknown to D; for P, however, the sin offering is primary. Wellhausen ascribes the change to the altered mood of the people after the Exile: the natural, spontaneous, joyous element of Israel's religion was suppressed by an overpowering feeling of guilt and sin. P's sacrifices thus reflect the postexilic mood.

Israelite festivals in early times were popular and linked with agricultural and pastoral life. Their essence was rejoicing and sacred banquets; it is so represented in JE and D, which mention only the three nature festivals. For P, however, the festivals have become historical reminiscences and cultic ceremonies. Their popular features disappeared when Israel became, as it did in postexilic times, a church.

The early historical books do not attest to a sharp division of priests and Levites in temple personnel. D's term, "the Levite priests," still reflects the view that all Levites are qualified to become priests. Ezekiel is the first to conceive of limiting the priesthood to one family; from him the idea passes into the literature of postexilic times. The beginning of the sacerdotal hierarchy was the Josianic reform, in which the priests of the high places were disqualified from service at the Jerusalem sanctuary. This degradation was later legitimized and made permanent by Ezekiel; the rural priests became an inferior caste of "Levites." The inferiority of the Levites is represented in P as dating to Moses' time. But since it did not, in fact, obtain until Second Temple times, P betrays itself here as a postexilic document.

In early times, the clergy received a share in the offerings sacrificed and eaten by the people in the temples, especially on holydays. It was the offerer, however, who consumed the chief part of the sacrifice. This custom is still reflected in D, where the tithe and firstlings are eaten by the owner in Jerusalem, the law merely exhorting him to give a share to the Levite. P transforms the clerical portion into priestly dues, levied from the people and the exclusive property of the clerical class. P also increases the number of gifts, again mirroring the change that occurred in Israel after the Exile; the people have become a church dominated by priests.

The ideal government of early times was monarchic; the priests were, under the monarchy, merely royal appointees. But P depicts Israel in the Mosaic age as a theocratic church, centered about a tabernacle and headed by the high priest, Aaron. For P, the monarchy was a deflection from the theocratic ideal. But a priestly theocracy did not exist in Israel before the Exile. It was the Persian domination that enabled it to develop. P, thus, reflects the situation and ideal of postexilic times.

The history depicted in the early historical books (Former Prophets) differs significantly from that of the later book of Chronicles. The earlier works portray a people waging a normal struggle for existence. Religion does not play an inordinate part in their lives; they are not dominated by a book; prophets guide and kings rule them. Chronicles, however, changes all this; the temple and its cult are central. David, the king, becomes a cultic hero. Priests and Levites occupy the center of the stage. All the laws of P are known and publicly observed. Between the writing of the early histories and the writing of Chronicles P was composed, and the complete Torah promulgated as the basis of national life.

The Torah came in between pre-exilic Israel and postexilic Judaism. The national collapse and exile was the great watershed of Israelite religion. In pre-exilic sources—JED—the life of a natural people is reflected; in P, the life of a theocratic church. P is thus the latest document: its composition began after the covenant made by Josiah upon Deuteronomy; it was completed in the age of Ezra-Nehemiah when a "sure agreement" was made upon the whole Torah.

The structure built by Wellhausen has great persuasiveness. Its mar-

velous internal cohesiveness and apparent success in fitting details into the
large picture are what have given it an enduring appeal. In spite of the
considerable inroads of subsequent criticism, this general view of the development, the mutual relation and dating of the sources remains the
foundation of modern biblical scholarship.[1]

Several of the conclusions of this theory may be considered assured.
To this category belongs the analysis of the three primary sources—JE,
P, and D—with their laws and narrative framework. The source JE
is manifestly composed of parallel accounts, even though their unraveling
cannot always be accomplished with certainty. The tripartite separation
is clearest in the legal material. There are three legal corpora, differing
from one another in their general style and juristic terminology, containing
parallel and at times contradictory laws. These differences were recognized
by early tradition and gave rise to harmonistic exegesis which is one of the
features of rabbinic midrash. Only by accepting midrash as the plain
sense of the text can the presence of separate legal compilations be denied.

The further analysis of the various editions or recensions of each source
rarely leaves the realm of speculation. Without having demonstrated that
ancient Hebrew writers ordered their writings in a logical manner, did not
include explanatory comments and repetitions, etc., text critics regard lack
of logical order, explanations, and repetitions as signs of compilation,
expansion, and edition. Furthermore, the degree of compositeness alleged
by extreme text-criticism gives cause to doubt that even the keenest
critic could successfully unravel so intricate a skein. Be that as it may,
such analysis has little bearing on the larger questions of the history of
Israelite religion.

A second established conclusion of classical criticism is that the present
Torah book was not in pre-exilic times canonical and binding upon the
nation. The literature that was to become incorporated in the Torah
existed in various documents and versions; a single book had not yet been

---

[1] Following Hölscher and Pedersen, and under the influence of Nyberg, the Scan-
dinavian school (Engnell *et al.*) reject the scheme of classical criticism with regard to the
chronological order of the sources and the manner of their composition, while accepting the
documentary analysis in itself. They assert that the "documents" were oral traditions
that existed side by side but which were reduced to writing very late. In their view
both Torah and prophecy were fixed in writing only in postexilic times. How this school
conceives the manner in which the Torah came into being is quite unclear in details.
Particularly erroneous is their view that Torah and prophecy became written literature
only in late times. There is ample and clear testimony (beginning with Exodus 17:14)
that there existed a written literature of Torah and prophecy in Israel from earliest times.
(The religio-historical views of this school are even more paganistic than those of the
classical criticism; the same may be said of the British school of Hooke and his adherents.)

crystallized. Before the book, there was an extended period of literary creation by priests and religious writers.

Third, there are sufficient grounds, as we shall see later, for maintaining that Deuteronomy was promulgated in the reign of Josiah, and that the Torah, as a whole, was promulgated and fixed in the times of Ezra-Nehemiah.

What requires examination is the dating of the bulk of the Torah, the Priestly Code, and the relation of the Torah to classical prophecy. The crucial question is: To what extent can the Torah be used as a source for the earliest stage of Israelite religion; is its monotheism preprophetic?

THE TORAH AND PROPHECY

The revolutionary concept of the Wellhausenian view in its classic formulation was that prophecy was the fountainhead of Israelite monotheism. The literary prophets, it asserted, created ethical monotheism, and the Torah is but the later popular-priestly formulation of prophetic teaching. In spite of the growing realization that factors independent of prophecy were at work in Israelite faith, modern scholarship still accords the literary prophets a dominant and decisive role in the formation of the universal and speculative monotheism that characterizes the later stages of Israelite religion. And, since monotheism prevails in the Torah, it is still believed to reflect, especially in its ethical emphasis (e.g., in Deuteronomy), the spirit of later prophecy. Is this view valid?

Beyond the distinctions of sources within biblical books, it is possible to group the books themselves into larger units. The bases of these groupings are the idea-constants that appear in various books, bringing them into connection with one another and distinguishing them from books of other groupings. The two groupings important for our purpose are (1) the Torah-group—including the historical books (Former Prophets), and (2) the Prophets. As we shall see, the ideas of each group are so different as to preclude the possibility that the former was inspired by the doctrines of the latter.

The conventional evaluation of literary prophecy as a factor in Israel's history tends to overdraw the effect of prophetic teachings. The impression is given that each new prophetic insight immediately opened a new period in the religious life of the people, and, more important, that there was no version of the monotheistic idea that developed independent of and unaffected by prophecy. Yet there is abundant testimony to the small influence that the prophets exercised on their own age; it was only later that their work became a decisive factor in national life. The historical books never mention literary prophecy at all. The book of Kings mentions, of all the literary prophets, only Isaiah—and then not as a teacher or exhorter, but as a foreteller and a wonder-healer. Not that the authors of Kings depreciate prophecy. Here, as elsewhere in the historical books, prophecy plays a central role in the life of Israel, attesting YHWH's nearness to and concern for his people through the ages. All the more remarkable, then, is the omission of even the names of Amos and Hosea, the fathers of literary prophecy who foretold the end of Ephraim; or of Jeremiah who prophesied for many years and heralded the destruction of Judah. Needless to say, Kings does not recognize literary prophecy as a distinctive religious phenomenon, the bearer of a new message and a new interpretation of history. Had the prophetic books not been preserved, we should have known nothing of the existence of literary prophecy, let alone its distinctive ideas.

This means that the literary prophets were regarded by their contemporaries as no different from the host of other prophets. Even among their supporters and opponents, the number of those who understood their ideas was surely few. To the people, the prophets (including the literary prophets) were first of all foretellers and wonder-workers; this is the view that prevails even in Kings. The new ideas of literary prophecy did not have a significant effect upon contemporary religious life. But the fact that the book of Kings takes no notice at all of literary prophecy means more; this book (along with the rest of the early historical literature) and its religious viewpoint could not have been inspired by the teachings of literary prophecy. Is it conceivable that disciples of the literary prophets, who undertook to memorialize forever the deeds of Israel's prophets, would not so much as mention the names of their great teachers? If literary prophecy goes entirely unnoticed in the historical books it can only be that they were not its offspring. Comparison of the leading ideas in the books of the Torah-group with those of the literary prophets bears this out.

THE VIEW OF ISRAEL'S HISTORY—The prophets denounce Israel for two types of sin, moral and religious; they regard both as grounds for the on-coming destruction. At times, as in the case of Amos, the moral sin is emphasized to the virtual exclusion of the religious. The Israel of the prophets is governed by robbers and corrupt officials; its rich have expropriated the property of the poor; its orphan and widow are oppressed and undefended. The historical books, however, make no mention—not even in the most general way—of this social decay; for them Israel's sin is the worship of foreign gods and the adoption of heathen customs, nothing more. Had the Prophets not been preserved, we should have known nothing of the moral corruption. This is not to say that the historical writers were insensible to moral matters. They frequently tell of moral sins and their punishments (Judg. 9:19; II Sam. 12:1–12; I Kings 21). But for them moral sin is not a historic, national sin that taints all Israel and is to be reckoned as a cause of its downfall. Among the factors that have shaped Israel's destiny they give no part to the moral factor. The historical scheme of the writer of Judges takes no particular notice of moral sins, nor do the generalized comments of the authors of Kings. In the itemization of the causes of the collapse of Israel and Judah in II Kings 17:7 ff., all manner of cultic sins are mentioned along with the fact that prophets and seers continuously warned the people of them, but that there were prophets who inveighed against social and moral corruption goes unnoticed.[2] In spite of the historiographer's view that YHWH is a moral and just God, moral sin plays no part in the historical books as a decisive factor in the destiny of Israel.

This is the view of the Torah as well. The God of the Torah is just and moral, and the Torah is filled with his social-moral injunctions. Yet, when the Torah speaks of the causes of national punishment and exile, these are not explicitly mentioned. The archetypal national sins of Israel are the cultic defection of the golden calf, and the lack of faith in YHWH shown in the episode of the spies (Num. 13—14; Deut. 1:22 ff.). Most important for our purpose are the chapters of admonition concerning the fate of Israel in future time. Leviticus, a work in which many socio-moral injunctions are found, specifies the punishment of exile for sins of "impurity" (chaps. 18; 20). In the monition of chapter 26, while "all the statutes and judgments" are spoken of, only the sin of idolatry and neglect of the sabbatical years are explicitly mentioned. Deuteronomy also contains a highly developed system of moral laws, yet exile is threatened only for idolatry (4:25 ff.; 6:10 ff.; 7:1 ff.; 8:19 f.; 11:16 ff.). The warning of Deuteronomy 28 includes "all the commands and the statutes"; but wherever sin is specified as a cause of exile, it is the sin of idolatry (vss. 14, 20, 47, 58). The idea that idolatry is the crucial national sin is repeatedly affirmed in the closing chapters of the book, 29–32. This is the theme of Joshua 23 and 24 as well.

The chronological priority of the Prophets to the Torah-group can be defended by assuming that the moral heights of prophecy were beyond

---

[2] It is typical that the one moral sin that is singled out in speaking of Judah's collapse—Manasseh's murder of the innocents (II Kings 21:16; 24:4)—is not only introduced by "and also," as if it were a subsidiary clause, it is counted as a personal sin of the king that was also attended to on the day of doom.

the reach of the popular-priestly writers of later times. Yet it is not easy to account for the total absence of the moral factor in the historiosophy of the Torah-group, especially since these writers too believe in the moral nature of YHWH and never repudiate the prophetic viewpoint. Moreover, the Torah does affirm that Israel's well-being in its promised land will be assured by the fulfilment of one or another of the moral laws (Exod. 20:12; Deut. 15:10, 18; 16:20; and elsewhere). It is just that in the books of the Torah-group, the moral principle does not reach the level of a historically decisive factor. The writers do not draw consequences for national history from their moral principles. For the Torah-group the moral factor is not, as it is for the literary prophets, equal in historical importance to the religious-cultic. Rather than reflecting a later development of the prophetic view, the Torah-group appears to represent a historical viewpoint that has not yet attained that of prophecy. At any rate, it is clear that this view derives from a separate, non-prophetic source.

CULT AND MORALITY—The great new doctrine of prophecy was the primacy of morality over the cult: "For I desire steadfast love, not sacrifice" (Hos. 6:6). Whether or not the prophets objected to sacrifice on principle, it is plain that they considered morality the essence of religion and valued it over the cult. Later writers do not follow the prophets in their more extreme formulations of this position. Yet, when speaking of the ultimate demand that God makes of men, they, too, stress the idea that the moral goodness is the chief part of piety. Extortion and violence cannot be atoned for by prayer and sacrifice, for the cry of the oppressed ascends to God and drowns out the prayer of the oppressor. Doing kindness and keeping far from evil are the sin and whole offerings that God prefers (Ben-Sira 34:21—35:15). The primacy of morality receives popular expression in such creations as Tobit (see especially chap. 4). And that is the prevailing view of the Pharisees, as Hillel's summary of the Law testifies: "What is hateful to you, do not to your fellow" (Shabbath 31a).

In the books of the Torah-group, however, this idea is never found. The religious and the moral are given equal emphasis, and are indiscriminately juxtaposed. Not that the Torah denies the primacy of morality; it is altogether silent on the issue. It cannot be said that a later priestly bias toward ceremonial is responsible for muting the moral stress in the Torah. Later Judaism, certainly fully taken up with ceremonial, did not, as we have seen, overlook the prophetic doctrine. The absence of this idea is a sign, not of a stage later than prophecy, but of an earlier stage. There is but a step from the moral outlook of the Torah to the doctrine of primacy of morality (cf. Deut. 10:17 ff.); but this step was never taken before prophecy.[3]

The historical books of the Torah-group likewise lack this idea. Not even those prophets who are charged with a moral mission (e.g., Nathan, Elijah) enunciate this characteristically prophetic doctrine. And yet something approaching it is found—just enough to point up the contrast between the outlook of the historical books and the prophets. God swears that the sins of Eli's sons, who "despised the offering of YHWH," should not be atoned for by sacrifice or offering (I Sam. 3:14; cf. 2:17, 29). And Samuel reproaches Saul with, "Does YHWH take delight in whole and peace offerings as in obedience to the voice of YHWH? Behold, obeying is better than sacrifice; hearkening, than the fat of rams" (15:22 f.). There is, then, something higher than sacrifice. It is not morality or goodness, however, but honoring the holy things and obedience to God's will as communicated by his prophet. It is not said that moral sin cannot be atoned for by sacrifice, or that righteousness and judgment are of greater value than whole offerings. The moral teaching of the Torah-group approaches, but fails to attain, that of the later prophets. The former can by no means be considered an outgrowth of the latter.

THE DOCTRINE OF CENTRALIZED WORSHIP—There is, on the other hand, an idea in the Torah-group that has no roots in prophetic religion: the idea of the chosen cult-site that appears in Deuteronomy and the related historical literature (principally Kings). Deuteronomy bans worship at the high places after Israel arrives at its "rest and inheritance" and builds a temple at "the place which YHWH will choose" (Deut. 12). This idea came to dominate Israelite thought from the end of the monarchy; it prevails throughout the book of Kings. Kings counts the sin of worship at the high places against every king of Judah except Hezekiah and Josiah; it is one of the causes of the Exile (II Kings 17:9 ff.). For later Judaism the doctrine of the chosen site became axiomatic; reflexes of it are visible even in Christianity.

This idea has no foundation in the thought of the literary prophets who precede the promulgation of Deuteronomy. No prophet asserts that God must be worshiped at a specific site. To be sure, the prophets regard the temple of Jerusalem as sacred and as the seat of the divine presence,

---

[3] Nor can the Decalogue be regarded as a product of later prophecy. The first commandments are cultic; they are singled out for paraenetic expansion in Deuteronomy 4:15–40, where the authoritative interpretation of them in the spirit of the Torah may be seen. Now this passage sets forth the historical view characteristic of the Torah literature: what is alone crucial to national destiny is the observance of these cultic commandments.

but this does not implicate them in a repudiation of the high places. It is decisive that neither Amos, Hosea, Isaiah, nor Micah reproach the north for not sacrificing at Jerusalem. For the manner of their worship, both Judah and Israel alike come in for denunciation. Worship at the high places was tainted with idolatrous rites that the prophets attacked, but so too was the worship of the Jerusalem temple. The sole conclusion that could be drawn from prophetic rebukes was that the worship at the high places (as at the Jerusalem temple) must be purged of its heathen elements, but not that the high places must be destroyed.

Centralization of worship is thus no consequence of prophetic teaching. The prophets taught that the glory of the one God fills the earth. Did this imply that he could be worshiped only at one site? The fact is that later Judaism, in the prophetic spirit, circumvented the law of centralization; adhering to the letter of the ban on high places, it nevertheless revived them in effect in the form of synagogues. Even a temple of sacrifice, like the Jerusalem one, was erected to God in the "impure land" of Egypt.

To be sure, the ban on high places in Deuteronomy and related literature is derived from the monotheistic idea. But it is clear that this is a specifically priestly version of the monotheistic idea without roots in prophetic teaching. The prophets never drew this conclusion from their own doctrines; post-Deuteronomic prophets accept the idea, but it is not their creation. As we shall immediately see, the removal of the high places in Josiah's time was not done on prophetic initiative. That so fundamental a doctrine of Israelite religion has no foundations in literary prophecy is clear testimony to the Torah's independence of literary prophecy. In this case, indeed, it is the Torah that influenced post-Deuteronomic prophecy. It had an independent influence on the people and led them eventually to an act that was not contemplated by the preceding literary prophets.

THE REFORM MOVEMENTS—That pre-exilic monotheism was fostered by priestly and popular circles, whose thought is reflected in the Torah rather than by the literary prophets, is manifest clearly in the accounts of the reforms of Hezekiah and Josiah. These, like the earlier reforms of Asa, Jehu, and Jehoiada, are purely cultic. The narrative shows no interest in portraying these pious kings as social reformers (although the writers of Kings are aware of the royal ideal of a just and righteous judge), and there is no reason to discredit it in this matter. Even the great reform of Josiah, which occurred during the later period of literary prophecy, affected only the cult. According to II Kings 22–23, Josiah purges the land of pagan cults and faithfully carries out the great command of Deuteronomy to do away with the high places. We search in vain for a specific prophetic element in his several acts. No trace of social reform, not even so much as was undertaken in the days of Zedekiah (Jer. 34:8 ff.) or Nehemiah (chap. 5), is to be discerned. Now the prophets did not oppose these reforms; but would they have been so devoid of a social element had the literary prophets been their inspiration? To the prophets, righteousness and justice were the burning issues of the hour; the fate of the nation hung in their balance. Josiah was dismayed by the warnings of the Torah book; he is spurred to action by the fear that they inspired in him. But the warnings of the Torah do not concern moral and social corruption; they threaten disaster for religious sins alone. Hence the direction taken by Josiah—the need of the hour as he understood it—was to purge the cult of YHWH of its dross.

Nor does the book of Kings represent any prophet as among the initiators of Josiah's reform; priests are its standard bearers. Not a prophetic message, but the book of Torah, found in the temple of YHWH, gave the initial impetus. To be sure, Josiah inquires of Huldah the prophetess concerning the book, and prophets are present in the covenant assembly—but theirs is not the role of actors and executors, let alone initiators. Furthermore, neither Huldah nor the prophets assembled can, with confidence, be counted among those imbued with the ideas of literary prophecy. The message of Huldah bears all the marks of the conventional Torah viewpoint: YHWH will bring calamity upon the nation because they have left YHWH and sacrificed to other gods. Huldah is silent regarding social corruption.

ESCHATOLOGY—Prophetic eschatology reaches its climax in the vision of the universal kingship of YHWH. In future time, the "knowledge of YHWH" will fill the earth; YHWH will reveal himself to all men, idolatry will cease, and all nations will call on the name of YHWH. Although this ideal underwent changes in later Judaism—particularly with regard to the destiny of the heathen—its essence, the vision of the end of idolatry and the universal kingdom of God, remained a permanent part of Israelite religion. The peak reached by prophecy was never lost sight of afterwards.

This vision is not yet known to the books of the Torah-group. The outlook of this literature may best be described as cosmic-national monotheism. YHWH is the one and only God, but he has chosen Israel alone of all the nations to be his people. He governs the entire world, but he has revealed his name and his Torah only to Israel; therefore, only Israel is obliged to worship him. The nations are judged for violations of the moral law, but never for idolatry. The ultimate expression of this cosmic-national religion is reached in Deuteronomy; YHWH himself has apportioned false gods to each of the nations (4:19; 29:25). The Torah, thus, divides mankind into two realms: Israel, who are obliged to worship God, and the nations, who have no part in him. The idolatry of Israel is a sin, but not that of the nations. These are apparently regarded as idolatrous from their beginning; this is the natural order of things. Hence, although YHWH is a cosmic God, he shows special favor to Israel, fighting its battles against the nations.

This view was a reflex of historical reality. The fact was that only Israel did know YHWH, and this religious distinction was naïvely ascribed to the working of YHWH himself. While the same viewpoint underlies the doctrine of the prophets, they regard the past and present dichotomy of mankind as a passing phase. At the end of days all men shall worship YHWH. In contrast, the faith of the Torah sees no end to this division. It has no dream of a universal kingdom of YHWH at the end of days, nor does it look for the end of idolatry. The eschatological visions of the Torah lack the motif of a universal religious conversion; even in the golden age of the future the distinction between the Israel and the idolatrous nations remains. The eschatological vision of the Torah is of an age in which Israel will dominate its enemies, or the heathen nations (Lev. 26:7–13; Deut. 28:7–14; 30:7; 32:34–43). The prophetic elements imbedded in the historical books likewise show no trace of the literary-prophetic ideal. The prayer of Solomon in I Kings 8:23 ff. is a case in point. The author of this chapter is a universalistic monotheist. YHWH is God of heaven and lord of all the earth; wherever men are, they may pray to this universal God, facing toward his city and his house. The universalistic ideal of the literature of the Torah-group is given its ultimate expression in verses 41–43. If a foreigner comes to pray before YHWH in his house, YHWH will hear his prayer, "so that all the nations of the earth will know your name to fear you like your people Israel, and to know that your name is called upon this house that I have built." Now the hope that YHWH will assert his authority before all the nations is expressed several times in the writings of the Torah-group (Exod. 7:5; 9:16; 14:4; Num. 14:13 ff.); it is a natural sentiment of every pious person. But this hope does not imply the end of idolatry; Egypt was given to know that YHWH is God (Exod. 12:32; 14:25); yet they remained idolatrous. Jethro acknowledges the greatness of YHWH (Exod. 18:11 ff.), yet he returns to his land and his priesthood (vs. 27, cf. vs. 1). Though the nations know the fame of YHWH and his mighty deeds, they remain idol-worshipers (Deut. 4:6 f.; 28:9 f.; cf. I Sam. 4:8). The prayer of Solomon is but a more developed version of this idea. Solomon asks that all the nations learn to know YHWH and fear him like Israel, that they may realize "that YHWH is God; there is none else" (I Kings 8:59 f.). It would seem that the prophetic ideal of the return of all the nations to YHWH is implied here, but just at this point of closest approach between the Torah-group and prophecy, the gulf that separates them is most apparent. The prophet announces the coming of an age when all the nations will abandon their idols and recognize YHWH as true God. The prayer of Solomon knows nothing of such a predetermined, final resolution of history. It knows nothing of the future glory of the temple as the center of a universal religion. It expresses only a pious hope. Such a hope cannot, of course, be said to be in opposition to the prophetic vision, but it is clearly unaware of it. It is ignorant of the prophetic promise that the knowledge of YHWH will fill the earth at the end of days, and his house will be a temple for all nations. The prophets promise a universal conversion as the outcome of a tremendous historical event in which God will reveal himself to all men. The prayer of Solomon asks that YHWH become known through his fulfilling the petitions of foreigners who come to his house and the daily requests of his people (vs. 49). The story of Naaman inevitably comes to mind: Naaman the Aramaean acknowledges the uniqueness of YHWH because Elisha, his prophet, cured him of his leprosy. This is how the creators of the Torah literature conceived that knowledge of YHWH would spread among the nations. They have a universal vision, but the spirit of the literary prophets never rested upon them.

The preceding paragraphs have shown, then, that

1. in the historical books of the Torah-group, literary prophecy is never mentioned;

2. in none of the books of the Torah-group is there an awareness of the ideas originated by the literary prophets regarding the history of Israel, the relation of morality to cult, and eschatology;

3. the idea of a central chosen sanctuary, one of the pervading themes of the Torah literature, is absent in pre-Deuteronomic prophecy. The Josianic reform has, therefore, no roots in literary prophecy, though it does in the Torah literature.

Therefore, the literature of the Torah-group and the literary prophets must be regarded as distinct domains. The Torah cannot be understood as a later outgrowth of prophetic faith. Literary prophecy cannot, then, be considered the fountainhead or "ideal source" of Israelite monotheism. The development of Israelite faith was, indeed, more ramified and intricate than either tradition or modern criticism has recognized. A stratum of tradition, independent of literary prophecy, is evident in the literature of the Torah-group. From the viewpoint of the evolution of Israelite religion this stratum belongs not after, but before literary prophecy. It is the literary product of the earliest stage of Israelite religion.

THE LAW CORPORA

There is an essential difference between the redactors' treatment of the narratives and that of the legal portions of the Torah. What criticism analyzes into originally separate narrative sources has been blended by the redactors into a fairly integrated whole that only the critical eye can resolve. The laws, however, have not been so blended. Duplications and contradictions have neither been eliminated nor harmonized; there is no attempt to systematize the law of the Torah into one integrated code. The compilers have evidently transmitted the legal material as they received it, corpus by corpus. No analysis is necessary to distinguish these corpora; they are found almost entirely separate in the Torah.

Except for a few laws imbedded in the narratives, the bulk of the legal material is comprised in three continuous codes: the JE code of Exodus; the Priestly Code (P), chiefly in Exodus, Leviticus, and Numbers; and thirdly, the laws of Deuteronomy (D).[4] The mutual independence of these codes is evident from their duplications, discrepancies, and distinct terminology and style.

Thus, the larger Covenant Code containing most of JE's laws, is composed in a terse and precise juristic style. The Priestly Code is distinguished by its developed cultic terminology. The Deuteronomic Code has much of the didactic and hortatory style of a sermon.

In the laws of JE and P, God addresses Moses; throughout D, Moses addresses the people in God's name. P's opening formula, "And the Lord spoke to Moses saying: Speak to . . . and say/saying. . . ." is never found in the laws of JE or D. P alone has concluding formulas, such as, "This is the law of . . . ," "an everlasting statute. . . ." The position of the particle *kī* ("if") after the subject is peculiar to P. The impersonal subject in JE and D is *ʾīsh* (*ʾishshā*, *ʾanāshīm*); in P, it is *ādām, nefesh, ʾīsh ʾīsh* as well; these are not found in JE or D. For P's peculiar "an everlasting statute unto

---

[4] The laws of JE comprise Exodus 12:21–27; 13:1–16; the Decalogue 20:2–14; the large Covenant Code 20:19—23:19; with its epilogue, verses 20–33; the small Covenant Code 34:17–26; with its prologue, verses 10–16. The laws of P comprise the rest of the legal material in Exodus (including 12:2–20, 43–49), all the legal matter in Leviticus and Numbers, and the isolated laws of Genesis 9:1–7; 17:10–14. Deuteronomy 12–27 contains the bulk of the laws of D, though there are a few in the introductory chapters (e.g., a version of the Decalogue in chap. 5) and the conclusion (e.g., 31:10–13).

their/your generations," JE and D employ such parallel expressions as "all the days," "forever," etc. P's "dwelling places" are D's "gates"; P's *rāgam* ("stoning") is JE and D's *sāqal;* P's "native born" (*ʾezrāḥ*) is paraphrased elsewhere by "you" or "you and your sons." "I am the Lord (your God)" is a concluding formula found only in P, as are the expressions "and you shall fear your God," "a holy convocation," "congregation," "sacrifice" (*qorbān*). D has the expressions, "which I command you," "therefore I command you," about forty times; JE, but once; P, never. Peculiar to D are such expressions as, "Hear, O Israel," "your eye shall not spare," "you shall exterminate the evil from your midst," "you may not. . . ."

Ideologically, too, the codes are distinct from one another. The command to love God is found some ten times in D; P lacks this idea, but commands, in its stead, to fear God. Profanation of God's name by man is an idea found only in P. No code other than P makes the alien and the Israelite equal under the law. D is alone in ascribing a deterrent function to punishment. Stoning is the sole capital punishment known to D; P speaks also of burning and stabbing (Num. 25:8). Stripes are mentioned only in D; "excision" only in P.

These few random examples, which could be multiplied many times, suggest that the three codes are mutually independent in origin. To be sure, they have in common a large fund of laws and ideas; there are also literary contacts between them, especially between the Covenant Code and D. Yet, the differences—especially the incidental, trivial ones for which no intent can be assigned—are sufficiently marked to cast serious doubt on the conventional theory of their evolution one from another.

Classical criticism views the Covenant Code as the source and substratum of D. To the extent that D is the latest stratification of biblical law, it is true that where its laws treat of the same matter, they take a form later than that of the Covenant Code. But can one say, with the regnant school, that D incorporated the Covenant Code, making in it certain changes in accordance with its spirit? Had D taken over all the laws of the Covenant Code excepting only those which did not suit its spirit, or had it incorporated only those laws in which it made innovations, relying for the rest upon the Covenant Code, the theory of literary dependence would be justified. But, in fact, some laws appear without change in both codes; many laws of the Covenant Code are unaccountably missing from D; many others appear with inconsequential changes that can in no wise be explained as dictated by the spirit of D.

Common to both the Covenant Code and D are, e.g., the prohibition of boiling a kid in its mother's milk (Deut. 14:21; Exod. 23:19; 34:26); the kidnaping law (Exod. 21:16; Deut. 24:7); the ban on accepting bribes (Exod. 23:8; Deut. 16:19). If D is assumed to have drawn these laws from the Covenant Code, what reason can be assigned for the failure to incorporate such of its other basic laws as those about striking parents, indemnity for loss of time and physician's expenses, killing of a slave, bailees, etc. Further omissions, inexplicable on the assumption that D derives from the Covenant Code, occur, e.g., in the law of the stone altar (Exod. 20:23), which Deuteronomy 27:5 f. sets forth without the ban on steps. D shows concern for defenseless classes, yet it omits the humane provision of the Covenant Code that the slave whose eye or tooth has been injured must be freed. Nor does it mention the social law (of P and the Covenant Code) regarding the sabbatical year of the soil. D condemns to death the rebellious son and damns the child who curses his parents, yet does not mention the Covenant Code's death penalty for cursing parents and overlooks entirely the case of the son who strikes his parent. D omits the law of seduction (Exod. 22:15 f.), but includes a law of rape (Deut. 22:28 f.); it omits the ban on eating the flesh of a torn animal (Exod. 22:30), but includes the parallel ban on the flesh of an animal that dies of itself (Deut. 14:21). The Covenant Code warns against wronging and oppressing the stranger; D, despite its solicitude for these classes, omits this, having, instead, a different law framed in positive form (10:19). D forbids perverting the rights of a stranger, orphan, and widow (24:17), but neglects to mention the poor (Exod. 23:6). Deuteronomy 22:1 ff. parallels Exodus 23:4 f., except that Exodus enjoins restoring the lost property and helping the fallen beast of "your enemy," while D speaks in both cases merely of the property of "your brother." This instance alone is enough to invalidate the theory that D revised and developed, in its more generous spirit, the ancient laws of the Covenant Code. Note, too, the lowered status of the bondwoman in D. In Exodus 21:2 ff., the bondwoman is treated as a concubine, her rights are safeguarded, and she must be freed if not married. D's law treats her no differently from the bondman (Deut. 15:12 ff.). No development or revision in the spirit of D is visible here.

Such haphazard divergences can be accounted for only on the assumption that D and the Covenant Code are independent crystallizations of Israel's legal-moral literature. The common content and stylistic affinities are due to the common source. They cannot, however, be regarded as indicative of a literary-historical relationship.

Has the JE code served as the source of P? Indeed, most of JE's laws are to be found in P, yet here again differences between them—especially those which cannot be explained on the basis of P's peculiar character—preclude the assumption that P has simply incorporated the laws of JE.

Thus, P's law of personal injuries fails to mention indemnity for loss of time and physician's costs, and the case of injury to a pregnant woman. And though P mentions bailees (Lev. 5:21 ff.), it has none of the detailed laws of bailees. It speaks of the case of a man who kills an animal, but omits the laws of a goring ox, an open pit, and fire. P fails to mention the ritual prescription regarding the memorial tokens on the arm and between the eyes, though these are part of the Covenant Code and D. The cultic prohibition of boiling a kid in its mother's milk, found both in D and JE, is missing in P. P fails even to mention the three annual appearances "before YHWH" found both in D and the Covenant Code. It fails also to prohibit intermarriage with the Canaanites. And while it bans divination, mediums, and necromancy, it is silent regarding magic (see Exod. 22:17). Cursing father and mother is punished by death, but smiting parents is not mentioned. P warns against wronging the stranger, but orphan and widow, coupled with the stranger in Exodus 22:21 ff. (and always in D) are not mentioned. P's law regarding slaves (Lev. 25:39 ff.) is entirely different from that of the Covenant Code and D.

Thus, notwithstanding points of contact, P cannot have drawn its laws from, nor revised and developed, the laws of JE. When both P and D were being composed, the laws of JE had not yet attained canonical status. The laws found in JE had various formulations, and appeared in various independent crystallizations. Two such crystallizations of ancient Israelite law are the legal corpora of P and D.

Equally groundless is the view that D is an earlier stage in P's development. The fact—which will be demonstrated below—that P knows nothing of D's laws of centralized worship is enough to confute this theory. But even apart from this a genetic connection of the two cannot be maintained. Had P taken over all or most of D's laws, revising or adding to them according to its lights, such a relationship might be assumed. But P's laws are, in fact, entirely different from those of D.

P's priestly gifts do not supplement, but differ completely from, those of D. To be sure, P's gifts are more numerous, but the crucial point, so far as literary history is concerned, is that they do not include those of D. P fails to mention the priestly dues listed in Deuteronomy 18:3, and the first shearings of 18:4. It lacks the ban against working a firstling or shearing it (Deut. 15:19), as well as other cultic laws: the memorial tokens on arm, forehead, and doorpost (Deut. 6:8 f.), the purification in the case of an unknown murderer (21:1 ff.), the ban on consecrating the price of a harlot or a "dog" (23:19). P has no law about the violation of a betrothed woman (Deut. 22:20 f.), although it does legislate regarding violation of a married woman and a betrothed bondwoman (Lev. 18:20; 19:20 ff.). While P condemns to death one who curses his parents (Lev. 20:9), it omits D's law of a rebellious son (Deut. 21:18 ff.). P contains many of the social-moral laws found in D, but it inexplicably omits many others: the law concerning bribes (Deut. 16:19), removal of boundaries (19:14; 27:17), or kidnaping (24:7). Nor does it enjoin the restoration of lost property, the lending of aid to overloaded animals (22:1 ff.), and so forth.

Parallel laws in P and D exhibit divergences that cannot be ascribed to differences in viewpoint. Numbers 33:52 parallels Deuteronomy 7:1–5, 25 f. (cf. 12:2 f.), without enjoining the burning of idols or banning their silver and gold ornaments. Treating of prohibited foods, D enumerates the clean animals (Deut. 14:4 f.), P the unclean only (Lev. 11). P knows the law of the sabbath of the soil, but is silent regarding the release of debts in that year. P's enumeration of idolatrous practices in Leviticus 19:26, 31; 20:1–6 leaves out sorcery and charming, which are listed in Deuteronomy 18:10 ff. Another divergence which can only be ascribed to distinct styles is P's stock phrase "the stranger and the poor," as against D's "stranger, orphan, and widow" (the latter two are never mentioned in P).

P cannot, then, be considered a revision or adaptation of D. Each of the three codes of the Torah is to be regarded as an independent crystallization of Israel's ancient juristic-moral literature. The evolutionary sequence and literary dependence assumed by Wellhausen has no foundation.

The several early law codes that have come to light since the laws of Hammurabi were discovered in 1902 testify to the rich legal tradition of the ancient Near East. Israel's obligation to this ancient, common tradition is evident from the patent relationship between the Covenant Code and Hammurabi's laws. It has been shown by D. H. Müller that the advanced state of Hammurabi's laws, relative to those of the Covenant Code, precludes the possibility of the biblical code having borrowed from the Babylonian. The Covenant Code is to be considered rather an early formulation and crystallization of the common Near Eastern law of which Hammurabi's laws are a more advanced development. The laws of the Covenant Code are for the most part entirely in accord with the nomadic stage of Israel's prehistory as reflected in the patriarchal narratives. Even such a primitive society has room for laws about slaves, murder, damages, bailees, seduction, and magic; only those of Exodus 22:4 f. are connected with agriculture. There is nothing that compels us to look to Canaan for the origin of these laws and to assume that Israel adopted them from the Canaanites only after they had settled. We may assume that these laws had their origin in the ancient legal traditions that the early Israelite tribes shared with the other tribes and peoples of that sphere of culture. Peculiar to Israel was the organic blend of what else-where constituted three separate realms: the juridical, the moral, and the religious. Israelite tradition knows of no secular legislative authority. Ideally, only the prophet, as the spokesman of YHWH, can legislate.[5] The belief that YHWH's covenant at the time of the Exodus involved matters of justice and law (cf. Jer. 34:12 ff.) served as the basis for the peculiar Israelite mixture of law, morality, and cult. Each of the three biblical codes bears this peculiar Israelite imprint, but their roots lie deep in ancient Near Eastern culture. That each is ultimately an independent development of the ancient legal tradition is further evident from the fact that each (not only the Covenant Code) has points of contact with the an-cient literature. And this contact is not made through materials found in the Covenant Code, but directly. The three codes are thus immediately linked to the ancient Near Eastern tradition; each is a primary Israelite formulation of elements of that common tradition.

THE FIXATION OF THE CODES—What is of crucial historical importance in the fact that each of the codes has its own characteristic style is that no cross-influences are in evidence. No traces of a priestly redaction can be detected in the laws of D or JE. More important, nothing characteristic of D's style can be seen in P. Nor is there warrant for the view that JE has undergone a Deuteronomic editing. None of the laws peculiar to D—viz., laws pertaining to centralized worship—can be found in JE. Compare the laws of Exodus 23:17 and 34:23 with Deuteronomy 16:16. In each case, the three annual "appearances" before YHWH are treated, but the idea of the chosen place is found only in D. Whatever be the case regarding the alleged Deuteronomic redaction of the narratives, no trace of such a redaction is visible in the laws. The monumental fact is that not a single peculiarity of one legal corpus has insinuated itself into either of the others.

This is all the more remarkable, since these corpora are themselves composites, as is clear from the variants, repetitions, openings, and conclu-sions that can be found in them. That the three codes nonetheless remain distinguishable in style and form testifies to a highly ramified literary development. Perhaps such variety was possible just because biblical law

---

[5] A regulation concerning the division of booty is ascribed to David (I Sam. 30:25), and it is likely that in reality kings did legislate. But to no king is the writing of a law book ascribed (Isa. 10:1 refers to inditing sentences, not laws).

was not made by kings and subject to royal standardization, but was believed to be divine and was transmitted and cultivated by circles of priests and men of God. The blending of law, morality, and religion also was a factor in the plurality of forms. This was a genuine, evolving literature, not a collection of official documents. The stylistic constants point to literary schools; the internal variations show that even within each school there was room for diversity. The deeper differences that distinguish the codes from each other point to an independent literary history for each of them.

The formal distinctiveness of each of the three law corpora of the Torah excludes the view that their composition was still in process even while the Torah book was being compiled—i.e., in exilic and postexilic times. From the manner in which the narrative sources were treated we see that the redactors had nothing in principle against the blending of various sources. If revision, expansion, and innovation were still going on as the codes were being compiled, why should such care have been exercised that nothing written in the style and spirit of P be attached to the laws of the Covenant Code or D, or that no law of the Covenant Code or P be revised in the style of D. The sharp distinction of styles and codes can be accounted for only on the assumption that the formation of the Torah book took place after the period of the fixation of the codes. The codes were fixed and closed by the time the various pentateuchal sources were being collected into one book. They were incorporated into the Torah book as finished entities and neither edited, revised, nor stylized. The narrative sources were blended, but the legal corpora—the heart and essence of the Torah— were preserved intact by the compilers. They were fitted into the narrative, but each corpus was incorporated as received.

Thus, two periods can be discerned in the development of the Torah: the period of the composition of the Torah literature and the age of the formation of the Torah book. The first is an age of variegated, many-styled creativity. The second is an age of collection and ordering. The legal corpora were composed and fixed before the formation of the book. The boundary between the two periods—the end of the creation of the Torah literature, and the beginning of the formation of the book—was the reform of Josiah, inspired and guided by the Torah book found in the temple.

THE BOOK OF DEUTERONOMY

The account of Josiah's reform in II Kings 22–23 is the sole testimony in the early historical books to the public influence of a Torah book. From other general allusions to laws, statutes, and covenants, no more may be inferred than the existence in pre-exilic times of legal traditions that went back to Moses, but these cannot serve as evidence for the existence either of a Torah book like our present one or of any one of its parts. The only other biblical attestation of the public effect of a Torah book is the account in Nehemiah 8–10 of the covenant made by the Restoration community. These two passages are our chief guideposts through the maze of problems concerning the formation of the Torah book.

The story of Josiah's reform contains two elements: actions taken against idolatry and actions taken against the cult of the high places, including the centralization of the paschal sacrifice in Jerusalem. The latter appears to have been a great innovation (II Kings 23:21 ff.). From the actions against idolatry, nothing can be learned as to the book that inspired the reform, inasmuch as all parts of our present Torah denounce idolatry. But the high places are banned explicitly only in the book of Deuteronomy. On this basis, De Wette, at the beginning of the last century, concluded that Josiah's book was Deuteronomy. This view has come to dominate the field of biblical criticism, though, more recently, some vigorous dissent has been voiced. The bases of this dissent, however, are not adequate and betray a misunderstanding of Deuteronomy's idea, as well as of the acts of Josiah.

The novelty of the Deuteronomic law is not the conception of a great central sanctuary of unique importance and holiness. From earliest times, the great sanctuaries of Shechem, Bethel, Dan, Gibeon, and Jerusalem overshadowed the smaller local altars. To these great temples, it was the custom to make pilgrimages three times a year (I Sam. 1; I Kings 8). The new feature of Deuteronomy is its emphatic interdiction of all sacrifice outside the one chosen site (Deut. 12:13 f., 17, 26 f.). According to the law of JE in Exodus 13:12 ff., 22:29, and 34:19 f., firstlings are to be "given over to YHWH"; no place is specified for this surrender. D, however, expressly prescribes that this be done at the chosen site (Deut. 12:6 ff.; 15:20). The law of Exodus 12:21–27 (JE) conceives the paschal sacrifice as a home ceremony; D makes it obligatory to celebrate the rite at the chosen site (16:1–8). The Deuteronomic law goes beyond the law of JE by restricting all cultic activity to "the place which YHWH will choose." In contrast to JE, it unconditionally and absolutely forbids all sacrifice outside the central sanctuary. To be sure, D recognizes that such sacrifice was once legitimate; only when Israel arrives at "the rest and the inheritance," says Moses, must they put the law of centralization into effect and cease doing "according to all that we do here today" (Deut. 12:8 ff.). It is, thus, a formerly legitimate cult (not, as is sometimes supposed, an idolatrous one) that D now deliberately prohibits.

Deuteronomy's view that the cult of the high places was once legitimate accords with the biblical histories which show that every generation to the time of Hezekiah worshiped YHWH at high places and temples. The editorial notice of I Kings 3:2 is an authoritative interpretation of Deuteronomy 12:8 ff., showing that the erstwhile legitimacy of the high places was regarded by the historiographer as having come to an end with the building of the Solomonic temple. But the whole of the narrative of Kings testifies to the legitimacy of the high places and the temples until the time of Hezekiah-Josiah. Neither prophets, priests, nor even pious kings raise a hand against them; nor do the early literary prophets attack them.

Thus, the laws of JE (and those of P, too, as we shall see) regarding the plurality of sanctuaries as legitimate, and the laws of D forbidding it, reflect the two periods in the history of the high places. Since the idea of centralization in its Deuteronomic form does not appear in the prophetic literature or the realities of the pre-Hezekiah age, it must be assumed to have arisen later. The stratum of D concerning the centralization of worship must be considered a product of the age in which it first appears as a historical factor, the age of Hezekiah and Josiah. Thus we have a fixed point for the dating of one element of the Torah, from their relation to which the dating of the others may be inferred.

While the composition of D is a problem in itself, it is not of crucial import to the history of Israelite religion. Certain it is that D contains ancient materials, although their precise dating cannot be fixed. But, except for its final chapters, D's style and character are its own. None of its peculiarities is to be found in the four preceding books of the Torah, and nothing of them has insinuated itself into D. No part of D requires a postexilic dating, not even those passages that speak of exile and restoration (see below). How early the materials of D go is a matter of question. But one thing is plain—before the days of Hezekiah, its effect was not felt. The book emerges as a historical factor in the actions of Hezekiah and Josiah.

Two purposes are manifest in Josiah's activity, the desire to centralize worship and the desire to establish a book of YHWH's Torah as the basis of national life. This latter, no less than the former, is a distinctive feature of the Deuteronomic reform. The idea of a book of Torah as a popular book and the idea of the study of the Torah are given unique stress in Deuteronomy. The books of earlier tradition were testimonies and memorials (cf. Exod. 17:14) rather than books of study. The book of the covenant was read to the people (Exod. 24:4–7); the stone tablets are a "testimony" (31:18, etc.) and are stored away in the ark (25:16; etc.). The priestly laws were "handled" and known only by the priests. Prophets attempted to influence the people through speech and deed. Deuteronomy is the first to conceive of a Torah book, the possession of the people, to be studied, taught by fathers to sons, its precepts to be bound on the hand and written on the doorposts and gates (Deut. 6:7 ff.; 11:18 ff.). Israel's king is to write a copy of the Torah and read in it all his life (17:18 f.). It is to be inscribed publicly on stones (27:3, 8); the priests are to read it to all Israel every sabbatical year (31:10 ff.). The very style of Deuteronomy, repetitive and hortatory, is inspired by this purpose.

With this end in view, the author reworked the narrative, hortatory, and legal material that he had at hand. How the book came to be in the temple, where Hilkiah found it, we do not know. Hilkiah's book contains both warnings (II Kings 22:16), as well as laws; apparently, all of Deuteronomy to 32:47 (and perhaps some special conclusion) was included.

Deuteronomy is, thus, the first stage in the development of the Torah as a book in which the word of God is fixed and becomes binding upon the people. Later, other literary units, comprising earlier narrative and legal literature, were added to D. With Deuteronomy, the period of Torah literature came to an end, and the formation of the Torah book began.

THE ANTIQUITY OF THE PRIESTLY CODE

The fact that in the first four books of the Torah, including the Priestly Code, there is no explicit law centralizing worship was taken by the earlier critics (De Wette and his followers) as evidence of their priority to Deuteronomy. But the school of Graf-Wellhausen rejected this conclusion. P, they held, is later than D; if it does not contain a law prescribing centralized worship this is because at the time of its composition (the Restoration) this law was taken for granted. Nevertheless, P is not utterly silent on centralization; its elaborate tent of meeting is nothing but an embodiment of the idea of centralization anachronistically dated back to the time of Moses.

Now it is true that the community of the Restoration apparently did not conceive of renewing the high places, yet the complete silence of P regarding them is somewhat strange. Other matters which were no less taken for granted by P's time—the exclusive right of priests to offer sacrifice, the ancient ban on eating blood—are not, for that reason, passed over in silence. Moreover, it is not at all clear that the high places were, in fact, a dead issue at that time. There was a temple at Elephantine;

the inhabitants of northern Palestine worshiped YHWH, certainly at high places (Ezra 4:2). The temple of Onias in Egypt illustrates what was still possible in this respect even later. Why, then, does P (and even the Holiness Code, which is dated by the critics between D and P) fail completely to ban the high places?

However, it is not only that P fails formally to prohibit the cult at the high places; none of the concepts that are peculiar to Deuteronomy are present in P.

THE CHOSEN CITY AND THE CAMP—The Deuteronomic concept of centralization is not merely the abstract idea of an exclusive cult place, but the idea of an exclusive cult place at one chosen site. D's concept involves both a chosen temple and a chosen city, the latter figuring in the laws no less than the former. The popular idea of sacred sites, such as were at Bethel, Gilgal, Beersheba, to which, before the Deuteronomic reforms, festal pilgrimages were made, naturally conferred an aura of holiness upon the entire temple city. Part of the sacred activities (processions, banquets, dances) took place, not at the temple, but in the city; such celebrations in the holy city were likewise considered to be "in the presence of YHWH" (I Kings 8:65). By virtue of its sanctuary or high place, nearly every Israelite town was regarded as, in a measure, holy. Hence, lepers were expelled outside the walls (II Kings 7:3), and the death sentence, too, was executed outside the city (I Kings 21:10, 13). When D concentrated sanctity in one chosen sanctuary, this naturally affected the sanctuary city as a sacred precinct. The chosen place of D signifies both the temple and the city. Just as one must not sacrifice anywhere but in the chosen temple, so one must not eat holy things anywhere but in the "chosen place," i.e., the city. This applies to the flesh of sacrifice, first fruits, tithes, and firstlings (Deut. 12:17 f.; 14:22 ff.; 15:19 ff.). The paschal sacrifice could no longer be performed at home, but that is not all: the Israelite is further commanded to roast it, eat it, and spend the paschal night in the chosen city (16:7). Similarly, the seven days of Tabernacles must be spent in the chosen city (16:15). The court of highest appeal is located in the chosen city (17:8), and the Torah is to be publicly read there on the sabbatical year (31:10 ff.). In this way, the distinctive Deuteronomic concept of the chosen city was fashioned: a sacred precinct within which alone could certain cultic duties be performed.

Nowhere in P is this basic and peculiarly Deuteronomic idea reflected. P's tent, in accord with the needs of the wandering tribes, is a portable sanctuary; but nothing is said regarding what is to be done with it upon entering the land. P does not in fact allude to a single one of the functions which D assigns to the chosen city. P does not even mention the law of appearing before YHWH on the three major festivals, let alone the requirement that this be done at a chosen site—although it does have many other laws that were to come into force only after the settlement. Is it conceivable that any work based on D should pass silently over this fundamental law, which is really vital to the whole institution of centralized worship?

P's own system of sacred and profane precincts makes it abundantly clear that the Deuteronomic concepts are unknown to it. P distinguishes three realms: the holy place (the tent and its court), the camp, and outside the camp—the last having a pure place (Lev. 4:12; 6:4; Num. 19:9) and an impure place (Lev. 14:40–45), both of which may be embraced in the term "everywhere" (Num. 18:31). The camp corresponds most closely to the concept of the city, so that in it we might expect to find parallels to D's idea of a chosen city. What is, in fact, the case? The central precinct— the holy place—is the primary cult site, yet cultic activity goes on outside the camp as well (e.g., Lev. 4:12; 6:4; 14:3 ff.; Num. 19:2 ff.). However, impurities are also expelled outside the camp (e.g., lepers). The camp, ordinarily considered a pure place, has several laws designed to keep it pure (see below); yet none of these endows the camp with the sanctity of the Deuteronomic chosen city.

This emerges clearest in P's laws regarding the place where sacred meals may be eaten. P ordains that the priestly portion of the peace offering be eaten in a pure place (Lev. 10:14); the same applies to the firstlings (Num. 18:15 ff.). That is to say, they may be eaten both inside and outside the camp. The rest of the peace offering is eaten by the lay Israelite in a state of purity; no fixed place is stipulated (Lev. 7:19). In all the detailed laws of P prescribing the nature, the manner, and the times of sacrifice there is no reference to the place where the sacrificial meal is to be eaten, neither for the desert period nor for the period after the entry into the land. P thus fails to take notice of a basic consequence of the centralization law, that sacred meals may be partaken of only at the chosen site (Deut. 12:6 ff.). In the distinctions it makes between the holy place, the camp, outside the camp, pure and impure places, there is no reflection of the concept of the chosen city.

What, then, does P's camp—the site of a sanctuary to which no Deuteronomic concepts are attached—represent if not every Israelite city in which a high place or temple was found? The laws of Leviticus 14 open in terms of "the camp" and close (vss. 33 ff.) in terms of "the land" and "the city." "Outside the city" in verses 40, 45, and 53 exactly parallels "outside the camp" of verses 2 ff. At least two of P's camp laws were applicable to all Israelite cities: the expulsion of lepers (Lev. 13:46) and the execution of criminals outside the camp (24:14 ff.; Num. 15:35 ff.; cf. I Kings 21:10, 13; II Kings 7:3 [cf. the formulation in Deut. 17:5; etc.]). Thus P's camp represents at once a temple site as well as any city; D's separation of the two concepts is unknown to it.

Not only is the ban on worship at the high places missing in P, then, but every element of D's conception of the peculiar status of the chosen site is missing in that document.

THE FESTIVALS—The preconceptions which led the Wellhausen school to regard the festival laws of P as late have no foundations in the reality of ancient times. Fixity in times and rites and absence of "natural spontaneity" characterize the festivals of ancient Babylonia, Egypt, and all known early civilizations. Annual purifications are likewise ubiquitous, alongside of nature festivals. None of these features need be taken as the melancholy effects upon Israelite religion of the Babylonian exile. As to the historicization of festivals, this, too, has its ancient analogue in the mythological rationales given to festivals by paganism. That these elements are found in P rather than in JE or D is, in itself, no indication of lateness.

Wellhausen's characterization of P's laws, in contrast with those of JE and D, as ritualistic, fixed, and unconnected with nature, is obtained only by the arbitrary connection of Leviticus 23 with JE and D, rather than with its present context, P. But Leviticus 23, part of the Holiness Code, not only has stylistic affinities to P, it was incorporated by the priestly editor and has, therefore, every right to be taken as representing the priestly conception of festivals. The gain to the Wellhausen view by this baseless procedure is patent. Leviticus 23 not only recognizes a natural as well as ceremonial side to festivals, it provides the Israelite calendar with an agricultural festival missing from both JE and D—the celebration of the first sheaf. As for the Day of Atonement, far from being a lugubrious memorial to Israel's historic sin, it is rather an annual purification of people and sanctuary, principally from ritual impurity. It has nothing to do with the sense of historic guilt which overwhelmed the Jews in the Babylonian exile.

P's festival laws unmistakably betray a pre-Deuteronomic viewpoint. It was pointed out above that P does not prescribe the three annual pilgrimages. Now, although this law does appear in earlier codes (Exod. 23:14 ff.; 34:23 f.), it is there but one of many festival laws and is not singled out as particularly significant. Pilgrimage to a great temple was an old and a popular custom, but it was not an indispensable element of the festival. Every settlement and high place was a fit place for celebration; no essential rites were connected with pilgrimage to a sacred city. The Deuteronomic law changed this. The exclusive site of all festal rites was shifted to the chosen city; the pilgrimage now became the very condition of a proper and full celebration. That P fails to take notice of the pilgrimage is understandable from a pre-Deuteronomic viewpoint; the pilgrimage law is just another of several laws found elsewhere but omitted by P. Not that P intended to abrogate the custom of appearing before YHWH; it merely overlooked what to it was not a fundamental aspect of festival rites. Is such an oversight credible after the Deuteronomic reform had made the pilgrimage an indispensable part of proper celebration?

The law of the paschal sacrifice of P (Exod. 12:2-20) stands in open contradiction to that of D (Deut. 16:1 ff.): P ordains that the sacrifice (it is a sacrifice to P, no less than to D [cf. Num. 9:7, 13]) be performed in the home with special rites; it belongs to the type of ancient home sacrifice. D forbids the paschal celebration "in your gates." At the Restoration (Ezra 6:19 ff.) and during Second Temple times the law of D was, of course, observed, and that of P (and JE) artificially brought into line with it. Each family had its lamb; the blood on lintels and doorposts was done away with, and, most important, the paschal lamb was sacrificed and eaten only in Jerusalem (cf. II Chron. 30:1, 15; Mark 14:12 ff.; Mishnah Pesahim 5.1 ff.; 9.5). The home sacrifice of P was unknown. Its antiquity is vouched for by the fact that it is the law of JE as well (Exod. 12:21 ff.). The conception of the house as a sanctuary and the ancient popular custom of smearing blood leave no doubt that P's law antedates D.

The custom of celebrating the feast of ingathering in booths is a local, rural practice, which naturally arose before centralization. Of this festival, D preserves only the name Tabernacles; it says nothing about dwelling in booths. The seven festival days are to be spent at the chosen site "in the presence of YHWH"; apparently this is regarded by D as taking the place of all the earlier customs associated with the holyday. P, on the other hand, says nothing about appearing before YHWH, but still speaks of celebrating in booths. In postexilic times, the people at first endeavored to combine the laws of D and P; Nehemiah 8:13 ff. tells of a celebration at Jerusalem, in booths. But since this was quite impracticable, the law of Deuteronomy 16:15 was eventually foregone, and the older custom of erecting booths everywhere (=P) was reinstated (cf. Sifre, *ad loc.*).

Exodus 23:19 and 34:26 show that anciently the first fruits were brought to the temple. Since the first fruits were given to the priest (cf. Deut. 18:4) in the form of loaves (cf. II Kings 4:42), we may assume that on the festival of first fruits, the latter were brought to the temple as baked loaves, just as we find in Leviticus 23:15 ff. This offering was naturally made by each individual farmer, the performance of the rite permitting him to enjoy his new produce. That it was an individual offering is clear from the terms of Leviticus 23:22 and the analogous law of first fruits in Deuteronomy 26. The terms of a parallel first fruits law of P itself, Leviticus 2:14 ff., leave no doubt that an individual offering is involved. The plain meaning of Leviticus 23:10 ff. (notwithstanding later sectarian controversies) is that on the morrow of the first Sabbath after reaping began, each farmer was to bring to the local sanctuary a sheaf for waving before YHWH to sanctify and bless his harvest. Seven weeks later, at the end of the reaping, having left the corners of the field and the gleanings to the poor (Lev. 23:22), he is to bring a "new meal offering" of the first fruits to YHWH. These agricultural rites were, in the first instance, celebrated in the local sanctuaries. Deuteronomy separates the first fruit offering from the festival, prescribing a special rite at the central sanctuary that is no longer related to the festival (Deut. 26). In later times, the laws of P and D were combined; the first sheaf and two loaves of the new meal offering were turned into communal offerings which were brought to the chosen site.

THE TENT OF MEETING—The theory that P symbolizes the idea of centralization by the Mosaic tent of meeting, as if to represent Second Temple conditions as Mosaic institutions, is groundless. P, as we have seen, does not contain a single law in which centralization in its Deuteronomic form is expressed. To insist that the later idea of the single sanctuary is the true meaning of the tent is arbitrary. P must be interpreted only in its own terms, and these are quite plainly unaware of the Deuteronomic idea of centralization.

P's tent is the realm of the holy. Unlike D's "place," it is not a fixed, chosen site, but a portable sacred inclosure, the dwelling place of the divine presence. Outside the tent is the realm of the profane and the impure. The contrast between these realms is the subject of Leviticus 17:3 ff. (P, Holiness Code): "Whoever . . . slaughters an ox, or lamb, or goat in the camp . . . or outside the camp, and does not bring it to the door of the tent of meeting to present it as an offering to YHWH . . . that man shall be cut off from among his people. To the end that the Israelites may bring their sacrifices which they sacrifice in the open field . . . to YHWH . . . and they shall no more sacrifice to the satyrs after whom they go astray." If this law were composed after, and in accord with, D, its effect would have been to ban that profane, non-sacrificial slaughter which is legitimized by Deuteronomy 12:15 ff. This is indeed how Wellhausen interprets it. Thus interpreted, the law in effect bans the eating of meat for the bulk of the people, who were unable to bring their animals to the Jerusalem temple (supposedly represented by the tent) for sacrificial slaughter. The absurdity of this law (conceded by Wellhausen) is heightened if it is further assumed that it was composed after the Exile when Jews were so scattered as to utterly exclude their bringing their sacrifices to Jerusalem. The only plausible interpretation of Leviticus 17:3 ff. is that it presupposes the existence of many legitimate local sanctuaries, each of which is represented here by the tent.

Where in the history of sacrifice does this law belong?

I Samuel 14:32–35 shows that profane slaughter was nonexistent in early Israel. To legalize the flesh eaten by the soldiers, Saul requires that the animals be slaughtered on an improvised rock altar. This does not mean that every slaughter was considered a genuine sacrifice. Note that Saul does no more than sprinkle the blood on the stone, whereas genuine sacrifice involved burning the fatty parts (I Sam. 2:16). It does mean that in early times every slaughter had a cultic aspect, the sprinkling of blood on a specially sanctified stone "altar" to YHWH. It was forbidden to let the slain beast's blood spill "to the ground" (ʔarṣā, I Sam. 14:32), to "eat upon the blood" (ᶜal haddām, vss. 32 f.). Stone field altars of this sort were presumably numerous, and the sprinkling rite not considered so solemn as to be forbidden to the laity. Hence, slaughter for eating is usually mentioned without reference to a ritual. P too forbids "eating upon the blood" (Lev. 19:26), agreeing in this with I Samuel 14:32 f. This prohibition is necessarily pre-Deuteronomic. For D's ban on sacrifice at the high places inderdicted the quasi-sacrifice of the type made by Saul as well. In the case of slaughter for eating, D commands, instead, to spill the blood "on the earth like water" (Deut. 12:16, 24), i.e., to "slaughter to the ground" and "eat upon the blood." That which P forbids categorically D expressly sanctions.

Before D, then, there was a distinction between genuine sacrifice (e.g., votive or festal offerings made usually in temples by priests) and quasi-sacrifice (of the type made by Saul for eating). Entirely profane slaughter was nonexistent, except for non-sacrificial game animals (e.g., the gazelle and the hart [cf. Deut. 12:15]) whose blood even Leviticus 17:13 permits to be spilled to the ground without ceremony. D's concentration of every cultic act in the central sanctuary necessitated its innovation of profane slaughter, performed without an altar and involving the spilling of the blood "to the ground." Now, since every beast became like the game animals of the early law, "pure and impure alike" could eat from every slaughter. D puts cattle and sheep, which could be slaughtered previously only with a quasi-sacrifice, on the same footing as these game animals, which were always eaten "upon the blood" (Deut. 12:15 f.).

Where does the law of Leviticus 17:3 ff. fit into this development? Leviticus 17:3 ff. warns against "sacrificing any longer . . . to the satyrs"; the slaughter spoken of was, therefore, sacrificial, if not always made to YHWH. What is banned by this law is, then, not the profane slaughter of D, but the quasi-sacrificial slaughter on field altars of the Saul type— slaughter without priest or temple. Such field rites were liable to lead Israel astray after the satyrs. To prevent this, all slaughter must be performed at a temple, by a priest. To Leviticus 17, all slaughter (except that of game) is sacramental, whether for food or for worship. It has a cultic side which is directed either to YHWH or to the satyrs. Thus P, like D, bans the Saul-type quasi-sacrifice, but for an entirely different reason. D bans it as part of its interdiction of the cult of the high places; hence, it sanctions profane slaughter at any place. P bans it to the advantage of the high places and temples; it does not provide for—because it does not need—profane slaughter. Leviticus 17 does not oppose one sanctuary to many, but sanctuary to no-sanctuary, YHWH to satyrs. It demands not that sacrifice be restricted to one sole sanctuary, but that sacrifice be made at a legitimate sanctuary, not "in the field."

The development of the sacrificial law was thus as follows: At first, eating "upon the blood" (i.e., without a quasi-sacrificial rite) was forbidden; Saul-type field altars were permitted for this rite (I Sam. 14). P also forbids eating upon the blood, but it does not countenance Saul-type sacrifice and field altars; it regards only legitimate temples and high places as qualified for slaughtering. D disqualifies the high places and restricts all sacrifice to the one chosen site; hence, it permits the "spilling of blood to the ground."

To be sure, P knows of but one legitimate sanctuary, the tent of meeting. But P's tent is not represented as a law, but as a historical fact. Anciently, there was but one tent in which YHWH revealed himself to Israel, hence it was the only legitimate cult place. There is no intention, however, to exclude the legitimacy of many temple sites in the land after the conquest. That is why P is silent about the sin of the high places; it recognizes no such sin.

P does, however, give full recognition to the legitimacy of many sanctuaries to YHWH. The stories about the concubine at Gibeah (Judg. 19–21), in which Wellhausen himself detects a priestly redaction, mention four legitimate cult places: Bethel, Mizpah, Shiloh, and an undefined place in the hill country of Ephraim. Since P contains no law concerning a new kind of central sanctuary to succeed the tent when Israel comes into its land (corresponding to the Deuteronomic law of the chosen site), it evidently regards the single desert sanctuary as no more than a phenomenon of the past. For the present and future the multiplicity of sanctuaries is taken for granted, as a passage of the Holiness Code incidentally reveals: "I shall make your temples desolate and no longer savor your pleasing odors" (Lev. 26:31). YHWH has many temples in the land at which "pleasing odors" are offered to him; these he threatens to demolish in the day of his wrath. Significantly enough, the post-Deuteronomic parallel to this passage in Ezekiel 6, omits "temples."

This local unity of worship that P depicts for Moses' time is not, however, a concept peculiar to priestly writings. JE also knows of only one camp, one tent, one ark, and one leader. P adds a priestly touch by insisting that only a sanctified precinct—and in the desert there was only one such precinct—is qualified for sacrifice. If this results in "centralization of worship" for the desert period, it is not as a demand and a law, but as a historical necessity. With the passing of the tent, the conditions of desert centralization pass away also. For the future, the uniqueness of the tent is no more a law than the uniqueness of the other archetypes of P: Moses, the archetypal prophet, Aaron, the archetypal priest, etc. Just as Moses was followed by other prophets, Aaron, by other priests, and the camp, by other "camps" (Israelite settlements), so the tent was succeeded by temples and high places. For P, it is the sanctity of a consecrated inclosure that is essential; in the desert period, there was only one such inclosure, built according to a divine plan and sanctified by the divine presence. In the future, however, when each "camp" has its own "tent," the "centralized worship" of the desert period will no longer exist. D's centralization, on the other hand, differs fundamentally in being linked with an exclusive site to be chosen in the future. This can only come to pass after Israel has come into "the rest and the inheritance." That is why D knows of no centralization, in its sense, in the Mosaic period, but only in the future.

The idea that the tent is a reflex of the Second Temple is a baseless contention of modern criticism. P's tent, like that of JE, is, as its very name (tent of meeting) suggests, the place where YHWH meets and reveals himself to men (see the interpretation of Exod. 25:22; 29:42 ff.). P adds to JE's conception the idea that YHWH gave Moses laws in the tent (Lev. 1:1 ff.). For P, the cultic activity in the tent, as it were, but provides the setting for divine revelation. It must be stressed that the chief sacrifices of P, the holyday offerings (Lev. 23; Num. 28), do not become obligatory until the settlement in the land (Lev. 23:10). In the desert, only the Passover (which had no connection with the tent) and the Day of Atonement (Lev. 17) are said to have been celebrated. The communal cult performed in the tent during the desert period was restricted, according to P, to the daily sacrifices, the candelabrum, the incense, and the atonement rite. Apart from this, only individual sacrifices were brought (not even these were to be offered outside the land according to Num. 15:2). P's tent, then, is a priestly-prophetic vehicle, with the prophetic, the oracular, predominating. The lustrations performed in the tent are designed to make it fit for divine revelation, for lawgiving, for judgment, for guiding the people through the desert, for the Urim and Thummim. None of this is a reflection of the situation in the age of the Second Temple.

For by postexilic times the ancient channels of divine revelation were all but stopped up. The Second Temple was never a priestly, let alone a prophetic, oracle (the Urim and Thummim were not remade). The detailed description of the tent and its vessels, the functions of its Levitical porters and guardians, the wood and metal altar (the Second Temple had a stone altar, Ezra 3:2) were entirely without practical application in Second Temple times. The roles of the porters and singers of the Second Temple, on the other hand, are not even hinted at in P (contrast the anachronism of Chronicles which predates them to David's time). P takes pains to describe the desert cult as part of its historical narrative, which served, like JE, as a framework for priestly legislation. To priestly historians, such details were intrinsically interesting. Whatever points of contact exist between the portable oracle-tent of P and the Second Temple are due to the later endeavor to put into effect as much as possible of the archaic legislation of P. However, the Second Temple is but a pale reflection of the desert tent, because the tent's oracular, military, and prophetic aspects have disappeared; nothing remains but the cult. And this cult, based largely on the ancient scrolls of P, was the basis of the Jewish church of Second Temple times. Even so, the resemblance is superficial. For what postexilic Judaism scrupulously adhered to was not the cultic prescriptions of P, but the harmony of the cult laws of P interpreted in the light of D. What made the Second Temple the center of the "theocracy" were just those festal pilgrimages, and the various obligations connected with the "chosen place" that belong to the program of D. But precisely these matters have no place in P, and have no connection with P's tent.

THE HIGH PRIEST AND THE CONGREGATION—Another sign of P's lateness is seen in the exalted role of the high priest in P's congregation. His purple dress, diadem (ṣīṣ), and anointing are the accouterments of a royalty that is otherwise absent in the camp of P. He appears as the symbol of holiness and of leadership. This picture is taken as mirroring the age of the Second Temple, in which temple and priesthood stood at the head of a kingless theocracy. Only under foreign rule could such a church community and a theocratic ideal as depicted in P have arisen.

This view, too, will not bear examination. To begin with, P's attitude toward the monarchy is plainly favorable, as Genesis 17:6, 16; 35:11 attest; the promise of royal offspring crowns God's blessings of the patriarchs. That the Israelites have no king in the desert is not a peculiarity of P's account; neither in JE are there stories or laws concerning kings. P's representation of the monarchy as a divine blessing and promise for the future is enough to show that its desert camp is not intended to depict the ideal form of Israelite society.

Nor does P's portrayal of the Mosaic age reflect the conditions of the Second Temple period.

P's camp is not a church, but an armed camp of the host of Israel (Exod. 6:26; 12:17, 51; cf. Num. 1:3, etc.). The order of march is exactly prescribed (Num. 2); rules of war (10:9) and the division of booty (31:25 ff.) are subjects of its legislation. The purpose of the armed camp is not cultic exercise under the protection of foreign rulers, but the conquest of Canaan. The land is spied out (the parts of Num. 13–14 belonging to P), and the request of the two and one-half tribes to settle in Transjordan is granted only on condition that they join in battle with their brothers (chap. 32). To be sure, the features of this camp are drawn unrealistically, but there is no essential difference here between P and JE.

At the head of this camp stands not the priest, Aaron, but the prophet Moses. The importance of Aaron is restricted to the realm of the cult. P—differing in this from D—does not even assign the priests a juridical function. Even in his own sanctuary, however, Aaron is not supreme; Moses apportions all tasks and consecrates both Aaron and his sons. All temple personnel, Aaron included, are answerable to the prophet for what goes on in the tabernacle (Lev. 10:16 ff.). In the camp itself, the priest has no authority. It is Moses who dispatches the spies, who sends Phinehas with the sacred vessels and trumpets to the war with Midian. Moses' successor, Joshua, stands in a similar relationship to the priest Eleazar who inquires for him by the Urim, in the same manner as priests of the early monarchy served their kings (Num. 27:21).

Beside the prophet, P recognizes the secular authority of chiefs, the clan heads. These appear to be P's archetype of the later kings. They endow the tabernacle (Num. 7), as later kings do the temple (II Sam,

8:11 ff.). In P's laws, the king is alluded to in the term *nāśîʾ* (Lev. 4:22 ff.).[6] That the high priest precedes the *nāśîʾ* in the order of sin offering in Leviticus 4 signifies nothing as to his political authority, but is due rather to his supreme cultic position. He is most holy, his sin is most dangerous, hence his purification precedes that of all others. The same applies to the law of Numbers 35:25 ff. which provides that the unintentional slayer reside in the city of refuge until the death of the high priest. It is to be observed that not the accession of a new priest—as in the case of royal amnesties—but the death of the incumbent priest is the decisive moment. This is because his death is regarded as atonement for innocent bloodshed; compare verses 31 ff.[7]

The priestly diadem (*ṣîṣ* "rosette," called *nēzer* "crown" in Lev. 8:9) and anointing are genuine points of contact between the priesthood and the monarchy. But these symbols are not in themselves signs of authority, but of sanctity and importance. The king's *nēzer* (crown) is a mark of his sanctity as is the hair of the Nazirite—likewise termed *nēzer* (Num. 6:7). Anointing of kings is similarly a sacrament that has been borrowed from the sacerdotal register by royalty. What tells decisively against the Wellhausen view is the fact that precisely in postexilic times high priests were no longer anointed.[8] That P makes unction a mark of high priesthood is thus a sign of its antiquity.

The idealized high priest of P stands, not in the place of, but beside the prophet-judge. His authority is founded on his oracle, the Urim, which is of crucial and living significance to P, as can be seen from Num. 27:21. P also assigns to the priest a role in war; at the command of the prophet-leader he accompanies the army into battle bearing the holy vessels and trumpets (Num. 31:6).

[6] Note that P interchanges *nāśîʾ* and *melek* in Numbers 25:18 and 31:8; *nāśîʾ* means "king" in I Kings 11:34 too. The law of Exodus 22:27 was later understood to include the king, as can be seen from its application in I Kings 21:10. That Ezekiel frequently uses *nāśîʾ* for "king" proves only his debt to P. There was no *nāśîʾ* in postexilic times, and certainly it cannot be supposed that anyone thought then of reconstituting the long defunct office of tribal chief. Not even Ezekiel, who revives the tribal division of the land, contemplates resuscitating the chiefs. P's attention to the *nāśîʾ* is another indication of its remoteness from the realities of post-exilic times.

[7] The high priest referred to belongs to the manslayer's home town, just as "the congregation" of verses 24 f. refers to his community. There is no warrant for assuming that the Deuteronomic chosen city or its priest is referred to, beyond the desire to read into this text a correspondence to the conditions of postexilic times.

[8] Unction, like the Urim and the ark, was not reinstituted in Second Temple times. Neither the books of Maccabees nor Josephus mentions the anointing of priests or kings. The "anointed" of Daniel 9:25 f. is an archaism. A tannaitic tradition (Yoma 52b) counts the anointing oil among the features of the Solomonic that were lacking in the Second Temple. The high priest of later times was distinguished only by his apparel.

This is precisely the status the priesthood aspired for and achieved in pre-exilic times. The priests of the early monarchy stand at the right hand of kings. State decisions are made according to their oracles—as in Babylon, Egypt, Rome, etc. In war, they march with the army to sanctify the armed camp (I Sam. 4; N.B. that here, as in Num. 31, it is the *sons* of the chief priest that go into battle). At times, the high priest had a voice in determining the royal succession no less than that of the army (I Kings 1:7 ff.; II Kings 11). The family of Eli at Shiloh seem even to have enjoyed a sort of autocracy over their temple. The ancient priesthood is, thus, faithfully mirrored in the ideal of P: an exalted status beside the political-military leader, based chiefly on the priestly oracle and the priest's role as sanctifier of the armed camp. This ideal disappeared in late times. The authority of postexilic high priests was not grounded on the Urim—which were non-existent (cf. Ezra 2:63)—nor on their role in wartime. There is, thus, no connection between the priestly ideal of P and the position of priests in the age of the Second Temple.

THE ENDOWMENT OF THE CLERGY—It has long been accepted that the Deuteronomic provisions for the endowment of the clergy antedate those of P. Wellhausen gave this view its classic formulation: D's sacred gifts—tithes and firstlings—are not given to the priests, but are eaten by the owners at the chosen place as peace offerings. This was the ancient popular custom. The idea of P to transform the sacral meal into an outright gift to the clergy is a product of the postexilic hierocracy. The transformation took place in the Exile, or at the beginning of the Second Temple period. P is, therefore, a postexilic document. Eissfeldt criticized this view in detail; yet he, too, conceded that the critical dating of P to exilic times and later "will remain a firm foundation of biblical criticism."[9]

Now it is true that P's gifts outnumber those of JE and D. But, this does not in itself signify lateness. Being a collection of priestly toroth, P naturally gives more room to priestly and temple matters. It must further be considered that P presents no harmonious and ordered system of priestly dues, but mentions various dues in various literary corpora. Presumably, local customs are represented here which did not form a single system of sacred dues until they were gathered together. P's laws are certainly not an expansion of those of D, for they do not include D's dues—P ignores the second tithe, the sacrificial portions that D assigns to priests,

---

[9] In *Erstlinge und Zehnten im Alten Testament* (1917) Eissfeldt showed that as regards heave offerings, firstlings, and tithes P demands nothing beyond what is in JE. He also concluded that already in pre-exilic times the offerings were priestly dues. Moreover, he takes exception to the view that P's dues are so numerous as is usually asserted. The citation is on p. 166 of this work.

the first shearings—but sets forth an entirely different enumeration. Furthermore, a comparison of what is common to the three legal codes reveals that P is closer to JE than to D.

All three codes agree that first fruits are given to priests and not eaten by the owner. Exodus 23:19 requires the farmer to bring his first fruits to the house of YHWH. Presumably, there was a rite of consecration, after which the produce was given to the temple priests, to be eaten by them. P, too, provides that first fruits be brought to YHWH (Num. 18:12 f.). They constitute a heave or wave offering (vs. 11), an allusion to the acts of consecration in the temple. Both laws assume the existence of local sanctuaries whose income was derived from the gifts of local farmers. In D, matters are quite different. The abolishment of local sanctuaries required that the delivery of first fruits to a priest be separated from the rites of consecration in a temple. D, therefore, legislates that the first fruits be given to the priest (Deut. 18:4), saying nothing about bringing to (the house of) YHWH. The ancient custom was preserved in a new, special rite of bringing first fruits to the chosen house (26:1 ff.). This new rite, however, has no fixity. Some of the first fruit (*mērēshīth*)—not all—is to be brought to the central sanctuary whenever the owner finds an opportunity. As a rule, then, the first fruits are to be given to the priests at large; on occasion, however, a basket of them is to be brought to the priest at the chosen house. Between the practice reflected in the law of JE and P on the one hand, and in that of D on the other came the idea of centralization of worship.

Deuteronomy enjoins that male firstlings be brought to the chosen city, and there be consumed by the owner in a festal meal (12:6, 17; 14:23; 15:19 f.). However, this was not the earliest view regarding the disposal of firstlings. JE prescribes that "on the eighth day you shall give him to me" (Exod. 22:29), "all that opens the womb first is mine" (34:19). The idea is that the firstling is the sacred property of God, like the first fruit which even D assigns to the priest. Human firstborn, which were also given to YHWH (sometimes literally, see Mic. 6:7), must be ransomed (Exod. 34:20 [JE])—evidence enough that the firstling was considered the property of God. The same idea motivates JE's law that the firstling of an ass must be ransomed (from the temple) or killed (*ibid.*). A trace of this taboo still lingers in D's injunction not to shear the firstling (15:19).

P's law agrees in principle with that of JE; the firstling is delivered to the priest who offers it as a peace offering and eats its flesh. The firstlings of all impure animals (like the ass of JE) must be ransomed (Num. 18:15 ff.). The ancient obligation to "make the beast over to YHWH" (Exod.

13:12 [JE]) is fulfilled by consecrating it and delivering it to YHWH's priest. That JE too knows the custom of redemption suffices to show that it as well regarded the firstling as contributing to the clergy's endowment.

In D only a faint trace of the ancient conception remains in the prohibition of shearing and working the firstling (15:19). The sanctity of the firstling is instead subsumed under that of the chosen place, and is embodied in the law requiring the owner to eat it in the sacred city. How great a departure this was from the early popular tradition of the sanctity of firstlings is clear from D's silence concerning redemption either of animal or human firstborn. D's conception may, perhaps, have been based on some local custom; clearly, however, it does not derive from the view that prevails in the earlier sources. In the earlier view, the firstlings even of impure animals and man were regarded as sacred, proof enough that D's idea of them as a peace offering to be eaten by the owners is not primary. The firstling law of P, then, is older than that of D.

Most illuminating, however, is a comparison of the tithe laws of D and P. Numbers 18:21–32 prescribes that a tithe be levied for the Levites; from this, a tenth again is set aside for the priests. The latter "tithe of the tithe" alone is holy; the rest is profane, and may be eaten by the Levite "anywhere." D requires that annually a tithe of produce be levied. This tithe is holy and, though eaten by Israelites, must be eaten only in the chosen city and in a state of purity (Deut. 14:22–27; 26:13 ff.). Still another tithe law occurs in Leviticus 27:30–33, according to which all tithes, animal and agricultural, are holy and belong to the sanctuary or priest.

What is the relationship of these laws to one another?

It must first be recognized that these are three distinct tithe laws, notwithstanding the efforts of tradition and modern criticism alike to reduce them to two by identifying the priestly tithe of Leviticus 27 now with the Levitical, now with the lay tithe of D. The context of Leviticus 27 deals with divine property, use of which may not be enjoyed by the laity without redemption. This, together with the absence of a provision requiring that it be consumed in the chosen place, makes it plain that the tithe of Leviticus 27 has nothing to do with that of D. To identify it with the Levitical tithe is equally mistaken. Levites are nowhere mentioned. Moreover, this tithe—unlike the Levitical—is entirely holy; no distinction is made between a profane portion belonging to Levites and a sacred portion belonging to the priest. In sum, there are no grounds for combining and reducing the three tithes to two.

Now the animal tithe of Leviticus 27 is taken to be a later hierocratic expansion of the agricultural tithe of Numbers 18. But tithing animals, far from being a sign of lateness, is a genuine mark of antiquity, being rooted in the early pastoral age of the Israelite tribes. On the other hand, the age of the Second Temple, as testified to by Josephus and the Mishnah knew of no priestly tithe of animals. Most important, that age knew of no tithe that properly belonged to priests at all. Only the early periods knew of such a tithe. Jacob, the herdsman, vows to erect in Bethel a "house of YHWH" and give a tithe of all his property to it (Gen. 28:22). Abram gives to the priest Melchizedek a tithe of all his booty (14:20). This early priestly tithe was not an annual obligation, but a votive or freewill offering. The votive tithe of Jacob in Genesis 28 was archetypal for the later Israelites who followed Jacob's example when petitioning God. Abram, too, gives a freewill tithe of booty to a priest. Later the sacerdotal share of booty was fixed by law (Num. 31). Amos 4:4 refers to such votive tithes. They belonged to the temple and the priest, and were regarded, of course, as holy and taboo to their lay owners. From the fact that this tithe is represented as levied from "all," not merely from animals or that which might be eaten, it is clear that the conventional notion that it originated as a sacred meal is mistaken. The early tithe was a gift to the temple or priesthood; it was a freewill or votive offering, not a yearly obligation.

This is the meaning of the law of Leviticus 27. The context deals with types of vows and devotions, and their redemption and exchange. The firstling, which is automatically holy and hence cannot be consecrated by man, is explicitly excluded from discussion (vs. 26), what is said about it being only incidental. As to tithes, the law is: if a man tithes produce (as a votive or freewill offering), it may be redeemed; not so animal tithes. Tithe (*ma‘asēr*) is here used—like valuation (*‘erek*) and devoting (*ḥerem*) in the preceding verses—to mean a voluntary consecration.

This priestly tithe was unknown to postexilic times. When necessity later forced the transfer of the Levitical tithe to priests (see below), it was not this passage that was invoked as a warrant. For this law was no longer understood by Second Temple times, much less could it have been written then. To the contrary, Leviticus 27 is one of the oldest passages of the Torah.

The Levitical tithe of Second Temple times was an annual obligation based in part on Numbers 18:21 ff. It was the amplest of all sacred gifts, and after having been appropriated by the priests, in contravention of the law, it was the source of wealth and power of the priestly aristocracy. Classical criticism dates this law to exilic or postexilic times. But is it credible that the priestly authorities of later times bestowed this most lucrative of all sacred gifts upon lowly temple servants? The fact is that the numerous priests of postexilic times (according to the lists in Ezra 2:36 ff. and Nehemiah 7:39 ff., they number in the thousands) were unable to live on the heave offering and the sacrificial portions that were assigned to them by the Torah. The latter especially became negligible when the many altars were done away with, and the entire priesthood had to share the sacrificial portions of the single postexilic altar. On the other hand, the Levites of the Restoration were few and powerless (Ezra 2:40 ff.; cf. 8:15 ff.). It was probably shortly after Nehemiah's time that, acting under the constraint of economic realities, the priests appropriated the tithe from them (cf. Josephus *Antiquities* xx. 8.8; 9.2; *Life* 15). For a long while the legality of this appropriation was in doubt, though the priests justified their action by "the penalty of Ezra."[10] In this manner the incompatibility of the tithe law of Numbers 18 with postexilic conditions was resolved. That the priests of those times should have created a tithe law which condemned them to penury, only to annul it in effect shortly afterward, is, of course, an absurd assumption. The Levitical tithe of Numbers 18 was, by the beginning of Second Temple times, an obsolete law, a relic of another age.

What are the terms of that law? By the time of Nehemiah the later Jewish interpretation of this tithe as an annual due was already in effect (Neh. 10:36–38; 13:10 ff.). But in itself the law of Numbers 18:21 ff. makes no such stipulation. Verse 21 speaks of "every tithe in Israel" belonging to the Levites just as verse 14 speaks of "every devoted thing in Israel" belonging to the priests; in neither case is a temporally fixed levy involved. The Levitical tithe need not be lifted from produce (as must the sacred levies given to the priest [Num. 15:17 ff.]) in order to release it for consumption by the laity. Hence there is no reason to take it as an annual obligation. It is rather a votive offering which is to be given to the Levites. As their "wages" (vs. 31) it is, on the one hand, profane and therefore may be eaten "anywhere"; on the other hand, as a votive offering it contains a holy element which must be separated before it may be eaten profanely. This holy part is the priest's and the Levite who eats it will bear guilt (vs. 32). The law provides for disposing of the votive sanctity by the "tithe of the tithe" which the Levite must give the priest, thus releasing the rest from the sanctity of the vow.

The Levitical tithe law obviously belongs to a time when the Levites were still numerous and served a significant function. The custom of

---

[10] Yebamoth 86b, Hullin 131b, and parallels. Ezra penalized the Levites for having refused to leave Babylonia by giving their tithe to the priests. It is significant that in the quest for a justification of this transfer it apparently occurred to no one to invoke the law of Leviticus 27:30 ff.

vowing tithes must have been widespread and served to maintain them. When the Levites afterward dwindled in numbers and importance the tithe law of Numbers 18 became obsolete. Tithes were brought, instead, to the temples in pre-exilic times. But this obsolete law still remained on the priestly scrolls and was to play a decisive role later.

In Second Temple times we find no trace of a votive or freewill tithe; nor do we find a priestly or temple tithe. The tithe has become a burdensome annual due, largely profane and belonging in law (according to Numbers 18) to the Levites (cf. Neh. 13:10 ff.). How can we explain this transformation which conflicted so with the realities of postexilic times? Even more puzzling, how can we explain the absence in P of a tithe law which would suit the then existing conditions? To the priesthood in particular the disposition of the tithe was a vital matter. Only one explanation is possible: by postexilic times P was a collection of ancient laws that later generations did not presume to alter by even so much as a letter. One could only interpret and harmonize midrashically. The annual Levitical tithe of Second Temple times, which was so remote from realities, is a product of midrashic exegesis.

It is in D that an annual tithe, to be brought to and eaten in the chosen city, first appears. This tithe is not based on popular custom; in its present form, it is one of the devices invented by the author of the law of centralization to link the people with the chosen city. We do not know to what extent it was put into practice in pre-exilic times. On the Restoration community, however, it had a decisive effect. For among the obsolete laws of P that the Jewish church sought to bring into harmony with D were the tithe laws. The early popular custom of vowing tithes had been forgotten or, perhaps, had been replaced by D's peculiar law. The priestly tithe law of Leviticus 27:30, no longer understood, was interpreted in connection with Deuteronomy 14:24-26 (see Sifre *ad loc.*). P's Levitical tithe was interpreted in the light of D as an annual due, and was accepted as such by the signers of the "sure agreement" of Nehemiah 10. This resulted in a law which was in profound disaccord with the economic conditions of the time. But inasmuch as it was "found written" in the Torah there was nothing to be done but accept it. Only later did this abstract legal creation give way before the realities of life. The newly born annual tithe was a burden that not even the pious generation of the Restoration could bear (Neh. 13:10). Nor did the mass of people throughout Second Temple times observe the tithes. Anciently the tithes were popular votive offerings; as fixed annual dues they were insupportable. Nor did the constitution of the temple personnel, with its thousands of priests, permit so rich an endowment to be squandered on the decimated Levites of postexilic times.

The annual Levitical tithe of Second Temple times is thus not found in the Torah at all. It was an impracticable result of the pious effort to harmonize the divergent laws "found written" in the ancient scrolls.

Of enormous significance is the fact that, despite the need of the hour, no explicit law providing for an obligatory priestly tithe made its way into the Torah. Such a law came into being by the "penalty of Ezra," but it was never introduced as a novel into the Torah. In spite of the long conflict over the tithe, the priests did not introduce a new law into Scripture that would decide this vital case. Instead, they kept on record obsolete laws, whose harmonization produced the unnecessary and unbearable annual Levitical tithe. Nothing proves more clearly how mistaken is the view that in postexilic times, the Torah book was still being added to and revised.

The history of the tithes confirms what has been inferred from the history of the law corpora in general: When the Torah book was being compiled (at the beginning of Second Temple times), the law corpora had already been crystallized. The founders of postexilic Judaism were not the composers, but merely the collectors of the Torah literature. They did not alter anything of what they "found written," much less add to it.

PRIESTS AND LEVITES—The one pillar of Wellhausen's structure that has not been shaken by later criticism is his reconstruction of the history of the Levites and the priesthood. The argument here seems to be conclusive. The early historical sources ignore the fundamental distinction that P makes between priests and Levites. D speaks indiscriminately of "Levite priests" and explicitly gives every "Levite" the right to serve in the temple (Deut. 18:6–8). It regards the whole tribe of Levi as consecrated to the holy service (10:8 f.) and knows nothing of P's distinction between priests who are "sons of Aaron" and "Levites" who serve in a lesser capacity and are not entitled to approach the altar. The inference appears unavoidable that before the Exile, no such distinction existed. Ezekiel still uses the phrase Levite priests (43:19 and elsewhere). But in the postexilic literature (Ezra, Nehemiah, Chronicles, etc.), the tribe of Levi is divided into two genealogically distinct classes, priests and Levites; here only do we find the expression "the priests *and* the Levites." This is to be explained by the assumption that the Levitical class was separated from the priesthood and became a distinct group of inferior temple personnel only after the Exile. More particularly, the Levites are the descendants of the priests of the high places who were disqualified by the Josianic reform from priesthood

(II Kings 23:9). Opinions differ as to the exact course of this degradation, but it is generally agreed that Ezekiel's demand to deny priestly status to any but the Jerusalem line of Zadok (44:6 ff.) provided the demotion of the rural priests with the necessary sanction. The Levites of postexilic times are, thus, descendants of the demoted priests of the high places. P, which alone of the pentateuchal sources carefully distinguishes priests from Levites, reflects the circumstances of Second Temple times and must, therefore, be postexilic.

This view, however, is beset by several difficulties. Neither D (cf. especially Deut. 18:6-8) nor the account of the reform in II Kings 23 indicates in any way that the rural priests were demoted. II Kings 23:9 speaks of a personal penalty that applied only to those who actually served at the high places. That these priests nonetheless eat of the consecrated wafers "among their brothers" shows that they retained their status as priests. But even granting, for the moment, that in defiance of the explicit law of Deuteronomy 18:6 f., the rural priests were unfrocked, when and by whose initiative did the Levitical class come into being? Only some ten or eleven years passed between the reform and Josiah's death. Did Jehoiakim and Zedekiah, who "did evil in the sight of YHWH," maintain Josiah's penalty in force? Did the pious men of the time support an act that clashed with the express law in the book of Torah? We know that the local priesthood of Anathoth, for example, who served at a rural altar, were counted priests, not "Levites," to the Exile and afterward.

Were the rural priests degraded to Levites after the destruction of the Temple? It is difficult to suppose so, since P, the very book that, *ex hypothesi*, confirms the demotion of the Levites, bestows upon them the munificent bounty of the tithe. Nothing can make plausible a theory that the very priests who demoted their colleagues saw fit to endow them with the amplest clerical due, a theory the more improbable when the great number of priests and paucity of Levites at the Restoration is borne in mind. The Levitical tithe law of P, which was faithfully observed by the community of the Restoration (Neh. 10:38-40; 13:10, 13), means (if Wellhausen's theory is correct) that the struggle over priestly status—for no unfrocking could have taken place without a struggle—was a struggle over poverty. The absurdity of this position is patent.

Other considerations, too, argue against the theory. It is quite remarkable that so important a matter as the disqualification and unfrocking of priests goes unnoticed in the Priestly Code. From Leviticus 21:1-15, it appears that only a blemished pedigree can deprive a priest of his sanctity. The priests who degraded their brethren thus apparently neglected to provide themselves any legal warrant in their own law for so doing. The attitude of the Bible, and particularly of P, toward the Levites also tells against the theory. To Ezekiel, Levitical status is a punishment and a disgrace. But Ezekiel is alone in his view. The Torah portrays the Levitehood as a distinction, a favored status close to God (Num. 3:11 ff., 40–51; 8:5–26; 16:9 ff.; 18:1 ff., 21 ff.). The priests preserved in their Torah a story telling how, when their ancestor Aaron made the golden calf, it was the sons of Levi who remained loyal to YHWH and his prophet. As their reward, they were consecrated by YHWH to the sacred service (Exod. 32:26–29). It must be supposed, then, that those who unfrocked their colleagues for the sin of the high places carefully removed any allusion to that sin. Instead, they awarded the Levites a glorious and honorable origin.

Thus, P's tithe law deprived the action against the rural priests of any material ground, while P's silence concerning the sin of the high places deprived it of its moral ground. If we add to this the fact that the postexilic Levites were a mere handful compared to the thousands of priests, the theory of a mass degradation of rural priests appears even more unlikely.

The history of the postexilic priesthood makes it clear that at least the bulk of the rural priests must have remained priests. This appears, first, from the fact that the four priestly clans that returned to Judah, according to the lists of Ezra-Nehemiah, comprised some four thousand souls; three other clans were disqualified for being unable to produce a satisfactory pedigree. Thus, about seven thousand priests returned from Babylonia. But these were not all, for the majority of priests still remained in exile. Later, Ezra was accompanied by three more clans, while twenty-one clans are listed as signers of the "sure agreement" (in Nehemiah 12:1, twenty-two clan-heads are named). At the beginning of Second Temple times, then, the total of priests who, at one time or another, migrated to Judah amounted to about twenty thousand (including those disqualified) —while still more remained in Babylon. All these could not have stemmed from the family of Zadok; the vast majority of them must have been descendants of rural priests.[11] Considering the smallness of pre-exilic Judah, it is clear that this number must represent most, if not all, of the Judean priesthood. At best, then, only a few of the rural priests could have been demoted. But if Ezekiel's program was ignored with respect to the vast bulk of the rural priests, what point was there in enforcing it against a mere handful, and in so peculiar a manner as to provide them with the tithe

[11] Note Nehemiah 11:10–14: only the minority of returned priests settled in Jerusalem, the remainder settling "in their cities, . . . each in his own possessions" (vs. 3)—i.e., in their ancestral lands where their fathers served at local altars.

in the present and glory in the past? Surely no connection exists between the postexilic Levites and the proposal of Ezekiel.

Not only with respect to degrading rural priests was Ezekiel ignored. His plan to replace the "heathen" Nethinim by the newly created Levites was also disregarded. The Nethinim returned to their tasks (cf. Neh. 10:29; 11:21). Alongside of them the handful of returned Levites were entirely supernumerary. Those who did not become farmers (Neh. 13:10) became, apparently, teachers and prayer-leaders (8:9 ff.; 9:4 ff.). In relying on Ezekiel, classical criticism has thus constructed an untenable historical scheme.

There is no reason to doubt the testimony that already in the Exile the Levites were a distinct class (separate from singers and porters) with their own ancient pedigree (Ezra 2:40 = Neh. 7:43; Ezra 8:15 ff.). They cannot, then, have come into being as a result of the centralization of worship, or in accordance with Ezekiel's demand. How could the Levitical class have originated in so short a time, without the hint of a struggle, and in a foreign land? What could have moved priests of venerable lineage quietly to surrender their ancient rights and accept an inferior status—with the temple in ruins and the cult suspended, so that the entire matter was purely academic? Indeed, the presence of Levites already in the Exile requires not merely a pre-exilic, but a pre-Josianic origin for the class.

The materials for reconstructing the early history of the tribe of Levi are meager. In Genesis 34 and 49:5⌐7 Levi is a secular, bellicose tribe. Later, in Deuteronomy 33:8-11, Levi appears as a sacerdotal class.[12] It had

---

[12] That the sacerdotal Levi was the same as the early secular tribe, and not (as has been argued) originally a professional order which only later became a synthetic tribe, is indicated by the following considerations:

Levites and priests are consistently represented as members of families and clans bearing an aristocratic lineage; they are never just isolated members of a professional group. Even the Levite of Judges 17–18 becomes the ancestor of the Danite priesthood.

The theory of a synthetic tribe that took "Levi" as its eponymous father confuses Israelite and Greek conceptions. Just as the Israelite conception of patriarchs is nearly unknown to the Greeks (Tros, Hellen, Dorus, etc. are not patriarchs but rulers after whom peoples were named), so the Greek conception of eponyms (heroes after whom tribes are named) is unknown to Israel. The Israelite tribe was conceived of literally as the descendants of one father. Hence the formation of a tribe was grounded on the natural conditions of close-knit association. Geographic proximity, unified organization, and common property were the bases of tribal formation insofar as they implanted in a given group the conviction of a common origin. But the common trade or calling of persons scattered throughout the country could never have become in Israel the basis of forming a tribe.

The geographic dispersion of the clergy would have tended to facilitate their assimilation into the various tribes they served; the priesthoods of Ephraim and Judah might have been expected to become separate groups. And why should all classes of temple personnel—priests, Levites, singers, porters—have been thrown together into one tribe? Only the assumption that the tribe was primary can explain all this. The strong tribal consciousness of the Israelite alone can account for the unity that priests and Levites

no tribal territory (Num. 18:23 ff.; 26:62; Deut. 10:9; 12:12 ff.), but its families did have private holdings—the Elides' fields in Benjamin (I Kings 2:26; Jer. 32:6 ff.; 37:12) and Nob, the city of priests (I Sam. 22:19); the possessions of the priests and Levites of the Restoration (Ezra 2:70; etc.) and their fields (Neh. 13:10). That is to say Levites were not considered *gērīm*. The tribe was divided into two groups: priests—who served actively in temples, and Levites—who, though qualified, did not hold priestly office (Judg. 17:12 f.; I Kings 12:31). This division is pre-exilic.

The various traditions regarding the origin of the Aaronic priesthood and the sacerdotal tribe of Levi agree on one point: from the beginning, there was a fundamental contrast between the priestly family (the Aaronides) and the tribe. In the story of the golden calf, the priest Aaron is opposed by the zealot Levites who are rewarded by consecration to divine service (Exod 32 [JE]; Deut. 9–10). In P, the contrast is set forth sharply in the rebellion of Korah (Num. 16–17). The same contrast appears to underlie the Elide-Zadokite conflict. The Elides are said to have been priests already in Egypt, in contrast to the Zadokites, who were consecrated as priests only in the time of the kingdom (I Sam. 2:27–36). This tradition, since it incorporates a curse on the house of Eli, must derive from a Zadokite source and shows that the Zadokites did not consider themselves descended from the ancient line that was chosen in Egypt. They were, presumably, Levitical priests of a family who served at first (in the time of David) alongside the Aaronides.

The Egyptian names that connect the Elides (Hophni, Phinehas, Hanamel) with the Aaronides confirm the tradition that at the Exodus the priesthood was already in the hands of the Aaronides. On the other hand, the consistent opposition of Aaronides to Levites (or Elides to Zadokites) makes it doubtful that the former considered themselves originally members of the tribe of Levi. It appears that the Aaronides are the ancient, pagan priesthood of Israel. Presumably, they were swayed by

---

felt despite their dispersion and difference in rank. This primary tribal unity could not be obliterated by all adverse factors, but these certainly would have prevented the formation of a late, synthetic tribe.

The theory is founded on a few obscure passages—Exodus 4:14, Deuteronomy 33:9, and Judges 17:7—of which the last is the clearest. The Levite is there said to be "out of Bethlehem of Judah, of the family of Judah," and so (it is argued) he was a Judahite. But the story evidently originated among the Danite priesthood, whose ancestor the Levite was, and they regarded themselves as descended from Moses (18:30). Even if the Levite were of Judahite origin the fact would surely have been obliterated by them in time. Again, this "Judahite" Levite is said to have been "sojourning" (*gār*) in Bethlehem—how so if he were a native of the place? The words "of the family of Judah" must perforce refer not to the Levite but to "Bethlehem of Judah," and they mean "in the territory possessed by the family [=tribe] of Judah" (cf. Judg. 18:11, and the territorial use of "tribe" in Deut. 12:5; II Sam. 15:2; 24:2).

the message of Moses, supported him, and influenced the people to follow him.

The golden calf episode marks the transformation of the old secular warrior tribe of Levi into militant defenders of the new faith. In what seems to have been a religious crisis, the Levites stand at the right hand of Moses against the house of Aaron. The Aaronic priesthood is too venerable to be set aside, but henceforth Levi shares with them the sacred service. The Aaronides demand the exclusive privilege of serving the altar and consent to Levi's being only hierodules; this demand is embodied in P. Accordingly, the role assigned to the Levites in the stories of P and in Deuteronomy 10:8, is the charge and guarding of the sacra of the people—especially the ark that was carried into battle and must be defended by the sword.

During the conquest, the Levites presumably remained with the ark, which needed protection especially during the period of constant warfare; hence, they did not acquire tribal territory of their own. In return, part of the sacred offerings was assigned permanently to them. After the settlement, when the ark was deposited in the Shiloh temple, the Aaronides (= the house of Eli) kept its charge. Now local sanctuaries sprang up throughout the land, and the Levites dispersed to take up priesthoods in them. This situation is vividly portrayed in the story about the Levite of Judges 17–18. Not all Levites could have gained priesthoods; many must have settled on the land and become farmers and herdsmen (cf. the program of priestly cities and pastures of P).

Although the cult could be performed by the laity in early times, Levites were even then considered to be the only ones fully qualified for priesthood; that is why Micah considers himself blessed to have found a Levite to be priest in his shrine (Judg. 17:13). They alone knew how to make offerings and inquire of YHWH properly—as we learn from Moses' blessing (Deut. 33:8 ff.).

But not every Levite was a priest. His lineage qualified him over any lay Israelite, but he attained fully to priesthood only upon being consecrated ("having his hands filled") to the office in a temple (Judg. 17:12 f.; I Kings 12:31). Thus, while every Levite was a candidate for priesthood, many remained mere "Levites," performing the menial work of temples. In time, there developed an amalgam of Aaronide and Levite priests, all of whom, of course, traced back their ancestry to Aaron.[13] For the Levite

[13] Moses was viewed as the father of one, isolated priestly line—that of the Danites (Judg. 18:30). But had he been considered the father of the priesthood as a whole, there is no accounting for the fact that later he was set aside in favor of the calf-maker Aaron.

priests may be presumed to have adopted the same exclusive attitude as the Aaronides toward their less successful confreres. The desire to suppress the non-priestly Levites gave rise to the genealogical fixing of priestly families; Levites were thus excluded from the priesthood. This struggle is echoed in the story of Korah; it ended with the expulsion of the Levites from the sanctuaries in which older priestly familes were entrenched.

When the period of sanctuary building came to a close, the Levites passed from the scene. Their ancient role of guarding the ark had long since ended. Menial tasks were now performed by other temple servants, who constituted, as it were, a new class of "Levites": the Nethinim, singers and porters. By later times there were no Levites in the temples. Hence, they are scarcely mentioned in the pre-exilic literature. In common usage, Levite became synonymous with priest. Only the old priestly writings preserved a record of the ancient Levites. The tithe law of Leviticus 27, giving the tithe to priests, now came into being. The old Levitical tithe, corresponding to the earlier situation when there was a large class of Levitical temple guardians and servants, was henceforth preserved only in the ancient scrolls.

But this was not the end of the Levites. In the exile, Ezekiel demanded the creation of a new Levite class by degrading the non-Zadokite priests who served at the local altars to the rank of the Nethinim. His program was ignored in this, as in most other, respects. The sudden reappearance of Levites in the postexilic period had other grounds entirely. The fundamental mood of the Restoration was repentance; convinced that the cause of their distress was their violation of God's will, the people resolved to observe his commands meticulously in order to assuage his wrath. This mood led, in the first place, to the creation of the Torah book. All the ancient scrolls that had transmitted the divine commands through the generations were assembled into one book. Most important was the restoration of the proper form of the cult, and for this the priestly writings served as the guide. To be sure, not everything that was found written could be renewed; ark, Urim, and anointing oil were not restored. But the system of P gave the Levites a crucial buffer position between the laity and the priesthood; this, the restored community was unwilling to forego. To avoid the terrible dangers of contact with the holy, the meager remnants of the old Levites were ferreted out and joined to the temple personnel. Ezra anxiously seeks out a handful of Levites, even though he has a large number of priests and Nethinim in his caravan. Levites were indispensable for restoring the proper sacred hierarchy; that is why Ezra considers it a token of divine favor that he has been provided with a few to bring back to

Jerusalem (Ezra 8:15–19). Only the desire to fulfil as faithfully as possible the commands of the Torah—in this case, the obsolete provisions of P—explains the renovation of the forgotten class of Levites, despite the fact that, at first, they have no proper function in the new community.[14] Thus, the history of the priests and Levites too confirms the antiquity of P.

THE ANTIQUITY OF THE TORAH LITERATURE

It was noted earlier that the Torah contains religious ideas that are distinct from and prior to those of literary prophecy. There are many other attestations of the antiquity of the Torah literature.

The covenant idea of the Torah literature stresses the pact with the patriarchs and God's promise to them. The covenant with the patriarchs guarantees YHWH's eternal grace toward Israel; it also figures prominently in the Torah's eschatology (Exod. 32:13; Lev. 26:42; Deut. 9:5, 27 ff.). This idea is not prophetic. It is alluded to only by Jeremiah (post-Josiah) and the prophets who follow him (Jer. 32:22; Ezek. 20:42; Isa. 51:2). In prophetic thought the covenant with the people at the Exodus is uppermost. It is this covenant with the people that the prophets promise will be renewed at the end of days.

The faith of the Torah has a naïve, popular character quite different from that of prophecy. Its image of deity is highly anthropomorphic; its conception of apostasy is primarily as disbelief in God's ability to conquer the obstacles of the desert and the Canaanites. Contrast the prophetic idea of apostasy as the forgetting of God's past kindnesses, straying after the lusts of the heart, and lack of faith in his prophets. Only in the Torah is the idea of a public theophany in broad daylight or a theophany to a foreigner (Abimelech, Laban, Balaam) to be found.

The historical background of the Torah is authentic. Although its history is legendary, it is grounded on a tradition that has a sound basis. The Torah correctly represents Israel as a young nation. The cosmogonies of Babylonia, Assyria, Egypt, and Canaan place the founding of their countries, peoples, cities, and temples at the beginning of time. The Hebrews, though they adopted much of Babylonian cosmogonic material, did not extend Israel's past to primordial times. Neither the people, its religion, nor its cities and temples are represented as primeval. The Babylonian antediluvian

---

[14] Eventually, they were assimilated into the singers and porters to whom they yielded their name. The lists of Nehemiah 12:8 f., 24 f. know of only two classes of Levites (cf. II Chron. 25–26; Bab. Arachin, 11b). Just as part of the tribe previously assimilated into the Aaronides and made them "Levite priests," so now the last of them assimilated into the singers and porters and made them "Levites." This was the final vicissitude of the ancient tribe.

kings became, in accord with Israelite conceptions, "patriarchs." These "patriarchs," however, are not the ancestors of Israel, but of mankind. Israel's monarchy is likewise correctly represented as late. The patriarchs are not transformed into kings who anciently ruled Canaan; they remain landless nomads with no claim to Canaan other than a divine promise for the future.

The tradition concerning the indigenous inhabitants of Canaan evidently dates to before the conquest. The Girgashite (not to speak of the Kenite and Kenizzite [Gen. 15:19]) were not in the land that Israel fought for at the time of the conquest. On the other hand, the Philistines were in Israelite Palestine and are counted by Judges 3:3 among the peoples left by God to test Israel. Yet, in spite of the long struggle with them, the Philistines are nowhere included in the Torah's lists of Canaanite nations. On the other hand, Tyre and Sidon, who were later to have a long history of peaceful relations with Israel, and whose land never came within the bounds of Israelite conquest, are included among the Canaanites whom the Torah condemns to annihilation (see below).

Especially significant in this regard is the matter of the boundaries assigned in the Torah and related portions of Joshua and Judges to the land of Israel. These cannot be explained by reference either to the ethnic settlement of the tribes, or to their political expansion under the monarchy. There is no congruence between the promised land and the real extent of Israelite territory, or between it and the land Israel aspired to rule over in later times. The boundaries of the promised land embrace Philistia, Lebanon, Tyre and Sidon, Byblos and Arwad. On the south, they reach the Red Sea, on the north, the river Euphrates (Gen. 15:18; Exod. 23:31; Deut. 1:7; 11:24; Josh. 1:4). Even the more modest claim to "the entrance of Hamath" includes Lebanon, Tyre, Sidon, and Byblos (cf. Josh. 13:5 f.; Judg. 3:3) which Israel never conquered or aspired to conquer at any later time. On the other hand, the eastern limit of the promised land is the Jordan River. The spies are sent to reconnoiter only the western side of the Jordan (Num. 13); Israel skirts Edom, Moab, Ammon, and wishes to traverse the land of Sihon to cross over the Jordan to its promised land (Num. 20:14 ff.; Deut. 2–3; cf. 11:8 f.). The request of two tribes to settle in Transjordan is considered a trespass against God, for that land is not included as part of Canaan (Num. 32); on one occasion, it is even called "impure" (Josh. 22:19). Since only the western side of the Jordan belongs to the promised land, only it is apportioned to the tribes by Ezekiel in his vision of the ideal territory of Israel (Ezek. 47).

To appreciate fully the problem raised by this notion of the promised land, it must be remembered that the Torah's boundaries are not given as the political limits of the Israelite empire (modern scholars casting about for a historical basis for these boundaries have generally seen in them a reflex of the Davidic empire), but as the limits of Israel's ethnic settlement. They are the bounds of Israel's "inheritance," its "possession," promised to the patriarchs together with the promise of numerous offspring (Gen. 17:6 ff.; 26:3 ff.; 28:3 ff.; cf. Exod. 23:29 f. and Deut. 7:22 where complete possession of the land is conditioned on Israel's increase). At no time, however, did the limits of Israel's ethnic settlement even approach these far-flung limits. Its real extent was approximately "from Dan to Beersheba." Even in Solomon's heyday, Phoenicia remained outside of the land Israel. Moreover, if the Davidic empire is the model, why does the promised land not include Ammon, Moab, and Edom? Equally without merit is the suggestion that these boundaries represent late patriotic dreams. They are promised not for the end time, but for the conquest and settlement of the tribes. The language of Joshua 13:1 ff. makes this unmistakably clear; the conquest of Lebanon and Sidon will complete the work begun by Joshua. Moreover, we know at first hand what the later patriotic dreams of Israel were. There was a vision of a world empire that would embrace all the nations even to Kush and Tarshish—but these far-flung dominions are not regarded as part of the land of Israel. When the territory of the future land of Israel is specified it never includes Tyre, Sidon, Byblos, etc. (Jer. 31:4 ff.; Obad. 19; Zech. 10:10). The prophecies of Tyre and Sidon's fall (Isa. 23; Jer. 47:4; Ezek. 26–28) do not promise that Israel will inherit their land. Nor does Ezekiel 47:15 ff. extend the northern boundary to the Euphrates. On the other hand Edom, Moab, and Ammon are incorporated in some dreams of the future (Obad. 19; Isa. 11:14), yet these are not part of the "promised land."

Every explanation based upon actual historical circumstances or later hopes is wrecked upon the hard fact that the promised land does not include Transjordan. Why should territory conquered by Moses, settled by Israelite tribes, united ethnically, culturally, and politically with the western tribes have been excluded by patriots from their dreams and hopes for the future?

There is but one adequate accounting for this. The boundaries of the promised land are a legacy from before the conquest. There existed an ancient oracle promising the land of Canaan to Israel. By the time of the conquest, this oracle was formulated in fixed terms, which Israel's actual settlement and later political expansion never fulfilled (a matter that perplexed early historiographers; cf. the several attempts to explain this failure in Judg. 2—3:5). Literary prophecy has nothing to do with this ancient oracle, but it dominates the world of the Torah, another evidence of the antiquity of the material that has survived intact in the Torah literature.

The patriarchal narratives contain much that is manifestly ancient. The connection of Simeon and Levi must be quite early, for at the conquest, Simeon amalgamated with Judah and is not heard of thereafter (Judg. 1:3). Ancient, too, is the record of Simeon and Levi's battle at Shechem— later belonging to the Joseph tribes. The primogeniture of Ishmael, Esau, Reuben, and Manasseh corresponds to nothing in later times. Ancient also is the notion of Edom's fraternity with Israel, which has no ground in later events. The whole political background of the Torah's narratives, laws, and songs points to the preconquest period. There is a promise of kingship, and a few allusions to events of the first days of the monarchy. But this is the limit of the Torah's historical horizon.

The national enemy of Israel in the Torah is Amalek (Exod. 17:8–16; Deut. 25:17 ff.)—an attitude that has no roots in the postconquest history, when Amalek is but one of many enemies, until its defeat by David. P speaks also of Midian as a national enemy; the last recorded battle with Midian was in the days of Gideon. Aram, the bitter enemy of Israel from David's time, is still part of the family in the patriarchal narratives. Not only do Abraham and Isaac seek wives for their sons from Aram, but Jacob concludes a covenant of peace with the Aramaean Laban (Gen. 31:44 ff.). Edom's later enmity is nowhere foreshadowed. The farthest look into the future occurs in Balaam's oracles, where David's conquests are alluded to (Num. 24:7). But here, too, Amalek is still "the first of the nations" (vs. 20), and the Israelite king's glory is his exaltation over Agag (vs. 7). There is no reference to the kingdoms of Aram, Assyria, Egypt, or Babylon.

Among the laws of the Torah, we find but one dealing explicitly with the monarchy, the law of Deuteronomy 17:14–20. (Exodus 22:27 [JE] and Leviticus 4:22 [P] probably apply to kings, although they speak only of the *nāśî*.) This law permits Israel to elect a king according to the dictate of YHWH (apparently by means of a prophet); he may not be a foreigner, and may not amass horses, women, silver, or gold. He must always study the Torah and fulfil it. These few moral-religious rules do not even touch upon the law of the monarchy: the rite of anointing, the royal privileges of taxation, tithing, dispensing justice, appointing officials, confiscating, etc. (cf. I Sam. 10). Excepting this passage, the Torah legislation reflects not the monarchy, but the early "kingdom of God" based on the primitive democracy that existed in premonarchic Israel. The tribes are headed by chiefs; the people, by a prophet-judge. Deuteronomy 16:18 makes the people responsible for the appointment of judges; the king's role in this vital matter is not mentioned. The property laws of the Torah know only the tribal and familial basis; the right of acquisition of property by royal grant is not mentioned. There is, then, no doubt that the Torah literature was crystallized at the latest by the beginning of the monarchy. It alludes briefly to the new political institution of kingship, but did not flourish on its soil.

The ideas, the religious and political symbols of the Torah were fully formed by the time of the early monarchy. The literature continued, of course, to develop and pass through successive formulations; but, the symbols and ideals of early times remained intact.

This conclusion is not contradicted by the prophecies of exile that are found scattered through the monitions of the Torah (Lev. 26:23 ff.; Deut. 28:36 ff.; etc.). For these monitions—like those at the end of the Code of Hammurabi—include so many threats and imaginary curses that it is hardly justifiable to single out, as having a real historical basis, the threat of exile (and promise of return).

National collapse and exile are found in Amos and Hosea as a visionary threat; they were conceived of long before the Assyrian and Babylonian exiles. Such notions no more required a basis in historical reality than Amos' threat of Aram's being exiled to Kir (Amos 1:5) or Ezekiel's prophecy of Egypt's forty-year exile and subsequent restoration (Ezek. 29:12; 30:23, 26). The peculiar emphasis on the punishment of exile in the Torah is grounded, perhaps, in the feeling that Israel was not autochthonous in Canaan, that it was "given" the land and might, therefore, be deprived of it by an angry God.

The descriptions of the exile in the Torah are, indeed, the most eloquent advocates of their antiquity, for they show clearly that their authors had no idea of the actual condition of Israel's historical exile (the Babylonian exile). The authors imagine the exiles as dispersed bands, wandering in the lands of their enemies, harried and persecuted. Their lives hang daily in the balance, they find no rest, and pine away in their misery and suffering. In foreign lands they will worship wood and stone gods. Palestine will be a desolate waste, "the whole land brimstone and salt and a burning" (Deut. 29:22).

Jeremiah and Ezekiel, the prophets of the fall, use the same frightful language to describe the exile which is about to come. But when they speak of the exile already in existence, they speak not of flight and terror, but of "building houses and dwelling therein, planting vineyards and eating their fruit" (Jer. 29:4 ff.). Ezekiel, too, reflects a relatively tranquil community, far removed from the terrors of his visions. The exiles, we know, settled down in the lands of their dispersion and found rest there. Many were not willing to return home when the opportunity presented itself. That is why the literature after Ezekiel bears no further allusions to these terrible visions. The horrors of the destruction are mentioned (Isa. 42:22 ff.; 51:17; Ezra 9:7; etc.), but nothing suggests that the exiles suffered physical distress. In later times, the exile was regarded as a disgrace and profanation of YHWH's name. But as to suffering, the Second Isaiah knows only of the misery of Zion and Jerusalem (Isa. 64:9 f.); this is the dominant note in later literature. Not the exiles, but those who remained in the land and who returned to it were "in great misery and disgrace" (Neh. 1:3).

The Torah knows nothing of all this. The later conception of the exile as a disgrace and profanation of YHWH's name (Ezek. 36:19 ff.) is unknown. The mood of the real exile is not reflected at all, nor are any of the later prophetic motifs alluded to: the gradual destruction, first of Israel then of Judah, or the destruction of the temple. The image of exile in the Torah must, therefore, be an ancient one, antedating the historical experience of destruction and exile.[15]

The Strata of the Torah Literature—The idea of centralization is the touchstone by which we can distinguish the two major strata, Genesis-Numbers (JEP), and Deuteronomy-Kings (the Deuteronomic stratum). Only in D and related literature is there a clear and unmistakable influence of the centralization idea. In the time of Hezekiah the idea began to gain favor; Josiah drew its ultimate conclusions. Thereafter, Judaism was enthralled by the image of the central sanctuary and chosen city. It is incredible that a priestly law which evolved at this time should pass over this dominant idea in silence. It has been shown above that there is no trace whatever of D's centralization idea in P; P must, therefore, have been composed before the age of Hezekiah.[16]

[15] It is this negative fact, that in the Torah nothing of later historical events is reflected that speaks decisively for its antiquity. The opponents of the Wellhausen school have often pointed out that the Torah contains old and reliable historical documents. But this argument is still not conclusive; late books can utilize ancient materials. Only the fact that the Torah shows no knowledge whatever of later historical conditions fixes the date of its sources between termini different entirely from those postulated by the prevailing view.

[16] All supposed tokens of P's lateness are overshadowed by this monumental fact. Wellhausen's idea that the early religion of Israel was spontaneous and rite-free is persuasive only so long as the cuneiform literature (that already in his time was being studied with reference to the religion of Israel) is not taken into account. To Wellhausen, the cultures of Babylonia, Assyria, and Egypt are irrelevant for the history of biblical religion. Israel's culture is taken as the direct outgrowth of primitive Bedouin origins. The error of this view will be shown below.

The idea that P is dominated by the exilic mood of national guilt is wrong. That mood

In every detail, P betrays its antiquity. Its narrative preserves bold anthropomorphisms ("Let us make man in our image," "I have set my bow in the cloud," etc.); its cult presupposes the existence of local altars, as pointed out above; its tithes are ancient; its thousands of Levites are a reflex of a distant past; its view of the prophets as the civil and military leaders of the people is archaic. Not only does P contain the harsh law of devoting (*ḥērem*), it alone of all the codes provides for the private devoting of the person of a human being (Lev. 27:29, illustrated in the story of Jephthah). P's position is far from that taken by the age of Ezra-Nehemiah, which refused to accept proselytes. Its concept of the *gēr* is a social-territorial one. The *gēr* of P is a free man, a foreigner who has settled in the land of Israel and has been assimilated culturally, and hence religiously. Such assimilated "proselytes" are, for P, on a par with Israelites in all matters of the cult. The exilic and postexilic problem of purely religious conversion, without a territorial and cultural basis (cf., e.g., Isa. 56), is unknown to P.

P is ignorant of Jerusalem's significance. None of the patriarchs visit it and no ancient theophany consecrates it. (If Genesis 14 is to be assigned to P, and if Salem is Jerusalem, it is most remarkable that its priest is a non-Israelite.) However, Bethel (the site of a northern calf-temple) is honored as the site of an ancient pillar set up by Jacob (Gen. 35:14 f., arbitrarily denied to P by the Wellhausen school to save its system). To this are to be added the archaisms of P (e.g., the name Kiriath-arba for Hebron) which are not to be explained away as artifices—as though the supposedly late authors of P thought it necessary to be more archaic than J or E. The story of the Gibeahite concubine, with its many cult sites (Judg. 19–21), would in itself be sufficient evidence for the antiquity of P, were the school of Wellhausen able to read it without prejudice.

As the law of the local sanctuaries, then, P crystallizes a stage of religious evolution earlier than D. The tradition that placed P before D thus correctly reflects the historical development.

Within JEP, the book of Genesis holds a peculiar position. Though composite, it has an overall distinctive character that must go back to the peculiar nature of its original elements. The materials of Genesis deal with the

---

brought into prominence the new cult forms of confession and prayer without sacrifice, often illustrated in Daniel, Ezra, and Nehemiah. These are not found in P. The sins that P's sacrifices atone for are unwitting transgressions of the individual and the community, especially sins involving impurity (Lev. 4–5; Num. 15:25; cf. Lev. 16:16 ff.). The sin offering, an innovation of P according to Wellhausen, is brought only for unwitting sins and has no reference to the historical sin of the nation. P knows of no special rite for atoning national sin.

establishment of the permanent order of the cosmos and the relationships among men. It is the book of formative acts and words. It closes, fittingly, with the blessings of Jacob, foretelling the destiny of the tribes at "the end of days." After Genesis we find only isolated instances of this literary genre (the blessing of Moses, the monition of Joshua, and the like; Balaam's oracles belong rather to the genre of prophecy than to that of blessing). While Genesis is the book of creative acts, the rest of the Torah provides a series of archetypes, ideal Israelite forms: Moses, the archetypal prophet; Aaron, the father of the priesthood; the tent, the archetype of the local sanctuary; the golden calf, the archetype of Israelite idolatry; the Urim, the ideal form of technical oracle; "the stiff-necked people," and so forth. Genesis is peculiar also in its form of theophany. Hardly one of its theophanies possesses an external framework, fire, clouds, or the like. God appears to the naked eye, mostly by day; Jacob even wrestles with a "man"—a unique story, with which only the story of the "sons of God" who consorted with women (also in Genesis) is comparable. Only in Genesis does an angel call to man from heaven (22:11, 15). P's theophanies are also marked by the same naïveté; God appears to man, speaks with him, and then "goes up" from him (17:1, 22; 35:9, 13). Genesis lacks entirely the peculiarly Israelite concept of the prophet: a man to whom God reveals himself continually, who serves as his messenger and intermediary.

Nor does Genesis allude in any way to Israel's unique religious status. Abraham is a God-fearing, just man; but neither in the promises made to him nor in those made to his descendants is the distinction of possessing YHWH's Torah, or the fact that Ishmael and Esau will be idolaters mentioned. The religious rift that separates Israel from the nations, so prominent in the rest of the books of the Torah, is never hinted at in Genesis. Here, Israel's distinction is purely one of lineage; it is "lord over its brethren" (27:29). True, there is a covenant between God and Israel's ancestors; but its promises are purely ethnic: numerous progeny, territorial possessions, and kingship.

There are, besides, many matters that are peculiar to Genesis, or that have a parallel only in the earlier literature: marriage to one's paternal sister (Gen. 20:12; cf. II Sam. 13:13); or to two sisters; the custom of barren women giving concubines to their husbands (cf. Code of Hammurabi 144–6); the custom of the father acting as levir to his childless daughter-in-law (paralleled in Assyrian and Hittite law). The (Egyptian) custom of putting the dead in a coffin is recorded only here (50:26); only here is the oath ceremony of placing the hand beneath the thigh mentioned (24:2, 9; 47:29). Moreover, the narrator is as little embarrassed by Rachel's theft of the teraphim, as by the embalming of Joseph and Jacob—although embalming was associated with the Osiris cult.

Genesis may, therefore, be regarded as constituting a stratum in itself whose material is on the whole most ancient. Within Genesis, again, several strata are to be discerned. Chapters 1–11 have long been recognized as drawing upon ancient Near Eastern materials. It may be further observed that these early legends are characterized by an almost unique folkloristic naïveté; God, for example, moves among men almost as one of them; there is neither revelation nor an angel of God. P's materials share these features, if to a lesser degree. It is P, after all, that speaks of man's creation in God's image, of God's bow, that has God speaking in the plural ("let us make"), and uses the expression "to walk with God."

In sum, then, the following literary strata are to be distinguished in the Bible:

1. Genesis 1–11 (Near Eastern materials; folkloristic naïveté; no revelation)
2. Genesis 1–49 (the book of formative acts and words; no prophecy)
3. JEP (Genesis-Numbers; no trace of Deuteronomic ideas)
4. Deuteronomy–II Kings (the influence of the idea of centralization is apparent)
5. The laws of JE
6. The laws of P
7. The laws of D
8. The Torah-group (Genesis–II Kings; no trace of the influence of literary prophecy)
9. The literary prophets (the climax of biblical religion)
10. The Hagiographa, the postexilic portions of which show a synthesis of the ideas of the Torah and prophets.

THE TORAH BOOK

The first book of Torah that was the occasion of a religious reform was the book found in the temple at the time of Josiah. This book was, as has long been recognized, Deuteronomy. The law of JE and P is the background of the account of Josiah's Passover (II Kings 23:21–3); in accord with D's provisions Josiah did away with the ancient home sacrifice of JE and P. A covenant was concluded with the people to observe the newly discovered Torah book; henceforth, the book was accepted as binding divine law.

Now the composition of D, we have seen, was quite independent of

P or JE. This means that before Josiah's covenant, none of the three legal corpora was recognized as binding law. Only this can explain their divergences and mutual contradictions. Why D should have been the first composition of the Torah literature that became binding Torah cannot be determined with certainty, owing to the insufficiency of our data. However that may be, Josiah's age marks the beginning of the emergence of the Torah book out of the Torah literature.

The Torah book of the time of Ezra-Nehemiah included both D and P. An effort is clearly discernible on the part of men of that age to combine the provisions of the codes and establish binding law on their basis. The laws of three corpora are interpreted in the light of each other; legal midrash springs into existence. While the general organization of the community of the Restoration is Deuteronomic—i.e., centered about Jerusalem and its temple—the ancient class of Levites, known only to P, is also on the scene. Tabernacles and Passover are celebrated in Jerusalem, according to D (Ezra 3:4; 6:19 ff.; Neh. 8:14 ff.); at the same time, the bringing of olive branches (Neh. 8:15) and the eighth day of assembly (vs. 18) are prescribed by P. The expulsion of foreign women is grounded in D and JE (cf. Neh. 13:1 f.), but the idea behind it—that the heathen have defiled the land (Ezra 9:11)— is P's (Lev. 18:24 ff.; 20:22 ff.). The law to let land lie fallow in the seventh year (Neh. 10:32) belongs to JE and P; but the extension of the idea to the release of debts (*ibid.*) is D's. The commitment to levy tithes annually is D's, along with the expression "year by year" (Neh. 10:35). First fruits are brought to the house of YHWH according to D (Neh. 10:36), but the heave offering and the tithe are given to priests and Levites everywhere, according to a midrashic interpretation of P. Firstlings are given to priests (vs. 37), as stipulated by P, but they are brought to Jerusalem, as prescribed by D. Clearly, by the Restoration, the Torah comprised all three corpora.

The distinction of styles in the three corpora, the absence of the idea of centralization in JE and P, and their independence of one another in matters of law point to the conclusion that they were combined only after their formation was completed. The laws are not alone, however, in displaying a tendency toward early fixity. The fact that Genesis 1–11 preserves a unique series of anthropomorphisms, that Genesis as a whole is palpably different from the other books, that it contains stories and expressions certainly offensive to later religious tastes (the story of the "sons of God" and the daughters of men, God's walking in the garden "at the cool of the day," etc.) means that already in early times the sources were quasi-canonical, so that later one hesitated to alter them. This diffidence reached its peak in the age of the compilation of the Torah book.

For the compilers were confronted by materials that collided not only with their religious sensibilities, but with the very laws they had determined to observe scrupulously. The patriarchs erect pillars, marry forbidden relatives, and act at times in a vile manner (Reuben with Bilhah, Judah with the "harlot"). If the literature was still in flux, indeed, was even then still being composed (as the prevailing view has it), how could this embarrassing material have survived unaltered? To say that later ages retained this matter out of pious veneration is no answer. Reverence would rather have dictated—according to the lights of those times—withdrawal and suppression of the offensive matter (a procedure seriously contemplated in the case of Ezekiel because of its divergences from the Torah). Only the assumption that by then the elements of the Torah had become fixed and hallowed is adequate to explain the reluctance of the compilers to revise and emend.

Still more instructive is the treatment of the laws. Here the repetitions and dissensions were even plainer, and the anxiety of the age to act in accordance with God's law made them all the more disconcerting. Yet repetitions, dissensions, and obsolete laws were all allowed to remain. No attempt was made to integrate the three law corpora as was done in the case of the narrative sources. If composition and compilation went on concurrently, such glaring defects would hardly have been permitted to stand. There can be but one conclusion. The age of the Restoration was an age of compilation, not of edition and revision, let alone of innovation.[17]

The nucleus of the Torah book was Deuteronomy, born out of the conviction that Israel could redeem itself only by steadfast adherence to the Torah of God. Out of the earlier Torah literature (with the addition of the law of centralization) a popular book, from which the people could learn the will of God, was fashioned. After the destruction and exile, remorse and contrition seized the people, rising out of their sense of sin and estrangement from God. The simple faith in God's nearness and immanence

---

[17] That the Day of Atonement happens not to be mentioned in Nehemiah 9:1 ff. is no evidence for its lateness. The rite of Leviticus 16 is an annual, fixed purification of temple, altar, and people from everyday sins and impurities. It has no historical aspect, and can in no way be brought into connection with the fast of Nehemiah 9, on the 24th of Tishri. That was a non-repeated day of national confession connected with the ratification of the "sure agreement." No temple rite was performed; the gathering did not even take place in the temple court. It was an altogether unique convocation, marked by a Torah lection and a public confession of present and past sin; no ritual riddance of sin is mentioned. P's rite is performed by the priest; in Nehemiah 9, priests play no part— Levites manage the affair. The rite of Nehemiah 9 is palpably the later of the two, displaying affinities with the nascent synagogal liturgy. That the Day of Atonement goes unmentioned in Nehemiah 8–10 is accidental, or, more likely, owing to the fact that the day had not yet achieved the popular significance it had later.

in Israel's history was shattered. It was as if the ancient covenant had been broken. By acts of repentance the people sought to heal the breach that had opened between them and God and to renew the covenant. This meant, first, to observe the Torah that was given the people as the basis of the ancient covenant. By this alone could Israel hope to be reinstated in divine favor. The idea of collecting all the ancient traditions into one book which could serve as the constitution of the penitent community came into being. The leaders of the community undertook to finish the task begun by the creator of Deuteronomy: to compile and complete the Torah book.

Precisely what was the condition of the material now preserved in JEP, we cannot know; apparently it was still on individual scrolls. P was probably also extant in several versions, one of which was the basis of the laws of Ezekiel. Concerning the principles of selection, no more can be said than that whatever was believed to be the genuine word of God was incorporated, intact and unrevised, into the new book; the rest was suppressed. The ancient priestly materials transmitted from early times were added to the corpus of Deuteronomy. Since Deuteronomy claimed to have been the last words of Moses, the priestly corpus was arrayed before it.

Thus, the Torah book was formed out of the desire of a penitent community to know and keep the law of God. Israel fastened naturally upon its early literary traditions, which contained the history and laws of its ancient covenant. The literature of Torah became the first stratum of the Bible, sealed and canonized at a time when prophetic literature was still unordered and still without decisive influence on the life of the people. The entire book is a testimony to the first age of Israelite religion, the age prior to literary prophecy.

CHAPTER VI

The Origins of Israelite Religion

APOSTOLIC PROPHECY AND THE RISE
OF ISRAELITE RELIGION

There is one cycle of legends in the Bible that has no parallel elsewhere: the legends concerning the divine revelation made to Israel in the desert, at the heart of which is the Sinaitic theophany. God descended upon the mountain before all the people, let them all hear his voice, and commanded them ten things. With this unique legend are allied others concerning the appearance of God in fire and cloud at the Exodus and during the Wandering. The fundamental purpose of these legends is to surround the prophecy and mission of Moses with supernal glory. They are an essential part of the Torah's picture of the ideal, archetypal prophet and their function in the story is to confirm Moses' message and mission—like the miracles performed in Egypt and at the Exodus (see e.g., Exod. 4:1–10; 14:31). At Sinai, God speaks with Moses; the people hear God's voice only that they may believe in Moses and his mission (19:9). The Sinaitic theophany is thus the source of the people's belief in prophecy; in Deuteronomy, it is said to have been the occasion of the founding of Israelite prophecy.

These stories underscore the distinctive feature of Israelite prophecy: the prophet is sent to the people to bring it the word of God and his command; he is charged with a mission. The role of apostle of God is what sets the Israelite prophet apart from all pagan analogues. And what makes the history of Israelite prophecy *sui generis* is the succession of apostles of God that come to the people through the ages. Such a line of apostle-prophets is unknown to paganism. Not even those great souls that arose among the nations to found religions and teach the good way are of a type with the prophets of Israel. Buddha, Zoroaster, or Apollonius of Tyana act by a di-

vine power which has become embodied in them. Buddha is the redeemer
of gods and men; Zoroaster is Ormazd's indispensable ally in the battle with
Ahriman. He possesses superhuman virtue because of his divine origin. Because of this, paganism does not know of a continuous, generations-long succession of prophets. Paganism created a mantic science that had permanence
and fixity. But the pagan prophet, legislator, or founder of a religion was
conceived of as endowed with a charism which was his alone. He incorporated a unique, self-contained divine power; therefore his "mission" ended
with him. Zoroaster was unique; Ormazd himself awaited his coming, and
could not afterward raise up others like him to fill his place.

It is otherwise with Israelite prophecy, which was conceived of as a continuous commissioning of men of God throughout the ages. Here the prophetic calling is entirely dependent upon the will of God. He is a prophet
whom God wishes to send to his people. Prophets are not embodiments of,
and cannot inherit or acquire, any special virtue; but each is a new creation
of the will of God. The difference between the two conceptions arises out of
the difference between the pagan belief in a multiplicity of divine powers
and the Israelite idea of the one, absolute divine will.

The Bible speaks of a long chain of messenger prophets—apostles of God
—who were sent to Israel. The commission of Moses, Isaiah, Jeremiah, and
Ezekiel is described in legends. In no case does it consist in the conveyance
of a special virtue or talent, but in the call to be a messenger of God. In the
theophany of the burning bush, the mission is the dominant theme: "Come,
let me send you to Pharaoh. . . . This is your sign that I have sent you. . . .
The god of your fathers has sent me to you. . . . EHYEH has sent me to
you." Isaiah hears, "Whom shall I send," and answers, "Here am I, send
me." Jeremiah is charged, "To wherever I send you, you shall go." Ezekiel is
told: "O man, I send you to the house of Israel." The verb "send" is the
heart of the divine call to an Israelite prophet.

The prophet acts on behalf of God, not of man. His function is not to
answer men's inquiries, like the pagan prophet and diviner, but to do and
say only that required by God. He may be sent against his will, coming
before the people unasked, and bearing a message they do not wish to
hear. There is no flight from his task, and he must often be specially fortified
to endure it. The idea is that apostolic prophecy is entirely the product
of a transcendental cause: God's desire to reveal himself and his will to men.

There is an ideological continuity in apostolic prophecy. The messages of
the apostle-prophets are not disconnected, they are not charges given merely
for an occasion and having but momentary import; nor are they diverse
personal teachings. Prophetic pronouncements have an ideological consist-

ency, a unity of doctrine not the less for their variety of styles and complexions. The apostolic prophets speak the absolute will of God, his constant and abiding demand of men. Israelite law derives from prophecy: the Torah was mediated to Israel by Moses; Samuel tells the rule of the monarchy to the people and writes it in a book.

There is a historical aspect to the work of apostolic prophecy. Ever and from its beginnings it belongs to the religion of YHWH. No apostolic prophet comes to Israel in the name of another god. Apostolic prophecy was always the standard bearer of the faith of YHWH, and its champion in the battle with idolatry. Every large step in the development of the religion of YHWH in Israel took the form of prophecy: the stress on the moral demand of God, the idea of a universal redemption, with Israel playing a central role. Early prophecy is also represented as the source of torah which it was the priesthood's task, however, to transmit.

Apostolic prophecy does not arise out of the personal faith of these men in itself; it has a historical-social basis. The prophet is sent to a people. His appearance depends, therefore, upon the belief of the people that God habitually sends it messengers. Indeed, this was the belief of Israel through the ages; it expected the coming of apostles of God, pined for them after prophecy ceased, and had faith in their reappearance in messianic times. It was never certain as to who was truly "sent," but for centuries it did believe that YHWH sent messengers. Apostolic prophecy was grounded on this popular belief.

Both ideally and in fact apostolic prophecy was limited to the people of Israel. Although eventually it attained to a universal religious viewpoint, prophecy conceives of itself essentially as a divine gift to Israel alone. This exclusiveness is based on the notion that the pagans are not obliged to worship YHWH and are not punished for idolatry. The universalism of prophecy is eschatological; for the present, it could fulfil its task of speaking on behalf of YHWH only in Israel. Accordingly, no missionary tendency is to be found in biblical religion. No prophet was ever sent to preach monotheism to the nations. The task of being "a witness" to the nations (Isa. 55:4) is the people's; through Israel, the name of God will be made known to men. Israel, then, is sent to the nations; the prophet is sent only to Israel. So deeply rooted was this idea that even Jesus, who considered himself an apostle of God, declares himself sent only "to the lost sheep of the house of Israel" (Matt. 15:21-8; cf. Mark 7:27).

Apostolic prophecy is an Israelite creation. The analogies that have been proposed with Canaanite or Asian prophetism obscure the basic distinctions. Precisely in the survivals of an ancient *kāhin*-type of prophecy the profound transformation that took place in Israelite prophecy can be discerned. What is the nature of that transformation? The clairvoyant, the "seer," possessing a personal charism, is replaced by the prophet, the servant of God. In place of the diviner and interpreter of signs appears the messenger of God who proclaims his will. This change is coeval with the monotheistic transformation of ancient Hebrew religion.[1]

[1] [Several texts have come to light from the eighteenth century B.C. kingdom of Mari (a West Semitic kingdom on the middle Euphrates) exhibiting mantic phenomena which have been compared to Israelite prophecy (see e.g., Martin Noth, "Geschichte und Gotteswort im Alten Testament," *Gesammelte Studien zum Alten Testament* [Munich, 1957], pp. 230–47, esp. pp. 242 f.). High officials report to Zimri-lim, king of Mari, that men have come to them with messages to the king from various gods. In three cases the messenger is a *maḫḫū*—a priest-ecstatic—of the god Dagan, and the message concerns delinquency in making certain offerings and in building a gate. A fourth case involves a dream in which Dagan appeared to a man (not specified as a religious functionary) and sent him to ask the king why he had failed to give an account of his activities to the god. Yet another text speaks of oracles concerning the delinquency of the king in regard to the delivery of certain beasts, which were communicated by a spokesman (*āpilu*, "respondent") of Adad.

In the following note (communicated by letter, November 8, 1959) Kaufmann assesses the bearing of this new material on Israelite prophecy.]

The idea of a messenger is so commonplace—even mythology knows of messenger-deities (Papsukkal, Hermes, etc.)—one is surprised that it figures so rarely in pagan manticism. Yet the conception does appear here and there. Some oracles to Esarhaddon and Ashurbanipal appear to be divine messages conveyed through prophets. Among the Mari texts are several containing oracles expressly attributed to messenger-prophets. The fact remains, however, that in pagan manticism the idea of commission is of minor importance. It does not appear as something special, opposed to the other techniques, but merely as another one of the many types of manticism, and a peripheral one at that.

In Israel the advent of apostolic prophecy is a turning-point, a new phenomenon of tremendous import for the future. The first apostle of God, Moses, makes his appearance in an aura of glory. He is not a priest or a temple prophet, but a shepherd. An unknown God who has no cult among men sends him to Pharaoh, the mighty king, with the demand to release the Israelites. He sends him to smite Egypt with plagues, to perform great wonders so that Egypt may know that the whole earth is his. He sends him to bring Israel to the land of Canaan, to root out Israel's idolatry, and make Israel enter an eternal covenant with the one God. From the time of Moses apostolic prophets continued to appear in Israel for generations. Among them are the classical prophets, who created a whole new world of religious and moral ideas. Christianity counts Jesus, and Islam, Mohammed, as belonging to their number. The mission of these prophets fills their lives, and they are ready to give their lives for it. This prophecy transformed the whole mantic realm of Israel. It involved a new conception of the revelation of the word of God, and it ousted the earlier forms of manticism. The distinctive feature of apostolic prophecy is that it champions a religious and moral doctrine. These prophets are stirred by a religious-moral passion. The continuity of their line is grounded on the continuing evolution of the religion of Israel, which found expression in their utterances. Upon the soil of pagan manticism an entirely new phenomenon, ideological prophecy, sprang into existence. Nowhere else was the *mantis* the bearer of a religious-moral ideology. Nowhere else did apostles of a god appear in an ages-long, unbroken succession. Israel's apostle-prophets, the first of whom was Moses, are, therefore, an entirely new phenomenon. An external, merely formal resemblance to this or that element in pagan manticism cannot alter this fact. Noth's estimate of the Mari material as leveling the qualitative difference between the Bible and its historical milieu in an essential point is greatly exaggerated.

What is the latest date that can be assigned to the religious revolution in which Israelite prophecy was born? Not after Israel's entry into Canaan, for in the life of the settled tribes the apostolic idea appears as a vital force from the very start. It pervades the period of the judges; the very institution of judges and its underlying concept of the "kingdom of God" rests on the faith in a succession of messengers of God. The early kingdom of God is founded on the expectation that what happened once—God's sending a savior to Israel—will be repeated when the need arises (cf. e.g., Judg. 6:13). The source of this expectation must lie in the period before the judges, that is, in the period before the settlement.

Apostolic prophecy is an intrinsic part of the historical religion of YHWH. Apostolic prophecy, the faith in YHWH, the battle with idolatry, and the covenant-confederation of Israelite tribes are inseparable elements in Israel's consciousness. Only the assumption that they have one and the same historic root can explain the continuous combination of these phenomena throughout the ages. It was an apostolic prophet, the first in history, who proclaimed the faith of YHWH to the tribes of Israel, made them enter into a covenant concerning this faith and implanted in them the expectation that other messengers would come after him. Moreover, his appearance must be placed before the entry into Canaan.

The biblical historians place the origins of Israel's relation with YHWH in patriarchal times. We must therefore examine the patriarchal traditions first for the historical nucleus that underlies them.

THE PATRIARCHAL AGE

Biblical tradition begins Israelite history with the patriarchal age, an age of wandering and transition lasting four or five generations.[2] The patriarchs are portrayed as heads of large households. What characterizes their condition is their status as protected aliens, *gērim*. There is as yet no people which possesses its own land. There is a "land of promise," but its conquest and settlement are still in the future.

---

[2] Abraham, Isaac, Jacob, his sons, and grandsons—Ephraim and Manasseh. This would amount to about 100 to 150 years, contradicting the chronological data given in the Bible (but these are not in harmony with each other either). Exodus 6:16 ff. makes Moses the fourth generation after Levi, separating him from Abraham by seven generations, or about 200 years. If the Exodus took place under the reign of Merneptah at about 1230, the beginning of the patriarchal age would fall at the end of the fifteenth century. These calculations are conjectural, of course, but the biblical numbers are evidently schematic, and self-contradictory as well. Relative to them an estimate based on generations would appear to be more reliable.

THE HISTORICAL BACKGROUND—The dating of the patriarchal age involves the extremely complex problems of fixing the date of the Exodus and the conquest. The available data in extra-biblical sources do not speak as clearly as we should like, yet some inferences may be drawn from them with a measure of confidence.

The Egyptian priest-historian Manetho connected the descent into Egypt and the Exodus with the advent and expulsion of the Hyksos.[3] His view has attracted some modern scholars, primarily owing to the desire to find reflexes of the biblical story outside the Bible. There is no real similarity, however, between the Hebrew shepherds-turned-slaves who flee Egypt and the Hyksos ruling class who, after a century of rule, were expelled by the Egyptians in a violent struggle. The Hyksos military and political organization, with its horse and chariot and city-state, contrasts sharply with the ass and camel pastoral culture of the patriarchs. The Joseph story depicts Egypt as already in possession of horse and chariot (Gen. 41:43; 46:29; etc.); the scene of that story is, then, the New Empire that arose after the expulsion of the Hyksos. Israel, on the other hand, did not possess war horses and chariots till the time of David and Solomon. The Bible tells nothing about the reign of the Hyksos in Egypt. If the Israelite tribes were already in existence, they must have stood entirely outside the stream of these events.

A widely held view sees in the activities of the Palestinian Hapiru[4] one stage or another of the Hebrew invasion of Canaan. But, even if we admit that Hapiru and Hebrew are related terms, that Hapiru could also signify an ethnic group, and that the Israelite tribes were connected with them, it is still unlikely that the data on the Hapiru have anything to do with the history of Israel. The Bible speaks of tribes; the Hapiru in Palestine and elsewhere are, for the most part, only mercenaries or slaves. They are rootless migrants, never represented as ethnic units on the move in search of tribal territory. What they conquer is for the kings and princes who hire them or for the sake of plunder. At times, a city is "given" to them by their masters as quarters; nothing suggests an ethnic settlement. Unlike the

---

[3] [A mixed horde of Asiatic invaders, marked by their military organization (they brought the war horse and chariot into Egypt and excelled in city fortification), the Hyksos conquered Egypt about 1720, built their capital in Tanis-Avaris-Rameses in the delta, and were driven back into Palestine by Pharaoh Aahmes in 1580.]

[4] [A soldier class mentioned in the el-Amarna letters written by Canaanite vassals to the Egyptian court during the fifteenth to fourteenth centuries. The correspondents seek Egyptian help against "rebels" and "traitors," among whom the Hapiru play a leading role. An oft-repeated complaint is that "the whole land is going over to the Hapiru."]

Israelite tribes they are thoroughly enmeshed in the intrigues of the Canaanite kings against each other and against Egypt.

A Hebrew settlement in Palestine before the conquest is a figment of scholarly imagination. In the inscriptions of Seti I, Ramses II, and the kings who follow them nothing is heard of the Hapiru as a general hazard or as an element of the settled population, nor does the Bible ever speak of a settlement in preconquest times.

Nonetheless, the probable identity of the terms Hapiru and Hebrews does permit the important inference that from the beginning of the second millennium B.C., there was a movement of Hebrews into the culture lands of the Near East. Many came as slaves and mercenaries and, in the course of time, assimilated into their surroundings. These are the Hapiru of the extra-biblical sources. But the same path was trod by others who preserved their tribal organization, their pastoral way of life, and their cultural tradition. The biblical record concerns tribes of this category.

Together with his three sons Terah, the father of Abraham, leaves Ur of the Chaldees for Harran in northern Mesopotamia. In Harran, Terah settles, but Abraham and his nephew Lot continue to journey southward to Canaan. In Canaan the band of Israelite tribes takes shape, separating gradually from their "relations" (Amon and Moab, Edom and the Arabs). Ethnically, they are a conglomerate; Aram is Abraham's homeland, from which he and his descendants take wives for their sons. Judah and Simeon take Canaanite wives; Joseph marries an Egyptian who bears him Ephraim and Manasseh. Israel is thus depicted as an ethnic mixture of Hebrew, Aramaic, Canaanite, and Egyptian elements. Moreover, it did not consider itself a desert tribe; its ancestors originated in the high civilization of Babylonia and wandered for centuries through the culture lands of the ancient Near East. When the tribes later flee in desperation to the desert, their ultimate goal is settlement in Canaan. Biblical tradition regards even the genuine Bedouin as fugitives from civilization. Ishmael becomes a "wild ass of a man" when he leaves Canaan for the desert; the "sons of the East" are sent away by Abraham from Canaan. So far goes the biblical picture of the patriarchs.

It must be assumed that in reality the tribes preceded the "patriarchs," the tribes being the seedbed for the growth of the patriarchal legends. If the *Banū-yamīna* of the Mari letters are related to their biblical cognomens (Benjamin)—they inhabit the region in Mesopotamia in which the biblical Terahides settled—this will, on the one hand, cast doubt on the biblical distinction between a patriarchal and a tribal stage of Israelite origins. On the other hand, it will mean that the tribes were in existence long before the conquest. Presumably they were part of a larger group that also included the descendants of "Lot," "Ishmael," and "Esau." The patriarchs themselves are not tribal symbols but historical personages enveloped in legend. They were "princes of God," the venerated leaders of the Hebrew tribes. That they are represented as aliens in Canaan reflects the fact that during this period the tribes were still landless wanderers. The patriarchal age, then, is the period of the confederation of the Israelite tribes. It was the period in which the ethnic unit of the *Benē-Yiśrāēl* was formed.

At that time the interrelationship of the tribes was established. Reuben was the "first born," but he declined early to be replaced by Joseph and Judah. Joseph was envied its leading position; perhaps because of this, it was harried so that it was the first to wander into Egypt. The division of the tribes into sons of wives and of concubines also belongs to this period; it reflects distinctions that were already obsolete by the period of the judges. Some social distinction is probably referred to; perhaps the sons of concubines were late adherents to the tribal band and were still in client status at the time. The allusion to the "brothers," Simeon and Levi, and their mischief (Gen. 49:5 ff.), and the account of their massacre of Shechemites refers to events of this period. Judah attempted to settle in the south of the land and intermarried with the Canaanites (Gen. 38); later, however, it too joined the movement to Egypt.

The historical allusions of Genesis 14 do not offer much help in fixing the date of this age. Not only are they obscure, but the story, though old, has peculiar features which are without parallel in the patriarchal narratives. The circumstances mirrored in the stories as a whole are a surer guide. The patriarchs live in almost idyllic peace, linked to their neighbors by covenants of friendship. Neither the wars of Egypt with the Hyksos, nor the internal convulsions of the el-Amarna age find any echo in their lives.[5] The post-Hyksos—indeed, the post–el-Amarna—age seems to be indicated. The stories presuppose an extended period of peace in Palestine, such as the reigns of Seti I and Ramses II, most of whose wars were waged in Syria. After Seti I's war with the Shasu the southern kings were submissive to Egypt, and southern Palestine is the main arena of the patriarchal stories.

[5] Not even the military campaigns of Genesis 14 violate the tranquillity of the land; the militant Abram of Genesis 14 fights beyond the borders of Canaan. The Dinah-Shechem episode, on the other hand, is isolated and accidental and utterly untypical of the patriarchs' situation. The motive of the conflict is typical of the feuds which abound among nomad tribes. The massacre disturbs the peace and frightens Jacob, thus underlining the idyllic setting of the story.

At least the greater part of the patriarchal age, then, is to be placed in the nineteenth dynasty, after 1350 B.C.

THE CULTURAL CONDITION OF THE ISRAELITE TRIBES—Although the tribes were not absorbed by the peoples among whom they wandered, they were deeply influenced by their high culture. Israelite religion bears the impress of these various cultures.

There is the primary Hebrew-Aramaic element, reflected first in the tribal organization, and the concept of the nation as descended from a patriarch. Among Israel's neighbors in antiquity, only the Arabic tribes share this idea with Israel. It is, therefore, to be regarded as a legacy of the most ancient period. The *kāhin*-type of seer, who prophesies under the influence of a familiar spirit, who is unconnected with sanctuary or cult, who participates in wars, and, at times, becomes the leader of his tribe has also left his mark on early Israelite prophecy. The lot-oracle, connected both in Israel and Arabia with temples, belongs here too. Israelite wisdom literature has, according to the testimony of the Bible itself, points of contact with the wisdom of the "sons of the East."

Babylonian civilization left a profound impression on Israelite culture. Biblical legend (especially concerning primeval times), law (especially the Covenant Code, Exod. 20:19—23:33), hymnody, and wisdom literature are manifestly indebted to Mesopotamia. There is no reason to assume (as is often done) that this debt was transmitted to the Israelites by way of Canaan. The tribes lived in the sphere of Babylonian culture; the impression it left on Israel doubtless goes back to patriarchal times.

In Canaan the Aramaic dialect of the tribes was exchanged for "the language of Canaan" (Isa. 19:18). This linguistic transformation occurred before the conquest, indeed, before the Israelites had parted from their Ammonite, Moabite, and Edomite kin; for the languages of the latter, who never settled in Canaan, underwent the same transformation. The recovery of Ugaritic literature has revealed to what an extent biblical poetry is rooted in Canaanite models. The Genesis legends have a Canaanite element in them, as does biblical psalmody. The divine epithets, ᶜelyōn, baᶜal, ᵓāḏōn, are Canaanite; the legend of the wise Daniel, who is mentioned in Ezekiel 28:3, and, with the righteous Noah and Job in 14:14, 20, is also Canaanite. From the Canaanites such Dionysiac features of the cult as the wine festival, libation, and ecstatic prophecy were adopted. Israel's sacrificial terminology (and surely its practice as well) was influenced by the Canaanites. These influences may be assumed to have been absorbed by the tribes during their wanderings in Canaan in patriarchal times.

There is, third, an Egyptian element discernible in Israelite culture.

It is visible in the local color of the Joseph stories and the Egyptian names of the priestly tribe: Moses, Aaron, Phinehas, Hur, Hanamel, Pashhur, etc. To be sure, the influence of Egyptian culture was less than that of Babylonia and Canaan. Yet Egyptian sapiential literature had a considerable influence on Israelite wisdom. Egyptian hymnody too, has left its traces. The technical magical wonder of the Bible is ultimately Egyptian; it is, perhaps, the most significant Israelite adaptation of Egyptian material. The Egyptian technical wonder became in Israel the wondrous sign that testified to the truth of the apostolic prophet, and thus was one of the chief expressions of the Israelite idea.

Amidst this high cultural environment, Israelite religion was born. Its prehistory is not to be sought in primitive or Bedouin religion, but in the mellowed civilizations of the ancient Near East. Its initial level was not magical, totemistic, animistic, or demonistic; it originated among developed theistic religions. The gods of Babylonia, Egypt, and Canaan were world creators and rulers, founders of culture and society, guardians of justice and morality. Israel did not have to develop these concepts; it inherited them. Moreover, by the end of the second millennium B.C., the religions of the Near East had evolved far beyond mere ethnic or collective ideas. The individual and his fate were the subjects of constant speculation. Egyptian thought knew the idea of a judgment after death. A universalistic tendency is also evident in these religions. The great gods were cosmic and sustained all living things. Religious expression in psalms, laments, and prayers had reached a high artistic level. The wisdom literatures of Babylonia and Egypt give voice to lofty moral sentiments. On this soil Israelite religion sprang up.

THE RELIGION OF THE PATRIARCHAL AGE—Biblical tradition represents the patriarchs as monotheists. Can this tradition be credited?

It is the view of the Bible that primeval men were monotheists. In Genesis 1–11 there is no trace of idolatry. Apparently—though this is not made explicit—biblical tradition conceived the origin of idolatry as coeval with the origin of nations at the confusion of tongues. For from Genesis 12 the worship of the one God is maintained by Abraham and his descendants alone, while the rest of the world—aside from such individual exceptions as Melchizedek—are idolaters. Abraham is thus not represented as the founder of monotheistic religion. He is but a link in the chain of monotheists that goes back to Adam. What distinguishes the patriarchs is their role as ancestors of the nation that was destined to become monotheistic. The biblical view gives no support to the theory that Abraham originated the idea of the one God or founded a congregation of monotheists.

Now there is no evidence for the biblical notion that the religion of primitive men was monotheism. Empirical history knows only of a monotheistic people in antiquity. That individuals in early ages were monotheists is a notion rooted in the Israelite narration of primeval history in monotheistic terms. It goes without saying that Israel's patriarchs were also included in this monotheistic history. Biblical legend could hardly have regarded them as different in this respect from Adam, Enoch, Noah, and the rest.

However, the Bible itself attests indirectly to the fact that Israel's monotheism is postpatriarchal. Historical monotheism is associated always with certain phenomena which serve as its organic framework: apostolic prophecy, the battle with idolatry, and the name of YHWH. Patriarchal times know none of these. Genesis records divine manifestations and prophecies, but there is no trace of apostolic prophecy. No patriarch is charged with a prophetic mission; the first apostolic prophet is Moses. Nowhere in Genesis is there reference to a battle with idolatry. The divine covenants with the patriarchs promise personal protection and future material blessings. But they never involve a fight with idolatry, nor do the patriarchs ever appear as reproaching their contemporaries for idolatry. Indeed, there is no religious contrast between the patriarchs and their surroundings. The tension between Israel and the pagan world arises first with the appearance of Moses. Finally, both JE (Exod. 3:13 ff.) and P (6:2 f.) preserve the tradition that the name YHWH was unknown to the patriarchal age, having been disclosed for the time to Moses at the burning bush. This is confirmed by the absence among early Hebrew names of the element YHWH.

Hence it must be assumed that Israelite monotheism arose after the patriarchal age. The monotheism of the patriarchs, then, is the child of later conceptions—the same that produced the monotheist cast of the primeval legends of Genesis. It is significant that while the God of Moses is termed "God of the fathers," the people are not said to have known or worshiped him in Egypt. The people—the real bearers of historical monotheism—even according to biblical tradition, did not inherit their faith from the patriarchal age.

What, then, is the historical kernel in the tradition that calls YHWH "God of the fathers," and Abraham the father of the Israelite nation? Although the Bible does not portray Abraham as a fighter for YHWH, it does depict him as a God-fearing and moral man. He pursues peace (Gen. 13:8 f.), is generous (14:21 ff.), hospitable (18:1 ff.), and intercedes on behalf of the Sodomites (vss. 23 ff.). He charges his descendants to observe "the way of YHWH" to do righteousness and justice (vs. 19). In Genesis 22, he is said to have substituted animal for human sacrifice. Abraham may thus be regarded as a pious "prince of God" among his tribe, who aspired to a noble, moral faith which he bequeathed to his descendants. To what extent this ancestral faith may have influenced Moses we cannot say. Later legend seized upon Abraham and made him the father of Israelite religion. But the absence of the essential motifs of Israelite religion in patriarchal times indicates that it was not then that the monotheistic idea came into being. In the patriarchal age the tribes were formed and absorbed the culture of the lands through which they wandered. Their leaders and artists cultivated song and legend, wisdom and morality, righteousness and justice. But it was in Egypt that the new religious idea sprang forth that was to transform their life and the lives of many nations.

THE BEGINNING OF ISRAELITE RELIGION

The Torah is, as we have observed, a folk literature, and it is pervaded by the monotheistic idea. The quest for origins cannot, therefore, concern itself merely with the author of the monotheistic idea; equally pressing is the question of the origin of that environment within which the popular monotheistic legends found in the Bible could have been created. The birth of the idea was not sufficient to produce such an environment; the idea might well have remained the private property of a spiritual elite. Only by uprooting the pagan popular religion could it have become the property of a people. And only men of the people, not philosophers or sages, could have succeeded in such an enterprise. The problem of origins, then, is this: When was the battle against the pagan folk religion joined, out of which a monotheistic people emerged?

The Torah literature testifies that this battle took place not only before the time of the literary prophets, but even before the formation of the Torah literature itself. This is the meaning of the fact that every level of the Bible, even the very earliest, views the pagan world as godless. That no story of a battle with paganism is recorded before the age of Moses suggests a terminus *a quo*. Only with Moses does the contrast between the faith of YHWH and paganism appear. Needless to say, it was not the intention of the biblical writers to make this distinction between the pre-Mosaic age and all that followed; nor, indeed, do they ever indicate that they are aware of such a distinction. The difference between the ages is, then, a historical one; the struggle with paganism began with Moses.

THE HISTORICAL TESTIMONY TO MOSES—The historicity of Moses is vouched for by trustworthy historical facts. It is a historical fact that while Israel, from its beginnings, regarded itself as the people of YHWH, this tie between people and YHWH did not exist in patriarchal times. It is a fact that apostolic prophecy is formative for the history of Israel from its beginnings. The political organization of the period of the judges is founded on belief in this institution. It is a fact that in early Israel a struggle was waged on behalf of YHWH, the jealous God. The setting of this struggle is a monotheistic people; its heroes are the apostolic prophets. When and where did belief in the jealous god YHWH, whose cause is championed by apostolic prophets, arise? Inasmuch as neither Babylon, Egypt, nor Canaan know of these phenomena, their origin must be sought within Israel itself. Moreover, the spiritual revolution, that gave historic moment to these ideas, must have been, like all similar events in history, the working of a creative genius and leader of men. Following the biblical saga, we call this pioneer creative spirit by the name Moses.

Every feature of the biblical Moses bespeaks a pioneer. The beginning of his activity is related in the legend of the burning bush (Exod. 3—4:17). Here, for the first time in history, a prophet is commissioned by a god to redeem men. The theophany takes place in the desert, at a site without cultic significance before or after. Neither the patriarchs nor later generations build altars or temples to YHWH at Sinai or Kadesh. The desert has prophetic sanctity only, and this originates in the theophany to Moses. Moses comes to the place ignorant of its holiness. He beholds something for which he was totally unprepared. He was not informed by Jethro either of the sanctity of the place, or of the name of the God who revealed himself there. The theophany of the bush has no roots in any existent cult, Kenite or Midianite, nor does the Hebrew people know of the sanctity of the place or the name of the God who manifested himself there. Moses is the first to discover both. He is called upon to proclaim a God heretofore known only to individuals to an entire people. The first prophet with a mission to a people was Moses.

The legend of the bush is the first in which signs play a part; Moses is given signs to confirm his mission. The Egyptian technical wonder is fundamentally recast; Israel's prophet performs miracles by the word of God. Moses learns YHWH's name, but not for magical purposes. This is typical of the entire saga; Moses never acts as an independent magician. On the contrary, he is helpless until the word of God comes to him. Moses is the archetype of the wonder-working prophet.

The redemption of Israel creates a clash between Moses and the heathen empire of Egypt. Pharaoh does not acknowledge YHWH, and so YHWH acts to glorify his name in the sight of Egypt. For the first time the line is drawn between the people of YHWH and a heathen world that is ignorant of him. Moses is the one who draws the line.

There can be no doubt that there is a connection between the rise of that popular monotheistic environment within which the early biblical legends grew and the life of Moses. The religious transformation of Israel is the lifework of that colossus of the spirit.

Biblical tradition connects the commandment "You shall have no other gods before me" with the Sinaitic theophany, the climax of YHWH's revelation to Israel. And doubtless it was at Sinai that pagan beliefs were dealt their final blow and belief in YHWH was confirmed in the hearts of the people forever. But that battle must have started in Egypt; indeed, it must have occurred at the very outset. In the account of Moses' activity in Egypt the front against idolatry faces Egypt. The battle is already at full tilt, having as its presupposition the faith of Israel in YHWH and his prophet. The millennial-long contrast between Israel and the nations is already full blown in these stories. The struggle ends with the fall of the pagan king and his magicians. Egypt is not converted to belief in YHWH, but Israel's faith is confirmed. This was the ultimate purpose of all the signs given Moses at the bush (Exod. 4:1–31). The narrative of the wonders closes with: "The people feared YHWH and believed in YHWH and in Moses, his servant" (14:31). The legends of Moses in Egypt do not tell explicitly of his battle with Israelite paganism, but the testimony to this battle is implicit in these stories throughout. The revelation of the name YHWH at the bush opens the battle with paganism and establishes the contrast between Israel and Egypt. It is the beginning of the monotheistic revolution in Israel.

Since the basic idea of Israelite religion has, as we have seen, no roots in paganism, Moses must have been the first to conceive it. Can his creation be explained? The birth of every original idea is a mystery which defies attempts to account for it. The task of the historian is not only to account for what he can, but also to see clearly what is beyond his capacity to explain. Now, if to explain a new idea means to show its historical-cultural derivation, we must assert that the Israelite idea has no source in paganism. This assertion does not, however, disengage Israelite religion and the appearance of Moses from the framework of history. It seeks solely to distinguish between cultural-historical antecedents and the innovation that appeared within their framework. To say that Israelite religion was a novel creation, essentially different from every form of paganism, does not deny the many threads that connect it with the cultures in whose midst it was born. We have repeatedly affirmed that Israelite religion incorporated a legacy from paganism, materials into which it breathed a new spirit. It is of utmost importance to bear in mind that the general level of Israel's culture derives from its environment. But against this background, an idea that paganism never contemplated sprang forth. This is what cannot be explained in terms of evolution, no more than any new cultural idea can be so explained.

Did Moses know the speculations of the priests of Babylon and Egypt, or of the "solar monotheism" of Akhenaton? Was he an Egyptian? These matters are neither here nor there. Moses is the historical person who first envisioned the peculiar ideas of Israelite religion. His racial stock is of no consequence, the only significant fact being that his new idea was neither Egyptian nor Babylonian. His thought cannot be related to any "monotheistic tendencies" in Egypt or Babylon without distorting it. Those tendencies did indeed aspire to a sort of monism, but it is not a question of number that distinguishes the Israelite idea of God. Belief in "one Marduk" or "one Re" or "one Aton" is, for all that, no less pagan.[6] It is not an arith-

---

[6] The great hymn to Aton, for example, regards the physical sun itself as a divine being, or the embodiment of a divine being. It addresses the rising, setting, and warming sun; the creative force of the sun is conceived of in wholly pagan terms of incorporation or generation. The sun's rays nourish and suckle the plant. Out of itself the sun has created many beings. The king is the sun's son, born out of his limbs or inner parts. Aton himself begat him. Though Aton appears to have created all, it is never said, for example, that he created the sea, or the moon and stars. In the great hymn, Aton's fatigue when he sets is alluded to, and in the phrase "who rejoices on the horizon (at sunrise)" lurks an allusion to his reinvigoration. The Aton disk is always portrayed with the divine serpent—the protector of gods and kings. In Atonism, the king retains his divine role. Akhenaton is still "the good god" who "creates what the entire earth needs," thus continuing the ancient tradition of divine kingship. And he worships his dead father as well. Atonism shows no tendencies either to abstraction or symbolism; attempts to minimize its normal pagan features by interpreting them symbolically are, therefore, unwarranted. It does not represent the god in human and animal form, because it adhered rather to the realistic image of the sun disk. Its abandonment of the more "futuristic," Egyptian mythological images may also be referred to this tendency to realism which is evident in all the art of the era. In language, too, it aspired to realistic plainness. If we find in its art the picture of the serpent, the symbol of life (*ankh*) and the symbol of *maat*, we must understand these as real magical forces. The deification of the king is sufficient to show that the basically pagan idea of apotheosis was alive in this religion.

It is of crucial importance that the king introduced the worship of Aton and celebrated the thirty-year festival of the new god (and himself) at a time when he still did not repudiate the cult of other gods. Inscriptions on boundary stones of Akhetaton (el-Amarna) even tell of the king's intention to build a sepulcher to Mnevis, the sacred bull of Heliopolis. Aton was thus at first one of many gods; his exclusiveness came about only gradually. It had at first a political basis, the king's quarrel with the priests of Amon. Akhenaton's zeal was a personal phenomenon, but his idea—the exaltation of the worship of the sun—is not necessarily bound up with zealotry. Akhenaton did make room, after all, for another god beside Aton—himself. It may be surmised that if his religion would have been permitted to develop, it would have evolved its own mythology, as singular and original as its style in art.

metical diminution of the number of gods, but a new religious category that
is involved, the category of a God above nature, whose will is supreme,
who is not subject to compulsion and fate, who is free of the bonds of myth
and magic. This idea, which informs all of biblical creativity, is what paganism never knew. As Moses must be considered the initiator of a religious
revolution, so he must be considered the creator of an original idea.

Why and how this idea arose in his mind we do not know. We should
not know even if we possessed more than those remarkable legends relating
the revelation made to Moses. It is possible, however, to delineate the social
and historical background of that revelation.

The prophetic type of Moses belongs to the earliest stage of Israelite
prophecy. Moses is an antique model of an apostolic prophet; he is a leader
and judge having political authority. Like Deborah, Gideon, Samson,
and Samuel he makes his appearance in time of trouble. Like them, he
"judges" Israel all his life. Like Gideon, Elijah, and Elisha he fights idolatry
and personally works judgments on idols and their worshipers.

But there are also peculiar features about Moses. He is accompanied
by two other prophetic figures, his brother Aaron (his "mouth" and
"prophet" to Pharaoh), and his sister Miriam, a prophetess and poetess.
YHWH speaks through the three (Num. 12:2 ff.); the three were sent to
Israel in Egypt (Mic. 6:4). Such a family of prophetic personages is never
again found in Israel. But pagan prophecy—and this is particularly true
of Arab *kāhins*—often manifested itself as the property of a family of seers.

Like the *kāhin*, Moses is not connected with an established temple or
cult. Whether Moses was ever himself a *kāhin* or not, he seems to have grown
up among a family of such seers, and this surely affected him. The ancient
Hebrew *kāhin*-clairvoyant was the social type that served as the vehicle
of his appearance as prophet and leader. The case of Mohammed in later
times is an instructive parallel. Mohammed was not an actual *kāhin*,
but his visions and poetic expression grew out of the soil of *kāhin* prophecy.
At first Mohammed feared that he was nothing but a possessed *kāhin*,
until he became convinced that an angel was speaking with him. If the
content of his prophecy was not *kāhin*ic, its form was, and his influence
and acceptance among his contemporaries were founded on the current
belief in *kāhin* prophecy. Similarly, the new message of Moses clothed itself
in a form familiar to the people of those times. That a divine spirit revealed
itself to a lonely seer was not an incredible thing; that this man should
become leader of his people was also not unheard of. And, since the ancient
Hebrew seer was not bound by a specific cult or temple, Moses enjoyed
the freedom necessary for the expression of a new idea. To this seer, however,

there appeared not a familiar spirit but a supernal, omnipotent God. Moses returned to his people not a clairvoyant, but a messenger of God.

The legends about Moses are peculiar in the vividness of their Egyptian coloring. For the first time, the Egyptian type of technical wonders appear: a fixed magical instrument (the staff), the transmutation of substances (staff-serpent-staff), the creation of animals out of matter. Despite earlier contacts with Egypt (in patriarchal times), such motifs appear first here, and henceforth they become fixed adjuncts of prophecy. These features constitute a faithful historical record of Egyptian influence upon Israelite prophecy at its very birth.

The figure of Moses possesses a feature of Canaanite prophetism as well; contact with him brings about Dionysiac behavior. Such a collective frenzy as described in Numbers 11 is peculiar to the cultural area of Canaan and Greece. Thus three cultures have left their mark on the life and legends of Moses. The historical situation mirrored here is the time after the Hebrew tribes had entered into Egypt following their sojourn in Canaan.

All the traditional sources depict Moses as a messenger; he is the first of the historic series of apostolic prophets. The beginning of his work was a prophetic experience. He did not learn a priestly doctrine in Egypt, Midian, or elsewhere; he did not arrive at his insights through meditation, nor did he seek to communicate to a circle of disciples a new theological truth that had dawned upon him. He was sent; his God revealed himself to him and let him hear his voice. Intuitive insight took the shape of a prophetic vision. The legend of the burning bush is the necessary prelude to Moses' appearance as a messenger of God. It is no less historical in its essence than later legends about prophetic visions, or, for that matter, than the legends concerning the visions of Mohammed.

THE UNIVERSAL AND THE NATIONAL IN MOSES' MESSAGE—The narrative of Exodus represents national liberation as the object of the wonders that were performed in Egypt. But another motif is also present: the battle between the God of Israel and arrogant heathendom. The redemption of Israel is at the same time the victory of YHWH over Pharaoh and his empire. Pharaoh's refusal to listen and his hardness of heart enable YHWH to reveal his might "that you may know that the earth is YHWH's" (9:29), "that Egypt may know that I am YHWH" (14:4; etc.). The God of the legends controls all of nature, bringing on evil as well as good. That he is not conceived of as a merely national deity is clear from the fact that there is no tension between him and other gods. The opposing forces are not various national gods, but defiant heathen men. Pharaoh ends by recognizing YHWH and submitting to him; here the ideal universalism of early Israelite religion comes to light. Clearly, YHWH in these legends is a cosmic and unique God, notwithstanding the special national purpose of his acts.

Many theories have been advanced concerning the primary meaning of the name YHWH and its derivation. All that can be known beyond doubt is the value of the name since the time that Moses brought it to the Israelite tribes. Henceforth, YHWH was the symbol of the monotheistic idea for the Torah literature, as for the prophets. YHWH is *"the* God," one and supernal, but he is also "the holy one of Israel." The national and universal are united.

The new religious idea took effect immediately in the realm of human events. Its national element gave it body. The new God did not reveal himself to found a new cult, to gain support in his cosmic struggle for existence; he did not consecrate a priest or arch-magician. He sent a messenger to reveal his will to men. His first appearance was as redeemer and savior; his demand was for an unremitting battle among men for faith in him. To initiate this battle is the task of the messenger. Moses first aroused the tribes with the message of the transcendent God, the invisible lord of all the earth, whom no man knew, and who showed himself to him in a wondrous vision in the desert. This God sent him to make a covenant with Israel, to make them his people, and promised them the land of Canaan. The new religious content of this message alone is what made the events that befell the tribes— petty in themselves—"signs" testifying to the One. In its light their troubles became "trials" and their impatience and weakness rebellion and faithlessness. It transformed their history into a religious drama of unique significance.

THE MONOTHEISTIC REVOLUTION

The tradition of the Torah and Prophets represents the first period of Israelite history until the time of the judges as a monotheistic period, in which Israel did not yet worship the gods of the nations.[7] The sin of the desert age is obduracy and faithlessness, grumbling, and trial of God. Despite the presence of God in fire, cloud, and tent, and a continuous series of wonders the people are fickle. But that Israel is joined to YHWH by an eternal covenant whose violation entails grave penalties is an idea that even

[7] Deuteronomy 32:15 ff.; Joshua 24:31 ff.; Hosea 9:10; Jeremiah 2:2. The golden calf is represented either as dedicated to YHWH (Exod. 32:5) or as a fetishistic god-image in itself (vss. 1, 4); in neither case is it a foreign god. The apostasy to Baal Peor is an isolated episode, with which weakness of flesh had as much to do as weakness of faith (see Num. 25:1 ff.). Ezekiel's claim (20:7 ff.) that Israel worshiped idols in Egypt even after YHWH's call is unfounded—part of the rebuke scheme of the whole chapter.

the most contentious of them do not challenge. The people as a whole never once suggest exchanging their God for another. The stories concerning the sin of idolatry in the desert are highly instructive. While the sin of the golden calf is attributed to the whole people, only 3,000 out of a total of 600,000 (Exod. 32:28) are said to have been punished for it. Again, while the worship of Baal Peor is counted as a national sin it is plain from the command made to the judges—"Execute each of you those of your men who joined Baal Peor" (Num. 25:5)—that only part of the people sinned. Israel made war upon the Midianites for having inveigled them into this apostasy (Num. 25:16 ff.; 31:1 ff.). If so, then, why does the narrative speak as though all the people had fallen away? Because it assumes that since Israel is the covenant people of YHWH they are all answerable for violations of the covenant. Collective punishment for the sins of a few implies that though some sin of idolatry is found among the people, the people as a whole never apostatize. They never made a covenant with another god—certainly not in the desert period, when YHWH was in their midst.

With Moses the sin of idolatry—particularly as a national sin—comes into existence. Before, idolatry was nowhere interdicted and punished. The stories depicting idolatry as a national sin presuppose the existence of a monotheistic people. Since such stories begin only with Moses, we infer that it was in his time that the great transformation took place. By making Israel enter a covenant with the one God, he made it a monotheistic people that alone among men was punishable for the sin of idolatry.

THE DEATH OF THE GODS—We do not have a reliable account of the original content of Moses' message. Although the whole of biblical literature is a product of the deep transformation that it brought about, the Bible tells nothing of the course of that transformation. In the first stage of the new religion there was doubtless a battle against the gods of the Hebrew pantheon and their myths. The various proclamations of the oneness of God, "YHWH, he is the God," "YHWH is one," "The earth is YHWH's," presumably include a judgment on pagan beliefs. The command "You shall have no other gods before me" must have had real substance at this time. Moses may have polemized against belief in theogony, divine sexuality, and death and resurrection of deity. If all traces of this battle have disappeared, it can only mean that it was brief and quickly won. The image of the one God captured the heart of the people; beside it, there was no room for other gods. The ancient gods either became impotent shades, or disappeared, leaving their name as epithets of the One. Their domain became the realm of impurity, without any power at all. The idea of a God who works wonders, rules all destinies, controls good and evil, light and darkness, wind and water, life and death ruled out a battle of divine forces. In place of mythological drama came the drama of God's will working itself out in human history.[8]

THE EXODUS AND THE COVENANT

Although potentially and essentially universal, the historical sphere of the new faith was a small group of shepherd tribes.

At the beginning of Pharaoh Merneptah's reign, Egypt's energies were taken up with an invasion from Lybia and rebellions in Palestine. The moment seemed propitious for the tribes to escape, and under Moses' leadership, they succeeded in gaining their freedom.[9] There is little prospect of retracing with any precision the path of the Exodus, since scarcely any of the places named in the Bible on this route have been identified. This much, however, seems clear: Rameses is to be identified with Tanis, in the northern part of the delta, and it is in that vicinity that Goshen, the place of the tribes' settlement in Egypt, is to be located. It is, therefore, unlikely that the tribes traveled to the southern extremity of the Sinai Peninsula, as tradition has it. The Red Sea cannot be either Lake Timsah, or the gulfs of Suez or Aqaba, nor can Mount Sinai be in the southern tip

[8] Such great upheavals have occurred more than once in history. In Mohammed's time, the Arab tribes were polytheistic in spite of having been influenced in some measure by Judaism and Christianity. They met Mohammed's message with hostility; his own tribesmen sought to kill him. Yet, within the short space of twenty years Mohammed effected a religious revolution among his people. By the end of his life, Arab tribes were streaming to his standard; his apostles passed through the land, demolishing heathen temples and breaking their idols. At his death a great army of fanatical Moslems was already on the march into many lands. The Arabs never again relapsed into idolatry. The same is true of the several peoples who subsequently adopted Islam, willingly or by force. Christianity spread much more slowly. Yet here too several peoples underwent a forced conversion that quickly worked a fundamental change in their religion, so that paganism never again showed itself among them.

Islam and Christianity both labored in a much larger field than Moses and among peoples who had a venerable religion, with temples, priesthoods, and political interests. Moses worked only with a few pastoral tribes, who were strangers in a foreign land. Their culture and religion was an amalgam having no established center of influence, nor did they have a stable political organization. The national-religious message of Moses is what first consolidated them into a people. For at bottom, the tribal confederation was a free band of believers. Whoever accepted the message of the new God could join the covenant; there were no definite territorial or ethnic qualifications at the beginning.

[9] The time of these events appears to be the end of the thirteenth century B.C. in the reign of Merneptah (1235–1227). Although no names of kings are given in the biblical account, Exodus 1:11 relates that the Israelites built the cities of Pithom and Raamses. Inasmuch as Ramses II built cities by this name, presumably he was the king of the oppression. Moses' activity occurred, then, during the reign of his son Merneptah.

of the peninsula. The immediate aim of the tribes was doubtless to escape the Egyptians and—bearing in mind the decisive importance of kinship—to make contact with the Midianites, Moses' relations. This suggests that their route led from northern Egypt into the nearby desert of the isthmus— between Egypt to the west, and Edom to the east. This desert is "great and terrible," but it also has wells and cisterns, pasturage, and some land suitable for tillage, so that it can sustain a considerable population.

The tribes, numbering several thousand persons, assembled in the land of Rameses and marched southeast to Succoth and Etham—"the edge of the desert." From there they turned northward toward Lake Sirbonis, perhaps because the seaside has more wells. This lake, separated from the Mediterranean by a thin sand strip, is a spot ripe for disasters. The sand strip is sometimes submerged, and the shores of the lake are swampy. Whole armies have perished here. It was in this region, apparently, that a clash between the fugitives and an Egyptian force took place. A triumphal stele of Merneptah speaks of the destruction of a nomad group of "Israel." It would seem that part of the Egyptian army, on its return from a campaign in Palestine, met the fleeing tribes and pressed them seaward toward Lake Sirbonis. During the night the fugitives managed to escape, but the pursuing party was drowned at the treacherous site. The Israelites commemorated their deliverance in legend and song. Merneptah, on the other hand, relates that he smote "Israel," the nomad people, in "Khuru" (for this region was considered by Egypt as part of Syria-Palestine), and "destroyed its seed."

The tribes escaped into the wilderness. There is no doubt that this was merely a temporary refuge for them, a station on their way to another goal. Modern criticism, discounting biblical tradition, suggests that Moses wished to bring the people to Kadesh, presumably their place of origin, where some of the tribes may have established themselves even earlier. Only later, it is supposed, when their numbers grew, did the people think of moving northward into Canaan. This theory is groundless. No shred of biblical tradition locates any of the ancestors of Israel at Kadesh nor, indeed, anywhere in the desert. The Israelites were not desert nomads and did not trace their origin back to the desert. They have none of the love of the desert that is found, to this day, among true desert nomads. While their most exalted religious memories are associated with the Wandering, this period is uniformly represented as one of hardship and suffering. The harsh decree of the forty-year Wandering is a result of sin; only by the grace of God did Israel survive it. Moses could hardly have stirred a people who had lived for generations in Canaan and Egypt by the promise of bringing them into the wilderness. Their prolonged stay at Kadesh can only have been an unavoidable necessity.

Moses' immediate goal, however, was the "mountain of God," where YHWH had first revealed his name to him.

THE COVENANT AT SINAI—The account of what occurred at Sinai has been preserved in several versions, all wreathed in legend. Exodus 24 seems to be the principal source. At one of the mountains in the desert of the isthmus, between Egypt and Midian-Seir, Moses assembled the twelve tribes and made them enter the covenant. At the foot of the mountain he built an altar and erected twelve pillars, one for each of the tribes. He made a sacrifice and sprinkled blood over the altar and the people. He read the terms of the covenant to the people. After the ceremony, there was a sacred feast before YHWH. The heart of the Decalogue, upon which the covenant was made, is in the first commandment which prohibits the worship of other gods, the host of heaven, and idols. Since the memory of paganism was still alive, it was necessary to combat it and uproot it. "You shall have no other gods before me," "He who sacrifices to a god . . . shall be destroyed" (Exod. 22:19) are echoes of that battle. By entering the covenant, the people as a whole accepted the faith in the one God and abandoned the gods forever.

The covenant also contained a moral-legal element. Moral commands form the bulk of what the legend represents God as proclaiming to the people from amidst fire. The book of the covenant, upon which the covenant was made (Exod. 20:19—23:33), is nearly entirely a collection of laws and judgments. It is a basic presupposition of biblical tradition, shared by the prophets as well, that YHWH gave Israel laws and judgments in the desert. Some prophets declare the legal-moral commandments to have been the very heart of the covenant (Amos 5:25; Jer. 7:21 ff.; 34:13 ff.).

The distinctively new element in the laws of the Sinaitic covenant was not their content. The cultures which the Israelite tribes had absorbed and out of which they had emerged had highly developed notions of law and morality. What innovation was it, centuries after Hammurabi, to ban murder, theft, adultery, or false witness? The Bible itself recognizes the existence of a universal moral law from primeval times, to which all men are subject. Cain, the generation of the Flood, and Sodom are punished for violations of this law. The Sinaitic covenant comes late in the history of man, even according to the biblical story. What point was there to YHWH's giving such ancient and elementary commands to Israel in an awful theophany at Sinai?

The novelty was in the very giving. For the first time morality was represented as a prophetic revelation, an expression of the supreme moral will of God. It was not the doctrine of sages, or the command of rulers, nor even the wisdom of a god who revealed laws along with other matters of art and science (like the laws of Thoth, Oannes, etc.). This law was the command of a God, his absolute will. The idea was expressed in an unparalleled legend: God revealed himself not to a visionary, a priest, or a sage, but to a whole people. Men heard the command from the mouth of God. Morality was thus transferred from the realm of wisdom to the realm of prophecy, the realm of the absolute divine command.

All the laws of the Torah are given to the nation, and the nation as a whole is answerable for their violation. This does not reflect a primitive moral sense, as yet bound to the conception of the collectivity of the tribe or the people. The cultural environment of Israel had long since passed the stage of collective morality. Babylonian, and especially Egyptian, wisdom deal constantly with the individual; this is the level of biblical wisdom as well. It is more ancient than the morality of Torah and prophets. The Sinaitic covenant superimposes upon the ancient individual obligation a new, national one. Morality ceases being a private matter. Because the covenant was accepted en masse, by all, all become responsible for its observance. When the Israelites stood together and heard the command "I am YHWH your God," a new moral subject was created: the community of persons that know YHWH. The religious-cultic distinction of Israel is complemented by a moral distinction. Both are equal in rank, according to the conception of the Torah, and fundamentally connected. YHWH did not elect Israel to found a new magical cult for his benefit; he elected it to be his people, to realize in it his will. The religious covenant was, therefore, by its nature a moral-legal one as well, involving not only the cult but the structure and rules of society. Thus the foundation for the religion of the Torah was laid, including both cult and morality and conceiving both as expressions of the divine will.

One tradition speaks of stone tablets of the covenant (Exod. 31:18; 32:15 f.; 34:28 f.; Deut. 4:13; I Kings 8:9, 21), another of a book (Exod. 24:4 ff.). Both may be historical, since both stone and scroll were used in making covenants or establishing new orders.[10] The tablet tradition, connected with the ark, appears primary, but it is possible that, as in the case of the Shechemite covenant, both stone and book were used. These stones were the "tablets of testimony" that the tribes bore with them as a memorial of the covenant. They became a permanent symbol of Israelite religion.

[10] See, for the first, Genesis 31:44 ff.; for the second, I Samuel 10:25; and, for both, Joshua 24:25 ff.

The new religious idea stirred the popular imagination and brought about the creation of a new genre of legends, whose subject was the life and destiny of the people. First were the legends of the Exodus and Wandering, the Sinaitic theophany, and the conquest. Their central figure was the messenger-prophet—a stirring, new religious type, not a powerful magician, not a priest or a conqueror, but a messenger of God. Such a thing had never been heard of before. We may judge of Israel's enthusiasm and excitement from the tremendous impression made nearly two thousand years later by Mohammed upon men of the same culture area. This first apostle of God in history became the subject of the first saga of Israelite religion.

The new faith also expressed itself in song. Song, music, and dance were part of popular festivity. In Israel, they were vehicles of adoration of YHWH, telling the tale of his triumphs. "Sing to YHWH, for he has been greatly exalted" (Exod. 15:21) was the first song to the new God that broke the desert stillness. The most ancient creation of Israelite religion, "the book of the Wars of YHWH," was a collection of songs relating what happened to Israel in their journeyings through the desert (Num. 21:14 ff.). From the same period come the song to the well (vss. 17 f.), the sentence concerning Amalek (Exod. 17:16), and perhaps also the song of the ark (Num. 10:35 f.). The character of the new religion can already be seen here; it sings not of the wars of the gods but of the wars of Israel, the people of God.

The popular festival also began to take shape in the desert. The giving of the Torah at Sinai was not commemorated in biblical times in a fixed annual festival. Its public ceremony did serve, however, as the prototype of later popular assemblies for covenant purposes (in the days of Joshua, Josiah, Ezra-Nehemiah, etc.). The first annual festival of the new faith was the celebration of the Exodus. We may assume that at the first encampment of the tribes after escape, when they felt themselves secure, they celebrated their first holyday in song and dance to YHWH. They baked *maṣṣōth* —a favorite quick dish in these lands to the present—out of the provisions they brought with them from Egypt. And this became an annual celebration thereafter.[11] Already in the first years of its existence the festival absorbed an older pagan spring rite of sacrifice of firstlings. Firstlings had been sacrificed and their blood smeared on doorposts to ward off evil spirits. In

[11] According to Numbers 9:1 ff., Passover was the only festival that was celebrated during the Wandering; Exodus 12:1 ff. (P) represents it as first celebrated in Egypt, but 12:21 ff. (JE) portrays the paschal sacrifice as an apotropaic measure taken against the plague of the first born, *maṣṣōth* being baked only after the Exodus (vss. 34, 39), and the command concerning the festival applying only to the future.

Israel the pagan festival lost its magical-natural basis and became as-similated to the historical legend of the rescue of Israelite firstborn in Egypt and the Exodus. This was the beginning of a new, non-mythological cult.

At the center of the new religion was the messenger-prophet. Out of veneration for him sprang the ancient Israelite idea of a "kingdom of God." Transcending the old tribal organization, beyond the elders, was the supreme authority of the aspostle of YHWH. Moses was leader, judge, and legislator (Exod. 18:13 ff.). Which were the laws that were given to the tribes in the desert cannot be ascertained, but there can be no doubt that Israel's moral-legal literature, grounded in ancient Semitic law, began to take shape in the desert. Its beginnings were the decisions and judgments of the messenger-prophet.

The phenomenon of Moses impressed upon the tribes a sense of the near-ness of God. The belief that God was in the midst of the camp, revealing himself from time to time to the prophet, could not but have affected the people deeply. In popular festivities about the altar, in the whirl of dance, in rapturous song to YHWH for his mercies and miracles, many must have seen visions. At the meal of the covenant, the "nobles of the Israelites" saw God (Exod. 24:10 f.); at the inauguration of the tabernacle, the glory appears to the people, who fall shouting upon their faces (Lev. 9:23 f.). "To see YHWH" remained forever the ideal climax of Israelite festive celebration. Ecstatic phenomena are also attested to in the desert period. Dionysiac ecstasy was known to the tribes from their sojourn in Canaan. Although apostolic prophecy was utterly different—Moses is not accom-panied by a band of ecstatics but by his faithful servant Joshua—we do hear of ecstasy having been produced on one occasion by Moses' "spirit" (Num. 11:25). Later, ecstasy was sometimes an adjunct of Israelite proph-ecy, but always as a subsidiary phenomenon, a by-product of the revelation of the divine word.

CULT AND PRIESTHOOD—Moses did not repudiate the accepted belief of his age that man's relation to God expresses itself through a cult. Nor did he espouse an abstract, aniconic, and asymbolic cult. To be sure, Mosaic religion did not have images of YHWH, but this is not owing to a radical rejection of images. The fact is that neither in the Torah nor in the prophets is the matter of representing YHWH a crucial issue. Both the desert calf and the two calves of Jeroboam are considered by their opponents to be fetishes, not images of God. The ban on making idols and other figures (Exod. 20:4 f.) follows as a separate prohibition the ban on having other gods The images are thus not conceived of as representations of the other gods, but as objects which in themselves belong to the category "other gods"; they do not symbolize, they *are*, other gods. Israelite religion never knew of nor had to sustain a polemic against representations of YHWH.[12] Intuitively, it rejected representations of God because such images were regarded in paganism as an embodiment of the gods and, as such, objects of a cult. This idea was to Israelite religion the very essence of idolatry; hence from the very outset it rejected without a polemic representations of YHWH. This tacit decision was the crucial moment in the battle against idol-worship.

But the biblical objection to the employment of figures in the cult is not primary or fundamental. Later zealots objected to every sort of image, but this was evidently not the early position. Israelite religion rejected from the first figures worshiped as gods; it did not forbid cultic figures which were not objects of adoration. Moses is said to have made a brazen serpent (Num. 21:8 f.; II Kings 18:4); the cherubs, too, were legitimate and likewise ascribed to Moses. This dual attitude toward images opened the way to inner conflict which, in the course of time, led to the branding of certain practices (e.g., Jeroboam's calves) as idolatrous. But this very conflict indicates that the most ancient traditions of Israel, going back to Moses, did not forbid every type of figure. There is, then, no reason to doubt that the cultic provisions of the Torah, in spite of all their legendary embellishment, have a historic basis.

The desert cult centered about the "tablets of testimony." To guard and bear them on the way required specially consecrated persons, the kernel of the sacerdotal class. The tablets were in an ark, and this was kept in a tent, concerning which there are various traditions. To judge from the information about the tent and ark preserved in the historical books, it appears that P's version of a tent which served both cultic as well as oracular

---

[12] Deuteronomy 4:12 ff. has been understood as combating representations of YHWH and as arguing for an abstract concept of deity. Idol-worship is banned on the ground that Israel saw no form in the fire on Mount Horeb. But if the text wished to assert YHWH's abstractness, it would not have limited it in such a way as to say that no form was seen just at Mount Horeb; it would have said that God has no form. Moreover— and this is decisive—the sequence shows that the chapter deals with the worship of idols and the host of heaven (which YHWH has allotted to the nations, vs. 19) in general, not with the worship of YHWH in images. Now clearly there could be no point in interdicting the idol-gods of the nations on the ground that YHWH has no form. This passage, then, cannot refer to the cult of representational figures, but to the cult of fetish images (see vs. 28). Its ingenuous argument is: there is no basis for worshiping any form in the world, because the people saw no form at Horeb.

Isaiah 40:18 means simply: "To whom shall you liken God, and with what image shall you compare (*taᶜarḵū*) him," as shown by the parallel expression of 40:25 "To whom shall you liken me that I should be like him"; and 46:5 "To whom will you liken me and make me equal, and compare me that we should be alike." For this usage of ᶜāraḵ cf. Psalm 89:7; Job 28:17, 19.

purposes gives the most complete picture, though P's generous legendary embellishments must, of course, be discounted.[13] There was a connection between the prophecy of Moses and the ark and tent. But the ark and tent became naturally also a cultic site; before the tent stood an altar where the people sacrificed to YHWH. Here prophecy and priesthood met.

We must imagine the tent cult as extremely simple, with that of the Shiloh sanctuary as our model. Like Samuel, young Joshua guards the ark in the tent (Exod. 33:11). Since the tent was portable, it needed porters and guardians. This task fell to the Levites, the fellow tribesmen of Moses. In all likelihood, they served also as a guard for Moses himself; to this day, kinship is the strongest support a leader can have in the East. Levi, which had been a bellicose tribe, notorious for mischief with Simeon its "brother," now consecrated its arms to guard the prophet and sacra of the new religion (Exod. 32:26 ff.). Levi's service became a tribal prerogative, and thus partook of the nature of a sacerdotal calling.

Priesthood proper was reserved to the family of Aaron. The priesthood of this family may well antedate the religion of YHWH. Its Egyptian names—Aaron, Hophni, Phinehas, Hanamel, Pashhur—point to an origin in Egypt. Its special connection with the lot oracle suggests an ancient Hebrew derivation. It was perhaps a priestly family that had wandered with the tribes and absorbed the various cultures of the lands through which they passed. Possibly, it was related to Levi and Moses. The family head, Aaron, was among the first who received Moses' message; he used his influence to rally the people to Moses' cause, acting as Moses' "mouth" and "prophet." The element of technical magic, native to Egypt, may stem from the priestly tradition of this family. The priestly regulations of the Torah are given to Moses and Aaron together; thus did the Aaronides demand and receive a special position in the cult of the new faith.

Although the priesthood is generally denigrated in the Bible (particularly by the prophets), the Israelite priesthood bore the standard of the new re-

---

[13] The basic elements of P's cultic establishment are evidenced in the early literature: the "ark of the covenant of YHWH who sits upon the cherubs" in Shiloh stands in a temple at which priests of Egyptian derivation (=Aaronides) serve (I Sam. 1–4). The people of Beth Shemesh as well as David and Solomon sacrifice before the ark (*ibid.* 6:15; II Sam. 6:13; I Kings 8:5). The ark resting in the adytum under the wings of cherubs is also the most holy thing in the temple of Solomon. David erects a tent for the ark (II Sam. 6:17; 7:2), a cultic sanctuary before which he sacrifices, and in which are anointing oil and an altar (I Kings 1:39; 2:28 ff.). The gorgeous tabernacle of P is an exaggeration, but the tribes, long settled in an artistically highly developed country, must have had some idea of how to embellish their sacra. The ephod, connected with the Urim, is likewise associated with the ark in the later history. Samuel, the guardian of the ark, wears a linen ephod (I Sam. 2:18); David wears a linen ephod when dancing before the ark (II Sam. 6:14). Ark, tent, cherubs, altar, ephod, and priests are thus always found in close conjunction.

ligion with hardly less fervor than prophecy. Aaron performs technical wonders in Egyptian style, but it is of utmost significance that he did not bequeath this function to his descendants. The Israelite priest, unlike the pagan, does not perform wonders, heal, utter incantations, or interpret omens. That nowhere in the Bible is there a trace of a battle over any of these functions indicates that the Israelite priesthood instinctively relinquished them from its beginning. At the very outset it gave up every sort of magical art.

What the contribution of the Israelite priesthood was specifically in the desert period is difficult to determine. Inquiring of God through the Urim-ephod is among its oldest functions.[14] A public cult also must have existed in the desert period, including fixed lustrations, a daily sacrifice, a lamp (cf. I Sam. 3:3), and shewbread (*ibid.* 21:7). The ritual of the Day of Atonement, with the scapegoat being sent away into the desert (not into the land of an enemy, or into a river, or to slaughter as in parallels elsewhere) may also go back to this period.

An ancient creation of the priesthood is the ark and cherubs, rooted, it would seem, in the Egyptian tradition of the Aaronides. In paganism, arks are employed to house or bear the deity. The Israelite ark too is a receptacle, but for the tablets of the covenant, not for YHWH (P, and Deut. 10:5; I Kings 8:9, 21). Upon the ark are two cherubs with outspread wings; unlike their Egyptian prototypes, however, they guard the tablets which are in the ark, not the God. Cherubs are also said to be the bearers of YHWH—"He who sits upon the cherubs" (I Sam. 4:4; II Sam. 6:2; Pss. 80:2; 99:1). But the cherub images upon the ark were not considered to be the bearers of deity, nor was the carrying of the ark conceived of in a pagan sense as bearing YHWH. The ark cherubs stood with their faces toward the ark-cover (Exod. 25:18–20), upon which God manifests himself, between, not upon, the cherubs (Lev. 16:2; Num. 7:89); they look toward the place of his appearance. They merely represent the celestial cherubs upon which God rides. Because of this the ark served as a military sacrum. The song of the ark in Numbers 10:35 f. points to a belief that when the ark went out to battle, YHWH, who sat upon the celestial cherubs, went out too before the armies of Israel. The ark was thus a double symbol. It housed the stone witnesses to the covenant of Israel with YHWH, guarded by the outspread wings of the cherubs. The pagan motif of guarding the god was transformed into the guarding of the god's covenant. At the same time representing the heavenly chariot, the cherubs symbolized the omni-

[14] It is present already in the time of Joshua (Num. 27:21; Josh. 7:13 ff. —referring doubtless to the Urim) and Samuel (I Sam. 10:17 ff.).

presence and authority of God. The antiquity of these motifs speaks for the antiquity of the ark. The close connection of the ark with the house of Aaron (in the desert, at Shiloh and Jerusalem) points to the Aaronic priesthood as its designer.

The new religion thus had two sacerdotal classes from its beginning. By the Levites the sacred service was newly acquired through kinship and loyalty to the prophet. The Aaronides had an ancient, but pagan, tradition. While this priesthood was devoted to the new idea and became the partner of prophecy in its development, it was unable, apparently, to purge itself of its pagan heritage sufficiently for zealots. In Exodus 32 (= Deut. 9–10), Aaron is said to have made the golden calf for which YHWH nearly destroyed him. It was the Levites who rallied to Moses and avenged God. Whatever be the historical kernel of this story, it gives clear expression to a fundamental opposition between Aaron and Levi. Though Levi appears as the more loyal to Moses, Aaron's sin is extenuated, and God does not, after all, do away with him. The venerable house of Aaron retained the exclusive privilege of altar service and refused to grant this right to Levi. A bitter rivalry continued over this matter for many generations.

THE NEW DIVINE DRAMA

From the debris of pagan mythology, a new kind of divine saga emerged. It told of the wonders of YHWH, of his messenger-prophet, of the "eschatological" hope of conquest, and of the establishment of a "kingdom of God" in the promised land. The new faith, notwithstanding its national garb, was universal in essence and therefore sought to comprehend the entire world in its view. The world was the domain of its one supreme God, yet within this domain there were still struggle and tension. This could no longer be interpreted mythically as the clash of divine forces. Instead, a new dimension was called into being: the historical-moral, expressed in the saga of man's defiance of God. History was conceived of as a struggle between the wills of God and man. There is no principle of evil alongside of the one supreme benevolent power, but the necessary consequence of the freedom that was given man is that he can defy God and choose to sin. With the transference of the divine drama from the realm of myth to the realm of history, pagan mythology evaporated. There is no polemic in the Bible against pagan myth, for when historical saga was born, the sources of myth dried up and it withered away.

This saga originates with the appearance of Moses. The God who appears to Moses is opposed not by other gods, but by a defiant pagan empire, symbolized by Pharaoh and his magicians. This God controls all nature; no room remains for a battle of gods. But man does not yet know him and refuses to heed his command. "Who is YHWH that I should hearken to his voice," "I do not know YHWH," says Pharaoh. Man's will is a "kingdom" unto itself, a domain that encroaches, so to speak, upon that of God. The conflict between the will of YHWH and the defiant pagan is the starting point of the biblical saga of human defiance. The existence of a pagan world flouting God is historically the first problem of Israelite religion. Before the legends about Moses this theme is not to be found. It follows that the Exodus legends, in which the motif first appears, are the prototype of all the rest. They were the beginning of the end of pagan myth in Israel.[15]

THE PROMISED LAND

The desire of the tribes to return to Canaan, memories of which were still alive among them, was at bottom an ethnic-political one. Yet under prophetic inspiration, it too became a religious ideal. Possession of the land is the earliest eschatological motif of Israelite religion. It is the ultimate goal of the people, and its attainment is promised by God. But it is more; the land is the sanctuary of YHWH, his dwelling place on earth (Exod. 15:17). The divine promise of a land thus became part of the larger idea of Israel as the elect of God, as his "possession."

As with Islam and Christianity, Israelite religion possessed a powerful social motive in its promise for the future. Christianity announced the advent of the Messiah, prophesied the end of this world and the coming of the kingdom of heaven. Islam preached to its believers a last judgment and a personal paradise and hell; messianic movements also arose within it. The caliphate embodied its ideal of establishing a sort of kingdom of God on earth. Israel's eschatology was neither universal nor personal, but national. It envisioned the conquest of a land and its sanctification as the kingdom of God.

After the events at Sinai, an attempt was made to invade the land from the base at Kadesh. But owing to the strength of the Amalekites and southern Canaanites, the Israelites were defeated. Fear seized the tribes, and a rebellion against the leadership of the prophet broke out. Moses was able to weather the storm and preserve the tribal confederation from

[15] In the legends about Moses' life the motif of Israel's defiance is central. Out of the constant tension between the people and the prophet some imaginative modern poets and scholars have spun the romance of Moses' murder by the people. Since Israel's sinfulness is the basis of the biblical interpretation of history, the Bible would surely not have kept silent about such an event had it occurred. A murder of the father of all the prophets would not have been hidden in obscure allusions which require all the resources of text emendation and modern midrash to decipher.

dissolution. But the invasion of Canaan had to be put off until a new and disciplined generation had matured. For the present it was necessary to secure a base for a long stay. The tribes established themselves at Kadesh, and spread out from there to find pasturage. That the confederation really spent this period united, and not as individual tribes, is attested by the absence of friction between them and the Bedouin tribes of the desert. During the generation of the Wandering, no tribe attacks them or contends with them over water and pasturage in the oases, because the small desert tribes were no match for the Israelite confederation that "covered the face of the earth" (Num. 22:5). Since our sources know of only two leaders—Moses and Joshua—between the Exodus and the conquest, the sojourn at Kadesh must have lasted about one generation. Disturbances that arose in Transjordan caused the tribes, apparently, to circuit Mount Seir and Moab to find a new base for invasion in Transjordan. They successfully engaged the Amorites and conquered their land. Here the prophet died, and in his stead came Joshua, who had been a military leader even in Moses' time. From the base in Transjordan, Joshua carried on the national enterprise that Moses had begun.

NOTE ON THE THEORY OF A KENITE-MIDIANITE ORIGIN OF MOSES' RELIGION

Inasmuch as several scholarly theories would connect Moses with the cult of a god of Sinai or Kadesh and find the origins of Israelite religion in such a cult, the question must here be clarified for a proper appreciation of the work of Moses.

Biblical (and Jewish) tradition distinguishes two sharply separate territorial realms of sanctity: one prophetic only, the other cultic and prophetic. The fixed boundary between the two is Beersheba. Northward from Beersheba extends the realm of cult and prophecy, southward to Sinai, the realm of prophecy (= revelation) only. There YHWH revealed himself to Israel and from there he appears, but he has no cult sites in this area. The distinction begins with the patriarchal narratives. At the sites of later Israelite sanctuaries throughout Palestine the patriarchs build altars and erect pillars, but no patriarch worships God anywhere south of Beersheba. The narrative tells of the descent of Abraham and Jacob to Egypt, yet they do not even stop at Kadesh or Sinai, let alone build altars there. Later tradition is the same. Throughout the Bible, the southern district is an area of revelation, but no Israelite ever went south to visit any ancient cult site. Elijah goes to Horeb to hear the word of God; he does not build an altar or offer sacrifice there. Nor do the narratives of the Wandering depict the Israelites as going from one cult site to another; on the contrary, they carry with them their sacra—the ark and the tent. To be sure, they worship one time at Sinai, but during the rest of the forty-year Wandering, they never again go back there to worship. In general, the desert generation is not regarded by the tradition as practicing a cult at sacred sites at all. So far was the desert period associated in the consciousness of Israel with revelation only that later prophets adduce it as an example of a cultless age (Amos 5:25; Jer. 7:22).

This consistent dichotomy of realms which runs through all of biblical tradition indicates two things: that the sanctity of the desert had no pre-Mosaic roots in Israel, and that this sanctity is limited to the domain of revelation and prophecy. This means that the religious movement that centered about Moses had no earlier cultic roots, and that it was not connected with any local sanctity, or linked with the cult of some god or other that was worshiped in the area of Moses' work. For it is hardly reasonable to suppose that such a background once existed but became totally effaced in the religious consciousness of the people at the same time that the sites themselves remained fixed in their memory forever.

The stories about Moses attest to this also. Moses performs no cultic rite at the spot where God reveals himself to him; that is, the legend knows nothing of any cultic holiness of the revelation-site. Moses asks Pharaoh to let Israel go to worship God in the desert, not at some fixed site, but at an indefinite place "three days' journey from Egypt." He rejects Pharaoh's suggestion to worship in Egypt not because Israel must sacrifice at a certain spot, not even because Egypt is unholy ground, but because of the fear of "sacrificing the abomination of the Egyptians in their sight." None of the altars built during the Wandering are permanent cult sites. The Rephidim altar appears to be a memorial; no sacrifice is mentioned (Exod. 17:15). At Sinai, Moses makes a sacrifice only for the purpose of ratifying the covenant. Even that altar had no priority, since Aaron builds a new one for the golden calf. The only permanent cult site of the desert age is the portable tabernacle, and even that was designed primarily as a sacred area for revelation.

All this indicates that the stories about Moses incorporate no cult-legends in the proper sense of the term: no legends that told of some ancient, local sanctity, no primarily etiological legends. For none of these stories are intended to account for a place of worship. Whatever local sanctity they know of has its basis in revelation. None of these stories, then, is grounded in the cult of any local deity—neither of a volcano nor of a bush. The absence of a cultic-etiological element in them shows that the Mosaic revelation is the source of the sanctity of the desert in Israel; this sanctity has no roots in pre-Mosaic times.

From the connection of Moses with Jethro, the Midianite priest, the theory of a Midianite-Kenite origin of the God and religion of Israel has developed. This theory is related to another making Kadesh the center of the Kenite god, and the Levites the original priests of this god at Kadesh Has this view any real grounds?

The biblical data on the Kenites show that a Midianite tribe, who traced their line to Moses' father-in-law, joined Israel and its God. But nothing justifies the theory that Israel learned their religion from them. Jethro is a priest "of Midian," not of YHWH. If he and the Midianites really were worshipers of YHWH, there is no reason why the biblical tradition should have obscured the fact. Biblical legends tell as much concerning Adam, Cain, Abel, Enoch, Noah, Balaam, Job and his companions, and Melchizedek. Yet the legend of Exodus 3 seems to indicate just the contrary. Moses comes unwittingly with his sheep to the "mountain of God"; he does not know it is holy ground. He has to ask the name of the deity who revealed himself there to him. None of these things were told to him by Jethro. Jethro's confession of the greatness of Israel's God is no more than the biblical stories tell of several other pagans (II Kings 5:15–17; Jonah 1:16; Dan. 2:47; 3:28–33; cf. Exod. 9:20; 14:25). And while other pagans are explicitly said to have offered sacrifice to Israel's God, the text of Exodus 18 does not even say that much expressly about Jethro. The Bible does not hide Moses' obligation to Jethro with regard to judicial procedure, why should it have hidden other of his teachings to Moses if there were any? If the narrative does not explicitly refer Moses' knowledge of YHWH to Jethro, it can only be that it regards the revelation to Moses as an absolute beginning.

The argument that Moses saw his vision in Midian, because he was shepherding a Midianite's sheep, and that the "mountain of God" was also in Midian breaks down in the face of the decisive fact that nowhere is Israel ever said to have entered the territory of Midian. The contact with Jethro and the Kenites is made in the desert between Egypt and Midian; from "the mountain of God" Jethro *returns* "to his land" (Exod. 18:27; cf. Num. 10:29 f.). Returning to Egypt from Midian, Moses meets Aaron, who is coming to greet him, at the mountain of God. Nor is there any shred of evidence in the later history which points to a religious affinity between Midian and Israel (for the contrary, cf. Num. 22:4, 7; 25; 31).

The history of Kadesh exposes the baselessness of the whole theory. Kadesh was on the boundary of Midian-Kenites-Amalek, and it played an important role in the life of the tribes during the Wandering. It was reckoned as part of the land of Israel, and was not so far away from the settled Israelites as the Sinai desert. And yet it plays no role whatever in the later religious life of Israel. Is it conceivable that Kadesh should not have been mentioned even once as a site of worship, if it were in fact the original home of the cult of YHWH?

There is even less warrant for regarding Kadesh as the home of the Levites or taking the Levites as Midianite in origin. Jethro and Levi have nothing in common. The Kenites, who traced their descent to Jethro, lived as *gērīm* in Israel, and did not join the Levites. The Rechabites (of Kenite ancestry) assimilated into Judah. No Levite is ever connected with Kadesh. In Deuteronomy 33:8 Levi is linked with Massah and Meribah, which are possibly references to Kadesh. Some lost legend appears to be alluded to, one which, at any rate, is but one among many legends, and is hardly enough to justify making Kadesh a Levitical center. Moses' special connection with Kadesh is a romance of modern midrashists.

CHAPTER VII

The Conquest and Settlement

THE NATIONAL PLAN OF CONQUEST

The transfer of prophetic authority from Moses to Joshua was untypically consecutive. But this transfer, too, is conceived of as a special divine act. God commands Moses to lay his hands upon his servant Joshua, "a man in whom there is spirit" (Num. 27:15–23). Before Moses' death, God appears in a cloud to charge Joshua with leading the invasion of Canaan (Deut. 31:14 f., 23). By virtue of this unbroken succession, the early "kingdom of God" was able to succeed in its primary undertaking, the conquest of the land.

It is the accepted view that Canaan was conquered gradually, in several unrelated stages, by individual tribes or tribal bands. The evidence, however, argues for the unified conquest of Canaan by a confederation of tribes that fought to carry out a national plan of conquest.

The consciousness of unity that the Israelite tribes display throughout their history cannot be explained as a late development. For the isolation and separate destinies of the Israelite tribes once settled in Canaan and Transjordan would have been sufficient under normal circumstances to dissolve even a united people into separate fragments. The Jordan divided the area of settlement in two. The absence of Judah in the wars of Barak, Gideon, and Jephthah speaks for a long period of its complete isolation. Amalgamation with Ammon and Moab would have been the normal course for the Transjordanian tribes. Judah and Ephraim might have been expected to develop independently of each other, yet they have a feeling of common origin and destiny. The political and territorial history of postconquest times was hardly favorable to promoting the feeling among the tribes that they were a national entity of twelve tribes. The fact is that after only three-quarters of a century of not unbroken political unity during the reigns of Saul, David, and Solomon the united kingdom fell apart. Yet the sense of common origin and destiny outlived all these divisions. It survived even the destruction of the northern kingdom. Inexplicable on the basis of later history, this sense of unity must have had its roots in the period before the entry into Canaan. The tribal confederation is therefore primary.[1]

We have already observed that the ideal boundaries of the promised land correspond neither to historical reality nor to later messianic hopes. The far-flung limits of the northern boundary and the exclusion of Transjordan in the east prove that these limits of the promised land were already fixed before the entry into Canaan. This implies a national ideal that preceded the individual wars of the tribes each for its own territory (Judg. 1).

That the conquest was indeed guided by such a national program is indicated by Judges 1. This chapter, though composite, contains ancient materials that date to various times during the very course of the wars of conquest.[2] The repeated notice of populations that certain tribes failed to dispossess signifies that the author regarded the tribes as following a prearranged plan, each fighting for its own allotted territory; they failed to take possession of land that they should have, according to plan. Where could this plan have originated? Not from the real ethnic and political demands of the tribes. For surely at no time in postconquest history did Asher ever aspire to take possession of Acco, Sidon, Ahlab, and Achzib, up to Rehob, thereby surpassing the ambitions even of David and Solomon. Now if the unpossessed land is combined with the conquered area, the sum comprises the complete land of Canaan. The ideal of the tribes, then, according to Judges 1, was to inhabit a continuous territory. But the territory actually occupied by Israel at the conquest was, in fact, not continuous; whence this ideal? No such neat parceling of Canaan with no overlapping boundaries, and comprising in sum the whole land, could have resulted from combining the achievements or even the hopes of tribes fighting individual uncoordinated actions. A continuous territory is the standing ideal of a national conquest. A preconceived, national plan of conquest and settlement is the

---

[1] The interrelationships of the tribes as set forth in Genesis also presuppose a preconquest period of confederation; see above, p. 219.

[2] The antiquity of the chapter is vouched for by its ignorance of the Philistines. Verse 9 has the Canaanites still inhabiting the coastal lowland; the datum of the conquest of Gaza, Ashkelon, and Ekron (vs. 18) also fails to mention the Philistines, who were there by the time of Samson. Furthermore, Dan's territory is located in the south (vss. 34 f.); during the period of the judges, however, Dan moved to the north (Judg. 17–18).

presupposition of the tribal battles as described in Judges 1. Of Judah and Simeon it is said explicitly that they go up to fight "for their share."

The conquest and settlement are marked by a striking absence of intertribal territorial disputes. The period of the judges, filled with internecine strife, fails to produce a single boundary dispute or even boundary agreement. Israel's settlement of Canaan did not follow the pattern of the Hellenic or Teutonic invasions. The Israelite tribes did not follow and encroach upon one another. The course of events thus supports the tradition that the land was divided by lot, by an oracle, before the conquest. It is plain, in any case, that the settlement followed a prearranged national plan.[3]

THE "H̱ĒREM"

For the history of Israelite religion the question of Israel's treatment of the Cananites has especial significance. Did the tribes settle down among the Canaanites, adopt their culture, and amalgamate ethnically with them? Or is the tradition of the wholesale destruction of the Canaanites historical?

To see clearly through the apparent contradictions in our sources, we must first distinguish the two conceptions of "the land of Israel." There is, first of all, the ideal land, of which we have spoken before, including Philistia, Tyre, Sidon, Lebanon, and Hermon. There is, second, the real land, the area actually occupied by Israelites by the end of the period of judges. The boundaries of the real land are approximately "from Dan to Beersheba." If

[3] [On the basis of earlier excavations the fall of Jericho to the invading Israelites was placed as early as 1400 B.C. (Garstang), antedating considerably the main wave of destruction of the Canaanite cities, which falls toward the end of the thirteenth century. This gave rise to the theories of a double invasion. However the most recent excavations (by Kenyon) have shown that the walls which served as the basis of this dating belong in fact to the Early Bronze, rather than the Late Bronze city. On the basis of pottery, opinion, after many vicissitudes, appears to be arriving at a consensus which would place the destruction of the Late Bronze city at the end of the fourteenth or the beginning of the thirteenth century. Compare Avigad's discussion in the Hebrew *Encyclopaedia Biblica* (Jerusalem, 1958), III, 852–55, which concludes as follows· "To tell the truth, the archeological findings upon which it is possible to lean are meager enough. Only new discoveries will be able to supply the data needed for a more trustworthy and authoritative dating. The most recent diggings at Jericho have not contributed anything to the solution of the problem and have only disclosed the error of the earlier conclusions regarding the alleged wall of the fourth city; it now is clear that we know nothing about it really. Yadin has conjectured, perhaps rightly, that the late Canaanite city had no wall of its own, but depended for its defense upon the Hyksos glacis, which was, then, the wall that fell before Joshua."]

It must, finally, be said that the view taken here of the nature of the conquest does not flow from the assumption that the stories of the Bible are historical reports. The general considerations that have been advanced above are not founded on the denial that the stories are merely etiological legends. On the contrary, it is they that prove that these stories do contain a historical substratum. This conclusion cannot be undermined by showing this or that element to be legendary.

the sources are examined with this distinction kept in mind, no evidence of an amalgamation of Canaan and Israel can be discovered.

The earliest records (Josh. 15:63; 16:10; 17:12–18; Judg. 1), dating from before the Philistine conquest and the song of Deborah, know nothing of alliances and intermarriage with the Canaanites or their influence on the religion of Israel. The attitude of Israel toward them is represented as uniformly hostile. Israel seeks, not always successfully, to dispossess them; those that remain are eventually impressed into forced labor. Later sources, however (e.g., the schematic framework of Judges and related portions), relate how Israel failed to drive out the Canaanites, but made alliances and intermarried with them, and thereby fell into idolatry. Judges 2:2–3, Joshua 23:13, and Numbers 33:55 have in common the idea that the Canaanites who remain in the land will be a cause of distress and religious apostasy for Israel. The context of Joshua 23 leaves no doubt, however, that the "remaining nations" are Philistia, Sidon, Byblos, etc., who occupy part of Israel's ideal, but never were in Israel's real, land. That Judges 6:8 ff. also refers to Israel's defection to the gods of the *surrounding* Amorites is the only interpretation of the passage consonant with the prevailing view of the framework of Judges. That view regards Israel's distress as stemming always from their straying after the gods of "the peoples that were round about them" (Judg. 2:11 ff.): Aram, Sidon, Moab, Ammon, the Philistines (10:6). Nowhere are Canaanites who remained within the conquered area specified as a cause of Israelite apostasy.[4] This is not to deny that there was intermarriage between Israel and Canaan. It does mean, however, that the biblical records give no support to the view that a general ethnic and cultural amalgam of peoples took place in Israelite Palestine.[5] Nor is there any trace of a mass assimilation of Canaanites into Israel. Such ethnic units as the Calebites, Jerahmeelites, Rechabites and the like were assimilated culturally, yet continued for generations to retain their ethnic individuality. *Gērīm*, though culturally assimilated, remained socially distinct. We hear of

---

[4] Judges 3:5 f. is to be interpreted accordingly as referring to those Canaanites, Hittites, Amorites, etc. who remained within the ideal boundaries of Israel, but outside the occupied territories. Since their settlements surrounded the real land, Israel is said to dwell "in their midst."

[5] Judah's marriage with a Canaanite (Gen. 38) reflects events preceding the tribes' migration to Egypt. From the conquest on, all recorded intermarriages are with nations that surround the real land of Israel. Samson marries a Philistine; David takes a Geshurite; Uriah is a Hittite; Solomon takes Egyptian, Moabite, Ammonite, Edomite, Sidonian, and Hittite women; Ahab takes a Sidonian; Ruth is a Moabite, and so forth. The view that Gideon's Shechemite concubine was Canaanite is groundless; Abimelech is born of a bondwoman, as Jephthah is of a prostitute; this not does make either woman a Canaanite.

other foreign groups—David's Gittite guard, the Cherethites and Pelethites —but never, in any period, of a Canaanite class. Had Canaanites assimilated in the normal fashion, it is strange that no vestige of this should have been left anywhere in the literature.

This silence accords with the fact that nowhere are Canaanites within the real land blamed for Israel's apostasies. None of the religious battles of Israel is directed toward Canaanites from within. The view everywhere is that the Canaanites within the Israelite area of settlement were destroyed; Israel was seduced by those who remained outside and surrounded them (cf. further II Kings 17:15). The prophets take the same view. The Amorites were destroyed (Amos 2:9 f.); idolatry entered Israel from the Philistines and the other surrounding nations (Isa. 2:6; 12:14 ff.). Ezekiel counts only Egypt, Babylon, Assyria, and other neighbors among those who led Israel astray (16:15, 26 ff.; 20:7, 32). Jerubbaal demolishes an altar to Baal in Ophrah; but nothing is said about a battle with local Canaanites. The great battles against Canaanite idolatry in the times of Elijah-Jehu are waged against Sidonian influence. Nothing is said about the influence of Canaanites within Israel. It is, on the contrary, plain that whatever Canaanites did remain in Israel must have assimilated Israelite culture like the rest of the *gērīm*.

Yet there are documents that list populations that Israel failed to evict; do these not contradict the tradition that the Canaanites were destroyed? And could these not have served as centers of Canaanite cultural influence on Israel? When later texts speak of nations that Israel left in its "land," there is no contradiction; the sense is that Israel destroyed the Canaanites who lived in the real land of Israel; it failed to evict those who lived outside it, but still within the ideal boundaries.

The case of the early records of unconquered cities is different. Here an early stage in the conquest, before the time of Deborah, is reflected, when not even the whole of Israel's real land had as yet been occupied. And what do we find? In the main area of tribal settlement—the territories of Joseph and Judah—only Jerusalem and Gezer remain Canaanite (the Gibeonite cities were taken earlier, under Joshua, and are not mentioned in Judges). There are few Canaanite cities in the territories of Zebulun, Naphtali, and Dan. The main Canaanite settlement in the lowlands encircles the Israelites. In the north, then, the boundary was spotty, but in the central highlands, from southern Manasseh through Ephraim, Benjamin, and Judah, there was, already at the beginning of the period of judges, a continuous Israelite settlement, within which there were only Canaanite enclaves. Such a continuous settlement at so early a time implies the destruction or expulsion of the original population.[6]

Several other lines of evidence point to the eviction and destruction of the natives of Palestine by the Israelites. Everywhere in the Bible the settlement is described in terms of expulsion (*gērash*) or destruction (*hishmīd*)— both implied in the verb *hōrīsh*. This is the language of the early song of Deuteronomy 33:27, of Amos 2:9 f., and of the several passages in which the early sources depict specific conquests. The population of Bethel (Judg. 1:25) and Laish (18:27) are "slain by the edge of the sword." Judges 1 uses the same language throughout. No word or phrase is employed that suggests peaceful relationships, like those between the patriarchs and their neighbors. That a tradition which told of peaceful relationships with foreign nations and even reported the pact with the Gibeonites would have at some later period invented the wholesale destruction of Canaanites in fulfilment of an imaginary law of *ḥērem* is not likely. Had there been a genuine ethnic amalgam this would have been mentioned as was done in the case of the Kenites and Calebites. The prevailing images of dispossession, destruction, and expulsion are inexplicable if not taken to be historical.

How the Canaanites fared at the hand of Israel is illuminated by the history of a group of them who did survive for nearly 1,500 years, the Gibeonites and their descendants. From the time of Joshua to the reign of Solomon, the Gibeonites were free men.[7] They lived among the Israelites and were culturally absorbed by them. By David's time, they worship YHWH and desire a place "within the borders of Israel" (II Sam. 21:5).

---

[6] That the population of these "undispossessed" settlements and enclaves was exclusively Canaanite is to be inferred from what is known about one of them, Jerusalem. Between its first, temporary conquest (Judg. 1:8) and its last, by David, it was a Jebusite city in which an Israelite fears to spend the night (Judg. 19:11 f.). Our sources never speak of mixed populations, and there is no reason to believe that in central Palestine such existed. The current opinion that Shechem remained Canaanite until the time of Abimelech, when it became mixed, is groundless. "The citizens of Shechem" of Judges 8–9 are not Canaanites. They are contrasted with the "men of Israel" whom they fight, but this no more makes them Canaanites than the contrast of "Benjaminites" with "the men of Israel" in Judges 20–21 makes the former Canaanite. Abimelech, whom they make king, rules "over Israel" (9:22). And there is no reason why, if in Abimelech's time a battle between Israelites and Canaanites did occur, this fact should have been obscured by a later author or editor. Judges 9:28 is defective; it implies no more than that there were some Canaanite survivors of the *ḥērem* still living in Shechem at that time. Moreover, Shechem is never counted among the Canaanite cities, an inexplicable omission, if such an important city had really been Canaanite.

[7] Joshua 11:19 f. suggests that the *ḥērem* was invoked upon all the Canaanites because they did not make peace with Israel. The Gibeonites did make peace and were therefore not destroyed; the legend of their deception is probably later. Again, Joshua 10:1 ff. shows that the Gibeonites remained in their cities; apparently, they did not at that time become hierodules.

Nevertheless, they do not lose their ethnic identity or name. When Solomon impressed the remnants of the native Canaanites (I Kings 9:20 f.) into his service, he included them too in spite of their ancient exemption. The Gibeonites and the rest of the Canaanites did not become private slaves; they were royal slaves and hierodules. Even then, however, the Gibeonites appear to have retained their identity. Among those who return from the Babylonian exile are two classes of hierodules: Nethinim and the descendants of the "servants of Solomon" (Ezra 2:43–58; Neh. 7:46–60). Talmudic tradition doubtless correctly identifies the Nethinim with the descendants of the Gibeonites (Yebamoth 78b–79). The Nethinim survived to the destruction of the Second Temple and are still mentioned as a distinct social group in the Mishnah.

Of all the Canaanites only the Gibeonites remain for centuries as an identifiable element in Israel (beside those who were not evicted but lived on within the enclaves). The rest are an anonymous remnant termed "the remaining people." Only the Gibeonites are said to have made peace with Israel. They were saved from extinction in the time of the conquest by the oath made to them, but they never mingled with Israel. They remained an inferior caste of hierodules even after becoming God-fearing Jews who returned from the Exile to Jerusalem. Can we suppose, in the light of this, that the Israelites intermingled amicably with the other Canaanites who are never reported to have made peace with Israel? Such a supposition would make the segregation for generations of the Gibeonites and "servants of Solomon" utterly unfathomable. Why did the others mix with Israel, but these not? Why did Saul seek to destroy them? How could Solomon have enslaved them all after they had been peacefully absorbed into Israel? Clearly, the special status of the Gibeonites and Canaanites, distinct from that of *gērīm* (who were not slaves) and private slaves (who constitute a distinct class alongside the Nethinim among the returning exiles), points to the historicity of the *ḥērem* law. The *ḥērem* status alone kept them apart and prevented their absorption into the class of *gērīm* or even slaves, let alone the free men of Israel.

That the Canaanites in the areas conquered by Israel were destroyed or evicted is also indicated by their absence as a military factor in the wars of the judges and the early kings. Only one of the wars described in the book of Judges is with Canaanites: the war of Barak and Deborah (Judg. 4–5), fought on the disputed boundary of Israelite-Canaanite occupation. But after this battle none of Israel's enemies is Canaanite. This is the great difference between the battles of Joshua and those of the judges: the former are Canaanite, the latter, non-Canaanite. Never did the Canaanites rise from within against their conquerors; never did they unite with their brethren on the boundaries and rise against the invaders, not even when the Israelites were weakened by internecine wars during the period of judges. The supposed amalgamation of Canaan and Israel must, therefore, have been completed in a twinkling.

The domestic Canaanites of the period of the judges and early monarchy are concentrated in the valley of Jezreel, in Jerusalem, and in Gezer. Whatever Canaanite points of resistance remain are thus precisely those that the records of Joshua and Judges 1 indicate to have been Canaanite enclaves in Israelite territory. Outside of these enclaves there was no "Canaanite problem." The main phase of the Canaanite wars thus came to an end in the time of Joshua. By the beginning of the period of the judges, the conquest of the highlands was complete; Barak defeated and expelled the Canaanites in the valley of Jezreel. Henceforth, only pockets remained that could no longer serve as a political or military factor. That there are no Canaanites at large in central Palestine by the period of the judges can only have resulted from a battle to death, or expulsion.

Another historical fact is the absence in Israel of a recognizable class of Canaanite slaves. Judges 1, and parallels in Joshua, record the impressment into forced labor of certain Canaanite settlements in the course of time. This was a mass impressment of whole communities for specific public or royal service. There is, however, no trace of the formation of a class of Canaanite private slaves. Israel's relation to Canaan, according to our sources, is one of annihilation, destruction, expulsion, dispossession, or impressment of entire communities—never of sale into slavery or private enslavement. The foreign slave of biblical law is not captured in war, but purchased (Exod. 21:21), either from the nations which are round about, or from among the aliens who reside in the land of Israel (Lev. 25:44 f.). Indeed, the tradition of the annihilation of the Canaanites by the *ḥērem* would have been inexplicable had there existed in Israel a class of Canaanite private slaves.

Israelite culture though indebted to Canaan in many ways yet shows such profound differences from it as to exclude being viewed as the successor to the culture of Canaan.

We know from Egyptian and biblical sources that the Canaanites used the war horse and chariot. With Israel's occupation of Canaan both disappear. The pastoral Israelite tribes had no knowledge of this highly specialized weapon; they were sword-bearing foot-soldiery, who could not deal with the valley people "for they had iron chariotry" (Judg. 1:19). The horses that Joshua captured he hamstrung; when he captured chariots, he burned them (Josh. 11:6, 9). David still does the same (II Sam. 8:4). Not before the time of Solomon do these weapons appear as part of the Israelite arsenal.

Now the passage to agricultural civilization did not require Canaanite mentors. Many peoples have developed farming without guidance. Moreover, Israel appears to have been acquainted with agriculture before the conquest. Note that Isaac sows in the land of the Philistines (Gen. 26:12). The Israelites were half-nomads who knew farming as well as herding. Hence it is unnecessary to invoke Canaanites to explain Israel's transformation into an agricultural society. But to learn the use of war horse and iron chariots a specially trained class and special political conditions were necessary. If Israel had been under the influence of Canaanite culture, we should expect the first evidences to be its adoption of the high military culture of the Canaanites. This was a vital advantage which would have helped Israel enormously in its wars with its neighbors. Yet Israel remained for generations on its early primitive military level. What would the course of history have been had David, Israel's sole military genius, possessed trained horse and chariotry! Why was this indispensable weapon not adopted by Israel from the Canaanites, if not because the *ḥērem* had destroyed the only class that could teach Israel its use?

An equally profound rift separates the political organization of Israel from that of Canaan. The el-Amarna letters and the book of Joshua show that the city-state was the basic form of Canaanite political organization. Each state had its own king, whose domain was territorial, not tribal. For Israel, however, the political unit was the tribe; the people was a federation of tribes, united by (real or fictitious) blood relationship. After the conquest, the territorial allocation was made on the basis of the tribes. For several generations thereafter there is no king in Israel, nor any other established general authority. And when kingship finally comes to Israel, it owes nothing to Canaanite predecessors. It does not involve the merging of several petty rulers under the authority of a single king, or of several cities under the rule of one. The Israelite king rules over tribes. (Even the abortive kingship of Abimelech is "over Israel," not over the city of Shechem alone.) He is elected by the desire of the tribes to be united under one leader. The tribal feeling outlasted the Davidic empire. The very division of the kingdom after Solomon's death sprang from tribal rivalry.

Thus, within the area of Israelite settlement the Canaanite form of city-state disappeared. But if Israel had absorbed Canaanite culture, we should expect to see the effect in the political life of the people, as happens wherever cultures mix. Nothing of the sort occurs. Again this can only be explained on the assumption that Israel did not amalgamate with, but destroyed and expelled, the Canaanites.

THE "ḤĒREM" AND ITS EFFECTS—We have seen that biblical sources do not refer Israel's apostasy to the influence of domestic Canaanites. This has been shown to be in harmony with other lines of evidence pointing to the historicity of the biblical tradition that the Canaanites were subject to the *ḥērem*. What do we know of the origin and working of this practice?

The high antiquity of the *ḥērem* law is vouched for by the absence of the Philistines from its list of condemned nations (cf. Deut. 7:1 ff.) notwithstanding their occupation of "promised land"(Josh. 13:2 f.).[8] It originated, apparently, in the Canaanite refusal to make peace with Israel (see Josh. 11:19 f.). As a religious-political measure, it is well attested to both in biblical and extra-biblical sources. The *ḥērem* is applied to Amalek (Exod. 17:8 ff.; Deut. 25:17 ff.; I Sam. 15), to the Canaanites of the Negeb (Num. 21:1 ff.), and to Sihon and Og (*ibid.* vss. 21–35). Abimelech made Shechem *ḥērem* (Judg. 9:45). The term is found in the Mesha inscriptions; Mesha destroys the population of Ataroth as *ḥērem* to Chemosh, and of Nebo as *ḥērem* to Ashtar-Chemosh. The account of the special *ḥērem* of Jericho seems to preserve a reminiscence of the fact that at first the *ḥērem* was not comprehensive. Only after the tribes had penetrated the land and encountered lively resistance did they apparently extend the *ḥērem* to all the inhabitants. Later a religious justification was supplied (Exod. 23:33; 34: 11 ff.; Deut. 7:1 ff., 16 ff.), just as "the sin of the Amorite" and the "wickedness" of the peoples of Canaan served to justify the conquest as a whole (Gen. 15:16; Lev. 18:24 ff.).

Terrible as it was, the *ḥērem* had important social and religious consequences; Israel did not assimilate to the indigenous population. Materially this brought about a marked decline. At the same time, it provided Israel's new religious idea with an environment in which to grow free of the influence of a popular pagan culture.

THE COURSE OF THE CONQUEST

Since the invading Israelites encountered neither Egyptians nor Philistines, their entry into Canaan must have taken place when the Egyptian rule was near its end, but before the Philistines had become a military power.

---

[8] The idea that the *ḥērem* law is a product of later patriotic zeal is untenable. The later enemies of Israel were its neighbors, but these are explicitly excluded from the *ḥērem* (Deut. 20:10–18). Later religious fanaticism has also been suggested as the motive of the law. But that late fanatics should direct their fury against peoples who, according to the evidence of our sources, no longer exercised any influence at all on the life of later times is highly unlikely.

The time of Egyptian weakness between the reign of Merneptah (1235–1227) and Ramses III (1195–1164), or perhaps during the reign of the latter is indicated. The Canaanite city-states were disunited. Although they surpassed Israel in material and armaments, the Israelite tribes were united and animated by the zeal of a new religion. At first the Canaanites do not appear to have sensed the danger; even after the initial reverses, they did not unite against their common enemy. Nor did they come to terms with Israel, thinking, apparently, that they could easily dispatch the crude shepherd-warriors. As a result, the tribes had to fight only isolated city-states or local coalitions. The Canaanite resistance was sufficiently serious to cause the invoking of a *ḥērem;* it was unable, however, to prevent the Israelite occupation of the country.

After the fall of Jericho and Ai, the Gibeonite towns were terrified into submission. Centrally located, they served as the base for further campaigns. The narratives of Joshua indicate that the issue was decided in two great battles: one with a southern, the other with a northern coalition of kings. The central highlands were conquered; their population was annihilated or expelled. The Joseph tribes and Judah (to whom Simeon attached itself) settled this area. After the back of Canaanite resistance had been broken, the central camp was disbanded, and the period of settlement began. Each tribe endeavored to occupy its "portion" and carried on the war of dispossession with the remaining Canaanites on its own. The Canaanite iron chariotry was not sufficient to fend off forever the persistent attacks of the land-hungry tribes. In time the tribes were able to secure the possession of what became the real land of Israel; the Canaanites ceased thereafter to be a military menace.

Since the aggression of the tribes aimed at satisfying their need for land, when this was accomplished by the conquest of Transjordan and central Palestine, their desire for expansion came to an end. The hope of conquering the ideal land of Israel gradually came to be a utopian dream. When the task of conquest passed from the united camp into the hands of the individual tribes, the ideal of the complete conquest of "the land of Canaan" was in effect foregone. At the invasion, it was expected that Joshua would conquer all the land to the sea and the Euphrates (Josh. 1:2–6). Later it was hoped that after his death, the tribes would complete the conquest (*ibid.,* 13:1–6). But the course of events belied this hope too. The historiographers of the early monarchy explained that the ideal was not attained because of the sin and rebellion of Israel in the time of the judges (Judg. 2:11–23). With this explanation, the ideal of the complete conquest was consigned to the lumber room of hopes that failed, existing henceforth only on the ancient books.

THE UNION OF THE TRIBES UNDER
THE KINGDOM OF GOD

The great events of the period of Moses and Joshua consolidated the tribes and created between them a strong national feeling. Israel had a political organization before the monarchy, though it is difficult to detect because of its excessively "spiritual" character. It was a confederation of independent tribes whose unity became visible only under certain conditions. The fact that no Israelite tribe ever fought with Canaanites against its kinsmen —as Greek fought Greek during the Persian wars—shows that the confederation felt itself to be a political-national entity.

Authority was vested in two institutions. There was, first, the secular, "primitive democracy" of the elders. This authority, unlike that of the Greek amphictyony, was not religious in any way; it was not connected with any temple and had no sacral functions. It arose out of the ancient tribal council of elders—the clan heads, of whom the chief was the *nāśiʾ*. During the days of Moses and Joshua, an intertribal authority of elders came into existence. Its composition and function are not well delineated in our sources, but we do have clear testimony to its operation. (See, for example, I Sam. 4; 8:4; 30:26 ff.; II Sam. 2:4; 5:1 ff.; 19:10, 12, 15, 44; I Kings 12:1 ff.)

Above this primitive democracy there arose from time to time the "judges," men of the "spirit," messengers of God. It is in this unparalleled political institution that the religious essence of the period was manifest.

The time was marked by a strong and simple faith in the nearness of YHWH, a direct continuation of the feeling in Moses' time. The God who had revealed himself to Israel in a mighty act of redemption continued to show himself near. The concrete expression of this faith was the succession of saviors raised up by YHWH in Israel—prophets, Nazirites, and mighty men. The whole period of the judges is an embodiment of this idea. The tribes do not go the way of their neighbors and establish a monarchy, because they believe simply and strongly that YHWH rules them through his messengers. From Moses to Samuel, apostles of God hold national-political leadership; they represent the kingdom of God, the visible embodiment of God's will in the world.

The most important national enterprises were carried out by these men of the spirit. In normal times the primitive democracy of elders functioned, but in time of trouble the people looked for the appearance of an apostle-savior and confidently expected that YHWH would raise up such a man by his spirit. Hence, while the judges follow one another, they do not constitute an unbroken chain. Non-consecutiveness was the very essence of prophetic authority; it depended upon the action of the divine spirit, upon the combination of personal qualities and external circumstances. Since the times after the Canaanite wars were relatively uneventful while each tribe settled and endeavored to establish itself, the line of prophetic authority comes to an end after Joshua. But afterward trouble broke out from a new quarter. Israel's neighbors began to press in on its border, and the need for a central national authority again arose. As they had been taught by the experience of Moses and Joshua, the people cry out to YHWH and look for the appearance of his messenger-savior. And he always appears: a prophet like Deborah, a visionary like Gideon, an intrepid fighter like Jephthah, or a Nazirite like Samson. Each is raised up by the divine word or spirit; each rescues his people as an agent of the divine king.

The circle of influence of the judges was dependent on their personality and on circumstances. There is no reason to suppose that they were merely local heroes who were later given national status by the editor of the book of Judges. At that early time, there was no definite boundary between local and national events. Under certain conditions a famous prophet, seer, or fighter might extend his influence among several or even all of the tribes. A local distress might become a general one; a local deliverance could be felt as a national one. Deborah is a case in point. Sisera's pressure was aimed primarily at the tribes of Zebulun and Naphtali (Judg. 4:6, 10), but this woman, whose activity was between Ramah and Bethel in the highlands of Ephraim (vs. 5), roused the whole confederation to do battle. This battle, which in Judges 4 appears as a local affair, becomes, in the ancient song (chap. 5), an event of national significance in which nearly all the tribes, "the people of YHWH" (vs. 13), participate; Deborah is "a mother in Israel"; those who did not come "to the aid of YHWH" are cursed.[9] Gideon's battle with Midian and Amalek also begins as a local war, but it ends by involving Manasseh, Asher, Zebulun, Naphtali, and even Ephraim. Centuries later, a Judean prophet can still speak of "the day of Midian" as a national memorial (Isa. 9:3; 10:26). The Ammonites of Jephthah's time harass not only the Transjordanian tribes, but Judah, Benjamin, and Ephraim as well. Jephthah, with his Gileadite freebooters, defeats them and delivers all these tribes. Such men as Samson, even when they did not muster the tribes to battle, could still become national heroes and central figures. Some of the judges appear to have been contemporaries, and some were surely famous only locally. But this does not change the general character of the period as reflected in the stories of Deborah, Gideon, and Jephthah. It

---

[9] Judah is not mentioned in the song, presumably, because by then it had become subject to the Philistines.

was a kingdom of the spirit, a theocracy whose divine king exhibited his rule through apostle-saviors, one of the most remarkable manifestations of the idealism of the early religion of YHWH.

THE CULT AND PRIESTHOOD

With the settlement a new cultic factor came into being: the sanctity of the land, which was capable of encroaching upon the heretofore unique sanctity of the desert tent. Joshua 22:9–34 reflects the perplexity of this period of transition. Inasmuch as the ideal eastern boundary of the promised land is the Jordan, only Canaan can be regarded as "the land of YHWH"; there "the tabernacle of YHWH stands" (vs. 19). The other side of the Jordan is "impure" land. Yet, notwithstanding this view of the sanctity of the whole land, sacrifice is still restricted to the altar before the tabernacle (*ibid.*). When the people became rooted in the land, this restriction became obsolete; the sanctity of the land overshadowed that of the tent, and throughout the towns and settlements of Israel sanctuaries arose.

Despite the opposition of the Aaronides (expressed in Lev. 17 [P]), earth or stone altars were erected everywhere (Exod. 20:21 ff.). Alongside of them, it was customary to set stone pillars or to plant trees. Among the pagans these were conceived as lodgings for the deity; in Israel the pillar became a memorial and a witness (Gen. 28:18; Exod. 24:4; Josh. 4); the tree provided shade where the deity was apparently wont to reveal himself to man, especially in the form of a wayfarer (Gen. 18:1 ff.; Judg. 6:11–24). These symbols met with opposition, and eventually were banned.

High places were to be found everywhere (II Kings 17:9); temples were built in larger cities or at particularly sacred sites. It was presumably the size of the establishment that distinguished the former from the latter. In the temples there was doubtless a fixed daily cult. Festive throngs filled the temples on holydays; the larger temples were also visited by individuals and families on private occasions (I Sam. 1:3–21). Around the high places bands of ecstatics congregated, accompanied by musicians (I Sam. 10:5 ff.). High places and temples were also places of private and public prayer (I Sam. 1:9–18; 7:6).

Such sanctuaries as those at Bethel, Shiloh, Shechem, Gilgal, Mizpah, Gibeon, Hebron, and Beersheba were more venerated than the rest. Popular legend crowned them with an ancient sanctity. But it is a widespread misconception that temples and even priesthoods were taken over by Israel from their Canaanite predecessors. None of the prophets ever reproach Israel with having worshiped YHWH in pagan temples. The Deuteronomic command to destroy the many cult places of the Canaanites is framed: "You shall not do so [i.e., worship at many sites] to YHWH your God" (Deut. 12:4); it does not read, "You shall not worship YHWH your God there." The particulars of the conquest also speak against this notion. The Josephides slaughtered the entire population of Bethel, save for one family which they expelled (Judg. 1:24 ff.). Here, then, there was no possibility of continuing the local cultic tradition. The Danites treat the population of Laish in the same manner, burning the city as well (18:27). The city of Dan, and, of course, its sanctuary (with its Israelite priest [17–18]) are newly built by the settlers (vs. 28). The Jerusalem temple is erected on the threshing floor of Araunah the Jebusite; the altar there was newly built by David (II Sam. 24:24 f.).

Nor does the nature of the temple legends of Israel support the view that Israelite sanctuaries preserved the local sacred traditions of the Canaanites. Whereas the tendency of pagan myth is to link the history of sacred sites to the lives of the gods—gods built and lived in the temples; in some cases the temples housed their graves—biblical temple legends date the origin of the sanctity of the sites to late times. Not one Israelite temple has a history antedating the patriarchs. It is only the sanctity of the site, however, that goes back to the patriarchs; they erect altars and pillars, but do not build temples. Israelite temples have, thus, no Canaanite history at all; local sanctity has no autochthonous roots, but originates in the revelations of YHWH made to Israel's ancestors while they were alien sojourners in Canaan. There is no natural, primordial sanctity in the land. Even the closest biblical approach to a pagan temple legend, the Bethel theophany (Gen. 28:10–22), is thoroughly Israelite in all its symbols. Jacob discovers that he has been lodging at a place that, unbeknown to anyone, is the "gate of heaven." A ladder connects heaven and earth—a familiar pagan motif; but while the pagan idea represents the ladder as a link between men and the gods and a means to apotheosis, this ladder serves the angels and agents of YHWH who ascend and descend it. While the holiness of the site is, then, "primordial," it is not by virtue of being (like the Babylonian Esagila temple) an ancient dwelling place of the deity, but as the portal of God's rule over the earth.

In Canaan, Israel's cult became the cult of farmers, and the bulk of its rites were related to the land and its produce. This does not necessarily imply a fundamental change from the religion of shepherds to that of farmers. For the tribes had been half-nomads; they also tilled the soil, though not bound to a specific territory. Presumably they farmed occasionally in Egypt and in the wilderness, which has tillable soil and in which agricultural festivals are celebrated to the present time. The agricultural element in Israel's cult need not, therefore, be less primary than the pastoral.

In any event, the shape the agricultural element in the cult of YHWH took betrays no Canaanite influence. YHWH, as God of all, blesses the produce of the field and is the source of fertility; that does not make him a Canaanite Baal. The pagan Baal is a god whose life processes are bound up in the soil. For him, the fertility of the earth is a vital matter; his festivals are designed to revive and reinvigorate him. In the biblical materials dealing with the period of the judges, such motifs are entirely absent. Nor is there a hint of a struggle against such ideas and rituals. The early Israelite pattern of agricultural rites, crystallized in the Torah literature, faithfully reflects Israel's non-mythological religion and lends no support to the theory that its religion became Canaanized on Canaan's soil.

THE FIRST IDOLATROUS PERIOD

Biblical historiography distinguishes four periods in Israelite history. The first, that of Moses, Joshua, and their generation is (except for two isolated instances) non-idolatrous. It is followed by the first period of continuous national idolatry, the period of the judges. This ends abruptly with the second period of loyalty to YHWH: the days of Saul, David, and the young Solomon, to be succeeded in turn by the second idolatrous period, lasting from Solomon's last days till the Exile. The artificiality of this period division is apparent; its historicity has been discussed above (chap. iv). Some additional comments may here be made regarding the age of the judges.

The evaluation of this age as idolatrous is part of the historiosophic idealism of the Bible, according to which every national distress is the result of apostasy. The truth is that even the schematic framework of the book of Judges knows only of a generalized worship of Baals and Ashtoreths, without being able to supply further details. What this means has been fully discussed in chapter iv: a vestigial fetishistic idolatry that was found among the ignorant masses throughout the entire pre-exilic period, and to which women seem to have been particularly addicted. Zealots regarded the toleration of this idolatry as sufficiently sinful to provoke the troubles that befell the people. The historical significance of these general allegations can be gauged from the testimony regarding the age of Joshua. Since this age enjoyed victory and success, the biblical historiographer could not regard it as guilty of idolatry. Hence, we hear nothing of idolatry during Joshua's time; to the contrary, it is an age loyal to YHWH (Judg. 2:7). Nevertheless, even

Joshua, in his parting address, demands that the people "remove the foreign gods which are in your midst" (Josh. 24:23).

Equally mistaken is the accepted view that Israel was still pagan and worshiped YHWH along with other gods. The religious revolution is attested to, first of all, by the institution of judges which, as we have seen, is a unique embodiment of the new religious idea. The prophetic apostle-saviors of Israel come in the name of YHWH only; no other god raises prophets or judges to challenge the sole dominion of YHWH over the national life of Israel. No trace of any creative influence of paganism can be found in our sources for this period. There is no battle against mythological beliefs. There are no temples or priests to any foreign god. The whole life of the people is animated, and all creative effort inspired, by the religion of YHWH alone.

EARLY ESCHATOLOGY

The military success and the settlement gave rise to pride and a sense of well-being. The period had an eschatological quality; ancient promises were being fulfilled. This was "the end of days," the final, permanent bliss. All the ancient visionary and prophetic literature is informed by this sentiment. The blessings of Jacob (Gen. 49) and Moses (Deut. 33) give it clear expression (the former is the earliest vision dealing expressly with the "end of days"). Both reflect premonarchic conditions. The tribes fight, but are always victorious; they have settled and enjoy the bounty of the earth. YHWH has driven out the enemy and has commanded, "Destroy!" He has given Israel a land of grain and wine, and has settled it in insulated security. Happy Israel! There is none like God, nor any like Israel, "a people saved through YHWH." Its enemies will dwindle away before it and Israel will tread on their backs (Deut. 33:26–29). This is the ultimate vision; the horizon is bright, despite an occasional cloud.[10]

---

[10] [Kaufmann has dealt in detail with the problems of the conquest and early settlement in two further publications: *The Biblical Account of the Conquest of Palestine* (Jerusalem, 1953), and *Sēfer Yehōshūaᶜ* (Jerusalem, 1959)—a commentary to the book of Joshua.]

CHAPTER VIII

The Monarchy

The early Israelite theocracy did not on principle repudiate kingship in favor of the rights of the people, God, priest, or prophet. It was the natural effect of the idea of apostolic prophecy on ancient Hebrew society, whose government—a primitive democracy of tribal elders—left room for the leadership of men of God. The activity of these men of God lessened, but could not obviate, the need for a monarchy, for their emergence was conditioned upon a religious-national enthusiasm that was not always present. Moreover, their authority lacked the stability necessary for the political survival of the tribes. Hence, in spite of the faith in the kingship of YHWH the desire for a monarchy developed. In the time of Gideon and Samuel the glimmerings of a dynastic form of authority appear. Gideon refuses the people's request to rule them; YHWH, he says, rules them—i.e., through his apostle-saviors (Judg. 8:22 f.). Nonetheless, government is concentrated in his hands and, after his death, in the hands of "seventy men, all the sons of Jerubbaal." At this point kingship is not regarded as a sin, but as a new experiment—an experiment that failed. The rule of the seventy men collapses in family strife. It was the Philistine oppression that underlined Israel's failure to achieve political stability. The prophetic kingdom of God was unable to meet this challenge. Pious men laid the failure to the sin of the people; this attitude is reflected in the stories concerning the founding of the monarchy. But opposition to the monarchy was ephemeral, for the need was all too evident. Prophecy itself finally crowned the king. Samuel, a prophet-judge who was himself not a warrior, was charged with the task. Henceforth, the apostle was no longer sent to "judge" and deliver, but to anoint YHWH's elect, to rebuke him, or oppose him. Thus the ancient prophetic theocracy came to an end.

THE FOUNDING OF THE MONARCHY

The tradition of Saul's election to kingship has been preserved in two versions. The first, "theocratic" version (I Sam. 7; 8; 10:17–27; 12), depicts the people's request for a king as a rejection of the kingship of YHWH. At first Samuel will not hear of it; only at YHWH's bidding does he finally acquiesce in the people's proposal "to be like the other nations." The king is chosen by divine lot, Samuel writes down the severe "rule of the monarchy" and warns people and king to be loyal to YHWH. The other version (9; 10:1–16; 11) represents the monarchy as a gracious gift of God. Samuel is commanded by YHWH to anoint the Benjaminite Saul who will deliver Israel from the Philistines. Saul, looking for the lost she-asses of his father, comes to ask directions of the seer Samuel and is privately anointed king of Israel. After his victory over Nahash the Ammonite, he is publicly crowned and joyfully acclaimed by all the people. The two versions are intertwined in the present text, the fruit of the author's desire to combine and harmonize the various traditions of Saul's rise to kingship.

Classical criticism regards the antimonarchic version as a reflex of the "theocratic ideal" of the postexilic age, when monarchy had given way to priestly rule. Hosea 8:4 and 13:10 f. are taken to be the first expression of this repudiation of the monarchic principle. The fact is, however, that later ages never were hostile toward the institution of kingship. The biblical histories, compiled during the Exile and afterward, portray kings as sinning and inciting to sin, but the monarchy itself is never regarded as a sin to be atoned for or repudiated. From I Samuel 13 to the last chapter of the book of Chronicles, the monarchy is represented as a grace of God. To be sure, the prophets opposed some kings, but they are so far from rejecting the monarchy that their opposition takes the form of raising new dynasties to replace the old. The age of the Restoration pinned messianic hopes on the Davidide Zerubbabel. The "theocratic" history produced in Second Temple times, the book of Chronicles, contains an extravagant idealization of the Davidic dynasty. Priestly rule under Persian and Greek domination was for the Jews of Second Temple times a bitter reality, not an ideal. They never left off hoping for the speedy end of that rule and the re-establishment of the Davidic line.

Moreover, the negative assessment of the monarchy expressed in the "theocratic" version of Saul's election is based not on priestly, but on prophetic claims. Not priests, but Moses, Gideon, Jephthah, and Samuel are opposed to the royal ideal (I Sam. 12:11). At stake is not priestly rule, but the kingdom of apostolic prophet-judges. Later times knew of no aspiration to establish this sort of prophetic authority over the people. Once introduced, the monarchic principle became firmly rooted in Israel. Kings were deposed and slain, but not even the prophets attacked the institution of kingship. Their own ideal of the future kingdom of God was intimately associated with a king of the line of David.

The isolated passages in which kingship is opposed do not, therefore, represent an ideology that prevailed in Israel at any time after the establishment of the monarchy. The origin of this hostility must be sought in the premonarchic period. That Hosea 13:10 f. cannot be its source is clear not only because the attitude there expressed bore no ideological fruit in later literature and thought, but also from the very language of the passage. The people's request for a king is cited in the phraseology of I Samuel, but with one telling divergence: Hosea's Israel asks for "king and officials" (*śārīm*) (cf. also 8:4). Alongside the king, sharing his authority, appears the bureaucracy of the later monarchy. To the writer of I Samuel 8, however, *śārīm* do not yet hold any important position in their own right; they are merely the king's "servants" (*ᶜabādīm*, vs. 14). The people ask only for a king, and in the sequel, the king alone is spoken of. Here the conditions of the early monarchy are reflected.

All the antimonarchic passages refer to the historical moment of the beginning of the monarchy. A historical reminiscence alone is involved, not an ideal or a demand of later times. These passages preserve the mood of a specific occasion that—save for Hosea's evocation of it at the collapse of the northern kingdom—found no echo subsequently. It remained forever linked with that occasion, without further ideological issue. These passages reflect the mood of the crisis when the ancient prophetic kingdom of God gave way to a secular monarchy. Opposition to a king in favor of the rule of prophet-judges can have had its origin only in the premonarchic age, and at this crisis.

Both versions of Saul's election are correct, then, in the sense that each faithfully reflects an aspect of the historical situation. The standard bearers of the kingdom of God were distressed by what appeared to them as an open rejection of their divine ruler. But there was another viewpoint. A king was desperately needed; would YHWH ignore this need? Samuel's attitude is, therefore, divided; he opposes a king, but he is the one who in the end anoints Saul in the name of YHWH.

The monarchy is the direct successor to the apostolic kingdom of God. Saul does not seize the monarchy (he is of the smallest family of the smallest tribe [I Sam. 9:21]) but is elected by God. Like Gideon, he is a quiet man whom the spirit of God rouses to action in time of trouble (I Sam. 11). He emerges in public view, like the judges before him, as a product of the popular faith that God raises up saviors for Israel in every distress. However, Saul is the last judge, for he is the first king. Samuel's failure as military leader split in two the figure and function of the ancient prophet. Political leadership was taken from him; he retained only the gift of spirit and vision.

The "spiritual" element in Saul is still very marked. Not only is his rise to kingship due to a prophet, but he himself is an ecstatic (I Sam. 10:5 ff.; 19:23 f.; cf. 16:14 ff. and 18:10). In I Samuel 10:9, Saul's inspiration is conceived of as an effluence from Samuel. The oracle that Samuel communicated to him gave Saul "another heart" and qualified him for "prophesying." The story is a kind of parallel to Numbers 11:16 ff. There the elders prophesy by virtue of the word of God that came to Moses; this temporary gift prepares them for the permanent rank of leaders. In Saul, however, a greater change took place; the touch of prophecy prepared him for kingship. Thus he was a fit successor to the authority of prophets.

It is surely no accident that the first king is at the same time a man of the spirit. Nor is it likely to be a mere coincidence that each of the first three kings is a man of spirit. Saul is an ecstatic; David is a poet in whom "the spirit of YHWH" speaks (II Sam. 23:2); Solomon is a sage in whom there is "the wisdom of God" (I Kings 3:28). We do not find this quality in any of the later kings. Does this feature reflect the momentum of the early kingship of God, the spiritual kingdom, out of which Israel's secular monarchy sprang?

THE CONCEPTION OF KINGSHIP

Samuel's opposition to the monarchy was a passing cloud. Israel's king was the "anointed of YHWH"; even in the moments of fiercest antagonism toward Saul Samuel never again suggests that the monarchy itself is a sin. On the contrary, it is viewed as the supreme expression of God's grace. Under the kingship of YHWH Israel took possession of their land, but the kingdom of YHWH's anointed brought victory and dominion over its enemies. The historiosophy of the framework of the book of Judges portrays the premonarchy as a time of constant relapse into idolatry, whereas the early monarchy is portrayed as non-idolatrous. Thus speaks the proud and confident voice of the time. Compared with the imperial glory of David and Solomon the period of the judges seemed faltering and weak—religiously interpreted as the effect of sin. The grace of God shone on Israel in its fulness only with the coming of kingship.

That Israel's monarchy was an emulation of a pagan institution is candidly admitted by the biblical narrator. The people ask for a king to rule them "like all the nations" (I Sam. 8:5, 20; Deut. 17:14). But the pagan materials were radically transformed on Israelite soil. In the cultures surrounding Israel the king was in some way endowed with divine qualities. Pharaoh is a god, the son of Re. The kings of Assyria and Babylonia are the sons and brothers of the gods, or have been suckled by goddesses; they are the consorts of Ishtar in certain cultic rites. It is true that the Mesopotamian king also conceives of himself as chosen by the gods to rule justly and maintain the cult, but this is only an adjunct to the basic idea. The Israelite conception rejected all the divine aspects of kingship and based itself exclusively on the idea of divine election (I Sam. 10:24; 16:1 ff.; II Sam. 6:21; Deut. 17:15; etc.). There are linguistic vestiges of the idea that the king is a "son" of God (Pss. 2:7; 89:27 f.). But that these are purely figurative (cf. II Sam. 7:14) is evident from the absence of any mythological motifs. There is no allusion to the divine origin of the reigning dynasty. No Israelite king is condemned for having vaunted himself a god or for instituting a cult celebrated in his honor.

In pagan society the king was the head of the cult. The Egyptian cult was performed by priests in the name of, and as agents of, the Pharaoh. Mesopotamian kings always retained the title of priest. It was their prime responsibility to maintain the temples and their proper cults; the gods elected them to maintain the service which mankind was created to perform for the gods. Israel's monarchy is grounded not in the priesthood, but in apostolic prophecy. Israelite kings had the right to perform altar service and were charged with the maintenance of altars and temples. But they never bore the official title "priest"; their priestly function was but a by-role. The Israelite king succeeded to the task of the prophet-judge, not of the priest; the latter never bore secular authority in Israel. The ideal king of the future is a just judge, God-fearing and mighty; he has no priestly features (cf. Isa. 11:1 ff.). Modeled after the apostolic prophet-judge, the king is the elect of God. He does not incorporate any divine essence; he does not control the destiny of the cosmos through the cult; he is but the bearer of God's grace, appointed to office by his messenger-prophet. The king is thus another embodiment of the idea that it is God's will that rules on earth.

DAVID AND SOLOMON

The tragic figure of Saul could not serve as the symbol of the blessing of YHWH. This symbol was fashioned by the popular hero, David. The tradition that makes him author of the Psalms, and the appellation "servant of YHWH" (e.g., II Sam. 3:18; I Kings 3:6; Ezek. 34:23; Ps. 36:1), indicate that besides being a military and political genius, he was a deeply religious man. This alone can explain the creation in his time of new permanent symbols of Israelite religion.

David's first act as king of all Israel was to capture Jebus-Jerusalem, previously outside the area of Israelite settlement. The founding of a new capital in Jerusalem was an apt symbol of the new period he was inaugurating in the nation's history. David fortifies the Jebusite city, renaming it "the City of David." Then he ventures to do what Saul never did: he conveys the ark, which had lain in obscurity since the destruction of the Shiloh sanctuary, to his new capital. The City of David became the home of the ancient national symbol of YHWH's covenant and election of Israel. But that was not all. Having built himself a palace, he conceived the plan of building a temple for the ark. Saul built altars (I Sam. 14:35); David envisioned a royal temple which would be the final resting place of the ark. Such a royal temple would, of course, possess extraordinary sanctity and would reflect glory upon the City of David as well. It would serve as a cultic symbol of the divine favor shown toward the king and his capital. With David the idea of a city and temple chosen by YHWH originated, though, since he did not intend to do away with the local altars, David's idea is not Deuteronomic.

The aspirations of the Davidic dynasty are given classic expression in the vision of Nathan in II Samuel 7:5–16. The kingship of David is viewed as initiating a new era in Israelite history, whose glory would last forever. The troubled age of the judges is over; henceforth, Israel would be planted securely in its land, "and it shall dwell there, and not be disturbed any longer." It is almost as if the land were "given" anew to Israel, this time for good (vss. 10 f.). The favor shown to David is not merely personal; his house would be firmly established before YHWH "forever." If his sons sin, they will be punished, but the kingship will not be taken from them. The eternity of the Davidic dynasty is also the central theme of David's prayer, which immediately follows. At the height of his career, the Israelite king is far from pretending to divinity; he asks, "Who am I Lord YHWH, and what is my house that you have brought me thus far?" His kingship is the product of the divine will and word (vs. 21).

In the conception of his kingship, however, the profound difference between David and Saul is manifest. David is more than just another savior of Israel; he is the ultimate savior, his kingship is the final expression of God's grace. David's successes and victories signify that YHWH has chosen him to be the vehicle through which Israel and the name of God will be exalted. His kingdom is eternal, for the will of YHWH is eternal. The inner motif of David's kingship is the creation of lasting symbols. The people, the land, and the line of David are to become the three eternal expressions of YHWH's favor. Similar conceptions are found in the Davidic psalms of II Samuel 22 (=Ps. 18) and 23:1-7.

SOLOMON'S TEMPLE—Solomon, too, regards his kingship as the fulfilment of the divine promise made to his father (I Kings 3:6; 6:11 ff.; 8:15 ff.). At the threshing floor of Araunah the Jebusite, where David built a new altar, Solomon erects the temple. He does not ban the rural cults, but it is plain that he conceives the "chosen house" as especially sacrosanct. To this temple he brings the ark, which is never afterward removed from there, not even to go out to war. Its sanctity and that of the temple lent an aura of holiness to the site that no destruction or political collapse was ever able to dissipate.

The art and architecture of the temple drew on pagan models. Its builders and designers were hired from Hiram of Tyre. Was more involved than a borrowing of external forms?

For the answer to this it is crucial to observe that in the *debir*, the adytum, there was no genuine mythological symbol. No image represents the resident God. More important, there is no trace of the mythological cult that was connected with such images. No rites are performed in the adytum; it contains only the ark and the cherubs, symbols of God's relationship to, and government of, the world. There is no bed for sleep or cohabitation. There is a table of shewbread; however, it is not for the divine repast, but only a symbol of piety: man consecrates some of the toil of his hands to God as a token of servitude and homage.

The meaning of the temple in Israel is strikingly set forth in the prayer ascribed to Solomon in I Kings 8:12-53.[1] It is not a house for the deity,

[1] This prayer is not a later creation. It contains nothing of the Deuteronomic idea that the temple is the sole legitimate place of worship. In fact, the Deuteronomic emphasis on the central sanctuary as the sole place of sacrifice has no echo at all in the chapter; sacrifice is not even mentioned. The calamities that are the occasion of prayer in the temple are all of the sort that befall a people living on its own soil. War and captivity are mentioned, but not national exile. Verses 44 f. speak of an offensive war to which God "sends" the people—a reference to the ancient custom of consulting oracles before going to battle. The captives of verses 46 ff. are only part of the people (those who went out to war). The sin of the nation—violation of the covenant and apostasy—and its

carefully guarded against the attacks of evil powers, in which man performs the cult necessary to protect and strengthen the deity. This prayer inaugurating a house of sacrifice and uttered before an altar, contains not a word concerning cultic functions. Not even worship through hymn and psalm is mentioned. This temple is solely a house of prayer. Man does nothing on behalf of God, but God hears and answers, judges and pardons, shows compassion to and delivers man. Since both the early and later religion of Israel accepted and hallowed the sacrificial cult, it cannot be assumed that originally sacrifice had a place in the prayer, but was later intentionally dropped out. The present formulation appears to be original and must be interpreted as the product of a deep religious insight. Alongside the Canaanite blueprint of the house in chapters 6–7, this remarkable prayer was placed as a sort of Israelite commentary to that document. The whole temple serves one idea: man's dependence upon and submission to the one, omnipotent God.

THE SECOND IDOLATROUS PERIOD

Solomon's reign was the turning point of the political fortunes of the monarchy. It is the testimony of the Bible that a religious decline too set in. I Kings 11:4 states that the private chapels that Solomon built outside Jerusalem for his pagan wives, at first out of a politic toleration, ultimately brought about his own involvement in their cults. This was not a public, aggressive pagan influx, as later in the days of Jezebel, but it was the first time that Ashtoreth, Milcom, Chemosh, etc. had altars built to them on the soil of Israel—and at the hands of an Israelite king! Northern prophets foretold the destruction of Solomon and his line for this sin (I Kings 11:11–13, 29–31, 33); this ferment was possibly the beginning of Jeroboam's rebellion.

For biblical historiosophy, I Kings 11:4 divides the history of the monarchy into two. From the reign of Saul to the last days of Solomon there was no national sin of idolatry; at this point the sin begins, and continues, with considerable lapses, to the fall. This view, however, is a dogmatic necessity for the biblical historians and cannot be taken at

---

collective punishment, standard themes of later times (cf. the prayers in Ezra-Nehemiah), are nowhere alluded to. On the contrary, the whole prayer is couched in terms of individual petitions and individual troubles. Its form is the individual prayer of Solomon; four times God is asked to hear his supplication, "maintain his right" and the right of his people "as each day shall require" (vss. 28, 30, 52, 59). It is basically a prayer for the age of Solomon and the daily needs of his time. For the supposed traces of prophetic universalism, see above, pp. 164 f.

face value. There can be no doubt that the religious condition of the bulk of the people after Solomon's reign did not change substantially from what it was before. Vestigial idolatry existed among the vulgar, both before and after. But the biblical narrative ignores these phenomena during the period of the monarchy's glory. It raises them to the rank of national sin to explain the political decline that set in at the end of Solomon's reign. Some justification for this can be found in the effect the foreign wives had on the king in his old age. But this private defection of the court did not, of course, initiate a new religious period in the life of the people. The idolatrous color that the biblical history of this period bears is the result of the writers' generalization of responsibility. If there is idolatry in the land, it is everybody's fault. But the fact is that the Bible does not know a popular cult of any foreign god. The post-Solomonic age cannot, therefore, be regarded as a period of the paganization of the national religion.

THE SINS OF JEROBOAM

With the division of the kingdom, a certain breach was opened between the religious life of north and south. In the view of the biblical historian, the secession involved nothing less than the apostasy of the northern ten tribes. Jeroboam sets up two other gods—golden calves—in Dan and Bethel to wean his people away from Jerusalem. This is his chief "sin." Besides, he invents a festival in the eighth month and appoints non-Levite priests (I Kings 12:26–33; 14:9). This black picture of Jeroboam is from a Judean hand; northern sources give an altogether different assessment of Jeroboam's work.

It is perfectly plain that Jeroboam and the kings of Israel who perpetuated his "sins" did not "cast YHWH behind their backs" or regard the calves as "other gods" (I Kings 14:9). Jehu, the prophetically appointed extirpator of Canaanite Baalism does not remove the calves. Nor do Elijah and Elisha utter a word against them (the denunciation ascribed to Ahiah in I Kings 14:9, 15 expresses the southern viewpoint and is late). The interpretation given in the book of Kings is Judean polemic designed to denigrate the calves as fetish-idols. The story itself testifies obliquely that the calves were not "other gods." It blames Jeroboam for inventing a festival and appointing non-Levite priests. But what additional sin can possibly consist in worshiping golden calves in this manner? What has Israel been commanded by YHWH concerning the festivals and priests of a calf-cult?

The story does not link the calves with any foreign deity; hence, they must have belonged (like the image of Micah) to the cult of YHWH. They were not conceived of as representations of YHWH—such a notion would have been too blasphemous for the biblical historian to have passed over in silence. The calves were, therefore, not idols of Israel's god, worshiped as symbols in the true pagan manner. What were they, then?

Moved by political considerations, Jeroboam built for his kingdom royal sanctuaries after the manner of the Jerusalem temple. His buildings, too, were presumably inspired by pagan models. Jeroboam needed a symbol that would replace the southern ark, and in this also he was guided by pagan motifs. The calf or bull commonly served as the pedestal of Near Eastern gods, particularly of Hadad, the storm god; the winged bull served also—like the cherub—as a guardian genius. Jeroboam, however, adopted only the calf, without the figure of a standing or riding god. Corresponding to the cherubs of the ark, they represented only the vehicle, not the divine rider. Jeroboam's calves were perhaps of the winged type and thus no more than a variation on the theme of the cherub. In essence, then, there is no difference between the calves and the cherubs. We must not be misled by the biblical polemic to think that the latter somehow imply purer religious ideas than the former. The rejection of the image of a divine rider upon the calf is the crucial evidence for the transformation worked by the Israelite idea on the calves of the north, no less than on the cherubs of the south.[2]

The historian of Kings asserts that Jeroboam appointed non-Levite priests; whence, then, the patent link between Jeroboam's calves and the desert calf made by Aaron, the father of the priesthood? It is difficult to avoid the conclusion that Jeroboam's calves were designed by Aaronide priests, some of whom doubtless served at the large local sanctuaries of the north. The calves belonged to the same priestly tradition from which the cherubs of the ark stemmed. Northern tradition doubtless related the golden calf episode of the desert in a manner entirely different from that of the south. This priestly tradition may also have furnished a basis for the new festival. From a dogmatic Jerusalemite viewpoint, calves and a new festival were rebellion against the command of God. In essence, however, they have absolutely no paganism in them.

What separated the religion of the north from that of the south, then, was a superficial heresy which orthodox zealotry exaggerated beyond all bounds. It is decisive that even the biblical writer depicts the division as purely cultic. It had no effect in the realm of prophecy. Jeroboam

---

[2] For this interpretation of the calves, cf. H. Th. Obbink, *Zeitschrift für die alttestamentliche Wissenschaft*, XLVII (1929), 268 f.

has no special "calf prophets"; only YHWH is the source of northern, as of southern, prophecy. Micaiah, Elijah, Elisha, and the other northern prophets before Hosea do not denounce the calves or call upon the people to worship in Jerusalem. Yet they are not stigmatized as idolatrous by the Bible.

Israel and Judah were one national-cultural realm. Common to both were their world view, legends, prophecy, laws, and morality. Their literary creativity was common; the patriarchal legends in which Joseph is central as opposed to the sons of Leah became the property of all the tribes. Legends about the postsecession prophets of the north were preserved in the literary store of the south. Prophets passed freely between the two kingdoms. Both realms felt themselves sharing a common destiny. Even in the cult we see a great common idea. The entire land—Israel and Judah—is sacred soil, the dwelling place of YHWH; "impure ground" is beyond the territory of both kingdoms. Sabbath and new moon, tithe, peace and whole offering, sin offering and libation belonged to north as well as south. The festivals of Ephraim were appointed seasons of YHWH to the southern prophet Amos (5:21).

The northern monarchy, like that of the south, was an embodiment of the Israelite idea of prophetic election. In each kingdom, however, the idea took a distinctive shape.

There are two aspects to the idea of divine election. On the one hand, the decision of God is everlasting—"God is not man, that he should lie, or human, that he should repent." A king chosen by the divine word is, therefore, ideally the founder of an enduring dynasty. On the other hand, kingship is conceived of as an expression of God's favor; hence it is forever conditioned upon the king's submission to the will of God. Divine election consecrates the king with a conditional permanence; his rebellion annuls the election. Saul was elected with a view to founding an everlasting dynasty (I Sam. 13:13); he is rejected for his failure to carry out a divine command. David is elected "forever," but after the scandal with Bathsheba, Nathan prophesies the destruction of his line. Ahiah foretells the end of Solomon's kingdom for the sin of idolatry. Eternal favor or annihilation are the alternative poles of divine election.

In Judah the concept of legitimacy took so firm a hold that no man ever challenged the exclusive right of the Davidides to kingship. Prophecy did not forego its right to defy the king, but its defiance was directed against the man, not against the line. In this way the south established a synthesis between the idea of eternal election and the prophetic right of challenge. This synthesis ultimately gave rise to the hope for an ideal

"David" of the future. The historic kings were failures; at the end of time, however, God would send a king in whom the royal ideal would be realized. This king would be a "shoot from the stock of Jesse."

The north did not develop such a synthesis. Here there were no bounds to prophetic defiance. Samuel's defiance and rejection of Saul was the prototype of northern prophecy; not the man alone but his entire line may be rejected. Ahiah prophesied the end of the line of Solomon and Jeroboam; Jehu condemned Baasha and his house; Elijah dooms Ahab's line, and Elisha incites Jehu to annihilate the Omrides; Amos condemns Jeroboam II and his house. Palace revolutions here, as everywhere, were motivated by personal rivalries and ambitions. But there is no doubt that the constant challenge of the prophets was what undermined the loyalty of the people to any given dynasty. Politically, such unrestricted challenge was dangerous; it probably contributed to the collapse of the northern kingdom. But in it is revealed most starkly the uniquely Israelite character of the northern monarchy. One may say that the prophetic conception of the monarchy was given fuller expression here than in the south, for the defiance of northern prophecy knew no legitimistic check to the freedom of YHWH's word.

THE BAAL WORSHIP OF THE NORTH AND ITS SCOPE

In chapter iv, it was pointed out that the Baal worship of the north was limited to court circles and that no evidence for syncretism in the religion of YHWH during the period of the Omrides exists. These conclusions are bolstered by an examination of the prophetically inspired attack on the Omride dynasty.

Elijah's victory over the Baal worshipers on Mount Carmel (I Kings 18) was not decisive; directly afterward he was compelled to flee the wrath of Jezebel. Yet it is significant that Baal worship no longer appears in the subsequent chapters of I Kings as a factor in the relations between Elijah and Ahab. When he goes out to battle the Aramaeans, Ahab is surrounded by YHWH prophets; he has no magicians or diviners; he does not take omens, nor does he inquire of Baal prophets (chap. 22). His battles with Aram are fought in the name of YHWH (20:13, 23 ff.). The new conflict between Ahab and Elijah arises, not over Baal, but over the murder of Naboth the Jezreelite. This foul deed is the occasion of Elijah's prophecy of doom for Ahab and his house (21:19 ff.). Ahab is terrified; he rends his garments, fasts, puts on sackcloth, and "goes about softly." The dynasty's doom is sealed, according to this, not by Baal worship, but by the murder of Naboth.

Ahaziah's brief reign is marked by a recrudescence of court paganism. Fallen sick, the king inquires of Baal-zebub, god of Ekron (II Kings 1:2), for which apostasy Elijah prophesies death.

Joram the son of Ahab is charged by the biblical record only with "the sins of Jeroboam." Joram's removal of a "pillar of Baal" that Ahab had made (II Kings 3:2) attests to a religious purge. Henceforth, Baal worship was an exotic out-of-the-way cult. Since it was not until Jehu's accession that the Baal temple of Samaria was destroyed, it must still have stood throughout Joram's reign. But the worshipers in it were a mere remnant of survivors from Ahab's time (10:18). The narratives concerning Elisha furnish glimpses of life throughout the north and involve persons of various condition; nowhere do we meet with Baal worship. Nor is Baal present in the history of Joram. When Joram seeks an oracle, he turns to Elisha, who is portrayed as a familiar of the king (6:12, 21; 8:4 ff.). What paganism he taxes Joram with pertains to his father and mother (3:13).

No sin of Joram plays any part in the account of Jehu's revolution. Elisha's servant anoints Jehu for the purpose of avenging Ahab's murder of the prophets and "servants of YHWH"; Jehu's response to Joram's greeting (9:22) suggests plainly that Joram is being held to account for the guilt of his parents. Even more important is the fact that destruction of the house of Ahab is not represented as punishment for apostasy, but for murder (vss. 6 f., 25 f., 30–37). Baal worship is invoked only indirectly, as the occasion for the murder of YHWH's prophets and servants. To be sure, Jehu eradicates the remaining vestiges of Baalism along with the house of Ahab, but the story of the revolution indicates that by that time they had become almost entirely a thing of the past. Jehu's revolution cannot be interpreted as a life struggle of the religion of YHWH against the menace of Baalism. Whatever menace may have existed in Jezebel's time had evaporated by the time of Joram. The religious aspect of the revolution expressed itself chiefly as the demand for satisfaction of the bloodguilt that lay on Ahab's house. There was, besides, the matter of lopping off the aftergrowths of Baalism in Israel and its transplant in Judah. Not even these withered remains could be tolerated by the devotees of YHWH. No menace of "syncretism," but the strength and zealotry of the religion of YHWH are what demanded that the last vestiges of Baalism be eradicated, even after Baal had long since ceased being a living issue.

What roused prophets and zealots into action was the national distress after the death of Ahab. Mesha, king of Moab, defected and withstood the attempt of a coalition of Israel, Judah, and Edom to subjugate him (II

Kings 3). The accession of Hazael as king of Aram opened a new and a more bitter phase of warfare with Israel (10:32 f.). To the God-fearing, these calamities were the hand of YHWH. YHWH was chastening Israel because of the sin of the house of Ahab—that was the meaning of events. YHWH's favor would be rewon only after the innocent victims of Jezebel were avenged, only after the seed of Jezebel and every memorial of her were extirpated.

That Jehu's revolution was not directed particularly against the Baal cult is clear enough from the account of II Kings 10:18 ff. When Jehu announces his intention to outdo Ahab in his zeal for Baal, all the worshipers of Baal flock to his summons, filling the Baal temple of Samaria from door to door. Having thus craftily assembled them all in one building, the king signals his men to fall upon them. Now this deceit could have been successful only because in its first stages Jehu's revolt did not appear to have as its chief end the annihilation of Baalism.

In sum, then, the Baal cult was far from constituting a vital danger to the religion of YHWH in the time of Elisha and Jehu.

THE POPULAR PROPHETS

By the ninth century, prophets are numbered in the hundreds and are found everywhere (I Kings 18:4, 13; 22:6). After the time of David, ecstatic bands are no longer heard of; in their stead a new phenomenon appears, the *benē nebīʾîm*—groups of prophetic "orders." These have nothing to do with the ecstatics of Samuel's time. They are not ecstatics, nor do they infect others with ecstasy. Unlike the ecstatics of Samuel's age, who have no other function but to "prophesy," the *benē nebīʾîm* act as mantics and messengers. They cluster about the great prophets; the relation between them and their leader, however, is not Dionysiac, but rational and ordered.

The *benē nebīʾîm* are the plural of the ancient servant-disciple of Joshua's type. They are styled the prophet's "servants" and "lads" (II Kings 5:22; 6:3; 9:4; etc.). With their families and households (4:1 ff.; 5:27), they live with him (4:38; 6:1), wander with him (6:1 ff.), and share his food. They tell his wonders (8:4 f.), do his bidding (4:29; 9:1 ff.), and are his agents in his work as a messenger of God. The prophet appears as the head of an order, although the membership of these orders appears to have been somewhat fluid.

In all likelihood, the prophets and *benē nebīʾîm* were, for the most part, psychically abnormal: men of wild imagination, visionaries, neurotics, epileptics. Like "men of God" everywhere, they differed from the rest of the people in behavior, dress, and speech. They wore a hairy mantle (Zech. 13:4) and a leather girdle (II Kings 1:8). It was not unusual for them to appear bruised and bleeding (Zech. 13:6; I Kings 20:35 ff.); at times, they ran as if possessed (I Kings 18:46). They were popularly regarded as madmen and fools (II Kings 9:11; Hos. 9:7; Jer. 29:26). But this madness had its method; it made an impression and inspired fear as well as scorn. Notwithstanding the prophet's madness, the people believed and feared him.

The popular prophet of this period is, on the lowest level, a seer, healer, and wonder-worker whose services are for hire. But this very prophecy can on occasion rise to become a political and moral force of the first rank. It is a fact that such major prophets as Samuel, Ahiah, and Elisha worked for hire. Elijah is never said to have accepted wages, but he is nonetheless to be accounted one of the popular prophets, the master of Elisha. For all that, he was a champion of YHWH and the moral order. The Israelite popular prophet is at once a seer, a wonder-healer, and a militant apostle of YHWH. The characteristic intertwining of functions is evident in several instances. Saul, having prepared his "gift," goes to the seer Samuel to inquire about some lost asses; Samuel appears to him, however, not only as a seer but as a messenger of YHWH, sent to anoint him king and savior of Israel (I Sam. 9). The wife of Jeroboam disguises herself, takes wages, and goes to Ahiah to inquire about the fate of her sick son. Ahiah foretells the death of the boy, but he does so as a messenger of YHWH who announces the doom of people and king as well (I Kings 14). Naaman comes to Elisha to be healed of leprosy. He regards the prophet as a wonder-healer, for whom he brings wages. Elisha effects a cure through a wondrous sign that converts Naaman to belief in YHWH. The magic healer is suddenly transformed into the servant of YHWH whose mission is to attest the might of the one God (II Kings 5). In Damascus, the Aramaean Hazael consults Elisha on behalf of his ailing king Ben-hadad. The two pagans turn to Elisha as a clairvoyant "man of God" whose services are worth a gift of "forty camel loads" to them. Elisha utters a cryptic message in true oracular fashion. But all at once, a new image appears. Weeping, Elisha announces to Hazael that he is destined to be king of Aram and oppress Israel. Here Elisha is no longer speaking for hire. Dropping the cloak of a seer, he is revealed as a messenger of God who has been sent to impart a fateful message. Specifically, he carries out here the mission intrusted to his master Elijah (I Kings 19:15 f.). The mantic suddenly takes on the role of an apostle; he makes Hazael, the rod of YHWH's wrath, king (II Kings 8:7 ff.).

Even more interesting is the story of II Kings 1. The ailing king, Ahaziah, sends men to inquire of Baal-zebub, god of Ekron, whether or not he will recover. Elijah is commanded by YHWH to intercept the embassy and send them back with the message that the king would die. "Thus said YHWH: Is there no God in Israel that you send to inquire of Baal-zebub? . . ." Elijah champions the mantic function of Israelite prophecy; it is the duty of the Israelite to inquire of prophets of YHWH concerning private as well as public matters. He defends this mantic function as a messenger of God. The mantic and the messenger are two sides of the same prophet.

These stories shed light on the conception that Israelite prophecy had of its mantic and healing functions. These were not viewed as powers inherent in persons, spirits, or materials, but as effects of and witnesses to the favor and might of Israel's God. Through Elisha's cure Naaman comes to recognize "that there is no God in all the world but in Israel" (II Kings 5:15). Israel's mantic and iatric prophecy thus serves an ideological end; it testifies to the power of Israel's one God. Thus it too has an apostolic role.

THE POLITICAL ROLE OF POPULAR PROPHECY—Out of the prophets and prophetic orders emerged men who played an active part in the political and spiritual life of the people. During the stormy reign of Ahab we hear of anonymous prophets who, while acting as individuals, nonetheless are partisans of a common ideology. In the Aramaean wars, they appear on their own as messengers of YHWH (I Kings 20:13 ff.). They are patriots, though not in the service of the king. Ahab does not inquire of them; in fact, they sometimes oppose him (vss. 35 ff.). These anonymous prophets initiated the fight against Baal. Before Elijah came upon the scene, prophets of YHWH had already been slain by Jezebel (18:4, 13, 22; 19:10, 14). Obadiah hides a hundred of them in two caves; there were, then, hundreds involved of whom Elijah is but the outstanding figure. These anonymous prophets were the first martyrs for the name of YHWH. God-fearing persons were stirred by their example, and these "servants of YHWH," too, paid with their lives for their devotion (II Kings 9:7). There now appears for the first time the figure of the suffering prophet, the prototype of the later martyr. Elisha's battle with the house of Ahab too must have involved the prophetic circles. The avenging purpose of the revolution (*ibid.*), as well as Elisha's particular mission—to mop up after Jehu (I Kings 19:17)—could hardly have been accomplished without the help of these zealots.

In this way the popular mantic prophet fulfilled an apostolic role as well. The boundary between mantic and apostolic prophecy was never sharply drawn. And it was from among the "professional" prophets that the first martyrs of the one God arose.

TRUE AND FALSE PROPHETS—In Ahab's time, the dichotomy of "true" and "false" prophets makes its first historical appearance. While the theoretical distinction is elementary and ancient (see Deut. 13:2 ff.; 18:15 ff.), what is new is the division into what seem to be two parties of prophets, each marked by a distinctive outlook and ideology. In I Kings 22, Micaiah son of Imlah is portrayed as Ahab's nemesis; he is opposed by four hundred prophets, headed by Zedekiah son of Chenaanah, who "prophesy good things to the king." At issue between the two parties is the truth of their prophecy. During the age of classical prophecy, this dichotomy reached its climax. Beyond falsely claiming to speak YHWH's word, the false prophet is a glutton, a drunkard, a liar, and an adulterer (Isa. 28:7; Jer. 23:14; 29:23); he is avaricious and prophesies only for money (Mic. 3:5); he promises only what the people wish to hear—prosperity and peace (Mic. 3:5; Jer. 4:10; 8:10 f.; 14:13; 23:17; 27:14 ff.; 28–29; Ezek. 12:24; 13:10). The true prophet is the contrary of all these.

This distinction made by the prophets themselves is, of course, not disinterested and cannot be accepted at face value. Historically and psychologically we must distinguish first between persons who prophesy out of an internal conviction and those who do so purely for an external end. The latter alone merit the title "false prophets" and are not a religious phenomenon at all. The former are "true prophets," whatever moral and religious differences are discernible among them. Crucial for the history of Israelite religion is the distinction that develops during this period between the prophet of weal and the prophet of woe. Prophets of weal appear first in the time of Ahab's Aramaean wars and thereafter in every time of stress. National crises gave rise, on the one hand, to a mood of penitence, the expression of which was the prophecy of woe. But it also aroused the hope of deliverance; the prophet of weal was the organ of this mood. Both types of prophecy are rooted in Israelite faith. This faith enunciated a religious-moral doctrine, but it was also linked with a national-territorial promise. The prophet of weal spoke for the latter; the prophet of woe, primarily for the former, though he also gave voice—as we shall see—to Israel's national aspirations. Thus, while the prophet of weal was one-sided, the prophet of woe gave full expression to the essence of Israelite religion.

For it is a mistaken notion that the classical prophets were exclusively prophets of woe. The superiority of these prophets lay in their moral alertness, in contrast to the moral complacency of the prophets of weal. But the prophetic monition does not regard punishment and destruction to be the last word of God. Warning, punishment, and deliverance are interwoven in the fabric of Israelite thought from earliest times. Though God twice threatens to annihilate the generation of the desert, he qualifies this threat with the promise of making Moses "a great nation" (Exod. 32:10; Num. 14:12; Deut. 9:14). The generation of the Exodus dies in the wilderness, but their children inherit the land. The period of the judges is made up of repeated cycles of sin, punishment, and deliverance. The apostolic prophets always combine these motifs. Even the extremism of northern prophecy goes beyond sterile threats of doom. It defied kings and overthrew dynasties, but its destructiveness aimed at salvation. Its agent of divine wrath was the new king, whom it regarded as a sort of savior and redeemer (see below on eschatology). The Elijah of wrath is the same who runs before Ahab's chariot in the hour of favor (I Kings 18:41 ff.). Elisha rejects Joram, but prophesies victory for him (II Kings 3:16 ff.). Isaiah, the great arraigner of Israelite society, appears in II Kings 19 as a prophet of weal. The grace and favor of God are no less fundamental to Israelite religion than its religious and moral demand.

It follows, then, that a sterile and hopeless prophecy of doom never existed in Israel as the ideology of any party of prophets. There was, however, a party who prophesied only weal. Since the classical prophets emphasized the moral-religious demand, reproach and warning are prominent in their writings. Their particular outlook could not find expression in prophecies of weal only. But the soil of Israelite religion as a whole did permit the rise of such a prophecy. The prophets of weal whom we meet in the writings of the literary prophets thus represent a type that belongs to the stage of Israelite religion prior to the rise of classical prophecy.

THE NEW ESCHATOLOGY

Before the Aramaean wars the possibility that YHWH would really break his covenant with Israel and expel it from its land could hardly have been seriously contemplated. The oldest warnings of the Torah, Joshua, and Judges include the imaginary threat that the remnant of the Canaanites will drive Israel off its land (Num. 33:55 f.; Josh. 23:13; Judg. 2); but these have no reference to real events. During the terrible century between the reigns of Ahab and Jeroboam II, however, a significant change took place in the mood of the people. The incessant Aramaean wars ravaged and impoverished the land; and with them came famine and plague (Amos 4:6 ff.; Isa. 1:5 ff.). To the religiously sensitive, it seemed as if YHWH were withdrawing his favor, as if a turning point in Israel's destiny had been reached. This mood is reflected in the last creations of early prophetic literature.

In these writings the earlier curses and threats become an eschatological certainty. This is evident especially in the late monitions of Deuteronomy, in those passages that deal expressly with what is to happen in the "end of days" (4:25 ff., cf. vs. 30; 31:16 ff., cf. vs. 29). Coming into the "rest and the inheritance" are no longer the final promise. After a period of well-being, Israel will stray from YHWH to serve other gods; then a time of punishment and distress will come. The scheme of these chapters is: Israel grows old, fat and secure, and violates the covenant; YHWH then "hides his face" and brings on the doom of the last days. The reference is unmistakably to the sin and punishment that are to follow the golden decades of the early monarchy.

In the Song of Moses (Deut. 32) and its introductory chapter (31), enslavement to a "no-people," a "foolish nation" (the Aramaeans) drought, famine, plague and wild animals, and death by the sword (32:21 ff.) are envisioned. After this chastisement, God will have compassion on his people and make atonement for their land. Exile is not mentioned. In the monitions of Leviticus 26 and Deuteronomy 4:25–28 (cf. 28:36 f., 63 ff.; 29:27), exile appears as the final calamity. Among the nations, Israel will find no peace. Continual affliction will expunge its sin, and it will repent, after which God will recall the covenant and restore Israel to its land. These monitions, which reveal acquaintance neither with the conditions of the real exile nor with the historiosophy of classical prophecy (pp. 158 ff. and 204 f. above), belong to the stage of Israelite religion prior to the rise of classical prophecy. They show clearly the radical change that took place in Israel's eschatology. Whereas earlier times believed that they were experiencing the fulfilment of the ancient promises (p. 261 above), these writings reflect an age that saw itself living in troubled and bitter times of YHWH's wrath—YHWH had "hidden his face." Only a new act of divine grace could save Israel. The hope for a new, eschatological restoration to God's favor was born. The "end of days" was transferred from the present to the future.

Although we cannot, with certainty, fix the time of these chapters, the contacts between Deuteronomy 32:36 and II Kings 14:26, and between the descriptions of Israel's distress in Deuteronomy and those in Amos and Isaiah, suggest that the Song of Moses dates from the time of the Aramaean wars. The chapters alluding to exile and dispersion date possibly closer to the collapse of the north. Since not even in the monitions of Deuteronomy is any allusion made to the sin of the high places, these chap-

ters antedate the time of Josiah. They are among the earliest creations
of the new eschatology.

More precisely datable is the brief prophecy attributed to Elijah (I
Kings 19:15 ff.). Hazael, Jehu, and Elisha are charged with eradicating
the sin of Baalism. This done, it is expected that the mission of Hazael
(his victories over Israel) will be ended. Since the prophecy is unaware
of the fate of Jehu's line, it may be dated around 840, the time of Hazael's
first ravages. The vision is imbedded in a unique narrative framework.
Unlike the other prophets who counterbalance their threats with prayers
for divine mercy (this is the task of the prophet according to I Sam. 12:23),
Elijah is all accusation (I Kings 19:10, 14). It is as though he wished to
excite God's wrath against his people. Here the idea glimmers forth that
religious faith, not national existence, is the ultimate value. Israel has
value only insofar as it is YHWH's people. YHWH is "the God," not a
symbolic extension of the national being of Israel. If Israel does not fulfil
its duty to YHWH, Israelite prophecy demands, even invites, its punishment. This idea, too, belongs to the old popular religion; it underlies
the new eschatology. In the crucible of affliction, sinful Israel will perish;
for the purified, the new era of "the end of days" will emerge.

Several of the main features of later prophetic eschatology are already
present in Elijah's vision. Aram is YHWH's "rod of anger"—though the
Isaianic phrase (Isa. 10:5) has not yet been coined. The prophetic notion
of the remnant makes its appearance in the form of the "seven thousand"
who will be saved by YHWH. Jehu is evidently conceived of as a prototypal
Messiah—the king, anointed by YHWH through his prophet, in whose
time Israel will be redeemed. The main lines of later eschatology are found
here in a northern setting: sin and wrath, a ravaging enemy, the remnant
and the ideal king. In the south, such visions centered always about the
house of David; this was the reason of their enduring importance.

In these times, too, the concept of "the day of YHWH" mentioned
by Amos (5:18 ff.) took shape.

Hazael's victories over Jehu and Jehoahaz were a great puzzle to the
pious. Ahab's house and the last traces of Baalism had been destroyed:
why did YHWH continue to chastise Israel?

The puzzlement and disappointment were resolved in the expectation
of a day when YHWH would wreak vengeance upon Israel's enemies.
This expectation was shared not only by the popular religion and the patriotic "false prophets," it was an integral part of all the great prophecies
of warning. A good example from the age prior to literary prophecy is
the Song of Moses, the final scene of which is a "day of vengeance and pay-

ment" that YHWH will enjoy against his enemies (Deut. 32:35 ff.). Almost all of these early prophecies of deliverance have been lost, because they were associated with the ill-fated last kings of the north. But a few allusions to them have survived.

The successes of Joash encouraged Elisha to prophesy before his death that Joash would smite Aram "to the end" (II Kings 13:14–17). Later the prophecy was expanded (vss. 18–25) to explain why it failed. A turn for the better came in the days of Jeroboam II when Assyrian pressure weakened the Aramaeans. Jeroboam II restored Israel's boundaries; Jonah son of Amittai brought him YHWH's promise of triumph (14:25). Elisha and Jonah evidently looked for a savior to arise from the line of Jehu who would put an end to national distress and disgrace. The editor of the book of Kings has preserved only scraps of their prophecies of salvation. But it is not difficult to reconstruct the spirit of the originals from which these meager excerpts are drawn: northern prophecy expected that through these kings YHWH would deliver his people. There is no suggestion that this deliverance would be transient. The belief appears rather to have been that the hour of renewed, eternal grace was at hand. These fragments thus hint at a lost literature of the new eschatology that was created during the dynasty of Jehu.

THE BOOK OF JONAH

It was during this period that the book of Jonah was composed.

The critical opinion that Jonah is a late work, that Nineveh represents the pagan world, and that the universalism of classical prophecy reached its highest peak here in the repudiation of Jonah's narrow outlook— supposedly a reflex of Jewish national sentiment in postexilic times—is a tissue of errors. The Nineveh of the book of Jonah is not the capital of a great pagan empire; its king is not the ruler of Assyria, but "king of Nineveh"; its sin is not the oppression and enslavement of Israel or any other land, but "the violence" of its citizens, reminiscent of the sin of Sodom. Is it likely that to a Jewish author of late times Nineveh could have become so remote and unreal that he no longer was aware even that it was the capital of the empire which enslaved and destroyed Israel? Of the universalism of literary prophecy there is not a trace in Jonah. That YHWH visits sins of "violence" on the nations is taken for granted by the earliest legends of the Bible—the Flood story, the legend of Sodom, etc. Prophetic universalism introduced the idea that the nations would abandon idolatry at the end of days. This idea has, of course, no echo in Jonah. On the contrary, the book carries the stamp of the early universalism of preclassical prophecy; YHWH judges the nations, but not for idolatry. Jonah does not call on the Ninevites to abandon their idols. The Ninevites' faith in the prophet's God is of the same sort as the pagan "fear of God" that figures in many early narratives (Gen. 20:11; 39:9; 42:18; etc.); its real meaning involves moral behavior only. This view, far from being a climax of universalism, regards the nations as a sort of inferior breed who are not obligated to accept monotheism. Yet God has compassion upon them, since they are "persons who do not know their right hand from their left," like the "much cattle" with which the narrator ingenuously lumps them (Jonah 4:11).

The significance of Jonah cannot be appreciated without the recognition that it contains no national-historical element, and has nothing to do with Israel's quarrel with the gentiles. The interest of the book comes out clearly in chapter 4, where Jonah explains why he fled, and God explains why he compelled him to prophesy and why he did not punish the city. The issue is wholly moral: sin, punishment, repentance, forgiveness—justice versus mercy. God's universal rule and even Jonah's rebellion are not motifs essential to the speculative fabric of the book. The purpose of the story is to set forth a moral problem and suggest a solution. It is similar, in this, to the narrative framework of Job which likewise propounds and answers a moral problem; it may be compared also to the story of Sodom with its colloquy—an integral part of the story—concerning the indiscriminate dooming of righteous and wicked. Jonah belongs, then, to the early literature of moral speculation. That is why it has a non-Israelite background like Job, the Sodom story, the primeval history of Genesis (which deals with the fundamental moral problems of sin and evil), and the wisdom literature of the Bible in general. Even Ezekiel, when treating of the problem of God's justice in society at large, frames his discourse in general terms: "If a land sins. . . ." and in it are the three exemplary righteous men, Noah, Daniel, and Job—all of whom are gentiles (Ezek. 14:13 ff.).

The Nineveh of the Jonah story is not the capital of a world-conquering empire, or a symbol of the heathendom despised by postexilic Judaism but a legendary "great city" with its own king. The doom that Jonah announces ("Forty days more and Nineveh shall be overthrown" [3:4]) also is legendary and calls to mind the fate of Sodom. This fabulous principality could have been conceived only before the reign of Sennacherib, who made Nineveh a glorious imperial capital. The dynasty of Jehu and even the Omrides had contact with the Assyrian kingdom; Jehu bore tribute to Assyria. Yet Assyria was still on the distant horizon in those times, at least in the popular consciousness. The book of Kings does not mention it until the reign of Menahem son of Gadi, when Tiglath-pileser III overran the northern kingdom. Prior to that, during the period of the Jehu dynasty, it was still possible for an Israelite to conceive of Nineveh in unreal terms.

The hero of the book is Jonah son of Amittai, who lived at the time of Jeroboam II (784–744), i.e., before the time of Tiglath-pileser (II Kings 14:25). Just as stories about "the great things" of Elijah and Elisha already circulated during their lifetime (II Kings 8:4), so this remarkable story about the reluctant prophet could well have arisen during his lifetime or shortly after his death. And like the Elijah and Elisha pericopes, the story of Jonah is also part of the literary legacy of Ephraim.

In a manner similar to the primeval legends of Genesis the book of Jonah clothes a lofty moral message in a disarmingly simple dress. It is the classic statement of the Israelite idea of repentance, one of the sublimest creations of the religion of Israel.

Paganism knows of expiation, confession, and atonement, but is ignorant of repentance in the biblical sense: atonement made solely by a change of heart and action. The pagan idea regards sin as charged with a baleful impure force, rooted in a transcendent evil principle, and requiring the counteractivity of expiation to check its injurious effects. Expiatory rites are directed toward the sin committed and involve always a magical element designed to combat its evil powers. Israelite religion did away with the magical-metaphysical principle of evil and transferred sin to the moral realm, regarding it a product of man's free will. Accordingly, it viewed punishment not as an effect of the baleful power inherent in sin, but as an act of God's will. This makes room for repentance, conceived of as an act of will, a change of heart in man which is answered by a change of the will-to-punish on the part of God. Mercy and compassion overbalance justice. Israelite religion did not give up atonement rites, but they became secondary and symbolic; the turn of heart and its reflection in deed were the core of atonement. This idea is expounded in the book of Jonah; it was arrived at only after a long and hard struggle.

To appreciate the achievement of Jonah, it must be borne in mind that the earliest biblical stories give no place to repentance. The generations of the Flood and the tower of Babel, the men of Sodom, and the Canaanites are not called upon to repent. Nor does Moses avert God's wrath from Israel by rousing them to repentance; he intercedes on their behalf, invoking God's promise to the patriarchs, and the glory of his name (Exod. 32:11 ff.;

Num. 14:13 ff.; Deut. 9:26 ff.). Something of the early, magical character of sin survives in the notion that can be found throughout the Bible that sin is atoned for only by punishment. Thus David's remorse after his adultery—the first instance of repentance for a moral sin—does not suffice to avert punishment (II Sam. 12:13 ff.). Nor does Ahab's repentance do more than postpone punishment (I Kings 21:27 ff.).

The Israelite concept of repentance receives its full expression in the book of Jonah. Nineveh is another Sodom, a city of wickedness whose doom has been sealed. Jonah is sent to announce this doom, but as a result of his prophecy the people repent and God annuls his decree. Jonah is outraged, not because he is a narrow-minded zealot, but because he is a champion of divine justice. He is the voice of the ancient idea that sin must be punished. Can a change of heart turn a wicked man into a righteous one? Is it the task of the prophet to rescue the wicked from their just deserts? How, then, will their sin be expiated? His view is here challenged; a change of heart and action is itself capable of atoning for sin. The wicked man who turns is forgiven by God as an act of mercy; there is no need for any other sort of expiation. Repentance is the greatest triumph of good over evil; moving men to repent is the highest achievement of the prophet. Thus Israelite prophecy formulated its task among men.

The choice of a non-Israelite background for the story may also have been motivated by the writer's desire to give maximum play to his new conception of the power of repentance. The Ninevites have no true religion and cannot, therefore, atone for their sin with any proper rite. As far as they are concerned, the God of the prophet is unknown. Consequently, they do not resort to their priests or their temples; they do not even ask the prophet how to expiate their sin. Instead they fast, cry out, cover themselves with sackcloth, and sit in ashes—these being, in the view of the narrator, elemental and universal expressions of sorrow, remorse, and fear of heaven. Even the animals participate in the fast and entreaty. This fasting has, then, no claim to be considered "magical." The fact is that only their repentance is decisive. "When God saw their acts, how they had turned from their evil ways, he repented of the evil" (3:10). In this foreign setting, repentance has necessarily been freed from any admixture of magical or quasi-magical rites.

The road to this idea was long. Anciently it was said: "A merciful and gracious God ... but who will by no means clear the guilty" (Exod. 34:6 f.); Jonah's formulation is "A merciful and gracious God ... who repents of evil" (4:2). Two diverse concepts of sin are here expressed, the latter truer to Israelite thought, though unable to oust the former throughout the biblical period. The book of Jonah shows what heights the religious-moral consciousness of Ephraim reached in the days of Jeroboam II.

REFORM MOVEMENTS

Toward the end of the eighth century, the exhausting Aramaean wars and the beginning of Assyrian menace brought about a religious ferment in Israel and Judah. A movement of inner reform of the cult of YHWH set in. The Judean evaluation of Jeroboam's calves as objects of fetishistic "idolatry" took root in the north. Hosea, prophesying in the reign of Jeroboam II, is the sole northern prophet to voice this view (8:4–6; 10:5 f.; 13:2). At approximately the same time, a similar attitude toward the brazen serpent Nehushtan appears in Judah (II Kings 18:4). Everything that savored of "idolatry" was marked for destruction. How did the cherubs of the ark fare? Nothing is said of their removal. What differentiated them from the calves and Nehushtan was perhaps the fact that the latter were popular sacra, to which the people had access (the calves could be kissed, Nehushtan was sacrificed to). Hence, they were liable to become objects of the sort of fetishistic adoration that the folk so readily fall into. The ark and its cherubs, on the other hand, were hidden in the adytum, away from the sight and touch of the vulgar. The notice in II Kings 17:2 that the last king of Israel, Hoshea, did not act as wickedly as his predecessors may signify that during his reign the calves were finally removed. The fact is that when Josiah later demolished the Bethel temple it is not recorded that he found the calf there (II Kings 23:15), nor does the Bethel priest imported by Cuthaeans instruct them in a cult that involves calves (17:28 ff.).

At the same time Judah experienced Hezekiah's reform (18:3–6, 22; 20:3) in which not only the brazen serpent, but even the local altars were removed, and pillars and asherahs that stood by the altars were cut down. This is the first historic record of the influence of the Deuteronomic movement on the cult.

As if to counterbalance these developments, however, Assyrian influence becomes more and more marked from the days of Ahaz (16:6 ff.). The long period of Manasseh's paganism followed Hezekiah. At this time, the dark cult of child sacrifice comes into prevalence. It is found in the time of Ahaz (16:3), Manasseh (21:6), and is attested to by Jeremiah (7:31 f.; 19:5 ff.; 32:35). It was Manasseh, apparently, who erected high places for it in Topheth, in the valley of Ben-Hinnom (II Kings 23:10;

Jer. *ibid.*). This cult flourished under the influence of foreign paganism, but was not in itself the worship of a foreign god. The immolation was made to YHWH as the ultimate token of veneration resorted to in times of distress (Mic. 6:7). No doubt some tradition was at hand to support the practice, hence Jeremiah's emphasis that YHWH did not command it (*ibid.*; cf. Ezek. 20:25 f.). Sacrifice of children to YHWH is banned as a pagan custom in Deuteronomy 18:10 (cf. 12:31), but an ancient law already regards such offerings as a pagan sacrifice "to Molech";[3] so Jeremiah, too, chooses to regard it. Since as a public cult it was linked with the valley of Ben-Hinnom, near Jerusalem, it does not seem to have been more than a local practice sponsored by Manasseh.

During this time, too, the worship of "the queen of heaven" (Ishtar) gained adherents. Cakes, sacrifice, and libation were made to her (Jer. 7:18; 44:15 ff.). This was a private cult, with no priests or temples, to which women in particular seem to have been addicted.

As in the time of Jezebel, opposition to these pagan inroads appears to have broken out first among prophetic circles. Manasseh suppressed it by force, shedding "very much innocent blood till he had filled Jerusalem from one end to the other" (II Kings 21:16; 24:4; cf. also Jer. 2:30). On the other hand, as in the time of Athaliah, the countermovement that brought about the purge of Judah was led not by prophets, but by priests.

THE JOSIANIC REFORM

There are two versions of the great reform of Josiah, one in II Kings 22–23, the other in II Chronicles 34–35. A critical reading of the account in Kings reveals that it is not chronological, so that we must resort to conjecture to reconstruct the actual course of events. It is probable that the purge was gradual, more along the lines of the narrative in Chronicles. During Josiah's childhood (he was eight years old at his accession), the nobles were the real rulers. Among them were the high priest Hilkiah—the moving force behind the reform—and Ahikam son of Shaphan, later the

---

[3] Leviticus 18:21 and 20:1–5. This is, according to I Kings 11:7, the name of the Ammonite god (also found as Milcom). However *meleḳ* "king" (of which *mōleḳ* is apparently a pejorative distortion, with the vowels of *bōsheth* "shame") was an epithet of YHWH, and child sacrifice was made to him, it seems, as a wrathful, domineering king. The epithet appears to have been interpreted early as referring to the pagan god, and the sacrifice taken as an offering to the idol Milcom (so Lev. 20:1–5). Eissfeldt (in *Molk als Opferbegriff im Punischen und im Hebräischen und das Ende des Gottes Moloch* [1935]) seeks to interpret Hebrew *mlk* as a kind of vow referred to in Punic inscriptions as well. A sacrifice *lmlk* is one offered in fulfilment of a *mlk*-vow to YHWH; it consisted of a whole offering. But the expression of Leviticus 20:5 "to go astray after Molech" argues against this theory; against Eissfeldt compare Bea, *Biblica*, 1939, p. 415.

rescuer of Jeremiah (Jer. 26:24). Can we suppose that these men educated their royal ward to paganism? Or that they maintained the pagan cult of Manasseh? Did Hilkiah serve as priest before Baal and Asherah? When Hilkiah and Shaphan come to the prophetess Huldah to ask about the meaning of the new-found book of Torah, she tells them that YHWH will bring calamity on the land "because they forsook me, and sacrificed to other gods, to provoke me with all the work of their hands" (II Kings 22:17), all in the third person. She blames neither the nobles nor the king personally. Hence, it seems that after Amon's assassination the idolatrous cult of the temple was stopped. A thorough purge of Jerusalem and Judah, however, had to wait upon a royal decision. Josiah's first move was to slay the pagan priests and their entourage. Later, the Torah book was found in the course of cleansing the temple, whereupon the high places of Judah and cities of Samaria were demolished, and their priests brought to Jerusalem. But the sensation created by the book had even more far reaching effects. All manner of vestigial idolatry that prevailed among the vulgar from time immemorial was rooted out: the mediums and necromancers, the teraphim, and so forth (23:24). Ahaz' altars (vs. 12) and the high places of Solomon (vs. 13) were also destroyed at this time.

The covenant spoken of in 23:1 ff. presumably followed upon these measures; it must have come after the purging of the temple at any rate, for it was solemnized there. Its object was to seal the end of the rural cults. Afterwards, Josiah enjoins the people to celebrate the Passover in Jerusalem. This was a great innovation. Heretofore, the paschal sacrifice was performed at home; it had nothing to do with the cult at the high places; hence Hezekiah's reform did not affect it. Josiah's reform went further; it aimed at concentrating all cultic activity in the one chosen temple.

The Doctrine of Centralization—To the extent that Josiah's measures were directed against paganism and "idolatry," they have precedents in the actions of Saul, Asa, Jehoshaphat, Jehu, and Jehoiada. The popular religion had always harbored various manifestations of vestigial idolatry. From time to time, these stirred up a wave of zealotry which swept the land, especially when distress called out feelings of penitence. The idea of centralization, however, involving the destruction of ancient sanctuaries flew in the face of sacred traditions hoary and venerable with age. From where did the idea of this bold innovation come?

Nothing in the doctrines of literary prophecy implied centralization of the cult, nor is it a logical inference from the monotheistic idea (see above, pp. 161 f.). It cannot be regarded as striking against Canaanite elements in the popular worship, because the rural altars were not the prime source of Israelite deviations into paganism. The waves of foreign influence that occasionally swept over Judah and Israel radiated from the royal centers— Samaria and Jerusalem. Manasseh converted the Solomonic temple itself into a heathen pantheon. Centralization was, therefore, no guarantor of a pure cult. Nor can the interests of the priesthood, or any party of priests, have been served by the reform. Rural priests were, of course, hit hardest. The Deuteronomic law assured them the right to serve at the central sanctuary (Deut. 18:6 f.), but in fact it was impossible for so many priests to find employment at one temple. The same law encroached upon the monopoly of the Jerusalem priests; they cannot, then, have been served by the new doctrine. Above all, it must be borne in mind that the immediate and most far reaching result of centralization was to empty the daily religious life of the people at large of all priestly influence. The Josianic reform drastically restricted the domain of the priesthood; needless to say, this did irreparable harm to the material interest of the entire class.

The Deuteronomic idea must perforce be regarded as one of the intuitive symbols through which Israelite religion sought expression. It is not a means to some didactic or material end, but an end in itself. Nor is it merely a reaction to the paganizing tide that overwhelmed Judah in Manasseh's time. The idea is at work already in the time of Hezekiah; it must, therefore, have been conceived during the non-idolatrous century between Joash and Hezekiah.

The Deuteronomic idea founds the entire cult on the idea of divine election. Deuteronomy 12 forbids worshiping YHWH at "every place," "on the high hills and under every leafy tree." The ban is not grounded on the fact that these were pagan cult sites, or that such worship would lead to paganism, but on the view that this very manner of worship was pagan: "You shall not do so for YHWH your God" (Deut. 12:4, 30 f.). Pagan sanctity is rooted in nature and may therefore be found everywhere. Israelite sanctity is a creation of the will of God; it originates always in a historical election, a revelation of God's word. The earlier embodiments of this concept are the idea of the sanctifying election of the people and land of Israel, of Jerusalem, the temple, and the house of David. The idea of the election of Jerusalem and the temple did not at first imply the prohibition of the rural altars. But in the course of time the Judean priesthood drew this ultimate inference.

The ancient sanctuary of the Aaronic priesthood was the tent, a portable sanctuary unconnected with any sacred site. Although later the priesthood adopted the popular idea of the holiness of the land of Israel and, consequently, acquiesced in the worship at rural altars, the tension between the two concepts was dormant rather than dead. The idea that the land in general, and specific sites in particular, were holy savored strongly of the idea of natural sanctity. Popular temple legends sought to overcome this pagan savor by dating the holiness of sacred sites to patriarchal times, explicitly providing a historical-revelational, rather than a natural basis for their sanctity. In time, however, a more extreme idea developed. Cultic sanctity is not to be found anywhere and everywhere, not even in places that were consecrated by an ancient theophany, but only in the place that would be chosen by YHWH in the future. The Deuteronomic temple of the future is diametrically opposed to the pagan temple whose sanctity is "prehistoric," mythological. It is an eschatological temple, to be established only after Israel arrives at "the rest and the inheritance." It will be entirely new, its sanctity a creation *ex nihilo*, unrelated to any ancient holiness. This historical-eschatological conception of the temple is the ultimate negation of pagan ideas of sanctity.

It appears that already in Hezekiah's time the idea had gained sufficient priestly backing to move the king to a cultic reform. During Manasseh's reign the movement had to go underground, but the ferment went on. The great problem was: What would take the place of the local altars in popular worship? The reformers had to develop a whole new system of cultic regulations which would centralize religious life around the temple. The new system—incorporated in the Torah book—was probably completed in the time of Manasseh-Josiah. Stages in its development can be glimpsed in the fact that a centralized Passover celebration occurs for the first time in Josiah's time when the book, too, made its first appearance. Both elements are as yet wanting in Hezekiah's reform. It was the production of the book that gave the movement for reform a firm basis.

The ultimate implication of the Deuteronomic reform was a new, popular cult without temple, sacrifice, and priest; this, however, could become clear only after the Exile. More significant is the fact that for the first time in history a religious reform was based on a book. The covenant of Josiah was the first attempt to make the Torah the law of the land. To what extent a moral-religious book like Deuteronomy could have become a political constitution is difficult to say; the experiment was made too near the collapse of Judah to tell. What can be said is that in the Josianic reform, the priestly idea of a book of Torah as the basis of national life took its first great step toward realization. This is its lasting historical significance.

CHAPTER IX

Some Aspects of the Popular Religion

In the preceding chapter we sketched the major stages in the development of the priestly-popular religion to the close of the pre-exilic period. What has been recorded in the historical books lends itself to dating. The age of most of the material in the Torah, the Psalms, the books of Proverbs and Job, however, cannot be precisely determined. We cannot say exactly when in pre-exilic times JE, or the ground form of D, or P were composed. The various forms of ancient Israelite creativity developed alongside each other; they cannot be forced into an artificial pattern of evolution. Renan long ago observed that Palestine was like Greece and Tuscany, and all lands in which an original culture developed, in that within a small area the most varied creations were produced. Each valley of Greece had its distinctive style of myth, art, and thought, though all were expressions of a common culture; so too in ancient Palestine.[1] The literature of Israel has Judean and Ephraimitic, popular and priestly, early prophetic and sapiential elements. It is futile to attempt to fix the date of this material by comparing the customs and beliefs which have accidentally been preserved in the historical books with those of the Torah. For what seem to be the products of various ages may in fact have been concurrent developments of different places and circles.

This does not mean that broad lines of evolution are not discernible. Comparison of the ideas of the Torah literature with those of literary prophecy indicates the priority of the former. The period in which this literature was composed overlaps the age of classical prophecy, but classical prophecy had not yet become a factor in the national culture and did not exert any influence on the popular-priestly religion or on the wisdom writers. Thus

[1] Ernest Renan, *Histoire générale ... des langues sémitiques* (1855), p. 235.

even if the material of the Torah and wisdom literature cannot be precisely dated in detail, it is still possible to speak with certainty regarding the stage of Israelite religion which they reflect. It is the stage prior to literary prophecy, though the works in question were composed during the whole of the pre-exilic period—from the beginning of Israelite religion to the Babylonian exile.

SIN AND EVIL

The legends of Genesis 1–11 contain an ancient non-Israelite substratum. Like the wisdom literature, these legends do not deal with matters touching Israel as a nation; like the wisdom literature again, these chapters belong to the legacy inherited from pre-Israelite civilization. The transformation of the material in these chapters is particularly illuminating, for it shows that Israelite religion conceived not merely a new national god, but a new religious idea, a new metaphysical insight. In these chapters Israelite thought seeks to answer universal questions and, in so doing, lays the foundation of a non-pagan world view.

The new religious idea of the One entailed the problem of theodicy—not the Jobian question of the suffering of the innocent, but the more primary issue of the origin of evil in general. To paganism, with its plurality of divine principles, the presence of evil was no particular problem; to Israelite religion it was. The legends of Genesis 1–11 tell how all the evils that beset men began: natural (death, pain, etc.), moral (murder, violence, etc.), and religious (idolatry). The narrative is couched not in philosophic language, but in picturesque, naïve imagery.[2] Yet the symbols fashioned by these legends have proven tremendously fertile, for the ideas involved are universal and timeless.

Both JE and P represent the world as a product of God's benign will. Genesis 1 (P) pronounces each act of creation good. The high point is reached in the creation of man in God's image. JE's story (Gen. 2:4—4:26) portrays man as a unique creature, the darling of God, set in God's garden to cultivate and enjoy it. Animals are created to keep him company and be his

---

[2] For a discussion of the demythologization of the cosmogonic materials, see above, pp. 67 ff. It is no accident that in the principal cosmogony, Genesis 1–11, allusions to YHWH's battle with Rahab and the dragon are not found. Biblical legend did not regard these events as crucial for the fate of the cosmos. They were merely episodes, evidences of divine power that were suitable embellishments for hymns. The legends of Genesis 1–11, however, aim to interpret the order of the world; the issue they deal with is the corruption of that order. It is, therefore, highly significant that biblical legend did not root sin and evil in Rahab or the dragon—conceived of as a Satanic figure—and did not make of them embodiments of cosmic evil that YHWH had to subjugate.

help. Woman, too, is given him not for procreation, but to be "a help meet for him." Only one restriction was placed upon him: he must not, on pain of death, eat of the fruit of the "tree of knowledge of good and evil." What is the meaning of this? The intention cannot be to represent God's favorite as bereft of knowledge. To the Bible wisdom is a gift of God; its pursuit is nowhere considered sinful. The Genesis legend itself portrays Adam as having knowledge. From his creation he knew how to work the soil, he could speak, and was able to give names to the animals. Moreover, God's threat and Adam's fear of it presuppose the capacity of distinguishing right from wrong. Eve desired the fruit, not merely for its taste, but because it could make her wise. Such a desire in itself bespeaks an intelligent recognition of knowledge as a good to be sought after. From the beginning, then, man had knowledge of the good and desired it. He knows the difference between life and death, and that death is something to be avoided; but evil is still veiled from him, because he has never tasted it. His knowledge is less than that of the celestial beings (ʾelōhīm), for they have divine knowledge of both realms. The tree is conceived, then, not as the source of knowledge in general, but of the knowledge of, and desire for, evil, without which man's comprehension is incomplete. The serpent plays the role of the seducer who reveals evil to man and rouses in him the desire for it. The legend, whose object it is to tell the origin of sin, could not place Adam entirely and essentially beyond the knowledge of evil, because the Bible conceives of sin as a consequence of human freedom, and this has meaning only if good and evil are both within the range of man's experience from the beginning. With great art it symbolizes evil as the tree of knowledge; the tree harbors all evil, for to approach it means to sin, to violate a divine prohibition. Rebellion lay within man's power from the very beginning, and he was unable to stand the test. Defying God, he laid bare the realm of evil, which God had concealed from him without, however, blocking his way to it.

After eating the forbidden fruit, the eyes of the two "were opened, and they knew that they were naked." Sexual desire appears here as the archetypal sin, the characteristic mark of the evil impulse. Only afterwards did Adam have intercourse with his wife and beget children. According to this view, procreation is not a blessing (as it is in Genesis 1:28), but the outcome of sin. So, too, speaks the psalmist (Ps. 51:7): "In sin did my mother conceive me." Man was created by grace, but is born through sin. The legend expresses a lofty view of woman and family; she was created as man's help and companion. The sexual act, however, is the child of sin. Offspring was given to man only after he had sinned and became subject to death. Then he ceased being one and unique and became the progenitor of humankind. The race was born from sin. Adam was condemned to toil and death; Eve, to the pains of birth; man's toil was cursed; the peace between him and the animals was broken.

Man did not thereupon become absolutely evil, but, having tasted evil, his sinful impulses raged ever more fiercely. With Cain, envy, murder, and the lie came into the world. In the generation of the Flood "every imagination of the thoughts of [man's] heart was only evil continually" (6:5). So God destroyed man and beast, saving only Noah and those with him. But Noah discovered the intoxicating property of wine, exposed his son Ham to sin, and brought the curse of slavery upon his descendants. Then came the tower of Babel; mankind was dispersed, its tongue confused, and all the evils of a divided humanity were entailed.

No story is dedicated to the origin of idolatry. One thing, however, seems clear: with the confusion of tongues there comes an end to the monotheistic period of history. The nations never knew God. Individuals continue intimate with God—Melchizedek, Balaam, Job and his friends—but outside of Israel (and its ancestors) no nation knows him. Apparently, then, the legend of the tower implies more than it says. Man's rebellion reached its peak. He wished to storm heaven, to be "like God," to rule the world. For this he was doubly punished; his language was confused, and nations with their wars and rivalries sprang up. But God also hid himself from man and abandoned him to his defiance and soaring ambitions. Because man wished to storm heaven, the Lord of heaven left him alone. In this way the Bible expresses its view of idolatry as a godless cult, a worship of man-made divinities produced by man's boundless arrogance. This conception goes to the very heart of paganism, to its magical basis. The pagan does conceive himself to be on a par with his gods, insofar as the knowledge and use of magic are concerned. He does view himself as the helper and partner of the gods, as their sustainer, redeemer, and reviver. The Bible represents this as a presumptuous worship of no-gods, in which man imagines himself to be the conqueror of heaven.

Yet the Bible does not regard the idolatry of the nations as a sin for which they must be punished. The absence of a story about the origin of idolatry seems to reflect the feeling that, although an abomination, idolatry is the fruit of sin, a punishment, rather than a primary sin itself. God deprived man of knowledge of him, allotting to him idolatry in its stead (Deut. 4:19; 29:25). Later he showed his graciousness toward Israel by revealing to them his name. However, if Israel sins, God threatens that he will reimpose idolatry on them (Deut. 4:28; 28:64; Jer. 16:13;

cf. 5:19). Like death, pain, and toil, idolatry is the consequence of rebellion.

The religious division between Israel and the pagan world does not arise, then, from a plurality of gods, or a struggle between two opposing divine realms. The nations are in ignorance; they have fallen from man's primeval eminence by the decree of God. The pagan world is without God. Genesis 11 is tantalizingly silent concerning the beginning of idolatry, but its position at the division of epochs is in itself eloquent. After the confusion of tongues there suddenly appears the world of idolatry, but not as the work of gods, spirits, or demons—before this no gods or spirits are mentioned. The meaning is plain; idolatry originated in a forgetting of God, and is the worship of no-gods.

The early legends of Genesis embody two great achievements of Israelite religion. First, myth is conquered with the suppression of the idea of a metadivine realm, with the absence of theogony and theomachy, with making God's grace the basis of creation, and the eradication of a primordial evil principle. Second, in place of myth Israelite religion conceived the historical drama of human rebellion and sin.

The idea of man's rebelliousness, by which Genesis explains the origins of the human condition, is a fundamental idea of biblical literature and of Israelite religion in general. One might call the Bible a chronicle of human rebellion. The history of Israel from beginning to end is motivated by defiance of God. The idolatrous world trusts in its strength and wisdom and ignores God. Out of this grand idea the prophets were to create their vision of a last judgment, when human rebelliousness would come to an end. These legends are not late creations, the product of scholastic speculation. They are primary, the very foundation stone of the biblical world.

ISRAEL AND THE WORLD

Israelite religion was national in its forms and in the scope of its activity from its beginnings to the end of the Second Temple period. Ideally, however, YHWH was not a national, but a cosmic God; the area of his special grace was restricted to Israel, but his dominion extended everywhere.

This ideal universalism finds clear expression in the conception of world history found in the legends of Genesis. Not only is YHWH alone creator, but the first men are portrayed as monotheists. The special favor bestowed later upon Israel was universal in primeval times. The very notion that God later withdrew himself from the world and decreed idolatry for mankind is essentially universalistic. Although it excludes the nations from the realm of YHWH's holiness, it regards them as nonetheless subject to his will.

The early view, however, did not entirely remove men from the sphere of divine concern. The monotheistic viewpoint prevented it from so doing. All men continued in God's image, continued enjoying dominion over nature and the arts of civilization. Moreover, God's providence and judgment were believed to be world wide. YHWH fixes the destiny of all nations (Gen. 9:26 f.), disperses mankind over the face of the earth (11:1 ff.), dooms Sodom and Gomorrah for their wickedness (18–19), gives nations their possessions (Deut. 32:8; cf. 2:5, 9, 19, 21 f.).

The ancient Psalm 104 (whose resemblance to Akhenaton's solar-hymn has long been recognized) praises YHWH as world creator and sustainer. This view pervades all of the book of Psalms, the bulk of which is a product of the early religion (e.g., 33:5; 36:7; 145:9). Amos treats it as self-evident that YHWH looks after all nations (1:3 ff.). Neither he nor any other prophet emphasizes the idea as a new one. The classical prophets look for an even greater revelation of God's goodness in the future, but nowhere do they represent it as a new thought that God shows kindness to all his creatures, even to idolaters. The conception of divine providence as universal is not a later development, but an ancient element of Israelite religion.

In the moral realm, too, the early religion knew a certain universalism. Although YHWH did not give men a religious law, he did impose moral obligations upon them. The Noachides are forbidden to murder, "because man was made in the image of God" (Gen. 9:6)—a broad, universal motive. They are also enjoined not to show cruelty to animals by eating them alive (vs. 4).[3] The general notion throughout the Bible is that there is a universal moral law that even the gentiles are obliged to obey. (This notion apparently goes back to the idea of a time when all men knew God and his moral will. When later they forgot him, their moral obligation still remained in force.) Cain is punished for murder, and the earth, too, is cursed for having "opened its mouth" to accept Abel's blood (4:3 ff.). For committing homicide, even beasts will be held to account (9:5).

---

[3] "But flesh with its life, its blood, you shall not eat" (Gen. 9:4) is not a prohibition against eating blood. The formula of that prohibition is always "you shall not eat blood" or the like (cf. Lev. 3:17; 7:26 f.; 17:10 ff.; Deut. 12:23 ff.). Moreover, such a prohibition would have been fictional so far as the Noachides were concerned; contrast the preceding ban on murder which was really universally recognized. The biblical ban on eating blood is connected with its consecration to the altar (Lev. 17:11), something which has no significance to a Noachide. Genesis 9:4 is to be understood rather as follows: while verse 3 permits the eating of flesh, verse 4 prohibits eating it "with its life, its blood," i.e., while its life and blood are still in it. Like the ban on murder, then, this too is a fundamental moral interdiction of a barbarous practice that was really no longer in vogue by biblical times, except in certain cultic survivals. Rabbinic exegesis correctly saw in the passage a ban on eating animals alive (Sanhedrin 59a).

The generation of the Flood perished for its "violence" (6:11). The Sodomites were annihilated for being "very wicked and sinful toward YHWH" (13:13; see 19:1 ff.). Violating a married woman brings calamity upon a whole kingdom (20:9; 26:10); the pagan regards it as worse than murder (12:11 f.; 20:11 ff.; 26:7, 9). Pagan morality is grounded in a "fear of God"; it keeps them from murder (20:11), adultery (39:9), and breach of faith (39:8 f.), and makes them benevolent (42:18). Amalek is condemned for the lack of "God-fearing" displayed in its dastardly attack on Israel's weak and weary (Deut. 25:18). The Canaanites are expelled from their land for sexual immorality (Lev. 18:24 ff.; 20:23 f.). And though idolatry itself is not punishable, the cruelty of Molech-worship is held against the nations (Lev. 18:21; Deut. 18:10–12).

Monumental testimony to the conception of YHWH as a universal God of justice and morality is the fact that purely moral questions, unrelated to the destiny of Israel, are always discussed against a non-Israelite background. This is the case with the early legends of Genesis, the story of Sodom, the book of Job, Proverbs, and Ecclesiastes, the sapiential psalms, the book of Jonah, and Ezekiel 14:13–20. Since in biblical thought such questions were essentially bound up with the view of God, this means that the idea of YHWH as a universal judge was primary and ancient.

Even in the purely nationalistic stories of YHWH's deeds in Israel, a certain universalism appears. The wonders done in Egypt aim at confirming Israel's faith in YHWH, but they also intend to show the Egyptians the might and uniqueness of YHWH (Exod. 7:5, 17; 8:6, 18; etc.). To this end, the Exodus occurred "in the sight of the nations" (Lev. 26:45); its fame was international (Num. 14:13, 15; Josh. 2:9 f.; I Sam. 4:8; 6:6). The nationalistic book of Joshua, too, speaks of YHWH's dividing the Jordan as designed to make all the peoples of the earth know that "the hand of YHWH is strong" (4:24).

This is, of course, a purely theoretical universalism. It does not go so far as to conceive of the actual conversion of the idolaters. Little more seems to be intended than an expression of the strong national feeling of religious distinctiveness. The idolater sees, acknowledges, even brings offerings to YHWH; yet for all that he remains an idolater (Jonah 1:7–17). The thought is found even in some of the classical prophets and in the Apocrypha. Ezekiel envisions YHWH's revelation before the eyes of all nations at the end-time; but he will still be only the God of Israel. The theoretical universalism of early times thus survived long after the vision of an eschatological conversion of the nations was created by the prophets.

The early religion had no vision of a new divine act which would dissolve the barrier between Israel and the nations. But its universalistic aspirations occasionally brought it to the point of ignoring the existence of the barrier. Though the nations are and will remain idolaters, they do, or shall, recognize the greatness of Israel and its God. The psalmists call upon all nations to acknowledge God's universal bounty, his providence, his justice, and the wonders he performed in Israel. All the world will acclaim him: "From the rising place of the sun to its setting place the name of YHWH is praised" (113:3). "Is," not "shall be!" This is not an eschatological vision, but a present reality in the imagination of the psalmist.

These purely theoretical universalistic ideas of the early religion served as the basis for the later prophetic conception of an eschatological return to YHWH.

THE NATIONAL ELEMENT IN ISRAELITE RELIGION

Unlike the faiths of Akhenaton, or Buddha, or early Christianity, Israelite religion was from the first a national religion, the expression of a national culture. But national elements eventually became supranational religious symbols. Israel's land became the Holy Land of many peoples; Jerusalem became the Holy City; the people of Israel, the symbol of the community of believers; Israelite history, sacred history. This transmutation could not have occurred had the national values not from the first been at least potentially universal.

Thus the sanctity in the national life of Israel was not conceived of in pagan terms. Israel did not descend from gods; YHWH is not Israel's kinsman; Palestine is not his natural habitat; Israel's cult is not the source of his vitality. The relation between Israel and YHWH is a covenant relation. This notion was not the matrix of the monotheistic idea; to the contrary, it was the monotheistic idea that precluded every conception but this. YHWH's relation to Israel could be conceived of only in terms of election and free choice. The covenant has no pagan meaning; it does not unite the two parties in any natural or mysterious way. Its sacredness consists in being the realization of God's plan. "You shall be holy" (Lev. 19:2)—sanctity is a command, something to be achieved, not a natural or supernatural racial quality.

Eloquent testimony to this is the disparity between the exalted status of YHWH and the lowly position of Israel among the nations. YHWH is the most high God; Israel is "the fewest of all peoples" (Deut. 7:7). This disparity is not grudgingly admitted; it is reiterated and emphasized throughout the whole of the literature.

The scheme of Genesis makes Israel the youngest of peoples. It entered a world full of nations; YHWH was the creator and sustainer of a world that existed long before Israel came into being. But Israel is not only the youngest, it is the smallest of the nations as well (Deut. 7:7; Amos 7:2, 5; cf. Isa. 41:14 "worm Jacob"). Legend glorified the history of Israel, but since its purpose was to extol the wonders of YHWH, it could incorporate the sufferings, the humiliations, and the failures of the people as well. The ancient sagas of Israel are not heroic: the people is weak and timorous; at its head stand not warriors, but men of God.

This is not to say that ethnic ambitions did not motivate Israel. There was the drive to conquer and settle Canaan, to overcome the "enemies of YHWH"; there was the glory of the early monarchy. But these national achievements are not conceived of as exhibiting in full the might of Israel's God, nor are they the final end of Israel's election. Israel's portion was eclipsed by what YHWH gave to the other nations. Egypt was like "the garden of YHWH" (Gen. 13:10); "YHWH's trees" in Lebanon (Ps. 104:16) never belonged to Israel. There was always the consciousness that "YHWH's possession" was inclosed by a great and wealthy pagan world. The earliest promises to Israel do not include that of world empire. The tribes attempted at first to found a modest "kingdom of God" on earth, without kings or heroes. This means that YHWH's special favor to Israel was not regarded as manifesting itself in great political and national achievements.

One thing only distinguished Israel: it knew YHWH; to it alone did he send messenger-prophets with his Torah and commandments. Israel had a gift of the spirit. The destiny of the idolaters was not determined by their relation to YHWH, but Israel's was. That was the "divine" element in its history. Israel's national prowess was not sacred or divine; divine was the favor, YHWH's presence, the election to be a vehicle of God's manifestation. The Bible's stress on Israel's smallness and weakness enables it to represent all of Israelite history as a wondrous sign. Just as Israelite wonder-working bespeaks the hand of God, not the power of man, so, too, the history of Israel. Small, weak, and powerless in itself, Israel's success attests the power of YHWH; its history is thus a wonder and a sign, the actualization of God's word and will. This alone was the purpose of its election.

Hence, the moments of greatest glory are the Exodus and the Wandering, not the conquest. The liberation from Egypt did no more than put Israel on a par with the other free nations of the earth. But the great signs and wonders that attended these events made them evidences of a special grace. Israel was led into a "great and terrible wilderness," where it ate "wretched food" and quail, while the other nations already dwelt secure and prosperous in their lands. But these meager rations were given to Israel by God's word, hence they, too, were evidences of a special grace. The wanderers suffered from thirst, famine, plague, fire, and serpents. A whole generation was condemned to die in the desert. But even these troubles became trials and signs of God's manifestation in Israel. This was the prototype of all Israelite historiosophy. In good times and bad the people saw "the finger of God." Famine and plenty, life and death, rain and drought, kingdom and collapse, all were the will of God and all were decreed for Israel as bearer of the divine word.

The values, customs, history—indeed the entire being of the nation—are, therefore, symbols of the supreme rule of the divine will. Through this the national element is divested of its particularity. Israel is not merely a national entity, but the historical dimension of YHWH's revelation, over against the mythological-magical dimension of paganism. Israel serves as the stage for an essentially historical—rather than a national—drama. That the setting is national was necessitated by circumstances. But because the national elements of biblical religion are symbolic of a universal religious idea, they too could serve as supranational, universal symbols.

Israelite religion has no fixed ideal ethnic boundaries. The biblical prohibitions of intermarriage with foreigners are not grounded on the idea of racial superiority. Ammonites and Moabites are excluded for historical reasons (Deut. 23:4 ff.). Egypt, on the other hand, is favored for historical reasons (vss. 8 f.). Intermarriage with the Canaanites is forbidden on religious grounds (Exod. 34:12 ff.; Deut. 7:2 ff.; Josh. 23:7 ff.; Judg. 3:6). In general, intermarriage is banned on a religious (Num. 25:1 ff.; 31:15 f.; I Kings 11:1 ff.; etc.) or a cultural-national-religious basis (Gen. 34:14 ff.; Judg. 14:3; cf. Gen. 24:2 ff.; 27:46—28:9).[4] The sources speak continually of mixture between Israel and the nations (see above, p. 218; cf. 248, n. 5). The rule was that the third generation of those who settled in Israel was permitted to join "the community of YHWH" and was considered Israelite (Deut. 23:8 f.). Female captives could be taken to wife immediately (Deut. 21:10 ff.).

The early religion of Israel does not know of religious conversion in the later sense of a deliberate, formal act immediately conferring equality with the native-born. Foreigners become Israelites by settling in the land and becoming assimilated in the course of time. This in itself demonstrates

---

[4] The denigration of the Ethiopians (Amos 9:7; perhaps also Num. 12:1) is not peculiar to Israel in antiquity.

that Israelite religion was not ideally limited to one ethnic realm. It is especially significant that even foreign groups who retained their identity were incorporated into Israel. Moses asks Hobab the Midianite to join Israel and promises him a share in the good that YHWH will do for Israel (Num. 10:29 ff.). Gibeonites and "servants of Solomon" were of alien origin, yet they became Israelites in religion. *Gērīm* were an ethnically distinct group as indicated by the discrimination practiced against them in the matter of slavery (Lev. 25:45 f.). Yet they are made equal to the native-born Israelites in all that pertains to the laws of the Torah (Exod. 12:19, 49; Lev. 16:29; 17:15; 24:16, 22; Num. 9:14 [all P]). Moreover, it was believed that the *gērīm* took part with Israel in the covenant with YHWH (Deut. 29:10 ff.) and the blessing and curse at the time of Joshua (Josh. 8:33, 35). From the beginning, then, the Torah was given to non-Israelites too.

For generations, "conversion" was conditioned on territorial and cultural assimilation. It is so in P, in the book of Ruth (1:16 f.), and in the story of the Samaritans who become quasi-Israelites by virtue of their settlement in the land (II Kings 17:24 ff.). But already in early times the idea of a purely religious conversion is foreshadowed; Naaman, who returns to his land and his people, becomes a worshiper of YHWH. A foreigner may offer a sacrifice to YHWH (Lev. 22:25) and can pray in the Israelite temple (I Kings 8:41 ff.). As noted above, the hope that Israelite religion would extend beyond the national bounds already appeared in preclassical prophecy. Later it became an eschatological certainty and led, in the time of the Second Temple, to the institution of proselytism.

PRIEST AND TEMPLE

YHWH elected the Aaronides and Levites to be the hereditary priesthood of Israel (Exod. 28:1 ff.; 32:26 ff.; Num. 8:5 ff.; 16:5 ff.; etc.). The priesthood played a decisive role in the formation of Israelite religion; an ancient poem praises it as the tribe of YHWH's devoted and loyal men (Deut. 33:8 ff.). The ark and tent of the Wandering, the temple cult in the land, the symbols of holiness and impurity, and, finally, the centralization of worship are its great contributions. Priestly literature is represented by Deuteronomy and the Priestly Code.

What can be learned of the character of the Israelite priesthood from the functions of pagan priesthood that it rejected has already been set forth above (pp. 107 ff., 239). Here the priestly conception of the temple and cult will be discussed.

While in the popular view the cult was designed to secure the blessing and favor of God (Gen. 28:18 ff.; Exod. 20:21; I Kings 8:29 ff.), this idea is ignored in priestly literature. Instead, P enlarges upon the popular idea of the temple as the place where God revealed himself and manifested his election of Israel. God commanded Israel to make a sanctuary that he might dwell in their midst (Exod. 25:8), not that he might hear their prayer and attend to their wants. The very name is telling: the tent of meeting—the place appointed by God for "meeting" Israel. The aim of the cult is to hallow the sanctuary, to guard it from all impurity, to surround it with a cordon of awe, so that it should be a fit place for God's revelation. P also retains the notion of the tent as an oracle. The heart of its archetypal temple is the ark of the covenant, upon whose cherubs God appears in a cloud and between which he speaks. Each Israelite temple is a replica of the ancient tent. Each holy of holies is conceived of as a place of God's revelation, as if the ark were there. Ezekiel says nothing about an ark in his future temple, but it has a *debīr* (41:3 f.), which is the ideal site of the ark. Nor did the Second Temple have an ark, yet the entire cult was performed as though it lay in the holy of holies (Mishnah Yoma 5.1–3). Even the terror that surrounded the ancient ark prevailed in the empty adytum of the Second Temple. Later Judaism inherited this symbol; the heart of every synagogue is its "holy ark," in which the Torah scrolls are housed.

The priestly writings describe the cult in great detail, probably combining the practices of various temples. Yet not only is there no magical or mythological rite designed to heighten the power of the deity, there is no rite designed to call down on man God's material blessings. No ritual is mentioned whose object is to bring down the blessing of rain or fertility. Festivals are marked by an additional sacrifice (whole and sin offerings, with their meal and wine adjuncts) for atonement and for a "pleasing odor" (Num. 28). The first sheaf is waved before YHWH, so that Israel will be acceptable before him (Lev. 23:11). This, with the accompanying offerings, permits enjoyment of crops (vs. 14), but is not interpreted as a fertility rite. On the festival of first fruits, the priest waves two loaves and two lambs (vss. 17 ff.), but here, too, thanksgiving for past blessings rather than an appeal for the future is implied. The rite of the Day of Atonement is the priestly rite par excellence. For later Judaism, it was the day of judgment on which the fate of each man was determined for the coming year. In the priestly ritual of the Bible, however, only the notions of purification and atonement figure. There is no activity aimed at seeking a good decision for the individual or the people, for priests or laity.

Needless to say, both priesthood and people hoped for divine blessing. YHWH's presence in Israel presumably implied a guarantee of his tangible favors. The priest blesses the people after the sacrifice (Lev. 9:22 f.) and sets YHWH's name upon Israel for a blessing (Num. 6:23 ff.). But these activities are on the periphery of priestly ritual, mere adjuncts to the main rites. Within the temple itself, at the altar and in the holy of holies, all is directed toward the sanctification of YHWH's dwelling place and the purification of whatever comes near it. Not *do ut des*, not even supplication and entreaty, but the awe of holiness.

The priestly temple is the kingdom of silence.

In Egypt, Babylonia, and in the pagan world in general word and incantation were integral parts of the cult; act was accompanied by speech. The spell expressed the magical essence of cultic activity. In more developed form, pagan rituals might be accompanied by mythological allusions relating to events in the life of the gods. Speech thus articulated the magical-mythological sense of the rite.

P makes no reference to the spoken word in describing temple rites. All the various acts of the priest are performed in silence. He kindles the altar fire, removes the ashes, tends the lamp, burns incense, arrays the shewbread; he daubs some sacrificial blood on the corners of the altar, pours out the rest at its foundation, burns the fatty parts, the limbs, and the meal offering, makes libations, eats the flesh of sin and guilt offering, burns bulls and goats outside the camp, sprinkles blood to atone and purify, waves consecrated objects in the temple, and so forth. None of these activities is accompanied by speech. Not only have spells and psalms no place in the priestly cult, even prayer is absent. The rite of bringing first fruits, described in Deuteronomy 26:1 ff., is typical. It is the farmer who recites a thanksgiving formula at the temple; the priest merely takes the basket of fruit and places it before the altar. Priestly speech is found only outside the temple or apart from the essential cultic act. On the Day of Atonement, the priest makes confession over the head of the scapegoat for "all the sins of the Israelites" (Lev. 16:21). After the offering is made, the priest blesses the people (Lev. 9:22 f.; Num. 6:23 ff.). In Deuteronomy 27:12 ff., the Levite priests are to recite the blessing and curse toward the mountains Gerizim and Ebal. The priest exhorts the army going out to war (Deut. 20:2 ff.). But throughout the course of the temple rite itself, speech is altogether wanting.

This silence is an intuitive expression of the priestly desire to fashion a non-pagan cult. It is the same intuition that removed psalmody from the realm of the Israelite priesthood. Song is no part of the priestly cult—not one of the biblical psalms is attributed to priests (see above, p. 110). Though the detail of priestly rites, magical in origin and essence, could not be done away with, the magical motivation made explicit in the accompanying utterances was eliminated. Therewith the Israelite cult became a domain of silence. The details of ritual lost their intrinsic meaning and became a vehicle expressive of human submission to the command of God. The silence of the temple cult also served to heighten the awe of holiness. A parallel development took place in the cult of Islam, in which song was excluded because it was believed by the pagan Arabs to be inspired by spirits.

There is no musical or orgiastic element in the priestly cult of Israel,[5] nor is there any sexual element; priestesses were nonexistent. The Dionysiac element of Israelite religion is found outside the priesthood. Prophetic frenzy and ecstasy are effects of the divine spirit—in the Israelite view, a gift of God that has nothing to do with human activity. "Prophesying" as a fixed cultic phenomenon, as a goal of sacerdotal rites, was therefore intuitively excluded by Israel's priesthood along with every element of enthusiasm and ecstasy.

There is no Israelite parallel to the funerary cults of paganism. The priestly laws of the Bible raise especially high barriers between the priest and the realm of death. He is severely enjoined from becoming defiled by the impurity of a corpse. No priest may attend to the dead who are not his kin; the high priest may not even attend his kin. Nor may the priest show signs of mourning (Lev. 21:1–12). In the temple there is no motif connected with death, nor is there any vestige of self-castigation or mutilation, through which the pagan priest sought to participate in the suffering of his dying god.

The Israelite priesthood excluded every activity that in paganism reflected the cycle of the life and death of the gods. Nothing remains of sexual and resurrection motifs. The pagan cult represents the course of the gods' lives; Israelite religion has no symbols of a life course. Its temple is to a being without change. Hence, its cult lacks drama as well (see above, pp. 116 ff.).

The priests were in charge of torah, but this torah was not an esoteric lore of cosmic magic; it consisted of law and statutes, cult and morality. The priest keeps the word of God and guards his covenant; he teaches YHWH's judgments to Jacob and his torah to Israel (Deut. 33:9 f.). He does not, ideally, receive God's law at his mouth; this is the prerogative of the prophet. The priest merely "handles" and transmits it (Jer. 2:8). In the torah, the prophetic and priestly elements join hands.

---

[5] The horn and the trumpet are the two instruments of the priesthood—both alarms, and employed as such, not as musical instruments (Num. 10:1–10; Josh. 6:5 ff.).

THE POPULAR CULT

The priestly cult in the temple of silence could not contain the abundance of popular religious sentiment. Around the silent sanctuary throbbed the joyous popular cult, all tumult and passion. The rapture and enthusiasm that were rejected by the priesthood found their place here. Having thus been sharply separated from the priestly cult, what might otherwise have savored of magic became innocuous. The folk did not enter the temple, but remained outside and around it, hence their activity was not linked with any specific symbol of sanctity.

The great national festivals were celebrated in fixed priestly rites inside the temples, but their essence lay in the popular celebrations outside. Of all the holydays, the Day of Atonement alone is essentially sacerdotal; the people fast and stop work, according to P, but all the activity of the day is priestly (Lev. 16; 23:26 ff.; Num. 29:7 ff.). For the other festivals, however, the only temple rite is an additional sacrifice, differing in composition from festival to festival, but in no way expressing their distinctive characters (Num. 28). It was the popular cult that gave each festival its particular flavor.

The popular, not the priestly, cult reflected the historical rationales of the three great festivals. The paschal sacrifice with its dramatic element commemorated the deliverance of the Israelite firstborn on the eve of the Exodus. It is a home sacrifice, entirely apart from temple. Within the temple the occasion was marked by an additional offering that suggests nothing of this commemorative aspect. The eating of *maṣṣ̄ōth* has nothing to do with the temple, but belongs entirely to the popular cult. Later, the bringing of the first sheaf to the temple was connected with the Passover festival. The sheaves—like the first fruits—were probably brought in a festive procession which was the main part of the festival for the people. At the end of the reaping, the Festival of Weeks was celebrated, and the first fruits were brought to the temple. Waving and offering of fruit were priestly rites, but the joyous procession of the people bearing their produce is what gave the festival its distinctive tone. The chief popular festival was Tabernacles, celebrating the ingathering of the crops. Its distinctive features were entirely outside the temple. Booths were erected out of prescribed materials (Lev. 23:40; cf. Neh. 8:15 f.) to celebrate the ingathering. A historical connection with the Exodus also was provided, which again had no reflection in the temple cult.

The three cosmic festivals—Sabbath, new moon, and new year—also were given color by popular rather than priestly rites. The "myth" of the Sabbath finds no reflection in the temple worship (Num. 28:9 f.), but only in the people's rest. The social-moral rationale of the Sabbath, set forth in Exodus 23:12 and Deuteronomy 5:14 f., is linked with national history; the Sabbath is a sign of Israel's covenant (Exod. 31:13 ff.) and a memorial to the Egyptian bondage (Deut. 5:15). The people embody the cosmic significance of the day in their rest; the repose of slave and beast represents the social-historical rationale; the perpetual observance of the day by Israel testifies to the covenant between it and the eternal God. The new moon holyday, too, was distinguished by its popular features. The people refrained from working (Amos 8:5) and made it the occasion of a solemn family feast (I Sam. 20:5, 24, 27 ff.) or a visit to the man of God (II Kings 4:23). The blowing of trumpets over the sacrifice was the distinctive cultic feature (Num. 10:10; Ps. 81:4).[6]

Ancient Israel appears to have had two new year days: one in the spring, the other in the autumn. According to Exodus 12:2, the spring month in which the Exodus occurred was the first of the year's months, and wherever months are counted in the Bible, Abib-Nisan is the first. But according to Exodus 23:16 and 34:22, the feast of the ingathering takes place at the "end" or "turn" of the year, that is, at the beginning of the new year. It is not necessary to suppose that the spring new year is a late importation from Babylonia. The antiquity of the spring counting of the months is vouched for by the fact that all the sources count the *maṣṣōth* festival as the first of the three agricultural festivals (Exod. 23:14 f.; 34:18 [JE]; Deut. 16:1 ff.). If the spring new year is Babylonian, it must have been adopted in very early times.[7]

The spring new year was a priestly festival, while the autumn new year in the harvest time was the festival of the popular religion. The development of this festival and that of the Day of Atonement, with which it is connected, show the influence of the priestly and popular realms upon one another.

The month of the Exodus is P's first month (Exod. 12:2). On the first day of the first month, the tabernacle was erected (Exod. 40:17); i.e., this day begins the cultic year. According to P, Israel entered Canaan in the first month (Josh. 4:19); Passover was the first festival celebrated in

---

[6] There is evidently a connection between the Sabbath and the new moon (II Kings 4:23; Isa. 1:13; Hos. 2:13; Amos 8:5), which originates in Mesopotamian culture. But in Israel, the conception seems to have been that the moon is created anew, so to speak, every month. Like the Sabbath, then, the new moon recalls the Creation. (This idea was reflected in the later benediction over the new moon; Sanhedrin 42a).

[7] Babylonia, too, knew of two new years. From the time of Hammurabi, it was the custom to celebrate Marduk's new year in Nisan, but the Tishri new year continued in various places. See Charles F. Jean, *La Religion sumérienne* (Paris, 1931), pp. 170 f.; Bruno Meissner, *Babylonien und Assyrien* (Heidelberg, 1920–25), II, 95 ff., 396.

the land (5:10 f.). The Second Temple, too, was inaugurated at the beginning of the cultic year (Ezra 6:14 ff.). Later also the first of Nisan was considered the start of the cultic year (Mishnah Rosh Hashanah 1.1). On the other hand, the month of ingathering was the beginning of the agricultural year. A combination of both reckonings is found in the ancient calendar of Exodus 23:14 ff. and 34:18 ff.; the first festival is *maṣṣōth*, yet the ingathering festival falls at the end or turn of the year. A similar combination is found in Leviticus 25:8 ff.; the seventh month of the cultic calendar (Tishri) is the start of the sabbatical and jubilee year, since these are connected with agriculture. I Kings 6:1 shows that there was a counting of years from the Exodus, i.e., by the priestly year. Notwithstanding, both Solomon and Jeroboam inaugurate their temples at the autumn festival, because the spring festival was a family affair during which not as many people came to Jerusalem. Thus the kings bowed to popular custom.

The tenth days of Nisan and Tishri were also sacred. The paschal lamb was selected out of the flock and consecrated on the tenth of the month (Exod. 12:3). P's tradition makes the tenth of the first month the day of Israel's entry into Canaan (Josh. 4:19). The tenth of the seventh month was a great fast day (Lev. 16:29, 31); according to Leviticus 25:9, the jubilee year is proclaimed on that day.

In early times, both new year days were apparently marked by temple purifications. This was their priestly side. According to Ezekiel 45:18 ff., the temple is to be purified on the first day of the first month and also (according to the Greek reading of vs. 20) on the first of the seventh month. (A reminiscence of this is, perhaps, to be found in the Second Temple practice of whiting the altar stones on Passover and Tabernacles, and the entire temple on Passover [Mishnah Middoth 3.4], a procedure which must have had purificatory significance.) P, on the other hand, speaks only of one day of purification and atonement, the tenth day of the seventh month. It is difficult to determine the relation between Ezekiel and P on this point. One thing is clear: it is naïve to speak of an "evolution" of the law of Ezekiel into that of P. Ezekiel did not invent these purifications. They pertain to a building with doorposts, not a tent (as in P); they touch only its exterior, the doorposts and altar. P's rite, on the other hand, centers on the interior and has at its heart the ancient idea of the ark's sanctity and God's appearing upon the ark. Ezekiel's purification is of the temple only, while that of P is of the people as well. These practices might very well have been concurrent. On the first of the new year, the doorposts and the altar corners were purified; on the tenth was the great general purification. Or there may have been differing customs in the various temples.

The people have no role in P's great purification; it is entirely the work of the priests. Presumably, the people did not come to the temples; they fasted and gathered in "vineyards" to watch the festive dance of maidens—conceived, doubtless, as a sacred dance (cf. Judg. 21:19 ff.)—happy that its sins were to be forgiven by YHWH (cf. Mishnah Taanith 4.8). That it was a joyous day is evident from the law that the jubilee year is to be consecrated then (Lev. 25:9 ff.).

Already in pre-exilic times the popular cult exerted an influence on the new year day and the Day of Atonement. The cultic new year (first of Nisan) is not even mentioned as such in P, but the popular new year, the first of Tishri, is a solemn rest day, a sacred convocation, proclaimed with trumpets, and having its special additional offering (Lev. 23:23 ff.; Num. 29:1 ff.). Several psalms, in which the motif of blowing horns and shouting joyously in honor of God is prominent (e.g., 47; 81:1–5; 89:6–19; 95–100), may refer to the popular new year. The whole earth shouts to honor God, the angels laud him, all creatures praise him, declaring him king. The joyous tidings are: YHWH has become king. Creation is referred to in these psalms only in the background; the central theme is God's rule, his kingship over all. From eternity God has established his throne, and thenceforth has ruled his world in righteousness. The phrase "for he comes, for he comes to judge the earth" (96:13; 98:9) suggests a fixed season, a day that was thought of as a cosmic judgment. Apparently, the new year day was conceived of as a time when God decreed life and sustenance for his creatures. He shows his goodness to Israel, too, on the day of his kingship: "He crushes peoples under us and nations under our feet" (47:4 ff.).

On the assumption that these are new year psalms, it seems that the new year festival was conceived of already in early times as the day when the destiny of the world was fixed. Since the new year celebration in Babylon involved a similar motif, there is a point of contact here between the two cultures, though not necessarily a late contact. The idea is an ancient one and is usually combined with the deliverance of the gods from some danger, and the divine marriage. Of these three motifs, only that of fixing destinies could be adopted into the religion of Israel; this was naturally attached to the autumn new year's festival, when the agricultural outlook for the future was a primary concern.

Later, the day became a day of divine retribution. The new year and the Day of Atonement turned into "days of awe," with prayers for forgiveness and repentance. In the Bible, this process is only incipient; the two are not yet joined as days of retribution. They are still separate and festive, in expectation of God's beneficent decisions.

Prayer belonged almost exclusively to the popular religion; it is not mentioned in P. Ordinarily, the individual prays for himself. When, on occasion, an intercessor appears, he is not a priest, but a righteous man or prophet (Gen. 20:7, 17; Num. 12:13; Deut. 9:10; Jer. 15:1). The only prayer formulated in the Torah is the tithe-confession (Deut. 26:12 ff.), which is non-priestly.

The sanctuary ("before YHWH" e.g., Josh. 7:6 ff.; Judg. 21:2 f.; I Sam. 1:10 ff.; II Sam. 7:18 ff.; I Kings 8:22 ff., 44; II Kings 19:14 ff.) is the preferred, but not the exclusive, site of prayer. There was never a controversy over legitimate places of prayer, as there was in the case of sacrifice. When the Bible tells of a person praying, it rarely takes note of his specific location. Unlike sacrifice and cultic song, prayer may be offered to YHWH outside of the land (Lev. 26:40; I Kings 8:46 ff.; Pss. 42–43). Jonah prays from the belly of the fish; Daniel, Ezra, and Nehemiah, from Babylonia and Persia. There were no fixed forms or seasons of prayer. It was a spontaneous "cry" and "shout" to God for mercy. Prayer developed as an independent, non-priestly religious realm; in the Bible it is almost entirely separate from sacrifice (the two appear together only in I Sam. 7:9; Job 42:8).

Confession, benediction, curse, and song, however, do show a tendency toward formulation. Public confession took the form, "We have sinned against YHWH" (I Sam. 7:6; cf. 12:10; Judg. 10:10, 15; Num. 21:7), "We have sinned, we have been perverse, we have been wicked" (I Kings 8:47), and the like. A popular parental blessing was, "May God make you like Ephraim and Manasseh" (Gen. 48:20). A priestly benediction is formulated in Numbers 6:24 ff.; a priestly curse in 5:19 ff. The hearer responded with "Amen," or "Amen, may YHWH so command," or the like (Num. 5:22; Deut. 27:15 ff.; I Kings 1:36). As formal artistic creations, song and psalm, like legend and dance, are especially liable to become public property. Along with the dance and the procession, song and psalm were part of the popular cult. The festive throng celebrated its holydays with the sound of song and the music of psalteries—the popular adjunct to the temple ritual (Amos 5:23)—hence psalmody tended to become formalized more like cultic forms and less like prayer.

That psalmody existed in pre-exilic Israel and Judah is beyond all doubt. Amos speaks of song and music in Ephraim's worship (*ibid.*).

Among the exiles in Babylonia are singers who still carried their harps and whose profession was to sing "the songs of Zion" and "of YHWH" (Ps. 137). Psalmody had begun to be stylized early. Originally the product of a personal need and a private sentiment, a given psalm might be adopted by others as articulating better than they could their own feeling. Such a psalm acquired fixed form and was utilized time and again on similar occasions and in like situations. The telltale sign of such stereotyped usage is disagreement between the content of the psalm and the occasion of its use. A composition made to order, even if it utilizes set formulas, will fit the occasion for which it is intended. But the use of a standing composition prescribed for set occasions often involves a divergence between what is said and the circumstances of the sayer. Yet this does not stand in the way of the devout. For two thousand years, Jews and Christians in the most varied circumstances have poured out their souls to God through the Psalter. What have the faithful of the centuries not read into these 150 chapters! There is reason to believe that such formalized usage of psalms began early in Israel.

There is a striking difference between the prayers and psalms of the Bible. Every word of prayer is appropriate to the situation in which it is spoken; this is not the case of the psalms whose life-context is known. Hannah's prayer (I Sam. 1:11) accords with her condition, but her hymn of thanksgiving has only one verse (vs. 5, "the barren woman gave birth to seven") applicable specifically to her. This one verse was enough for the narrator to have Hannah recite the whole psalm, although verse 10 shows plainly that it is a royal thanksgiving hymn. Jonah's prayer (4:2 f.) fits his condition; the hymn of chapter 2, however, is obviously a thanksgiving connected with the payment of vows in the temple. In verses 3 ff., the poet employs such figures as "from the belly of Sheol I cried out," and these were enough to justify ascribing the psalm to Jonah in the belly of the fish. In Joel's prophecy about locusts, there is a psalm (1:16–20) that has more to do with drought than with locusts. But since the prophet speaks of the locust-plague in figures of fire and flame, a psalm describing scorched earth could be appropriated to describe the locusts. Such instances —and there are others—of incongruity between a psalm and the occasion in which it is uttered are not editorial mistakes. Once a given psalm has become public property, its application to various situations is obviously considered justified if even a non-essential element can be conceived as relevant. This phenomenon—repeated countless times through the centuries with the psalms of the Psalter—appearing already in pre-exilic literature testifies to the fixation of psalm stereotypes, and hence of psalm literature in general, in early times. The collections that eventually comprised the book of Psalms are all pre-exilic. There is no psalm whose plain sense (as distinct from the midrashic romancing of modern exegetes) requires a dating later than the exilic Psalm 137.

THE LIVING AND THE DEAD

The realm of the dead, the rites connected with death and burial, as well as the destiny of the soul in the other world, play no part in the religion of YHWH. This is one of the most astonishing features of Israelite religion. That the spirit of the deceased lives on apart from the body is the belief of the people, but biblical faith draws no religious or moral inferences from this notion.

The spirit of the deceased descends beneath the earth to Sheol, "the pit" (Isa. 14:15 ff.; Ezek. 32:18 ff.), the world of the shades (Job 26:5), where it joins its departed ancestors and kin (Gen. 25:8; II Sam. 12:23). Although kings sit there on their thrones (Isa. 14:9 ff.), there is equality in Sheol; small and great, king and captive, master and slave sleep together (Job 3:11 ff.). It is a land of deep darkness (Job 10:21 f.), a land of no return (Prov. 2:19; Job 7:9; 10:21).

Alongside this conception is another that links the soul with the grave and the interred body. Rachel weeps for her children in her sepulcher at Ramah (Jer. 31:15). Necromancers spend the night in graveyards (Isa. 65:4). Care of the corpse is crucial for the fate of its ghost. It made a difference with whom one was buried (II Sam. 4:12; I Kings 13:31; Isa. 53:9). The patriarchs are concerned to buy a family graveplot (Gen. 23:3 ff.; 25:9 f.; 49:31); Jacob asks to be brought up from the land of Egypt to be buried with his ancestors (47:29 ff.). Burial away from the family grave is a punishment (I Kings 13:22). It is an act of loyalty and kindness to bury the dead (Gen. 47:29 f.; II Sam. 2:5); to go unburied is a terrible calamity. The men of Jabesh-gilead rescue the mutilated bodies of Saul and his sons from exposure by the Philistines and bury them (I Sam. 31:11 ff.), and for this David commends them (II Sam. 2:5 f.). The worst fate was to die and be abandoned to wild beasts and birds of prey (I Sam. 17:46). Rizpah faithfully sits guard by the bodies of her sons to ward off preying creatures (II Sam. 21:10). Rebels and usurpers exposed the bodies of the royal family to dogs and birds—the ultimate divine punishment (I Kings 14:11; 21:23 f.; II Kings 9:25 f., 34 ff.). Exhumation, too, is considered a punishment (Isa. 14:19; Jer. 8:1 f.).

Mourning in Israel followed the custom of all peoples. Upon receiving the report of death there was weeping and crying, clothes were rent, and sackcloth was girded on (Gen. 23:2; 37:34; II Sam. 1:11). The mourner fasted, and sat and slept upon the ground (I Sam. 31:13; II Sam. 1:12; 13:31; Isa. 3:26), went about bareheaded and barefoot, with his upper lip covered (Ezek. 24:17). It was the practice to inflict wounds and baldness upon oneself (Jer. 16:6; Ezek. 7:18; cf. Isa. 22:12). Apparently, it was also customary to shave the hair of the face (Jer. 41:5; cf. the prohibitions of Lev. 19:27 f.; 21:5; Deut. 14:1). The meal of the mourner—"bread of mourners" (Hos. 9:4; so read in Ezek. 24:17)—was provided for him by others (II Sam. 3:35; Jer. 16:7). Mourning lasted for seven days (Gen. 50:10; I Sam. 31:13); Moses and Aaron were mourned over for thirty (Num. 20:29; Deut. 34:8), and the captive woman was given a month to mourn over her parents before being taken to wife (Deut. 21:13). A wife mourned for her husband a long time; she refrained from anointing herself, but wore mourning or widow's dress (II Sam. 14:2, 5; Gen. 38:14, 19). Over the dead there were cries and laments (II Sam. 1:17 ff.; I Kings 13:30; Amos 5:16). Professional mourners (often women—cf. Jer. 9:16 ff.) probably had fixed forms of lamentation. For kings of Judah, a large burning was made (Jer. 34:5; II Chron. 16:14; 21:19). It was a popular custom, an expression of solicitude, to give food to the dead (Deut. 26:14).

Belief in some connection between the living and the dead was prevalent. Necromancy was practiced (I Sam. 28), although it was under ban (Lev. 19:31; Deut. 18:11; I Sam. 28:3; Isa. 8:19). The anxiety of biblical man to produce offspring, to have "a name and a remainder on the face of the earth" (II Sam. 14:7), is grounded on this belief. The levirate duty is motivated by a concern for "carrying on the name of the dead man in Israel" (Gen. 38:8; Deut. 25:5–10; Ruth 4:5, 10), not (as has been supposed) by the need for maintaining an ancestor cult of whose existence we hear nothing in the Bible. That this is not a later idea is shown by Absalom's motive in erecting a monument during his lifetime, "For he said, 'I have no son to keep my name in remembrance' " (II Sam. 18:18). A monument can fill the role of a son only because it was not for carrying on ancestor-worship that sons were desired (cf. also Isa. 56:5, in which eunuchs are promised "a monument and a memorial better than sons and daughters"). To ancient man a name was a substantial matter; keeping up its memory after death gave vitality to the soul in the other realm. The deceased who is buried among his people and whose name is kept alive among them still shares, as it were, in life upon the earth. Muffled sounds of the tumult of life may be heard below (the extreme position taken in Job 14:21; 21:21 is not representative of the thought of the age). The fate of one's progeny is, in a sense, one's personal fate. Rachel weeps for her exiled children and is consoled by the promise of their return. Hence, in spite of the defilement of the realm of death the ghost may still be in touch somehow with earthly holiness. That would seem to be one reason for the patriarch's wish to be buried in the land of Israel, and it is the point of Amos' threat to Amaziah that he would die in an "impure land" (Amos 7:17).

Were these customs and beliefs a religious matter? Did they express some relationship toward a divine or demonic realm? Doubtless the origin of many of these customs is in a cult of the dead or an ancestor cult. The question is whether this was still their meaning in biblical times. To be sure, the Israelites were accustomed to give food to the dead, but not every gift of food is a sacrifice or an offering to a divinity. It is of crucial significance that nowhere is ancestor-worship or a cult of the dead referred to.[8] What is forbidden in Deuteronomy 26:14 is the gift to the dead of consecrated food. There is no offense taken at giving him profane food, from which it is clear that the law does not regard such gifts in the light of offerings. Such concern for the well-being of the deceased in the grave, grounded in the belief that it is possible still to be in touch with and benefit him, is not a cult of the dead.

Indeed, of all the forms of contact between the living and the dead, only necromancy is banned. The dead is *ᵓelōhīm*, insofar as he is a disembodied spirit whose existence is unlike that of the living. This term itself is restricted to the spirit as invoked by the necromancer (I Sam. 28:13; Isa. 8:19). His "divinity" is solely mantic and, as such, is recognized by the Bible, although recourse to him is forbidden. No other divine quality is referred to, either as a recognized belief or as a condemned popular error. The dead have no power to help the living or to deliver them from trouble. No cultic rites at the graves of national heroes and ancestors are mentioned.[9] Nor do the dead have any baleful, demonic power; they are tranquil, at peace, and asleep in their graves or in Sheol (Job 3:13; 14:12; Dan. 12:2). To raise them by necromancy is to disturb them (I Sam. 28:15). Doubtless, the Israelite had an instinctive horror and fear of the dead; nonetheless he did not imagine that ghosts haunted the earth seeking to harm mankind. Indeed, the very concept of an autonomous realm of demonic power is altogether lacking in the Bible. To be sure, some of the funerary rites of Israel had their origins in demonic conceptions, but

[8] "Sacrifices of the dead" in Psalm 106:28 refers to feasts arranged for pagan gods; cf. Gunkel's commentary *ad loc*.

[9] There is no cultic significance attached by the Bible to the annual mourning over Jephthah's daughter.

by biblical times, these notions are no longer in evidence. The rite of the heifer, performed to expunge the bloodguilt of an untraceable murder, no longer aimed at appeasing or warding off the ghost of the murdered man, but was directed wholly toward YHWH (Deut. 21:1 ff.). The famine in David's time is not conceived of as the revenge of the murdered Gibeonites, but comes from the wrath of God over Saul's violation of their rights. David hangs and exposes Saul's sons to propitiate YHWH, not the ghosts of the murdered man (II Sam. 21). The blood of a murdered man "cries out" to YHWH, it does not seek vengeance on its own; the avenger is YHWH (Gen. 4:10).

The original meaning of mourning customs having been forgotten, they became no more than expressions of sorrow and grief. This accounts for the fact that the Bible did not ban them as pagan. Self-mutilation, shaving, and tattooing (apparently connected with burial rites) were banned, but not rending clothing, wearing sackcloth, fasting, and the rest. Why this distinction was made is not clear; perhaps enduring bodily marks made as memorials to the dead were abhorrent for being constant reminders of the realm of impurity.

While the rest of paganism's religious legacy was transformed and assimilated into the religion of YHWH, rites of the dead, though transformed, never became part of the new religion. Apart from banning certain customs, the Torah laws have nothing to say about such rites. Whatever we know about them comes from the narratives and prophetic literature. No special customs were prescribed for Israel. The Bible, it seems, considers the treatment of the dead and mourning a matter of universal, human culture and regards them as altogether secular. It does not hesitate to tell that Jacob and Joseph were mummified (Gen. 50:1 ff., 26), although this rite was connected with the Osiris cult; or that the Egyptians performed mourning rites for Jacob (vss. 3, 10 f.). The afterlife of the soul, too, is outside the sphere of the religion of YHWH. To be sure, YHWH rules Sheol, yet there is no relation between him and the dead. The dead do not praise him; those who go down to the pit do not call upon him or wait for his kindness (Isa. 38:18; Pss. 6:6; 30:10). Biblical religion knows nothing of a judgment of souls in an afterlife, a central motif of Egyptian faith and one that is found in Babylonia as well. The realm of the dead in Israelite religion is godless.

Such a conception empties the rites of the dead of all religious significance. Burying the deceased in a family grave, giving him food, raising a monument for him, and the like, are deeds of devotion toward the dead through which the living maintained a connection with them. These acts of familial piety were devoid even of a magical element. Their purpose was not to fortify the soul for its new existence or to provide it with apotropaic devices. Biblical religion regards these rites rather in the light of ethical behavior than as religious acts. Caring for the dead is "steadfast loyalty" (Gen. 47:29; II Sam. 2:5; Ruth 2:20). The propitiatory or apotropaic element of mourning rites lost their pagan meaning in Israel without striking fresh roots in the new faith. Only the status of impurity of the dead survives as a last vestige of the primary cultic-magical notion.

This de-religionization of rites of the dead is not a necessary consequence of Israelite monotheism. Later Judaism did, in fact, reintroduce God in the idea of a judgment in the afterlife. Burial and mourning rites did become invested with religious significance; the soul was aided by them and strengthened in the other world. Why did biblical faith not make over in a new, monotheistic form the pagan conceptions of afterlife and funeral rites? The new faith was surely less satisfying here than the old pagan beliefs. By excluding the realm of the dead from its concern, it ran the risk of driving the people—in this vital area at least—to the ancient, forbidden practices.

The explanation of this remarkable circumstance lies, it would seem, in the especial intransigence of these pagan materials. To paganism death was an introduction to the divine or demonic realm. The kingdom of the dead is an autonomous divine-demonic realm with its own laws and its own ruling god. Entering this kingdom, the soul becomes "divine"—a good or evil spirit empowered to work good and evil and fit to become an object of religious activity, to be propitiated or warded off. The higher pagan religions link redemption from death with the death of a god or his descent into the underworld; by rituals the god is delivered from death and resuscitated, and these same rituals open the way for men, too, to escape death's clutches. In Egypt, the dead were identified with Osiris, the dying and reviving god; the mysteries of Adonis and Demeter-Persephone have a similar purpose: through death man becomes god.

When Israelite religion concentrated all divinity in YHWH, the spirits of the dead ceased being "gods." A trace of the early notion of the deified soul survived in the belief that it could be invoked to tell the future. A memorial of the cult of the dead is the impurity that attaches to all contact with death. Because it was impossible to do away with the activity performed upon the body of the deceased—the actual object of the ancient cult—its impurity was declared the most virulent of all. Thus the corpse and the ghost became farthest removed from the realm of God. The soul could not become a god, but only a shade. And, inasmuch as the activity performed upon the deceased was defiling, no religious content or value could be ascribed to it. Consequently, the soul was deprived of all means of deliverance from death, since such deliverance could then be conceived of only in terms of apotheosis or identification with a dying god—both of which were rejected by Israelite religion. Not even the idea of a judgment in the afterlife was adopted, since such a judgment involved—in the thought of the times—gods of the underworld as judges, and apotheosis as a reward for righteousness. A tendency to ignore even the notions of the ghost and Sheol can be discerned in the conception of Genesis 2–3 that the soul is the breath of God, the body, dust of the earth; death is but a return of dust to dust after God has withdrawn the breath (Gen. 3:19; Ps. 104:29 f.). The problem of the deliverance of the soul from death remained unsolved in the Bible. The only escape allowed was ascension alive into heaven—as in the singular instances of Enoch and Elijah (Gen. 5:24; II Kings 2:11).

What distinguishes the faith of later Judaism from that of the Bible is not, then, the idea of immortality. It is rather that the biblical age had not yet succeeded in forming a conception of a judgment of the soul and its deliverance from death that would not be vitiated by the images of an infernal god, a dying god, or the apotheosis of the dead. Having surrounded death with impurity, it was unable to find a way to introduce holiness into that realm. And because the holy, the divine, has no place among the dwellers in Sheol, there is no judgment, no reward, and no punishment there. It was not the belief in immortality that came later, but the breakthrough of the soul to God from the realm of death. This transformation occurred only after many centuries.

JUSTICE AND MORALITY: INTRODUCTORY

The moral conceptions of the Bible have been crystallized in two parallel but distinct traditions: Torah and prophecy on the one hand, and the wisdom literature on the other. Prophetic morality is rooted in that of the Torah and is its culmination. Biblical wisdom literature exhibits hardly a trace of the influence of either; it runs as a parallel and independent stream of thought. These traditions differ fundamentally with regard to the source, the ground, and the bearers of moral responsibility.

For Torah and prophecy, the source of morality is the will of God, and the basis of moral obligation is the command of God communicated to man through prophecy. God gave man a just and moral law and made a historical covenant with him, binding him to observe it. With Israel, God made a national covenant involving a special moral-religious law which is the basis of Israel's special obligations. The prophetic denunciations of Israel take their departure from this notion.

Biblical wisdom literature is pervaded with the idea that morality stems from wisdom. Its source is not prophetic revelation, but understanding and discernment. To be sure, morality is rooted also in the fear of God, who requites men according to their deserts. Yet, for all that, it is primarily conceived of as the child of wisdom, human and divine. This viewpoint dominates Proverbs, which, as the book of wisdom's instructions, may be regarded as a counterpart to the Torah, the book of divine laws. In Job, God's providence is a speculative problem which it is the task of wisdom to solve. In prophecy, it is a matter of faith and trust (Jer. 12:1 ff.; Hab. 1:2—2:4; cf. Ps. 73; Lam. 3). Wisdom literature makes no allusion to covenants having moral content between man and God. It conceives of morality rather as a kind of natural law that God implanted in the hearts of men.

Conceptions of morality thus crystallized in two distinct literary corpora: a prophetic—humanistic and national, and a sapiential—humanistic alone. The one speaks in categorical imperatives; the other appeals to prudence and utilitarian considerations. The Torah legislates and commands; the prophets exhort and censure; both call for faith and trust in God. Proverbs counsels and warns on the basis of observation and experience; it does not know of any disturbing problems. Job (like the later Ecclesiastes) speculates upon the moral order. Psalms contains something of the sapiential outlook, but by and large it is a book of faith and trust.

THE MORALITY OF THE TORAH

THE SANCTITY OF LIFE—The Decalogue (Exod. 20:1 ff.; Deut. 5:6 ff.), doubtless part of the earliest Israelite traditions, lays down broad principles of justice and morality that are detailed and elaborated upon in the other law corpora: the inviolability of life and person, the sanctity of marriage, of one's utterance, and of property rights. Exodus 21:12 ff. distinguishes the murderer from the accidental homicide, condemning the first to death and providing the second with asylum. Numbers 35:9 ff. and Deuteronomy 4:41 ff.; 19:1–13 institute cities of refuge for the accidental slayer, though outside the laws only the altar-asylum is referred to (I Kings 1:50 ff.; 2:28 f.). The murder of a slave, even by his owner, was to be avenged (Exod. 21:20 f.). For goring a slave to death, a bull known to be a gorer was stoned, and its owner compelled to pay a fine. If the slain was a freeman, the owner was put to death (Exod. 21:28–32). Even indirectly causing death imposes guilt on a person (Deut. 22:8). Maiming is punished by the *lex talionis:* "an eye for an eye, etc." (Exod. 21:24 f.; Lev. 24:19 f.). According to Deuteronomy 19:21, this law was applied to the false witness as well. A man who maims his slave must set him free (Exod. 21:26 f.).

FREEDOM AND SLAVERY—A man's freedom is his supreme right. Kidnaping for sale into slavery is punishable with death (Exod. 21:16; Deut. 24:7). In the conception of Adam—the progenitor of all men—as created in God's image, the idea of the equality of all men is implicit. This idea, however, never attains full expression; women are subservient to men, and—what is worse—slaves to their masters. Slavery is regarded as a curse laid especially on the offspring of Canaan (Gen. 9:25 ff.), though by no means limited to them. A Hebrew who sells himself into slavery must be released after six years. If he refuses to be freed, he is formally branded as a perpetual slave (Exod. 21:2 ff.). Leviticus 25:39–43, on the other hand, does away with Israelite bondage entirely, for Israelites are "slaves of YHWH," whose lordship excludes subservience to human masters. This lofty conception, unparalleled elsewhere in antiquity, is, however, limited in its application to Israelites and does not embrace foreigners (vss. 44 ff.). Moreover, it seems that in pre-exilic times it was a utopian ideal without practical effect. From the equality of all men before God, Job 31:13–15 infers only that justice and compassion must be shown to slaves; it does not repudiate slavery in principle. A foreign slave who fled to the land of Israel must not be surrendered to his owner (Deut. 23:16 f.), although it appears that there was in fact an international convention to surrender fugitive slaves (I Kings 2:39 f.). Israelite slaves could acquire property and might even have slaves of their own (II Sam. 9:2, 9 f.). Bondwomen usually became concubines of their master or his sons (Exod. 21:7 ff.).

MARRIAGE AND SEX LAWS—In Israel, as elsewhere, the sanctity of the family and the relations between the sexes were regulated by powerful sanctions (Lev. 18; 20; Deut. 22:13–29; 27:20–23). But the sexual prohibitions of the Torah are more comprehensive and their violations more severely punished. Sodomy and bestiality were punished by death (Lev. 20:13, 15 f.). Relations with father's wife, daughter-in-law, a woman and her daughter, are similarly punished (*ibid.* vss. 11, 12, 14). Noteworthy is the wider scope of the later laws of incest, compared with the customs of the patriarchs: with Genesis 20:12 and II Samuel 13:13 compare Leviticus 18:9 and Deuteronomy 27:22; with Genesis 29:16–30 compare Leviticus 18:18.

Owing to the biblical view of the bleak destiny of the soul after death, it values the pleasures and blessings of this world. And yet in sexual matters it demands severe chastity. Though polygamy is not banned, the basic view is that the proper end of sexual relations is procreation and that pursuit of pleasure alone is sinful. The non-pagan quality of the biblical view finds particular expression in its attitude toward harlotry. Paganism could not lay down an absolute prohibition of harlotry, since it sanctified and even deified sexual desire. It consecrated men and women to cultic prostitution. By repudiating the divinity of desire the Bible did away with the religious basis of promiscuity and prepared the way for a new moral evaluation. Paganism, of course, bans adultery and incest; it counsels against wantonness and praises chastity. But it offers no parallel to the absolute command: "You shall not defile your daughter by causing her to be a harlot" (Lev. 19:29). Sexual license, even when not adulterous or with prohibited relations, is per se defiling. Nor is there any law outside of Israel that corresponds to the absolute ban upon cultic prostitution (Deut. 23:18); the very terms *qedēshā* and *qādēsh* (lit. "holy person") are a monument to the transformation of pagan sanctity into Israelite impurity.

SANCTITY OF THE SPOKEN WORD—An oath or vow taken in the name of God imposed the greatest of obligations (Exod. 20:7; Lev. 19:12). Jephthah must sacrifice his daughter because he "opened his mouth to YHWH" (Judg. 11:30–39). Such an oath could be counteracted only by another (II Sam. 19:24; I Kings 2:8, 42 f.). To delay in fulfilling one's vows is counted as a sin (Deut. 23:22 ff.). Bearing false witness is especially condemned (Exod. 20:13; 23:1); the perjurer who is discovered is dealt with "as he had schemed to do to his fellow" (Deut. 19:16 ff.). Lying and denying the truth are prohibited (Exod. 23:7; Lev. 19:11).

JUSTICE AND RIGHTEOUSNESS—To do what is right and just is the way of YHWH (Gen. 18:19). In Israel, as elsewhere, justice was the special virtue of the king, the quality in which he gloried (II Sam. 8:15; I Kings 3:6 ff.; Pss. 45:5, 8; 72:1 ff.). But every Israelite is enjoined from showing partiality, taking bribes, and perverting justice (Exod. 23:3, 7 ff.; Lev. 19:15, 35; etc.). The duty of dealing rightly with the poor and helpless is emphasized (Exod. 23:6; Deut. 24:17; 27:19); God himself is the model of this virtue (Deut. 10:18; Ps. 10:18). Equality before the law is implicit in biblical justice. It was long ago observed that the Covenant Code does not discriminate between men and women and recognizes that even slaves have certain basic rights. P enjoins equal treatment of alien and native-born in religious, as in non-religious, matters (Lev. 24:16 and elsewhere; Num. 35:15). Despite the existence of class divisions among the people, particularly in late monarchic times, Israelite law—as distinct from other ancient Near Eastern law—recognizes no class privileges. Slaves apart, the law makes no distinction between patrician and plebeian, rich and poor, propertied and proletariat. There are no restrictions on inter-marriage between classes. The king is ideally chosen "from among his brothers" (Deut. 17:15) and is charged not to let his "heart be exalted over his brothers" (vss. 19 f.). His rule is based on a covenant with the people (II Sam. 5:3; II Kings 11:17).

REVERENCE—Going beyond the demands of strict justice is a class of laws aimed at placing the relations between men on a footing of propriety and mutual respect. Patriarchal society was founded on the respect shown to parents and other persons of experience, wisdom, or age. Honor and reverence of both father and mother is one of the basic commands (Exod. 20:12; Lev. 19:3; cf. Exod. 21:15, 17). An insubordinate, dissolute son is punished with death (Deut. 21:18 ff.). Chief and king must not be cursed (Exod. 22:27; II Sam. 16:5–13; 19:22; I Kings 2:8 f.). Respect is due to gray hairs (Lev. 19:32). Concern for the dignity of persons in general is expressed in the proscription of dealing out excessive stripes, lest "your brother become despised in your eyes" (Deut. 25:3). A captive woman taken to wife may never afterward be sold, "inasmuch as you have humili-ated her" (Deut. 21:14).

LOVE AND COMPASSION—Compassion is a quality of YHWH who is "a merciful and gracious God" (Exod. 34:6; Ps. 86:15; etc.). A creditor must not keep the pledged garment of a poor man overnight, for "if he cries out to me I will hear him, for I am gracious" (Exod. 22:26). Both compassion and love are embodied in the social legislation. "You shall love your neighbor as yourself"—a positive extension of "You shall not hate your brother in your heart"—is the climax of biblical morality (Lev. 19:17, 18). What is meant by this is not a mere state of mind, but its actualization in deeds of generosity and kindness. This becomes clear from verses 33 f., "You must not wrong the alien . . . but love him as yourself." Repeated in Deuteronomy 10:19, its meaning is elucidated in verse 18 where God, who "loves the alien," is said "to give him bread and clothes." All the laws that obligate men to stand by each other in the time of need, or which forbid exploiting poverty and distress, are based on this law of love. The Israelite is required to go out of his way, if necessary, to restore lost property or help unload an overburdened ass, even one belonging to his enemy (Exod. 23:4 f.). He is repeatedly bidden to aid the poor, the alien, the orphan, and the widow, as, e.g., in the obligation to be open-handed toward the needy; the ban upon taking interest on loans (Exod. 22:24; Lev. 25:35 ff.; Deut. 23:20 f.); the (surely utopian) sabbatical cancellations of debts (Deut. 15:1 ff.); the right of redemption of real property and the jubilee law (Lev. 25:8 ff.); the poor dues—the spontaneous growth of the fallow year (Exod. 23:10 f.), the corners of the field, and gleanings of vineyard and field (Lev. 19:9 f.; cf. Deut. 24:19 ff.).

Related to the law of love is the proscription of revenge, grudge-bearing, and talebearing (Lev. 19:16, 18). Compassion forbids cursing the deaf and placing a stumbling block before the blind (*ibid.* vs. 14). Beasts, too, are embraced by biblical compassion. They must be given rest on the Sabbath (Exod. 20:10; 23:12); the ox may not be muzzled while threshing (Deut. 25:4). Hospitality is not expressly enjoined, but it is considered an ancient and universal obligation. Abraham and Lot are depicted, in contrast to the Sodomites, as exemplary hosts (Gen. 18–19). Ammon and Moab are excluded from the Israelite community, because they refused to show elementary decency to the wandering tribes on their journey through the wilderness (Deut. 23:4 f.). The Israelite took care to be hospitable (II Sam. 12:1 ff.; cf. Job 31:32: "No stranger had to lodge outside, I opened my door to the wayfarer").

MEEKNESS—Meekness is one of the virtues of Moses (Num. 12:3); in prophetic and wisdom literature, the meek are the mass of simple folk, over against the wealthy and luxurious classes.

DRUNKENNESS—Wine is not forbidden in Israel. It was employed in the cult and was celebrated for its virtue of cheering the heart (Judg. 9:13; Ps. 104:15; Prov. 31:6). Yet winebibbing is at times linked with harlotry (Hos. 4:11, 18; 7:4 f.; Amos 2:7 f.), and the drunken woman is called "base" (I Sam. 1:16). In the tales about the intoxication of Noah (Gen. 9:20 ff.) and Lot (19:31 ff.), it becomes the occasion for heinous sins. The moral obloquy attached to winebibbing was reinforced by the liberation from the ideal of Dionysiac intoxication. Just as it rejected cultic prostitution, so the Bible rejected cultic intoxication—though room was left for wine as a "gladdener."

THE PROPHETIC AND NATIONAL CHARACTER OF THE TORAH MORALITY— While Torah and prophecy know of a universal moral law, the basis of Israel's moral obligation is the covenant, with its special moral-legal code. Several prescriptions of the universal moral law were given anew to Israel as national-religious obligations. Biblical morality is societal and national. Nation and society are responsible for its maintenance; their welfare is conditioned upon its observance.

Even the fundamental moral injunction, "You shall not murder," which in Genesis 9:5 f. has a general sanction ("for man was made in the image of God"), was given anew to the people of Israel at Sinai and supplied with a national motive: bloodshed defiles the land of Israel in which God dwells (Num. 35:31 ff.). A hanged man must not be exposed overnight lest the land be polluted (Deut. 21:22 f.). Several social laws are grounded in the fact that Israel was "a stranger in the land of Egypt" and knows what it means to be helpless: the injunction against wronging an alien (Exod. 22:20; 23:9); the duty to love him (Lev. 19:34; Deut. 10:19); bestowal of gifts on the emancipated slave (Deut. 15:13 ff.); the sharing of the festal banquet with the poor (16:11 f.); the injunction against perverting the cause of alien and orphan and taking a widow's pledge (24:17 f.); the poor dues (vss. 19–22). Even the Sabbath rest is supplied with this national motive (5:12 ff.). Violations of the sexual prohibitions of Leviticus 18 and 20 defile the land so that it will spew Israel forth. To take back a divorced wife after she has remarried also brings guilt upon the land (Deut. 24:4).

Various moral laws are grounded on Israel's religious distinction. Israelites may not be enslaved, because they are the slaves of God (Lev. 25:42, 55). The law of land redemption is linked with the sanctity of the jubilee year and with the fact that the land belongs to God (vss. 10 ff.). Some laws are framed in language applicable to Israel or Israelites only: the Sabbath law, the poor dues, the ban on cultic prostitution, those which speak of "your neighbor," "your brother" or which explicitly exclude the non-Israelite. The produce of the seventh year is set aside for "the poor of your people" (Exod. 23:10 f.); "you shall not go about as a talebearer among your people . . . you shall not hate your brother in your heart . . . you shall not take vengeance or bear a grudge against the members of your people" (Lev. 19:16 ff.). Boundary stones "in the inheritance which you hold in the land" (Deut. 19:14) must not be removed. The slanderer is guilty for having defamed "a virgin of Israel" (22:19). It is a duty to lend aid to "your needy brother" (15:7 ff.). Usury may be exacted from the foreigner (23:20 f.). Only the Hebrew bondman is freed after six years (Exod. 21:2; Deut. 15:12 ff.), while the slavery of the foreigner is perpetual (Lev. 25:44 ff.).

In sum, then, the morality of the Torah is prophetic, given by God in a revelation. Though basically universal, it is fixed in a national framework.[10]

[10] The plain meaning of "You shall love your neighbor as yourself" is national in scope. Jewish apologetic argues that the "neighbor" is not limited to the Israelite, while Christian exegesis maintains that it was Jesus who was the first to embrace all men in this law of love (Luke 10:29 ff.: the "neighbor" is the good Samaritan). Yet Jesus was, in fact, imbued with an intense national feeling. It was he who said that the gentiles were dogs and who hesitated to aid a sick child of a gentile (Matt. 15:21–27). Moreover, Luke 10:29 ff. deals with a Samaritan, not a gentile; the Samaritans were regarded as proselytes by the Jews. On the other hand, the New Testament nowhere enjoins

THE MORALITY OF THE WISDOM LITERATURE

The morality of biblical wisdom is catholic and humanistic, without any national or distinctly Israelite coloring. Its monotheism is the legendary monotheism of primeval times. Job is a patriarchal monotheist (Ezek. 14:14, 20). Proverbs speaks of the non-Israelite Agur and Lemuel (30:1; 31:1), both apparently conceived of as early monotheists (cf. Agur's lofty credo 30:5 ff.). The cult reflected in this literature consists of sacrifice, vow, and prayer. Like the cult of patriarchal times, it lacks priests, temples, and national festivals. Biblical wisdom retains the style and mood of ancient Near Eastern wisdom out of which it sprang. Like its antecedents, it grounds morality on prudence and "God-fearing," rather than on a historical covenant. Its doctrine of individual retribution resembles that of general Eastern wisdom; like the latter, it too has little to say about cultic matters.

The nature of biblical wisdom stands out clearest in the book of Proverbs, the book of wisdom's teaching—a counterpart to the Torah, the book of divine commands.[11]

---

love of idol-worshipers. Christianity zealously annihilated idol-worshipers whenever and wherever it could. The question is, then, not one of priority, but of historical fact. The fact is that the plain meaning of "neighbor" or "brother" in the Bible is Israelite. The law of Leviticus 19:18 was given to and framed for Israelite society. It is not a theoretical maxim, but a practical law. It demands that every man show compassion toward those among whom he lives, and help them; and the Israelite lived among Israelites.

However, there is no reason to suppose that the Bible intended to exclude other peoples from the basic law of love. That it embraced non-Israelites too is clear from the injunction to love the alien (Lev. 19:34; the *gēr* of the Bible has not necessarily adopted Israelite religion; note the ground of the law: "for you were *gērīm* [surely not proselytes!] in the land of Egypt"). Any alien who lived within Israelite society, then, came under the law of love.

[11] Proverbs is composed of several corpora, stemming from various authors and times. There is no reason to reject out of hand the tradition that it has a Solomonic basis. The image of Solomon as a parable-making sage is doubtless historical. His wisdom is described as comparable with that of Egypt and the "men of the East"; people of all nations come to hear him (I Kings 5:9 ff.). The catholic nature of biblical wisdom as represented by Proverbs accords with this description. In all likelihood, the wisdom element of the cultural legacy that Israel inherited from its environment began to take literary form in the time of Solomon. Proverbs was not completed before the time of Hezekiah (25:1— 29:27), but nothing in the work reflects Second Temple times. It betrays no trace whatever of the doctrines of classical prophecy. The dogma of individual retribution (found in chaps. 10–22) is no sign of lateness; the idea is found throughout the wisdom of ancient Egypt and Mesopotamia. The personification of wisdom in the early chapters has its pagan counterpart in the embodiments of wisdom in such deities as Thoth, Ea, etc. Moreover, the book of Ahikar (line 95) preserves a fragment speaking of personified wisdom as established in heaven and dear to the gods. On the other hand, there are points of contact between Proverbs 1–9 and the wisdom of Ptahotep, one of the earliest Egyptian works. The Aramaisms in the vocabulary of Proverbs are insufficient to establish its lateness. Contact was early established between Israel and Aram; when Aramaic really began to influence Hebrew, its effect was visible in whole structure of the language. Such a pervasive influence is not to be found in Proverbs.

Proverbs is suffused with optimism and complacency; it knows no real problems. God's just providence and a moral world order are presuppositions it does not question. Do not envy the prosperous wicked man, it exhorts, for "the lamp of the wicked will be extinguished" (24:19 f.). If the righteous suffers, he is being chastened by God as a son by his father; let him not reject God's reproof or hold himself wise or be lax in devoutness (3:5–12). An unmistakable utilitarianism pervades Proverbs, as in the wisdom literature of the ancient East in general. Morality is the way to success. Thus adultery is, of course, a sin (2:17); but it is also ruinous to one's substance (29:3). Drunkenness involves one in blows and wounds (23: 29–35). Even the religious basis of Proverbs' exhortations—the fear of God who requites men according to their deserts—is tinged with a certain utilitarianism. Since God oversees all the acts of men and knows their innermost thought, doing good will benefit man, while doing bad will harm him. How can man know what is good and bad? Wisdom teaches him. Not personal wisdom—"Rely not on your understanding" (3:5; etc.)—but traditional wisdom tried and tested through the ages. It is a spark of the same divine wisdom through which God created the world (3: 19 f.), which indeed preceded creation (8:22 ff.). And its first teaching is "fear of YHWH."

Sapiential morality coincides in many ways with that of the Torah. All of the rules of the Decalogue, excepting the ban on idolatry and the law of the Sabbath, are to be found here. Murder is an abomination to God (6:17; etc.); adultery is evil and disgraceful, a disregard of the divine convenant between husband and wife (2:16 ff.; 5:1 ff.; 6:20 ff.; 7:1 ff.; etc.). Theft is despicable (6:30 f.) and a profanation of God's name (30:9). False testimony is frequently condemned (6:19; 12:17; etc.). Following Egyptian models, the obligation of obedience to parents is dealt with even more fully than in the Torah.

There are points of contact with the other law corpora as well. False weights are an abomination to YHWH (11:1; 20:10, 23), for fixing weights is the work of his hands (16:11). Perversion of justice, biased judgment, taking bribes are also loathsome to YHWH (15:27; 17:15, 23, etc.). To do what is right and just is preferred by YHWH to sacrifice (21:3). The perversion of the poor man's cause is severely censured (22:22 f.; 31:5, 9). The king above all is bound to be righteous in judgment (8:15; 16:10, 12 f.).

Among the virtues of the righteous sage are compassion and kindness (11:17; 14:22; 16:6; etc.). The righteous man withholds no good from his fellow (3:27 f.), gives unstintingly (21:26), has compassion even on beasts (12:10). He does not oppress the poor, for God is their avenger (14:31;

21:13; 22:16; etc.). He does not return evil for evil (20:22; 24:29). He regards it a sin to deride the poor and rejoice in another's misfortune (17:5), to go about as a talebearer and betray confidences (11:13; 20:19). If he can, the God-fearing man saves his fellow from death and does not turn a blind eye to those in distress (24:10 f.). Humility characterizes the righteous man, as pride does the wicked (6:17; 8:13; 14:3; etc.).

The slave is mentioned in Proverbs alongside of the poor, the orphan, and widow. One must not inform on a servant to his master (30:10); at the same time, servants must not be overindulged (29:21); an occasional beating is in order (vs. 19). Only "patriarchal" slavery is mentioned, in which the slave is a permanent part of the household, at times shares a patrimony with brothers (17:2), may even rise to rule over nobles (19:10) and become king (30:22). The "Hebrew bondman" in the sense of the laws of Exodus is unknown.

Many maxims are intended to educate sons (daughters are unmentioned). The entire first collection (chaps. 1–9) and fragments of other collections are formally pedagogical. The son is warned away from women and wine; he is exhorted not to be greedy and gluttonous. An application of the rod is frequently recommended to lead youth into good ways.

THE ANTIQUITY OF ISRAELITE WISDOM MORALITY—In later wisdom literature (from Ben-Sira onward), Torah and wisdom were identified. This has not yet occurred in biblical times. Proverbs speaks of torah and commandment, but they are (as always in oriental wisdom) the instruction and commands of father, mother, sage, or of wisdom personified. There is nothing about a revealed Torah, concerning which a covenant has been made. The first chapters of Proverbs are full of the image of a father instructing his son, exhorting him to obey wisdom and get understanding. But according to Exodus 13:3 ff., Deuteronomy 4:9, etc., what the Israelite must teach his children is the story of the Exodus and the laws given Israel at that time. Proverbs 1:9; 3:3, 22; 7:3 urge the wearing of wisdom as a graceful chaplet on one's head, as a necklace, writing them on the tablets of one's heart, binding them to one's fingers. Nothing is said of binding the words of God on the hands or placing them as "frontlets" between the eyes and on doorposts (Deut. 6:8 f.; 11:18 ff.). In striking contrast with the Torah, the moral rules of Proverbs are never provided with a historical or national motive. Not only is the cultic aspect of the Sabbath never referred to, its social-moral aspect of giving rest to slave and animal is equally ignored. The poor dues, the sabbatical cancellation of debts, the jubilee, the gift to the emancipated slave, all go unmentioned. Proverbs frequently warns against the "strange woman" and her wiles, but it has not a word for the duty of the Israelite to guard the chastity of his daughter (Lev. 19:29; Deut. 23:18). Despite its solicitude for depressed classes, Proverbs lacks the great command of loving the stranger—in fact, there is no word at all about *gērīm*, that class which the Torah takes pains to protect. Biblical wisdom altogether lacks the national-religious basis which is the distinctive feature of Israelite morality.

The abundant material of cognate cultures at our disposal today shows beyond question that Israelite wisdom belongs to the common sapiential legacy of the ancient Near East. Hardly anything in biblical wisdom (apart from its monotheistic viewpoint) cannot be paralleled in the literatures of Egypt and Mesopotamia. Inasmuch as oriental wisdom was individual, universal, and humanistic, the presence of these features in Israelite wisdom must not be taken for signs of lateness, as if they were the end product of a long, internal development, showing the influence of classical prophecy, the national calamity, the Exile, and so forth. The very contrary is to be inferred: individual and universal morality was the earlier, and the societal-national morality the offspring of a later, inner Israelite development.

Indeed, biblical wisdom has preserved its ancient character intact far more successfully than have the materials of the Torah. Like its non-Israelite counterparts, biblical wisdom is not a prophetic revelation, but the teaching of reason. Nor is it addressed to the people as a whole or linked with the national destiny. Biblical, like Egyptian, wisdom displays slight interest in cultic matters—an indifference which has nothing to do with prophetic influence. The materials that have entered the Torah, on the other hand, have been fundamentally recast. Just as state law was transformed in the Torah into a national-religious law, so the ancient individual and universal morality was given a national framework. The people became collectively accountable for its observance, and national destiny is made to depend upon the fulfilment of this moral-legal Torah. Special prescriptions affecting Israel and related to its land develop. The whole is given a religious cast, the old framework of rulings by a king or sage being replaced by prophecy. The laws of the Torah are the word of God through his prophet. Legal-moral prescriptions are frequently interspersed with a cultic element.

Such a profound transformation did not take place in the wisdom literature. Hence, the absence of a distinctively Israelite element in wisdom morality. That the moral covenant of God with Israel has no echo in biblical wisdom indicates the antiquity of the style of that literature. To be sure it was so far inspirited with Israelite conceptions as to bear the imprint of the monotheistic idea. But throughout the biblical period, wisdom remained a self-contained realm, and until the time of Ben-Sira scarcely a single national, or cultic, recognizably Israelite element penetrated it. True to its ancient forms, it maintained its similarity to the wisdom of Egypt, Mesopotamia, and the "Easterners." It was in the Torah and prophets that the creative force of the Israelite idea found fullest expression. The individual, universal wisdom of the sapiential literature is thus the crystallization of an earlier style, whatever be the date of its final compilation.

THE IDEA OF MORALITY AS A NATIONAL COVENANT

Torah and prophecy, then, distinguish two moral realms: Israelite and universal; wisdom knows only the latter. Beside the special obligations laid on Israel by the covenant, Torah and prophecy recognize a primeval moral law obligatory upon all nations. This peculiar duality of moral realms, which is ignored by Israelite (as by oriental) wisdom, is further evidence that the conceptions of Torah and prophets are the later. Far from being primitive, it is a new, national version of the ancient, individual-universal morality. What new idea is embodied in this national version?

The conception of morality and justice as a branch of wisdom is part of the mythological world view of paganism (see above, pp. 37 f.). While paganism roots moral and natural law alike in the primordial realm and understands it as the task of human and divine wisdom to discover and teach it, Israelite religion conceives of all law as an expression of the will of God, his absolute command. Israel's God created not only the realm of the *is*, but the realm of the *ought* as well. Whether goodness is intrinsic and therefore willed by God, or whether it is so only because God willed it, is not discussed in the Bible. Goodness is simply a quality of God ("YHWH, a God merciful and gracious . . . and abounding in love and fidelity" [Exod. 34:6]). While the Bible does not recognize the subjection of God to any compulsion, it does depict him as observing the moral law. But this is not conceived of as an autonomous law, to which God is subject, but rather as itself a manifestation of God's will. What is has been created by the goodness of God. This goodness has been revealed to man, and man has been commanded to realize it in his own life. Man must "create" here on earth the world of moral goodness that ought to be. But he has the freedom to defy God's will, and this freedom is the root of sin and evil. The moral demand thus reaches its highest intensity as an expression of the will of God; at the same time, the moral responsibility of man reaches its full justification in the idea of human freedom.

The new idea is embodied in the concept found in the Torah and prophetic literatures that morality is a covenant between God and man. Since morality is now a statement of the divine will, all men ought to be obliged to observe it. Hence the biblical notion, expressed most clearly in P, that primeval man (Noah and his sons [Gen. 9:1-7]) had already received a moral law. But this was, after all, only a legend. A historical covenant with a real people was made with Israel alone; of Israel alone, then, could the new covenant morality be required.

Because of this historical reality, the new morality was incorporated in a national-moral law, given together with a new religious-cultic law. Because Israel alone knows YHWH, it especially is obliged to recognize and obey his will. The divine dictate is to be a kingdom of priests and a holy nation (Exod. 19:6); the reward is national well-being. In the account of the Sinaitic covenant, the moral-legal element is the very core. Exodus 18 relates the establishment of a judicial procedure for the people. In the Decalogue, the moral imperatives are the end and purpose of the initial declaration of God's sovereignty and the demand to be loyal to him. In the larger book of the covenant, too, the moral-legal element predominates. There is no need to look for later prophetic influence to account for this. The prophets' insistence that God's covenant had a moral-legal, rather than a cultic purpose (Amos 5:25; Isa. 5:7; Jer. 7:22; 34:13 f.), was not their own invention; it is implied as well in this early literature.

The covenant calls into being a new moral entity: the people Israel. The laws of the Torah are given to the whole nation at once; all as one are obliged to carry them out. The community to which God manifested hmself becomes corporately responsible, becomes, as it were, a new moral person. The individual's responsibility derives from his membership in the Israelite community; as such, the covenant binds him personally. On the other hand, the community as a whole is accountable for each of its members. The Torah addresses not the family, the tribe, the state, but the people of the covenant. The people are commanded to be just and righteous, must appoint judges, and extirpate evil out of their midst; must keep sanctity of the land from being profaned by bloodshed, sexual immorality, and violence. The "you" of the laws shifts imperceptibly from the individual to the people; at times, both are meant.

In the conception of the entire people receiving as a man the moral-legal covenant at the mouth of God, the unique essence of the Israelite idea of morality found its ultimate expression; it is the absolute command of God, revealed and imposed on mankind by him. Its presupposition is the freedom of the human will. Sin is not a tragic necessity; it is always the fruit of will, and its guilt is always deserved. True, there is suffering for the sin of another, but such suffering—let it be noted—is always attendant upon some deserved punishment; it has, moreover, a counterpart in God's dispensation of grace, with which it is combined (Exod. 20:6; 34:7). The important point is that the ultimate causes of sin and punishment lie always in the will and act of man. Because man can choose to do good, he is answerable for his evil-doing. Hence the unparalleled moral passion of the Bible. Pagan morality and biblical wisdom utter their sage and prudent counsels in deliberate, reasonable accents. The Torah and prophets, however, speak impassionedly of guilt and the consequences of wrongdoing and demand that Israel choose life. Punishment is not merely a danger or threat, but a necessary part of the moral order. This moral passion is evident in the admonitions of the Torah, in the stories concerning Nathan (II Sam. 12:1-12), Elijah (I Kings 21:17-24), and especially in the writings of the literary prophets. Not the individualistic morality of wisdom literature, but the national morality of Torah and prophets is the sphere of the sublime prophetic passion.

The intense passion of the national morality is the final demonstration that is not primitive, but rather the highest stage of a morality transcending the individual. It is no longer satisfied with individual responsibility; morality is not " a private matter." Society has a duty to educate each member and look after his deeds, not because there are crimes that produce a *miasma* and rouse the fury of the Erinyes against men, but because society as a whole is under a covenant obligation to eradicate evil from its midst and cause justice to prevail. Communal responsibility springs from the ardent desire to realize the demands of morality—a societal task which lies beyond the power of any individual to accomplish. This new moral conception, especially as it was expressed by the prophets, was beyond the scope of the ancient, sapiential morality that had never heard of a claim upon society as a whole.

THE DOCTRINE OF RETRIBUTION

It is a widespread opinion that the doctrine of individual retribution is a late development of Israelite religion. Ezekiel is thought to have been the first to transcend the "primitive, collective morality" of the old religion and discover the significance of the individual. Since Proverbs and Job deal with the individual and his fate, these works must necessarily come later than Ezekiel and be based on his revolutionary idea. This opinion is a compound of errors. The notion of individual retribution is to be reckoned among the ideas that Israel inherited from the ancient cultures. It is found, alongside the idea of collective punishment, in Egypt and Mesopotamia as well. That a man is requited for his own deeds is a theme of the earliest sources. He is not, however, conceived of as an isolated entity, but as inextricably bound up with his family, tribe, people, city, and land. And since his life extends in effect beyond his own person, the scope of his reward and punishment may also.

The first mention of retribution in the Bible is individual. Adam and Eve, who were, as we have seen, created not as ancestors of the race, but as individuals, are warned they will die if they sin. (Indeed Adam is warned of death even before Eve is created.) Strictly individual requital is meted out to Noah and his generation. The individual members of Lot's family are requited variously in accord with their deserts: some are saved; Lot's wife is turned to salt for violating the angel's command; Lot's scoffing sons-in-law are destroyed with Sodom and Gomorrah. The Egyptian midwives who saved the Hebrew children (Exod. 1:20 f.), the generation of the wilderness, Caleb and Joshua (Num. 14:20–34), Zelophehad (see Num. 27:3), and David (in the opinion of Shimei, II Sam. 16:8) are all rewarded or punished individually—to mention but a few instances. When all of a group are involved in sin all are punished, as, e.g., the generation of the Flood and the Sodomites. Various laws of the Torah, though set in a national framework, reflect the concept of individual requital (e.g., the individual sin and guilt offerings, laws of vows and dedications, nearly all of the moral injunctions).

However, there is also a belief in collective retribution and in collective responsibility. The stories about the ancestors of the race and of Israel assume collective retribution. The punishments of Adam, Eve, and the serpent were individual, as were the rewards of the tribe of Levi and of Phinehas, yet their effects endured throughout the generations. Especially close are the bonds of collective responsibility between members of the family. Children and wives are embraced by the retribution meted out to fathers and husbands. Although the custom of punishing children for fathers was eventually abolished (Deut. 24:16; II Kings 14:6), in Israel, as elsewhere in antiquity, this custom seems to have been practiced (Josh. 7:24 ff.; Judg. 21:10; I Sam. 22:19; II Sam. 21:6 ff.; cf. Code of Hammurabi, par. 210).[12] The collective responsibility of the family before God remained

[12] Just when the law of Deuteronomy 24:16 came into being is impossible to say. There is no question but that divergent laws and customs might exist concurrently. Typical is Herodotus' story (ix. 88) of how the Thebans delivered to Pausanias the sons of Attaginus, a pro-Persian who fled after the Greek victory. Pausanias freed them, saying that sons were not guilty because of their father's Persian leanings. Thus contradictory concepts existed side by side.

fundamental. God visits the iniquity of parents on children and keeps mercy to the thousandth generation (Exod. 20:5 f.; 34:7; Deut. 5:9 f.; 7:9). Amos prophesies to Amaziah not only that his children would die, but that even his wife would play the harlot in the city (7:17).

The scope of collective responsibility before God might extend even to a large group, a city or kingdom. A king's sin is particularly apt to bring calamity on his entire realm (Gen. 20:9; 26:10; etc.). Many of the calamities that befell Israel are explained as caused by royal sin. Saul's sin occasioned the subjection of Israel to the Philistines (I Sam. 28:19); David's sin with Bathsheba brought on the rebellion of Absalom; Solomon's sins were the cause of the division of the kingdom.

The people of Israel constitute a special sphere of collective responsibility. The basis of this responsibility is not natural, like that of the family or tribe, but artificial; it is the covenant that God made with the people and which was made in terms of eternal obligations (Deut. 29:13 f.). There is, therefore, a common responsibility not only among all members of a given generation, but among all generations as well. This idea underlies the whole historical outlook of the Bible. Every sin committed by part of the people is counted against Israel and serves to explain the fate of the entire people.

Yet there is the feeling that the most fitting and just retribution is that which befalls the sinner himself; the more restricted the scope of collective responsibility, the more just the deserts meted out. Complaints are lodged against collective responsibility: "Will one man sin, and you be angry with the whole congregation?" (Num. 16:22); "Lo, I have sinned and I have acted wickedly, but these sheep, what have they done?" (II Sam. 24:17). In the stories about Jonathan (I Sam. 14:24 ff.) and Jonah, only the strictest individual retribution is regarded as just; yet even in Jonah, one finds the notion that the doom of one man is liable to envelop so random an assemblage as the travelers on a ship.

Biblical thought attempted to account for the workings of divine justice by setting up various circles of retribution. Each man's destiny is bound up with that of his fellow; the course of his life may be influenced by distant events. The deeds of his father, his relatives, his countrymen, and his king can all affect him. Other auxiliary assumptions were also at hand to explain God's ways. God afflicts men in order to test their loyalty to him; this was the case of Abraham, of Job, of the people Israel in the wilderness and in the land. Evil may go unpunished because God is patient with the wicked, or because he changed his mind about destroying them (Exod. 34:6; Jonah 4:2). At times, he waits until the measure of sin has been filled before inflicting punishment (Gen. 15:16). One way or another, biblical man justified his belief in a morally ordered world. Because he knew of no judgment after death, only this world could serve as the scene of divine justice. If the righteous suffer and the wicked prosper, he prays to God and entreats him to manifest his judgment.

Yet the contrast between reality and the religious-moral ideal could not be disregarded, and ever disturbs biblical thought. The Bible as a whole may well be called the book of the justification of God. To biblical writers, the fate of the righteous and the wicked is a distressing and perplexing problem. They question the disaccord between what befalls men and the religious-moral demand. But more often than ask, they answer. They always justify God; they always feel the need to justify him.

Theodicy is confronted with three basic issues. The first, the origin of primary, natural evils—death, sickness, pain, and toil—is dealt with in the legends of Genesis. Second is the issue of religious evil—idolatry and its corollary, the weakness of Israel among the heathen empires. Third is the issue of moral evil. This last has two aspects: social evil—the prevalence of violence and wickedness among men, the crushing of the righteous by the wicked; and second, divine evil—the sufferings of the righteous at the hand of God. How can faith in a beneficent, just providence be maintained in the teeth of these phenomena?

Complaints about the evil in the world, especially about moral evil, are voiced by pagan thinkers as well. Job and Ecclesiastes have their counterparts in the literatures of Egypt and Babylonia. Here, too, men vacillate between faith in a just providence and doubt and despair, to the point even of denying a moral order. Only in Israel, however, does the question touch the very essence of God. The existence of evil is not in itself a problem to paganism, which posits primordial evil principles. The presence of evil does not, therefore, condemn the good gods. Indeed, evil may also overwhelm the good gods themselves. They too are subject to its onslaught, and combat it like men; they fall into sin and are punished. The pagan, faced by undeserved suffering, can suppose that the gods envy man and, therefore, injure him; or out of caprice, they destroy him, or stand aside, indifferent to his fate. Pagan man complains, becomes embittered, and reviles the gods, or resigns himself in despair to their decrees. It was otherwise in Israel. On the one hand, there was no evil principle; good and evil came from YHWH. On the other hand, Israelite religion tolerated no fault or blame in God. He was altogether good and just. When harsh reality challenged the conventional view of divine justice, concern for the honor of God violently disturbed the devout. They could not break out in insults or surrender to despair; they could only complain and question and go on seeking an answer. At bottom, it is not so much the human side of undeserved suffering that agitates the Bible as the threat it poses to faith in God's justice. Hence the tremendous pathos of Israelite theodicy that has no pagan parallel.

The foundation of Israelite theodicy is the idea of human sin and rebellion. In the absence of divine sin, it is necessarily human sin which is forever at the root of all evil. In the stories of Genesis the sins of primeval man accounted once for all for the existence of natural and religious evil. But the problem of the continual national-religious distress and the problem of ever present moral evil had constantly to be wrestled with anew at every fresh encounter.

The destiny of Israel among the nations was a perplexing enigma. Did not Israel's material failure before the eyes of the pagans discredit its religion as well? The problem is ancient. It is given naïve, direct expression in the prayers of Moses in Exodus 32:11 ff., Numbers 14:13 f., and Deuteronomy 9:28 f.: Israel's fate and the fate of YHWH's name in the world are inseparable. Several psalms, stemming no doubt from some period of war and suffering in pre-exilic times, give voice to the same concern. The enemy has humiliated Israel; YHWH's name has been desecrated. The psalmist fears for the honor of God; for the sake of his name, he begs for deliverance (Pss. 44:16 f.; 74:10, 18, 22 f.; 79:10 ff.; 115:1 ff.). This enigma gave birth to the legend of the national sin of Israel, whereby God was invariably justified. This sin is more a requirement of biblical theodicy than a historical reality (see above, pp. 134 f.).

In the individual moral sphere, it was equally impossible to escape the gap between what was and what should have been. The prosperity and success of the wicked flew in the face of belief in divine justice. Like their counterparts in Egypt and Babylonia, the poets and sages of Israel decry this wrong, but their plaint has a peculiar religious motive—concern for the good name of God. The prospering villain boasts, "There is no God," and denies divine providence and justice (Pss. 10:3 ff.; 12:5; 14:1 ff.; 36:2; 73:4 ff.). At times, even the faithful man falters; envy of the wicked overcomes him; what sense is there in his righteousness and integrity (Ps. 73:2 ff.)? Yet, in the end, nothing can shake the faith in divine justice. Even the prophet who complains of the tranquillity of the wicked knows that God is "right" (Jer. 12:1 f.). Biblical man has no refuge other than faith (Pss. 37:1 ff.; 73:17 ff.; cf. Hab. 1:2—2:4).

JOB

Two elements have combined to form the book of Job: the prose framework (1–2; 42:7–17) and the poetic cycle of dialogues (3—42:6). The legend of Job's trial at the instance of Satan is surely early. The story belongs, with the stories of the Flood, Sodom and Gomorrah, and Jonah, to the ancient moralistic literature of Israel. Job is a righteous non-Israelite, a hero of popular legend mentioned together with Noah and Daniel in Ezekiel 14:14 ff. The wisdom author of the book of Job utilized this early story for his own purposes. Hence, there are two elements in the book, one legendary, the other sapiential.

The Job of the legend is a righteous man, not a sage. The problem of the legend is to what extent a righteous man can withstand trials. It also teaches that suffering may aim only at testing men. Job's successful resistance is put forward as a model for all.

Passing to the poetic dialogue, we enter the realm of wisdom. Job, like his companions, is now a sage who speaks in parables and figures. The problem of the dialogue is a speculative one—how to interpret the fate of Job in the light of the wisdom dogma of just retribution. The question involves more than the suffering of the righteous; it is whether there is at all a moral order in the world. In the course of the dialogue Job eventually denies the existence of the moral order. Apparently, then, there is a contradiction between the legend and the wisdom chapters. The Job of the legend stands the test and does not sin with his lips, whereas in the dialogue, he accuses God. However, if we bear in mind the two levels on which the book moves, the conflict disappears.

The issue of the legend is the character of Job, not his world view. Satan claims that Job will "bless" God—that is, come to hate him, and no longer be "blameless and upright and God-fearing." And, in fact, his wife does urge him to "bless God and die," but Job withstands all trials and remains righteous. He does no less in the dialogue. To the very end, he speaks as a profoundly moral and religious man. He is not cynical; he does not curse God; nor does he draw impious conclusions from his accusations. Throughout the argument he remains God-fearing and good. Even in despair, he prays, exalts God, yearns for him and puts his trust in him. He even threatens his companions with divine judgment for having spoken falsely about God (13:7 ff.). A dual personality thus appears, Job the righteous man of the legend, and his twin, Job the sage. The sage, notwithstanding his blameless heart, cannot escape the conclusions to which he is led by his mind. The tragic conflict between heart and mind climaxes the troubles that have come upon him. With wonderful subtlety the poet lets Job the sage finish the work of Satan and deal Job the righteous man the final blow: to deprive him of his dearest treasure, faith in divine justice. This lost, all is lost. Yet even out of the depths of his anguish, what does he cry?

> "By the life of God, who has deprived me of justice,
> And Shaddai, who has embittered my life!
> As long as my breath is in me,
> And the spirit of God is in my nostrils,
> My lips shall not speak wrong, nor my tongue utter deceit.
> Far be it from me to justify you,
> Till I die I shall not deny my innocence,
> I hold to my righteousness and will not let it go!" [27:2 ff.]

His final word is this great oath. Though his world has collapsed, he clings to the one value that is left him, his righteousness. That has become an intrinsic value, without hope of any reward. Thus the poet raises Job to the bleak summit of righteousness bereft of hope, bereft of faith in divine justice.

Job is portrayed as righteous out of love of God alone. He challenges God only because he considers it a moral duty to speak the truth before him. To the end, then, Job the sage, like Job the righteous man, remains firm in his moral character. His friends, however, follow an easier path. Armed with the conventional clichés of wisdom, they acquit themselves with these empty phrases. That is why God ultimately rebukes Eliphaz and his friends for not having spoken rightly concerning Job.

Only gradually does Job arrive at the repudiation of the moral order. All his arguments take their departure from the primary conviction of his righteousness. He knows with an immediate, unshakable knowledge that he is innocent; that is his Archimedean point. He has feared God and loved goodness all his life, and continues to do so now. He does not deny that he has sinned, but what man born of woman is blameless? His sins are failures and weaknesses; they are not enough to make him "wicked." He argues repeatedly the injustice of an almighty God holding to account so weak a creature as man for petty moral failures.

Step by step, he passes from his own case to generalized observations. In his second response to Zophar (chap. 21) and his third response to Eliphaz (chap. 24), he asserts that not only does God fail to distinguish the righteous from the wicked, he fails wholly to requite men. The wicked man prospers and goes unpunished. The idea that righteousness is rewarded in the end is wrong; the wicked crushes the good man, despoiling and killing him with impunity. Job has reached the climax of his denials. Distress has opened his eyes to see what he was blind to before: the absence of a moral providence in the world. This is the shattering conclusion to which he is led.

Job's companions have but one argument: wisdom teaches the infallible truth that there is just retribution. Job must have sinned to deserve his misery; if he does not know what his sin is, God in his wisdom does. To the companions, everything is quite plain: Job has suffered, *ergo* he is wicked. This they repeat with endless variations from beginning to end. Only in Job's responses can a development in the argument be discerned.

At the end of the discussion between Job and his friends, a new speaker, Elihu, comes upon the scene. Elihu is not mentioned in the narrative, because he was not a figure of the ancient legend. But the Elihu chapters are nonetheless an organic part of the book. They are a transition from the final charges of Job to the manifestation of YHWH. Elihu is an additional figure, apparently a reflex of the poet himself. He begins with the last point reached by Job, the repudiation of a moral providence. He does not argue, like the three companions, that Job's suffering was caused by his wickedness. For him the issue is not the personal one of Job, but the terrible conclusion that Job has reached.

Through the many obscurities in the text, it is possible to discern in Elihu's chapters a certain direction, and even a certain form. Elihu argues for divine providence from evidence that even Job must allow. He calls on the testimony of events that befall nations and men, and on the evidence of the ordering of the world. Three examples of the former and three of the latter are adduced alternatively. Of happenings to men, he adduces: (1) the providential promptings to repentance, in the form of dreams or sickness, which rescue man from divine doom (33:14–33); (2) the sudden collapse of tyrants which can be ascribed only to God, and explained only as punishment for their tyranny (34:16–37); (3) a continuation of (1) mentioning other sufferings by which God rouses man to repent of sin and be saved from punishment (36:2–21). From the order of the world, he adduces: (1) First, God's perpetual maintenance of the cosmos; can God, who in his kindness maintains the world perpetually, be indifferent to it? Creation itself speaks against the denial of providence (34:13–15). (2) Next Elihu points to the moral consciousness of man as evidence of God's love; through this alone is he elevated above the brutes. Can a God who implanted in man moral consciousness be himself indifferent to moral demands? Job's very sense of moral outrage is an outcome of God's goodness (chap. 35). (3) The last of Elihu's arguments is chapter 28 (to which 36:22–37:24 are an introduction), an argument from man's wisdom and fear of God. Man's wisdom "searches out to-the farthest bound"; "his eye sees every precious thing." This too testifies to God's grace and his concern for man. Yet God has given man only human wisdom, and if that is not enough to penetrate even the secrets of nature, how much less ought it to pass judgment on the gracious God. For although God has kept divine, cosmic wisdom from man, he has endowed him, in its stead, with a unique and precious gift, the fear of God. This again is a sign of grace and a token of divine solicitude. Thus human wisdom leads us to the final conclusion: the recognition of God's graciousness and of man's nothingness in the face of God's wisdom. Therefore it subjects itself to the fear of God, and its expression—the moral law—as the end of all wisdom and understanding. Wisdom and the fear of God are the supreme evidences of the divine providence and concern that Job has too rashly denied.

There follows immediately the final, conclusive evidence of God's graciousness to man: YHWH speaks to Job out of the whirlwind. In a series of vivid pictures the thought that Elihu has already stressed is repeated. How can man presume to judge God if the world, which is merely his handiwork, is filled with mysteries he cannot fathom. Once again, Job's special case is not dealt with. The foundations of the moral universe are at stake; God's providence has been impugned. In view of this, the special plight of Job falls into the background.

Is the whole answer, then, that God's ways are hidden from man? Surely the poet desired to say more. It is noteworthy that in these final chapters wisdom and legendary elements commingle. God's words are sapiential, but their framework is a legend: God speaks in a daytime theophany out of the storm. Is this not the embodiment in legend of wisdom's maxim, "He has said to man: Behold, the fear of the Lord, that is wisdom ..."? In the theophany and the discourse with man, God's ultimate grace shines forth, the grace of revelation. This is his supreme favor. Not what he said, but his very manifestation is the last, decisive argument. "I had heard of thee only a report, but now my eye beholds thee, therefore I despise myself and repent in dust and ashes." These are Job's last words (42:5 f.). If the almighty God has consented to reveal himself to mortal man and instruct him, what further room is there to question his providence and his concern for the world?

God's answer is the beginning of Job's restoration. In itself, it restored his last and severest loss, his faith in God's providence. God's reproach of the companions next restores his honor and good repute which were lost consequent to his afflictions. Lastly, God restores his material possessions which were the first to perish.

The answer of the book of Job is, then, religious to its very core. It comes from the realm of revelation, not wisdom; this is the distinctive Israelite feature of the book. A tragic conflict broke out between the righteous man and the sage in Job. The righteous man believed in the existence of God; the sage does not argue with this belief, but seeks to separate God from the idea of morality and justice. God exists but his rule is not moral. This separation is rejected by the book; the idea of God necessarily includes the moral idea. The Israelite sage contends with God, but in the end, he, like the righteous man, "lives by his faith."

THE CONQUEST OF PAGAN WISDOM—While pagan wisdom never denied the existence of the gods, it did come to a repudiation of their moral character (see, e.g., the Babylonian "Dialogue of Master and Servant"). Thus it reverts to its mythological matrix: the gods are symbols of natural forces to which morality is not essential. To the faith of Israel, belief in a god without a moral nature, who "follows [the sacrificer] like a dog" (*ibid.*, viii) is the very essence of paganism. Job combats this image of the deity.

Job's repudiation of providence cannot be the last word of the book. Leaving the problem of retribution unsolved, its final theme is the wonder of creation that reflects the glory of God. Here (and in chap. 28) heathen pride of wisdom is rejected. Pagan wisdom asks and answers; it presumes itself capable of solving the problem and proceeds to pass a negative verdict concerning the gods. Israelite wisdom asks but does not answer; it knows that man is dust and ashes.

Although the book of Job cannot be precisely dated because of its non-historical character, nothing stands in the way of considering it a creation of the pre-exilic age. The antiquity of the prose framework is vouched for by its highly naïve images of God and its notion of revelation in the full light of day (such a revelation is last spoken of in I Kings 19). What we can still comprehend of the poetry of the book is classical Hebrew of the best. Contacts with Ugaritic, Aramaic, and Arabic are most naturally understood as arising out of the antique literary dialect that the author employed; it is this that makes the reading of the book so difficult. The author may also have known and been influenced by the wisdom of the "Easterners." However that may be, the book was composed in the golden age of Israelite creativity, the age before the Exile.

IDEAL AND REALITY

The moral ideal of early Israel makes piety and God-fearing the basis of a life of righteousness, truth, love and compassion, humility and toil. Happiness and the pleasures of life are valued; fertility—human, animal, and agricultural—is the supreme blessing of God; to rejoice is a divine command. The flesh becomes evil only when it leads man astray and makes him forget God.

The honest man toils; he is a herdsman or a farmer. The morality of the Bible is that of a folk living off its soil. Charity takes the form of produce of farm and orchard; money is never mentioned. "The woman of valor" (Prov. 31) raises her own crops, buys a field, and plants a vineyard. Poverty, mendicancy, and suffering are not considered moral or religious virtues. The sage prays: "Give me neither proverty nor riches ... lest I be full and deny, and say, 'Who is the Lord?' Or lest I be poor, and steal, and profane the name of my God" (Prov. 30:8 f.). Integrity and closeness to God are absolute values to be desired even more than prosperity (Pss. 37:16; 73:25 ff.; etc.). To judge from the Bible, commerce played a negligible role in the life of the people. It is a foreign characteristic (Canaanite = merchant), though it is not considered sinful.[13]

The ancient narrative sources (the Torah and histories) count one religious-cultic sin against the people: straying after foreign gods. Violations of other religious laws are not mentioned there, nor in the psalms, and only incidentally in the latter prophets. Sabbath and festival, sacrifice and sacred dues, matters of purity and impurity were all part of popular life and popular piety. Sins were committed, of course, intentionally and unintentionally, but their remedy was also at hand in rites of propitiation and atonement. For this, one turned to the priest and his torah. Certain of the moral prescriptions were supported by antique taboos. The early narratives illustrate how great was the fear of violating oaths (e.g., the story of Jephthah). Sexual taboos also doubtless inhibited grosser crimes

[13] There is no nomadic ideal in the Bible. Israel was never a genuine desert people; the desert was but an episode in its history. It originated in culture lands, and never aspired to nomadic life; at the Exodus it is promised "a land flowing with milk and honey." The Rechabites were a peculiar order; no prophet or any other biblical writer takes them as ideal types of the people as a whole. In all eschatological visions the land is central. The ultimate ideal is a people farming its land and enjoying its fruits in peace (Mic. 4:4). Once upon a time, Israel was "a fugitive Aramaean," wandering in the culture lands without national territory; thanks to God they were delivered from that wretched status (Deut. 26:5 ff.). The "terrible desert" of the Wandering was remembered, despite its hallowed religious associations, for the suffering and privation that were endured there. Hosea 2:4 ff. warns of a return to the desert as part of Israel's punishment for idolatry. God will withhold the land's wealth, will put an end to Israel's festivals and Sabbaths, and take the people out again into the desert there to purge them. Once purged, Israel will return and resettle the land. John W. Flight, *JBL* XLII (1923), 158–226 (with detailed bibliography) sets forth the argument for the "nomadic ideal." As elements of it he includes opposition to city life, civilization and culture, sacrifices and cult, temple and idolatry, aspiration to the simple life, longing for a golden age, etc. All these can, indeed, be found in the Bible. Only evidence for the nomadic ideal in the real sense of the word is missing.

under this head. The violation and murder of a concubine touched off a bloody intertribal battle (Judg. 19–20). David's adultery with Bathsheba stirred up a storm. Later, the morals of the aristocracy degenerated, but the common folk seem to have preserved their old ways.

In the relationships between man and man, however, the rift between ideal and reality was very great. One need only read what is narrated of Abimelech, Saul, David, Absalom, Joab, or Solomon to see how far the admonition "You shall not bear a grudge nor take vengeance" was from being a reality. Before the reign of Amaziah, the law "Fathers shall not be put to death for sons, nor sons for fathers" appears to have had no legal force (II Kings 14:5 f.). The literature of the Torah takes its departure from the life of the people, but it contains a large idealistic and utopian element. Though it championed the weak and poor, it was not the law of the land; it was merely an edifying literature to which were joined some legal elements. The basic social laws of the Torah were essentially no more than moral sanctions and exhortations, as is clear from the fact that no penalties are prescribed for their violation. The Torah provided no real legal recourse for the oppressed.

Moreover, the fact that the social background of the Torah was the early tribal and patriarchal polity tended to render it obsolete as the centuries passed. It says next to nothing of the monarchy; it wholly ignores the royal officialdom; its concept of land ownership is based exclusively on tribes and clans. No wonder, then, that actual practice was quite at variance with its idea. The Torah forbids taking usury or the clothes of a poor man in pledge. Yet, in the time of the monarchy, a creditor could take the children of his debtor as slaves! (II Kings 4:1). The Torah provides for a sabbatical emancipation of Hebrew slaves; but when, in the time of Zedekiah, this law was (obviously as a novelty) put into effect by a special covenant, the slaves were soon re-enslaved by their owners (Jer. 34:8 ff.). Even the community of the Restoration took debtors' children into slavery (Neh. 5:1 ff.). There were many varieties of exploitation and expropriation, persecution and oppression. This provided the basis of the division between "righteous" and "wicked" in ancient Israel; in the Torah, prophets, wisdom and psalm literature the distinction is a socio-moral, not a religious one.

In the twilight of the northern kingdom, the social cleavage and the evils that it entailed grew more acute. Masses of people became impoverished, and the rift between ideal and reality became critical. Out of this rift, classical prophecy was born.

CHAPTER X

The Literature and the Age

THE LEGACY OF THE EARLY RELIGION

In the middle of the eighth century B.C., the creative force of Israelite religion gave birth to literary or classical prophecy.

From its socio-historical side, classical prophecy is rooted in the early popular religion. Like their predecessors, the classical prophets are moved by an individual call; they, too, are poets as well as reprovers and visionaries. Also like the popular prophets, they have a purely mantic element in their work. They do not only interpret the grand design of history; they also predict future events, petty and great, for individuals as well as for the nation. Indeed, it was belief in the mantic power of classical prophecy that ultimately determined its place in biblical literature. Ages of men have searched the writings of the prophets for clues to their own future and answers to the riddles of their time. Furthermore, the classical prophets were wonder-workers; even Isaiah is depicted as working wonders and miraculous cures (Isa. 7:11; 38:7, 21; II Kings 20:7 ff.).

Yet classical prophecy cannot be considered essentially mantic. Not one of the classical prophets is said to have prophesied for pay. Amos denies that he is a prophet by profession (7:14); Micah disdains prophets who make a living by prophecy (2:6 f., 11). The classical prophets are exclusively apostles of God; even the mantic utterances that are ascribed to them are related to their mission. With the literary prophets, apostolic prophecy reverts to its pristine level, to the level of Moses and Joshua, when, too, it was not for hire. The classical prophets come of their own accord to a people who have not sought them. They regard themselves as links in the chain of divine messengers that began with Moses. They believe in the prophetic election of the people of Israel. Each prophet actualizes anew this idea of prophetic election and confirms the popular faith that God reveals his word to Israel through his apostles. If, despite the lack of an established succession, Israelite prophecy is consistent ideologically, it is by virtue of this constant faith in the presence of the prophetic spirit in Israel which periodically raises up new spokesmen for YHWH. Prophecy is a personal grace, but through it the divine favor toward the whole nation comes into expression. All Israelite prophecy was nurtured upon this historic, national faith.

Classical prophecy sprang from the soil of Israel's popular monotheism. To be sure, it went so far beyond the religion of the people that a rift appears between prophets and people. Popular-priestly religion goes its own way during this age, unaffected by the ideas of literary prophecy. Tension between the two becomes so great that at times the prophets suffer violence at the hands of the people and the priests. Yet classical prophecy was rooted in and grew out of the early religion. It does not so much repudiate the popular religion as rise above it.

From the popular religion classical prophecy received its idea of the one God, sole creator and judge of the world; a non-mythological, non-magical deity, a supreme will, unfettered by fate or compulsion. Classical prophecy does not recognize or combat mythological or magical beliefs. It arose among a people out of which genuine paganism had been uprooted centuries before.

The historical and moral presuppositions of the prophets are those of the popular religion. The one God made his name known only in Israel. Israel and its land are holy; the pagan lands are "impure." Israel alone is judged for idolatry; the nations are held accountable only for gross moral sins. And though the prophets speak about the nations, their mission is only to Israel. Classical prophecy shares with the popular religion the belief that Israel is subject to the moral and religious obligations of a covenant made with YHWH in ancient times. It adopted essential features of the eschatology of the popular religion, especially the later form of eschatology that arose during the wars with Aram.

How closely bound classical prophecy is to the popular religion is manifest from their having in common the name of YHWH. The new prophets do not announce a new God or teach a new concept of the nature of deity. They bewail the lack of "knowledge of God" in the land, but the God they speak of is the God of the people, and the bases of their demand are the popular legends telling of his wonders in Israel.

The classical prophets create a new literature, but they are steeped in the literature of the past. At times, one must ascend to ancient Canaanite poetry for the antecedents of their literary allusions. Motifs of the narrative traditions of the Torah are widely utilized, and Israelite legal literature is also drawn upon. Jeremiah is strongly influenced by Deuteronomy, Ezekiel, by the Priestly Code. The prophets are familiar with psalmody and compose in its style. Their creations also evidence an acquaintance with the themes and forms of wisdom literature. The poetic expression of their prophecy followed traditional models. Ancient mantic prophecy was rhythmic and poetic, this being regarded as the work of the divine spirit that rested on the prophet as an adjunct to the revelation of the divine word (see above, pp. 97 f.). Early prophecies (e.g., the blessings of Jacob and Moses) had already been embodied in literary form and were so transmitted from generation to generation. There was also literature ascribed to Moses and Joshua which contained prophecies and warnings. This traditional material was known by the prophets and served them as a pattern for their own creations.

In the work of the literary prophets, Israelite religion reached a new height. They were the first to conceive of the doctrine of the primacy of morality, the idea that the essence of God's demand of man is not cultic, but moral. This doctrine regards human goodness as the realization of the will of God on earth. It negates the intrinsic, transcendent value of the cult. The first to express this idea was Amos; he was followed by Isaiah, Micah, Jeremiah, the Second Isaiah, and Zechariah; Hosea, too, expresses it in his own way. But even those prophets who did not utter the doctrine explicitly are affected by it. In the course of time, it came to be a fundamental idea of Israelite religion.

This doctrine provided a new basis for prophetic reproof. Morality was regarded by the prophets as decisive for the destiny of Israel. The older view was that the fate of the people was determined by their religious practice; idolatry entailed national punishment. But the prophets conceived the idea that moral corruption too was a national historical factor. Moreover, they have a new evaluation of social morality: not merely bloodshed and sexual crimes, but injustice, taking bribes, and oppressing the poor and defenseless are crucial for the fate of the nation. The moral factor is taken account of in eschatology as well.

This moral-religious view results in a re-evaluation of state, society, and culture. Not all, but some of the prophets repudiate the power state, military culture, and the trust in fortifications and armies. A kingdom founded on righteousness is their political ideal. At the same time they repudiate the luxury of palaces and pleasure-seeking. Their ideal is not "nomadic," and does not involve a return to the desert, but a life of simple, humble farmers, a life of peaceful labor and trust in God. The realization of this religious-political idea is envisioned for the end of time.

The prophets transformed the vision of the end of days. To the popular religion, the "day of YHWH" was to be a day of victory over enemies. The prophets gave it a new character as a day of judgment in which God would call Israel to account as well as Israel's enemies. Israel would be judged not only for idolatry, but for moral corruption. The psalmists' call for judgment upon the wicked became for the prophets an eschatological vision, unfolding against a background of tremendous historical events. A "remnant" of loyal and righteous men would be saved out of Israel; then the eschatological kingdom of God would be established.

Classical prophecy is the first to conceive of the disappearance of idolatry at the end of days. This idea is not found in all the prophets, but it looms large in the literature as a whole. The ancient idea of a primeval monotheism was complemented by the prophetic idea that monotheism would again prevail among all men at the end of time. Linked with this is the vision of the future reign of peace.

Thus the concepts of Israel and its land, of Jerusalem, the temple, and the dynasty of David became religious symbols of supranational significance. When first conceived, these were national expressions of an essentially universal idea. The universal presuppositions of the early religion stand out clearly in the legends of primeval monotheism at the beginning of time. Yet, since knowledge of God was believed to have later become the property of Israel alone, the national limitations of the early religion were basic and real. The prophets, while accepting and employing national symbols (they are not "cosmopolitan" or "citizens of the world"), gave them universal significance by their new eschatological vision of the return of the nations to God. Israel, the elect of God, is the arena of God's self-disclosure to all the nations. The national symbols became supranational, eternal, beyond the power of any political collapse to destroy. Classical prophecy created the idea of universal history in its conception of the kingdom of God as ultimately destined to extend over all mankind.

Why did classical prophecy come into being both in Israel and in Judah at this time? The primary sources of human creativity are beyond our ken and power to explain. An Amos or an Isaiah is not entirely accounted for by historical or social circumstances. Nonetheless, it is true that classical prophecy was born in a certain historical situation, that it addresses itself to a given people, and that it has roots in the culture and history of Israel. To that extent, then, one may speak of social and historical conditions which shaped its character.

The distinctive feature of classical prophecy is its vehement denunciation of social corruption. Amos, Isaiah, Micah, and Hosea accuse the wealthy and aristocratic class of dispossessing and impoverishing the masses, of living wantonly and luxuriously. This sort of societal decay was something new in Israel. It not only introduced a sharp cleavage into Israelite society, but harbored a threat to national existence as well. Early Israel was founded on an agricultural economy, land being owned by families and tribes. With the coming of the monarchy and the consequent rise of a royal bureaucracy, a great change took place. The king's right of confiscation became a new means of acquiring property alongside of the ancient method of inheritance. The new non-patriarchal class of royal officials began to play a crucial role, it seems, in the period of the Aramaean wars.

These wars lasted over a hundred years, beginning in the time of Ahab (875–854) and coming to an end in the reign of Jeroboam II (784–744). Like all wars of attrition, they impoverished the bulk of the nation, while giving the opportunity to a few elements of the ruling class to amass great wealth. These war profiteers bought out the lands and the houses of the poor masses. Many persons were forced into slavery; the rest became a miserable proletariat. The famine, drought, plague, war, and captivity that harassed Israel in those days (Amos 4:6 ff.) were thus capped by the gravest evil—social dissolution. This condition obtained both in Judah and in Israel.

Religiously sensitive men looked on in dismay. Was this the people whom YHWH had brought out of Egypt, had given a land and laws of justice and righteousness? Soon, it seemed, the wealthy classes would submerge the land of YHWH in wanton self-indulgence. After the victories of Jeroboam II over Aram, a frenzy of celebration diverted attention from the moral and social decay. No one appeared to realize that such living and such celebrations in YHWH's temples were a violation of the covenant and a profanation of the divine name. Indignation reached white heat among prophetic circles; the rift between the ideal and reality had reached its critical point. The new prophecy of the classical prophets welled up out of this crisis.

THE CHRONOLOGICAL LIMITS OF CLASSICAL PROPHECY

Biblical tradition ascribes the whole of classical prophecy to fourteen prophets[1] from Amos to Malachi, who produced books called by their name. Criticism makes it clear that this tradition cannot be maintained

---

[1] Not counting Jonah, a book of prophetic narrative rather than prophecy.

in detail. Isaiah 40–66 are not from the hand of Isaiah son of Amoz, nor do chapters 9–14 of the book of Zechariah belong with chapters 1–8. The basic question, however, is whether the chronological limits set to classical prophecy by tradition, especially the lower limit—in the middle of the fifth century—are correct. Current opinion maintains that they are not. Prophecies dating from the end of the Persian period (fourth century), and even some from the Greek period (third and second centuries), are alleged to have made their way into the corpus of the literary prophets. Many critics assign Joel, Habakkuk, Zechariah 9–14 and Isaiah 24–27, together with various other passages, to a time later than Malachi. These prophecies are classed with the later apocalyptic literature, with which they have in common vague historical backgrounds and fantastic symbolic visions. No sharp break, then, divides classical prophecy from apocalypse. The periods of the two literatures blend into each other—prophetic literature not having been crystallized before the fourth century, and thus having absorbed much of the creations of later times.

This view, however, is groundless. The distinctive feature of apocalypse is its anxious inquiry and research into the secrets of the cosmos. The literary prophet, on the other hand, is first of all a messenger whose task is not to reveal hidden things, but to command or reprove in the name of God. To be sure, he is privy to "the secrets" of God; he knows and reveals the future; he sees visions and symbols and interprets them. Yet all these are subordinate to his message and his mission. In apocalypse, the chief task of the visionary is to reveal hidden things. He possesses occult knowledge by which he searches out the predictions of ancient prophecies, investigates history and seeks to disclose its secret to men. Disclosure of secrets is the very essence of apocalypse as is shown by its name, the meaning of which is "revelation."

Apocalyptic visions are of two types: cosmic and historical. The visionary may be transported to unearthly realms and behold the mysteries of the cosmos—the divine palace, paradise and hell, etc.; or he may be shown the sequence of generations and ages to the end of time. In both types, a tour in time or space is the dominant feature. The apocalypse is a moving picture of places or ages, a succession of scenes. This perspective vision, as we may call it, is the very heart of apocalyptic. Through it the motivating purpose of the visionary to disclose the secrets of time or space to the reader is achieved. In perspective visions, then, the basic nature of apocalyptic finds expression.

Now to be sure, classical prophets see visions of God and his entourage, but never as ends in themselves; such visions are always either an introduction or an adjunct to a message. Hence, there is never a succession of scenes; the vision stands alone, and is followed by the word which the prophet is charged to convey to men. Even the description of the divine vehicle in Ezekiel 1 and 10 is not a revelation for its own sake, but serves only to preface the commissioning of the prophet by God. It is true that Ezekiel is taken on tours in space. He is the first prophet to move in spirit from place to place with God or a "man" as guide; to that extent, then, Ezekiel may justly be regarded as the father of the apocalyptic tour in space (though Ezekiel, too, is not taken into extra-mundane realms).

Nowhere in the entire corpus of classical prophecy, however, can there be found a vision with historical perspective. No succession of ages and events ever unfolds before our eyes. The classical prophet knows only of two ages: the kingdom of his time and the visionary kingdom of God at the end of days, which follows directly upon, and flows out of, the prophet's vision concerning his own time. There is no mantic interpretation of a sequence of events. All the detail that a prophet may amass adds up to one picture of what will happen "on that day," when the next and final age will be inaugurated.

The literary prophets are thus quite distinct from the apocalypses. The fact that the former contain visionary elements which the latter utilized has misled many into obscuring this distinction. But the complete absence in the prophets of perspective visions testifies that the two are essentially different; no literary commingling of the two realms has taken place. The two are products of different ages; classical prophecy does not gradually blend into apocalypse. This supports the tradition that classical prophecy came to an end at the beginning of Second Temple times.

THE COMPOSITION OF THE PROPHETIC BOOKS

It is commonly held that prophetic literature is the product of a development involving (a) the prophets themselves; (b) their disciples, who transmitted their words and added other traditions concerning their master; and (c) generations of prophetic writers, compilers, and annotators who continued enlarging the prophetic tradition until the time of canonization. It is, of course, clear that the prophetic literature has not reached us in its primary state. It contains material composed by later compilers and editors, and scribal errors have considerably corrupted the tradition as well. The crucial question is, however, whether disciples and later editors had a hand in the composition of the prophecies themselves, and not merely in the narrative framework or the arrangement of the books. Was there an oral tradition of the words of the prophets which was first committed to writing by circles of disciples, who may be assumed to have colored them with their own viewpoint? Did generations of scribes and glossators continue to alter the body of written prophecies, adapting them to new conditions and ascribing to the ancients later ideas?

Later revisers would have been anxious, first of all, to doctor the political and historical background of the prophecies. Adaptation would have made of the ancient seers authors of visions concerning far off ages and empires that were to rise long after their time. It would necessarily have turned the ancient prophecies into perspective, historical visions. In annexing Isaiah 40–66 to the words of Isaiah son of Amoz, tradition did lend to the present book of Isaiah something of perspective vision. The essential point, however, is to note that such "adaptation" can be found only in the work of the arranger of the book, but never in the text of the prophecies themselves. Later ages searched the prophets for hints of events of their own day. But these hints did not then, nor do they now, lie on the surface. The plain meaning of no classical prophecy contains allusions to historical events that occurred after the age of the prophets.

THE HISTORICAL BACKGROUND OF THE PROPHETS—The historical background of the material of literary prophecy is not always clearly defined. In the prophecies whose setting is obscure, and only in these, hints and allusions have been found to events of late Persian and Hellenistic times. Neither the kingdom nor the kings of the Greeks are ever mentioned explicitly, but ingenious modern midrash has discovered veiled hints to Alexander the Great and his successors. It is noteworthy that when in Daniel the Greek kingdoms are spoken of, it is in express terms which require no ingenuity to interpret.[2]

When the historical purview of each of the prophets is examined, it proves to belong to a definite setting and to reflect the events of one period only. The historical horizon of each prophet is always a natural one.

[2] While the country and people of Javan (Ionia-Greece) are referred to in Isaiah 66:19; Ezekiel 27:13, 19; Joel 4:6; and Zechariah 9:13, their empire is not mentioned. Inasmuch as Greeks are referred to in the annals of Assyrian kings, it may be inferred that they were known to Israel too in Assyrian times.

The idea that in certain passages (e.g., Isa. 11:11–16; 19:19–25; 27:12 f.; Zech. 9–14) Assyria is to be understood as Seleucid Syria, and Egypt as Ptolemaic Egypt has no basis in Hebrew (as distinct from Greek [Herod. vii. 63]) usage. In late biblical literature the land that is *east* of the Euphrates may be called Assyria and Babylonia; Persia is called Assyria in Ezra 6:22; Babylonia, in Ezra 5:13; Nehemiah 13:6. But no Jewish author styles the land *west* of the Euphrates Assyria or Babylonia. And since the Seleucid capital, Antiochia, was in the west, the Seleucid kingdom is never styled Assyria (cf. Dan. 11, where the Syrian king is called "king of the north" as opposed to the Egyptian "king of the south").

The prophecies of Amos date from the time of Jeroboam II. They were composed before the reign of Tiglath-pileser III (before 745), when the Aramaean kingdoms were still in existence. Amos foretells the exile and destruction of Israel, but he never mentions Assyria. The nation in whose hand Israel is to fall (6:14) is some undefined northern one. Later his prophecies were, of course, referred to the Assyrian conquest of 722. Yet his words were preserved in their original vagueness; Assyria was nowhere explicitly inserted. Amos' prophecies are a faithful document of the Aramaean–early Assyrian period. What happened after Jeroboam II is beyond their horizon.

Hosea, who prophesied in the reign of Jeroboam II and the Israelite kings after him, couples Egypt with Assyria and reproves Israel for having sought help from them. Hosea, too, foresaw destruction and exile, but he gives no indication that Assyria would be Ephraim's scourge. He hints that Egypt would have a hand in Israel's fall (9:6), but of Assyria he says only that to trust in it is futile. Later generations, of course, understood Hosea's words about the destruction as referring to the Assyrian conquest. Yet not one verse of his book was reworked to make this interpretation explicit.

The book of Isaiah reflects several historical backgrounds. Chapters 40–66 are set against the decline of Babylonia and the rise of Persia. In 13:1—14:23; 21:1-10 Babylon is mentioned, and what is signified thereby must be further investigated. For the rest, there are some chapters whose background is undefined (e.g., 24–27); these have provided scholars with material on which to exercise their imagination. But the bulk of it reflects clearly the situation of the eighth century. The empires of Aram, Egypt, and Assyria are locked in battle; Israel and Judah are caught in between. Egypt is once coupled with Assyria as an enemy (7:18), but for the most part, it appears as the kingdom from which Judah seeks help against Assyria. Assyria, the rod of YHWH's wrath, is destined to rule the earth, and then be broken on the mountain of Israel (10:5 ff.). Assyria is believed the final enemy; that it in turn was to fall before and be succeeded by Babylonia is nowhere indicated. This silence is all the more remarkable in view of the fact that that tradition did supplement the prophecies of Isaiah son of Amoz with later ones of the Babylonian-Persian period. But these later chapters were kept entirely separate from the Assyrian prophecies. No suggestion of a succession of empires was interpolated into the early visions.

The explicit background of Micah, too, is the Assyrian menace—the fall of Samaria, the deliverance of Judah, the coupling of Assyria and

Egypt. There is to be found a later, "Babylonian" adaptation of one passage: "and you shall come to Babylon" (4:10). This is one of the few instances in the whole corpus of prophecy of a genuine revision in the light of later events. It is characteristically obvious, no exegetical subtlety being required to detect it. The glossator doubtless imagined that he was doing no more than making explicit the vague terms of the ancient prophecy—note that Assyria is nowhere mentioned here. Where Assyria is named, however, there is not a word about the empire which is to succeed it.

The historical setting of Zephaniah—the reign of Josiah—is also clearly Assyrian; there is no allusion to Babylonia or the Chaldeans. Nahum prophesies at the collapse of Assyria. For him the Assyrian domination is the last; there is no hint of a new heathen empire. Habakkuk's setting is the rise of the Chaldeans. The prophet comforts himself that their empire will speedily collapse; he knows nothing of Persia which was to follow.

The historical reflexes of the book of Jeremiah are particularly illuminating. Jeremiah began to prophesy in 625, when Assyria was already showing signs of dissolution. In chapters 2–19, he speaks of "a nation from the north" which is to destroy the land. The year 605 is the turning point in his prophecy (25:1–3; 36:1–32); henceforth, Babylonia is identified as the future conqueror of Judah and all the nations. From that year on (chap. 21 to the end), the Babylonian theme prevails. Yet in the main prophetic corpus, from 1 to 19, Babylonia is not referred to once. In 20:4–6, there is evidence of a Babylonian reworking, but this has occurred in narrative matter. The text of the prophecies of 1–19 has not been penetrated by the Babylonian motif, even though Jeremiah himself later interpreted the "nation of the north" of his earlier prophecies as the Chaldeans. Thus the prophecies of Jeremiah faithfully reflect the political changes of his time. For Jeremiah, too, Babylonia is the last kingdom. In 50–51, he foresees the collapse of Babylonia, but there is not a word concerning Persia, its successor.

The historical setting of Ezekiel is the reign of Nebuchadnezzar. Until chapter 24, Ezekiel speaks of the destruction of Jerusalem; from 33 on, after word of the fall reaches him, he concerns himself with the future Israel. Chapter 21:33–37 is a prophecy concerning the fall of Babylonia,[3] but nowhere is there a hint that Persia would have a hand in this. Persia appears only incidentally in 38:5 as one of the auxiliaries of Gog. No later hand insinuated any suggestions of the upheaval that occurred shortly after these prophecies were uttered.

---

[3] As recognized already by Ehrlich, *Randglossen zur Hebräischen Bibel*, V (1912), 84 f.

The explicit historical setting of Isaiah 40–66 is the rise of the Persian Empire. This empire is the background of Haggai, Zechariah 1–8, and Malachi. No allusion to its destruction by yet another heathen empire is to be found in these books.

Thus each literary unit of prophecy has a unified and natural historical horizon which—save for a few obvious instances—has nowhere been extended artificially by editors, interpolators, or supplementers.

But the historical horizon of the prophecies was surely the element most in the interest of later generations to revise. In these ancient oracles of God they hoped to discover, prefigured or foretold, the great events that agitated their time. If they did not revise prophecies in this respect, if they did not write into them allusions to events beyond their natural historical purview, it must be concluded that they did not substantially revise them at all. The redaction of prophetic tradition was a work of compilation and arrangement. Alongside of genuine material there were doubtless some spurious elements that insinuated themselves into prophetic traditions. Technical errors of transmission were also operative. But a purposeful, continuous, large-scale revising of the ancient prophecies themselves is nowhere in evidence. It is clear that the transmitters considered it their duty to preserve the text of prophecies as they received them.

Especially significant in this respect is the rift between prophecy and historical reality.

The lasting value of the prophets resides in the noble religious and moral ideas to which they gave voice. The people, however, set equal store by their mantic powers. Generations of believers searched the biblical prophets for allusions to contemporary and future events. The collection and preservation of these prophecies must also have been motivated, to an extent, by this belief. Prophecies that were considered to have been fulfilled were preserved; hence the predominance of prophecies of woe.

But the accord of prophecy and reality is indeed only a very general one, which does not extend to details at all. The rift between the plain sense of prophecies and the actual course of events passes through the whole of the literature. In some cases, the prophets' words became antiquated during their own lives. Yet, most remarkably, no effort was made to mend this rift by altering the antiquated prophecies in accord with events, although often the change of a mere phrase or a word would have sufficed. The problem cannot have escaped the early transmitters; later generations found a way out through midrashic exegesis. How is the intact transmission of prophecies that failed, with all the disaccord between them and historical reality, to be explained except by the assumption that already during the time of the prophets themselves their words had become sacred? They cannot have been in a fluid state, yielding to the needs and moods of the times, being added to and subtracted from at the discretion of editors. Were it so, how could the gap between them and events have maintained itself? The facts can be accounted for only by assuming that the commonly held view of the transmission of prophetic literature is wrong.

How the Prophecies Were Transmitted—The fixity of the text implies that prophecies were written down by the prophets themselves. Their admirers, followers, and disciples preserved and transmitted them. Presumably, the prophetic narratives, in which the prophet is the hero and is spoken of in the third person, also arose in these circles. But the disciples were not themselves prophets, nor did they have a hand in the creation of the prophecies.

The one pertinent fact that can be elicited from the scanty data concerning the formation of prophetic literature is that the classical prophets acted as individuals, not as heads of prophetic guilds or circles of disciples. Not one of them moves among or works through "sons of prophets." In contrast with the prophets of I Kings 20:35–43; 22:6–25, the literary prophets perform their symbolic acts alone before an audience of the people. Amos prophesies at and is expelled from Bethel alone. Hosea and Isaiah use their children as symbols, but no disciples accompany them in their activities.[4] Among the information given in the book of Ezekiel about the life and activity of the prophet, there is not a trace of a prophetic company. Ezekiel's audiences are the exiles, the elders, and so forth. Nor does the book of Jeremiah speak of a circle of disciples. Jeremiah's well-wishers and helpers are not a prophetic band, but officers and priests. Jeremiah does have a companion who at times acts for him—the professional scribe, Baruch (36:26, 32). But Baruch is not a prophet or a "son of the prophets," and he is the sole permanent companion that Jeremiah had.

---

[4] The rendering of Isaiah 8:16 as "seal up instruction among my disciples" is altogether uncertain in spite of the efforts of commentators old and new. All Isaiah's prophecies are directed to the people or the court; it is nowhere suggested that he "sealed up" anything among a circle of disciples, who are otherwise never mentioned. But even granting that *limmūdīm* here means disciples, they are heirs and witnesses to the prophecy only, not themselves prophets or "sons of prophets." The obscure verses in Zechariah 11:7, 11 f. may refer to a band of "poor men" who participate in the prophet's activity, but these too are at bottom only onlookers, whose essential purpose is to witness the fact that the actions of the prophet "are the word of YHWH." They are not sons of prophets or prophets.

There are, then, no grounds for assuming that the literature ascribed to the prophets was cultivated by circles of disciples who eventually wrote it down, formulated according to their lights. There is even less reason to believe that the sermons of the prophets were transmitted at first orally and only after generations set down in writing. We know nothing about "circles" who could be credited with the cultivation and transmission of such traditions, written or oral.[5]

Wherever a prophet's words are known to have been committed to writing, it is the prophet who writes (or dictates) them (see below, p. 360). Especially instructive is the account of Jeremiah 36, telling how Jeremiah's prophecies were indited. Jeremiah himself dictates his sermons to his scribe, Baruch; he has no circle of disciples who know his prophecies by heart. Baruch, unmentioned previously, seems to have joined the prophet only in that year. Doubtless he had a hand in the compilation of the prophecies. But examination of the result of Baruch's work shows how faithfully the words of the prophet were transmitted. Despite the fact that henceforth (after 605) Jeremiah's entire prophecy was dominated by the theme of Babylonia, in setting down all the earlier prophecies the scribe does not insinuate into them a single line of the new theme.

At a point not long before the appearance of Baruch, the consecutive narrative in Jeremiah sets in (from the beginning of the reign of Jehoiakim [chap. 26]), continuing until the descent of Baruch and Jeremiah to Egypt.

[5] Nyberg, in *Studien zum Hoseabuche* (Uppsala, 1935), 5 ff. argues for a long period of oral transmission of biblical literature on the analogy of other oriental parallels. Only in postexilic times, he claims, was the text of most of the Bible set down in writing. This is an untenable opinion. Egypt and Babylonia were scribal cultures from earliest times. And it was not only economic texts and memoranda that were written, but literary and religious works as well. Temples were great libraries. Pre-Israelite Canaan, too, had a written literature. Nyberg's parallels from Arabia and other oriental cultures are not apt, since Israel was not at its inception a "primitive" people, but one that had lived for centuries among the high civilizations of the ancient Near East. Only by confusing the manner in which the Koran is taught with the manner of its composition can Nyberg find support in Islam for his views. The fact is that while the Koran is recited and taught by heart, what is taught and recited is a written work. The theory is that the Koran was written even before its revelation to Mohammed. As to biblical literature, the witnesses to its early writing are clear and reliable. The earliest poetic collection is entitled "the book of the Wars of YHWH" (Num. 21:14); another ancient collection is "the book of Jashar," which in two places is expressly described as a written work (Josh. 10:13; II Sam. 1:18). Moses records the battle with Amalek in a book (Exod. 17:14), and writes the book of the covenant (Exod. 24:4, 7), the book of Torah (Deut. 31:9, 24), and the song (vs. 19)—which last he thereupon proceeds to teach by heart. Samuel writes the rule of the monarchy in a book (I Sam. 10:25), and Solomon's history and wisdom are written in "the book of the acts of Solomon" (I Kings 11:41). Hosea mentions written laws (8:12), and so forth.

Presumably, this narrative was written or revised by Baruch. Hence, the difference between Jeremiah 19 and 20:1–6. In the prophecy of doom concerning Topheth and pagan worship on the rooftops in chapter 19 (and in the Topheth prophecy of 7:29–34), there is no mention of Babylon. But in 20:1–6, the third-person narrative appendix to 19, there is a Babylonian adaptation (vss. 4–6). Only later does Jeremiah himself interweave these motifs in a Babylonian prophecy (32:26–35), but in the prophecies of chapters 7 and 19, composed before 605, Babylonia is absent. Thus the text of the prophecies, transmitted faithfully, reflects the new departure after 605. Only the narrative, formulated more freely, anticipates and thus obscures the change; doubtless we see here the hand of Baruch.

Prophetic narrative, then, is the creation of the prophets' surroundings. The prophetic stories and legends of the Torah and the books of history (and those of later times, too) are not, of course, the work of the prophets themselves, but of their admirers, and perhaps even the folk. Similarly, the legends and stories that grew up around the literary prophets arose among those who venerated them and received their teaching; in time, they assimilated a folk element as well. The rule is: the prophecies are to be regarded as the work of the prophets, the narratives, as the work of their admirers (except where the prophet speaks in the first person, e.g., Isa. 8:1–4; Jer. 28:1–4; etc.; these are to be taken as basically the work of the prophets themselves). While keeping the written word that they inherited intact, they felt free in composing the narrative and any prophetic utterances that were fixed within its framework. In such cases, there was doubtless an ideological difference between the narrative and the authentic prophecies. Such a difference is evident between the prophecies about Assyria in the book of Isaiah and the Isaianic prophecy imbedded in the story of II Kings 19 (reproduced in Isa. 37), as also between the image of the prophet that emerges from the stories, and that emerging from the prophecies themselves.

Further indication that the prophetic books are far from being a collection assembled in the course of centuries is the distinctive ideological cast of each; Amos, Hosea, Isaiah 1–33, Zephaniah, Jeremiah, Ezekiel, and the rest, each bear the stamp of one creative personality. Isaiah 1–33 is an entity unique in the literature for its disregard of the motif of national revenge. The book of Jeremiah is altogether rooted in the ideas, symbols, and language of Deuteronomy; Ezekiel is under the influence of P. Such homogeneity cannot be naturally explained on the assumption of a generations-long accretion of glosses, revisions, and supplements.

PROPHECIES OF CONSOLATION

The basis of early Israelite eschatology is faith in the perpetuity of Israel as the kingdom of God, of the covenant and its concretizations: the land, the people, national independence, and the monarchy. It is rooted in the idea that YHWH dominates all, and no other divine power opposes him or limits his rule. In essence, the kingdom of YHWH is not something to be achieved in the future as a result of YHWH's triumph over forces of evil in the end of days, but has already come into being through his covenant with Israel. However, through the sin of Israel and by the decree of God, its glory is departed and it verges on collapse. Yet, by virtue of being the will of God and his promise, it exists ideally even now. Through chastisement and suffering, Israel's sin will be expiated, and then it will return to its former state, or be even more glorious than in time past. This faith is the ground of prophetic eschatology as well. No less than the popular religion do the prophets believe in the unique role of Israel as the earthly arena in which God manifests himself. They, too, regard the land, the people, the temple, Jerusalem, and the monarchy as the visible symbols—in the future, no less than in the past—of God's kingdom. They affirm that chastisement is temporary, and that afterwards the monarchy will again arise, because they, too, share the faith in the perpetuity of God's kingdom in Israel. Destruction does not come from demonic sources whose defeat is a condition of YHWH's kingship. YHWH himself brings it on to expunge sin, and thereby to reconstitute his kingdom. He remains king during the period of chastisement. To the prophets the past glory, the present distress, and the future glory are all manifestations of one and the same kingdom.

There is no need, then, to look for a special source of Israel's prophecies of consolation (e.g., the Gunkel-Gressmann view that it stems from popular mythological-eschatological beliefs). Both the reproof and the consolation of the prophets spring from the same ground—the perpetuity of the kingdom of God. The prophets are sent to denounce Israel for profaning the covenant. By so doing, Israel calls down on itself divine punishment; the result is the humiliation of God's kingdom. The denunciation cannot, then, be an end in itself; it aims at arousing the people to repentance so that the glory of the divine kingdom may be restored. To the prophets, the splendid visions of the future kingdom are the necessary complement to their prophecies of doom. Just as in the past the kingdom of God was concretized in the people, the land, the city, the temple, and the Davidic monarchy, so it will be in the future. In classical prophecy as everywhere in the Bible, the material blessings of God are made the vehicles of a religious idea. To separate the religious-moral from the national-messianic elements of prophecy reflects a modern prejudice which cannot serve as a criterion for the ideological analysis of Israelite prophetic literature (see above, pp. 278 f.).

Prophecies concerning the ingathering of the dispersion do not necessarily imply a date after 586. From the times of Tiglath-pileser an ever growing Israelite dispersion existed. Sennacherib exiled large numbers of Judeans. This was no mere captivity, but a genuine "exile." These exiles kept faith with YHWH and, with their countrymen who remained in the land, awaited the day of his redemption.

THE NEW HISTORIOSOPHY

The ancient religion as set forth in the Torah and the other literature prior to classical prophecy distinguished two periods in the history of mankind: prior to the tower of Babel, a primeval monotheism reigned among men; subsequently the nations came into existence with idolatry as their "portion." When YHWH revealed himself to Israel, the world became divided into two camps: Israel, who knew God, and the rest of the nations who did not know him. Israel alone was henceforth the subject of history. The nations, deprived of the supreme human value—knowledge of God—stood outside; events befall them, but except as it impinges upon the history of Israel, what happens to the nations generally has no divine meaning, and is ·therefore not history in the biblical sense. The early religion conceived this division of mankind as perpetual; it did not expect a merging of realms in some future age.

The new eschatology that came into being during the Aramaic wars did conceive of a universal "day of YHWH," a judgment of all nations, but it was left for classical prophecy to give full expression to this new idea. A reconstituted universal history first appears with Isaiah's vision of the ultimate return of the nations to YHWH in the future (Isa. 2). At the culmination of history mankind is reunited, all sharing the divine grace which heretofore had been the portion of Israel alone. With Habakkuk and Jeremiah, the idea that Israel's historical mission is to combat the idolatry of men is born. Idolatry has no right to existence; the ideal is one humanity under God. This is the background of the prophecies of the Second Isaiah.

The concept of a universal history attains its final form in apocalyptic literature. Daniel formulates the classic symbol of four pagan monarchies to be succeeded by the kingdom of God. The idea that idolatry is a sin for which the nations also are punished dominates that literature; the heathen realm is the kingdom of Belial, of Satan. This view is at once the climax of universalism and particularistic intolerance. Knowledge of the one God becomes a universal human obligation; all men must become Israel in spirit. There is no longer room for two historical realms. History is one, and it moves toward the kingdom of God, when idolatry will be utterly cut off.

In this ideological development classical prophecy stands between the level of the early religion and that of apocalyptic literature. Again we see that there is no promiscuous mixing of realms, as current opinion would have it.

SPEECH AND WRITING

As apostles of God, the prophets could fulfil their primary task only through speech or action. In the stories of the Torah and the historical books there is a direct confrontation of prophets and people; doubtless the literary prophets also confronted their audience directly in the first instance. The prophets communicated to their hearers the word of God that they received. When the message was simple and pragmatic, the prophet spoke prosaically. But the prophet was also a poet, and he lived in a cultural environment in which poetic improvisation before an audience was a customary practice. In appropriate circumstances, the prophet might "sing" his words with poetic passion, working on his audience with images and melody, often accompanying his utterance with gestures or dramatic action. Some prophets were masters of the pithy phrase: "Have you murdered and also taken possession?" (I Kings 21:19); "Go up and prosper!" (22:12). Others were orators, who could on the spur of the moment compose a finished and complex piece before their audience. Several styles and forms might be employed according to the circumstances. The prophet might begin with reproof, continue with impassioned warnings of punishment, and end with an elegy. Nathan opens his discourse to David with a disarming parable; afterward, he vehemently denounces the king, ending with a warning (II Sam. 12). Isaiah opens with a parable, interprets it, and then utters a series of "woes" to add force to his interpretation (chap. 5). Ezekiel relates a parable, explains it, then announces punishment, and ends with a promise of restoration couched in the terms of the parable (chap. 17). A criticism which atomizes the prophets by analyzing them into tiny, discrete literary units is founded on a completely erroneous conception.

It is, of course, possible to isolate various literary forms that may have been combined in a given prophecy (parable, reproof, lament, etc.), but there is no reason to suppose that in so doing one has also isolated primary literary units. The prophets freely and frequently combined various literary forms in a single composition.

But the prophets were not only speakers, they also created a written literature. There is no internal conflict between speech and writing, nor is there any basis for the view that only in Second Temple times were prophecies set down in writing. Neither is it true that the literary prophets began writing only in late times when a general tendency toward writing prevailed. The references to ancient books of poetry ("the book of Jashar," "the book of the Wars of YHWH") show that poetic works were early indited in Israel. Classical prophecy was poetry and considered divinely inspired; there is no ground for asserting that such poetry was not collected and indited. Some prophecies doubtless had too transient a value to be set down in writing. But prophecies embodying substantial poetical or ideological creations were certainly preserved in writing. To be sure, the historical books do not mention written works of prophecy, but neither do they mention the names of any literary prophet except Isaiah.

The writing of prophecies is referred to several times in the Latter Prophets. Isaiah is commanded to write certain words "on a large tablet" (8:1 ff.), again he is commanded to write "on a tablet" and inscribe "in a book" a testimony "for the last day" (30:8). Habakkuk is commanded to write his vision clearly "on tablets," so that the reader might read it easily (2:2). Jeremiah writes prophecies of consolation in a book (30:1 ff.). Another time he is bidden to write "in a book" the prophecies of woe concerning Israel, Judah, and all the nations (36:1 ff.). He sets down the Babylonian prophecies "in a book" and dispatches them to Babylonia (51:59 ff.). Another book is mentioned in 25:13. Beside this, Jeremiah writes a letter to the exiles (chap. 29). Ezekiel is given a "scroll" upon which prophecies are written (2:8—3:4); his prophecy is, as it were, written by "the finger of God"; cf. also 43:11. Isaiah 34:16 mentions a book of prophecies.

It has been suggested that the prophets resorted to writing only under special circumstances. It is true that Isaiah uses writing for a sign and witness against non-believers, but Habakkuk writes for any reader who wishes to learn the word of God. Jeremiah is charged to write in the twenty-third year of his prophetic activity; but there is no reason to assume that previously he had written nothing. The reason for his writing at that time was in order to have all his prophecies recited at once before the people, in the hope that they would have a greater impact on them in this form than before (36:3). For in that year (605, the year of the battle of Carchemish), he discovered that the referent of all his earlier prophecies was Nebuchadnezzar. That his prophecy of consolation was written "in a book" (30:2) had nothing to do with his detention.

It may therefore be said that when the prophets wrote, they did not indite merely short notes, nor were they moved to it only by emergencies or special circumstances. Writing was a means of communication hardly less customary than speech. It was particularly likely to be employed by the literary prophets, for it is naïve to assume that the prophets could really convey their message "to the people" through speech alone. In fact, they addressed only a limited audience—even when in the temple court or the market. There were doubtless people scattered far and wide who wished to know what a prophet said but could not come to hear him. The limited circle of listeners was supplemented by the broader circle of readers.

The writing and reading (reciting) of prophecies had different purposes. Written prophecies might be preserved "for the last day" as signs and witnesses. But prophecies were also written to be read aloud in a solemn ceremony. Jeremiah charges Seraiah to recite the content of his scroll before sinking it in the Euphrates. Such ceremonial reading originated in the custom of reciting the word of God when making a covenant (Exod. 24:4, 7; II Kings 23:2 f.). Its chief purpose was to impress the audience, as when Deuteronomy commands to read the Torah before the people in sabbatical years (31:10 ff.).

The story of Jeremiah 36 suggests that only new prophecies were "sung" or spoken by the prophet to an audience. Old prophecies were not recited by heart, but were written down and read from writing. It is the rule in the case of important utterances that speech is followed by writing; God first speaks the Decalogue and only later sets it down on the tablets. Moses rehearses the laws to the people, then writes them in a book (Exod. 24:3 ff.). Samuel tells the people the rule of the monarchy before writing it down in a book (I Sam. 8:9; 10:25). Ezekiel is charged first to tell Israel the plan of the temple, and afterward to write it in their sight (43:11). Isaiah and Jeremiah also write after speaking. This does not mean that some prophecies—such as the wisdom chapters of Habakkuk 1–2—were not written down from the first.

Why were the sermons of the prophets preserved *in extenso* beginning only with Amos? The chief reason is surely the new level of thought that was reached in these writings. Unlike their predecessors, the classical prophets were important for what they said more than for what they did. It was not enough, in their case, merely to incorporate a few of their utterances in a story about their lives. Their lives were subordinate to their words. Furthermore, it is to be noted that this literature clusters about the two falls: it arises just before the fall of Ephraim and ends not long after the fall of Judah. This literature contained the answer to the question, why did God destroy what he had established? In the prophecy beginning with Amos the word of God concerning the most fateful events in the life of Israel was embodied. Here were presaged the rise of Assyria, of Babylonia, and of Persia; the destruction of Ephraim and Judah, as well as the Restoration. The people eagerly awaited the "end of wonders," but the end never came. Then prophecy was stilled, the song of redemption frozen on its lips, a divine enigma for the ages.

CHAPTER XI

Amos and Hosea

AMOS

The first of the new prophets was Amos, a shepherd of Tekoa, who lived during the reigns of Jeroboam II of Israel (784–744) and Uzziah of Judah (774–739). Taken by YHWH "from behind the sheep" he goes north to the kingdom of Ephraim. He utters his harsh prophecies in Bethel, and possibly elsewhere. Amaziah, the priest of Bethel, regards his prophecies of doom concerning the king and the kingdom as treason and expels him from the country (7:9 ff.).

Amos was an original poet and thinker, yet he utilized styles and material that were ready at hand. It has been recognized that his work reveals a degree of culture far higher than that of a simple shepherd. He feels himself a link in the succession of Israelite prophecy (3:7 f., cf. 2:12), and employs the standard formulas of prophecy ("Thus said YHWH," "Hear. . . ." "Ah. . . ." "In that day . . . ," etc.). He draws upon the ancient narrative tradition in allusions to the destruction of Sodom and Gomorrah (4:11), the plagues of Egypt (vs. 10), the Exodus (2:10), the forty-year wandering (*ibid.*; 5:25), YHWH's Torah and laws (2:4), and so forth. He reflects knowledge of wisdom and psalm style: ascending numbers (three . . . four; 1:3—2:6), Canaanite in origin, are found in biblical wisdom (e.g., Prov. 30:15 ff.). Amos composes an elegy in the *qīnā* meter (5:1 f.). The epigram in question form (3:3 ff.) has wisdom parallels (e.g., Prov. 6:27 f.). The phrase "With shouting and the sound of the horn" (2:2) is found in Psalm 47:6, and so forth.

From the early religion he inherits the conception of YHWH as lord of history—it is, for example, the presupposition of the ancient popular legend concerning Sodom and Gomorrah which he cites. From the early religion he derives the notion that the nations are punished only for gross moral offenses (particularly against Israel; compare the sins of Egypt and Amalek in the popular legends), but not for idolatry. That the destiny of all nations was decided by YHWH (9:7) was an old idea that Amos does not have to argue. His taunt, "Are you not to me like the Ethiopians, O house of Israel," is a satirical hyperbole. For to Amos, YHWH's bringing up Israel from Egypt differed radically from his bringing up Aram from Kir. In Israel only did YHWH act as a known God, as Amos himself tells us explicitly: "Only you have I known out of all the families of the earth ..." (3:1 ff.). This idea underlies all his work. In Israel alone did YHWH raise up prophets and Nazirites (2:10 ff.), them alone did he chastise in order to make them repent (4:6 ff.), to Israel alone did he give statutes and laws (2:4). Only Israel worships YHWH, and only against Israel's cult does Amos inveigh; for only in Israel can YHWH's name be profaned (2:7). The gentiles are not required to know YHWH, indeed their very land is impure (7:17).

The book is evidently a composite of various collections. The prophecies concerning the nations (1:3—2:3), contain historical allusions to events before the time of Amos.[1] The latest element in the book is the prophetic narrative of 7:11 in which the death of Jeroboam "by the sword" is (wrongly) predicted. The book was composed, then, before Jeroboam's death in 744; there is no reflection of the tumultuous events that occurred afterward. Inasmuch as the collections out of which the book is composed each have a distinct form and are evidently arranged according to a plan not necessarily chronological but stylistic, and since the last element was added before 744, nothing stands in the way of assuming that Amos himself was responsible for this arrangement.

Concerning the doctrines of Amos three questions are crucial: How did he regard Israel's past? What was his view on religion? What did he demand for the present and envision for the future?

It has been pointed out above that Amos shares the view of early tradition that Israel has been elected by God and has a unique position in the divine order of the world. His view of the cult, however, appears to be a sharp break with the past: "I hate, I despise your feasts ... take away from me the noise of your singers.... Come to Bethel and sin ...,"

[1] E.g.: Ben-hadad son of Hazael was a contemporary of Joash (799–784), and was defeated by him (II Kings 13:24 f.); Aram's cruelties in Gilead therefore must have preceded his time. The hostility of Philistia and Edom against Judah occurred in the time of Joram son of Jehoshaphat (850–843); see II Kings 8:20 ff. and II Chronicles 21:16 f. The cremation of Edom's king must have occurred during the war of Joram son of Ahab, Jehoshaphat, and the Edomite king against Moab (II Kings 3), after the defeat of the coalition.

etc., etc. The extreme position of 5:25—"Did you offer me sacrifices and oblations forty years in the desert?"—has given rise to the opinion that Amos unconditionally rejected the cult, especially the cult of sacrifice. This is quite out of the question. A wholesale repudiation of the cult would have meant a rejection of tradition which grounded it on an express command of YHWH. That Amos did not reject tradition is evident alone from the fact that 5:25 itself is based on it.[2] Moreover, he calls foreign lands "impure" and regards giving wine to Nazirites a sin (2:11). Again, his condemnation extends, beyond sacrifice, to song and psalm as well (5:23). The positions of Isaiah, Jeremiah, Second Isaiah, and Zechariah are comparable. Amos and Isaiah reject the people's feasts and Sabbaths as well as their sacrifices. Now there is no question but that the prophets—most of whom express veneration of the Jerusalem temple, and, even while foretelling its destruction, look for a future restoration of its cult—did not conceive of a religion without prayer, festival, and Sabbath. On the other hand it is equally plain that Amos is not directing his attack specifically against a corrupted cult, for he rejects even the legitimate worship of the people. (Idolatry goes unmentioned except for the almost incidental notice of 5:26.) As in Isaiah 1:11–17; Micah 6:6–7a; Jeremiah 7:21 f.; Isaiah 58; and especially Zechariah 7:5–14, it is the legitimate, national cult of YHWH that is rejected in its entirety. It is rejected in favor of morality; God desires righteousness, not sacrifice! What is the source and meaning of this attitude?

Social Morality as a Factor in National Destiny—The prophetic demands for social justice echo, for the most part, the ancient covenant laws. But they go beyond the early religion in raising these matters to the level of factors decisive for the national destiny. In the literature prior to classical prophecy, national doom and exile are, as a rule, threatened only for idolatry. The idea that God dooms a whole society for moral corruption is not altogether absent in the early literature, but it is for particularly heinous sins which the whole society has committed or is responsible for that the doom comes. The Flood annihilates a mankind in which "all flesh corrupted their way." Sodom and Gomorrah lacked even ten

---

[2] In order to accept this verse at face value it is not sufficient to say that Amos did not know of P's tabernacle and cult laws. One must also assume that he was ignorant of JE: cf. Exodus 3:12, 18 (and related verses in 8:21 ff.; 10:8 ff., 24 ff.); 12:21–27; 13:1, 12–15; 17:15; 24:1–11; see also 32:4–6, 8; Deuteronomy 12:8. Once again it is a matter of hyperbole, but the meaning is clear enough. Amos wishes to contrast the present multitude of offerings that the people daily "give" to God and by which they set great store, with the age of the Wandering, when God had to lead them and sustain them in direst need. Yet that age, when they were unable to make daily offerings to him, was the time of favor and grace! Amos does not fundamentally depart from tradition even here.

righteous men, and the story specifies in detail the extent and atrocious nature of their corruption (Gen. 19:4 ff.). Degeneracy had become the norm, and the divine moral law had sunk into oblivion. The Canaanites were dispossessed for their sexual corruption which had become "the law of the nation" as a whole (Lev. 18; 20). Whenever God's judgment falls upon the nations specific gross sins are the cause: murder, sexual immorality, oppression of strangers, inhuman cruelty. This is the view of preclassical prophecy as well. Violations of everyday social morality—perversion of justice, bribe-taking, exploitation of the poor, and the like—are never mentioned. These are regarded as "venial sins," subject to the regular process of God's judgment and his individual providence.

Classical prophecy radically alters this view; it threatens national doom and exile for everyday social sins. While Nathan inveighs against David's adultery and murder, Elijah against Ahab's judicial murder, neither regard these sins as determining the fate of the nation. Amos is the first to evaluate social morality as a factor in national destiny. The gentiles are to be judged for particular enormities, in line with the early view (1:3—2:3). But Israel and Judah will be judged "for selling the righteous for silver, and the needy for a pair of shoes" (2:6). Moreover the new reproof is here given its most pointed expression. Unlike the other prophets who tend to generalize, and, by comparing Israel to Sodom, to imply that the whole nation is involved in especially horrendous sins, Amos makes it plain that it was the ruling class in particular that was involved, and in the everyday moral sins. He never speaks of murder, but only of exploitation, oppression, and perversion of justice, such wrongs as can be done only by the rulers and the rich. They crush the poor, carouse on pledged clothing in temple courts, fill their mansions with violence and plunder. They raise the price of bread; they defraud and impoverish the people. For this Amos threatens destruction and exile. What underscores the novelty of this evaluation is Amos's almost complete silence regarding idolatry, the chief offense which the early literature held crucial for the destiny of the people.

The new stress on morality has as its concomitant a new attitude toward the cult. It was the prophets who expressed for the first time the idea that the cult of the nation as a whole, the entire YHWH cult, has no intrinsic value.[3] The Torah literature, as we have seen does not distinguish cultic from moral prescriptions, but indiscriminately juxtaposes them. The proph-

---

[3] This is not the same as the view, expressed already in Egyptian wisdom, that the god prefers goodness to the sacrifice of the evildoer. Could the pagan gods have declared the entire cult of man without intrinsic value?

ets, taking their departure from the tradition of Israel's election, declare that its object was to publish the "knowledge of God" and realize his moral will. In this way they draw the ultimate conclusions of the Israelite idea. That idea, essentially non-mythological and non-magical, could conceive of the relation of God and the world only in terms of free grace. All that is—both the physical and the moral universe—came into existence as the realization of God's gracious will. The absolute and autonomous value that paganism placed on the cult thereby vanished. God is in no way dependent on the cult of men; on the contrary, the cult is a manifestation of his grace to man. Its purpose is to serve as a symbol and expression of the "knowledge of God," a memorial to his covenant. Hence its value is conditional, not absolute. But through the sin of man, even this conditional value is lost and it becomes an empty and broken vessel, an abomination of YHWH.

Morality, on the other hand, is an absolute value, for it is divine in essence. The God who demands righteousness, justice, kindness, and compassion is himself just, gracious, kind, and compassionate. Moral goodness makes man share, as it were, in the divine nature. Classical prophecy established a hierarchy of value; both cult and morality are God's command and part of his covenant, and both are expressions of "knowledge of God." But while the cult is sacred only as a symbol, morality is essentially godlike, being a reflection of the qualities of God.

Doom and Consolation—The conception of the "day of YHWH" was part of the popular eschatology that antedated Amos. It was imagined as a cosmic judgment amidst thunders and earthquakes and great natural convulsions, "The day of YHWH is dark, and gloomy without light" (5:18 ff.). The popular conception was that the day would inaugurate Israel's deliverance from, and vengeance upon, its enemies. Amos turns the day into a dismal one for Israel too. The land will quake, the sun will set at noon, altars and mansions, houses large and small, will collapse. "Fallen, not to rise again, is the virgin Israel" (5:2). The people will go into exile "beyond Damascus," with the decadent, self-indulgent aristocracy at their head, for God will destroy the sinful nation from off the face of the earth (9:8a).

Before 9:8b there is no promise of consolation. Amos calls for repentance, and interprets the distresses that Israel has suffered as spurs to repentance (4:6–11). If the people return, "perhaps YHWH, God of hosts, will show grace to the remnant of Joseph" (5:4–15); if not, only complete destruction awaits them.

In a peculiarly abrupt transition 9:8b introduces a prophecy of consolation. While the idea of consolation is not inherently contradictory to the prophetic viewpoint (see above), the unparalleled suddenness of the transition has raised critical doubts as to Amos' authorship of these last verses. What must be stressed is that even if Amos did not prophesy consolation, this is no more than a personal idiosyncrasy, from which no generalization may be made touching classical prophecy as a whole.

As to the prophecy itself, all signs point to its earliness. It speaks entirely in terms of the early literature and has nothing of the distinctive ideas of the new prophecy. The remnant of 9:8–10 is no different from that of Elijah (I Kings 19:18); it consists of those righteous persons who will survive the holocaust to inherit God's blessings. Classical prophecy conceived of "the remnant that shall return" to YHWH, chastened by suffering; here the chastisement destroys the wicked, it does not bring about repentance. The future of the gentiles is also described in typically antique terms. Classical prophecy envisaged the inclusion of the gentiles in God's future grace, and the removal of the division between Israel and the nations at the end of days. Of this, the prophecies of Amos know nothing. There is no historical connection between the judgment of Israel and that of the nations. The conqueror of Israel has no role in the vision of salvation (cf. the position of Aram in Elijah's vision; I Kings 19:15–18). When Israel will be restored, those nations which were formerly part of the Davidic empire, will be repossessed by the new Davidic king (9:12). Nothing is said about a turn of nations from idolatry (cf. the early visions and psalms about Israel's future domination of the heathen). In characteristic Judean fashion the prophet, while envisioning the destruction of Israel, looked for the restoration of the Davidic dynasty; this, of course, necessitated the collapse of the northern dynasty.

In sum, then, Amos was first to conceive the idea of the primacy of morality, and to give sins against social morality decisive weight in determining the national destiny. He is as yet unaware of the new eschatology, and the new concept of universal history.

FIRST HOSEA

The first three chapters of the book of Hosea are distinguished from the rest so radically as to justify the assumption that the present book contains two distinct literary units, whose authors lived at different times. Chapters 1–3 develop an ordered series of events; except for 2:4–6 the style is almost mantic. The prophet sets forth the people's sins and their consequences objectively; there is no lyrical strain. In chapters 4–14 on the other hand, there is no chain of events, but a formless aggregation of impassioned reproof, argument, threats, pleading, and hope. The metaphor of marriage for God's covenant with Israel, and adultery for Israel's idolatry, does not recur in these chapters.[4] Here the relation between God and people is symbolized altogether differently; Israel is "grapes in the wilderness" (9:10), "a trained calf" (10:10 f.; cf. 11:4), an adopted son (11:1 f.). Perhaps the most deep-rooted difference between the two parts is that in 1–3 the moral corruption of the people—concern with which is the hallmark of classical prophecy—never figures. As in the early literature, only one national sin is referred to: idolatry. Moreover, while Baal worship is depicted in chapters 1–3 as a present sin, in chapters 4–14 it is a sin of the past (9:10; 13:1). The present sin of 4–14 is Samaria's calves; these, however, are never mentioned in 1–3.

The book of Kings relates that Jehu destroyed Israel's Baal cult once for all upon his accession (II Kings 10:28). Amos, Isaiah, and Micah make no mention of Baal; and Hosea 4–14 speaks of his cult only as a sin of the past. The setting of Hosea 1–3 is necessarily, then, the time before Jehu. The dates of the superscription in Hosea 1:1 (the reigns of Uzziah to Hezekiah of Judah, and Jeroboam II of Israel) refer only to chapters 4–14.

The misconception concerning Israel's syncretism has hitherto prevented scholars from appreciating correctly these obvious differences between the First and Second Hosea. It is assumed that syncretistic worship of YHWH-Baal continued in Israel after Jehu extirpated the cult of the Sidonian Baal. However, no passage in the book of Hosea lends support to this view. There is no confusion of gods. On the contrary, First Hosea speaks clearly of two distinct realms. The people have turned to other gods (3:1), have forgotten YHWH and gone after "lovers" (2:15), foolishly imagining that it is to the Baals that they owe their prosperity (vss. 7 ff.). After being chastened, errant Israel will return to "its first husband." The prophet distinguishes the festivals of YHWH from the "days of the Baals" (2:13, 15). Because they celebrated "days of the Baals," YHWH will take from the people their crops, and will put an end to their festivals, new moons, Sabbaths, and all appointed times. That is to say, he will punish Israel by depriving them of the observance of their legitimate festivals (for the idea compare Amos 8:10, Hos. 9:2–5). We know of only one period of Israel's history when "days of the Baals" were publicly celebrated: the reign of Jezebel. Then only was there in existence a temple to Baal with its own priests and prophets. This worship on Israelite soil is considered

---

[4] Two passages (4:12; 9:1) contain generalized allusions to Israel's "straying" from God—but such language is found several times in the Bible (e.g., Exod. 34:15 f.; Lev. 20:5 f.; Deut. 31:16).

by the First Hosea—as by Elijah and Elisha before him—a national sin, for which the entire nation is to suffer. These chapters were composed, then, before the destruction of Ahab's dynasty.[5]

THE MARRIAGE OF HOSEA—The narrative of chapters 1–3 has perplexed exegetes from earliest times. Hosea is commanded to take "a wife of harlotry" and "children of harlotry" as a sign that the land is unfaithful to YHWH. Hosea takes Gomer and she bears him three sons who are given names symbolic of sin and divine rejection. Later, Hosea is charged again "to love" an adulterous woman. The prophet buys an unnamed woman and makes a condition with her that she "sit solitary" for him many days.

The key to these stories must be sought in what is told regarding the children, for their history at least is complete and unambiguous and does not require imaginative reconstruction. They were born to Hosea legitimately, for there is no hint that Gomer played the harlot after her marriage, or that the children were not Hosea's. In what sense, then, are they "children of harlotry," and why do they bear names symbolizing hatred and estrangement? It must be supposed that they play the role of "children of harlotry" in a dramatic representation. Like the wounds and bandage of the prophet in the days of Ahab (I Kings 20:35 ff.), the nakedness of Isaiah (20:2), and the bands and bars of Jeremiah (27:2; 28:10 ff.) their import is representational. Gomer too is not "an adulterous wife" but "a wife of harlotries"; in 2:4 it is said: "Let her remove her harlotries from her face and her adulteries from between her breasts." The "harlotries" seem to be something material, some cosmetic or face covering, and some whorish ornament on her breast. Gomer must play the role of a harlot, going about with the appearance of a harlot to symbolize the apostasy of

---

[5] Only this assumption makes sense out of 1:4 where it is said that God will punish the royal house for "the blood of Jezreel." The massoretic reading "the house of Jehu" cannot be maintained. If the reference is to Jehu's slaying of Ahab's house in Jezreel, then the symbol of the adulterous wife which fills the sequence has nothing to do with this supposed sin. Moreover it is highly improbable that this zealous prophet would hold the destruction of Jezebel's family against Jehu, especially since it was viewed as just retribution for Ahab's murders (II Kings 9:7—10:10). The "blood of Jezreel" can only be that of Naboth for which Ahab's dynasty was accountable. This bloodguilt is interwoven in the narrative of Kings with the motifs of Baal worship and the murder of prophets (I Kings 18–19; 21; II Kings 9–10). It would therefore serve to evoke the sins of Ahab's house in general, including all of Jezebel's "harlotries."

The LXX reading here is "Judah" instead of "Jehu" which is, in turn, graphically close to "Jehoram." Read, accordingly, "the house of Jehoram"—Jehoram son of Ahab in whose time the sins of Ahab's house were punished (cf. "the house of Jeroboam" [Amos 7:9], referring to a dynasty of which Jeroboam was not the founder). Hosea 1–3 is, then, a prophetic narrative from the time of Jehoram (853–842). How this scroll became annexed to the prophecies of the Second Hosea, who lived about a century later, we do not know. It is not, however, the only instance in the prophets of a mistaken combination of prophecies belonging to two distinct periods (cf. the books of Isaiah and Zechariah).

Israel. As such her children are "children of harlotry," and are called by names expressing hatred. Here, as in all prophetic theatrical acts, the appearance is the essence, not the objective truth.

The actions of chapter 3 are also theatrical. The prophet is not commanded to "take" (i.e., marry) but to "love" a woman; i.e., to play the lover. His "mistress" does not bear him children. On the contrary, she symbolizes the break in the life of the nation—a forlorn interval in which the nation will be without king or cult. The prophet buys the woman, but on condition that she "sit solitary" for him, apart from all men— himself included. This is the sign of the desolate time that is about to come upon the people.

THE PROPHECIES—Chapter 1 contains a prophecy of the fall of the northern kingdom—doubtless a reflex of the Aramaean wars. Both here and in chapter 3 Israel's chastisement will be followed by the rise of a new united kingdom under a Davidide: "They will seek YHWH their God and David their king." Chapter 2 describes Israel's whoring after Baal; for this sin God will bring drought and famine. Then he will lead Israel into the wilderness, and from there give them their land in possession anew. The very name of Baal will be forgotten; Israel's God will not be called by that name any longer. A new covenant will be made with the beasts of the land, and the people will dwell in it secure from war. God will betroth Israel to him again, will bless the land, and will legitimize the "children of harlotry." Israel and Judah will be united under one king.

These prophecies appear to be from a Judean prophet; they recall those at the end of Amos, which give voice to the Judean hope of the restoration of the Davidic monarchy after the fall of Ephraim. If the prophecies are from the time of Ahab's successors, it is pertinent that Jehoshaphat, who then ruled Judah, was regarded as a righteous king (I Kings 22:43–47; II Chron. 17:3 ff.; 19). The prophets probably looked for great things in his time, as they later did in the reigns of Hezekiah and Josiah.

The chastisements of chapters 1–3 follow early motifs, echoing at times the phraseology of Leviticus 26:3–46; idolatry alone is the cause of doom. The prophecy of restoration follows the pattern of the ancient promises of peace and prosperity. There is no universal ideal. A new idea appears in the concept of eschatological repentance (2:9; 3:5). The faithless nation will realize its error and return to God; then God will renew his relations with the people. But the idea is expressed most naïvely; the motive seems to be longing for material blessing, and the repentance is cultic only.

All signs point to these three chapters being a product of preclassical prophecy.

SECOND HOSEA

In chapters 4–14 we enter the realm of classical prophecy. The Second Hosea is a lyrical poet of genius, whose writings are rich in color and imagery. Disjointed and at times obscure, they reflect the confusion and depression of the time. The northern kingdom is faltering under the rule of adventurers who no longer command the respect of the people. Its officers are drunkards. Ephraim is sick and old, shifting desperately between Egypt and Assyria in a vain endeavor to survive. Hosea does not mention Aram, or the Judean alliance with Assyria. Hence chapters 4–14 were composed after 732, when Tiglath-pileser destroyed Damascus, but before 725 when it became clear that it was Assyria, not Egypt, which was destined to destroy Israel.

Hosea's roots in Israelite tradition are manifold. He often alludes to the legends and history of Israel. Connections with wisdom literature are clearest in his fundamental images—*ḥesed*, *ʾemeth*, and "knowledge of God." He builds on the popular traditions of the Exodus, the Wandering, the covenant and Torah (4:6; 6:7; 8:1). God's special love for Israel is a central theme of his thought (9:10, 15; 11:1 ff.). Like Amos, he considers Israel's land "the land of YHWH," and all other lands impure (9:3). The land, the temples, and the festivals of YHWH are as much elements of his own faith as of the popular religion.

Hosea has been regarded as a mine of information concerning the syncretistic worship of ancient Israel. But chapters 4–14 have as little to say about syncretism as chapters 1–3. Baal worship is mentioned explicitly only twice (9:10; 13:1), both times as a sin of the past. The current sin of Ephraim—for Ephraim has "continued to sin" after having "died" for its Baal worship (the reference must be to the extirpation of Ahab's line)—is that of the calves (13:2).[6] Of a continuous historical sin of YHWH-Baal syncretism Hosea knows nothing. To the contrary, at first Israel was loyal to YHWH; apostasy set in only when Israel became fat and full (13:6; the idea was current then; cf. Deut. 31:20; 32:15). Formerly beloved, Israel has now been rejected by God (10:11; 11:4; 9:15). All prophecies of doom are based on the present guilt. Hosea knows of no punishment for past periods of sin; the past furnishes him only with sporadic examples of sin: Gibeah (9:9; 10:9) and Baal Peor (9:10). The Second Hosea is as silent as the First regarding syncretistic, mythological cults. Chapters 4–14 make no reference at all to worship of "other gods" as a sin of the present.

---

[6] The Baals of 11:2, in parallelism to images, are, as often in Jeremiah, no more than a derogatory reference to idol-worship in general, not to actual Baal worship.

THE GODLESSNESS OF ISRAEL—In the opening words of his prophecy Hosea formulates his indictment of the northern kingdom: "There is no loyalty [ᵓemeth], and no steadfastness [ḥeseḏ], and no knowledge of God in the land" (4:1). This is the core and essence of the prophet's message. The time was ten to fifteen years after Amos. The decadence of the bureaucracy had become aggravated by the dissolution of the monarchy, and the vassaldom to Assyria. Politically the country was split between pro-Assyrian and pro-Egyptian factions. The future appeared gloomy, and the demoralization of an era's end had set in. Pursuit of pleasure and a brave front was the order of the day among the aristocracy. Hosea observed this wealthy, arrogant, despairing society and was not deceived by its bravado. To this sensitive, lyrical dreamer and man of faith, the evil had begun not in Ephraim's senescence, but earlier, in its age of satiety and prosperity. Israel, grown fat and haughty, had lost the precious gift given to it in the wilderness; faith in God, "knowledge of God" had disappeared. Temples, altar, pillars, priests, sacrifices, feast and appointed times there were in abundance but "the spirit of harlotry is in their midst, and YHWH they do not know" (5:4). Not that the people turn to gods of the nations or to Baal—Hosea does not mention these—but their worship is without devoutness (ḥeseḏ), and therefore "idolatrous." To Hosea the moral corruption is but an expression of the radical evil, the forgetting of God. The presence of this evil is the chief object of his indictment: "For I desire ḥeseḏ, not sacrifice, and the knowledge of God more than burnt offerings" (6:6). It is an original conception of Hosea that these qualities, which the Torah and wisdom literature urge on the individual, must become realized in the national life of Israel. Everyone pays lip service to these virtues; they are written on stones, in books, and sung by poets, but they are not found in the life and heart of man. Because Israel does not possess them, they suffer the wrath of God. The fate of the nation depends upon ḥeseḏ, ᵓemeth and knowledge of God. Ḥeseḏ is the foundation of the religious life. It means love of God and devotion to him, and it includes love of the good (6:4 ff.; 10:12; 12:7). But more than that, it implies complete and exclusive trust in God, with the refusal to look for support and help except to him. Hosea insists that what the earlier literature acknowledged as a private virtue be made the policy of national life. Against this demand he re-evaluates the state and its armed might and condemns the cult. Without ḥeseḏ and knowledge of God what is the cult if not a lie and a profanation of God's name?

The source of the national disorder and decay is the forgetting of God. Man, governed by his lust and pursuit of power has become the center of all things. The ancient foundations of authority have gone: "We have no king, yea we fear not YHWH, and what will the king do to us?" (10:3). Cynicism and wantonness pervade Israelite society. The people continues to practice its cult, but this too is thoroughly demoralized. The priests want the people to sin so that they might eat more sacrificial meat (4:8); and the joy of the sacrificial celebration is debased by the presence of harlots (vs. 14).[7] Such a cult is an abomination, and Hosea rejects it with disgust. He discerns in this godless worship a pagan evaluation: as if the cult were intrinsically valuable, even when not animated by *ḥeseḏ*. Trust in temples, sacrifices, and priests as if they were innately effective is a pagan trust in human work. This view, it seems, underlies Hosea's repudiation of the calves, to which neither Elijah nor Elisha nor even Amos objected. The man-made calves epitomize the entire impious cult. The people no longer address God; "My people inquire of its wood, its stick instructs it" (4:12). During this decadent age the calves may have become fetishistic objects of popular worship. They are the work of human hands, argues Hosea, and not gods (8:4 ff.; 13:2). He mocks them (10:5 f.) and regards them as similar to the Baal worship of Ahab's time (13:1 f.). When the people eventually repent they will no longer say, "Our god" to the work of their hands (14:4).

HARLOTRY AND WINE—The Israelite desanctification of sexuality and intoxication (see above, pp. 319, 321) finds its clearest exponents in the prophets. Amos denounces harlotry and drunkenness in connection with his social protest: the aristocracy oppresses the people in order to pursue a dissolute life. But Hosea regards them as in themselves religio-moral sins. Harlotry and wine enthrall the heart and close it to the knowledge of God (4:11). There is a direct connection between them and forgetting God; the man governed by his appetites no longer has God and can only worship "idols" (4:10-18; 5:1-4; 6:8-10; 7:3-7). Because a "spirit of harlotry" is in the people, they cannot know YHWH (5:4); because king and officers fornicate and drink, none of them calls on YHWH (7:3-7). The harlotry spoken of in these passages is no more symbolic than the drunkenness with which it is linked; it has nothing to do with Baal worship (a misconception which has been furthered by the failure to separate the two Hoseas).

Of Israel's past sins, Hosea singles out only Baal Peor and Gibeah since both involve the sin of harlotry. In 9:1 ff. he blames Israel for their immorality "on every threshing floor," meaning that the celebrations of threshing

---

[7] This licentiousness does not appear to have anything to do with the Baal-Ashtoreth cult. Hosea says nothing concerning pagan rites in the worship of YHWH. The word *qeḏēshā* means "harlot" (cf. Gen. 38:15, 21 f.).

and vintage, like the festivities at the temples, were marked by sexual license. Women went from one threshing floor to another collecting "hire" from the new grain. Because God's blessing of fertility has been converted into harlot's wages Israel will eat "impure" in the land of their enemies.

ON THE MONARCHY, THE MILITARY, AND POLITICS—Hosea is the sole biblical author to echo Samuel's wrath at the monarchy and to revive the notion that it was born in sin and rebellion (13:10 f.). There can be no doubt as to what inspired Hosea's protest: "All their kings have fallen, not one of them calls upon me" (7:7). The monarchy has failed, just as have priesthood, prophecy, and the cult. One might say that Israel as a whole has been a failure. The current opinion that Hosea repudiates the monarchy in principle would be tenable had he advocated another political principle in its stead, as does Samuel. But Hosea does not call for a government of judges or prophets. His political ideal can only have been a monarchy guided by the word of God from the mouth of prophets (cf. his complaint in 8:4: "They made kings, without asking me; officers, without my knowing"). Hosea's disillusion is caused by the anarchy of the times, promoted by military adventurers who usurped the throne without even a pretense of divine election, and who were surrounded by drunken officers. The kings offer themselves as "saviors" of the people—with the support of Aram, Assyria, or Egypt. As is usual with Hosea, the phenomenon recalls to him a moment out of the past. When the people ages ago first clamored for a king-savior, there was already a glimmer of idolatrous trust in man's power. Now that the monarchy had severed itself entirely from the word of God, it becomes another symbol of Israel's trust in no-gods.

The first biblical author, indeed the first man in history, to condemn militarism as a religious-moral sin was Hosea. "Israel has forgotten its maker, and built palaces, and Judah has multiplied walled cities" (8:14). Israel has been unfaithful, sowed evil and reaped iniquity, "For you have trusted in your chariotry,[8] in the multitude of your mighty men. Therefore tumult will arise among your people, and all your fortresses will be ravaged" (10:13 f.). In the confession that Hosea places in the mouth of the repentant people they say: "We will not ride on horses nor say, 'Our god' to the work of our hands." Trust in chariotry and fortresses is as idolatrous as trust in an idol. How far Hosea intended to go in his condemnation is not clear. Since he speaks of the "multitude" of mighty men and walled cities, it may be only exaggerated militarism and the cult of power that he was denouncing. Even so, such a reproof in the days of Tiglath-pileser and Shalmaneser must be regarded as a climax of religious-moral idealism.

[8] Reading *brkbk* for *bdrkk* "in your way."

Hosea finds the clearest evidence that Israel has forgotten God in its reliance on heathen powers. Israel knows it is sick but instead of returning to God it looks to Assyria and Egypt for healing (5:13). Hosea recognizes the political folly of this—Israel is among the nations "like a vessel in which there is no value" (8:8)—but above all it is the breach of faith with YHWH involved in this maneuvering that he denounces. By seeking the protection of heathendom, Israel has surrendered to heathen values and the heathen world view. In the confession to be made by the people in the future they will say: "Assyria shall not save us . . . nor will we say, 'Our god' to the work of our hands" (14:4).

PUNISHMENT AND CONSOLATION—A spirit of gloom pervades Hosea 4–14; the prophet has no confidence that his reproof will avail. Both Ephraim and Judah have stumbled and fallen into the deepest corruption. For this YHWH "has become like the moth to Ephraim, and the rot to the house of Judah" (5:12); the sword, plague, drought, and fire will devour Ephraim (11:6; 13:14 f.; etc.). Punishment will be spiritual as well: YHWH will abandon Israel and Judah; men will seek him in vain (5:6; cf. Amos 8:12 f.; Mic. 3:6 ff.; Ps. 74:9; Lam. 2:9). Yet Hosea does not speak of deportation and exile by a conquering nation, but of returning to Egypt and going to Assyria for help (7:11 ff.). Those who escape God's net and reach these countries will live there desolate, eating "impure," without festivals and appointed times, and there they will die (9:3 ff.). This may reflect a current of migration to Egypt and Assyria that the prophet regarded at once as sin and punishment.

Hosea calls for repentance. If the people return and pray to God, "it will blossom like the lily and strike root like Lebanon" (14:2 ff.). But since there is no line of development in the prophecies of chapters 4–14 the calls for repentance and the visions of salvation appear rather as exhortings and hopes, than as events whose time is fixed. There is no explicit eschatological promise. In 11:8 ff. a kind of prophecy of salvation appears in the form of a divine soliloquy. God, out of grace, will not again destroy Ephraim, and will gather those who went to Assyria and Egypt. Chapter 12:10 may also be considered as a promise of blessing. God will again make the people dwell in tents (in the land, not in the desert; N.B. "their houses" of 11:11); i.e., he will restore them in their land to the simplicity and innocence of early days. This is the most explicit messianic vision in Hosea 4–14.

The Second Hosea sounds a new religious note. God requires of man not fear, humility, or submission but unconditional love and loyalty, human *ḥeseḏ* answering God's grace to man. From *ḥeseḏ* arise hope and trust, a life of holiness, conquest of appetites, and love of neighbor. The cult has no value, indeed it is loathsome, if it does not express *ḥeseḏ*. Hosea is the father of all utopians who believe in the power of love to bring salvation to man. He is the first to repudiate the power state.

The setting of Hosea's prophecy is national; his universal ideas are couched in national terms. He speaks in the name of the national covenant that YHWH made with Israel; the individual's duty of *ḥeseḏ* derives from the national obligation. Hosea has not a word for the nations. YHWH is, of course, the ruler and judge of all men, but the realm of his grace is Israel. Even his eschatological visions, such as we have of them, do not embrace the nations. Universal prophetic eschatology was born only after him.

CHAPTER XII

Isaiah, Micah, Habakkuk

ISAIAH

The year Jeroboam II died the empire-builder Tiglath-pileser III (745–727) came to the throne of Assyria. Ten years later Pekah of Israel and Rezin of Aram tried to coerce Judah into joining them in an anti-Assyrian front (II Kings 15:37 f.; 16:5 ff.). Ahaz, king of Judah, preferred instead to buy the aid of Tiglath-pileser, who proceeded to overthrow Rezin and detach the northern and western provinces of Israel (734); in 732 Tiglath-pileser took the Aramaean capital of Damascus. Pekah's successor, Hoshea, was encouraged by promises of Egyptian aid to rebel against Assyria. After a prolonged siege Samaria fell to Sargon in 722, and "Israel was exiled from its land."

During the reign of Hezekiah son of Ahaz, Judah's prospects of making a stand against Assyria improved. The Ethiopian dynasty which reinvigorated Egypt came into power in 714; Merodachbaladan of Babylonia was making a serious bid for independence. In 713–711 Judah and its neighbors, expecting Egyptian aid, revolted, but in 711 and 710 both the Palestinian and the Babylonian rebels were crushed. The accession of Sennacherib (705–681) was again the occasion of a general insurrection stirred up by Babylonia and Egypt (the story of II Kings 20:12 ff. may refer to these times). In 701 Sennacherib attacked the Palestinian-Syrian rebels, compelling the Egyptian army that came to their aid to retire. The countryside of Judah was subdued and Jerusalem came under siege. Hezekiah paid a heavy tribute to relieve the city (II Kings 18:14–15), but refused to open it to the Assyrians. Sennacherib failed to conquer the city or exile its inhabitants as he had hoped (II Kings 18:31 f.; Isa. 36:16 f.) but returned to his land, never again to set foot in Palestine.

This stormy and fateful period is mirrored in the prophecies of the First Isaiah (chaps. 1–39).

THE COMPOSITION OF THE FIRST ISAIAH—The book of Isaiah is generally regarded as the most composite and disordered of the prophetic books. Its composition and revision are held to have extended through generations of disciples and later prophetic writers down to the time—some think—of the Hasmoneans. Against this may be urged not only the general considerations adduced above (pp. 347 ff.), but, for Isaiah in particular, the rift between prophecy and reality that is in evidence throughout. The prophecies of Assyria's fall (10:5–34; 14:24 f.; 30:27—31:9) foresee the rout and collapse of the heathen empire upon the mountains of Israel. There is no inkling of the actual fate of Assyria at the hands of the Babylonians and Medes. Zion's remnant will live to see the glory of the new age (1:8, 25 ff.; 4:2–6; 10:32 ff.; etc.); not a word hints at Jerusalem's destruction by the Babylonians. The Davidic dynasty is promised an eternal and glorious kingdom (9:6; 11:1 ff.; etc.); no account is taken of the cessation of the kingdom in Nebuchadnezzar's time. None of the great historical changes that the Near East underwent during the seventh and sixth centuries are reflected in the prophecies of Isaiah 1–39. By the middle of the sixth century, then, a gap already existed between the predictive content of Isaiah and reality. Not only were the great events of 150 years (between Sennacherib and Cyrus) utterly ignored, but that which was promised never came to pass. Such a gap between prophecy and reality could hardly have arisen had the prophecies been constantly subject to revision. The historical horizon of Isaiah (leaving aside for the moment chapters 13–14) is perfectly natural, reaching to about the year 700. The momentous upheavals that occurred later are beyond its scope. The "allusions" scholars have found to later events are to such minor matters as the capture of Tyre by Artaxerxes Ochus, or the spread of the Nabateans in Moab, and the like. This speaks strongly for the imaginary nature of these allusions; there is no convincing evidence at all that the prophecies have been revised.

The rift between prophecy and history began to manifest itself already during Isaiah's lifetime. Damascus and Samaria did not fall together (as predicted in chapters 7, 8, 17). Nor did they fall before Immanuel could know "how to reject evil and choose good" (7:16) or before Maher-shalal-hash-baz could know how to cry "father" and "mother" (8:3 f.); Samaria fell ten years after Damascus, when both lads were already grown up. Ahaz did not suffer the fate threatened in 7:17; he was not attacked either by Egypt or Assyria (7:18 ff.; 8:5 ff.); Moab was not desolated "in three years" (16:14), and so forth. Such discrepancies might have been removed with but minor textual alterations. The fact that they were not indicates that the prophecies were published close upon their composition; from the outset they possessed such a fixity that not even the prophet himself changed them.

Especially instructive is the difference between the Assyrian prophecies in the body of the book (1–33), and the narrative and prophecy about Sennacherib's attack in chapters 36–37. According to the narrative the king and his messengers blaspheme Israel's God by name and argue that he will not save Jerusalem. Isaiah then prophesies that Sennacherib will not enter the city, that he will return to his land and there die. All these predictions came true. Presumably the present form of the narrative is not earlier than 680 (the accession of Esarhaddon); there is no reason to date it much later. Now it is remarkable that not one of the motifs of the narrative has entered the Assyrian prophecies in the body of the book. Into none of the prophecies in chapters 1–33 were references to Sennacherib's blasphemy, his retreat, or his murder insinuated. On the other hand, the theme of these prophecies— that YHWH will ravage Assyria's armies and shatter them on the mountains of Judah—has no echo in the narrative or its prophecy. The conclusion imposes itself that by 701 the Assyrian prophecies were so fixed that they could not receive any new motifs. The existence of such fixed, closed complexes of prophecies argues against the assumption of an "organic" growth of material through centuries.

Criticism, notwithstanding its preoccupation with the ideology, the style, and the historical allusions of Isaiah 1–33, has failed to take account of the monumental fact that the whole bears a unique ideological stamp that sets it apart from the rest of biblical literature. Alone in the Bible these chapters show no trace of the motif of national revenge. It is unnecessary to pass in review the references in the early literature to the motif of national militance and vengeance. The image of YHWH as "a man of war" (Exod. 15:3) underlies all the early narratives of the Exodus, the Wandering, the conquest, the period of the judges and the kings. Nationalism and militancy pervade the royal and war psalms (e.g., Pss. 18, 21, 45, 68, etc.). In time of stress the motif took the form of lament over the religious disgrace attendant upon Israel's political misfortunes, and entreaty for help and revenge. This motif is the basis of the popular conception of "the day of YHWH," which prevails in all of prophetic literature (except Isaiah 1–33) as well. Amos foretells the destruction of Israel's neighbors for their atrocities against Israel (1:3–15). In Amos 9:12 Israel is promised it will "inherit" the remnant of the nations (cf. Num. 24:18). (Since Hosea does not deal with the nations, he has no occasion for this motif.) Micah has a good measure of national revenge (4:13; 5:6 ff.; 7:9 ff.); Nahum is wholly devoted to it. The rest of the minor prophets, too, display this motif (Zeph. 2:7 ff.; 3:19; Hab. 3; Joel 4:1–21; Obad. 10–21). Jeremiah incorporates elements of a "day of YHWH" psalm (10:25), and prophesies retribution against the neighbors of Israel (12:14). See also the theme of national revenge in his prophecies against Moab (48), Ammon (49:1–6), Babylon (50–51), and compare 30:11; 46:28. Ezekiel predicts the destruction of the nations because of their glee at Israel's fall, and their part in its collapse (Ezek. 24–32; 35; 36:1–7). Haggai prophesies that "the treasures of all the nations" will flow into the temple (2:6 ff.). Zechariah looks for God's wrath against "the nations that are at ease" (1:14 f.; 2:1–4; 12 f.). The Second Zechariah prophesies the destruction of the hostile neighbors of Israel (9:1 ff.) and predicts Zion's sway over the entire earth (vs. 10; cf. also 12:1 ff.). Malachi breathes hatred of Edom (1:2 ff.). Isaiah 34–35, written in the style of the Second Isaiah and not from the hand of Isaiah son of Amoz, contain a sanguinary prophecy against "all the nations." The Second Isaiah is full of vengeful prophecies of all types (41:11 ff.; 42:13; 43:3 f.; 47; etc.).

Not so the prophecies of Isaiah 1–33. There are oracles against Assyria, Philistia, Moab, Aram, Ethiopia, Egypt, Babylon, Edom, Arabia, Tyre, and Sidon. But since the harm these nations did to Israel is never referred to, their punishment is not conceived of in terms of national revenge. "The king of Babylon" will be judged for his heathen arrogance and his cruelty. In the other visions no explicit ground is given for judgment, but the background is the same: general wickedness and moral corruption. Not even Assyria's fall is depicted as retribution for oppressing Israel, but as punishment for heathen pride and murderousness (10:5–34; cf. 30:27–33, 37:21–32, where the motive of national revenge is likewise absent). In chapters 25–26 and in 29:5 the condemned heathens are "ruthless nations," "a multitude of the ruthless"; wrongs against Israel are not specified. Isaiah's eschatological thanksgiving hymn (chap. 12) has many contacts with the Song of the Sea (Exod. 15) and with Psalms 47, 99, 105, 149; but while the latter abound with elements of revenge, retribution, and aggressiveness, Isaiah's psalm lacks these entirely. Deuteronomy 32:35 ff. is employed in Isaiah 1:24–31; in the latter, however, God's enemies are the wicked of Israel, not the nations.[1]

---

[1] In Isaiah 25:8 we find the motif of national disgrace. It is characteristic of Isaiah, however, that this disgrace is not conceived of in national terms, but involves "the whole earth," i.e., Israel's disgrace is a cosmic blemish. The only real passage of revenge in Isaiah 1–33 is 14:1 f., but this passage is out of context, and is surely an addition (see note 3), as is 11:14. Spoliation of the fallen enemy is mentioned in 9:5; 33:4, 23, but only as incident to the general holocaust.

Chapters 1–33 must be read after 34–35, 40–66, and the prophecies concerning the nations of the rest of the prophets, to appreciate the contrast. That a collection of prophecies bearing such a unique stamp could have resulted from an ages-long accretion of diverse prophecies and prophetic fragments is incredible.

The prophecies concerning idolatry also speak against the conventional view. The First Isaiah contains but seven verses on idolatry: 2:8, 18, 20; 17:8; 27:9; 30:22; 31:7²—all in Isaiah's characteristic style. Now the battle with idolatry is a theme of the Bible that recurs over and over again in many various formulations. Yet not one non-Isaianic verse on idolatry has penetrated Isaiah 1–33, in spite of centuries of alleged addition and revision.

The current view rests to a large extent on the fact that the book contains whole units (e.g., chaps. 15–16, 24–27) which differ literarily from the admitted creations of Isaiah. Yet it must be stressed that these chapters, like the rest of the book, lack the motif of national revenge. The literary argument would have weight only on the assumption that the prophets created *ex nihilo*. But the fact is that the prophets were heirs to a rich literary legacy, elements of which they freely drew upon and adapted for their own purposes. Differences in literary genres are most naturally explained as arising from the variety of the underlying material used by the prophet. It is also to be assumed that the prophets used differing literary forms in the various periods of their career. The decisive question is this: Are there prophecies in chapters 1–33 that reflect historical events after 701, or whose literary genre necessitates a late dating?

The vision of Babylon in chapters 13–14 has been interpreted from earliest time as predicting the fall of the Neo-Babylonian Empire; on that ground it is declared non-Isaianic. Now it has long been recognized and wondered at that these chapters contain no allusion to Babylon's destruction of Judah and Jerusalem. The "king of Babylon" is to be punished only for what he did to "peoples and countries" at large. Moreover the description of the king in chapter 14 ill suits the Babylonian rulers, who were not notorious as universal scourges (the sole warrior among them, Nebuchadnezzar, speaks in his inscriptions only of his elaborate building operations). Least of all does it suit the archeologist-priest Nabonidus, in whose reign Babylon fell; contrast also the descriptions of the late Babylonian Empire

² In 1:29 the reference is to gardens of the wicked built with money extorted from the poor (cf. Amos 5:11; Mic. 2:2). The *niṭʿē naʿamānīm* of 17:10 is taken by some to refer to gardens of Adonis. Even if the phrase did once bear this meaning, there is no evidence for it in biblical times. Here at any rate it seems to denote no more than a kind of plant; the reference is not to its idolatrous nature, but to its transitoriness.

in Isaiah 47 and Jeremiah 50–51, and especially in Daniel. On the other hand the characterization in chapter 14 suits well the kings of Assyria who were cruel destroyers, and who pursued world dominion with a ruthlessness they never tire of describing in their inscriptions. Chapter 14, notwithstanding some ancient elements, seems to have come from the same hand as chapter 10:5 ff.

Both the Assyrian and the Persian kings vaunted themselves "kings of Babylon," the proud mother of an ancient civilization. Some "took the hand of Marduk," formally receiving from him Babylon's world dominion. Tiglath-pileser III, a contemporary of Isaiah took a special name, Pulu, as king of Babylon. When II Kings 15:19 calls him Pul it therefore represents him actually as king of Babylon (though calling him king of Assyria). It is no wonder, then, that the poet of Isaiah 13–14 entitles the Assyrian tyrant king of Babylon.

But what of "Media" in 13:17 ff.? It is a common mistake of biblical scholarship to endeavor to interpret every prophecy in historical-realistic terms. Allusions to events that occurred subsequent to the purported date of the prophecy are "discovered," and thus poetic visions are transformed by critics into insipid postevent prophecies. Now Isaiah 13–14 do not speak of any historical destruction; though placed in a historical setting, the vision is a product of poetic imagination. The cruel and destructive Media of 13:17 is far removed from the Medo-Persian Cyrus who entered Babylon peacefully and announced himself king by grace of Marduk. These barbarians who do not know the value of money (contrast the real Media and Persia of Isaiah 45:3) are some nation from "afar," from "the north," whom the prophets like to envision swooping down on civilization from their remote haunts. For the author of Isaiah 13, Media is a representative of those northern barbarians whom Jeremiah 51:27 f. enumerates in detail: Media, Ararat, Minni, and Ashkenaz.[3]

The "Babylon" vision of Isaiah incorporates various older entities (e.g., a "day of YHWH" song [13:2–16], a *māshāl* composed in the form of a taunt-elegy [chap. 14]) that the prophet made over his for own use. In 14:24–27 he has appended his own explanation of the vision (just as in 16:13 f. he adds an explanation to the ancient oracle concerning Moab), expressly identifying this kingdom with Assyria, concerning whom he spoke before.

[3] The Chaldeans of 13:19, and the prosaic verses 14:1–2 (containing the only revenge motif in First Isaiah) are doubtless additions, made on the basis of the later interpretation of this chapter as referring to the collapse of the Neo-Babylonian Empire. The real continuation of 13:22 is 14:3 in which the fall of "Babylon" is said to put an end to Israel's subjugation. Cf. 9:3; 10:27; 14:25.

What Isaiah has to say concerning the real Babylon is contained in chapter 21. The vision of the city's fall shocks and stuns the prophet; since Babylon has not wronged Israel there is no joy at its fall. Indeed it is no world empire, but a city, conceived of as a metropolis of pagan culture, that is described. The fall of this center of culture into the hands of a "traitor and destroyer" arouses the sympathy and sorrow of the prophet. Obviously this has nothing to do with Cyrus' peaceful capture of the city. It has been surmised that the capture of Babylon by Sargon in 710 is the background of the vision. While the location of the prophecy after chapter 20 (fall of Ashdod, 711) supports this view, we must beware of seeking a historical allusion in every detail. This vision is a free poetic creation; it contains non-Isaianic elements (the ecstatic visions, the terror and trembling). Again an ancient oracle has been borrowed by Isaiah. Babylon was captured several times before Sargon; the fate of the city worked on the imagination of earlier writers; one of these earlier creations served as the framework of Isaiah's prophecy.

Chapters 24–27, usually entitled "the Isaiah apocalypse," are assigned to late times, though there is no agreement as to how late. However, nothing of the essence of apocalyptic—the perspective vision of historical ages—can be found in them. The vague, non-historical character of these chapters contrasts sharply with the wealth of allusion to historical persons and events that characterizes apocalypse. The judgment of "the host of heaven in heaven" (i.e., the stars [24:21]) refers neither to the fallen angels (who are not in heaven), nor to the angelic patrons of the nations (who are never conceived of as stars, nor called "host of heaven"); the reference is simply to eclipses, as part of the terrors of the day of doom—a motif of early literature (e.g., Amos 4:13; 5:8; Hos. 4:3; Isa. 13:10, 13), which the later apocalypses borrowed. If, as it seems, the monsters of Isaiah 27:1 represent heathen kingdoms (besides being real sea monsters; cf. Amos 9:3), the symbol is unparalleled both in biblical and apocalyptic literature. For precisely Leviathan, the sea serpent, and the dragon never are utilized as symbols for nations in apocalypse. The image and the language have a Canaanite background that had entirely disappeared by the age of apocalypse. Now that we know the Canaanite basis of such eschatological imagery there is no reason whatever to date it to late times.

In 25:8 and 26:19 reflexes of the later doctrine of resurrection have wrongly been seen. That God makes the dead live again is a theme of ancient doxologies (Deut. 32:39; I Sam. 2:6; Ps. 30:4). The antiquity of this theme is vouched for by its occurrence in Babylonian literature (cf. *I Will Praise the Lord of Wisdom*, end). Sick, suffering, and persecuted persons are said to "have descended into the pit" (Pss. 88:4 ff.; 143:3; Lam. 3:6, 54 f.); the nation too may be covered with "deep darkness" (Ps. 44:20), walk in "darkness" and live in the land "of deep darkness" (Isa. 9:1). Ezekiel depicts the exile and restoration of the nation in terms of death and revival (chap. 37). The Isaiah passages are to be viewed in the same light. The "death" that God will put an end to in 25:8 is the carnage of war (and perhaps plague, famine, and other visitations on sinners); at the end of days, when heathendom will vanish, God will do away with this manner of death—and thus "will remove the disgrace of his nation from the whole earth." The revival of the dead and the shades of 26:19 is but a figure for the deliverance of those who are in dire distress, who have come down to dust. Upon these "the dew of light" will descend and redeem them from darkness (cf. 9:1).

ISAIAH'S PROPHECY—The first collection of prophecies (chaps. 1–12) sets forth the foundations of Isaiah's world view. Composed during the twenty or twenty-five years from the end of Uzziah's reign to the beginning of Hezekiah's, these chapters were presumably selected and ordered by the prophet himself. The ideas of chapters 13–33 build on this foundation.

Various prophecies have been skilfully woven together to form the majestic introductory chapter which gives voice to the new prophetic doctrines that appeared almost simultaneously in the works of Amos, Hosea, and Isaiah. Isaiah condemns the legitimate national cult of YHWH as practiced in Jerusalem, not only its sacrifices, but its festivals, Sabbaths, and prayers (vs. 15) as well. To this empty cult is opposed the new idea of the absolute value of morality (vs. 17). Here, if anywhere, it is plain that the demand is not for a cultless religion; not only because prayer too is rejected by the prophet, but because Isaiah manifestly reveres the temple. Its courts are YHWH's courts (1:12); its future glory is the core of the vision of 2:2–4, and it is the location of the vision of chapter 6. There can therefore be no doubt that Isaiah's meaning is to deny the worth and sanctity of a cult that is not morally informed.

Isaiah underscores the decisive weight of the moral factor in determining Israel's fate by ignoring idolatry and enumerating only moral and social sins. From their nature it is plain that the culprits are the ruling classes; like Amos, Isaiah speaks for the downtrodden in the name of YHWH's covenant. God will be avenged of his enemies in Israel (vs. 24), and a new Jerusalem will emerge from the crucible of affliction, "the city of righteousness, the faithful city." All of Isaiah's prophecy, except his universal eschatology, is foreshadowed in this chapter.

The themes of the first collection recall Amos: the appalling corruption of the upper classes; the cleavage between the luxurious rich and the miserable poor; the pleasure-seeking aristocracy and their wanton women. These sins are conceived of in religious terms, as the forgetting of God. The Israelite has ceased to feel "the kingdom of God"; he no longer sees the world religiously, he cannot comprehend the divine meaning of events. (1:3; 5:12 f.; cf. Hosea's complaint of the absence of "knowledge of God"). Through political and military reverses God has given repeated signs of his wrath at Israel's corruption. But Israel "does not perceive the work of YHWH," it does not fathom the significance of its material distress. In 5:25 the earthquake during the time of Uzziah is alluded to as another manifest token of divine wrath. Yet the people complacently continue "business as usual"; this blindness and arrogance can lead only to worse chastisement.

In these chapters, punishment does not take the form of specific political events; it is panic and confusion (3:1 ff.), sickness and plagues (3:24 ff.), a far-off nation which will ravage and take captives (5:13 ff., 26 ff.). Surviving the catastrophe will be a righteous remnant who have been written in the book of life (4:2 ff.). Isaiah recasts the old remnant idea (see above, pp. 281, 368); not only the sinless, but also the repentant will survive. Going beyond the purely cultic repentance of Hosea 1–3, Isaiah understands God's intent to be the purging of the religious-moral dross of Israel. Chastisement will spur the people to repentance: "Zion will be redeemed by justice, and those in it who repent, by righteousness" (1:27). This is the prophetic touch. Redemption comes through a life of righteousness, innocence, and humility.

THE VISION OF THE END OF DAYS—The climax of the young Isaiah's prophecy is his vision of the end of days in chapter 2. This sublime vision, unparalleled in the earlier literature, ushers in a new phase in the history of Israelite religion; it is the beginning of prophetic eschatology.[4]

Though complex, the chapter is a unit. The vision of the temple mount anticipates the condition of mankind at the end of days, after God will bring low all that is "proud and lofty" on "that day" of which the rest of the chapter speaks. It is the climax of the chapter, all of which treats of one theme, the end of idolatry. After the prophet depicts the end-time,

---

[4] The prophecy of 2:2–4 is found again in Micah 4:1–4, a circumstance that has led to denial of its Isaianic authorship. Since there is no universal eschatological vision in the earlier literature (including Amos and Hosea) there is no ground for assuming an earlier prophet from whom both Isaiah and Micah might have borrowed the vision. In Micah the vision is solitary and entirely out of keeping with the rest of the prophecy (see below on Micah). Isaiah, the book of universalistic eschatology, is the natural context for the vision. The language is also characteristically Isaianic. The theory that Isaiah is too early for such a universalistic vision has no merit whatever.

he turns to reproach the house of Jacob for having forsaken their God (read *ᶜōsekā* "your maker" for *ᶜammekā* "your people") and having filled their land with heathenish things. This leads into a vision of the universal doomsday of YHWH, in which the idolatry that has dominated men will be crushed before the supreme majesty of YHWH "when he comes to judge the earth."

This vision is one of the noblest expressions of Israelite religion. It is the first to envisage the end of idolatry, and thus marks the beginning of prophetic universalism. Idolatry is conceived of as arising out of human pride. The wisdom through which man is creative and can control nature has become his stumbling block. Trusting in his power he makes himself gods; in adoring them, he worships himself. Here the prophet (like all biblical writers) has fastened upon the magical essence of idolatry. Man's pride expresses itself especially in aspiring to height; he conquers mountains and builds towers and high walls. An echo of the tower of Babel legend can be heard—indeed Isaiah's vision is the prophetic complement to that legend. The sin of the tower led to the rise of idolatry (see above, pp. 294 f.); when "towers fall" (cf. 30:25), idolatry will come to an end. But idolatry also has moral consequences for Isaiah; it not only flouts God, it nourishes the ambition to domineer over men. The thought pervades Isaiah that moral evil originates in idolatrous pride and love of power. The proud Assyrian king, trusting in his power and wisdom, seeks to destroy nations and possess their wealth. In Israel too wealth and idolatry go hand in hand (2:6 ff.). Haughty eyes, Tarshish-ships, horses and chariots, luxury and oppression, warfare and fortresses, idol-making, and worship of man's handiwork—all are manifestations of one and the same sin: idolatry, the forgetting of God. Since Israel has fallen prey to this sin, it too will suffer speedy punishment. But this punishment will be different from all that came before, for out of the ruins of the old order a new will emerge, in which idolatry, pride, wealth, and militarism will be no more. Then Israel will bear the word of God to all the nations, realizing at last the universal purpose of its divine election.

After God's judgment on "all that is proud and lofty," the mountain of YHWH's house will be exalted above all mountains, and all nations will come to it to learn YHWH's ways. Zion is depicted not as the seat of the Davidic dynasty, not as the capital of an Israelite empire, but as the center of God's universal kingdom. The cultic aspect of the temple is completely ignored; it is not a site of worship for all mankind (contrast 56:7), but the place from which justice and law go out to all men (cf. I Kings 8:41 ff.). From his temple God will instruct and arbitrate between nations, "so that they will beat their swords into plowshares and their spears into pruning-hooks; nation shall not lift up sword against nation, neither shall they learn war any more." Because the lust for power and domination has come to an end, warfare will cease, and men will return to the simple life of farmers. Enduring peace will reign among nations.

This vision is the first adumbration of the idea of an international morality. Going beyond the older conception of a universal individual morality, the prophet envisions a morality which will be binding upon the nations in their relations with one another. To this day the sword, recourse to which is forbidden to individuals by law, still remains the recognized arbiter between nations; murder is a crime, war is not. For Isaiah, social and international evil are equally the offspring of idolatrous pride and lust for power. War, no less than murder, is heathen. With the passing of heathenism and the establishment of the divine moral law among men, there will also be peace among nations. In this unprecedented vision, the early theoretical universalism of Israelite religion became an eschatological certainty. The legend of a primeval monotheism was rounded out by the vision of an eschatological monotheism of all men. What is to unite mankind in lasting peace is no Babylonian "tower whose top is in heaven," but the moral law of God that comes forth out of Zion.

THE THRONE VISION—Though the sublime beauty of the prophet's words may have affected his audience, his reproof worked no changes in society. His dejection at this failure is reflected in the bitter vision that closed his first period: the throne vision which he saw "in the year of the death of the king Uzziah" (chap. 6).[5] Standing before the temple the prophet sees the throne of God surrounded by seraphim in some cosmic height; the hem of the divine garment fills the temple. An angel purifies his mouth and prepares him for a new mission: "Make the heart of this people fat, and their ears heavy and shut their eyes. . . ." Here the frustration of the prophet finds poignant expression. To change the heart of the people is impossible; they must all perish in the impending doom except a remnant of "holy seed" who will survive.

POLITICAL PROPHECIES—During the subsequent forty years of his mission, Isaiah held fast to the vision of his youth. The land will suffer terrible

[5] This is not Isaiah's inaugural vision. It does not exhibit the characteristic dread and resistance to the divine call that mark other inaugural visions, e.g., that of Moses (Exod. 3–4) Jeremiah (chap. 1) or Ezekiel (chaps. 1–2). Here God appears to Isaiah surrounded by his suite; it is to these that the question, "Whom shall I send?" is addressed. Isaiah, who attends this solemn gathering of the divine court as one of God's agents, speaks up much like the spirit of Micaiah's vision (I Kings 22:19 ff.). It is with that vision that Isaiah 6 must be compared, rather than with any inaugural vision. In the throne vision Isaiah is already one among other messengers of God.

chastisement, but a remnant will survive in Zion through which Israel and all mankind will be saved. His political prophecies are grounded on this religious idea; they are not the product of shrewd statesmanship. But this idea gave him a peculiar ability to perceive the meaning of events in a realistic sense too. One thing is plain to Isaiah: pursuit of plunder and trust in power is ungodly, hence it cannot establish any lasting order; what it builds today it demolishes tomorrow. To be sure, Assyria is the rod of YHWH's wrath, but Assyria is at the same time the epitome of heathenism, the symbol of pride and presumptuousness. Heathendom's fall means first of all the fall of Assyria. That is why Isaiah rejects both Ahaz' policy of reliance on Assyria as well as Hezekiah's attempt to muster force against it. Hezekiah's coalition is in essence an Assyrian means to fight Assyria; several little "Assyrias" have banded against the giant. But their purpose too is nothing but plunder, wealth, and domination; in joining them Israel falls into the idolatrous pattern. But Israel cannot win at Assyria's game. To be sure Zion will be delivered, but not by Assyrian means. Only those who redeem themselves from "Assyrianism," from idolatry, will be saved in Zion.

Isaiah's political prophecies (chaps. 7–12) set in during the reign of Ahaz. Ahaz' refusal to join the Israelite-Aramaean coalition against Tiglath-pileser (734)—a coalition foredoomed to destruction in Isaiah's view—won Isaiah's praise (7:3–4; 8:1–4). But far from trusting in God, Ahaz proceeds to seek help from Assyria, whereupon Isaiah adds Judah to those who will suffer divine chastisement: "If you will not trust, you shall not stand" (7:9, and the Immanuel pericope 7:10–25; 8:5–15). The remnant that will survive the calamity which will come upon Judah from Egypt and Assyria (7:18) will live humbly as farmers and shepherds, eating the plain food of a simple society (vss. 22–25).

Isaiah's harsh prediction gradually became reality. The northern and Transjordanian provinces of Israel were seized by Assyria (8:21 ff.), but the destruction of Aram afforded partial solace (9:1 ff.). Promise of a better future was seen in the young successor Hezekiah (= $^{\jmath}\bar{e}l$ *gibbōr* of 9:5 f.). For the gloom of the present, however, the prophet saw no relief; the people continue heedless, and learn nothing from their distress. During the troubled last decades of the eighth century Isaiah composed the Assyria-Israel trilogy (10:5—12:10) that ends the second collection of prophecies. In it the new conception of universal history was crystallized.

In the first phase (10:5–15) Assyria appears as the agent of God's wrath against all the nations that have angered him (Aram, Philistia, Egypt, Tyre, etc. [cf. 8:4; 14:29 ff.; 17:1 ff.; 20:23; etc.]). But Assyria, unmindful of its divine mission, regards only its own interests, "for to destroy is in its heart, and to cut off not a few nations" (vs. 7). It boasts of its conquests; its arrogant king, ignoring God, exalts himself. Through Assyria, heathendom attains to its peak of power and universal dominion.

In the second phase (10:15–34) Assyria is destroyed—not for oppressing Israel, but for its universal cruelty and arrogance, for its disregard of God. The doom of Assyria is depicted as a judgment upon idolatry as such. While the vision of the temple mount is not provided with a historical setting, here the end of paganism is historically defined as the collapse of Assyria. To achieve his purpose God leads Assyria from triumph to triumph to the land of Israel. Only if it occurs there will the collapse of the heathen empire be recognized by all men as proof of YHWH's supremacy. When God's work has been accomplished in Zion (vs. 12), and the remnant of Israel have returned, he will shatter Assyria and remove its yoke from their shoulders. But this is not to be merely a local deliverance of Israel. "This is the plan planned for the whole earth, and this is the hand that is stretched forth upon all the nations" (14:24–27).

The final phase (11–12:6) is the rise of a new Davidic king. In chapter 2 after "high mountains" are laid low the humble temple mount is exalted; here after the fall of mighty Lebanon (Assyria), a shoot will sprout from the stock of Jesse. Again a political-historical setting is furnished the purely spiritual vision of chapter 2. The future king is not depicted as a redeeming Messiah, but as the culmination of God's grace to Israel: the founder of a line animated by "the spirit of wisdom and discernment, the spirit of counsel and bravery, a spirit of knowledge and fear of YHWH." He will be a king of the meek, a just and righteous ruler—unlike the present leaders of Judah. The natural order also will be reformed:

> The wolf shall lie down with the lamb,
> The leopard will couch with the kid. . . .
> And a little child shall lead them. . . .
> The suckling shall play at the den of the cobra. . . .
> They shall not hurt or destroy
> In all my holy mountain
> For the land will be full of the knowledge of YHWH
> As the waters cover the sea.

Thus the enmity between animals and men that sprang up after the sin of Adam will disappear.

Notwithstanding its national framework, the redemption has universal scope. The scion of Jesse is not a conqueror; he rules in Israel only (11:9). Just as the future authority of the temple over men is purely spiritual so also is that of the new king. He is a paragon for the nations, "an ensign of peoples, whom nations will seek" (vs. 10). The miraculous gathering of Israel's dispersed, which will be accomplished in the sight of all men, will likewise be "an ensign for the nations" (vs. 12). No mention is made of the removal of idols, but other prophecies leave no room for doubt that this feature of the vision of the temple mount was associated by Isaiah with the fall of Assyria (17:7 f.; 31:7). The fall of Assyria, the rise of a new Davidide, and the gathering of Israel's dispersed are all elements in the denouement of that period of distress.

Isaiah is the first prophet to affirm that all men would worship the one God at the end of days. This belief implies an idea of universal history, the hope of a reuniting of the strands of mankind that had been separated after the confusion of tongues. The abstract ideal is expressed in the vision of the temple mount; it is embodied in a real historical setting in the vision of the stock of Jesse. For the first time the idea of divine plan for mankind's future is conceived. The destiny of pagan Assyria is linked with that of Israel, the people of God. Israel is envisioned as the arena for the climax of world history; Jerusalem takes on universal significance. Classical prophecy after Isaiah adopted the concept of one history for all mankind; it remained for apocalyptic to give the idea its complete expression.

THE BURDENS OF THE NATIONS—In the burdens of the nations the prophet carries this new idea further. Often employing older materials, Isaiah composes a series of prophecies embracing all the nations: "Babylon"-Assyria, Philistia, Moab, Aram, Cush, Egypt, Babylon, Elam, Media, Edom, Arabia, Tyre and Sidon, Tarshish and Kittim. The old prophecies were adapted to their new setting by being related to events of the time; these are interpreted as episodes in the realization of a general divine plan.

Thus, for example, the burdens of Ethiopia and Egypt (chaps. 18–20): After prophesying the destruction of Ethiopia, the prophet voices his eschatological hopes; swift messengers are dispatched to Ethiopia with a message to all men, "When the ensign is raised on the mountains, look! When the trumpet is blown, hear!" God's kingdom is established; even the far-off nation will bring gifts to him in Zion (18:1 ff.). The peak of universalism is reached at the end of the burden of Egypt (chap. 19). After punishing Egypt, YHWH will send them a savior and reveal himself. An altar and pillar will be set up near the border, at which the Egyptians will sacrifice to YHWH. Egypt with Assyria will worship YHWH, with Israel the "third." Then YHWH will say: "Blessed be my people Egypt, and Assyria my handiwork, and Israel, my possession" (vs. 25). This remarkable prophecy has no equal in biblical literature; nowhere else is YHWH represented as calling a foreign nation "my people."[6]

THE DAYS OF HEZEKIAH—The religious-moral reformation that the prophet had demanded did not come about. To be sure, Hezekiah "did that which was right in the eyes of YHWH" (II Kings 18:3), and the religious movement led by the priesthood that was to terminate in the Deuteronomic reform already had begun its work (vss. 4 ff.). But neither king nor priest had it in their power to realize the moral ideal of the prophet. Nor could Hezekiah follow the political policy that Isaiah laid down. He could not "wait for YHWH" tranquil and trusting; instead he looked to Egypt and the coalition of anti-Assyrian states for help in throwing off Assyria's yoke. Isaiah warned of impending punishment, but he never prophesied the destruction of Jerusalem. He had believed in the inviolability of the city in the time of Ahaz and held fast to his belief in the time of Hezekiah also. This made him popular, but the people ignored entirely the moral and religious basis of his faith. Isaiah's prophecies during the days of Hezekiah therefore combine unshakable faith in Jerusalem, with bitter denunciations of the moral blindness of the people who are the subject of his hopes (22; 28–29).

The Egyptian policy of Hezekiah comes in for even stronger censure than Ahaz' reliance on Assyria. Isaiah views it as rebellion against God (30:1, 9). Echoing Hosea, he condemns Judah's reliance on Egypt's horse and chariotry as a disgrace for the kingdom of YHWH. He perceives, too, the practical futility of this policy (30:1–7). Yet, in contrast to Hosea, who yields to despair, Isaiah creates out of his anguish a wonderworld of vision; for unlike Hosea, Isaiah had an Archimedean point, his faith in Jerusalem and the Davidic dynasty. Inspired by a new intuition—the idea that Israel has a universal mission, that Israel's religion is to conquer the world—he cannot but believe that there will be a remnant in Jerusalem. But through the eyes of such a faith the request for Egyptian protection appeared all the more ignominious. How could Israel make known to all men the supremacy of the One with Egyptian horses and chariots? (chaps. 30–31).

[6] Notwithstanding the opinion of some scholars that these verses are late, the images of verses 19–21 must be pre-Deuteronomic, since neither high places nor pillars are yet considered illicit. Verse 19 was already interpreted by Josephus (*Antiquities* xiii. 3. 1 f.) to refer to the Onias temple at Leontopolis, and there are some moderns who concur in this view and imagine the verse to be a late addition. This is out of the question. The prophet speaks of an altar, not a temple (Josephus transforms Isaiah's "altar" into "temple" for his interpretation). A late supplementer would not have written "altar," and certainly would not have furnished his altar with a pillar!

The emptiness of Hezekiah's policy was exposed when Sennacherib invaded Judah. King and court surrender in terror to the Assyrian's demands. Only when Rabshakeh orders that the city be opened does Hezekiah draw the line. In despair he turns to his last resort, to YHWH and his prophet. The figure of Isaiah towers above the crisis; unlike Jeremiah later, he bids the king resist. Amidst panic and despair Isaiah alone stands firm in his faith, and with incredible assurance hurls taunts at the Assyrian:

> The virgin daughter of Zion despises and mocks you;
> The daughter of Jerusalem nods her head after you.
> Whom you have taunted and blasphemed,
> Against whom have you raised your voice
> And lifted your eyes aloft?
> Against the Holy One of Israel! [37:22 f.]

After the northern kingdom had collapsed, after Judah's allies and Judah's countryside had been ravaged, after Hezekiah had submitted to all but the last of Sennacherib's demands, Isaiah hurls taunts in the teeth of the Assyrian king! This audacity carried the day; the profound faith of the prophet won out. Hezekiah did not open the city and Sennacherib was not able to crown his campaign with the conquest of Jerusalem.

What was Isaiah's mood as his career drew to an end after more than forty years of struggle and vision? He had composed his visions out of the stuff of contemporary history. The Zion and Assyria of the eighth century were his subjects, yet he could not urge the literal meaning of his visions. As a poet and a visionary he sought truth in his visions, but he did not cease believing in them for not having found it. Such faith is what has kept them forever among the sacred possessions of Israel. Every Assyrian king might be the "king of Assyria" who was to fall on the mountains of Israel. Hezekiah should have been the "prince of peace"; but reality decreed otherwise. How and when the vision was to be fulfilled remained a divine mystery, but there could be no doubt that the great drama would eventually be played out between Israel and heathendom. Such must have been the conviction of Isaiah and those who preserved his prophecies. Not that the prophet was unmoved by the failure of his vision; when he gazes on the reality of "the valley of vision" he weeps bitterly and will not be consoled (22:4). Yet his last utterances express, through yearning and prayer, a steadfast faith. He still sees the visions of his youth in the fading light of old age.

THE IDEAL OF PEACE IN ISAIAH 1–33—The idea of universal peace broke upon the young Isaiah with full clarity and vividness in the vision of the temple mount. Its echoes can be heard throughout his prophecy. The vision of the triad of nations (19:23–25) not only heralds the end of idolatry, it also points to the concord that will prevail between the great empires. A "highway" will connect Assyria and Egypt, by which their peoples will have peaceful intercourse. The destruction of the "veil that is spread over all the nations" (25:7), and the slaying of Leviathan-tannin (27:1), are to be interpreted in this light. Destruction of the veil enables the nations to see the glory of YHWH; then "he shall destroy death forever" (25:8) i.e., an end will be made of the carnage of war. The slaying of Leviathan-tannin presages the disappearance of the ruthless domination of monster empires. The national prophecy about the stock of Jesse (11:1–9) shares the spirit of this vision. The future Davidide will not dominate other nations; he will impose on the world no *Pax Israelitica;* he will be rather "an ensign of peoples, whom nations shall seek."

Isaiah 1–33, that unique body of prophecies characterized by the absence of the theme of national revenge, is the natural setting of all these visions of peace. There can hardly be a doubt that they have not accumulated here by chance, as the product of a generations-long process of supplementing and revision.

THE HISTORICAL SIGNIFICANCE OF ISAIAH—The beauty of these prophecies is matched by their lofty moral content. With the insight of genius, Isaiah drew the ultimate consequences of the Israelite idea. His universal God is at the same time the Holy One of Israel; he believes in the election of Israel and the sanctity of Zion and the temple mount, yet he gives new scope to the universal essence of Israelite religion. God has set a reflex of his moral will in the soul of man; therefore mankind at large is the proper domain of his grace. God's purpose is not forever to remain hidden; he will be known to all men as he is to Israel. History moves toward the end of idolatry, the triumph of the divine moral law, the kingdom of righteousness and eternal peace. Idolatry is a passing phase; born of sin it will be purged away in the crucible of affliction. After the universal catastrophe, the veil will be removed from the face of the nations and the reign of arrogance will disappear.

Isaiah elevated the pious wish of ancient Israel, that the glory of the Lord should fill the earth, to an eschatological certainty. He placed the rest of mankind alongside of Israel as the recipients of God's grace and self-revelation, and thus burst the national confines of the early religion. Zion, until now a national and cultic symbol, became through Isaiah the symbol of the ultimate redemption of all mankind at the end of days. The vision of Isaiah heralds the new epoch in which Israelite religion was to become a factor in world history. Isaiah does not himself combat the idolatry of the nations, nor does he regard this as the task of Israel; idolatry will be destroyed, he believes, through a redeeming act of God. Nonetheless, his vision of the end of idolatry marks the beginning of the world mission of Judaism and Christianity.

Above this there rises as a yet unconquered peak the prophecy of universal peace. Isaiah was a visionary; he imagined that the end would come with the collapse of Assyria on the mountains of Israel. His vision of peace is associated with the peoples and events of his time, and it failed to come true in those terms. A thousand years passed and the paganism of antiquity died away, yet this vision remained a dream. But its truth endures and will endure forever. For Isaiah perceived that there can be no redemption for man unless he conquers idolatry as Isaiah understood it—his self-deification, the worship of his creations, his lust for power, avarice, class domination, the cult of the state. There can be no redemption unless man recognizes his moral obligation as transcendent and divine. No form of government, no level of material well-being will save man; he will be redeemed only when "towers fall," and Jerusalem triumphs over Babylon. Isaiah bequeathed a legacy of redemptive idealism; his vision has beckoned man through the ages as a bright star urging him to lift up his eyes on high. Even as a dream it has exercised a profound influence upon the human spirit. There is no doubt that its role in history has not yet been played out.

MICAH

Contemporaneously with Isaiah but before the fall of Samaria in 722,[7] Micah of the town Moresheth in Judah entered on his prophetic career. That he was a contemporary of Isaiah is clear from the superscription (1:1) and from the notice of Jeremiah 26:18 f. that the oracle of Micah 3:12 was uttered in the days of Hezekiah. Although none other of the prophecies has an explicit historical setting, there is no reason to reject as unauthentic any of the prophecies that are ascribed to Micah. The prophecies of salvation in chapters 4–5, the promise of an ingathering of the dispersion in 2:12 f. and 4:6 have, without adequate grounds, been dissociated from the reproof and warning of chapters 1–3. It must be borne in mind that Israelite prophecy was not merely "mantic"; it was not content merely to announce the inevitable decrees of fate, but had a religious-moral purpose. Its dooms are always contingent and may be averted by repentance and

---

[7] Micah 1:6 f. foretells Samaria's fall.

divine forgiveness. Hence a prophet may bear "contradictory" messages. As to the real background of the prophecies of ingathering, it is enough to recall that by Micah's time numerous Israelites were living in exile, especially after the fall of Ephraim. No passage in Micah reflects the collapse of Judah, the destruction of the temple, or the cessation of the monarchy. To be sure, the style of the book is composite and the connection of its chapters loose; it cannot be proved that all of it proceeds from the hand of one man. But neither is there any compelling reason to reject tradition, or to date any passage after the fall.

There are several points of contact between Micah and Isaiah, the vision of the temple mount (4:1–4; see below) being the most obvious. Yet the differences between them are too great for Micah to be regarded as Isaiah's disciple; both have common roots, but each prophesies in individual accents. Micah's social reproof, like Isaiah's, takes the part of the people against the upper classes; but he does not, like Amos and Hosea speak for the poor and weak in particular, but for "my people" (2:8, 9; 3:3) as a whole. A new note is the denunciation of false prophets. These men know how to reprove on occasion like the true prophets, but their reproof originates in selfish motives (3:5 ff.). They are hypocrites of the same stripe as those patriots who "build Zion" with crookedness and bloodshed (3:10). To Micah such persons are nothing but diviners for hire, a disgrace to true prophecy. The true prophet declares to the people its sin, and is endowed by YHWH with strength and courage to do so. His wages are hatred, rejection, even death. Against the priesthood, Micah hurls the reproach of teaching for money (3:11). There is a condemnation of trust in arms in 5:9 f. and possibly also in 1:13, where Lachish is branded "the beginning of sin" for Israel, apparently because it was the first station for the importation of horses from Egypt.

The doctrine of the primacy of morality is asserted with particular force in Micah, first because of the absence—except for 1:7 and 5:12 f.—of an attack on idolatry. Like Amos, Micah lays greatest stress on offenses against everyday morality (but unlike him he also speaks in 7:2 ff. and 3:10 of the gross offense of murder). In the wisdom-style soliloquy of 6:6 ff. Micah reaches an unprecedented position on the relation of cult to morality. No longer addressing himself to the nation, but to man as such, he enunciates three requirements of religious and moral goodness: "To do justice, to love kindness, and to walk humbly with God." The last is the antithesis of trust in the efficacy of a lavish cult—"thousands of rams, ten thousands of rivers of oil." It is not only the striking combination of sapiential elements (cf. Prov. 21:3, 15, 21; 22:4) that gives the passage its force; it is the unparalleled idea that these are God's *sole* demand of man that carries it beyond anything in wisdom. When combined with the extreme historical conclusion that Micah draws from the new moral doctrine, his prophecy may well be regarded as its climactic and ultimate expression·

This historical conclusion is reached in 3:12: "Therefore, because of you Zion shall be plowed as a field, and Jerusalem shall be ruins, and the temple mount a forested height." Here for the first time the possibility of the destruction of Jerusalem is envisaged. No one before Micah prophesied the destruction of YHWH's temple; to Isaiah its permanence is an article of faith.[8] With what impact this dreadful prophecy fell upon the ears of its hearers may be seen in the narrative of Jeremiah 26:17 f. A century after it had "lapsed" elders still knew of it. Thus Micah infers the final consequence of the new prophetic doctrine; he prophesies not merely punishment, but total destruction. Moreover, while Jeremiah and Ezekiel combine the religious with the moral factor in their prophecies of destruction, Micah insists that it will come for moral sins alone.[9]

Micah's prophecies of salvation are inspired by the popular image of the "day of YHWH." They are purely national, and are pervaded by the theme of national revenge. YHWH will succor his people not as reward for any change of heart, but for the sake of his name which was profaned among the nations (7:10; compare Deut. 32:26 ff. and Pss. 44; 74). No mention is made of repentance; it is rather an act of God's grace that Israel will survive; he will forgive "the remnant of his inheritance" and cast its sin into "the depths of the sea" (7:18 f.). In 7:20 the idea appears in classical prophecy for the first time that God will redeem his people for the sake of the patriarchs. The idea of an eschatological remission of sin is an innovation of Micah, and was to become a permanent feature of later eschatology.

How the Isaianic elements in the prophecies of salvation fared in Micah is an illuminating chapter in the history of transmission of prophetic ideas. The vision of 4:8—5:6 is doubtless influenced by the Ariel prophecy

---

[8] I Kings 9:6 ff. differs from Micah doubly: it merely threatens destruction, and does that for the sin of idolatry. Micah is the first who prophesied the destruction of the city, and that for its moral sins.

[9] How this oracle was understood by a later age illustrates well what of the new prophecy was assimilated in pre-exilic times by the people. The elders of Jeremiah's time consider the oracle to have lapsed because Hezekiah feared and entreated the favor of YHWH (Jer. 26:19). But it was precisely this sort of repentance that Micah rejected: "Then they will cry out to YHWH, but he will not answer them" (3:4). God will not be satisfied by entreating favor but only by "doing justice and showing mercy." The awful prophecy was remembered, but its radical moral ground was ignored. The same thing happened to Isaiah's prophecy of the temple mount in the very book of Micah itself.

of Isaiah. But while Isaiah links the miraculous deliverance of Jerusalem with the end of heathendom and idolatry, here it is a national prophecy only. The Davidic monarchy will return to its former glory, and the enemies of Israel will be crushed and despoiled by the new king, who is described as a ravaging bull or lion. Nothing remains of the Isaianic images of the righteousness and gentleness of the new kingdom. In this setting the Isaianic vision of the temple mount is particularly out of place; moreover, it has received an ending (4:5) that wholly contradicts it. Note, however, that it is not a technical, scribal error that has placed this vision here. It has been reworked—the phrases "many nations," "many peoples," "mighty nations" are characteristic of Micah 4–5. But despite this tie with the context, it is a foreign body in Micah. Too splendid for the author of chapters 4–5 to overlook, he was yet unable to assimilate its spirit. Does this mean that the author of these chapters was not Micah? Perhaps. But it may mean only that not every one of the new prophets could rise to Isaiah's heights. Neither Amos nor Hosea created an eschatology equal to their new doctrine of morality. The man who had the audacity to say "Zion shall be plowed as a field" still may not have had the vision of Isaiah in eschatological matters. Such a commingling of heterogeneous elements as we find in the book of Micah is characteristic of most of the works of literary prophecy.

When the predicted destruction became reality some centuries later the prophecy of Micah—the first to give voice to the idea of Jerusalem's fall—became a source of consolation for the shattered people because it combined the final act of God's wrath with the idea of an eschatological remission of sin—the ultimate act of divine grace. Collapse and ruin, it affirmed, were not the last word of God's plan. In the Babylonian period the words, "and you shall come to Babylon" were attached to 4:10. As late as Rabbi Akiba's time Jews were still drawing comfort from Micah's prophecy (cf. Sifre at Deut. 11:15b). For Christianity, the prophecy of a ruler who would come from Bethlehem had crucial importance. The idea of an eschatological remission of sin was decisive for Jesus as well; by his claim to remit sins he expressed his own belief that this was one of the redeeming tasks of the Messiah. Wondrous is the career of ideas.

HABAKKUK

The prophecy of Habakkuk reflects the period of transition from Assyrian to Babylonian hegemony of the Fertile Crescent; it inaugurates the Chaldean period of prophecy. Better than Jeremiah, who also prophesied at this time, Habakkuk gives voice to the perplexity of the age at the sudden rise of a new pagan empire. Not one of the prophets of the Assyrian period had foreseen a new heathen empire after Assyria; the rise of Babylonia was therefore a distressing riddle, like the rise of Greece and Rome afterward. The book of Habakkuk is a monument to the bewilderment and shock of that historical juncture.

The prophet begins with a complaint, sapiential in tone and style, about the success of evil in the world. The occasion of the complaint is specified in 1:5 ff. where, having called the world to witness, he says: Behold YHWH has raised up (read *hinnē hēqīm*) a new villain, a pillager and a ravager, whose success not only encourages wickedness, but promotes the cause of the false gods. Why does God suffer the success of the wicked, why does he deliver men into their hands, as if they were fish of the sea? Since the trouble of Judah is not singled out, it appears that the prophecy was uttered in the early days of Nebuchadnezzar (605), before Judah's subjection. The prophet does not believe that any nation deserved to be subjected to the Chaldean oppressor.

Habakkuk's response (chap. 2) is couched in terms of prophetic faith; it is a vision, a promise. God, he asserts, has set a limit to the sway of the oppressor; his time will come, it will not tarry. Habakkuk creates the terms *qēṣ* and *mōʿēḏ*, which became permanent features of later apocalypse. It is he who formulated the great principle: "The righteous shall live by his faith" (2:4). Faith in God's justice is the basis of his existence; he cannot abandon it and live on. The new tyrant will surely be repaid in his own currency. All his conquests will prove ephemeral and a new age will dawn when "the land will be filled with the knowledge of the glory of YHWH as the water covers the sea" (vs. 14; cf. Isa. 11:9).

Habakkuk is the only biblical author who deals with the Jobian problem of the success of the wicked in the historical-national realm. This prophetic Job is concerned, in first instance, as an Israelite; the success of the heathen confirms the faith in idols. The idolatry of the nations has suddenly become a problem for Israelite religion. Whereas the Bible generally conceives the success of the pagans as the source of arrogance or self-deification of king or people (see e.g., Exod. 5:2; Isa. 10:12 ff.; Ezek. 28:2 ff.; Obad. 3, etc.), Habakkuk considers it rather as the source of a metaphysical error. The pagan ascribes his power "to his gods" (1:11). To Habakkuk it is an issue of God against the gods; what distresses him is not so much the existence of the heathen empire as the ground its success gives to belief in idols.

Accordingly God's answer to the prophet sounds a new note: "Woe to the believer in dumb idols" (2:18–20) is directed for the first time to pagan ears.

These three verses open, if only in a vision, the polemic against idolatry addressed to the nations. In the political arena paganism triumphed. But behind the clash of political forces lay a more primary issue: the one God versus the idols. On this battlefield Israel did not admit that it could ever be vanquished. "The righteous shall live by his faith" has, in this context, a particular Israelite meaning: no political and military victories of heathendom can bring Israel to believe in "dumb idols." The wish for paganism's fall became detached from the dream of the fall of the pagan kingdom. The "faith" was not dependent upon the coming of the "end." The Israelite idea began to prepare to engage triumphant paganism on its own ground. This is the historical significance of the prophecy of Habakkuk.

CHAPTER XIII

The Prophecy of the Fall: Jeremiah and Ezekiel

THE PROBLEM

For the historian of Israelite religion the fall of Jerusalem poses two questions: What was the real historical cause of the fall? and what was the basis of the prophecy of doom that Jeremiah and Ezekiel prophesied? The two are not identical.

Empirically speaking, Jerusalem fell because the might of Babylonian arms overwhelmed the small state of Judah which was abandoned in the field by all its allies. Biblical tradition, of course, gives another answer. In the belief that the destiny of Israel is controlled by a special providence the Bible regards the fall as a unique event. It was a punishment, first for the sin of idolatry, and second for moral sin; both were violations of the covenant which entailed—as Israel had been forewarned they would—political collapse and exile. This view is justified from the standpoint of biblical faith, but it can hardly be of service to the empirical historian, who deals only with factors that operate equally in the history of all societies. Since idolatry or polytheism in themselves have nowhere been the causes of a national political collapse he cannot simply adopt the biblical theory and regard them in this case as causes of Israel's fall.

Nor can the moral factor be so regarded. To be sure, social dissolution is a real factor in history and has more than once contributed to political collapse. But the fact is that such dissolution did not exist in Judah at the time of its fall. Of this there is decisive proof. Jerusalem was not demoralized, did not suffer a failure of nerve, did not lack the will to fight. On the contrary, little Judah armed with an ardent faith went out boldly to battle the Babylonian Goliath. Jerusalem withstood a long and terrible siege and was finally brought to its knees only by famine and death. Its "wicked king" and officers were faith and fortitude incarnate. The record tells of but one voice raised against resistance: that of Jeremiah, who cannot at all be counted among the "sinners."

This is not to deny that the prophetic condemnations of Israel's moral sin were founded on some reality. However since prophecy, like the rest of the Bible, assumes that Israel is judged by a unique and special divine standard, its testimony alone is not enough to establish the fact that Israelite corruption had reached the proportions of a genuine historical factor. Violence, bribery, oppression, and murder are found everywhere and in every age. Nothing suggests that the extent of Judah's corruption was abnormal; it was surely no more than that of its conqueror. As a matter of fact, the denunciations of the last prophets indicate a change for the better since the times of Amos, Hosea, Isaiah, and Micah. By the end of the seventh century we hear no more of the dispossession and impoverishment of masses. The dispossessed had apparently been consolidated by then into a new industrial class, the "craftsmen and smiths" of Jehoiachin's exile (II Kings 24:14, 16). Nor was there a change for the worse in the matter of slavery. Jeremiah 34:8 ff. makes it clear that never before Jerusalem's siege were slaves emancipated in accord with the law of Exodus. The attempt to do so during the siege miscarried, owing to the fact that it had no economic foundation. But even Jeremiah, who condemns the failure of the people to abide by the covenant, does not speak of inhumanity in the treatment of slaves. The fate of Jeremiah himself argues against the supposition of a moral decay. During the very years of his nation's death struggle he can call for desertion to the enemy and yet live; surely nowhere in oriental antiquity but in "sinful" Jerusalem could this have happened. Officers save him in Jehoiakim's time; during the siege they decide to kill him, but, fearing to shed blood, they throw him into a miry pit! Later they come to talk with him, and finally he is placed in a guardhouse where he lives undisturbed.

It is the inner necessity of religious faith, of theodicy, that has produced the biblical doctrine of Judah's sin—a doctrine that was shared alike by Jeremiah and Ezekiel and their opponents (see Lam. 4, from the pen of a courtier who trusted to the end in God and his king). This doctrine does not assume that Judah had sunk into the depths of a degeneracy that would in the normal course of things have led to its collapse. To the contrary, Israel's doom followed its own special law: when Israel's "measure" was filled, God visited on it the sins of all the generations. To make this doctrine the foundation of a naturalistic-empirical interpretation of Israel's collapse is to be utterly naïve.

The real problem of the age is the prophetic doctrine of the fall. The people were sinning, to be sure, but they had sinned in Isaiah's time also, yet he had threatened chastisement, but never total destruction. Any man could plainly see that there were more regiments to Nebuchadnezzar's army than to Zedekiah's, but Sennacherib's forces were no less overwhelming, yet Isaiah steadfastly believed in Jerusalem's inviolability. The faith of the people in Jeremiah's time was one with that of Isaiah; without denying Israel's sin, it maintained a complete and wholehearted trust in YHWH. Not the people's faith, but that of Jeremiah and Ezekiel must be explained. Why could they not adopt the view of Isaiah?

Christian doctrine regards the two destructions of Jerusalem as merited by the continuous sin of Israel, which was climaxed by the rejection of Jesus. Israel's sinfulness, rooted in a constitutional tendency to rebellion, led ultimately to its being rejected by God. Whether consciously or not, this conception underlies the modern interpretation of Israelite history which has been formulated by Christian scholars. It is reflected in the scholarly axiom that the Israelite people was pagan, only the prophets and their circles transmitting the monotheistic idea. The god of the popular religion is described as a syncretistic YHWH-Baal, naturally connected with the people and the land. It was therefore necessary that Israel undergo a violent deracination in order to be sundered from its old territorial-natural religion. National collapse and exile was the precondition for the victory of prophetic monotheism over popular beliefs. It was consequently the inner demand and ultimate object of prophecy, although to be sure the prophets as individuals loved their people. In the prophecy of the fall adequate expression was finally given to the radical opposition between the particularistic, syncretistic faith of the people and the universalistic monotheism of the prophets. In the flames of his temple the god of the popular religion perished; the destruction was the victory of prophecy. In Second Temple times Judaism again became "national," and prophetic universalism was again opposed by the national particularism of the folk; the old struggle was renewed. The spirit of ancient prophecy found its new embodiments in John and Jesus. It was, therefore, but natural that Jesus should predict the destruction of Israel, Jerusalem, and the temple, and that Israel on its part should reject him and his doctrines.

This view necessarily assumes that the rift between prophecy and the popular religion reached its height in the age of the fall. The reforms of Hezekiah and Josiah are not to be thought of as having been accepted by the people; Josiah's tragic death heightened the power of the popular syncretism. Two images of YHWH were current; that of the prophets and that of the people. The fanatic, nationalistic belief of the people in their king and temple stemmed from their pagan faith. Jeremiah knew this well, and therefore recognized the collapse of the monarchy and the destruction of the temple as an ineluctable necessity. His prophecy of the fall thus poses no problem to Christian scholarship.[1]

The error of this view consists, first, in opposing Israel's nationalism to universalism, and then regarding it as pagan. Upon this foundation of confused ideas the entire structure is reared. It is not perceived that universalism has two senses (see above, pp. 127 f.), and that Israel always conceived YHWH as universal in his dominion and exclusive in his godhood, while at the same time confining the manifestation of his special grace to Israel. This level of national monotheism pervades all of the Torah literature and several of the prophets (e.g., Ezekiel) whose monotheism is beyond question. There is nothing essentially pagan in the popular belief that YHWH is particularly connected with Israel and its land. It is a fact that the popular, patriotic prophets who opposed Jeremiah were no less "universalistic" (in this sense) than he. Hananiah ben Azur prophesied in the name of YHWH, "Thus will I break off the yoke of the king of Babylonia ... from the neck of all the nations" (Jer. 28:11). Hananiah takes it for granted that it was none other than YHWH who made Nebuchadnezzar king over all the world, and that it would be he therefore who would redeem all men from his yoke. This same nationalistic faith animated Isaiah, who was as much a monotheist and a universalist as Jeremiah.

The reason that biblical scholarship lays such stress on the national aspect of the popular religion and insists so emphatically on its pagan character is that otherwise no real evidence is available that the popular religion of YHWH was pagan. Never—it cannot be too often repeated—do any of the prophets reprove the people for mythological beliefs; upon this rock all theories of popular syncretism or polytheism are shipwrecked. Not even Jeremiah and Ezekiel know of mythological beliefs; like all of the Bible they too rebuke the people only for pagan cultic rites. One cannot speak, then, of a struggle between two religious world views—a popular and a prophetic—which could be resolved only through the destruction of the nation.

Furthermore it is wrong to regard the prophecy of the fall as especially expressive of the prophetic aspiration to universalism. Jeremiah and Ezekiel are the prophets of the fall par excellence. Of the two it is Ezekiel who with

---

[1] For the classic statement of this view, see Julius Wellhausen, *Israelitische und Jüdische Geschichte* (Berlin, 1907), pp. 29 ff., 139 ff., 359 and Cornill, *Der israelitische Prophetismus* (Strasbourg, 1912), pp. 113 f., 177.

ruthless consistency predicts the fall as inevitable and necessary; Jeremiah promises to the very last that if the city will submit to Nebuchadnezzar there will be no fall or exile. Yet Ezekiel, is, of all prophets, the most archaic; his views, more than any other's, follow early models whose horizon was limited to Israel. The one prophet who preaches destruction most single-mindedly is thus the farthest removed from the universalistic spirit of classical prophecy. The irony of this has escaped modern theologians, but to the historian of Israelite religion it is a circumstance of the utmost importance for the understanding of the prophecy of the fall.

The threat of national collapse and exile appears in but four books of the Bible: Leviticus (chap. 26), Deuteronomy (chap. 28) and those parts of Jeremiah written under its influence, and Ezekiel. That is to say it appears precisely in contexts from which prophetic universalism is utterly absent and in which the viewpoint of the national religion prevails—contexts which regard temple and priestly holiness as central. This argues strongly for the unrelatedness of the prophecy of the fall to universalism. On the other hand, it is noteworthy that the universal visions of the prophets clothe themselves in prophecies not of doom, but of salvation, and they are always connected with the glorification of Israel, Jerusalem, and the temple. The highest expression of prophetic universalism is Isaiah's vision of the temple mount, which has nothing to do with the prophecy of the fall. All of prophetic universalism is suffused with national symbols.

These two facts expose the baselessness of the modern theory. National and prophetic faith were not radically opposed; they did not represent a clash between pagan and non-pagan religion. The prophecy of the fall did not arise out of a denial of the national religion and an aspiration toward a non-national universal monotheism.

IDOLATRY IN THE AGE OF THE FALL—The view that the prophecy of the fall was a reaction against the popular religion seeks support in the fulminations of Jeremiah and Ezekiel. It is supposed that after Josiah the pagan practices of Manasseh's time were restored, indicating that the reform did not have a popular basis. What is the evidence for such a reaction?

Neither Jeremiah nor Ezekiel censure their age for mythological beliefs. Vestigial, fetishistic idolatry, on the other hand, had existed in Israel from earliest times, alongside of the worship of YHWH in a pagan manner (e.g., by child sacrifice). These types of "idolatry" were present in the generation of the fall as well; the question is, to what extent? Were they nationwide and royally sponsored as in the time of Manasseh? Can they serve to account for the prophecy of the fall?

Jeremiah and Ezekiel reproach the people at large for the general sin of worshiping "other gods," the host of heaven, and so forth. There is no way of discovering the basis for these broad accusations. However, three passages (Jer. 7:30; 32:34; Ezek. 8) seem to imply that in the time of Jehoiakim and Zedekiah the public, royally sponsored pagan worship of Manasseh's time was restored. Again, Jeremiah 2:23, 7:31 f., 19:5 ff., and 32:35 condemn the burning of children in Topheth while Ezekiel 6 prophesies to the mountains of Israel that all their high places, at which a cult of "idols" is practiced, will be destroyed. Are these not evidences that the reforms of Josiah lapsed after his death?

That the Josianic reforms endured is attested to in the first place by the last chapters of II Kings. Not only are they silent regarding the supposed revival of Manasseh's cults after the death of Josiah, they report no particular form of idolatry at all during the reign of Jehoiakim or Zedekiah. The last kings of Judah "did what was evil in the sight of YHWH," but this cliché is not detailed in any way. Most significantly, the writer does not ascribe the fall to the wickedness of these kings. So far as the author of Kings knows, the fate of Judah was sealed by the sins of Manasseh (II Kings 21:10 ff.; 23:26 f.; 24:3 f., 20). The death of Josiah was the beginning of the end; the rebellion of Jehoiakim was a punitive decree of God (24:3); Zedekiah rebelled "owing to the anger of YHWH" (vs. 20), who thus executed his decision based on the earlier sins of Manasseh. It is obvious that the author of Kings would not have invoked the sins of Manasseh as the cause of the fall had he known of like outrages committed by Jehoiakim or Zedekiah. Nor does the author of Kings mention a recurrence of the high-place cults. His silence on this point, after carefully reckoning this sin against all the kings from Solomon to Josiah, can mean only that the high places were not rebuilt.

Ezekiel 8 is the only source from the time of Zedekiah that depicts pagan cults in the temple in the style of Manasseh. Ezekiel's picture—an idol of Asherah, women wailing for Tammuz, sun-worship, etc.—can be controlled and must be tested by the writings of Jeremiah. For while Ezekiel was wafted to Jerusalem by the spirit in "visions of God," Jeremiah walked its streets daily. Moreover Jeremiah supplies a corpus of vivid and circumstantial descriptions of the conditions prevailing in Jerusalem at that time. Now the utterances directed against Jehoiakim specifically (22:13 ff.; 36:29 ff.) do not allude in so much as one word to idolatry. The prophecies made "to the house of the king of Judah" (21:11—22:30, see also 17:19–25) do not censure the kings of Jeremiah's day for idolatry. Jeremiah knows of Baal and his prophets only in the past (23:13—the prophets of Samaria; cf. vs. 27). Priests, kings, officers, and the city of Jerusalem are accused of idolatry only in passages which survey all of Israel's history (2:26; 8:1 f.; 22:9; 32:32). Jeremiah never accuses contemporary Jerusalem and its inhabitants in Ezekiel's terms.

Jeremiah was accustomed to speak in the temple and visited it on other occasions during the reigns of Jehoiakim and Zedekiah. Yet he never sees what Ezekiel "saw," nor does he ever reproach the people for practicing in it the abominations mentioned in Ezekiel 8. Especially significant in this regard is the great arraignment of 7:1–16 (from the days of Jehoiakim, cf. 26:1–24). Jeremiah accuses the people of profaning the temple by entering it after committing various atrocious actions. Among these, however, are not the erection of idols in the temple. On the contrary, the sanctity of YHWH's house is intact insofar as it is not polluted by the sin of those who enter it—an entirely different position from that of Ezekiel.

In the fifth year of Jehoiakim, Jeremiah sends Baruch to recite the scroll of his prophecies in the temple on a fast day. The officers are stunned at hearing its contents. Did this solemn recitation take place in a temple housing a statue of Asherah, and women wailing for Tammuz, without anyone taking notice? At the end of Jehoiakim's reign Jeremiah brings the Rechabites into one of the temple chambers by command of God (chap. 35). Jeremiah is at home in the temple, and has free access to its chambers. Did he or the Rechabites find any of the "loathsome things" that Ezekiel saw there? Not once does Jeremiah demand of his priestly friends (e.g., Zephaniah, the overseer of the temple [29:26 f.]) or the kings, or the officers, that they cleanse the temple of abominations or Tammuz rites; this can only mean that they were not present in his time. That is why Jeremiah can promise the city and the king that if they but submit to Babylonia they will be delivered—a promise not likely to have been made to a city and temple polluted by idolatry.[2]

There was, then, no national, public pagan cult sponsored by kings and disposing of its own temples and priests. The real nature of the idolatry that so exercised Jeremiah is revealed in his denunciations of the one

---

[2] Hence it is plain that when Jeremiah speaks of the pollution of the house (7:30; 32:34), he refers to a sin of the past which still haunts the people. That Topheth was a sin of the past is clear from the circumstances of chapter 19. Topheth is deserted when Jeremiah comes to it; he brings along his own audience of elders and priests. The people are addressed only when he returns to the temple court (vs. 14). He never accuses his contemporaries of sacrificing children. The prophecies concerning high places must refer to the time before 620, for in the stories from the reigns of Jehoiakim or Zedekiah, they are never mentioned. The same is true of Ezekiel 6. Although the prophet speaks only of the destruction of high places, making no reference to the temple of Jerusalem, in the visions of 8–9 he sees the destruction of the city and temple alone; no high places are destroyed. Clearly there were no high places at that time; this sin too belonged only to the past.

genuinely idolatrous cult of his time: the women's worship of the "queen of heaven" (7:17 f.; 44). This cult is generally identified with the worship of Ishtar, Ishtar-Isis, or the like. Jeremiah, at any rate, does not call the goddess by name; did the women know the name of the "queen"? Jeremiah argues that this was a cult of gods whom they and their fathers "did not know" (44:3). He did not regard it, then, as having a history in Israel. The women who carry on this cult are old; they still remember the days of Manasseh (44:17 f.). Their goddess has no temple, priest, or animal sacrifices. Cakes and libations, which according to 44:17 were votive, were made for her, apparently at no set times. Her devotees are poor; children collect wood in the streets or the woods, fathers kindle the fire, and the women bake the cakes. It is a forlorn and debased worship, without benefit of temple, altar, or clergy. That this was "the popular religion's cult of Ishtar-Tammuz" is a romance of modern scholars. The cult of Ishtar-Tammuz as we know it from pagan sources had fixed nature festivals and was celebrated by throngs at temples with songs and processions. This private cult, lacking any definable mythological content, which some old women performed with the help of their relatives, is of a piece with the vulgar superstitions of the ignorant that are found everywhere down to this day. To the prophet, however, this vestigial idolatry constituted a grave sin and impurity of national proportions.

Another testimony to the character of the real idolatry of those days may be recovered from Ezekiel 8:7–18, after due allowance is made for the fantastic nature of the passage. The thought of the idolaters is remarkable; they commit these abominations not because they believe in the idols, but because "YHWH does not see us, YHWH has left the land" (8:12; 9:9). If this picture has historical value it reflects the mood of persons who had broken under the strain of the time. They act in the dark, because "YHWH has gone and cannot see . . ."! Whoever these men may have been, they were certainly not representative of the people or the leaders of Judah. Far from believing that YHWH had "left the land" the latter were supremely confident of his presence among them; they had a faith in the inviolability of his temple and the eternity of Jerusalem which Jeremiah deplored. On the basis of this faith they went out to battle the Babylonian conquerors of the world.

There is, finally, the evidence of the book of Lamentations. This book is the product of militant Jerusalem to which Jeremiah was opposed; its sympathies lie with the king and the officers. The poet attributes the fall of Judah to sin, of course; but he knows nothing of a widespread sin of idolatry—to him the temple remains to the end God's "footstool" (2:1).

Embattled Jerusalem appears here as it really was, wholly trusting in its one God.

The "sin" of Jerusalem at the time of its fall was much less clear-cut to men of that age than to the scholars and theologians of today. The people asked, "Why has YHWH decreed all this great misery upon us; what is our iniquity, and what our sin which we have sinned against YHWH our God?" (Jer. 16:10). Jeremiah himself is, in the end, compelled to fall back upon the sin of Manasseh (15:4), like the author of Kings. He cannot deny the bitter protestation of innocence, "Fathers have eaten unripe grapes, and children's teeth are set on edge" (31:29). Lamentations justifies God by confessing Jerusalem's "sin" (1:8, 18; 4:13), but is unable to define it satisfactorily (cf. 5:7). Rabbinic homilies added to the sins of that generation according to the inventiveness of the preacher; even then it was necessary to throw into the tally the sins of earlier generations back to the days of Solomon in order to justify God's judgment. The historians and theologians of today continue the process, and yet the measure of sin will not be filled. The source of Jeremiah's and Ezekiel's prophecy of doom remains to be elucidated.

JEREMIAH

In the year that Jeremiah began to prophesy—the thirteenth of Josiah (625)—Nabopolassar founded the Neo-Babylonian kingdom, and the death knoll of the Assyrian empire sounded. Allied with Kyaxares of Media and the barbarian tribes of the northern mountains, the Babylonians attacked Assyria in 616. In 612 Nineveh fell, and, although Egypt rushed north to help, the remnant of the Assyrian Empire collapsed within a few years. Egypt and Babylonia now prepared to contest the succession to Assyria's Syro-Palestinian domain. Nabopolassar having grown old, Nebuchadnezzar, the crown prince, led the Babylonian forces at the fateful battle of Carchemish (605). Egypt was forced to abandon its claim in Syria and Palestine, and Babylonia became mistress of the Fertile Crescent up to the borders of Egypt.

The Assyrian collapse had great political and religious consequences for Judah. For the devout, it opened the way to rid the country of Manasseh's idolatry. Young King Josiah gave them his full backing. The beginning of Josiah's purge is dated to the twelfth year of his reign (the year of Ashurbanipal's death) in II Chronicles 34:3. In his eighteenth year (about 620), the "book of the Torah" was found in the temple. In an unprecedented action, the king convened a national assembly and bound the people to the observance of the book in a new covenant; the Deuteronomic reform followed. Jeremiah witnessed and participated in this covenant, as will be shown below. During the death struggle of Assyria, Josiah appears to have thrown his support on the side of Babylonia. When Pharaoh Necho passed through Palestine in 609 on his way to aid Assyria, Josiah met him at Megiddo in an attempt to stop him; the venture cost him his life. His Egyptian-appointed successor, Jehoiakim, remained loyal to Egypt even after Carchemish (605), when Babylonia took over Palestine and Syria. Later, Jehoiakim rebelled against Nebuchadnezzar. Jerusalem suffered its first exile, and the temple was despoiled in the time of his successor, Jehoiachin, whose three-month reign ended in captivity (597). In his stead, Nebuchadnezzar enthroned Zedekiah, Josiah's third son.

The exile and captivity of Jehoiachin and the spoliation of the temple appeared to be the extremity of divine wrath; surely now, many hoped, YHWH would turn and favor his people and city. Both among the exiles and in Judah, prophets arose proclaiming that the exile and the rule of Babylon would soon end. Zedekiah, following the model of Hezekiah a century earlier, sought to enlist allies for an insurrection; the movement was encouraged by the accession of a new Pharaoh, Psammetichus II (594–588), though the revolt did not materialize until the accession of Pharaoh Apries (588–569). Then, Zedekiah, abandoned by his allies, had to face the Babylonians alone. An Egyptian relief force failed to break Nebuchadnezzar's siege of Jerusalem, and Zedekiah could hope only for a miracle from YHWH (Jer. 21:1 f.). Famine in besieged Jerusalem decided the issue, and the city fell in 587. The upper classes were sent into exile; those remaining in Judah were under the charge of Gedaliah ben Ahikam, appointed governor by the Babylonians. But Gedaliah was assassinated the very same year, whereupon many more people fled Judah to Egypt. Thus Judah went into exile.

JEREMIAH'S LIFE—Throughout this troubled and tragic period, Jeremiah prophesied. The burden of his prophecies was doom and destruction. Josiah's reform does not satisfy him; Assyria's fall evokes in him no rejoicing; mindful of the terrible fate that awaits the people of Judah, he does not marry and have children (16:1 ff.). The Chaldeans, who strike terror in Habakkuk, are messengers of God for Jeremiah. More than any other prophet he excites the animosity of his countrymen all his life. He curses them and is cursed by them; his kinsmen, the priests of Anathoth, plot to kill him. During Josiah's reign he was an obscure rustic visionary, an object of reviling and abuse by his neighbors. During the reigns of Jehoiakim and Zedekiah, he attains national prominence. He is consulted by royalty and attacked by the government officialdom; he is no longer abused by private individuals, but is now a "public enemy."

Jeremiah first collided with the authorities during the reign of Jehoiakim. After a terrible prophecy of doom uttered in Topheth and then repeated in the temple court, Pashhur, the temple officer, strikes him and puts him in prison (19:14—20:3). Later, another such prophecy spoken in the temple court enrages priests, prophets, and people. He is put on trial for his life, but is saved by some officers, of whom Ahikam ben Shaphan is singled out for mention (chap. 26).

The rise of Nebuchadnezzar in 605 supplied Jeremiah with the key to all his prophecy of doom (see below). In that year, he collected his prophecies, added a new one concerning the king of Babylon, and dictated them all to his secretary, Baruch. This record of prophecy and fulfilment is read to the people by Baruch in the court of the temple. The people listen respectfully to Baruch's recitation. Jeremiah's identification of the future destroyer of Judah as the Babylonian king arouses the interest of the court; the officers request and receive a private reading. When the king asks to hear it, however, they are terrified; knowing the king's temper, they advise Jeremiah and Baruch to hide. Jehoiakim listens to the prophecies, and, since he has already put one prophet to death (26:20 ff.), does not shrink from burning the odious scroll section by section. He orders Jeremiah imprisoned, but the prophet cannot be found (chap. 36). The prophet's withdrawal is only temporary, for later in the reign of Jehoiakim, Jeremiah appears and preaches publicly again in the temple, and has free access to its chambers (chap. 35).

In the reign of Zedekiah, Jeremiah becomes a consultant of the king. Zedekiah's relation to Jeremiah parallels that of Hezekiah to Isaiah. The king esteems the prophet as a man of God, but cannot regulate state policy in accord with his demands. In the fourth year of his reign, when Zedekiah invited representatives of neighboring countries to a conspiratorial meeting in Jerusalem, Jeremiah goes about openly denouncing the conspiracy against Babylon and predicting that all would be slaves of Nebuchadnezzar. It is likely that the effect of this subversion told years later in Judah's isolation during her final struggle. After the siege sets in, Zedekiah and his officers remain in contact with the prophet, asking him to pray for the city (21:1 f.; 37:3). But Jeremiah persists in his gloomy prophecies. When he publicly advocates that the people and the army desert to the Babylonians, official patience with him comes to an end. Caught under suspicion of flight to the enemy, he is imprisoned. Even then Zedekiah continues to inquire of him surreptitiously, and has him transferred to the court of the guard and supplied with ample rations (37:11 ff.). There Jeremiah carries on his seditious prophesying until the officers demand his death as a public enemy. Zedekiah is forced to yield, but arranges to have him extracted from the pit of mire into which he was thrown to die. Again the king inquires of him secretly, and again he is told that if he does not surrender, the city will be burned, and he will fall captive to the Babylonian king (chap. 38).

After the fall of the city, the Babylonians, who learned that Jeremiah opposed the rebellion, free him and bestow upon him a bounty (chap. 40). When Gedaliah is murdered and the people inquire of Jeremiah what to do, he urges them in the name of YHWH to stay in the land and live under the Chaldeans; they disregard his advice and go down to Egypt. Jeremiah and Baruch accompany them, and there his last prophecy against the idolatry of the Jews in Egypt is uttered. We do not know how and where he died.

Jeremiah is surely a tragic figure; his tragedy is the inner conflict between his national feeling and his prophetic mission. To be sure, he suffered at the hands of his contemporaries. But any tried and true revolutionary of modern times who fell into the hands of the police, was imprisoned, or was condemned to hard labor or banishment, suffered as much or more. For long years, Jeremiah prophesied a terrible fate for all that was sacred to the people. He foretold that its king would be buried with "the burial of an ass" (22:19). During the death throes of Jerusalem, he tried to persuade the people to surrender to the Babylonians. Yet during the reigns of both Jehoiakim and Zedekiah, he was permitted to prophesy and was imprisoned only for short periods. Judging by normal standards one must say that what he suffered at the hands of his contemporaries was as nothing compared with the gravity of his offenses against them.

THE COMPOSITION OF JEREMIAH—As in the case of the other prophetic books, it is assumed that Jeremiah has undergone a complex history of composition, with generations of revision, glossing, and expansion. Against this, however, must be urged the rift between prophecy and reality that manifests itself throughout the book. Moreover, the prophet was twice compelled by events to change the line of his prophecy, yet his earlier visions were left unrevised.

In the fourth year of Jehoiakim (the first of Nebuchadnezzar, 605), Jeremiah is charged to indite in a book all his prophecies from the time of Josiah (36:1 f.). The sum of these prophecies is: "The king of Babylon is surely coming to destroy this land" (vs. 29). But we search in vain for mention of the king of Babylon in the basic corpus of the prophecy—

chapters 1–19; not even the name of Babylon appears. Instead, Jeremiah announces the coming of a nation "from the north country," "from the uttermost parts of the earth," to ravage the land (6:22); in 1:15, he declares that he does not intend any specific nation, but "all the tribes of the kingdoms of the north." Opinion is divided concerning the identity of these northern nations—understandably so, since the prophet himself never specified them. One thing only is plain; he does not mean Babylonia.[3] In the first year of Nebuchadnezzar, Jeremiah realized that Babylonia was the correct interpretation of the "northern nation," and henceforth he prophesies about Babylon. Yet this solution did not penetrate a single one of the earlier prophecies. This can mean only that they were fixed and sealed by that time.

A second transformation occurred in the year when Nebuchadnezzar subjugated Judah. The "northerners" had not been represented as successors to Assyrian hegemony, but as pillagers and ravagers. Consequently, in the first Babylonian prophecy (25:3–11a, 13) and in 36:29 (year 604) as well, Jeremiah still portrays Babylon as a ravager. The king of Babylon will come and scourge the land, cutting off man and beast. The realization that Nebuchadnezzar was not at all a destroyer of nations, but the founder of a new world empire, brought about a deep change in the theme of Jeremiah's prophecies. The prophecies of subjugation and surrender come into being, with the new idea that God has decreed that all nations of the earth must accept the yoke of Babylon's king for a fixed term. Babylon is no longer the ruthless barbarian; on the contrary, the nation that submits to it will be well off. This new theme too failed to insinuate itself into a single one of the earlier prophecies.

The rift between prophecy and reality had developed already during the lifetime of the prophet and the generation immediately following. Many northern kings did not set up thrones at Jerusalem's gates (1:15); the people of Anathoth were not utterly destroyed (11:23; cf. Ezra 2:23). Jehoiakim did not receive "the burial of an ass," nor was his corpse thrown outside of Jerusalem (22:18 f.; 36:30; cf. II Kings 24:6); Zedekiah did not die in peace (34:5), nor did God ever remember him in Babylon (32:5); the exiles were not compelled to worship other gods "day and night" (16:13); Nebuchadnezzar did not destroy or exile Egypt (46:13 ff.); the seed of Jehoiachin—notwithstanding 22:30—was thought fit for kingship both by Ezekiel (17:22 ff.) and the Restoration community, who pinned their hopes on Zerubbabel, a descendant of Jehoiachin (I Chron.

---

[3] In chapters 50–51, the northern people destroy Babylon itself; compare 6:22 f. with 50:41 f.

3:15 ff.; Hag. 2:21 ff.; Zech. 3:8; 4:6 ff.; etc.). That these and other instances of disaccord with reality were left untouched speaks against the view that the book was subject to continuous revision through the ages. There have been technical errors, and the order of chapters has been confused, owing to the fact that the book was compiled from several collections over a period of time. A few marginal remarks may also have entered the text. But by and large the prophecies have retained their original form. The many changes in the Greek version (itself filled with peculiar errors) are remarkable, but do not always prove that the translators had a less "edited" text before them. Many of these changes themselves are "editings" of the translators, whose object is not always clear.

Wholesale excisions and condemnations of passages on literary and aesthetic grounds are certainly unjustified. Scholars have freely cut and altered the text of Jeremiah to make it conform with their preconceived notion of what a true prophet and poet would have written. Repetitions and expansions are declared the work of editors, commentators, or epigoni. The fact is rather that reiteration is the distinctive phenomenon of Jeremiah —one might almost say his original and peculiar form. Not only are words, phrases, and motifs repeated, but whole passages recur two, three, and four times. These repetitions are alleged to be the work of editors or accidents of transmission. But these factors were operative in the transmission of all biblical texts; how, then, can they explain the peculiar quality of Jeremiah? Did editors and expanders through the ages conspire to fill just this book with so liberal a measure of repetition? This peculiar feature can be explained only as the design of the original author. Jeremiah relished his figures and phrases and liked to employ them in various contexts. In the Topheth speech (chap. 19), he warns of punishment for immolation of children and sacrificing on rooftops. In the impassioned poem "Cut off your hair. . . ." (7:29 ff.), he mentions the abominations in the temple and immolation of children. During the last days of Jerusalem, he speaks of sacrifice on rooftops, immolation of children, and the temple abominations all together (32:29 ff.). The outstanding case of this phenomenon occurs in the chapters concerning the nations, 50–51. Here citations of other passages in the book are particularly numerous. Why? The content of the scroll—a curse against Babylon to be sunk in the Euphrates—certainly has something to do with it. Jeremiah follows the style of the Torah's curses and monitions in which an expansive, verbose style predominates—a common Semitic feature of this genre of writing (cf. the series of curses at the end of Hammurabi's code). That the Torah's style of reproof and warning is at the bottom of Jeremiah's repetitiveness as a whole is something that appears to have escaped the notice of the critics.

THE INFLUENCE OF DEUTERONOMY—The wisdom and psalm literature of Israel have left a strong mark on the book of Jeremiah. What attests to a turning point in the religion of Israel, however, is the influence of the book of Deuteronomy. Jeremiah is the first of the literary prophets whose work is organically linked with a source of the Torah. His age marked the beginning of the crystallization into a book of the Torah literature. As a priest, Jeremiah was one of the "handlers of torah," the tribe whose "craft" the Torah was. Phrases and even whole passages of Deuteronomy are interwoven into nearly every chapter of his book. The law reflected in Jeremiah is that of Deuteronomy, and there is a particularly manifest bond with the non-legal framework of D. Deuteronomy is cited in all more than two hundred times. The writings of Ezekiel, the Second Isaiah, Haggai, and Zechariah also show the influence of D, but not nearly so much as Jeremiah. The conclusion imposes itself that Jeremiah spoke the language of D because he lived and created in its atmosphere. Jeremiah is the prophet of Deuteronomy and the covenant that was made upon it.

The inaugural vision of the prophet and his conception of prophecy are drawn from the relevant passages in Deuteronomy. God touches Jeremiah and says, "Behold, I have put my words in your mouth" (1:9), thus materializing the expression of Deuteronomy 18:18—the only other occurrence of the phrase in the Bible. The various commands of God to the prophet—"All that I command you, you shall speak," "I am with you," "fear not nor be dismayed"—are taken from Deuteronomy (compare Moses' exhortation to Joshua in Deut. 31). The terms of the death penalty pronounced by Jeremiah upon Hananiah ben Azur and Shemaiah the Nehelamite for false prophecy (28:16; 29:32) are derived from Deuteronomy 13:2 ff. and 18:15 ff. Jeremiah's test of the true prophet (28:9) is that of Deuteronomy 18:21 f. In 11:1 ff., God's curse of him who does not obey "the words of this [the Josianic] covenant" and Jeremiah's response, "Amen," are inspired by the priestly rite of blessing and curse described in Deuteronomy 27. Not only does Jeremiah follow Deuteronomy in its condemnation of the high places, he even recasts the image of the past in accord with the Deuteronomic requirement. He calls the Shiloh sanctuary "My place . . . where I caused my name to dwell at first" (7:12), allowing, like Deuteronomy, only one place "which YHWH will choose to cause his name to dwell there" (Deut. 12:11; 14:23). Jeremiah apparently regards the Shiloh sanctuary as the first embodiment of the centralization law, thus laying the foundation for the later Jewish view set forth in the

Mishnah (Zebahim 14.4 ff.). The warning of 17:19 ff. concerning the observation of the Sabbath is couched in the terms of Deuteronomy. The reproof in 34:8 ff. concerning the failure to keep the law of manumission follows the formulation of the law in Deuteronomy 15:12 ff., rather than that of Exodus 21:1 ff.; Jeremiah, like Deuteronomy, gives equal treatment to female and male slaves (cf. also verse 13 [the liberation from Egypt] with Deuteronomy 15:15; there is no such allusion in the law of Exodus). The error of 34:14, "At the end of seven years" (instead of the correct "six"), is a lapse of memory based on Deuteronomy 15:1, the first of two social laws, of which the slave law is the second; Jeremiah recalled the Deuteronomic slave law in context, but, citing it from memory, he committed this error. No later glossator would have erred in this manner. The faithful transmission of the error is a further witness to the fidelity with which the prophet's words have been preserved. The "new heart" and the "new covenant" of Jeremiah's eschatology are rooted in Deuteronomy 29–30. Moses complains that Israel has not yet been "given a heart" to comprehend God's wonders (29:3); later he promises the people that when they repent in their exile, God will show them mercy and "will circumcise their heart and the heart of their seed to love the Lord with all their heart and soul" (30:1 ff.). The very ideas and expressions recur in Jeremiah; the prophet promises the exiles that if they return to God with "all their heart," God "will give them a heart" to know (24:7) and fear him (32:39). The figure of circumcising the heart occurs in 4:4; 9:25. The idea of the new covenant is woven out of the Deuteronomic injunctions to keep the words of the Torah in the heart, write them on doorposts, and teach them to children (Deut. 6:4 ff.; 11:20 f.); these become the basis of the eschatological promise that God will write the Torah in the heart of the people, and children will know it without being taught. The warnings of Jeremiah, as noted above, are repetitious like those of Deuteronomy. Not only are whole passages out of Deuteronomy 28 and 29–32 adduced, the motifs of punishment in Jeremiah are, for the most part, Deuteronomic. The destroyer-nation of 5:15 ff. is drawn from Deuteronomy 28:49 ff.; the symbol of the "iron yoke" (28:14) comes from Deuteronomy 28:48; Deuteronomy 28:53 is cited in 19:9. The threat that the exiles would worship "other gods" (16:13) against their will is found again only in Deuteronomy (4:28; 28:36, 64). Jeremiah himself reveals the origin of these visions of punishment when he says (11:8) that the evil comes as the fulfilment of "the words of this covenant," i.e., the Josianic covenant mentioned in verses 2–5.

This bond between Jeremiah and Deuteronomy is not accounted for merely by the influence of the book on the prophet's environment. The inaugural vision of the young Jeremiah antedates the discovery of the book in the temple, yet it is pervaded by the figures and language of Deuteronomy. The book must have been an element in Jeremiah's education; he studied it in his youth in the priestly school of Anathoth and absorbed its language and spirit. To him the book was "the Torah of God," and he regarded it thus to the end of his days. He is the prophet of Deuteronomy and of the covenant that was based on it. This alone explains the man and his work.

ANTECEDENTS AND ROOTS—Like all the prophets, Jeremiah inherited the foundations of his world view from the popular religion. He lives and creates in the atmosphere of a monotheistic people. His God is non-mythological; the cult he knows is non-magical. He shares with the people the belief in Israel's election and uniqueness and the faith in the everlastingness of YHWH's covenant, of Jerusalem, and of the Davidic monarchy. The destruction that he foretells is temporary; afterward YHWH will return the captivity and renew Israel's days as of old. Jeremiah is also the bearer of the great ideas of classical prophecy. His eschatology is a legacy from Isaiah, although he does not match Isaiah in his power of vision.

The common notion that Jeremiah is the father of individual religiosity is an error related to the other error that he is the founder of the individual psalm. The individual psalm had existed in Babylonia and Egypt for centuries and had reached the peak of its development in Israel long before Jeremiah; he merely utilized its forms and style for his own purposes. The individual element in Jeremiah's prophecy is not more pronounced than that in the stories about Abraham, Isaac and Rebecca, Jacob and Rachel, Moses, Samson, Hannah, David, Solomon, and so forth. The notion that he innovated the doctrine of individual retribution is equally groundless. An element in his messianic vision is that "each man will die for his own sin" (31:29 f.); however this is but one motif—not particularly emphasized—in a broad canvas of vision. The doctrine of retribution that pervades the bulk of his prophecy is essentially societal-national. He not only cites the verse "paying back the sin of the fathers into the bosom of their children" (32:18), this is his own view as well: the exile and destruction of his generation are "because of Manasseh son of Hezekiah" (15:4), his prayers of vengeance against the men of Anathoth include the plea that "their sons and daughters may die in famine" (11:22; cf. 18:21).

Jeremiah nowhere expresses the doctrine of the primacy of morality as an explicit contrast of morality versus cult. He emphasizes the idea that God delights in kindness and righteous judgment (9:23; cf. 22:15 ff.). He negates the value of the cult of his contemporaries, and in 6:20 and 7:21 f. appears even to deny the value of the cult as a whole—but only if his words are torn from their context. In 7:23, he opposes a positive demand to the cult: "I did not speak to your fathers on the day I took them out of Egypt concerning whole and peace offerings; but this thing I commanded them: 'Hearken to my voice . . . and walk in all the way that I command you.'" Moral conduct is not singled out for emphasis. The demand of Jeremiah (formulated in Deuteronomic style, and almost literally repeating the prophecy about the Josianic covenant [11:4 ff.]) is: not sacrifice, but observance of the whole of the covenant. External cult acts are rejected in favor of the faithful observance of the Torah.

That Jeremiah does not intend to abrogate the sacrificial cult is evident from 14:11 f., in which the people's cry and prayer are denounced along with their sacrifices. Jeremiah himself prays and urges to pray (29:7, 12). Moreover, far from speaking "against the temple," as liberal theologians would have it, Jeremiah speaks always on its behalf. The temple is the place in which YHWH has caused his name to dwell, upon which his name is called, and so forth. The assurance with which villains and idolaters enter its precincts is an affront to and a desecration of God's name (7:1–15). The climax of his indictment is, "Even in my house have I found their wickedness" (23:11). Jeremiah's visions of the future give a prominent place to the restoration of the joyous temple cult (30:19; 31:4 f.; 33:11, 18–22).

Consequently, when Jeremiah insists that God has no delight in the cult of this people (14:11 f.), it is only because of their wickedness. Their sacrifices do not please him, because they did not hearken to his words (6:19 f.), the implication being that if they hearken, their sacrifices will be acceptable. And when he says that God did not command them on the day of the Exodus concerning sacrifices (7:22), he does not intend thereby to deny the divine origin of the sacrificial laws, but, like Amos, he wishes only to emphasize that the cult has no absolute value. Jeremiah can hardly have had his own peculiar version of the story of the Wandering on which basis he argued against the popular notions. Indeed, what he says accords with the tradition of D (and P) that in the desert the temple cult of sacrifice was not yet performed. In the desert, "each did what was right in his own eyes" (Deut. 12:8); the national temple cult was established only in the land. The desert period of Israel's "youthful devotion" was really not a time of "whole and peace offerings." The prophecy that the ark will not be made in the future (3:16) does not imply a repudiation of the cult; it is connected with the prophecy of the new covenant, when the Torah will be written on the heart (31:31 ff.), and stone tablets and ark will no longer be needed.

THE PROBLEM OF THE FALL—Between Jeremiah and the people there was, then, no fundamental religious difference. His prophecy of destruction is not founded on a denial of the sanctity of Jerusalem and the temple. It must be borne in mind that the very book which centralized worship in Jerusalem itself warns of total destruction and exile (Deut. 28; cf. Lev. 26). The dread that seized Josiah and his court upon reading the book, and Huldah's prophecy of destruction (II Kings 22:15 ff.) originated in these warnings.

The idea of the fall was thus no innovation of Jeremiah, nor did his opponents deny what the book of the covenant explicitly threatened: that God would destroy temple and city, if they violated his covenant. The issue between prophet and people was, had they or had they not in fact violated it? The people, who had remained true to Josiah's reforms, did not believe that they deserved the threatened punishment; they believed that the God who had delivered the city from Sennacherib would deliver it again from Nebuchadnezzar. It was a question of evaluating the sin.

The gravity of the problem is revealed in Jeremiah's indictment. What sins does he enumerate? Public cults of idolatry were a thing of the past (see above). The private cults of his day were of the same vestigial type that had always existed in Israel. His indictment of morals is instructive for what it omits—frivolity and drunkenness, luxury, "eat and drink for tomorrow we die," cynicism, militarism, and trust in armies. Above all, Jeremiah's denunciation lacks a class basis; he does not fight the battle of the masses against the aristocracy and bureaucracy. On the contrary, Jeremiah attacks "the people" as a whole. His arraignment begins by addressing the "poor," from whom he then turns in despair to the "great"; "From the smallest to the greatest of them, all seek gain, from prophet to priest all deal falsely" (6:13; 8:10). Jeremiah lists public and private sins, the likes of which are prevalent in every age and in every society: lying and deceit, treachery and slander, adultery, love of gain, fraud, and perversion of justice. A major indictment is found in 7:5 ff.; the sins are oppression of the stranger, orphan and widow, murder, "other gods," stealing, adultery, false oaths. But the speech of most men to this day is lies; their favorite pastime, slander; their chief occupation, gain; bribe-taking and wickedness still pervade human societies everywhere. Jeremiah himself betrays his exaggeration. The indictment of 5:26 ff. opens with the words, "Wicked men have been found among my people"; it closes with, "Shall my soul not take vengeance against such a nation!" Because "wicked men are found" among the people, they become "such a nation."

Jeremiah's indictment is in fact milder than those of earlier prophets. Yet he, not they, prophesied destruction. How is this to be explained?

THE SHOCK OF MANASSEH'S AGE: EXTREME IDEALISM—Jeremiah's indictment springs from the same source as that of his predecessors: religious-moral idealism, coupled with a deep disappointment at the realization of the gulf that separated ideal from reality. Israel has been elected, but it has failed to become the nation of YHWH. The political decline shows that God is punishing Israel for its failure. The prophets condemned, threatened, and called for repentance; but the sort of repentance they demanded did not, could not, come about.

Between the ages of Isaiah and Jeremiah, however, something new had happened in Israel: the age of Manasseh, in which idolatry, for the first and last time, reached almost national proportions. The Jerusalem temple was turned into a pagan pantheon, housing "loathsome things." The faithful trembled and despaired. Would repentance or annihilation follow? Huldah's prophecy shows that at the beginning of Josiah's reign, the belief had already taken root that the fate of the people had been sealed. As soon as Manasseh died, the prophecy of wrath broke forth out of Zephaniah and the young Jeremiah. A program of reform was drawn up with the purpose of renewing the covenant with God by solemnly subscribing to a book of Torah. The Abiathar priesthood appears to have conceived the idea, and the book that was found in the temple was probably composed from their traditions. Jeremiah knew the book and became one of the advocates of reform.

Five years after Jeremiah began his prophetic career, the reform took place. In a solemn national assembly, the king and the people entered into a covenant made upon the book of the Torah in the temple. Since the days of Moses and Joshua such a thing had not occurred. To Jeremiah, this event had enormous significance; in a vision, he participates with God in making the covenant. God performs the ancient rite of adjuration according to Deuteronomy 27:1 ff.; he adjures and curses whomever will not fulfil the words of the covenant, and the prophet answers "Amen" after him (11:1–5). By this covenant, in which God himself plays the part of the adjuring priest, the people have pledged themselves anew to God and have gained a last chance to be reconciled with him. Woe betide them from the curses pronounced by God and the threats of the book itself should they violate it![4]

The reform had a profound effect. Public idolatry was eradicated, the temple was purified, and the high places were removed. Sages took pride in their knowledge of the book (8:8). King and people wished to believe that they had found the way to salvation; they wished to have confidence in their purified cult and temple. There seems to have been a betterment of public morality as well; Josiah did "judge the case of the poor and needy" (22:15 f.). Needless to say, however, the demand to observe "all that was written" in the book was not met. There was still vestigial idolatry for which, according to the book (Deut. 13:7), the people were no less accountable because it was private. The moral prescriptions of the book were especially ignored. Life went on as usual with the normal measure of daily sins.

To Jeremiah, however, there was no forgiveness for such sins. If there were still idolatry, lies, slander, oppression, what was the good of the covenant? He beheld with pain and outrage the complacency of his neighbors in Anathoth and of the prophets of weal. "A conspiracy has been discovered among the men of Judah and the inhabitants of Jerusalem: they have returned to the former sins of their fathers" (11:9 f.). The covenant had been made in vain: "Verily the pen has worked vainly, vainly the scribe" (so 8:8 is to be rendered). At this time, the warnings—based on Deuteronomy—of the coming of the "nation from the north" (5:15 ff.; 6:22 f.) set in. At this, his former friends turn upon him; the priests are particularly offended. The reproof of the young priest-prophet seemed to them presumptuous and false, and they plot against him. The failure of the nation from the north to materialize gave them grounds for taunting him (17:15). The bitter experiences of the young idealist are reflected in his poems of vengeance and execration.

Now Jeremiah begins to understand his role and historical position. "You will speak to them . . . but they will not listen to you; you will call to them, but they will not answer you" (7:27). The whole history of Israel has been one long series of provocations and rebellions. All its troubles have arisen from violation of the covenant, yet the people did not take notice, did not attend the warnings of prophets who were sent through the generations to warn them (7:13, 25 f.; 11:7 f.; 25:3 ff.; 26:5; etc.). Now they have failed the last test; they have violated Josiah's covenant in

[4] In 11:2 read "speak thou" (LXX and Syriac), and "hear thou" (Syriac). The words of the prophet to the people begin with "Thus said YHWH" and end with "Amen, YHWH." God commands Jeremiah to go and listen with the people to the words of Josiah's covenant, and then disclose to them that God himself was present and cursed its violators in the hearing of the prophet.

which God himself had participated. This idea produced the new prophecy of terror. The warnings of the Torah become predictions; what was conditionally threatened for a far-off future was announced by Jeremiah as close at hand. The prolixity of the Torah's warning style is adopted by the prophet; this is what makes his prophecy so dreadful.

Yet there was also another Jeremiah, a man who loved his people and his land, who believed in their election and sanctity. But precisely because he believed he raged; and because he raged, his heart was broken. This is the personal tragedy. Jeremiah supplicates God on Israel's behalf, but his prayer is rejected. He weeps "day and night" over the catastrophe which is about to overtake his people. In his laments, too, he is a man of extremes. The word of YHWH is his joy (15:16), yet he curses the day he was born (20:14 ff.).

The Prophecies of Subjection to Babylonia—After Jehoiakim's submission to Babylonia, a turning point came in the prophecies of Jeremiah; from about 604, he begins to demand surrender to Babylonia. This theme is the great paradox of Jeremiah. Under the very same circumstances in which Isaiah counseled resistance, Jeremiah demanded surrender. The kings who wished to follow the course of Isaiah and Hezekiah are advised by Jeremiah to go the way of Ahaz and Manasseh! What heightens the paradox is the absolute character of Jeremiah's demand: he does not condition Babylonia's conquest of Judah upon Judah's failure to repent. The call to surrender has nothing to do with sin and repentance; Israel, the nations, even the beasts of the field, have been fated to bear Nebuchadnezzar's yoke (27–28). During the very time that Jeremiah censured the people for their sin and called for repentance, he demands unconditional surrender to Babylon! If Zedekiah will but yield, the city, despite all its sins, will not be burned (38:17 f.). Jeremiah prophesied destruction, but at the same time, he counsels a way to avert the calamity—by surrender to the pagan tyrant. Such a prophecy was unheard of. That punishment would be meted out to them for sin was a warning the people found in the book, but they had never heard of a religious obligation to surrender their city and temple to a heathen king. They had made no covenant concerning that! One had to take it on faith from Jeremiah that such was God's will. Zealots considered this counsel—the path followed by the wicked Ahaz and Manasseh—the words of "a raving madman" who must be punished (29:26).

Jeremiah's prophecy of subjection can be understood only in the light of his new concept of a heathen world empire of predetermined duration. The Babylonian Empire inherits the chastening task of the "northern nation"; it is the bitter fruit of sin. But Jeremiah conceives it to be God's will that the pagan empire achieve world dominion. The rise of this empire has been foreordained; so has its fall: God has allotted it a term of seventy years. Once this view of Babylonia had broken upon the prophet, the punishment of Israel could be seen in a different light. An alternative to annihilation presented itself: subjection to the cruel yoke of Babylon, as an act of resignation to the divine decree, in the realization that it was just retribution for sin. Subjection thus becomes a token of contrition and repentance. The period of exile and subjection is at the same time a period of supplicating God (24:7; 29:12 ff.). By surrender, life in the land of Israel itself becomes "exilic," and can serve, like the exile, to expiate the sin of the generations and reconcile Israel with its God.

In this light, the battle for independence is an act of defiance of God. For it assumes that there is no national sin which requires expiation, but that, on the contrary, deliverance is at hand. Judah's rebels imagine that they will be saved without contrition and repentance; this is their grievous sin and rebellion against God. From Jeremiah's viewpoint, the exile of Jehoiachin, which already bears the yoke of suffering, has a chance for the future; it will find the way to repentance in exile. That is why he favors the exiles over those in Judah (chap. 24), and why he supports the puppet Gedaliah after the fall—Gedaliah has accepted the yoke of subjection. That is why, after Gedaliah is murdered, he advises the remnant of Judah to remain in the land (chap. 42); their desire to flee the rigors of Chaldean rule flies in the face of God's purpose. It is no wonder that Jeremiah's unprecedented prophecy was unacceptable to his generation.

To the exiles, Jeremiah speaks with two tongues. Drawing, on the one hand, upon the imaginary descriptions of the book, he foresees decimation of the exiles by sword, famine, and pestilence (9:15; 24:8 ff.; 29:17 f.; 42:16 ff.). From Deuteronomy 4:28 and 28:36, 64, he adopts the peculiar idea that the exiles will be forced to worship other gods (5:19; 16:13). Harried and persecuted, the exiles will be broken and repent, and then God will turn their fortunes and restore them to their land—for even the visions of Deuteronomy (and Leviticus 26) assume that Israel will live through and survive the exile. But the nature of life and the conditions of survival in the exile have also quite another aspect in Jeremiah. Alongside of the visionary terrors, the picture of the real conditions of Jehoiachin's exile appears. The real exile was not harried or persecuted. The exiles were impatient; they were encouraged by their prophets to believe that they would not be long in returning to Judah. The advice given by

Jeremiah in his letter to the exiles (chap. 29) lays the foundation of a radically different idea of exile.

Jeremiah fixes the exile in the framework of the divine plan for a universal pagan empire. Like the latter, it has a fixed, preordained term of seventy years; the task of the people in exile is to accept the necessity of living out that term, estranged from their land, without cult or access to the holy. They must patiently wait on God and hope for the end. In this way, Jeremiah outlined a program for the exile which was to come. About seventy years did elapse from the reign of Nebuchadnezzar to the fall of Babylon, and the exiles did, in fact, accept it on Jeremiah's terms. Their reaction to the catastrophe took the form of a heroic effort to "return" to God and his Torah.

THE PROPHECIES AGAINST IDOLATRY—Jeremiah strikes a new note in his prophecies about idolatry. For the first time, the idea is enunciated that the nations will arrive at a religious awareness of the vanity of idolatry. They will confess: "Our fathers inherited nothing but lies, vanity, and things in which there is no good. Can man make for himself God? . . ." (16:19 f.). This return to God will have a moral effect as well (3:17).

For the first time, too, the idea that idolatry is counted as a sin for which the nations will be punished appears. YHWH will teach Israel's neighbors to swear "by the life of YHWH"; if they will not learn, he will destroy them (12:14 ff.). Worship of YHWH thus becomes obligatory for the nations of the future. The same conception underlies the passage in the prophecy about Babylon, "a sword against the Chaldeans . . . for it is a land of images, and over idols they are mad" (50:35 ff.). For the first time, idolatry is given as a motive for punishing a gentile nation.

The most striking expression of this new idea is the Aramaic prophecy in 10:11 of the eschatological destruction of idols. "Thus shall you say to them: 'Gods that did not make heaven and earth will perish from the earth and from under these heavens.'" Ancient exegesis (cf. Targum Jonathan) is doubtless correct in taking this to be a fragment of a letter sent to the exiles and addressed to the pagans. Jeremiah speaks to the gentiles in their own language, Aramaic, underscoring the momentous novelty of the phenomenon. For the first time, and not in vision but in reality, a message on idolatry is addressed "to them." The prophet solemnly charges the exiles to warn the gentiles among whom they dwell of the imminent destruction of idolatry, because it is folly and flouts "the King of the nations" (vs. 7). Jeremiah carries the war against idolatry into its own territory. In this fragment, we witness the transformation of the purely visionary universalism of prophecy into practical universalism.

Jeremiah 10:11 is not only a vision for the future, but a charge to action. The exiles are bidden to speak to the nations in the name of "the living God and the everlasting King" (vs. 10). Jeremiah here adumbrates the idea of Israel's mission among the nations; he is the father of the missionary idea. Isaiah had heralded the end of idolatry in an eschatological act of God; Jeremiah charges Israel with the task of carrying this message to the nations and thus take part in bringing them back to God.

ESCHATOLOGY AND CONSOLATION: THE NEW COVENANT—During the desperate days of Jerusalem's siege, Jeremiah assumed the role of the great consoler. The theme that dominates his thought now is the eternity of God's covenant with Israel. God will as soon abolish the laws of heaven and earth as his covenant with Israel, with the priests and Levites, and with David (31:35 ff.; 33:17 ff.). This assurance is the rock upon which Jeremiah builds the future of Israel. Babylon will fall and the exiles of Israel and Judah together will come back to Zion, weeping as they go, to establish "an eternal covenant that shall not be forgotten" (50:4 f.). Farmers and shepherds will repopulate Judah (31:23 f.; 33:12); the sounds of rejoicing will again be heard in the countryside (33:10 ff.); a Davidic "shoot of righteousness" will be king; and Jerusalem will dwell secure under the watchword "YHWH is our vindication" (33:14 ff.).

The beginning of salvation will be Israel's repentance. When the people turn to God, they will find him and will be renewed (24:7; 29:10 ff.). This renewal will not be merely territorial or political, but spiritual as well. Following Micah, Jeremiah proclaims an eschatological forgiveness of, and purification from, sin (33:8; 50:20). But the jewel of his prophecy of consolation is the promise of a new covenant. Before Jeremiah, the end-time was envisaged as a time of righteousness and freedom from evil (Isa. 11:9; Zeph. 3:13; Hab. 2:14). Deuteronomy promised more: "YHWH your God will circumcise your heart . . . to love YHWH your God with all your heart and all your soul" (Deut. 30:6). Inspired by this promise, Jeremiah develops the idea of the new covenant. In time to come, God will give Israel "one heart and one way" to fear and know him all the days (32:39). Not only will they do no evil, they will love and cleave to the good. God will inscribe his Torah on their heart, so that they need no longer teach each other to know YHWH, for all will know him, young and old alike (31:31 ff.). Since this covenant will be written on the heart—not on tablets of stone—the ark that housed the old tablets will be no more in time to come (3:16). This covenant, unlike the old one, will be everlasting; it will never be violated (31:32; 32:40) or forgotten (50:5).

The vision of the new covenant completes Jeremiah's prophecy. The

prophecy of destruction arose out of the conception of Israel as habitually
backsliding from Sinai to the time of Josiah. Experience teaches that mankind as now constituted cannot keep God's covenant, hence a new mankind
must be created whose heart God has refashioned, and upon which he
has impressed his word as a seal. Jeremiah's prophecy of doom is a vindication
of God; his prophecy of consolation is an apology for man. Jeremiah
realizes that men cannot fulfil his radical demands without the gracious
help of God. What gives this vision its Israelite character is the precondition
of repentance. The redeeming act of God waits upon man's initiative;
man must take the first step by repenting.[5]

Jeremiah's consolations and the new covenant are for Israel. "They
shall be my people, and I will be their God" (24:7; cf. 31:33; 32:38).
For the rest of the nations, Jeremiah prophesies subjection to the yoke
of Babylon, the world empire. In the vision of the cup (25:15 ff.), he
symbolizes this idea. All the nations appear assembled before God in
some visionary place. God hands the prophet the "cup of the wine of
wrath," and charges him to give it to them to drink. All the nations appear
on one stage, all have a part in the divine world-drama. History has
now but one subject: the Babylonian Empire, founded by God and endowed
with dominion over the whole earth for seventy years. Jeremiah believed
that in the end-time, all nations would come to know Israel's God (3:17),
although this idea does not have a central place in his prophecy. Yet there
can hardly be a doubt that the new covenant with Israel has universal
significance. Not only the destruction and the subjection have universal
meaning, the redemption has too. Jeremiah's demand that all nations
willingly yield themselves to Babylon arises out of his faith that the
subjection of the world was the necessary prelude to its salvation.

EZEKIEL

Ezekiel began his prophecy in 592, the fifth year of Jehoiachin's exile
(Ezek. 1:2). The latest date in his book is 570—the twenty-seventh
year of Jehoiachin's exile (29:17). Since he speaks of "our exile" (33:21;
40:1), he is, according to the plain sense of the text, one of the exiles.
God revealed himself to him in Babylonia by the Canal Chebar; there

---

[5] Christianity regards itself as the fulfiment of Jeremiah's vision of a new covenant.
This covenant was made upon the sacrifice of the son of God; the bread and wine of the
mass are the symbols of this sacrifice, and enable man to participate in it. Liberal
Christianity has foregone this mystical element, but it too claims that Christianity, which
nullified the law and commandments and based itself upon goodness and love, is the true
fulfilment of Jeremiah's prophecy and that of the other prophets who demanded "stead-

he called him and sent him to the community of exiles that lived at nearby Tel-abib (3:11–15). This community is "the house of Israel" whom he addresses in reality, prophesying to them for six years concerning Jerusalem's fall. There is nothing artificial in this; under the circumstances, it was a perfectly natural thing.

Jeremiah's letter to the Babylonian exiles (Jer. 29) reveals that they were impatiently awaiting their return home. Both their own prophets as well as those in Jerusalem predicted an exile of short duration. The exiles did not cease feeling themselves part of Jerusalem; the fate of Jerusalem was the vital question for them as well, for if Jerusalem should fall, what future had they?

To this community, Ezekiel is sent with the shocking message that Jerusalem must perish. The nature of this message testifies to an exilic audience. Jeremiah calls for repentance, and in the days of Zedekiah even promises deliverance if the king submits to Babylon. But Ezekiel never calls upon Jerusalem to repent; his calls to repentance are addressed solely to the exiles.[6] For Ezekiel is not at all concerned with influencing Jerusalem; his one purpose is to persuade the exiles that they must separate their fate from that of Jerusalem, the abode and symbol of sin. Renunciation of the hope of return is the prerequisite of repentance. Jerusalem must perish; Israel will be regenerated from its exiles. This idea was alien to the exiles, and could never be accepted by them so long as any hope remained for Jerusalem's survival. Hence, the prophet's continuous insistence on the city's fall. Such an unconditional prophecy of destruction could have a point only among the exiles. Had Ezekiel brought this message to the people of Jerusalem he would have been merely a soothsayer; only in Babylonia could he serve as a prophet, a messenger of God whose task was to change the hearts of men.

Ezekiel knew well that the exiles' identification with their homeland closed their minds to his message. Hence, though he sets his hope for the future on them, at present, they are still part of the "rebellious house."

---

fast love and not sacrifice." This claim is put forth as an objective, historical evaluation, and on this ground it must be challenged. What the prophets demanded was not a particular doctrine, but a particular reality, not a teaching of love, but acts of love. And from this viewpoint, the church cannot be considered the fulfilment of prophecy. It is true enough that ritual piety is capable of masking moral corruption, but pious preachments may serve the same purpose, and with even greater success.

[6] That all the calls to repentance (3:16 ff.; 14:1 ff.; 18; 33:1 ff.) are addressed to the exiles is to be inferred from the fact that in no prophecy explicitly directed toward Jerusalem does a call for repentance appear.

Through them he can reprove "all the house of Israel," those in Jerusalem as well. Their ardent desire to return to the "city of blood" makes them share fully in the guilt of the sinful city. There was, in fact, no qualitative difference between the moral state of the exiles and those whom they left behind in Judah five years earlier. The captivity included the officers of Jehoiakim (II Kings 24:15) and members of the war party who were Jeremiah's opponents. Nebuchadnezzar did not single out the righteous men of the city for deportation. There was no ground for making any moral distinction between the exiles and those in Jerusalem. What Ezekiel said concerning the inhabitants of Jerusalem was equally true (or, as we shall see, false) for the exiles. Ezekiel distinguishes the exiles favorably only with regard to the future, for he believes that they will ultimately repent. There is, therefore, nothing unnatural in his failure to distinguish Jerusalemites from exiles in his terms of address.[7]

THE BOOK OF EZEKIEL: TIME, PLACE, AND INTEGRITY—Over and above the long process of expansion and revision that the current view ascribes to the book of Ezekiel along with the rest of the prophetic books, recent criticism has raised special questions regarding its integrity. The allegation most seriously affecting the conception of the nature of Ezekiel's prophecy is that it contains a Jerusalemite stratum. Prophecies originally uttered in Jerusalem, it is said, were later either recast into a Babylonian setting or supplemented with Babylonian prophecies. The dating of the prophecy has also been challenged; it has been suggested that the entire book is a late pseudepigraph (Zunz, Geiger, Torrey). What is the testimony of the book concerning its time and place?

The historical horizon of the book of Ezekiel is a natural one and accords with its given chronology. Assyria is mentioned only as an empire of the past (16:28 f.; 23:5 ff.; etc.). The ruling kingdom is Babylonia; the next heathen enemy after Babylonia will be Gog. The Persian Empire is

---

[7] The argument that denies to Ezekiel the title of "prophet" because he had no "people" to address in exile is utterly without merit. The size of the exile is beside the point, for not even in Jerusalem did the prophets actually address more than a limited audience. Some prophets never worked beyond the confines of one city or town. That there were popular prophets in the Exile is reported explicitly in Jeremiah 29:1, 8 f. 15, 21 ff. Ezekiel prophesied in Tel-abib, but this does not mean that his utterances did not have a wider hearing. Jeremiah hears of what is being prophesied in Babylonia; "the prophets" are among those addressed in his letter. The exilic prophet, Shemaiah, reacts to what Jeremiah says in Jerusalem (vs. 27). Ezekiel's words could thus certainly have reached Jerusalem, but this, too, is beside the point. The fact is that Ezekiel speaks and acts like a prophet: he addresses an audience, performs dramatic, symbolic acts before them; they inquire of him, and he responds (see especially 33:31). He is as much among a "people" as the prophets in Judah.

not mentioned.[8] There is no hint of the historical circumstances of the Restoration. Moreover, as in other prophetic books, there is a distinct rift between prophecy and reality which attests to a faithful transmission. The Judean exile lasted more than the forty years of 4:6; the exiles of 586 did not die by the sword (5:2, 12, etc.); Zedekiah was condemned in Riblah, not Babylon (17:20); Tyre was not destroyed (chaps. 26–28); Nebuchadnezzar did not destroy Egypt, nor were the Egyptians exiled and restored after forty years (29:8 ff.); "the horn of the house of Israel" did not sprout either at the time of Egypt's conquest (29:21) or at any other occasion in Egypt's history. Especially glaring is the rift between chapters 40–48 and the reality of Second Temple times. The cultic code of 40–48 is for a clerical establishment supported by an independent Davidic king such as did not exist in postexilic times. Jerusalem as there described never existed. The twelve tribes never returned; those who did, did not settle according to the prescriptions of Ezekiel. Neither was the temple rebuilt along his lines, nor were non-Zadokite priests made Levites, nor were the Nethinim removed from temple service. Ezekiel depicts himself as in charge of the inauguration of the new altar (43:18 ff.), and in 45:18 ff. he is commanded to purify the sanctuary. This is in accord with his vision that the redemption would come at the end of forty years of Jehoiachin's exile while he was yet alive—as it did not. The laws of chapters 40–48 contradict the Torah in so many ways as to have recommended to the later Rabbis withdrawing the book from public use. And yet later generations did not venture to alter a single passage to harmonize these divergences. This is perhaps the most telling evidence against the common notion that prophetic writings remained for centuries in a fluid state.

The more glaring inconsistencies between prophecy and reality were noticed already in the prophet's time. In 29:17 ff., the prophet himself takes account of the failure of his Tyrian prophecy to materialize. His procedure is most interesting. In a special oracle, received on a particular date, the prophet announces that Nebuchadnezzar will take Egypt in lieu of Tyre. This illustrates nicely what sort of "revision" Ezekiel's prophecy really underwent.

---

[8] The mention of Persians only as one among many elements in Gog's army (38:5) and among the Tyrian mercenaries (27:10) reflects the writer's ignorance of the late Persian Empire. The "twig" of 8:17 has nothing to do with the Persian *baresma*; see Kraetzschmar's commentary *ad loc.*, and S. Spiegel, *HTR* XXIV (1931), 300 f. Extending the twig is not one of the cultic abominations of Israel (the last of these is in vs. 16), but is merely a general act of challenge and provocation (read with the Massorah *ʾappī*, "my nose"). It follows upon the phrase "they have angered me yet the more," and is a figure taken, it would seem, from daily life, where to stretch out a stick to another's face or nose constituted an act of provocation.

The repetitiveness of Ezekiel borders at times upon the wearisome. The need to hammer the unwelcome message into the minds of a "stiff-hearted" people (2:4; 3:7) surely has had something to do with this. Repetition is not in itself ground for assuming a later expansion; only a clear literary or historical reason can justify such an assumption. A few obvious marginal notes and later expansions have entered the text,[9] but nothing that warrants the assumption of an extensive and continuous process of revision and supplementation.

The visions in chapters 8–11 have been invoked as evidence that Ezekiel prophesied in Jerusalem. According to 8:1 ff., the prophet is brought in a vision to Jerusalem where he witnesses various abominations going on in the temple precinct. The true character of these visions is suggested by 9—10:7, in which an imaginary destruction of the city and its inhabitants by heavenly beings takes place before the eyes of the prophet. That this is pure fantasy is manifest; neither was the city destroyed in the sixth year of the exile—the date of the vision, nor was it destroyed in this fashion in 586. Ezekiel has seen things that never happened; this is the key to the understanding of the rest of his visions.

Their fantastic nature is clearly evident in 8:7 ff. Seventy elders (cf. Num. 11:16) are in a temple chamber whose door is walled up. (How, then, did they enter?) It appears at first that they are all together making offerings to pictures on the walls, but it then develops that the prophet sees what each man does "in darkness, each in his image-rooms" (vs. 12). They say, "YHWH does not see us; YHWH has left the land"; if so, then, why do they act in darkness? Why do they gather surreptitiously in this God-forsaken temple? It is plain that Ezekiel sees shadows, not living beings; the entire vision is but a "parable." He specifies one man's name (vs. 11); hence it seems likely that the fantasy has some basis in a report of what took place somewhere in Jerusalem. One thing is certain: this was not the cult practiced in the temple, or the prevalent cult of the people of Jerusalem. Ezekiel who was carried to Jerusalem by his hair in a vision sees these things, but Jeremiah who frequented the temple and its courts does not. What Ezekiel really sees are shadows out of the past. He had heard in his youth of the dreadful abominations that took place in the temple during Manasseh's time. Ghosts of that time now rise before his eyes; they are still there, haunting the city and the temple. Retribution still clamors for satisfaction, and its claim will not be met until the city and temple are destroyed.

[9] Such as 12:13 f.—an expanded version of 17:20 f.; the mention of Babylon in the former passage is not original.

The vision of 11:1 ff. continues and terminates the scenes of chapters 8–10. The prophet sees twenty-five men at the east gate of the temple. He is bidden to prophesy against them, and while he is prophesying, one, Pelatiah ben Benaiah, falls down dead. Some commentators interpret the prophet's knowledge of Pelatiah's death as an instance of "second sight"; others assert that it is a postevent prophecy; still others take this as further evidence that Ezekiel prophesied in Jerusalem. Yet there is no suggestion in the text that Pelatiah really died at that moment or at any time thereafter (contrast the treatment in Jer. 28:17). The commentators have gratuitously verified Pelatiah's death, though it is not clear why this detail of the vision of 8–11 should be regarded as more real than the slaying of all the inhabitants of the city and its burning by celestial beings. We know nothing more than that Pelatiah died in the vision; here Ezekiel's word slays, in 37:4 ff., it revives—both times in a vision.[10]

To appreciate fully the imaginative character of Ezekiel's visions, his historical surveys (chaps. 16, 20, and 23) must be examined. Chapters 16 and 23 are similar in form and style: both represent Jerusalem as a harlot and enumerate her abominations from the beginning; both are filled with extravagant erotic imagery. These chapters furnish modern scholars with copious data on the paganism and syncretism of Israel's popular religion, but the fact is that they are nothing but fantasies in which it is difficult to find any substance whatever. As a source of history, they are worthless; to maintain their historicity, one must reject all of the rest of the biblical record. The high places of Israel were not idolatrous (save during the time of Manasseh); child sacrifice was not normally practiced (under foreign influence, it was present during the reigns of Ahaz and Manasseh [II Kings 16:3; 21:6; 23:10]; no northern king is ever blamed for this sin). In his view of the past, Ezekiel ignores the existence of such

---

[10] Another passage which has occasioned resort to the theory of "second sight," or to the assumption of postevent writing is 24:1 ff. The Hebrew text runs: "The word of YHWH came to me in the ninth year, in the tenth month, on the tenth of the month, saying: O man, write down the name of the day, this very day; the king of Babylon set siege [*sāmak*] to Jerusalem on this very day. And tell a parable, etc." This text is suspect. No date in Ezekiel begins "The word of YHWH came to me in the year. . . ." Moreover, while *sāmak* of verse 2 obviously begins a new clause, its position is strange. Again, "and tell a parable" (vs. 3) manifestly picks up and continues "write down" (vs. 2), though in the present text it is separated from it by "the king of Babylon," etc. Ezekiel's prescience is apparently a product of a confused text, which must be rearranged thus: "The word of YHWH came to me saying: In the ninth year . . . the king of Babylon set siege . . . on this very day. O man write down the name of the day, this very day, and tell a parable. . . ." No second sight or postevent writing is involved. When the report arrived in Babylon that Jerusalem's siege had begun, God commanded Ezekiel to record the day as a memorial to the beginning of the end.

pious kings as Saul, David, Solomon, Asa, Jehoshaphat, not to mention Josiah. It is characteristic of his exaggerated generalizations that he does not mention Topheth or the valley of Ben-Hinnom, but speaks as if the burning of children took place everywhere and at all times. Also characteristic is the way in which he minimizes the sin of Sodom; she was merely proud and refused to aid the poor (16:49; contrast Gen. 18:20 ff.; 19). The survey of chapter 20 takes its origin in the Torah's legends of Israel's rebellion, but it goes well beyond them in vilifying Israel. The Torah knows nothing of Israel's addiction to the idolatry of Egypt, of God's intention to destroy Israel in Egypt, or of a continual desecration of the Sabbath during the Wandering. (In the light of this penchant for inventing sins, how seriously can one take Ezekiel's charge [20:31] that the exiles worship idols and burn children "to this day"?) The political indictment of chapter 23 is most bizarre. Ezekiel interprets Israel's alliances with foreign nations as a lusting after them and their idols. In fact, of course, Samaria's "lust" after Assyria was the result of subjugation by an iron fist—eventually Samaria revolted and was destroyed by her "lover." The apogee of Ezekiel's "history" is reached in the arraignment of Jerusalem for "doting upon" Chaldea, whom she invited to "the bed of love." During Ezekiel's time, there was only one man in Jerusalem who "doted upon" the Chaldeans— Jeremiah. After Jehoiakim became a Babylonian vassal, the "doting" went on three years; thereafter Judah continuously plotted rebellion. Zedekiah spent all his days planning revolt; when he revolted, who denounced him for treachery toward his "lover"? Ezekiel! (cf. chap. 17).

Ezekiel's histories are of a piece with his visions of events in Jerusalem. They are products of an exuberant imagination and have no historical worth. The challenge to the integrity of Ezekiel from the Jerusalem visions is thus unsubstantial. They prove, if anything, that Ezekiel never left Babylonia.

A PREPROPHETIC IDEOLOGY—Alone among the prophets, Ezekiel foretells the unconditional destruction of Jerusalem. His prophecy of the destruction of the city, temple, and monarchy has no accompanying call for repentance. In Zedekiah's sixth year, he beholds the destruction of the city; to him the fall already has a kind of reality. His fierce antipathy toward Jerusalem —he alone calls it a "city of blood" (22:2; 24:6, 9) whose wickedness exonerated Sodom (16:51 f.)—leads one to suspect some personal provocation is involved.

The grounds of this ruthless prophecy are likewise singular. Ezekiel does not regard his generation as particularly wicked; except for Zedekiah's violation of his vassal oath, the sins he denounces have been with Israel from its beginning. A historical perspective is altogether lacking; he knows of no periods of faithfulness or repentance. This excessive generalization of sin dissociates his reproof from the reality of his times. The new moral idea of classical prophecy—"kindness and justice, not sacrifice"—has no echo in Ezekiel. He never enunciates the contrast of morality versus cult. It cannot, then, be zeal for the new idea that so excites his wrath. His contact with the ideology of classical prophecy is limited to the inclusion of social sins among the causes of the national collapse. But the social moment in Ezekiel has none of the gravity that it has in the thought of his predecessors, because, unlike them, Ezekiel never denies the absolute value of the cult. He alone among the classical prophets threatens national collapse for ceremonial sins (chap. 22). He alone is concerned with prescribing cult laws.

In short, Ezekiel's outlook is not so much that of classical prophecy, as of the Torah literature. His is the view of the early literature that idolatry, "Sodomic" sins, and particularly sexual immorality defile and bring on destruction (Lev. 18:24 ff.; 20:22; cf. Num. 35:33: bloodshed "pollutes the land"). Murder is ignored by Amos; other prophets mention it along with other sins; but Ezekiel gives it high prominence (7:23; 9:9; 22:1 ff.; 24:6 ff.; 33:25 f.; 36:18). Ezekiel is fond of describing Israel's sin in "Sodomic" terms. The land "has become full of violence" (7:23; 8:17; 9:9)—an echo of the Flood story (Gen. 6:11). The burning of Jerusalem by an angel recalls the fate of Sodom. Jerusalem is Sodom's sister, but viler than she (16:46 ff.). Of all the prophets, only Ezekiel justifies the punishment of Israel by producing a whole list of sexual offenses (chap. 22) based upon Leviticus 20.

That Jerusalem in the age of Ezekiel was no Sodom has been shown above on the basis of the other testimony of the times; a special ground must, therefore, be sought for Ezekiel's unconditional condemnation.

Ezekiel is rooted in the Torah literature more markedly even than Jeremiah. He is influenced by Deuteronomy, but more by the Priestly Code. The contacts with the Priestly Code—the whole of it, not merely the Holiness Code, which alone is allowed by critical dogma—are numerous and pervasive. That Ezekiel is the borrower is clear, for the matter in common has a natural context and fits into a larger framework in P, while in Ezekiel's context it is artificial or fragmentary, obviously adapted for a new purpose. Thus in Numbers 13–14, the forty-year wandering is a punishment corresponding to the forty-day duration of the spies' journey in Palestine. Ezekiel's forty years of Judah's exile (4:6), however, have no correspondingly long period of sin; the number is simply borrowed from

P. The punishment is borne by the prophet forty days, "a day per year"—a strained adaptation of the straightforward motif of P. Especially artificial is the procedure in 43:1 ff. Moses was shown the structure of the tabernacle in a vision, but only after it was erected did God's glory actually enter it (Exod. 40:33 f.) and speak to Moses from between the cherubs. In Ezekiel, however, the glory fills the house that the "man" shows Ezekiel in a vision, and speaks to the prophet out of an imaginary holy of holies. Again, P's Levites have a natural function; they are the guards and bearers of a portable sanctuary accompanying a camp of wandering tribes. Their rank is a dignity and sacred honor which qualifies them to be in charge of the sanctuary and live around it; their wages are the tithe. Long before Ezekiel's time, the early Levites had retired from the stage of history. Ezekiel's re-created Levites are, therefore, quite bizarre; they are idolatrous priests for whom Levitical status is a disgrace and punishment. Yet withal they "keep the charge of the sanctuary" and live with the priests around the temple (44:14; 45:5; 48:12 ff.). Because the Levites are degraded priests, Ezekiel is silent about the tithe. The image of the Levites is thus grotesquely distorted in Ezekiel. Although Ezekiel gives them and the priests a territory around the temple as large as one of the tribal portions (48:8), he still clings to the archaic language of P that they will not have a possession in the land (44:28; cf. Num. 18:20, 23 f. P gives them no continuous tribal land, but assigns them scattered cities in accord with the real status of the tribe in early times). Ezekiel mentions only incidentally, and without their peculiar features, terms which have an established usage in P, e.g., the divine epithet Shaddai (1:24; 10:5)—in P the fixed name of God in patriarchal theophanies.

Ezekiel 40–48 contains laws that contradict those of P. Could the authors of P have on the one hand so closely adhered to the style of Ezekiel as to have turned isolated phrases of his into fixed terms, while, on the other hand, ignoring his laws? Again, Ezekiel's concepts are influenced by those of D: he condemns the high places (which P ignores); he recognizes only one legal sanctuary of YHWH (P knows many, Lev. 26:31); he knows the idea of one sacred site in the land (P does not). How could P, which betrays no influence of D in these matters, have been derived from Ezekiel? The contradictions between Ezekiel and P show merely that in the prophet's time the priestly writings had not yet been crystallized in definitive, final form. A beginning had been made of the Torah book (Deuteronomy), but the process was not yet complete. Ancient collections of priestly writings, marked by distinctive style, terminology, and ideas, were in existence. Ezekiel's laws are part of this literature. He incorporated in his book an ancient priestly code which differs in detail from the Torah's P; this alone can account for the similarities and differences. Later it will be seen how Ezekiel composed a series of novellae with the purpose of bringing the ancient laws, including P's, up to date.

There can be no doubt that Ezekiel was educated on the Torah literature, especially the priestly literature. In him the zeal of the priest was superadded to that of the prophet. His prophecy gives voice to the mortal dread that surrounds the holy in P. That is why it is so ruthless.

THE SOURCE OF THE PROPHECY OF DESTRUCTION—The cloud of Manasseh's age hovers over the book of Ezekiel. The vision of temple abominations in chapters 8–10, the historical surveys of chapters 16, 20, and 23 paint the whole of Israelite history in the lurid colors of the age of Manasseh, indicating how far the memory of that age threw a pall over all that came after. The shock of "those who moaned and groaned" (9:4) over the abominations and the reign of terror introduced by Manasseh (II Kings 21:16; 24:4) was ineradicable. Some hoped to regain the favor of YHWH through a new covenant—the circle of men around Josiah represent this hope. Others were convinced that Manasseh's idolatry and bloodshed could not be atoned for except through the destruction of the city. This is the mood of II Kings 21:11 ff., 22:15 ff., and 24:3 f.; it is reflected in Jeremiah as well (Jer. 7:30 ff.; 15:4), although that prophet forever oscillated between hope and despair. The tragic death of the reforming king brought the pessimism out into the open; this was a sure sign that YHWH had not forgiven. Ezekiel grew up among those "who moaned and groaned." He was about fifteen years old when the death of Josiah took place; the impending doom that this betokened was thus part of his thinking from his youth. Adult priests could tell of the "loathsome things" they had seen with their own eyes in the temple; the air was still heavy with their odor. The impressionable lad absorbed the atmosphere of horror, revulsion, and despair of his surroundings. Josiah's death was not the last blow. Necho subjugated the land, then the Chaldeans; then came Jehoiachin's exile in which Ezekiel himself was exiled. Judah was rushing downhill into the abyss. Jerusalem was already cast aside; the decree had been sealed; the very hope of deliverance was rebellion.

The second constituent of Ezekiel's thought is the idea of the Torah. The faithful of the age believed that by founding the life of the people upon the book of Torah, they could heal the breach. The priesthood was particularly inclined to this idea, attributing the national calamity to violation of God's Torah. Ezekiel gives it prophetic expression. To Ezekiel, the legends of Israel's rebellion in the Torah are the pattern of

Israelite history. He is the only prophet who utilizes these legends of rebellion; the others view the Wandering as the time of Israel's espousals with YHWH. These legends form the foundation of Ezekiel's historical surveys. From its birth Israel has had an insatiable hunger to sin. Jerusalem, the sole survivor, has become filled to overflowing with the pollution of the ages; YHWH is about to spend all his wrath upon it and obliterate it from the face of the earth. Ezekiel transforms the Torah's legends of rebellion and its threats of destruction into the story of Israel's entire past and the prophecy of its future. All the curses of Leviticus 26 are about to be poured upon Jerusalem (chaps. 5, 6).

Why had his generation been singled out for the fulfilment of these threats? Not because they sinned more than their ancestors. The destruction is a necessity that arises out of the whole of Israelite history. Generation after generation have flouted God's good laws "obeying which a man shall live" (20:11 f.). Stroke after stroke has fallen upon them, without their taking it to heart. Now nothing remains but the ultimate punishment: destruction and exile. For Ezekiel (as for Jeremiah), the destruction is the only way to salvation. The people will not return to God with all their heart until they feel the full force of his wrath, and realize that their sin is unforgivable. When God looses his fury against Jerusalem and destroys it, all will know that he is YHWH. A call to repentance is of no avail; what is wanted is the final purging fire. "Because I would have purged you, but you would not be purged of your impurity, you shall never more be purged till I have satisfied my fury upon you" (24:13).

The radical demands of prophetic idealism gave rise to visions of punishment and a day of judgment. But the prophecy of destruction and exile as formulated by Jeremiah and Ezekiel was the child of the monitions of the Torah, and came into being concurrently with the idea of the Torah book. It is not a reflex of any particular excessive moral or religious decay of that age.

THE CHARACTER OF EZEKIEL'S PROPHECY—Ezekiel is the prophet of the early religion, especially of the ideology of P, but this does not mean that prophecy entered an age of decline with him. In some ways, Ezekiel brought prophecy to a new peak. His mission is the most dismal and difficult of all the prophets: to pronounce an unsparing and unconditional destruction. He feels himself almost the equal of Moses in prophecy; alone of all prophets after Moses, he is a lawgiver; none but Moses and Ezekiel see visions of the sanctuary of the future whose service they inaugurate. The dramatic acts of this prophet attain a fulness never reached before; he creates the genre of visionary dramatic acts (e.g., his prophesying against the twenty-five men in chapter 11, during which Pelatiah dies—all in a vision). Ezekiel is the great visionary of the Bible; no one equals him in power of imagination as it reveals itself in his dramatic acts, his parables, his laments, and his plan for the temple-to-be. None describes with such details the throne and chariot of God (chaps. 1; 10). His vision of the divine vehicle has had a profound influence upon the religious imagery of Israel and the nations. The details of the vision give expression to the idea that overwhelmed him at the moment of his call, the idea of the awesome and all-powerful God. God is borne on his chariot to Ezekiel, because the prophet is in exile on "impure ground" outside the land of prophecy. The vehicle itself is rooted in ancient imagery (cf. II Sam. 22:11 f. [=Ps. 18:11 f.]; Ps. 104:3 f.; Hab. 3:8, 15), but Ezekiel adds a host of detail: a "firmament" and "an earth," the four sides, the four "creatures" erect, with the faces of man, lion, bull, and vulture, supporting the "firmament" upon which a thronelike form stands. At each of the four sides, there is a wheel; wheels and creatures are full of eyes. The vehicle does not turn in moving, but can fly everywhere, the whole animated by one living spirit. The symbolism is cosmic; the vehicle has its own heaven and earth, has four sides (= the compass points), is made of fire, the all-consuming element. The creatures embody the chiefs of animate creation. Their brightness and eyes symbolize omniscience, their free movement symbolizes God's omnipresence. The throne and the irridescent image upon it symbolize God's universal kingship and judgment.

Ezekiel had an important role in shaping later angelology. He is the first to provide celestial beings with distinctive features: the six "destroyers" of chapters 9–10 and their linen-clothed officer, the heavenly scribe. Demonology adopted his idea of an apotropaic sign against destructive angels.

Ezekiel originates some elements characteristic of apocalyptic. He is the first to describe a journey of the spirit apart from the body (chaps. 8; 40). He is borne on the wind to various places, sees visions, and describes them afterward. Heavenly beings accompany him and guide him on his journeys. These set a pattern for apocalyptic tours. Yet Ezekiel cannot be said to have founded apocalypse. He lacks the essential feature, mantic research. Ezekiel does not reveal the secrets of heaven. The divine chariot of his vision is on earth, not in heaven; the vision is not an end in itself, but serves only as a framework for the revelation of a divine message. As in all classical prophecy, the stress is on a revelation of God's will, not a behind-the-scenes knowledge of the secrets of the universe. He has no perspective visions of the rise and fall of successive empires. The great problem of apocalypse is, why has the final redemption been so long in coming? Apocalypse strains to solve the riddle of the suffering of the right-eous; its indictment is directed against the idolaters and the pagan world. For Ezekiel it is quite different; if anything is overdue, it is the destruction of wicked Israel. Even in his prophecies of redemption there is no hint of an idea that Israel will deserve it through righteousness. Needless to say, the prophet's main indictment is directed against Israel; the sin of the nations is nowhere referred to. Apocalypse utilized Ezekiel's vision of the battle of Gog, but only after having made essential changes in it (see below).

Ezekiel's power of vision and imagery was the source of his lasting influence. With terrible accuracy, he foresaw what was to take place. But he does not merely predict the coming fall, as did Jeremiah; he actually sees God and his angels destroying Jerusalem, and relates this to his neighbors in the sixth year of their exile. This was more than an idea, it was the summit of faith. When disaster finally came, it had the appearance of fulfilling the prophet's vision. Now all believed "and knew that a prophet was among them." This faith in divine justice and providence harbored within it the seeds of a faith in a redemption to come. It was not the king of Babylon who destroyed the city and burned the temple; "a burnt temple did he burn, a slain people did he slay." The destruction was God's design; this belief is what turned defeat into a warrant of redemption.

THE CONCEPTION OF GOD—Like other biblical writers, Ezekiel conceives of God anthropomorphically, but in his visions the exaltation of God reaches its ultimate biblical expression. The entire book is suffused with the awe of holiness. This is doubtless owing to the priestly outlook of its author. Ezekiel's God is the God of sanctity, judgment, and law; love and com-passion do not figure in him. Man's duty is to obey God's law and sanctify his name. "Knowledge of God" as conceived by Hosea and Jeremiah (i.e., intimacy with, and love of God) is unknown to Ezekiel. His oft-repeated phrase, "And they shall know that I am YHWH," always follows upon some act of divine wrath or power. It means that man will then come to recognize God's majesty and stand in awe of him and his mighty will.

MORAL SPECULATIONS—Ezekiel conceived of God's justice as the dealing out to man of measure for measure (3:17 ff.; 14:12 ff.; 18; 33:1 ff.). He is impatient with all carping at "the way of YHWH," and insists upon what for him is an absolute dogma, the infallible justice of God. Like the writers of Proverbs, he is a moral optimist. He does not recognize the problem of the suffering of the righteous; he does not ask, "Why does the way of the wicked prosper?" (Jer. 12:1). His dogma is his reality. The way of the wicked does not prosper; the problem is nonexistent.

Does Ezekiel reject collective retribution and conceive of punishment in individual terms only? Does he deny that punishment comes upon society as a whole and strikes at innocent and guilty alike? One might think so on the basis of 14:12 ff., but the whole picture is not given there. For in 9:4 ff., although the righteous are saved by a mark, the command to destroy embraces even the little ones who are innocent; here collective and individual retribution are spoken of in the same breath! See also 21:8 f. Even in 14:12 ff., the little ones are not saved. The principal theme of chapter 14 is stated only in verses 16, 18, and 20: if the righteous are saved, it is they alone, but not their (grown) sons and daughters. What the prophet wishes to emphasize is that there is no retributive bond between generations. That this is so is confirmed by the discussion of chapter 18. Here the prophet deals with the parable, "Fathers have eaten unripe grapes and children's teeth are set on edge." The entire chapter hammers at one point: there is no transfer of guilt and retribution from one generation to another. Ezekiel does not deny that retribution may strike indiscriminately at the contemporaries of a given society.

The object of this emphasis is revealed by the idea of repentance that pervades these chapters. No decree of God concerning man is final; man need not pine away in sin. No generation suffers for the sins of its fathers—unless it is caught up in that sin. The task of the prophet is to warn men away from sin, and this warning has meaning, for if men repent they will not be held accountable for the sins of the past—not even of their own past. That this was a burning issue of the time is clear from the parable that stimulated this prophecy (cf. Lam. 5:7). Ezekiel's generation did not admit the justice of its fate. Not even Jeremiah can bring himself to reject the complaint of his generation that they suffer for the sins of their fathers. He can merely promise that in the future there will be just, individual retribution (Jer. 31:29 f.). Ezekiel takes an entirely different tack. He argues that children do not suffer for the sins of their fathers; the calamities of the age are thoroughly merited by the corruption of Jerusalem and Judah which he is at pains to describe.

The doctrine of the dissociation of generations in the matter of retribution seems also to be derived from P. For while the idea that God visits the iniquity of fathers on children appears in the other sources of the Pentateuch (Exod. 20:5; 34:7; Num. 14:18 [JE]; Deut. 5:9), it does not occur in P. On the other hand, P alone knows of the punishment of "excising"—a heavenly judgment on the individual. P's narratives also imply that children are not accountable for their father's sins. Korah's sons did not die (Num. 26:11); the children of the generation that came out of Egypt were not punished for the faithlessness of their fathers (Num. 14:31). Only if children of wicked men sin do they bear both their own and their father's guilt (Lev. 26:39 ff.). This is Ezekiel's standard, too; because his generation did not purify themselves from sin, they will harvest the punishment of all the generations. At the same time, he provides his audience with an opening for repentance. Destruction has already been decreed, but those who repent will be delivered from the judgment and will constitute the future house of Israel.

THE EXILE: VISION AND REALITY—Ezekiel, like Jeremiah, portrays two exiles: a visionary one, drawn from the warnings of Leviticus 26, full of terror and death (chaps. 4–7), and a real one, which is entirely different. The real exile was a veritable land flowing with milk and honey; the threatened terror and harassment failed to materialize. This perplexed the prophet, for according to the theory, it was the terror of exile that was to break the stiff neck of the people and bring them back to God. Redemption was to be a deliverance from the dreadful existence of the exile. Reality flew in the face of this vision. Out of Ezekiel's perplexity arose the prophecy of 20:32–44. This remarkable prophecy is unparalleled for its depiction of God's redemption, not as a longed-for release, but as a compulsory, wrathful redemption "with a strong hand and an outstretched arm." Willy-nilly the people shall be restored in the sight of the nations for the glory of God. The mood of the exiles at that moment is reflected with marvelous fidelity in this amazing passage. The elders who inquire of the prophet feel themselves rejected by God, but they have been welcomed by the idols. They open their hearts to the prophet: Why not be like the nations, mingle with them and settle down in their lands? To this the prophet responds vehemently: It shall never be! YHWH will be king over them, whether they will or no; "With a strong hand, with an outstretched arm, and poured-out wrath" he will bring them out of the exile, purge them in the "desert of the nations," and restore them to their land before the eyes of the nations.

The lesson of history is that the exiles did repent—though not because of terror; and they were restored (at least in part) to their land—but not by compulsion. Repentance was an internal process and the exodus from exile was a longed-for release. How did this come about? Because the people were not as they are portrayed in Ezekiel's vision. They were, at bottom, monotheists who could never adopt the religion of their environment. Ezekiel's own words provide the plainest evidence of their real spiritual condition. He blames them vaguely for "calling to mind their idols" (14:3) and for "thinking about" idolatry (20:32), even for defil-

ing themselves with all their idols and sacrificing their sons (20:30 f.)—
this in a people who, exiled amidst a great pagan culture, raised a generation loyal to YHWH, out of whom came those who returned to Zion at
the Restoration! But Ezekiel never issues a demand that they remove idols
from their midst; he never upbraids them for entering pagan temples, or
celebrating pagan festivals, or taking part in sacred processions. He has not
one word of polemic against mythological beliefs. The notion that Israelite
monotheism was threatened by a popular belief in the superiority of Babylonia's gods over YHWH, and that the chief task of the exilic prophets was
to combat this view, finds no support in the Bible. No exilic prophet fights
the idea that Jerusalem's fall is due to the pagan gods. The exiles believed
that YHWH would not destroy his city; Ezekiel prophesied that he would.
Neither side believed that any but YHWH would carry out the destruction.
Ezekiel 20:32–44 is monumental testimony to the real state of affairs.
These exiles who wish to be like the nations do not say: "Let us accept
the fact that Marduk created the world, that Ishtar is the source of fertility,
that thunder is the voice of Adad, and that Babylonia's gods overcame
YHWH." Being like the nations means "to serve wood and stone"! This
is not faith in new gods, it is no faith at all. This is the desperate counsel
of men whose spirit is broken and who have lost faith in the future. Despairing, they seek to live a life without God, like the nations. To this the prophet
answers, "It shall not be!"

This chapter of Ezekiel is one of the great visions of the Bible, a vision
for all time. The prophet speaks the innermost convictions of his people.
Israel are bound to God with an eternal, iron-bound covenant. The despair
of the moment may demoralize them, but they will never be able to serve
wood and stone. This is the meaning of the promise that God will be
king over them with a strong hand, an outstretched arm, and outpoured
wrath. Ezekiel's view is limited to the national religion of the priesthood,
but within these limits he gives voice to the full significance of the national
element, without which the ultimate battle with paganism at large would
have been impossible—the eternal, binding nature of YHWH's covenant
with Israel. There is no reversing the fateful election, for it is not for the
sake of Israel, but for the sake of God.

REDEMPTION FOR THE SAKE OF GOD: THE NEW HEART—Ezekiel's
message of redemption (chaps. 34–48) complements his prophecy of destruction; both spring from the same source, faith in the election and the covenant. Israel profaned YHWH's name by their deeds, therefore they were
destroyed. But the national collapse and exile themselves caused God's
name to be profaned by the nations among whom Israel came, "When

they said about them: 'These are the people of YHWH, and from his land have they come forth' " (36:20). This very profanation is a guarantee of redemption; God will redeem Israel to sanctify his name in the sight of the nations (the idea derives from the Torah legends; Exod. 32:11 f.; Num. 14:13 ff.; Deut. 9:28). Redemption for the sake of God overshadows the idea of repentance in Ezekiel's prophecies of redemption. It is the background of the prophecy concerning the new heart. Here Ezekiel was influenced by Jeremiah, but while Jeremiah conceived the new covenant and new heart as the divine response and reward for Israel's repentance, Ezekiel appears to leave no room for merit on Israel's part. Israel's heart has ever been stony, and has obdurately refused to keep God's commands. God's name was profaned in the land and profaned again in the exile. To avert further recurrence of this, God will remake Israel's heart and spirit. He will purify them with pure waters, plant in them his spirit, and give them a "heart of flesh" so that they will obey him forever (36:25 ff.; 37:23). All this will come about not for Israel's sake, but for the sake of YHWH's name. And yet Ezekiel's vision of a new heart does not entirely lack the element of repentance; in 18:31 he says, "Cast off all your sins, and make yourselves a new heart and new spirit." Thus man must strive to attain the new heart before God will bestow it.

THE KINGDOM OF THE FUTURE—Like the priestly writer of the Torah, Ezekiel views the monarchy as a supreme expression of God's grace toward Israel (cf. Gen. 17:6, 16; 35:11). He hints at the restoration of the kingdom by a descendant of Jehoiachin in 17:22 ff., and prophesies the rise of a righteous line of Davidides who will rule the people after their redemption (34:23 f.; 37:24 f.). The details of his portrayal of the future kingdom are drawn from Leviticus 26:3–13 with the difference that here they appear not as conditional, but as certain eschatological promises. Other changes reflect the altered conditions of eschatological times; since there will be no war, victory over neighbors (Lev. 26:7 f.) has no place in Ezekiel's messianic vision. A new promise not to be "prey" for the nations any more (34:28) reflects the fall and the exile that occurred between Leviticus and Ezekiel. New also are the promises of rebuilding ruins, restoring the monarchy, and establishing the unity of Joseph and Judah in the future kingdom (37:15–22). The king will not be a warrior, but a righteous and just shepherd who will protect the weak (34:1 ff.). The land will enjoy an everlasting covenant of peace. The monarchy that Ezekiel promises is not world wide. Israel will live at peace with its neighbors; it will possess no army or fortresses, but will live secure and prosperous, trading with the nations (38:12). This is the setting of the vision of Gog.

Ezekiel not only predicts the redemption, he envisions it, just as he envisioned the destruction before its coming. The great vision of the resurrection of the dry bones in 37:1–14, with its detail of the opening of graves and the restoration to the land of Israel anticipates the ingathering of the dispersion. The detail of revival, the emphasis that the bones are "very many," and that the revived are "a very great host," and the new motif of opening of graves suggest that perhaps there is more here than merely an ingathering. Is this an adumbration of the resurrection of the dead which was to become an accepted doctrine of Judaism only in the age of Daniel?

CHAPTERS 40–48—Chapters 40–48 are characteristic creations of Ezekiel. He appears as an architect, a cultic legislator, but above all as a messianic visionary. This is not a program for action, and anticipates nothing of what was actually carried out at the Restoration. The splendid temple; the wondrous life-giving stream that issues from it; the desalted Sea of the Arabah; the twelve tribes, each in its geometrically conceived plot in the promised land; the city in the center of the land; the temple removed far from the city; priests and Levites dwelling around the temple; the king— the whole of the picture is a flight of the imagination that could not be, nor ever was in fact, realized. Except for those parts of 44:17–31 that agreed with P, not one feature of Ezekiel's program was put into effect in Second Temple times. The idea that Ezekiel fathered the theocratic polity of later Judaism is absurd. He anticipated not a hierocracy, but a visionary kingdom of God. Priests have an important role as keepers of the temple and as teachers, but they have no more temporal authority than do the priests of P. Their dues are modest (44:29 f.; it must be borne in mind that since there is to be, in accord with Deuteronomy, only one sanctuary, these provisions are really quite meager) and do not include even the tithe. The high priest is not granted any privileges. The king, on the other hand, has officers (46:17; "servants" is the technical term), has his own large territory (45:7 f.; 48:21 f.), and receives tribute from the people (45:16). He is obligated to maintain the national cult (45:17), the ancient prerogative of kings both in Israel and the nations. Ezekiel details with particular fulness the sacral duties of kings (46:1–12), but he does not overlook the fundamental task of kingship, to "remove violence of robbery, and administer justly"; the duty of supervising weights and measures also falls to the king (45:9 ff.).

A MESSIANIC PRIESTLY CODE—The broad pattern of 40–48 follows that of P: first comes the plan of the sanctuary; then laws of the sanctuary and its personnel; finally the description of the boundaries of the land

and the tribal settlement. In both cases, too, the laws are preceded by an account of the deliverance of Israel.

The laws themselves are intended to bring up to date provisions of the Torah which had by then become obsolete; they contain a series of novellae to an archaic code.

Thus Ezekiel supplies a law of a temple to replace the obsolete tent-sanctuary of P. Ezekiel's temple, however, has no ark; the ark served no purpose after the stone tablets it housed were lost in the destruction. Ezekiel combines the sanctuary plan of P with D's idea of a fixed site, and for the first time specifies the site of the sanctuary. It is Jerusalem, as he says expressly in 40:1 f. (cf. 43:2).

P knows nothing of the Nethinim, a class which developed during the monarchy. It distinguishes only between priests and Levites; but since the Levites had gradually disappeared, Ezekiel was obliged to invent several novellae to restore matters to their ancient state. The alien Nethinim, he says, must be removed, and non-Zadokite priests who served idols at the local altars are to be degraded to Levites in their place (44:6–16). Now, in fact, these Nethinim, far from being "uncircumcised foreigners," were loyal temple servants who remained attached to the Jews all through the Exile, returned with them from the Exile (Ezra 2:43–58), and subscribed to the "sure agreement" of the restored community (Neh. 10:29). Long before Ezekiel's time, they had become thoroughly Judaized. Ancient tradition ascribed the institution of this class of temple servants not to the "rebellious house," but to Joshua (Josh. 9:27). The Jews of Second Temple times found no fault with the Nethinim and completely ignored Ezekiel's program for replacing them with degraded non-Zadokite priests.[11]

Also with regard to the privileges and the duties of the king, Ezekiel complements older laws. Samuel's "rule of the monarchy" made all the people "servants" of the king, and gave him unlimited authority over their person and property. Ezekiel adopts P's conception that land belongs to the tribes, and title to it can be acquired only by inheritance. Accordingly, he assigns the king an ample territory from which he may grant estates to his sons and officers, but denies him the old right to confiscate the lands of

---

[11] There is no reason to credit Ezekiel's assertion that all the priests except the Zadokites served idols at the high places. In II Kings 23:9 high-place priests (*kōhanīm*) of YHWH are spoken of; the same is implied by Deuteronomy 18:6. Ezekiel's failure to distinguish the legitimate high places from the idolatrous ones set up by Manasseh is typical of his distorted historical perspective. In view of what Ezekiel himself saw in the temple of the Zadokites (chaps. 8–10) it is not easy to understand why he differentiates them from the rest of the priests. No attempt was made later to degrade non-Zadokite priests. It is only modern criticism that has conceived the idea of deriving the Levitical class from Ezekiel's fantasies.

the people for his own use (45:8; 46:18). The Torah says nothing either about the duty of the king to maintain the cult or of the tribute which he may collect from the people. The various injustices and irregularities in these areas are corrected in 45:13–17 and 46:4–15. The king's right to set standards (45:10 ff.) belongs here, too.

A special law supplements P's law concerning aliens. P makes the alien equal to the native-born in matters of the cult, but fails to provide any territory for those who settled in Israel. This meant that they were permanently condemned to insecurity and poverty. Ezekiel corrects this by assigning them land among the tribes (47:22 f.).

P makes the eastern boundary of the land the Jordan; the real settlement included Transjordan. Ezekiel restores the old law and settles all the tribes on the west bank.

The detailed laws concerning the sanctuary, priests, and sacrifices diverge in many ways from those of the Torah, but the divergences do not appear to have any particular pattern. Here Ezekiel incorporated various bodies of the priestly literature which contained the same sort of divergences from P as can be found among the collections that make up P itself. This means only that at that time the literature of P had not yet been crystallized into one book.

THE PROPHECIES TO THE NATIONS—Ezekiel's horizon is national. His prophecies concerning the nations in chapters 25–32 do not contain a vision of the end of idolatry. In the spirit of the early literature, Ezekiel conceives of YHWH as ruling the nations, though manifesting his grace and holiness only in Israel. He does not condemn the nations for their idolatry.

What Ezekiel foresees for the nations is determined by their attitude toward Israel. Ammon, Moab, Edom, Philistia, Tyre, and Sidon (chaps. 25–28) are enemies of Israel; upon them the prophet pronounces destruction. Egypt is a disappointing ally, and will also be destroyed, but after forty years it will be restored as a lowly kingdom. Alongside the motif of revenge, the prophecies against Tyre and Egypt contain a denunciation of pagan pride. God will hold Pharaoh and the King of Tyre to account for their claim to divinity (29:3, 9; 28:1 ff.). All the prophecies to the nations are pervaded by the recognition of the new historical-religious configuration of the post-destruction era: Israel lies prostrate before a triumphant heathen empire. To Ezekiel this means profanation of YHWH's name. Ezekiel alone knows the truth that it was YHWH and his angels who executed the destruction of Jerusalem. The nations tauntingly say, "Behold the house of Judah is like all the nations" (25:8) and come to take possession of the land (35:10 ff.); Israel has become a mockery (36:4); YHWH is laughed at (35:13). For this God will wreak mighty judgments upon the nations and sanctify his name through their collapse.

THE VISION OF GOG—For the world-wide sanctification of God's name, Ezekiel provides a special eschatological battle to take place in the sight of the whole heathen world (chaps. 38–39).

Report of Israel's prosperity and defenselessness will reach the barbarian warrior nations of the north. Moved by avarice and lust for plunder, they will muster out their hordes and attack Israel. When they have overrun the land, God will destroy them with earthquakes, falling walls, tumbling mountains. Heaven will storm down hail, fire, and brimstone; the barbarian armies will slay each other in their panic, and cover the mountains of Israel with their corpses. Then all the nations will know that YHWH is true God. They will realize that Israel's exile was the work of YHWH, the result of Israel's sin, and that now out of jealousy for his name, he has restored them and will no longer hide his face from them (39:1–7, 22–29).

The motifs of this vision are pieced together from earlier tradition, undergoing a fundamental revision in their new form. Earlier prophets (Amos, Isaiah, Jeremiah) imagined a great attack by the heathen against Jerusalem directly before the final redemption. Since Ezekiel prophesied after the fall, he must place the attack after the restoration; what point was there in the barbarian falling upon a ruined desolation? The purpose of the heathen onslaught is now entirely different; the "northerners" come not to punish Israel for sin, but to satisfy their lust for plunder. But they cannot harm Israel; before reaching Jerusalem, they will fall by God's sword. The theme is derived from the rout of Pharaoh at the Red Sea (Exod. 14:2–4, 8, 17 f.); a defenseless people is set upon by armed pagan hosts and is miraculously saved for the glory of YHWH. This motif served Ezekiel as the basis of an eschatological world cataclysm. The vision of Gog had tremendous influence on later eschatology, but the apocalyptic version of the war of Gog and Magog altered Ezekiel's concept radically. It no longer leaves Israel unscathed, and, more important, it no longer follows, but precedes the final redemption.

While the vision of Gog has a universal setting, the dichotomy between Israel and the nations remains in full force even after Gog's fall. The nations will continue their separate ways. Ezekiel received much from his predecessors, but he did not inherit their vision of the return of the nations to God at the end of days.

Epilogue and Prospect

The fall of Jerusalem is the great watershed of the history of Israelite religion. The life of the people of Israel came to an end; the history of Judaism began. To be sure, the people lived on and were creative after the fall, but the form of their life and the conditions of their existence and creativity were radically transformed. Israel ceased to be a normal nation and became a religious community. This development was rooted in the ideas of the pre-exilic religion, both priestly and prophetic. Its manifestations are the crystallization of the Torah book, and the transformation of Israel into a "witness to the nations," the bearers of a universal religious mission.

The goal of the religious ferment that arose in the age of the fall was to found the life of the nation on the basis of the word of God. Earlier the word of God was but one of several manifestations of YHWH's presence in Israel. YHWH dwelt in Israel: its land, its sanctuaries, its monarchy, its prophecy were all vehicles of divine grace; Israel's history and life as a whole were the expression of the divine will. With the fall and the exile, however, the simple faith of the people in the working of the divine in their life, in the indwelling of God's presence among them, was shattered. YHWH had turned his back upon them. The life of Israel was no longer the arena of his mighty acts. With land, temple, and king gone, only one contact with the holy was left: the divine word. The people yearned to reconcile themselves with God; how could they do so if not by obedience to his word which they had continuously violated? Repentance was conceived of as compliance with YHWH's commands, fulfilling what he had revealed during the period of grace. Israel's religious self-confidence having been shattered, it sought to re-establish its relationship with God upon the written word. The sacred literary legacy of the past was collected and sifted; the age of compilation and canonization began. One after another, the Torah, Prophets, and Sacred Writings were ordered and fixed. Religious

creativity did not cease. On the contrary, it was destined to reach heights
that the pre-exilic age had never dreamed of. But it took on a new form,
an elaboration of and at all times a dependence upon the legacy of the past.

The collapse of religious self-confidence that attended the fall struck
a fatal blow at Israelite prophecy. Prophecy had been nurtured by the
simple faith in the indwelling of God in Israel's life and history. Now that
the feeling of God's nearness had been undermined, the spirit of prophecy
began to die. It was the priesthood, not prophecy, who could provide a
sure basis for the religious life of the people. The priesthood did not reveal
new words of God, but transmitted and taught the ancient toroth that
God gave Israel in antiquity. The priestly toroth answered the religious
need of the age—to found the life of the people on the fixed and eternally
sanctified word of God.

The return from Babylon, the building of the Second Temple, and the
crystallization of the Torah book all served to express the yearning to
heal the breach between God and people opened by the fall. The temple
symbolized God's presence in Israel in the past; the Torah symbolized
Israel's commitment to live by the divine word in the present. Compiled
from ancient scrolls, embodying divergent and at times mutually contradictory matter, it is a monument to the diffidence of an age which dared
not alter a jot or tittle of, much less add anything to, the ancient revelation.
Upon this book the Restoration community made a new covenant, pledging
themselves to obey all its commands. Henceforth, the book left the charge
of the priest to become forever the property of the people at large.

The effect of this momentous act was greater by far than its authors
could have imagined. In crystallizing and sealing the Torah, a way was
opened to overcome the ethnic-territorial limitation of the old religion.
The Torah was destined to leave the land and the temple and to accompany
Israel from exile to exile. The product of the mood of exile, it was well
adapted for the needs of a dispersed people. Although the religious consciousness of that time regarded the temple and the land as necessary conditions for the fulfilment of the Torah, the Torah book was a self-contained,
in itself adequate, embodiment of the religion of YHWH. Of itself the
Torah was a fountainhead of sanctity, an eternal expression of the will
of God. The idea of the Torah book thus harbored the seed of an ultimate
liberation of the religion of Israel from ethnic and territorial limitations.

Without the formation of the Torah book, the prophetic vision of the
universalization of Israel's religion could not have been realized.

How did that vision fare after the fall?

During the pre-exilic age, the religion of Israel, universal in essence, had embodied itself exclusively in national forms. As Israel's peculiar possession it fell to Israel to establish a "sanctuary" for the one God, a "place for his dwelling" on earth. Conquered Canaan was consecrated to YHWH as the holy land, where alone he could be worshiped with sacrifice and oblation. The people and land of Israel were considered the sole domain of YHWH's cult and prophecy. The gentiles' lands were impure; their idol-worship on their own soil was considered legitimate. Within Israel, idolatrous deviations were combated, but there was no battle against the paganism of the gentiles. The universalistic ideal of early times expressed itself in the pious wish that the nations would come to recognize the greatness of Israel's God, or at most, that individual gentiles would come to fear the God of Israel.

The early period is thus the age of the consolidation of Israel as the people of YHWH. The national covenant was the source of the obligation to destroy idolatry; it was the basis of the prophetic demands as well. This period does not address the gentiles; it knows nothing of missionary tendencies. The early *gēr* is a person who settles in the land of Israel and, as a matter of course, assimilates the culture and religion of his environment. It is characteristic that even in the story of Naaman, the one story in which a religious conversion is related (II Kings 5), there is no element of polemic against idolatry. Naaman acknowledges the God of Israel because of a miracle worked by his prophet, not because he realizes the vanity of manu-factured gods.

Isaiah, who first envisioned the end of idolatry, also speaks in terms of the national covenant. His indictment of Israel is based on the claim YHWH has on Israel's loyalty; Isaiah has unbounded faith in the eternal election of Jerusalem and the house of David. Like the other prophets, he does not regard idolatry as a sin for the nations; nonetheless, he envisages a time when the nations will forsake idolatry and cleave to the God of Israel. This prophecy set a new goal for human history. God has not destined the nations to be outside the scope of his grace forever. Here the idea that God has destined Israelite religion for the gentiles appears for the first time. With this vision, Israelite religion took the first step toward becoming a factor in world history. It was left for Habakkuk and Jeremiah to take the next step and declare the idolatry of the nations sinful. Now the theoretical basis of a mission to the gentiles was laid, although the way was still far to its actual realization.

Isaiah's vision that the end of idolatry would come with the collapse of the heathen empire on the mountain of Israel was not fulfilled. The road to the ultimate goal was far longer and filled with thorns and pitfalls. After the fall of Samaria came the turn of Jerusalem. Then came a succession of empires: Babylon, Persia, Greece, Rome. Jerusalem was destroyed again, and the Second Temple went up in flames. The bulk of the nation was exiled and dispersed, encompassed by derision and hate. The man who was to be the symbol of Israelite religion to the gentiles, who was to be their redeemer and Messiah, died ignominiously at the hands of the Romans with the taunt "King of the Jews" inscribed by Roman soldiers on his cross. It was a long path of suffering from Tiglath-pileser, to Pontius Pilate, to Nero, and to Titus. And yet Jerusalem prevailed over her conquerors. Throughout the world wherever the Jewish people were dispersed, paganism was destined to die.

How did this come to pass?

One thing is clear: Since the fall of paganism did not come about through a political or military collapse, this triumph of Israelite religion can only have been the product of its inner strength, the strength of a new religious idea. Its only weapons can have been ideological: propaganda, preaching, and missionaries. The necessary precondition for this victory was the emergence of the idea of a mission to the nations, the development of a resolve to combat the paganism of the nations. Israel had first to take upon itself the prophetic task of fighting for monotheism throughout the world.

In this respect, there is a basic difference between the periods of the First and Second Temples.

During the golden age of Israelite creativity in pre-exilic times, the religion of Israel exerted no influence whatever on its surroundings. Israel's soul remained a world in itself, *terra incognita* to the outsider. The entire period produced but one religious convert, Naaman.

During Second Temple times, however, Judaism agitates the gentile world wherever it is found. Its influence gradually spreads, until by Hellenistic times there are myriads of converts and "fearers of God" among the nations. An ideological battle rages between Judaism and paganism. The Jews have taken up the missionary task of eradicating idolatry from the world.

Between the two periods come the fall of Jerusalem and the Babylonian exile.

With the fall, Israelite religion was uprooted from the land which had nurtured it and given it life, the land to which it was bound by countless threads of rite and custom and culture. The fateful question was: Could Israel stand this separation; could they endure apart from the seedbed of their culture? The lesson of history is that they not only endured, but that it was precisely in exile that the full stature of Israelite religion began to manifest itself. It began to prepare the forms for its second stage of development, when it would challenge and finally overwhelm the triumphant gods.

Before Israel could declare war upon paganism, however, it had to eliminate the last vestiges of "idolatry" from its own midst. A jealous God must have a jealous people. The disappearance of idolatry in Israel took place in the first generations after the fall.

Next, the prophetic idea of the battle with idolatry had to be accepted by the people. It was not enough to be jealous; they must also be apostles, willing to endure the suffering involved in the fight. This transformation was conditioned upon the popular acceptance of the idea that idolatry was a sin for the nations as well. The idea had to take root in the heart of the people that heathenism had no right to existence.

The attack upon gentile paganism could become a reality only when the cult of Israelite religion evolved forms independent of the land of Israel. So long as Israel refused to sing YHWH's song on foreign soil, it was impossible for their religion to become in reality the religion of other peoples. The idea of the unique sanctity of the holy land was not done away with; in theory, everything remained bound to the city and the land. But life in exile necessarily gave birth to a radically new type of cult, a cult without sacrifice or priesthood: the worship of the synagogue.

The early religion knew how to assimilate foreigners only through a complete ethnic, cultural, and territorial amalgamation. This, too, had to be superseded before it could become the faith of the mass of gentiles. Accordingly, after considerable groping, Judaism evolved religious proselytism. Here was the clearest manifestation of the conquest of the early religion's national confines.

Great significance attaches to the fundamental change that was to take place in the doctrine of retribution. The belief in resurrection, in judgment, and retribution in the afterlife gradually came into being. The soul found a way to God after death. This doctrine remedied what was a serious defect in the early religion when compared with paganism. It provided tremendous attractive power to missionary Judaism.

The history of Israelite religion in the last generations before the Exile moves toward this goal: the molding of Israel into a prophet-nation, "a witness to the peoples." Its teachers instruct it to suffer patiently and have faith in the vision even if it should tarry; to live in the faith that YHWH is God, there is none else. The fruit of this faith was to ripen during the period of the Second Temple.

Indexes

Index to Passages Cited

(The letter *n* after a page number refers to a footnote)

Index to Subjects

(The letter *n* after a page number refers to a footnote)

Aaron, 13, 78, 82, 195, 221, 227, 238, 239, 240; Egyptian name of, 221, 238; figure of, in P, 183, 185–86; staff of, 81, 82, 83

Aaronic priesthood, 197–99, 238–40, 271

Abiathar, priesthood of, as composers of Deuteronomy, 420

Abimelech (son of Gideon), 248 n., 250 n., 254

Abraham, 74, 98, 121, 131 n., 190, 219 n., 321; in history, 216 n., 218; a monotheist? 153, 221–23; *see also* Patriarchs

Absalom, monument of, 312

Achan, 74

Adam (and Eve), 123, 292-94, 330, 390; image of God, 318; as monotheist, 153, 221, 222, 244

ʾĀḏōn, 136, 220

Adonis, gardens of, 382 n.

Adytum; *see Debīr*

Africa, religion of tribes of, 29–31

Agag, 137, 203

Agriculture, techniques and festivals of, not learned from Canaanites, 116, 253, 259–60

Agur, 323

Ahab, 135, 140, 273, 274, 275, 277, 285, 366, 370 n., 372

Ahaz, 140–41, 288, 378, 379, 389, 431

Ahaziah (king of Israel), 89, 135, 274, 277

Ahiah (prophet), 270, 272, 273, 276

Ahikam son of Shaphan, 287, 411

Ahikar, book of, 149, 323 n.

Akhenaton, 36, 226, 298; solar hymn of, 226 n., 296

Akiba, Rabbi, 398

Alien, resident; *see Gēr*

Altar(s), 112, 119; in Egypt, of YHWH, Isaiah on, 391, 392 n.; local 258, 286, 288–89 (*see also* Centralization of wor-ship; High places; Sanctuaries), of P not like that of Second Temple, 184; stone field, for slaughter, 181, 182; a "table," 111; with theophoric name, 138 n.; of Transjordanian tribes, 129–30

Amalek, 74, 203, 235, 241, 254, 257, 297, 355 n., 364

Amaziah (priest), 126, 313, 363

America, religion of tribes of, 29, 31, 54

Ammon, Ammonites, excluded from Israel, 300, 321

Amorite, "sin of the," 73, 254; *see also* Canaan and Canaanites

Amos, 98, 126, 162, 204, 273, 313, 354, 363, 374, 380; on cult and morality, 125, 158, 345, 365–67; date and composition of book of, 351, 363, 364; on idolatry and gods, 14, 143, 366; prophecies of con-solation in, 367–68; remnant idea in, 367, 368; against ruling class, 347, 366; symbolic visions of, 94; tradition in, 296, 363–64, 365

Amphictyony, 256

Anathbethel, 149

Anathiahu, 149

Anathoth, 410, 413, 417, 421

Ancestor cult, 77, 312, 313

Angelology, 63–64, 66, 437

Angels, 63–64, 77, 106; in dreams and prophecy, 94; eat, desire, 70 n.; evil, 64, 109; praise God, 121; princes (patrons) of nations, 66, 384; rebellious and fallen, 11, 63, 65–66, 384; see also ʾĔlōhīm; Sons of God

Anointing, of kings and priests, 186, 199

Apocalypse, 358–59, 384, 399, 437–38, 446; characteristics of, 348–49

Apollonius of Tyana, 36, 49, 53, 212–13

Apotheosis, 36–37, 40, 77–78, 315–16

Apries, 410